Random House

Italian Dictionary

Second Edition

Italian • English
English • Italian
Italiano • Inglese
Inglese • Italiano

Edited by
Robert A. Hall, Jr.
CORNELL UNIVERSITY

Revised by
Vieri Samek-Lodovici, Ph.D.

RANDOM HOUSE
NEW YORK

Abbreviations

abbr.	abbreviation	*math.*	mathematics
adj.	adjective	*med.*	medicine
adv.	adverb	*mil.*	military
Amer.	American	*n.*	noun
Brit.	British	*naut.*	nautical
coll.	colloquial	*num.*	number
comm.	commercial	*pl.*	plural
conj.	conjunction	*pred.*	predicate
dem.	demonstrative	*prep.*	preposition
eccles.	ecclesiastical	*pron.*	pronoun;
econ.	economics		pronunciation
f.	feminine	*refl.*	reflexive
fam.	familiar	*sg.*	singular
fig.	figuratively	*tr.*	transitive (used only
geom.	geometry		with verbs which also
gram.	grammar; grammatical		have reflexive use to
interj.	interjection		indicate intransitive
intr.	intransitive		meaning)
lit.	literally	*typogr.*	typography
m.	masculine	*vb.*	verb

Months and Days of the Week

January	gennàio	*Monday*	lunedì
February	febbràio	*Tuesday*	martedì
March	marzo	*Wednesday*	mercoledì
April	aprile	*Thursday*	giovedì
May	màggio	*Friday*	venerdì
June	giugno	*Saturday*	sàbato
July	lùglio	*Sunday*	doménica
August	agosto		
September	settèmbre		
October	ottobre		
November	novèmbre		
December	dicèmbre		

Concise Pronunciation Guide

Italian Letter	Pronunciation
a	Like English *a* in *father*.
b	As in English.
c	Before *e* or *i*, and sometimes at the end of words, like English *ch*. Elsewhere, like English *k*.
ch	Before *e* or *i*, like English *k*.
ci	Before *a*, *o*, or *u*, like English *ch*.
d	As in English.
é	("closed *e*") Like English *ay* in *day*, but with no final *y*-like glide.
è	("open *e*") Like English *e* in *bet*.
e	Like English *e* in *bet*.
f	As in English.
g	Before *e* or *i*, like English *g* in *gem*. Elsewhere, like English *g* in *go*.
gh	Before *e* or *i*, like English *g* in *go*.
gi	Before *a*, *o*, or *u*, like English *g* in *gem*.
gl	Before *i*, normally like English *lli* in *million*.
gli	Before *a*, *e*, *o*, or *u*, like English *lli* in *million*.
gn	Like English *ny* in *canyon*.
h	After *c* and *g*, indicates "hard" pronunciation of preceding consonant letter. Elsewhere, silent.
i	After *c*, *g*, and (normally) *sc*, before *a*, *o*, or *u*, indicates "soft" pronunciation of preceding consonant letter or letters. Elsewhere: When unstressed and before or after another vowel, like English *y*. Otherwise, like English *i* in *machine*, but with no final *y*-like glide.
j	At the end of words, when replacing *ii* in some noun plurals, like Italian *i*. Otherwise, like English *y*.
k	As in English.

Italian Letter	Pronunciation
l	Like English *l* in *like,* but with the tongue behind the upper front teeth.
m	As in English.
n	As in English.
ó	("closed *o*") Like English *o* in *go,* but with no final *w*-like glide.
ò	("open *o*") Like English *o* in *bought.*
o	Like English *o* in *bought.*
p	As in English.
qu	Like English *qu* in *quick.*
r	Not at all like American English *r;* a quick flap of the tip of the tongue on the gumridge.
s	Between vowels, like English *s* in *lease* (in southern Italy); like *s* in *please* (in northern Italy); sometimes like *s* in *lease* and sometimes like *s* in *please* (in central Italy). Before *b, d, g, l, m, n, r, v,* like English *z.* Elsewhere, like English *s* in *same, stick.*
sc	Before *e* or *i,* and occasionally at the end of words, like English *sh.* Elsewhere, like English *sk.*
sch	Before *e* or *i,* like English *sk.*
sci	Before *a, o,* or *u,* like English *sh.*
t	As in English.
u	When unstressed and before or after another vowel, like English *w.* Otherwise, like English *oo* in *boot,* but without final *w*-like glide.
v	As in English.
w	Rare; like English *v.*
x	Rare; like English *x.*
z	Like English *ts* in *cats* or like English *dz* in *adze.*

Consonant Length

All Italian consonants occur both single (short) and double (long); in the latter instance, the time of their pronunciation lasts from one-and-a-half to two times that of the single consonants.

Italian Accentuation

In most conventional writing and printing, spoken stress is marked by a grave accent (`` ` ``), but only when it falls on the last syllable of a word: *città, vendè, lunedì, cantò, tribù.* An accent is placed over the vowel letter of some words to distinguish them from others having the same spelling and pronunciation but differing in meaning: *è* "is" versus *e* "and." In other instances, stress is usually left unmarked, although it may fall on any syllable up to the sixth from the end.

However, Italians are very sensitive to misplaced stress, even though accent marks are not customarily used in Italian spelling. In this dictionary, therefore, as in most Italian dictionaries, the occurrence of stress is indicated with an accent mark whenever it does not fall on the next-to-the-last syllable, and also in all words ending in *-ia, -io.* In addition, the presence of the open varieties of *e* and *o,* to which Italians are also sensitive, is marked by a grave accent (`` ` ``) in all its occurrences, even in the next-to-the-last syllable.

Noun and Adjective Plurals

Virtually all Italian nouns form their plurals by changing the final vowel. The following are the principal patterns of noun plural formation:

Final Vowel		Examples	
Singular	**Plural**	**Singular**	**Plural**
-a *(f.)*	-e	ròsa	ròse
-a *(m.)*	-i	dramma	drammi
-o *(m.)*	-i	libro	libri
-o *(m.)*	-à *(f.)*	bràccio	bràccia
-e *(m., f.)*	-i *(m., f.)*	fiume	fiumi
		parte	parti

Nouns ending in unstressed *-i,* in stressed vowels, or in consonants; family names; and abbreviations are normally unchanged in the plural: *crisi, città, tram; Scaglione; auto, radio.*

Adjectives ending in *-o* follow the pattern of *libro* for the masculine and that of *rosa* for the feminine; those ending in *-e* follow the pattern of *fiume, parte* for both masculine and feminine.

Regular Verbs

Infinitive	Present	Future	Preterite	Past Part.
cantare	canto	canterò	cantai	cantato
dormire	dormo	dormirò	dormii	dormito
finire	finisco	finirò	finii	finito
temere	temo	temerò	temèi	temuto
véndere	vendo	venderò	vendèi	venduto

Irregular Verbs

Infinitive	Present	Future	Preterite	Past Part.
accèndere	accendo	accenderò	accesi	acceso
andare	vado	andrò	andai	andato
aprire	apro	aprirò	apèrsi	apèrto
avere	ho	avrò	èbbi	avuto
bere	bevo	berrò	bevvi	bevuto
cadere	cado	cadrò	caddi	caduto
cingere	cingo	cingerò	cinsi	cinto
cògliere	colgo	coglierò	colsi	colto
concèdere	concedo	concederò	concèssi	concèsso
condurre	conduco	condurrò	condussi	condotto
dare	do	darò	diedi	dato
difèndere	difendo	difenderò	difesi	difeso
dire	dico	dirò	dissi	detto
dovere	devo	dovrò	dovèi	dovuto
èssere	sono	sarò	fui	stato
fare	fàccio	farò	feci	fatto
fóndere	fondo	fonderò	fusi	fuso
giacere	giàccio	giacerò	giacqui	giaciuto
morire	muòio	morirò	morii	mòrto
nàscere	nasco	nascerò	nacqui	nato
parere	paio	parrò	parsi	parso
porre	pongo	porrò	posi	posto
potere	pòsso	potrò	potèi	potuto
rèndere	rèndo	renderò	resi	reso
salire	salgo	salirò	salii	salito
sapere	sò	saprò	seppi	saputo
scégliere	scelgo	sceglierò	scelsi	scelto
stare	sto	starò	stetti	stato
tenere	tengo	terrò	tenni	tenuto
trarre	traggo	trarrò	trassi	tratto
uscire	esco	uscirò	uscii	uscito
valere	valgo	varrò	valsi	valso
vedere	vedo	vedrò	vidi	visto or veduto
venire	vengo	verrò	venni	venuto
vivere	vivo	vivrò	vissi	vissuto
volere	vòglio	vorrò	vòlli	voluto

Numerals

Cardinal

1	uno, una	32	trentadue
2	due	38	trentòtto
3	tre	40	quaranta
4	quattro	50	cinquanta
5	cinque	60	sessanta
6	sèi	70	settanta
7	sètte	80	ottanta
8	òtto	90	novanta
9	nòve	100	cènto
10	dièci	101	centuno
11	ùndici	102	centodue
12	dódici	200	duecènto
13	trédici	300	trecènto
14	quattòrdici	400	quattrocènto
15	quìndici	500	cinquecènto
16	sédici	600	seicènto
17	diciassètte	700	settecènto
18	diciòtto	800	ottocènto
19	diciannòve	900	novecènto
20	venti	1,000	mille
21	ventuno, ventuna	2,000	duemila
22	ventidue	3,000	tremila
28	ventòtto	100,000	centomila
30	trenta	1,000,000	un milione
31	trentuno, trentuna	2,000,000	due milioni

Ordinal

1st	primo	15th	decimoquinto
2nd	secondo		or quindicésimo
3rd	tèrzo	16th	decimosèsto
4th	quarto		or sedicésimo
5th	quinto	17th	decimosèttimo
6th	sèsto		or diciassettésimo
7th	sèttimo	18th	decimottavo
8th	ottavo		or diciottésimo
9th	nòno	19th	decimonòno
10th	dècimo		or diciannovésimo
11th	decimoprimo	20th	ventésimo
	or undicésimo	21st	ventésimoprimo
12th	decimosecondo	30th	trentésimo
	or dodicésimo	40th	quarantésimo
13th	decimotèrzo	100th	centésimo
	or tredicésimo	1000th	millésimo
14th	decimoquarto		
	or quattordicésimo		

a, *prep.* at; in; to; by.

àbaco, *n.m.* abacus.

abate, *n.m.* abbot.

abbàcchio, *n.m.* lamb.

abbagliante, *adj.* dazzling.

abbagliare, *vb.* dazzle.

abbàglio, *n.m.* mistake.

abbaiamento, *n.m.* bark; barking.

abbaiare, *vb.* bark, bay.

abbaino, *n.m.* dormer.

abbandonare, *vb.* abandon, forsake, relinquish, vacate.

abbandonato, *adj.* abandoned.

abbandono, *n.m.* abandon, abandonment.

abbassamento, *n.m.* lowering, abasement.

abbassare, *vb.* lower, abase; debase; (*refl.*) stoop; subside.

abbassato, *adj.* lowered; downcast.

abbàsseo, *interj.* down with!

abbastanza, *adv.* enough.

abbàttere, *vb.* knock down, fell; dishearten; (*refl.*) droop.

abbattimento, *n.m.* disheartenment, dismay, dejection.

abbattuto, *adj.* despondent.

abbazia, *n.f.* abbey.

abbecedàrio, *n.m.* speller, primer; ABCs.

abbellimento, *n.m.* embellishment.

abbellire, *vb.* beautify, embellish.

abbeverare, *vb.* water (animals).

abbiente, *adj.* well-to-do, upper-middle-class.

abbigliare, *vb.* dress up, accouter.

abbigliamento maschile, *n.m.* menswear.

abbigliatura, *n.f.* accouterments.

abbonacciare, *vb.* becalm.

abbonamento, *n.m.* subscription.
biglietto d'a., season ticket.

abbonarsi, *vb.* subscribe.

abbonato, *n.m.* subscriber.

abbondante, *adj.* abundant, plentiful.

abbondantemente, *adv.* abundantly.

abbondanza, *n.f.* abundance, plenty.

abbondare, *vb.* abound.

abbordàbile, *adj.* accessible.

abbordare, *vb.* accost.

abborracciare, *vb.* bungle.

abbozzare, *vb.* sketch.

abbòzzo, *n.m.* sketch, draft.

abbracciare, *vb.* embrace, clasp, hug.

abbràccio, *n.m.* embrace, clasp, hug.

abbreviamento, *n.m.* abridgement.

abbreviare, *vb.* abbreviate, abridge, shorten.

abbreviatura, *n.f.* abbreviation.

abbronzare, *vb.* tan.

abbronzato, *adj.* sunburnt.

abbronzatura, *n.f.* sunburn, tan.

abbrustolire, *vb.* toast.

abbrutire, *vb.* brutalize, degrade.

abbuono, *n.m.* allowance.

abdicare, *vb.* abdicate.

abdicazione, *n.f.* abdication.

aberrante, *adj.* aberrant.

aberrare, *vb.* be aberrant.

aberrazione, *n.f.* aberration.

abete, *n.m.* fir.

abiètto, *adj.* abject.

àbile, *adj.* skillful, clever, able, adroit, capable, cunning, deft.

abilità, *n.f.* ability, skill, cleverness, adeptness, cunning.

abilitazione, *n.f.* qualification; license.

abilmente, *adv.* skillfully, ably, adeptly, capably.

Abissìnia, *n.f.* Abyssinia.

abissino, *n. and adj.* Abyssinian.

abisso, *n.m.* abyss, chasm.

abitàbile, *adj.* habitable, livable.

abitante, *n.m.* inhabitant, dweller, resident.

abitare, *vb.* live, dwell, reside, inhabit.

abitazione, *n.f.* dwelling, habitation, residence.

àbito, *n.m.* dress, suit, habit.

abituale, *adj.* habitual, usual, accustomed.

abituare, *vb.* accustom, habituate.

abituarsi a, *vb.* get accustomed to.

abitùdine, *n.f.* habit.

abiura, *n.f.* abjuration.

abiurare, *vb.* abjure.

ablativo, *n.m. and adj.* ablative.

abluzione, *n.f.* ablution.

abnegare, *vb.* abnegate.

abnegazione, *n.f.* abnegation.

abnorme, *adj.* abnormal.

abolire, *vb.* abolish.

abolizione, *n.f.* abolition.

abominare, *vb.* abominate, loathe.

abominazione, *n.f.* abomination.

abominévole, *adj.* abominable, loathsome.

aborìgeno, 1. *n.m.* aborigine. **2.** *adj.* aboriginal, native.

aborrimento, *n.m.* abhorrence.

aborrire, *vb.* abhor.

abortire, *vb.* abort; be abortive.

abortivo, *adj.* abortive.

aborto, *n.m.* abortion.

abrasione, *n.f.* abrasion.

abrasivo, *n.m. and adj.* abrasive.

abrogare, *vb.* abrogate.

abrogazione, *n.f.* abrogation.

àbside, *n.f.* apse.

a buòn mercato, *adv.* cheap; cheaply.

abusare di, *vb.* abuse, misuse.

abusivamente, *adv.* abusively.

abusivo, *adj.* abusive.

abuso, *n.m.* abuse.

acàcia, *n.f.* acacia.

acanto, *n.m.* acanthus.

àcaro, *n.m.* acarus, mite.

a cavalcioni, *adv.* astride.

accadèmia, *n.f.* academy.

accadèmico, *adj.* academic.

accadere, *vb.* happen, befall, occur, take place.

accalcare, *vb.* crowd.

accaldato, *adj.* hot.

accampamento, *n.m.* camp, encampment.

accampare, *vb.* camp, encamp.

accanire, *vb.* persist.

accanimento, *n.m.* animosity.

accanto, *adv.* beside, alongside.

accanto a, *prep.* beside, next to, alongside.

accantonamento, *n.m.* cantonment.

accaparrare, *vb.* corner.

accarezzare, *vb.* caress, fondle, stroke.

accattone, *n.m.* beggar.

accavallare, *vb.* cross one's legs; overlap.

accecare, *vb.* blind.

accelerare, *vb.* accelerate, speed up.

accelerato, *n.m.* local (train).

acceleratore, *n.m.* accelerator.

accelerazione, *n.f.* acceleration.

accèndere, *vb.* light, switch on, ignite, kindle.

accendisìgaro, *n.m.* cigar-lighter, cigarette-lighter.

accennare, *vb.* hint.

accensione, *n.f.* ignition.

accentare, *vb.* accent, stress.

accènto, *n.m.* accent, stress.

accentuare, *vb.* accent.

accerchiare, *vb.* encircle, ring around.

accertarsi, *vb.* ascertain.

accessibile, *adj.* accessible.

accèsso, *n.m.* access, approach; fit.

accessòrio, 1. *n.m.* accessory; attachment. **2.** *adj.* accessory; adjunct.

accetta, *n.f.* hatchet.

accettàbile, *adj.* acceptable.

accettabilità, *n.f.* acceptability.

accettabilmente, *adv.* acceptably.

accettare, *vb.* accept.

accettazione, *n.f.* acceptance.

accètto, *adj.* acceptable.

acciàio, *n.m.* steel.

accidentale, *adj.* accidental.

accidentalmente, *adv.* accidentally.

acciglìato, *adj.* frowning, glum.

acciuga, *n.f.* anchovy.

acclamare, *vb.* acclaim.

acclamazione, *n.f.* acclamation.

acclimare, *vb.* acclimate.

acclimatare, *vb.* acclimate.

acclività, *n.f.* acclivity.

acclùdere, *vb.* enclose.

accoglìenza, *n.f.* reception.

accògliere, *vb.* receive, entertain.

accòlito, *n.m.* acolyte.

accollata, *n.f.* accolade.

accomodante, *adj.* accommodating.

accomodare, *vb.* accommodate; mend; *(refl.)* make oneself comfortable; compromise.

accomodazione, *n.f.* accommodation.

accompagnamento, *n.m.* accompaniment.

accompagnare, *vb.* accompany.

accompagnatore, *n.m.* accompanist.

acconciare, *vb.* fix.

acconciatura, *n.f.* hair-do.

accondiscendénza, *n.f.* condescension.

accondiscéndere, *vb.* condescend.

acconsentire, *vb.* consent.

accontentare, *vb.* content.

accoppiare, *vb.* couple; mate.

accorciare, *vb.* shorten, curtail.

accordare, *vb.* tune.

accòrdo, *n.m.* agreement, accord; compact; concord; chord. **d'a.,** in agreement.

accosciarsi, *vb.* squat.

accostare, *vb.* bring near, approach, come alongside *(naut.)*; leave ajar (door).

accovacciarsi, *vb.* crouch.

accreditare, *vb.* accredit.

accréscere, *vb.* accrue, increase, boost, enhance, heighten.

accrescimento, *n.m.* increase, accretion, accrual, boost.

accucciarsi, *vb.* crouch.

accudire, *vb.* look after, attend.

accumulàbile, *adj.* cumulative.

accumulare, *vb.* accumulate.

accumulatore, *n.m.* battery, accumulator.

accumulazione, *n.f.* accumulation.

accuratamente, *adv.* accurately, carefully.

accuratezza, *n.f.* accuracy, carefulness.

accurato, *adj.* accurate, careful.

accusa, *n.f.* accusation, indictment.

accusare, *vb.* accuse, arraign, indict. **a. ricevuta di,** acknowledge receipt of.

accusativo, *n.m. and adj.* accusative.

accusato, *n.m.* accused.

accusatore, *n.m.* accuser.

acerbamente, *adv.* prematurely, bitterly, sharply.

acerbità, *n.f.* acerbity.

acèrbo, *adj.* sour, unripe.

àcero, *n.m.* maple.

acetato, *n.m.* acetate.

acètico, *adj.* acetic.

acetilène, *n.m.* acetylene.

aceto, *n.m.* vinegar.

acidificare, *vb.* acidify.

acidità, *n.f.* acidity.

àcido, *n.m. and adj.* acid, sour.

acidòsi, *n.f.* acidosis.

àcidulo, *adj.* acidulous.

àcino, *n.m.* berry, grape.

acme, *n.f.* acme.

acne, *n.f.* acne.

acqua, *n.f.* water.

acquafòrte, *n.f.* etching.

acquaio, *n.m.* sink.

acquarèllo, *n.m.* watercolor.

acquàrio, *n.m.* aquarium.

acquàtico, *adj.* aquatic.

acquavite, *n.f.* brandy.

acquazzone, *n.m.* heavy shower, cloudburst.

acquedotto, *n.m.* aqueduct.

àqueo, *adj.* aqueous.

acquiescenza, *n.f.* acquiescence.

acquietarsi, *vb.* calm down, acquiesce.

acquisitivo, *adj.* acquisitive.

acquistare, *vb.* acquire.

acquisto, *n.m.* acquisition.

acre, *adj.* acrid, acrimonious; tart.

acrèdine, *n.f.* acrimony.

acrimònia, *n.f.* acrimony.

acro, *n.m.* acre.

acròbata, *n.m.* acrobat.

acròstico, *n.m.* acrostic.

acume, *n.m.* acumen.

acùstica, *n.f.* acoustics.

acutamente, *adv.* acutely, sharply.

acutezza, *n.f.* acuteness, sharpness.

acuto, *adj.* acute, sharp, keen, pointed, shrewd.

ad, *prep.* at; in; to; by.

adàgio, 1. *n.m.* adage. **2.** *adv.* slowly; gently.

adamantino, *adj.* adamant.
Adamo, *n.m.* Adam.
adattàbile, *adj.* adaptable.
adattabilità, *n.f.* adaptability.
adattamento, *n.* adaptation; fitting.
adattare, *vb.* adapt.
adattévole, *adj.* adaptive.
adatto, *adj.* suitable, right for, fitting.
addèbito, *n.m.* debit, charge.
addensare, *vb.* densify, thicken.
addentrarsi, *vb.* enter into, penetrate.
addestramento, *n.m.* training, preparation, instruction.
addestrare, *vb.* train, prepare, instruct.
addetto, 1. *n.m.* attachè. **2.** *adj.* assigned, employed.
addìo, *interj.* hello; good-bye, adieu, farewell.
addirittura, *adv.* altogether, all in all, positively.
additare, *vb.* point out.
addizionale, *adj.* additional.
addizionare, *vb.* add.
addizione, *n.f.* addition.
addobbare, *vb.* adorn, decorate.
addobbo, *n.m.* ornament.
addolorare, *vb.* grieve, *tr.;* (*refl.*) sorrow.
addolorato, *adj.* sorrowful.
addòme, *n.m.* abdomen.
addomesticare, *vb.* tame.
addominale, *adj.* abdominal.
addormentarsi, *vb.* (*refl.*) fall asleep.
addottrinare, *vb.* indoctrinate.
addurre, *vb.* lead up, bring up, adduce.
adenòide, *adj.* adenoid.
adeguato, *adj.* adequate, satisfactory.
aderènte, *n.m.* adherent, member (of association, etc.).
aderènza, *n.f.* adherence, support; relation.
aderire, *vb.* adhere, cling, stick, support, join.
adescare, *vb.* allure, entice, lure.
adescatore, *adj.* alluring.
adesione, *n.f.* adhesion; adherence; assent. **dar a.,** join, support.

adesività, *n.f.* adhesiveness, adherence.
adesivo, *n.m. and adj.* adhesive.
adèsso, *adv.* now.
adiacènte, *adj.* adjacent, adjoining.
adibire, *vb.* designate, assign; use as.
adirarsi, *vb.* get angry.
adirato, *adj.* angry, cross.
adocchiare, *vb.* spot, glance at.
adolescènte, *n. and adj.* adolescent.
adolescènza, *n.f.* adolescence.
adoperare, *vb.* use.
adoràbile, *adj.* adorable.
adorare, *vb.* adore, worship.
adorazione, *n.f.* adoration, worship.
adornamento, *n.m.* adornment.
adorno, *adj.* adorned.
adottare, *vb.* adopt.
adozione, *n.f.* adoption.
adrenalina, *n.f.* adrenalin.
adulare, *vb.* adulate, flatter, fawn upon.
adulatore, *n.m.* flatterer.
adulazione, *n.f.* adulation, flattery.
adùltera, *n.f.* adulteress.
adulterante, *n. and adj.* adulterant.
adulterare, *vb.* adulterate.
adultèrio, *n.m.* adultery.
adùltero, *n.m.* adulterer.
adulto, *n.* (*m.*) *and adj.* adult, grown-up.
adunata, *n.f.* gathering, meeting.
adunco, *adj.* hooked.
aerare, *vb.* aerate, air.
aerazione, *n.f.* aeration.
àereo, 1. *n.m.* aircraft, airplane. **2.** *adj.* aerial.
aerodinàmico, *adj.* streamlined.
aereolinea, *n.f.* airline.
aeronàutica, *n.f.* aeronautics.
aeroplano, *n.m.* airplane.
aeropòrto, *n.m.* airport.
aeroscalo, *n.m.* airport.
afa, *n.f.* sultriness; mugginess.
affàbile, *adj.* affable.
affabilità, *n.f.* affability.
affabilmente, *adv.* affably.
affaccendato, *adj.* busy.
affamato, *adj.* famished, ravenous.

affare, *n.m.* affair, concern; **bargain, deal;** *(pl.)* business.
affascinante, *adj.* fascinating, glamorous.
affascinare, *vb.* fascinate, allure, captivate, charm.
affaticare, *vb.* fatigue.
afferènte, *adj.* afferent.
affermare, *vb.* affirm, state.
affermativamente, *adv.* affirmatively.
affermativo, *adj.* affirmative.
affermazione, *n.f.* affirmation, statement.
afferrare, *vb.* grasp, grip, seize, catch, snatch.
affettare, *vb.* affect; slice.
affettato, *adj.* affected; finicky, prim.
affettazione, *n.f.* affectation; frill.
affettuosamente, *adv.* affectionately.
affettuoso, *adj.* affectionate.
affezione, *n.f.* affection, attachment.
affibbiare, *vb.* buckle.
affidare, *vb.* entrust.
affiggere, *vb.* post.
affiliare, *vb.* affiliate.
affiliazione, *n.f.* affiliation.
affine, *adj.* related, akin, allied.
affinità, *n.f.* affinity.
affissare, *vb.* affix.
affisso, *n.m.* affix.
affittare, *vb.* lease, let, rent.
affitto, *n.m.* lease, rent.
affliggere, *vb.* afflict, distress.
afflizione, *n.f.* affliction, distress.
affluènte, *n.m.* tributary.
affluire, *vb.* rush.
afflusso, *n.m.* rush.
affollare, *vb.* crowd.
affollarsi, *vb.* come together in crowds, flock.
affondare, *vb.* sink.
affrancare, *vb.* enfranchise.
affrancatura, *n.f.* postage.
affresco, *n.m.* fresco.
affrettare, *vb.* hasten, haste, hurry, quicken, speed.
affrettatamente, *adv.* hastily.
affrettato, *adj.* hasty.
affrontare, *vb.* face, go to meet; affront, insult.

affronto, *n.m.* affront, insult.
affumicare, *vb.* smoke; blacken.
affumicato, *adj.* smoked.
aforisma, *n.m.* aphorism.
afoso, *adj.* sultry; muggy.
Àfrica, *n.f.* Africa.
africano, *n. and adj.* African.
afrodisiaco, *adj.* aphrodisiac.
afta, *n.f.* aphtha, mouth sore.
àgata, *n.f.* agate.
àgave, *n.f.* century plant.
agènda, *n.f.* note-book.
agènte, *n.m.* agent, representative, intermediary; (chemical) agent.
agenta di borsa, *n.m.* stockbroker.
agente di polizia, *n.m. or f.* police officer.
agenzia, *n.f.* agency.
agevolare, *vb.* facilitate, ease.
agèvole, *adj.* easy, comfortable.
agganciare, *vb.* clasp.
aggancio, *n.m.* docking; fastener, clasp.
aggettivo, *n.m.* adjective.
agghiacciare, *vb.* freeze; horrify, petrify.
aggiogare, *vb.* yoke; subjugate.
aggiornamento, *n.m.* adjournment.
aggiornare, *vb.* adjourn; bring up to date.
aggiùngere, *vb.* add.
aggiunto, 1. *n. and adj.* adjunct. **2.** *adj.* added, extra.
aggiustamento, *n.m.* adjustment.
aggiustare, *vb.* adjust.
aggiustatore, *n.m.* adjuster.
aggiustatura, *n.f.* adjustment.
agglutinare, *vb.* agglutinate.
agglutinazione, *n.f.* agglutination.
aggravamento, *n.m.* aggravation.
aggravare, *vb.* aggravate.
aggregare, *vb.* aggregate.
aggregato, *n.m.* aggregate.
aggregazione, *n.f.* aggregation.
aggressione, *n.f.* aggression.
aggressivamente, *adv.* aggressively.
aggressività, *n.f.* aggressiveness.
aggressivo, *adj.* aggressive.

ammezzato, *n.m.* entresol, mezzanine.

ammiccare, *vb.* wink.

amministrare, *vb.* administer, manage.

amministrativo, *adj.* administrative.

amministratore, *n.m.* administrator, executive, manager.

amministrazione, *n.f.* administration, management.

ammiràbile, *adj.* admirable.

ammirabilmente, *adv.* admirably.

ammiràglia, *adj.* **nave a.,** flagship.

ammiragliato, *n.m.* admiralty.

ammiràglio, *n.m.* admiral.

ammirare, *vb.* admire.

ammiratore, *n.m.* admirer.

ammirazione, *n.f.* admiration.

ammirévole, *adj.* admirable.

ammissìbile, *adj.* admissible.

ammissione, *n.f.* admission, admittance.

ammobiliare, *vb.* furnish.

ammollire, *vb.* soften, mollify.

ammoniaca, *n.f.* ammonia.

ammonimento, *n.m.* warning.

ammonire, *vb.* admonish, warn, caution.

ammonizione, *n.f.* admonition.

ammontare, *vb.* amount.

ammonticchiare, *vb.* collect; pile up.

ammorbidire, *vb.* soften; baste.

ammortare, *vb.* pay off, redeem.

ammortire, *vb.* deaden.

ammortizzare, *vb.* amortize.

ammucchiare, *vb.* heap, pile, stack.

ammuffito, *adj.* musty.

ammutinamento, *n.m.* mutiny.

ammutolire, *vb.* be struck dumb; strike dumb, dumbfound; silence.

amnesìa, *n.f.* amnesia.

amniocentèsi, *n.f.* amniocentesis.

amnistìa, *n.f.* amnesty.

amo, *n.m.* hook, bait; deceit.

amorale, *adj.* amoral.

amorazzo, *n.m.* love affair; intrigue.

amore, *n.m.* love.

amorfo, *adj.* amorphous.

amoroso, *adj.* amorous, of love.

ampère, *n.m.* ampere.

ampiamente, *adv.* extensively, diffusely.

ampiezza, *n.f.* breadth.

àmpio, *adj.* ample; extensive; broad, wide.

amplèsso, *n.m.* (sexual) embrace.

ampliamento, *n.m.* widening.

ampliare, *vb.* amplify.

amplificare, *vb.* amplify.

ampollina, *n.f.* cruet.

ampolloso, *adj.* stilted.

amputare, *vb.* amputate.

amputato, 1. *n.m.* amputee. **2.** *adj.* amputated.

amuleto, *n.m.* amulet, talisman.

anabbagliante, *n.m.* dimmed headlight.

anacronismo, *n.m.* anachronism.

anagrafe, *n.f.* registrar's office.

analfabèta, *n. and adj.* illiterate.

analfabetismo, *n.m.* illiteracy.

analgèsico, *n.m.* analgesic.

anàlisi, *n.f.* analysis, test.

analista, *n.m.* analyst.

analìtico, *adj.* analytic.

analizzare, *vb.* analyze.

analogìa, *n.f.* analogy.

anàlogo, *adj.* analogous.

ànanas, *n.m.* pineapple.

anarchìa, *n.f.* anarchy.

anatomìa, *n.f.* anatomy.

anca, *n.f.* haunch, hip.

ancella, *n.f.* handmaid.

anche, *adv.* also, too; even.

anchilòstoma, *n.m.* hookworm.

ància, *n.f.* reed.

ancora, *adv.* still, yet.

àncora, *n.f.* anchor.

ancorare, *vb.* anchor.

ancorràggio, *n.m.* anchorage.

andare, *vb.* go; fare; be (health). **a. bene,** *vb.* fit; become. **a a zonzo,** loaf, loiter, lounge; saunter.

andàrsene, *vb.* go away.

andatura, *n.f.* gait.

andazzo, *n.m.* the way things are going.

anèddoto, *n.m.* anecdote.

anelare, *vb.* pant.

anèllo, *n.m.* ring, link.

anemìa, *n.f.* anemia.

anestesìa, *n.f.* anesthesia.

anestètico, *n.m. and adj.* anesthetic.

anestetista, *n.m.* anesthetist.

anèto, *n.m.* dill.

anfibio, 1. *n.m.* amphibian. **2.** *adj.* amphibious.

anfiteatro, *n.m.* amphitheater.

àngelo, *n.m.* angel.

angolare, *adj.* angular.

àngolo, *n.m.* angle, corner.

angòscia, *n.f.* anguish, heartache.

anguilla, *n.f.* eel.

ànice, *n.m.* anise.

anile, *n.m.* anil, bluing.

anilina, *n.f.* aniline.

ànima, *n.f.* soul.

animale, *n.m. and adj.* animal.

animare, *vb.* animate.

animazione, *n.f.* animation.

ànimo, *n.m.* spirit, animus, mind.

animosità, *n.f.* animosity.

ànitra, *n.f.* duck.

annali, *n.m.* *(pl.)* annals.

annegare, *vb.* drown.

annegato, *n.m.* drowned man.

annerire, *vb.* blacken.

annessione, *n.f.* annexation.

annèsso, *n.m.* annex.

annèttere, *vb.* annex.

annichilire, *vb.* annihilate.

annidarsi, *vb.* nestle.

annientamento, *n.m.* annihilation.

annientare, *vb.* annihilate, destroy.

anniversàrio, *n.m.* anniversary.

anno, *n.m.* year.

annodare, *vb.* tie.

annoiare, *vb.* annoy, bore, harass.

annotare, *vb.* annotate.

annotazione, *n.f.* annotation.

annuale, *n.m. and adj.* annual, yearly.

annualità, *n.f.* annuity.

annullamento, *n.m.* annulment, cancellation, nullification.

annullare, *vb.* annul, cancel, nullify, void.

annunciare, *vb.* announce.

annunciatore, *n.m.* announcer.

annunciatrice, *n.f.* announcer.

annunziare, *vb.* announce.

annunzio, *n.m.* announcement, advertisement.

ànnuo, *adj.* annual.

ànodo, *n.m.* anode.

anomalìa, *n.f.* anomaly.

anòmalo, *adj.* anomalous.

anònimo, *adj.* anonymous.

anormale, *adj.* abnormal.

anormalità, *n.f.* abnormality.

anormalmente, *adv.* abnormally.

ansa, *n.f.* loop.

ansando, *adj.* panting, breathless.

ansante, *adj.* panting, out of breath.

ànsia, *n.f.* anxiety.

ansietà, *n.f.* anxiety, concern, worry.

ansimare, *vb.* pant, be out of breath.

ansioso, *adj.* anxious.

antagonismo, *n.m.* antagonism.

antagonista, *n.m.* antagonist, opponent, villain.

antàrtico, *n.m. and adj.* antarctic

Antàrtide, *n.f.* Antarctica.

antebellico, *adj.* prewar.

antecedente, *adj.* antecedent.

antenato, *n.m.* ancestor, forebear, forefather.

antenna, *n.f.* antenna; (radio) aerial.

anteprima, *n.f.* preview.

anteriore, *adj.* anterior, previous, fore.

antiàcido, *adj.* antacid.

antiaèreo, *adj.* antiaircraft.

anticamente, *adv.* in ancient times, formerly.

anticàmera, *n.f.* anteroom.

anticipare, *vb.* anticipate; advance (payment).

anticipato, *adj.* anticipated, foregone.

anticipazione, *n.f.* anticipation.

antìcipo, *n.m.* advance payment; down payment. **in a.**, beforehand.

anticlericale, *adj.* anticlerical.

antico, *adj.* ancient, antique.

anticoncezionale, *adj. and n.m.* contraceptive, birth control.

anticonformista, *n.m.* nonconformist.

anticòrpo, *n.m.* antibody.

antidoto, *n.m.* antidote.

antìfona, *n.f.* anthem.

antìlope, *n.f.* antelope.

antimònio, *n.m.* antimony.

antinucleare, *n.f.* antinuclear.

antipasto, *n.m.* hors d'oeuvres, appetizer.

antipatìa, *n.f.* antipathy, dislike.
antipàtico, *adj.* disagreeable, nasty.
antiquato, *adj.* antiquated.
antiquità, *n.f.* antiquity.
antisèttico, *n.m. and adj.* antiseptic.
antisociale, *adj.* antisocial.
antitossina, *n.f.* antitoxin.
antologìa, *n.f.* anthology.
antrace, *n.m.* anthrax.
antracite, *n.f.* anthracite.
antropologìa, *n.f.* anthropology.
antropològico, *adj.* anthropological.
anzi, *conj.* on the contrary.
anziano, *n.m.* senior citizen, elder; *adj.* senior, aged.
apatìa, *n.f.* apathy.
apàtico, *adj.* apathetic.
ape, *n.f.* bee.
apèrto, *adj.* open, overt.
apertura, *n.f.* opening, aperture, gap.
apiàrio, *n.m.* apiary.
àpice, *n.m.* apex.
apogèo, *n.m.* apogee, high point, heyday.
apologìa, *n.f.* apology.
apoplessìa, *n.f.* apoplexy.
apoplèttico, *adj.* apoplectic.
apòstata, *n.m.* apostate.
apostòlico, *adj.* apostolic.
apòstolo, *n.m.* apostle.
appaciamento, *n.m.* appeasement.
appannare, *vb.* tarnish.
appannatura, *n.f.* tarnish.
apparato, *n.m.* apparatus.
apparecchiare, *vb.* set the table; dress.
apparècchio, *n.m.* apparatus.
apparènte, *adj.* apparent.
apparènza, *n.f.* appearance, guise.
apparire, *vb.* appear.
appariscente, *adj.* showy, gaudy, ostentatious.
apparizione, *n.f.* apparition.
appartamento, *n.m.* apartment, flat.
appartato, *adj.* secluded; lonely.
appartenènza, *n.f.* belonging, appurtenance.
appartenere, *vb.* belong, pertain.

appassionato, *adj.* passionate.
appassire, *vb.* fade, wilt.
appellante, *n.m.* appellant.
appellare, *vb.* appeal.
appèllo, *n.m.* appeal, call, roll-call.
appena, *adv.* hardly, scarcely, just, barely.
appendectomìa, *n.f.* appendectomy.
appendere, *vb.* hang.
appendiàbiti, *n.m.* hook, peg.
appendice, *n.f.* appendix, appendage.
appendicite, *n.f.* appendicitis.
Appennini, *n.m.pl.* the Apennines.
appesantire, *vb.* weigh down; grow heavy.
appetito, *n.m.* appetite.
appezzamento, *n.m.* lot, plot.
appiattire, *vb.* flatten.
appicccicare, *vb.* stick.
applaudire, *vb.* applaud, cheer, clap.
applàuso, *n.m.* applause, cheer, plaudit.
applicàbile, *adj.* applicable.
applicare, *vb.* apply.
applicazione, *n.f.* application.
appoggiare, *vb.* support, back (up), lean.
appòggio, *n.m.* support, backing; foothold, footing; furtherance.
appollaiarsi, *vb.* roost, perch.
apportare, *vb.* bring, fetch.
apposito, *adj.* appropriate.
apposizione, *n.f.* apposition.
appòsta, *adv.* on purpose, advisedly, deliberately.
apprèndere, *vb.* learn.
apprendista, *n.m.* apprentice.
apprezzàbile, *adj.* appreciable.
apprezzamento, *n.m.* appreciation.
apprezzare, *vb.* appreciate, value, prize.
approfittare, *vb.* profit.
approfondire, *vb.* deepen.
appropriato, *adj.* appropriate.
appropriarsi, *vb.* appropriate.
approssimare, *vb.* approximate.
approssimativamente, *adv.* approximately.
approssimativo, *adj.* approximate.

approssimazione, *n.f.* approximation.

approvare, *vb.* approve.

approvazione, *n.f.* approval, approbation.

appuntamento, *n.m.* appointment, date, engagement, rendezvous, tryst.

aprile, *n.m.* April.

aprire, *vb.* open, unlock.

apriscàtole, *n.m.* can-opener.

àquila, *n.f.* eagle.

aquilino, *adj.* aquiline.

aquilone, *n.m.* kite.

aquilotto, *n.m.* eaglet.

aràbile, *adj.* arable.

àrabo, 1. *n.* Arab. **2.** *adj.* Arabic.

aràchide, *n.f.* peanut.

aragosta, *n.f.* lobster.

aràldica, *n.f.* heraldry.

aràldico, *adj.* heraldic.

araldo, *n.m.* herald.

arància, *n.f.* orange.

aranciata, *n.f.* orangeade; *adj.* orange.

arància, *n.m.* orange tree.

arare, *vb.* plow.

aratro, *n.m.* plow.

arbitrare, *vb.* arbitrate.

arbitràrio, *adj.* arbitrary, high-handed.

arbitrato, *n.m.* arbitration.

àrbitro, *n.m.* arbiter, arbitrator, judge, referee, umpire.

arbòreo, *adj.* arboreal.

arboscello, *n.m.* shrub.

arbusto, *n.m.* shrub.

arca, *n.f.* ark.

arcàico, *adj.* archaic.

arcangelo, *n.m.* archangel.

arcano, *adj.* arcane; supernatural; secret.

archeologìa, *n.f.* archaeology.

archetto, *n.m.* little bow. **gambe ad a.,** bow legs.

architetto, *n.m.* architect.

architettònico, *adj.* architectural.

architettura, *n.f.* architecture.

archiviare, *vb.* file.

archìvio, *n.m.* archives, file.

arcidiòcesi, *n.f.* archdiocese.

arciduca, *n.m.* archduke.

arcière, *n.m.* archer.

arcipèlago, *n.m.* archipelago.

arcivéscovo, *n.m.* archbishop.

arco, *n.m.* arc, arch; bow. **tiro con l'a.,** archery.

arcobaleno, *n.m.* rainbow.

ardènte, *adj.* ardent, burning.

àrdere, *vb.* burn.

ardèsia, *n.f.* slate.

ardimento, *n.m.* boldness.

ardire, *vb.* be bold, dare.

arditamente, *adv.* boldly.

ardito, *adj.* bold.

ardore, *n.m.* ardor.

àrduo, *adj.* arduous, difficult.

àrea, *n.f.* area.

àrem, *n.m.* harem.

arena, *n.f.* sand, arena.

arenària, *n.f.* sandstone.

arenarsi, *vb.* get stranded.

arenile, *n.m.* sandy beach, strand; sand pit.

argano, *n.m.* winch.

argènteo, *adj.* silver.

argenterìa, *n.f.* silverware.

Argentina, *n.f.* Argentine.

argentino, *adj.* silvery; Argentine.

argènto, *n.m.* silver.

argilla, *n.f.* clay.

argilloso, *adj.* clayey.

arginare, *vb.* embank, dam, stem.

àrgine, *n.m.* embankment.

argomento, *n.m.* argument, topic.

arguire, *vb.* argue; deduce, conclude.

ària, *n.f.* air, (music) aria.

àrido, *adj.* arid.

aringa, *n.f.* herring.

arioso, *adj.* airy.

aristòcrate, *n.m.* aristocrat.

aristocràtico, *adj.* aristocratic.

aristocrazia, *n.f.* aristocracy.

aritmètica, *n.f.* arithmetic.

Arlecchino, *n.m.* Harlequin.

arma, *n.f.* arm (weapon). **a. da fuòco,** firearm.

armàdio, *n.m.* clothes-closet.

armamento, *n.m.* armament.

arma nucleare, *n.f.* nuclear weapon.

armare, *vb.* arm.

armatore, *n.m.* shipowner.

armatura, *f.* armor.

armerìa, *n.f.* armory.

armistìzio, *n.m.* armistice.

armonia, *n.f.* harmony.

armònica, *n.f.* harmonica.

armònico, *adj.* harmonic.

armonioso, *adj.* harmonious, dulcet.

armonizzare, *vb.* harmonize.

arnese, *n.m.* tool, implement, instrument.

àrnica, *n.f.* arnica.

aròma, *n.m.* aroma.

aromàtico, *adj.* aromatic.

arpa, *n.f.* harp.

arpìa, *n.f.* harpy.

arpione, *n.m.* harpoon.

arrabbiarsi, *vb.* get angry.

arrabbiato, *adj.* angry.

arraffare, *vb.* grab.

arrampicarsi, *vb.* climb, creep, clamber up, scramble up.

arrampicatore, *n.m.* climber.

arrangiare, *vb.* arrange, settle.

arrecare, *vb.* cause; bring.

arredamento, *n.m.* furnishing; interior decoration.

arredare, *vb.* furnish; decorate, arrange.

arrèndersi, *vb.* surrender.

arrestare, *vb.* arrest, apprehend; (*refl.*) stall.

arrèsto, *n.m.* arrest.

arretrato, *adj.* out-of-date.

arricchire, *vb.* enrich.

arricciare, *vb.* curl.

arringa, *n.f.* harangue.

arringare, *vb.* harangue.

arrischiare, *vb.* risk.

arrivare, *vb.* arrive.

arrivista, *n.m. or f.* social climber.

arrivo, *n.m.* arrival.

arrogante, *adj.* arrogant.

arroganza, *n.f.* arrogance.

arrogarsi, *vb.* arrogate, assume.

arrossire, *vb.* blush.

arrostire, *vb.* roast.

arròsto, *n.m.* roast.

arrotolare, *vb.* roll up, coil.

arruffare, *vb.* ruffle, bristle.

arrugginire, *vb.* rust.

arrugginito, *adj.* rusty.

arruolare, *vb.* enroll; levy.

arsenale, *n.m.* arsenal; dockyard, navy yard.

arsènico, *n.m.* arsenic.

arte, *n.f.* art, trade, craft, craftsmanship, guild.

artèria, *n.f.* artery.

arteriale, *adj.* arterial.

arterioscleròsi, *n.f.* arteriosclerosis.

artesiano, *adj.* artesian.

àrtico, *adj.* Arctic.

articolare, *vb.* articulate.

articolato, *adj.* articulate.

articolazione, *n.f.* articulation; joint.

artìcolo, *n.m.* article, item. **a. di fondo,** editorial.

artificiale, *adj.* artificial.

artificialità, *n.f.* artificiality.

artifìcio, *n.m.* artifice.

artigiano, *n.m.* artisan, craftsman.

artiglière, *n.m.* gunner.

artiglierìa, *n.f.* artillery.

artìglio, *n.m.* talon, claw.

artista, *n.m. or f.* artist.

artìstico, *adj.* artistic.

arto, *n.m.* limb.

artrite, *n.f.* arthritis.

artrosi, *n.f.* osteoarthritis.

arzigogolare, *vb.* daydream, fancy.

arzillo, *adj.* spry.

asbèsto, *n.m.* asbestos.

ascèlla, *n.f.* armpit.

ascendente, *n.m.* ascendancy (over); rising; influence.

ascensionale, *adj.* upward, ascensional.

Ascensione, *n.f.* (*eccles.*) Ascension, Assumption.

ascensore, *n.m.* elevator, lift.

ascèsso, *n.m.* abscess.

ascètico, *n.m. and adj.* ascetic.

àscia, *n.f.* axe.

asciugamani, *n.m.* handtowel.

asciugapiatti, *n.m.* dishtowel.

asciugare, *vb.* dry, blot, wipe.

asciutto, *adj.* dry.

ascoltare, *vb.* listen to, hearken to, hark.

ascrivere, *vb.* ascribe.

asfalto, *n.m.* asphalt.

asfissìa, *n.f.* asphyxia.

asfissiare, *vb.* asphyxiate, smother.

Asia, *n.f.* Asia.

asiàtico, *adj.* Asian.

asimmetrìa, *n.f.* asymmetry.

àsino, *n.m.* ass, donkey.

asma, *n.m.* asthma. **a. del fièno,** hay fever.

asmàtico, *adj.* asthmatic.
aspàrago, *n.m.* asparagus.
asperità, *n.f.* asperity.
aspettare, *vb.* await, wait (for); *(refl.)* expect.
aspettativa, *n.f.* expectation, expectancy.
aspètto, *n.m.* aspect, appearance, look; meaning.
aspirante, *n.m.* aspirant.
aspirare, *vb.* aspire, aspirate.
aspiratore, *n.m.* aspirator.
aspirazione, *n.f.* aspiration, suction.
aspirina, *n.f.* aspirin.
asportare, *vb.* remove.
asprezza, *n.f.* harshness.
aspro, *adj.* harsh.
assaggiare, *vb.* test, try, assay, sample.
assaggio, *n.m.* taste, sample, small quantity.
assai, *adv.* a lot, much.
assalire, *vb.* assail, attack, beset.
assalitore, *n.m.* assailant, attacker.
assaltare, *vb.* assault.
assalto, *n.m.* assault, bout, round.
assaporare, *vb.* savor, enjoy.
assassinare, *vb.* assassinate.
assassinio, *n.m.* assassination, murder.
assassino, *n.m.* assassin, murderer.
asse, 1. *n.m.* axis, axle. **2.** *n.f.* board, plank.
asse a rotelle, *n.m.* skateboard.
assecondare, *vb.* go along with; agree with, favor.
assediante, *n.m.* besieger.
assediare, *vb.* besiege, beset.
assèdio, *n.m.* siege.
assegnàbile, *adj.* assignable.
assegnamento, *n.m.* assignment.
assegnare, *vb.* assign, allot, allocate.
assegnazione, *n.f.* assignment, allotment.
assegno, *n.m.* check; allowance.
assegno (per) viaggiatori, *n.m.* traveler's check.
assemblaggio, *n.m.* assembly.
assemblèa, *n.f.* assembly, gathering, meeting.

assembramento, *n.m.* gathering, crowd.
assennato, *adj.* sensible.
assènso, *n.m.* assent.
assente, 1. *n.* absentee. **2.** *adj.* absent.
assenteismo, *n.m.* absenteeism; indifference.
assentire, *vb.* assent.
assenza, *n.f.* absence.
assènzio, *n.m.* absinthe.
asserire, *vb.* assert.
asservire, *vb.* enslave.
asserzione, *n.f.* assertion.
assessore, *n.m.* assessor.
assetato, *adj.* thirsty; eager.
assetto, *n.m.* good order; trim.
asseverare, *vb.* asseverate.
asseverazione, *n.f.* asseveration.
assicurare, *vb.* assure, insure.
assicurazione, *n.f.* assurance, insurance.
assiduamente, *adv.* assiduously.
assìduo, *adj.* assiduous.
assimilare, *vb.* assimilate.
assimilativo, *adj.* assimilative.
assimilazione, *n.f.* assimilation.
assìoma, *n.m.* axiom.
assistènte, *n. and adj.* assistant.
assistente mèdico, *n.m.* paramedic.
assistènza, *n.f.* attendance, assistance, relief. **a. sociale,** social work.
assìstere, *vb.* be present.
asso, *n.m.* ace.
associare, *vb.* associate, affiliate.
associazione, *n.f.* association, affiliation.
assoggettare, *vb.* subject.
assòlo, *n.m.* solo.
assolutamente, *adv.* absolutely.
assolutezza, *n.f.* absoluteness.
assolutismo, *n.m.* absolutism.
assoluto, *adj.* absolute, complete, total.
assoluzione, *n.f.* absolution, acquittal.
assòlvere, *vb.* absolve, acquit.
assomiglianza, *n.f.* likeness.
assomigliare, *vb.* resemble, look like.
assonanza, *n.f.* assonance.
assonnato, *adj.* sleepy, drowsy.
assopirsi, *vb.* drowse.

assorbènte, 1. *n.m.* absorbent. **2.** *adj.* absorbent, absorbing.

assorbimento, *n.m.* absorption.

assorbire, *vb.* absorb.

assorbito, *adj.* absorbed.

assordare, *vb.* deafen.

assortimento, *n.m.* assortment.

assortire, *vb.* assort, sort.

assortito, *adj.* assorted.

assorto, *adj.* absorbed.

assottigliare, *vb.* reduce, make thin.

assuefare, *vb.* get used to, addict; inure.

assuefazione, *n.f.* addiction.

assùmere, *vb.* assume, take on.

assunzione, *n.f.* employment; assumption.

assurdamente, *adv.* absurdly.

assurdità, *n.f.* absurdity, nonsense.

assurdo, 1. *n.m.* absurdity. **2.** *adj.* absurd, preposterous.

astèmio, *adj.* abstemious.

astenersi, *vb.* abstain, refrain.

asterisco, *n.m.* asterisk.

asteròide, *n.m.* asteroid.

astigmatismo, *n.m.* astigmatism.

astinènza, *n.f.* abstinence.

àstio, *n.m.* grudge.

astrale, *adj.* astral, of the stars.

astrarre, *vb.* abstract.

astratto, *adj.* abstract, abstracted.

astrazione, *n.f.* abstraction.

astringènte, *adj.* astringent.

astro, *n.m.* star, aster.

astrofisica, *n.f.* astrophysics.

astrologia, *n.f.* astrology.

astronauta, *n.m.* astronaut.

astronave, *n.f.* spaceship.

astronomìa, *n.f.* astronomy.

astruso, *adj.* abstruse.

astuccio, *n.m.* case.

astuto, *adj.* astute, artful, clever, canny, cunning, designing.

astùzia, *n.f.* guile.

atassia, *n.f.* ataxia.

atelier, *n.m.* workshop; studio; fashion house.

ateneo, *n.m.* university.

àteo, 1. *n.m.* atheist. **2.** *adj.* atheistic, godless.

atìpico, *adj.* atypical.

atlante, *n.m.* atlas.

atlàntico, *adj.* Atlantic.

atlèta, *n.m.* athlete.

atlètico, *adj.* athletic.

atletismo, *n.m.* athletics.

atmosfèra, *n.f.* atmosphere.

atmosfèrico, *adj.* atmospheric.

atòllo, *n.m.* atoll.

atòmico, *adj.* atomic.

àtomo, *n.m.* atom.

atonale, *adj.* atonal.

atroce, *adj.* atrocious, heinous.

atrocemente, *adv.* atrociously, dreadfully.

atrocità, *n.f.* atrocity.

atrofìa, *n.f.* atrophy.

atropina, *n.f.* atropine.

attaccàbile, *adj.* assailable.

attaccamento, *n.m.* attachment.

attaccapanni, *n.m.* coathanger.

attaccare, *vb.* attach, fasten, hitch, tack, stick; attack, assail.

attaccatìccio, *adj.* sticky.

attacco, *n.m.* attack, onslaught.

atteggiamento, *n.m.* attitude.

atteggiarsi, *vb.* take an attitude.

attentamente, *adv.* attentively, carefully.

attènto, *adj.* attentive, careful, thoughtful.

attenuare, *vb.* attenuate.

attenzione, *n.f.* attention, carefulness, notice.

atterràggio, *n.m.* landing. **pista d'a.,** landing strip, runway.

atterrare, *vb.* land.

atterrire, *vb.* terrify.

attesa, *n.f.* wait. **in a. di,** while waiting for, pending.

attestare, *vb.* attest, vouch for.

àttimo, *n.m.* instant.

attìnio, *n.m.* actinium.

attirare, *vb.* attract, entice, lure, decoy.

attitùdine, *n.f.* apitude.

attivamente, *adv.* actively, busily.

attivare, *vb.* activate.

attivatore, *n.m.* activator.

attivazione, *n.f.* activation.

attivismo, *n.m.* activism.

attività, *n.f.* activity.

attivo, 1. *n.m.* asset. **2.** *adj.* active, busy.

attizzare, *vb.* stir, poke.

atto, 1. *n.m.* act, deed. **2.** *adj.* apt, fitted.

attore, *n.m.* actor; plaintiff.

attorno, *adv.* about, around.

attraènte, *adj.* attractive, engaging, fetching.

attrarre, *vb.* attract.

attraversare, *vb.* cross, go through, pass through.

attravèrso, *adv. and prep.* across, through.

attrazione, *n.f.* attraction.

attrezzare, *vb.* rig.

attrezzatura, *n.f.* rig.

attrezzista, *n.m.* gymnast.

attrezzo, *n.m.* tool, implement.

attribuìbile, *adj.* attributable.

attribuire, *vb.* attribute.

attribuzione, *n.f.* attribution.

attrice, *n.f.* actress.

attrizione, *n.f.* attrition.

attualità, *n.f.* reality, current significance; *(pl.)* newsreel.

attuare, *vb.* actuate.

attuàrio, *n.m.* actuary.

attutire, *vb.* silence.

audace, *adj.* audacious, bold, daring.

audàcia, *n.f.* audacity, boldness, daring.

audiovisivo, *adj.* audiovisual.

auditòrio, *n.m.* auditorium.

audizione, *n.f.* audition.

augurare, *vb.* augur; wish.

augùrio, *n.m.* greeting.

àula, *n.f.* hall; classroom.

aumentare, *vb.* augment, increase, raise, enhance; escalate.

aumènto, *n.m.* increase, raise, rise.

àureo, *n.m.* golden.

aurèola, *n.f.* halo.

auricolare, *adj.* auricular.

aurìfero, *adj.* gold-bearing.

auriga, *n.m.* charioteer.

aurora, *n.f.* dawn.

ausiliare, *n.m. and adj.* auxiliary.

auspìcio, *n.m.* auspice.

austerità, *n.f.* austerity.

austèro, *adj.* austere, severe; unadorned.

Austria, *n.f.* Austria.

austrìaco, *adj.* Austrian.

aut-aut, *conj.* yes or no; *n.m.* dilemma.

autenticare, *vb.* authenticate.

autenticità, *n.f.* authenticity.

autèntico, *adj.* authentic.

autista, *n.m.* chauffeur, (auto) driver.

àuto, *n.f.* auto.

autobiografìa, *n.f.* autobiography.

àutobus, *n.m.* bus.

autocarro, *n.m.* truck, lorry.

autoclave, *n.f.* sterilizer.

autòcrate, *n.m.* autocrat.

autocrazìa, *n.f.* autocracy.

autògrafo, *n.m.* autograph.

autolìnea, *n.f.* bus line.

autòma, *n.m.* automaton, robot.

automaticamente, *adv.* automatically.

automàtico, *adj.* automatic.

automòbile, *n.f.* automobile.

automobilista, *n.m.* motorist.

automobilìstico, *adj.* pertaining to automobiles, automotive.

automotrice, *n.f.* railcar.

autonoléggio, *n.m.* car rental.

autonomìa, *n.f.* autonomy.

autònomo, *adj.* autonomous.

autoparchéggio, *n.m.* parking area.

autopsìa, *n.f.* autopsy.

autoradio, *n.f.* car radio.

autore, *n.m.* author.

autorévole, *adj.* authoritative.

autorevolmente, *adv.* authoritatively.

autorimessa, *n.f.* garage.

autorità, *n.f.* authority.

autoritàrio, *adj.* authoritarian.

autoritratto, *n.m.* self-portrait.

autorizzare, *vb.* authorize, empower, entitle.

autorizzazione, *n.f.* authorization.

autosalone, *n.m.* car showroom, car dealer.

autostop, *n.m.* hitchhiking.

autotreno, *n.m.* trailer truck.

autunno, *n.m.* autumn, fall.

avambràccio, *n.m.* forearm.

avampòsto, *n.m.* outpost.

avana, *adj.* brown, beige.

avanguàrdia, *n.f.* vanguard.

avanti, 1. *adv.* in front, ahead, onward, forward, before; (clock) fast. **2.** *prep.* before, in front of. **3.** *interj.* come in!

avanzamento, *n.m.* advancement.

avanzare, *vb.* advance; be left over.

avanzato, *adj.* advanced.

avanzo, *n.m.* relic, left-over, surplus.

avaria, *n.f.* damage.

avariare, *vb.* damage.

avarizia, *n.f.* avarice.

avaro, 1. *n.m.* miser. 2. *adj.* avaricious, miserly, grasping, stingy.

avemmarìa, *n.f.* Hail Mary.

avena, *n.f.* oats.

avere, *vb.* have.

aviàrio, *n.m.* aviary.

aviatore, *n.m.* aviator, flier.

aviatrice, *n.f.* aviatrix.

aviazione, *n.f.* aviation.

àvido, *adj.* avid, greedy.

aviogètto, *n.m.* jet plane.

aviolìnea, *n.f.* airline.

aviorimessa, *n.f.* hangar.

aviotrasportato, *adj.* airborne.

avòrio, *n.m.* ivory.

avornièllo, *n.m.* laburnum.

avvelenare, *vb.* poison.

avvenimento, *n.m.* event, happening, occurrence.

avvenire, *vb.* future, futurity.

avventato, *adj.* reckless.

avventizio, *adj.* adventitious.

avvènto, *n.m.* advent.

avventore, *n.m.* regular customer.

avventura, *n.f.* adventure.

avventurare, *vb.* adventure; risk.

avventurière, *n.m.* adventurer.

avventurosamente, *adv.* adventurously.

avventuroso, *adj.* adventurous, enterprising, venturesome.

avverare, *vb.* realize, fulfil; verify; become true.

avverbiale, *adj.* adverbial.

avvèrbio, *n.m.* adverb.

avversare, *vb.* oppose.

avversàrio, *n.* adversary.

avversione, *n.f.* aversion.

avversità, *n.f.* adversity, hardship.

avvèrso, *adj.* adverse; averse.

avvertenza, *n.f.* warning.

avvertire, *vb.* warn, alert, advert.

avviare, *vb.* start, begin.

avvicinarsi a, *vb.* approach.

avvilimento, *n.m.* abasement.

avvilire, *vb.* abase, debase.

avviluppare, *vb.* envelop.

avvincente, *adj.* charming, engaging.

avvio, *n.m.* start, beginning.

avvisare, *vb.* inform, advise.

avviso, *n.m.* advice; news, information, notice, notification; warning.

avvitare, *vb.* screw.

avvizzire, *vb.* wither.

avvocato, *n.m. or f.* advocate, lawyer.

avvòlgere, *vb.* wrap up, enfold, wind.

ayatolla(h), *n.m.* ayatollah.

aziènda, *n.f.* firm, concern.

azione, *n.f.* action; share (of stock).

azionista, *n.m.* stockholder.

azzittire, *vb.* shut someone up.

azzuffarsi, *vb.* get into a scrap.

azzurro, *adj.* blue, azure.

B

babau, *n.m.* ogre, bogeyman.

babbeo, *n.m.* fool, idiot.

babbo, *n.m.* dad, daddy, pop, pa.

babbuino, *n.m.* baboon.

bacca, *n.f.* berry.

baccano, *n.m.* uproar, racket, row.

baccèllo, *n.m.* pod, shell.

bacchetta, *n.f.* wand, (conductor's) baton.

baciare, *vb.* kiss.

bacillo, *n.m.* bacillus.

bacino, *n.m.* basin, dock. **b. di carenaggio**, dry dock.

bàcio, *n.m.* kiss.

baco, *n.m.* worm. **b. da seta**, silkworm.

bada, *n.* a **b.**, at bay.

badare, *vb.* heed, look out, mind.

badessa, *n.f.* abbess.

badìa, *n.f.* abbey.

badile, *n.m.* shovel.

baffo, *n.m.* mustache.

bagagliaio, *n.m.* trunk.

bagàglio, *n.m.* baggage, luggage.

bagarinaggio, *n.m.* scalping.

bagliore, *n.m.* glare.

bagnante, *n.m. or f.* bather.

bagnare, *vb.* bathe, soak.

bagnino, *n.m.* bath attendant, life-guard.

bagno, *n.m.* bath.

bàia, *n.f.* bay.

baio, *adj.* bay (color).

baionetta, *n.f.* bayonet.

balaùstra, *n.f.* balustrade.

balaustrata, *n.f.* balustrade.

balbettare, *vb.* babble, stammer.

balbettìo, *n.m.* babble.

balbuziènte, *n.m.* stammerer, stutterer, babbler.

balcone, *n.m.* balcony.

baldacchino, *n.m.* canopy.

baldòria, *n.f.* carousing, revelry, spree.

balena, *n.f.* whale.

balenare, *vb.* flash.

baleno, *n.m.* flash.

bàlia, *n.f.* nurse.

balìstica, *n.f.* ballistics.

balla, *n.f.* bale.

ballàbile, *n.m.* dance tune.

ballare, *vb.* dance.

ballata, *n.f.* ballad, ballade.

ballatòio, *n.* catwalk.

ballerina, *n.f.* dancer, ballerina.

ballerino, *n.m.* dancer.

ballo, *n.m.* dance, dancing; ballet; ball.

balneare, *adj.* pertaining to baths or bathing.

balsàmico, *adj.* balmy, balsamous.

bàlsamo, *n.m.* balsam, balm.

baluardo, *n.m.* bulwark.

balzare, *vb.* bound, leap, dart.

balzo, *n.m.* bound, leap, dart.

bambina, *n.f.* child, little girl.

bambinaia, *n.f.* nurse.

bambinesco, *adj.* childish, baby-ish.

bambino, *n.m.* child, little boy.

bàmbola, *n.f.* doll.

bambù, *n.m.* bamboo.

banale, *adj.* banal, commonplace, hackneyed.

banalità, *n.f.* banality, platitude.

banana, *n.f.* banana.

banca, *n.f.* bank.

bancàrio, *adj.* pertaining to banks.

bancarotta, *n.f.* bankruptcy.

banchetto, *n.m.* banquet, feast.

banchière, *n.m.* banker.

banchina, *n.f.* pier.

banchisa, *n.f.* ice pack.

banco, *n.m.* bench; counter; desk; stall; bank.

banconota, *n.f.* bank note.

banda, *n.f.* band, gang; fillet.

bandièra, *n.f.* banner, flag, ensign.

bandire, *vb.* banish, exile.

bandista, *n.m.* bandsman.

bandito, *n.m.* bandit, outlaw.

banditore, *n.m.* crier, auctioneer.

bando, *n.m.* banishment, exile.

bar, *n.m.* bar, coffee shop, cafe.

bara, *n.f.* coffin.

baracca, *n.f.* hut; barrack.

baraonda, *n.f.* chaos.

barare, *vb.* cheat.

baratro, *n.m.* abyss.

barattare, *vb.* barter, swap.

baratto, *n.m.* barter, swap.

barba, *n.f.* beard.

barbabiètola, *n.f.* beet.

barbàrie, *n.f.* barbarism.

barbarismo, *n.m.* barbarism.

bàrbaro, 1. *n.m.* barbarian. **2.** *adj.* barbarous.

barbetta, *n.f.* little beard, goatee.

barbière, *n.m.* barber.

barbitùrico, *n.m.* barbiturate.

barbuto, *adj.* bearded.

barca, *n.f.* boat. **b. a remi,** row-boat.

barcollare, *vb.* stagger, totter.

bardare, *vb.* caparison, harness.

bardatura, *n.f.* caparison; har-ness.

barèlla, *n.f.* litter, stretcher.

barile, *n.m.* barrel, cask.

bariletto, *n.m.* keg.

bàrio, *n.m.* barium.

barista, *n.m.* bartender.

baritono, *n.m.* baritone.

barlume, *n.m.* glimmer, gleam.

baro, *n.m.* cardsharp.

baròcco, *adj.* baroque.

baromètrico, *adj.* barometric.

baròmetro, *n.m.* barometer.

baronale, *adj.* baronial.

barone, *n.m.* baron.

baronessa, *n.f.* baroness.

barricare, *vb.* barricade.

barricata, *n.f.* barricade.

barrièra, *n.f.* barrier.

barzelletta, *n.f.* joke.

basare, *vb.* base, ground.

base, *n.f.* base, basis, footing, ground.

basetta, *n.f.* whisker.

basilare, *adj.* fundamental; basilar.

Basilèa, *n.f.* Basel.

basìlico, *n.m.* basil.

bassezza, *n.f.* baseness.

basso, 1. *n.m.* bass. **2.** *adj.* low, vile, base; bass.

bassofondo, *n.m.* slum.

bastardo, *n.m. and adj.* bastard, mongrel.

bastare, *vb.* suffict, be enough.

bastione, *n.m.* rampart.

bastonare, *vb.* club.

bastone, *n.m.* baton, stick, club, staff, rod, bat, cane.

battàglia, *n.f.* battle.

battaglièro, *adj.* bellicose, warlike, combative.

battàglio, *n.m.* clapper.

battaglione, *n.m.* battalion.

battèllo, *n.m.* boat.

battente, *vb.* shutter.

bàttere, *vb.* beat, batter, hit, shoot?

batterìa, *n.f.* battery.

battèrio, *n.m.* bacterium. **battèri,** *pl.* bacteria.

batteriologìa, *n.f.* bacteriology.

batterìologo, *n.m.* bacteriologist.

battesimale, *adj.* baptismal.

battésimo, *n.m.* baptism, christening.

battezzare, *vb.* baptize, christen.

battibecco, *n.m.* squabble.

battìpalo, *n.m.* ram.

battista, *n.m.* Baptist.

battistèro, *n.m.* baptistery.

bàttito, *n.m.* beat.

battuto, *adj.* beaten.

batùffolo, *n.m.* wad.

baùle, *n.m.* trunk.

bauxite, *n.f.* bauxite.

bauva, *n.f.* drivel.

bazzicare, *vb.* hang around.

bavaglino, *n.m.* bib.

bavaglio, *n.m.* gag.

bazàr, *n.m.* bazaar.

bazzècola, *n.f.* trifle.

beatamente, *adv.* blissfully.

beatificare, *vb.* beatify.

beatitùdine, *n.f.* bliss, beatitude.

beato, *adj.* blissful, blessed.

beccare, *vb.* peck.

becco, *n.m.* beak, bill; burner; spout.

Befana, *n.f.* old woman who brings presents on Twelfth Night.

bèffa, *n.f.* gibe.

beffarsi di, *vb.* gibe at, jeer at, mock.

bèlga, *adj.* Belgian.

Bèlgio, *n.m.* Belgium.

bella, *n.f.* beauty; sweetheart; final draft; (sports) final game.

belletto, *n.m.* make-up.

bellezza, *n.f.* beauty. **salone di b.,** beauty parlor.

bèllico, *adj.* military, relating to war.

bellicosamente, *adv.* belligerently.

bellicoso, *adj.* bellicose, belligerent.

belligerante, *adj.* belligerent.

belligeranza, *n.f.* belligerence.

bellimbusto, *n.m.* dandy.

bellino, *adj.* cunning, cute, pretty, good-looking.

bèllo, *adj.* beautiful, fine, fair, handsome, lovely.

bellumore, *n.m.* way, wit.

belva, *n.f.* wild beast; (fig.) brute.

belvedere, *n.m.* observation post, lookout.

benchè, *conj.* although.

benda, *n.f.* bandage; blindfold; headband.

bendare, *vb.* blindfold.

bène, 1. *n.m.* good, asset. **b. mobile,** chattel. **2.** *adv.* well.

benedettino, *n.m. and adj.,* Benedictine.

benedetto, *adj.* blessed.

benedire, *vb.* bless.

benedizione, *n.f.* benediction, blessing.

benefattore, *n.m.* benefactor.

benefattrice, *n.f.* benefactress.

beneficare, *vb.* benefit.

beneficenza, *n.f.* charity.

beneficiàrio, *n.m.* beneficiary.

beneficio, *n.m.* benefit, advantage, profit.

benéfico, *adj.* beneficent.

benèssere, *n.m.* welfare.

benevolènza, *n.f.* benevolence.

benevolmente, *adv.* benevolently.

benèvolo, *adj.* benevolent, kindly.

bèni, *n.m.pl.* goods, estate.

benignità, *n.f.* benignity.

benigno, *adj.* benign.

benvenuto, *adj.* welcome.

benzina, *n.f.* benzine, gasoline.

bere, *vb.* drink.

beri-bèri, *n.m.* beriberi.

Berna, *n.f.* Bern.

berretto, *n.m.* cap.

bersàglio, *n.m.* target.

bestémmia, *n.f.* blasphemy, curse-word, expletive, oath.

bestemmiare, *vb.* blaspheme, curse, swear.

bestemmiatore, *n.m.* blasphemer.

bèstia, *n.f.* beast.

bestiale, *adj.* bestial, beastly.

bestiame, *n.m.* cattle; animals, livestock.

bèttola, *n.f.* (low-class) wineshop.

betulla, *n.f.* birch.

bevanda, *n.f.* beverage, drink.

bevìbile, *adj.* drinkable.

bevitore, *n.m.* drinker.

biada, *n.f.* fodder, forage.

biancherìa, *n.f.* linen, laundry.

bianco, *adj.* white, blank.

biancospino, *n.m.* hawthorn.

biascicare, *vb.* mumble, utter indistinctly; ramble.

biasimare, *vb.* blame.

biàsimo, *n.* blame.

Bibbia, *n.f.* Bible.

biberon, *n.m.* baby bottle.

bìbita, *n.f.* drink.

bìblico, *adj.* Biblical.

bibliografìa, *n.f.* bibliography.

bibliotèca, *n.f.* library.

bibliotecàrio, *n.m.* librarian.

bicarbonato, *n.m.* bicarbonate.

bicchière, *n.m.* glass.

bicentennale, *adj.* bicentennial.

bicicletta, *n.f.* bicycle.

bicìpite, *n.m.* biceps.

bidèllo, *n.m.* janitor.

bidone, *n.m.* large can.

biennale, *adj.* biennial; biannual.

biènnio, *n.m.* two-year period.

bietta, *n.f.* wedge, cleat.

bifocale, *adj.* bifocal.

biforcazione, *n.f.* crotch; junction.

bigamìa, *n.f.* bigamy.

bìgamo, 1. *n.* bigamist. **2.** *adj.* bigamous.

bighellone, *n.m.* gadabout, loafer.

bigliettàrio, *n.m.* ticket agent; (tram, bus) conductor.

biglietto, *n.m.* note; (money) bill; card; ticket. **b. di visita,** calling card.

bigotterìa, *n.f.* bigotry.

bigottismo, *n.m.* bigotry.

bigòtto, 1. *n.* bigot. **2.** *adj.* bigoted.

bilància, *n.f.* balance, scales.

bilanciare, *vb.* balance.

bilaterale, *adj.* bilateral.

bile, *n.f.* bile.

biliardo, *n.m.* billiards.

biliare, *adj.* bilious.

bilingue, *adj.* bilingual.

bilioso, *adj.* bilious.

bimbo, *n.m.* child, baby.

bimensile, *adj.* bimonthly (twice a month).

bimestrale, *adj.* bimonthly (every two months).

bimèstre, *n.m.* two months' period.

bimetàllico, *adj.* bimetallic.

binàrio, 1. *n.m.* track. **2.** *adj.* binary.

binda, *n.f.* jack.

binòcolo, *n.m.* binoculars, spyglasses. **b. da teatro,** opera-glasses.

binoculare, *adj.* binocular.

binòmio, *n.m.* binomial.

biochìmica, *n.f.* biochemistry.

biodegradàbile, *adj.* biodegradable.

biografìa, *n.f.* biography.

biogràfico, *adj.* biographical.

biògrafo, *n.m.* biographer.

biologìa, *n.f.* biology.

biologicamente, *adv.* biologically.

biològico, *adj.* biological.

biondo, *adj.* blond(e), fair.

biopsìa, *n.f.* biopsy.

biòssido, *n.m.* dioxide.

bipartitismo, *n.m.* two-party system.

bipede, *n.m. and adj.* biped.

biplano, *n.m.* biplane.

bipolare, *adj.* bipolar.

biposto, *n.m.* two-seater.

birba, *n.f.* rascal, scoundrel.

birbone, *n.m.* naughty boy, trickster.

birichinata, *n.f.* prank.

birichino, *adj.* naughty.

birra, *n.f.* ale, beer.

birraio, *n.m.* brewer.

bisbigliare, *vb.* whisper.

bisbiglio, *n.m.* whisper.

biscòtto, *n.m.* cracker, biscuit, cookie.

bisecare, *vb.* bisect.

bisestile, *adj.* **anno b.,** leap year.

bisettimanale, *adj.* twice weekly, biweekly.

bismuto, *n.m.* bismuth.

bisnònno, *n.m.* great-grandfather.

bisognare, *vb.* be necessary.

bisogno, *n.m.* need, want.

bisognoso, *adj.* needy.

bisonte, *n.m.* bison.

bistecca, *n.f.* beefsteak, steak.

bisticciarsi, *vb.* quarrel, argue, bicker.

bisticcio, *n.m.* quarrel, argument; pun.

bistrattare, *vb.* mistreat.

bivacco, *n.m.* bivouac.

bivio, *n.m.* (road) fork, junction.

bizzèffe, *n.f.pl.* **a b.,** galore.

blandire, *vb.* blandish, coax.

blando, *adj.* bland; suave.

blatta, *n.f.* cockroach.

bleso, *adj.* lisping.

blindato, *adj.* armored. **carro b.,** tank.

bloccare, *vb.* blockade.

blòcco, *n.m.* bloc; block; blockade.

blu, *adj.* blue.

blue jeans, *n.m.pl.* blue jeans.

bluff, *n.m.* bluff (at cards, etc.).

bluffare, *vb.* bluff (at cards, etc.).

bluffatore, *n.m.* bluffer.

blusa, *n.f.* blouse.

bòa, *n.f.* buoy.

bobina, *n.f.* bobbin, reel, spool; coil.

bocca, *n.f.* mouth. **a b. aperta,** open-mouthed, agape.

boccapòrto, *n.m.* hatch, hatchway.

boccheggiamento, *n.m.* gasp.

boccheggiare, *vb.* gasp.

bòccia, *n.f.* bowl.

bocciare, *vb.* fail, flunk.

boccone, *n.m.* morsel, swallow.

boemo, *n.m. and adj.* Bohemian.

boia, *n.m.* executioner.

boicottàggio, *n.m.* boycott.

boicottare, *vb.* boycott.

boliviano, *adj.* Bolivian.

bolla, *n.f.* bubble.

bollare, *vb.* stamp.

bollettino, *n.m.* bulletin.

bollire, *vb.* boil.

bollo, *n.m.* stamp.

bòlo, *n.m.* cud.

bomba, *n.f.* bomb; bombshell. **b. atòmica,** atom bomb. **b. al neutrone,** neutron bomb.

bombardamento, *n.m.* bombardment.

bombardare, *vb.* bombard, shell.

bombardière, *n.m.* bomber, bombardier.

bomboletta nebulizzante, *n.f.* aerosol bomb.

bonifica, *n.f.* reclamation.

bonificare, *vb.* reclaim.

bontà, *n.f.* goodness.

borbottamento, *n.m.* mumbling, gibberish.

borbottare, *vb.* mutter.

bordata, *n.f.* broadside.

bordèllo, *n.m.* brothel.

bordo, *n.m.* board (side of ship); edge, brink, rim. **a b. di,** *prep.* aboard, on board (of).

borghese, *adj.* bourgeois, middleclass.

borghesìa, *n.f.* bourgeoisie, middle class.

borgo, *n.m.* village, burg, borough.

bòrico, *adj.* boric.

borsa, *n.f.* bag, brief-case, pouch; purse; fellowship; stock exchange. **b. di stùdio,** scholarship.

borsaiòlo, *n.m.* pickpocket.

borsetta, *n.f.* little bag, purse, handbag.

borsista, *n.m.* scholarship holder.

borsistico, *adj.* stock exchange.

borsite, *n.f.* bursitis.

boscàglia, *n.f.* underbrush, thicket.

boschetto, *n.m.* grove.

bosco, *n.m.* wood.

boscoso, *adj.* wooded.

bòsso, *n.m.* boxwood.

bòssolo, *n.m.* cartridge-case.

botànica, *n.f.* botany.

botànico, *adj.* botanical.

bòtola, *n.f.* trap door, hatch.

bottaio, *n.m.* cooper.

bòtte, *n.f.* cask, hogshead.

bottega, *n.f.* shop.

botteghino, *n.m.* box-office.

bottìglia, *n.f.* bottle, jar.

bottino, *n.m.* booty, plunder, loot.

bottone, *n.m.* button.

bovaro, *n.m.* cattleman.

bovino, *adj.* bovine.

bòzze, *n.f.pl.* proof. **b. in colonna,** galley-proof. **b. impaginate,** page-proof.

bòzzolo, *n.m.* cocoon.

braccialetto, *n.m.* bracelet.

bracciata, *n.f.* armful.

braccio, *n.m.* arm; fathom.

brace, *n.f.* embers.

brache, *n.f.pl.* breeches, pants.

brama, *n.f.* ardent desire, craving, eagerness, longing.

bramare, *vb.* desire ardently, covet, crave, long for, yearn for.

bramino, *n.m.* Brahman.

bramosamente, *adv.* desirously, covetously, eagerly.

bramosìa, *n.f.* greed; avidity.

bramoso, *adj.* desirous, covetous, eager.

brànchia, *n.f.* gill.

brandire, *vb.* brandish.

brano, *n.m.* passage, excerpt.

Brasile, *n.m.* Brazil.

brasiliano, *adj.* Brazilian.

bravata, *n.f.* bravado.

bravo, 1. *n.* henchman. **2.** *adj.* fine.

breccia, *n.f.* breach.

brefotròfio, *n.m.* foundling hospital.

Brètone, *n.m.* Briton.

brève, *adj.* brief, short.

brevemente, *adv.* briefly.

brevettare, *vb.* patent.

brevetto, *n.m.* patent.

brevità, *n.f.* brevity, briefness.

brezza, *n.f.* breeze.

briccone, *n.m.* rascal, rogue.

bricconesco, *adj.* roguish.

brìciola, *n.f.* crumb.

brigantino, *n.m.* brig.

brigata, *n.f.* brigade.

briglia, *n.f.* bridle.

brillante, *adj.* brilliant.

brillare, *vb.* shine.

brillo, *adj.* tipsy.

brina, *n.f.* frost.

brindare, *vb.* toast.

brìndisi, *n.m.* toast, health.

brìo, *n.m.* vim, verve.

brioso, *adj.* lively, sprightly.

brìscola, *n.f.* trump (card).

britànnico, *adj.* British.

brìvido, *n.m.* shudder, shiver, chill.

brizzolato, *adj.* grizzled.

bròcca, *n.f.* jug, pitcher.

broccato, *n.m.* brocade.

bròcco, *n.m.* nag.

bròdo, *n.m.* broth, bouillon. **b. ristretto,** consommé.

bròglio, *n.m.* scheme, plot, intrigue.

bronchiale, *adj.* bronchial.

bronchite, *n.f.* bronchitis.

brontolamento, *n.m.* grumble.

brontolare, *vb.* grumble, growl; rumble.

brontolìo, *n.m.* rumble.

bronzo, *n.m.* bronze.

brucare, *vb.* browse.

bruciare, *vb.* burn, scorch.

bruciatura, *n.f.* burn.

bruciore di stòmaco, *n.m.* heartburn.

bruco, *n.m.* caterpillar, cankerworm.

brughièra, *n.f.* heath, moor.

bruna, *n.f.* brunette.

brunire, *vb.* burnish.

bruno, *adj.* brown.

bruscamente, *adv.* brusquely.

brusco, *adj.* brusque.

bruscolo, *n.m.* cinder.

brutale, *adj.* brutal.

brutalità, *n.f.* brutality.

bruto, *n.m. and adj.* brute.

bruttezza, *n.f.* ugliness.

brutto, *adj.* ugly, homely.

buca, *n.f.* pit, pot-hole.

bucato, *n.m.* laundry.

bùccia, *n.f.* hull, husk, peel, rind, skin.

bùccina, *n.f.* bugle.

buco, *n.m.* hole.

budèllo, *n.m.* bowel, intestine, gut.

budino, *n.m.* pudding.

bue, *n.m.* ox; beef.

bùfalo, *n.m.* buffalo.

buffonata, *n.f.* antic.

buffone, *n.m.* buffoon, jester.

bugìa, *n.f.* lie, fabrication, falsehood.

bugiardo, 1. *n.m.* liar. **2.** *adj.* lying.

bugigàttolo, *n.m.* cubbyhole.

bùio, 1. *n.m.* darkness. **2.** *adj.* dark.

bulbo, *n.m.* bulb.

búlgaro, *adj.* Bulgarian.

bulletta, *n.f.* tack.

bullone, *n.m.* bolt.

bungalò, *n.m.* bungalow.

buoncostume, *n.m.* morals.

buongustaio, *n.m.* gourmet.

buòn mercato, *n.m.* cheapness.

buòno, 1. *n.m.* bond. **2.** *adj.* good.

buonsenso, *n.m.* common sense.

buontempone, *n.m.* merry fellow.

buonumore, *n.m.* good mood.

burattino, *n.m.* puppet.

bùrbero, *adj.* gruff.

burla, *n.f.* trick, practical joke, prank.

burlone, *n.m.* joker.

burro, *n.m.* butter.

burrone, *n.m.* ravine, canyon, gulch, gully.

bussare, *vb.* knock.

bussata, *n.f.* knock.

bùssola, *n.f.* compass.

busta, *n.f.* envelope.

busto, *n.m.* bust; bodice, corset.

buttafuòri, *n.m.* bouncer (night-club).

buttare, *vb.* throw, toss.

C

C (on water faucets) — **caldo,** *adj.* hot.

càbala, *n.m.* cabala.

cabina, *n.f.* cabin, stateroom.

cablogramma, *n.m.* cablegram.

cacao, *n.m.* cocoa.

càccia, *n.f.* fighter plane.

càccia, *n.f.* hunt, hunting, chase.

cacciare, *vb.* hunt; chase; stick; shove.

cacciatore, *n.m.* hunter, chaser.

cacciatorpedinière, *n.m.* destroyer.

cacciatrice, *n.f.* huntress.

cacciavite, *n.m.* screw-driver.

cachi, *n.m.* khaki.

càcio, *n.m.* cheese.

cacofonìa, *n.f.* cacophony.

cadauno, 1. *adj.* each; apiece. **2.** *pron.* each one.

cadàvere, *n.m.* cadaver, corpse.

cadavèrico, *adj.* cadaverous.

cadènza, *n.f.* cadence, cadenza.

cadere, *vb.* fall. **lasciar c.,** drop.

cadetto, *n.m.* cadet.

càdmio, *n.m.* cadmium.

caduta, *n.f.* fall.

caffè, *n.m.* coffee; café; buffet.

caffeina, *n.f.* caffeine.

cagionare, *vb.* occasion, cause.

cagionévole, *adj.* sickly, weak.

cagna, *n.f.* bitch.

caimano, *n.m.* cayman.

calabrese, *n.m. or f. and adj.* Calabrian.

calabrone, *n.m.* bumblebee, hornet.

calafatare, *vb.* calk.

calafato, *n.m.* calker.

calamità, *n.f.* calamity, woe.

calamitoso, *adj.* calamitous.

calapranzi, *n.m.* dumbwaiter.

calare, *vb.* lower.

calcagno, *n.m.* heel.

calcare, *adj.* calcareous. **pietra c.,** limestone.

calce, *n.f.* lime.

calcestruzzo, *n.m.* concrete.

calciatore, *n.m.* soccer player.

calcificare, *vb.* calcify.

calcina, n.f. mortar.

càlcio, n.m. calcium; kick; soccer; butt (of gun).

calcolàbile, adj. calculable.

calcolare, vb. calculate.

calcolatore, 1. adj. calculating. 2. n.m. computer.

calcolatrice elettrònica, n.f. computer.

càlcolo, n.m. calculus; calculation. **c. biliare,** gallstone.

caldaia, n.f. boiler, caldron, furnace.

caldarròsta, n.f. roasted chestnut.

caldo, 1. n.m. heat. **2.** adj. hot, warm.

caleidoscòpio, n.m. kaleidoscope.

calendàrio, n.m. calendar.

caletta, n.f. joggle.

càlibro, n.m. caliber; calipers.

càlice, n.m. chalice; calyx.

calicò, n.m. calico.

callìfugo, n.m. corn-plaster.

calligrafia, n.f. calligraphy, handwriting.

callista, n.m. chiropodist.

callo, n.m. callus, corn.

callosità, n.f. callousness.

calloso, adj. callous, horny.

calma, n.f. calm, composure; stillness.

calmante, n.m. tranquilizer.

calmare, vb. calm, soothe; still.

calmo, adj. calm, composed; still.

calore, n.m. heat, warmth.

caloria, n.f. calorie.

calòrico, adj. caloric.

calorifero, n.m. heater.

calorìmetro, n.m. calorimeter.

caloroso, adj. warm.

calpestare, vb. tread on.

calùnnia, n.f. calumny, slander.

calunniare, vb. calumniate, slander, slur.

Calvàrio, n.m. Calvary.

calvìzie, n.f.sg. baldness.

calvo, adj. bald.

calza, n.f. stocking, (pl.) hose.

calzamàglia, n.f. tights, leggings, leotards.

calzare, vb. shoe.

calzascarpe, n.m. shoe horn.

calzatura, n.f. footwear.

calzetteria, n.f. hosiery.

calzettone, n.m. thick sock.

calzino, n.m. sock.

calzolaio, n.m. shoemaker, cobbler.

calzoncini, n.m.pl. shorts.

calzoni, n.m.pl. trousers.

camaleonte, n.m. chameleon.

cambiale, n.f. promissory note, IOU.

cambiamento, n.m. change, shift.

cambiare, vb. change, shift.

cambiavalute, n.m. money-changer.

cambio, n.m. change; relief. **c. di velocità,** n.f. gearshift.

cambrì, n.m. cambric.

camèlia, n.f. camelia.

càmera, n.f. room, chamber; (legislative) house.

camerata, n.m. comrade, buddy, pal.

cameratismo, n.m. camaraderie, comradeship.

camerièra, n.f. chambermaid, waitress; stewardess, flight attendant.

camerière, n.m. manservant; waiter; bellboy; steward, flight attendant; valet.

camerino, n.m. dressing room.

càmice, n.m. smock.

camìcia, n.f. shirt.

camiciòla, n.f. undershirt.

camiciòtto, n.m. smock.

camino, n.m. chimney.

camion, n.m. truck.

camioncino, n.m. light truck; utility.

cammèllo, n.m. camel.

cammèo, n.m. cameo.

camminare, vb. walk, step.

cammino, n.m. road.

camòscio, n.m. chamois.

campagna, n.f. country, countryside; campaign.

campana, n.f. bell.

campanèllo, n.m. (little) bell.

campanette, n.f.pl. glockenspiel.

campanile, n.m. bell-tower, belfry, steeple.

campeggiare, vb. camp.

campeggiatore, n.m. camper.

campeggio, n.m. camping.

campionàrio, 1. adj. pertaining to samples. **2.** n.m. sample.

campionato, n.m. championship.

campione, n.m. champion; sample.

campo, n.m. field.

camposanto, n.m. cemetery, churchyard, graveyard.

camuffamento, n.m. disguise, camouflage.

camuffare, vb. disguise, camouflage.

Canadà, n.m. Canada.

canadese, adj. Canadian.

canàglia, n.f. rascal, scoundrel; rabble.

canagliata, n.f. roguery, knavery, mean trick.

canale, n.m. canal, channel, duct, inlet.

canalizzare, vb. canalize.

canalone, n.m. ravine.

cànapa, n.f. hemp.

canapè, n.m. couch, sofa.

Canàrie, n.f.pl. Canary Islands.

canarino, n.m. canary.

cancan, n.m. clamor, uproar.

cancellare, vb. cancel, erase, delete, efface, obliterate.

cancellatura, n.f. erasure.

cancellerìa, n.f. chancellery. **oggetti di c.,** stationery.

cancellière, n.m. chancellor.

cancèllo, n.m. gate.

cancrena, n.f. gangrene.

cancrenoso, adj. gangrenous.

cancro, n.m. cancer, canker.

candeggina, n.f. bleach.

candela, n.f. candle. **c. d'accensione,** spark-plug.

candelabro, n.m. candelabrum.

candelière, n.m. candlestick.

candidamente, adv. candidly.

candidato, n.m. candidate, nominee.

candidatura, n.f. candidacy.

càndido, adj. candid.

candire, vb. caramelize.

candito, adj. candied.

candore, n.m. candor.

cane, n.m. dog, hound, cock (of gun). **c. poliziotto,** police dog, bloodhound.

cànfora, n.f. camphor.

canguro, n.m. kangaroo.

canile, n.m. doghouse, kennel.

canino, adj. canine.

canna, n.f. reed, cane.

cannèlla, n.f. cinnamon.

cannìbale, n.m. cannibal.

cannone, n.m. cannon.

cannoneggiamento, n.m. cannonade.

cannonièra, n.f. gunboat.

cannonière, n.m. cannoneer.

cannùccia di paglia, n.f. straw (for drinking).

canòa, n.f. canoe.

cànone, n.m. canon; rent.

canònico, 1. n.m. canon. **2.** adj. canonical.

canonizzare, vb. canonize.

canottàggio, n.m. rowing, boating.

canottièra, n.f. undershirt, tank top.

canovaccio, n.m. canvas.

cantare, vb. sing, chant; (hen, goose) cackle; (rooster) crow.

cantautore, n.m. singer.

canticchiare, vb. hum, croon.

cantina, n.f. basement; canteen.

canto, n.m. corner; song, singing, chant.

cantuccio, n.m. nook.

canuto, adj. grey-haired, white-haired.

canzonare, vb. mock, ridicule; banter.

canzone, n.f. song.

càos, n.m. chaos.

caòtico, adj. chaotic.

capace, adj. capable, able.

capacità, n.f. capacity, ability.

capanna, n.f. cabin, hut, shack.

capannèllo, n.m. small crowd.

capannone, n.m. large shed, depot.

capàrbio, adj. wilful.

capatina, n.f. brief visit.

capello, n.m. hair.

capestro, n.m. halter.

capezzale, n.m. **al c. di,** at the bedside of.

capézzolo, n.m. nipple.

capillare, adj. capillary.

capire, vb. understand.

capitale, 1. n.m. capital (city). **2.** n.m. capital (money). **3.** adj. capital.

capitalismo, *n.m.* capitalism.

capitalista, *n.m.* capitalist.

capitalístico, *adj.* capitalistic.

capitalizzare, *vb.* capitalize.

capitalizzazione, *n.f.* capitalization.

capitano, *n.m.* captain.

capitare, *vb.* happen, befall.

capitolare, *vb.* capitulate.

capitolo, *n.m.* chapter.

capitombolare, *vb.* tumble.

capitómbolo, *n.m.* tumble.

capo, *n.m.* head, chief, chieftain, head-man, leader, principal.

capobanda, *n.m.* bandmaster; gang leader.

capofitto, *adv.* **a c.,** headlong.

capolavoro, *n.m.* masterpiece.

capolìnea, *n.m.* terminus.

caporale, *n.m.* corporal.

capotreno, *n.m.* conductor (of train).

capovòlgere, *vb.* overturn, upset, capsize.

cappa, *n.f.* cape.

cappèlla, *n.f.* chapel.

cappellano, *n.m.* chaplain.

cappellièra, *n.f.* hatbox, bandbox.

cappèllo, *n.m.* hat, bonnet.

càpperi, *interj.* Wow!

càppero, *n.m.* caper.

càppio, *n.m.* loop.

cappone, *n.m.* capon.

cappòtto, *n.m.* heavy coat.

cappùccio, *n.m.* hood.

capra, *n.f.* goat.

capraio, *n.m.* goat-herd.

capretto, *n.m.* kid.

capriccio, *n.m.* caprice, whim.

capricciosamente, *adv.* capriciously.

capricciosità, *n.f.* capriciousness.

capriccioso, *adj.* capricious, fanciful, flighty, temperamental.

caprifòglio, *n.m.* honeysuckle.

capriòla, *n.f.* caper, somersault.

capriòlo, *n.m.* roe deer.

càpsula, *n.f.* capsule.

captare, *vb.* intercept; pick up.

capzioso, *adj.* captious.

carabina, *n.f.* carbine.

carabinière, *n.m.* Italian military policeman.

caraffa, *n.f.* carafe, decanter.

caramèlla, *n.f.* caramel.

caramente, *adv.* dearly.

carato, *n.m.* carat.

caràttere, *n.m.* character.

caratterística, *n.f.* characteristic.

caratteristicamente, *adv.* characteristically.

caratterístico, *adj.* characteristic.

caratterizzare, *vb.* characterize.

caratterizzazione, *n.f.* characterization.

carbónchio, *n.m.* carbuncle.

carbone, *n.m.* charcoal; coal.

carbonèlla, *n.f.* charcoal.

carbònio, *n.m.* carbon.

carbonizzare, *vb.* char.

carburante, *n.m.* fuel.

carburatore, *n.m.* carburetor.

carburo, *n.m.* carbide.

carcassa, *n.f.* carcass; hulk.

càrcere, *n.m.* jail.

carcerière, *n.m.* jailer.

carcinogènico, *adj.* carcinogenic.

carciòfo, *n.m.* artichoke.

cardellino, *n.m.* goldfinch.

cardìaco, *adj.* cardiac.

cardinale, *n.m. and adj.* cardinal.

càrdine, *n.m.* hinge.

carenare, *vb.* careen.

carestìa, *n.f.* famine.

carezza, *n.f.* caress; endearment.

carezzévole, *adj.* caressing.

cariarsi, *vb.* decay.

càrica, *n.f.* charge.

caricare, *vb.* load, charge; (watch) wind.

caricatore, *n.m.* loader; charger; cartridge.

caricatura, *n.f.* caricature.

càrico, 1. *n.m.* load, cargo, charge, freight. **2.** *adj.* loaded, fraught.

càrie, *n.f.* caries, decay.

carino, *adj.* cute, pretty, nice.

carisma, *n.m.* charisma.

carità, *n.f.* charity, charitableness.

caritatévole, *adj.* charitable, benevolent.

caritatevolmente, *adv.* charitably, benevolently.

carlinga, *n.f.* cockpit.

carnagione, *n.f.* complexion.

carnale, *adj.* carnal.

carne, *n.f.* meat; flesh.

carnéfice, *n.m.* executioner.

carneficina, *n.f.* carnage, slaughter.

carnevale, *n.m.* carnival.

carnìvoro, *adj.* carnivorous.

carnoso, *adj.* fleshy.

caro, 1. *adv.* dear(ly). 2. *adj.* dear, expensive.

carosèllo, *n.m.* carousel, merry-go-round.

caròta, *n.f.* carrot.

carovana, *n.f.* caravan, trailer.

carovita, *n.m.* high cost of living.

carpa, *n.f.* carp.

carpire, *vb.* seize, grab.

carponi, *adv.* a c. on all fours.

carretta per bagagli, *n.f.* baggage cart.

carrettata, *n.f.* carload.

carrettière, *n.m.* carter, drayman.

carrièra, *n.f.* career.

carro, *n.m.* car; cart, wagon; chariot; dray, van. **c. armato**, tank. **c. fùnebre**, hearse. **c. di scorta**, tender.

carròzza, *n.f.* carriage, coach, (railroad) car. **c. lètti**, sleeper. **c. ristorante**, diner.

carrozzèlla, *n.f.* baby-carriage, perambulator.

carrozzino, *n.m.* side-car.

carta, *n.f.* paper; card; chart; map; charter. **c. a carbone**, carbon paper. **c. assorbente**, blotter, blotting paper. **c. di crèdito**, credit card. **c. da léttere**, notepaper. **c. velina**, tissue-paper; onionskin. **c. da parati**, wallpaper. **c. intestata**, letterhead.

cartéggio, *n.m.* correspondence (mail).

cartèlla, *n.f.* portfolio; folder.

cartèllo, *n.m.* cartel; placard; poster, sign. **c. pubblicitàrio**, billboard.

cartièra, *n.f.* paper mill.

cartilàgine, *n.f.* cartilage, gristle.

cartina, *n.f.* map.

cartolaio, *n.m.* stationer.

cartoleria, *n.f.* stationery store.

cartolina, *n.f.* postcard.

cartomante, *n.m. or f.* fortuneteller.

cartoncino, *n.m.* thin cardboard.

cartone, *n.m.* cardboard, pasteboard; cartoon (picture).

cartuccia, *n.f.* cartridge.

casa, *n.f.* house, home. **in c.**, indoors. **c. colònica**, farmhouse.

casacca, *n.f.* coat; shirt.

casàccio, *n.m.* a c., haphazard, helter-skelter, at random.

casalingo, *adj.* home; homelike.

casamatta, *n.m.* bunker.

cascata, *n.f.* cascade, waterfall.

casèlla, *n.f.* pigeonhole; P.O. box.

casèrma, *n.f.* barracks.

casetta, *n.f.* cottage.

casimiro, *n.m.* cashmere.

casino, *n.m.* casino.

caso, *n.m.* case; happening; chance. **per c.**, by accident.

cassa, *n.f.* case; chest; box; cashier's office or desk. **c. da mòrto**, coffin. **c. di rispàrmio**, savings bank.

cassafòrte, *n.f.* strongbox; safe.

cassare, *vb.* overrule.

casseruòla, *n.f.* casserole.

cassetta, *n.f.* box; cassette.

cassettina, *n.f.* casket.

cassetto, *n.m.* drawer; till.

cassière, *n.m.* cashier; teller.

cassone, *n.m.* caisson.

casta, *n.f.* caste.

castagna, *n.f.* chestnut.

castagno, 1. *n.m.* chestnut tree. 2. *adj.* tan.

castèllo, *n.m.* castle, château. **c. di prua**, forecastle.

castigare, *vb.* castigate, chastise, chasten.

castigo, *n.m.* chastisement.

castità, *n.f.* chastity.

casto, *adj.* chaste.

castòro, *n.m.* beaver.

castrare, *vb.* castrate, emasculate; geld.

castrone, *n.m.* gelding, wether.

casuale, *adj.* casual; perfunctory.

casualmente, *adv.* casually.

casùpola, *n.f.* hut.

cataclisma, *n.m.* cataclysm.

catacomba, *n.f.* catacomb.

catàlogo, *n.m.* catalogue.

catapulta, *n.f.* catapult.

catarro, *n.m.* catarrh; cold.

catarsi, *n.f.* catharsis.

catasta, *n.f.* heap, pile, stack.

catastale, *adj.* land office.

catasto, *n.m.* land office, real estate register.

catàstrofe, *n.f.* catastrophe.

catechismo, *n.m.* catechism.

catechizzare, *vb.* catechize.

categoria, *n.f.* category.

categòrico, *adj.* categorical.

catena, *n.f.* chain; range.

catenaccio, *n.m.* bolt.

cateratta, *n.f.* cataract; floodgate.

catetère, *n.f.* catheter.

catino, *n.m.* basin.

càtodo, *n.m.* cathode.

catòrcio, *n.m.* piece of junk.

catrame, *n.m.* tar.

càttedra, *n.f.* teacher's desk; professorship.

cattedrale, *n.f.* cathedral.

cattivèria, *n.f.* badness, mischief.

cattivo, *adj.* bad, evil; mischievous.

cattolicismo, *n.m.* Catholicism.

cattòlico, *adj.* Catholic.

cattura, *n.f.* capture.

catturare, *vb.* capture.

catturatore, *n.m.* capturer, captor.

caucciú, *n.m.* rubber.

càusa, *n.f.* cause; lawsuit; case. **a c. di**, because of.

causalità, *n.f.* causality, causation.

causare, *vb.* cause, bring about; encompass.

càustico, *adj.* caustic.

cautèla, *n.f.* caution.

cautèrio, *n.m.* cautery.

cauterizzare, *vb.* cauterize.

càuto, *adj.* cautious; gingerly.

cauzione, *n.f.* bail; security.

cava, *n.f.* quarry.

cavalcare, *vb.* ride (horseback).

cavalcata, *n.f.* cavalcade.

cavalcavìa, *n.m.* overpass.

cavalcioni, *adv.* **a c.** astride.

cavalière, *n.m.* knight, cavalier, horseman, rider.

cavalla, *n.f.* mare.

cavalleresco, *adj.* chivalric.

cavalleria, *n.f.* cavalry; chivalry.

cavalletta, *n.f.* grasshopper.

cavalletto, *n.m.* easel.

cavallo, *n.m.* horse; (chess) knight. **c. a dòndolo**, rocking-horse; hobby-horse. **c. da guerra**, warhorse, charger. **c.-vapore**, horsepower.

cavatappi, *n.m.sg.* corkscrew.

cavèrna, *n.f.* cavern, cave.

cavezza, *n.f.* halter.

caviale, *n.m.* caviar.

caviglia, *n.f.* ankle.

cavità, *n.f.* cavity; hole.

cavo, 1. *n.m.* hollow; cable. 2. *adj.* hollow.

cavolfiore, *n.m.* cauliflower.

càvolo, *n.m.* cabbage; kale.

cazzòtto, *n.m.* punch, sock.

cazzuòla, *n.f.* trowel.

cecchino, *n.m.* sniper.

cece, *n.m.* chickpea.

cecità, *n.f.* blindness.

cèdere, *vb.* yield, cede, surrender, give in; back down; subside.

cèdola, *n.f.* coupon.

cèdro, *n.m.* cedar.

C.E., *acronym f.* (Comunità Europea), E.C.

cèffo, *n.m.* thug, snout. **brutto c.**, ugly mug.

ceffone, *n.m.* slap in the face.

celare, *vb.* conceal.

celebrante, *n.m.* celebrant.

celebrare, *vb.* celebrate.

celebrazione, *n.f.* celebration.

cèlebre, *adj.* celebrated, famous.

celebrità, *n.f.* celebrity.

celerità, *n.f.* speed, quickness, celerity.

celèste, *adj.* celestial.

cèlia, *n.f.* joke, banter, chaff.

celiare, *vb.* joke, banter, chaff.

celibato, *n.m.* celibacy.

cèlibe, *adj.* celibate; single, unmarried.

cèlla, *n.f./cell.

cellòfane, *n.m.* cellophane.

cèllula, *n.f.* cell.

cellulare, *adj.* cellular.

cellulòide, *n.f.* celluloid.

cellulosa, *n.f.* cellulose.

cèltico, *adj.* Celtic.

cementare, *vb.* cement.

cemento, *n.m.* cement, concrete.

cena, *n.f.* supper.

cenàcolo, *n.m.* coterie; Last Supper.

céncio, *n.m.* rag.

cencioso, *adj.* ragged.

cénere, *n.f.* ashes.

cenno, *n.m.* sign, hint.

censimento, *n.m.* census.

censore, *n.m.* censor.

censòrio, *adj.* censorious.

censura, *n.f.* censure; censorship.

censurare, *vb.* censor.

centenàrio, *n.m. and adj.* centenary.

centennale, *n.m. and adj.* centennial.

centésimo, 1. *n.m.* cent; 100th part. **2.** *adj.* hundredth.

centigrado, *adj.* centigrade.

centinaio, *n.m.* group of 100.

cènto, *num.* hundred.

centrale, *adj.* central.

centralino, *n.m.* switchboard.

centralizzare, *vb.* centralize.

cèntro, *n.m.* center. **c. da tàvola,** centerpiece.

centrocampo, *n.m.* (soccer) midfield.

ceppi, *n.m.pl.* fetters.

ceppo, *n.m.* log, stump.

cera, *n.f.* wax; beeswax; mien.

ceralacca, *n.f.* sealing-wax.

ceràmica, *n.f.* ceramics.

ceràmico, *adj.* ceramic.

cercare, *vb.* seek, look for, hunt for.

cérchia, *n.f.* circle (of friends).

cérchio, *n.m.* circle; hoop; ring.

cereale, *n.m. and adj.* cereal.

cerebrale, *adj.* cerebral.

cèreo, *adj.* waxen; pale.

cerimònia, *n.f.* ceremony.

cerimoniale, *adj.* ceremonial.

cerimonioso, *adj.* ceremonious.

cerino, *n.m.* wax match.

cernièra, *n.f.* hinge; clasp; zipper.

cèrnita, *n.f.* selection; choice; sorting.

cero, *n.m.* church candle.

certamente, *adv.* certainly.

certezza, *n.f.* certainty, certitude.

certificare, *vb.* certify.

certificato, *n.m.* certificate.

certificazione, *n.f.* certification.

cèrto, *adj.* certain, sure.

cèrva, *n.f.* doe; hind; roe.

cervèllo, *n.m.* brain.

cervellòtico, *adj.* preposterous; absurd; extravagant.

cervicale, *adj.* cervical.

cervice, *n.f.* cervix.

cèrvo, *n.m.* stag; deer.

cesellare, *vb.* chisel.

cesello, *n.m.* chisel.

cesòie, *n.f.pl.* shears.

cespùglio, *n.m.* bush.

cespuglioso, *adj.* bushy.

cessare, *vb.* cease, stop, quit.

cessazione, *n.f.* cessation.

cessione, *n.f.* cession.

cesta, *n.f.* basket; hamper.

cèto, *n.m.* class.

cetriòlo, *n.m.* cucumber.

che, 1. *pron.* who; which; what. **2.** *prep.* than. **3.** *conj.* that.

chè, *conj.* for, because, so that.

chemioterapìa, *n.f.* chemotherapy.

cherubino, *n.m.* cherub.

chi, *pron.* who; whom.

chiàcchiera, *n.f.* chatter, chat.

chiacchierare, *vb.* chatter, chat, gab.

chiacchierone, *n.m.* chatterbox.

chiamare, *vb.* call, summon.

chiamata, *n.f.* call, summons.

chiaramente, *adv.* clearly.

chiarezza, *n.f.* clarity, clearness.

chiarificare, *vb.* clarify.

chiarificazione, *n.f.* clarification.

chiarimento, *n.m.* enlightenment.

chiarina, *n.f.* clarion.

chiarire, *vb.* clear, clear up.

chiaro, *adj.* clear, bright, lucid, plain. **c. di luna,** moonlight.

chiarore, *n.m.* brightness.

chiaroveggènte, *n. and adj.* clairvoyant; fortune-teller.

chiaroveggènza, *n.f.* clairvoyance.

chiasso, *n.m.* uproar, fuss, hullabaloo.

chiassoso, *adj.* uproarious; obstreperous.

chiatta, *n.f.* barge.

chiave, *n.f.* key; clef. **c. inglese,** wrench.

chiàvica, *n.f.* sewer.

chiavistèllo, *n.m.* bolt, lock.

chiazza, *n.f.* spot, blotch, mottle.

chicca, *n.f.* sweet, candy; (coll.) gossip.

chicchessia, *pron. indef.* anybody, anyone.

chicco, *n.m.* grain; seed.

chièdere, *vb.* ask for, request, beg.

chièsa, *n.f.* church.

chìglia, *n.f.* keel.

chilocìclo, *n.m.* kilocycle.

chilogramma, *n.m.* kilogram.

chilomètràggio, *n.m.* distance in kilometers.

chilòmetro, *n.m.* kilometer.

chilowatt, *n.m.* kilowatt.

chìmica, *n.f.* chemistry.

chimicamente, *adv.* chemically.

chìmico, 1. *n.m.* chemist. **2.** *adj.* chemical.

chimono, *n.m.* kimono.

chinino, *n.m.* quinine.

chiocciare, *vb.* cluck.

chiòdo, *n.m.* nail; spike; clove.

chiòsa, *n.f.* gloss.

chiosare, *vb.* gloss.

chiòsco, *n.m.* kiosk.

chiòstro, *n.m.* cloister.

chirurgìa, *n.f.* surgery.

chirurgo, *n.m.* surgeon.

chitarra, *n.f.* guitar.

chiùdere, *vb.* close, shut. **c. a chiave,** lock.

chiunque, *pron.* whoever; whomever.

chiusa, *n.f.* lock.

chiusura, *n.f.* closure; fastening. **c. lampo,** zipper.

ci, *pron.* us; to us.

ci, *pro-phrase* (replaces phrases introduced by prepositions of place) here, there; to it; at it.

ciabattino, *n.m.* cobbler.

ciambellano, *n.m.* chamberlain.

cianfrusàglia, *n.f.* gimcrack; trash.

ciao, *interj.* hi!; so long!

ciarlare, *vb.* chatter, jabber, prattle.

ciarlatanismo, *n.m.* charlatanism.

ciarlatano, *n.m.* charlatan, mountebank.

ciarpame, *n.m.* junk.

ciascuno, *pron.* each one.

cibare, *vb.* intr. feed, nourish.

cibàrie, *n.f.pl.* food, groceries.

cibo, *n.m.* food.

cicala, *n.f.* cicada.

cicatrice, *n.f.* scar.

cicatrizzare, *vb.* scar.

cicca, *n.f.* butt.

cicchetto, *n.m.* nip, shot (of liquor); lecture.

ciccia, *n.f.* flesh, fat.

cicisbèo, *n.m.* gigolo.

ciclamato, *n.m.* cyclamate.

ciclista, *n.m. or f.* bicyclist.

ciclo, *n.m.* cycle.

ciclomotore, *n.m.* moped.

ciclone, *n.m.* cyclone.

ciclotrone, *n.m.* cyclotron.

cicogna, *n.f.* stork.

cicòria, *n.f.* chicory.

cicuta, *n.f.* hemlock.

ciecamente, *adv.* blindly.

cièco, *adj.* blind.

cièlo, *n.m.* heaven; sky.

cifra, *n.f.* cipher; figure.

cifràrio, *n.m.* code.

ciglio, *n.m.* eyelash, cilia.

cigno, *n.m.* swan.

cigolare, *vb.* creak, squeak.

cigolìo, *n.m.* squeak.

ciliare, *adj.* ciliary.

ciliègia, *n.f.* cherry.

ciliègio, *n.m.* cherry-tree.

cilìndrico, *adj.* cylindrical.

cilindro, *n.m.* cylinder.

cima, *n.f.* peak.

cimare, *vb.* clip, trim.

cìmbalo, *n.m.* gong.

cimèlio, *n.m.* relic, souvenir.

cìmice, *n.f.* bedbug.

ciminièra, *n.f.* smoke-stack; funnel.

cimitèro, *n.m.* cemetery; churchyard.

Cìna, *n.f.* China.

cincona, *n.f.* cinchona.

cinèllo, *n.m.* cymbal.

cìnema, *n.m.* cinema, movies; (movie) theater.

cinematogràfico, *adj.* cinematic, of the movies.

cinematògrafo, *n.m.* cinema, movies; (movie) theater.

cinese, *adj.* Chinese.

cinètico, *adj.* kinetic.

cìngere, *vb.* gird.

cìnghia, *n.f.* strap.

cinguettare, *vb.* chirp.

cinguettìo, *n.m.* chirping.

cìnico, 1. *n.m.* cynic. **2.** *adj.* cynical.

cinìglia, *n.f.* chenille.

cinismo, *n.m.* cynicism.

cinòfilo, *n.m.* dog lover.

cinquanta, *num.* fifty.

cinque, *num.* five.

cinta, *n.f.* fence, wall.

cintura, *n.f.* belt, girdle, sash; waist.

ciò, *pron.* this; that; it.

ciòcco, *n.m.* log.

cioccolato, *n.m.* chocolate.

cioè, *conj.* that is; namely.

ciòttolo, *n.m.* pebble, stone; cobblestone.

cipolla, *n.f.* onion; chive.

ciprèsso, *n.m.* cypress.

cipria, *n.f.* face-powder.

circo, *n.m.* circus.

circolare, 1. *n.m. and adj.* circular. **2.** *vb.* circulate.

circolatòrio, *adj.* circulatory.

circolazione, *n.f.* circulation; currency.

circolo, *n.m.* circle, club.

circoncìdere, *vb.* circumcise.

circoncisione, *n.f.* circumcision.

circondare, *vb.* surround, encompass.

circondàrio, *n.m.* district, surroundings, neighborhood.

circonferènza, *n.f.* circumference, girth.

circonlocuzione, *n.f.* circumlocution.

circonscrìvere, *vb.* circumscribe.

circonvenire, *vb.* circumvent.

circonvenzione, *n.f.* circumvention.

circospètto, *adj.* circumspect.

circostante, *adj.* surrounding, neighboring.

circostanza, *n.f.* circumstance.

circostanziale, *adj.* circumstantial.

circostanziatamente, *adv.* circumstantially.

circùito, *n.m.* circuit.

cirrìpede, *n.m.* barnacle.

cirròsi, *n.f.* cirrhosis.

ciste, *n.f.* cyst.

cistèrna, *n.f.* cistern.

citare, *vb.* cite; quote; summon.

citazione, *n.f.* citation; quotation; summons.

cìtrico, *adj.* citric.

citrullo, *n.m.* fool.

città, *n.f.* city, town. **c. universitària,** campus.

cittadella, *n.f.* citadel.

cittadina, *n.f.* woman citizen; small city.

cittadinanza, *n.f.* citizenship; citizenry.

cittadino, *n.m.* citizen.

ciucco, *n.m.* drunk.

ciuco, *n.m.* donkey.

ciuffo, *n.m.* tuft.

ciuffolòtto, *n.m.* bullfinch.

ciurma, *n.f.* crew; gang; mob.

civetta, *n.f.* owl; coquette, flirt.

civettare, *vb.* coquet, flirt.

civetteria, *n.f.* coquetry.

cìvico, *adj.* civic.

civile, 1. *n.m. and adj.* civilian. **2.** *adj.* civil; civilized.

civilizzare, *vb.* civilize.

civiltà, *n.f.* civilization; civility.

clàcson, *n.m.* klaxon; horn.

clamore, *n.m.* clamor.

clamoroso, *adj.* noisy, blatant, clamorous, obstreperous.

clan, *n.m.* clan, tribe.

clandestinamente, *adv.* clandestinely.

clandestino, *n.m. and adj.* clandestine, secret.

clangore, *n.m.* clangor.

claretto, *n.m.* claret.

clarinettista, *n.m.* clarinetist.

clarinetto, *n.m.* clarinet.

classe, *n.f.* class.

classicismo, *n.m.* classicism.

clàssico, *adj.* classic; classical.

classificàbile, *adj.* classifiable.

classificare, *vb.* classify; class; grade.

classificazione, *n.f.* classification.

claudicante, *n.m. and adj.* limping, lame.

clàusola, *n.f.* clause.

claustrofobìa, *n.f.* claustrophobia.

clausura, *n.f.* seclusion.

clava, *n.f.* cudgel, nightstick.

clavicémbalo, *n.m.* harpsichord.

clavìcola, *n.f.* collarbone.

clemènte, *adj.* lenient.

clemènza, *n.f.* clemency.

cleptòmane, *n.m.* kleptomaniac.

cleptomanìa, *n.f.* kleptomania.

clericale, *adj.* clerical.

clericalismo, *n.m.* clericalism.

clèro, *n.m.* clergy.

clessidra, *n.f.* sandglass; water clock.

cliènte, *n.m.* client, customer; guest.

clientèla, *n.f.* clientele.

clima, *n.m.* climate.

climàtico, *adj.* climatic.

clìnica, *n.f.* clinic.

clinicamente, *adv.* clinically.

clìnico, *adj.* clinical.

clistère, *n.m.* enema.

cloaca, *n.f.* sewer.

cloridrico, *adj.* hydrochloric.

clòro, *n.m.* chlorine.

clorofilla, *n.f.* chlorophyll.

cloroformio, *n.m.* chloroform.

cloruro, *n.m.* chloride.

coabitare, *vb.* live together.

coagulare, *vb.* coagulate.

coagulazione, *n.f.* coagulation.

coalizione, *n.f.* coalition.

coalizzarsi, *vb.* coalesce.

cobalto, *n.m.* cobalt.

còbra, *n.m.* cobra.

cocaìna, *n.f.* cocaine.

cocainomane, *n.m.* cocaine addict.

coccarda, *n.f.* cockade; bow.

cocchière, *n.m.* coachman.

còcchio, *n.m.* coach.

coccinèlla, *n.f.* ladybug.

còcco, *n.m.* coconut tree.

coccodrillo, *n.m.* crocodile.

coda, *n.f.* tail.

codardìa, *n.f.* cowardice.

codardo, 1. *n.m.* coward. 2. *adj.* cowardly, craven.

codeìna, *n.f.* codeine.

còdice, *n.m.* codex; code. **c. (di avviamento) postale**, zip code.

codificare, *vb.* codify.

coeguale, *adj.* coequal.

coercitivo, *adj.* coercive, compulsive.

coercizione, *n.f.* coercion, duress.

coerènte, *adj.* coherent; consistent.

coesione, *n.f.* cohesion.

coesistènza, *n.f.* coexistence.

coesistere, *vb.* coexist.

coesivo, *adj.* cohesive.

còfano, *n.m.* coffer; (auto) hood; *(Brit.)* bonnet.

còffa, *n.f.* crow's-nest.

cogitare, *vb.* cogitate.

cògliere, *vb.* pick, pluck, gather, cull.

cognata, *n.f.* sister-in-law.

cognato, *n.m.* brother-in-law.

cognizione, *n.f.* cognition, knowledge.

cognome, *n.m.* family name, surname.

coibente, *adj.* nonconducting.

coincidènte, *adj.* coincident; coincidental.

coincidènza, *n.f.* coincidence; (transport) connection.

coincidere, *vb.* coincide; connect.

coinquilino, *n.m.* co-tenant, one who lives in the same building.

coinvòlgere, *vb.* involve.

colare, *vb.* strain.

colatòio, *n.m.* colander.

colazione, *n.f.* light meal; lunch. **prima c.**, breakfast.

colèi, *pron. dem. f. sg.* that one; that woman, she.

colèra, *n.f.* cholera.

colino, *n.m.* strainer.

còlla, *n.f.* glue, paste.

collaborare, *vb.* collaborate.

collaboratore, *n.m.* collaborator.

collaborazione, *n.f.* collaboration.

collaborazionista, *n.f.* collaborationist.

collana, *n.f.* necklace.

collant, *n.m.* panty hose.

collante, *n.m.* adhesive.

collare, 1. *n.m.* collar. 2. *vb.* glue.

collasso, *n.m.* collapse.

collaterale, *n.m. and adj.* collateral.

collaudare, *vb.* test.

collaudatore, *n.m.* tester, inspector.

collàudo, *n.m.* test.

collazionare, *vb.* collate.

collèga, *n.m.* colleague.

collegamento, *n.m.* connection, liaison.

collegare, *vb.* connect, link.

còlle, *n.m.* hill.

Còlle, il C., *n.m.* the residence of the President.

còllera, *n.f.* choler, anger, wrath.

colèrico, *adj.* choleric.

collettivamente, *adv.* collectively, jointly.

collettivo, *adj.* collective, joint.

colletto, *n.m.* collar.

collezione, *n.f.* collection.

collezionista, *n.m.* collector.

collina, *n.f.* hill.

còllo, *n.m.* neck; package.

collocare, *vb.* locate; place.

colloquiale, *adj.* colloquial.

colloquialismo, *n.m.* colloquialism.

colloquialmente, *adv.* colloquially.

collòquio, *n.m.* colloquy; interview.

collusione, *n.f.* collusion.

colmare, *vb.* fill.

colombo, *n.m.* dove.

colònia, *n.f.* colony, settlement.

Colònia, *n.f.* Cologne.

coloniale, *adj.* colonial.

colonizzare, *vb.* colonize.

colonizzazione, *n.f.* colonization.

colonna, *n.f.* column; (*typogr.*) galley.

colonnato, *n.m.* colonnade.

colonnèllo, *n.m.* colonel.

colòno, *n.m.* colonist; settler; farmer.

colorare, *vb.* stain.

colorazione, *n.f.* coloration.

colore, *n.m.* color, hue; paint; stain; suit. **di c.,** colored.

colorifìcio, *n.m.* paint factory, dye factory.

colorire, *vb.* color.

colorito, *n.m.* coloring, complexion.

coloritura, *n.f.* coloring.

coloro, *pron. dem. m. f. pl.* those, those men, those women, they.

colossale, *adj.* colossal.

Colossèo, *n.m.* Coliseum.

colpa, *n.f.* fault, guilt.

colpetto, *n.m.* little blow, tap.

colpévole, **1.** *n.m.* culprit. **2.** *adj.* guilty, culpable.

colpevolmente, *adv.* guiltily.

colpire, *vb.* hit, strike, rap, smite.

colpito, *adj.* stricken.

colpo, *n.m.* blow; stroke; clout, hit, rap; shot.

colposo, *adj.* unpremeditated.

coltèllo, *n.m.* knife, **c. a serramànico,** jack-knife.

coltivare, *vb.* cultivate, till; grow, raise.

coltivatore, *n.m.* cultivator.

coltivazione, *n.f.* cultivation.

colto, *adj.* cultured, cultivated, educated.

coltre, *n.f.* blanket, layer.

coltrone, *n.m.* quilt.

coltura, *n.f.* cultivation.

còma, *n.m.* coma.

colui, *pron. dem. m. sg.* that one, that man, he.

comandamento, *n.m.* commandment.

comandante, *n.m.* commander.

comandare, *vb.* command, order, bid.

comando, *n.m.* command.

comare, *n.f.* godmother.

combaciare, *vb.* match, fit closely together, coincide.

combattènte, *n.m.* combatant, fighter.

combàttere, *vb.* combat, fight, battle.

combattimento, *n.m.* combat, fight, fray.

combinare, *vb.* combine.

combinazione, *n.f.* combination; union suit.

combrìccola, *n.f.* coterie.

combustìbile, **1.** *n.m.* fuel. **2.** *adj.* combustible.

combustione, *n.f.* combustion.

come, **1.** *adv.* how. **2.** *prep. and conj.* like; as.

cometa, *n.f.* comet.

còmico, **1.** *n.m.* comedian. **2.** *adj.* comic, comical, funny.

comìgnolo, *n.m.* chimney pot.

cominciamento, *n.m.* beginning; commencement.

cominciare, *vb.* begin, commence, start.

comitato, *n.m.* committee, board, commission.

commèdia, *n.f.* comedy.

commemorare, *vb.* commemorate.

commemorativo, *adj.* commemorative, memorial.

commemorazione, *n.f.* commemoration.

commentare, *vb.* comment.

commento, *n.m.* comment; commentary.

commerciale, *adj.* commercial.

commercialismo, *n.m.* commercialism.

commercializzare, *vb.* commercialize.

commercialmente, *adv.* commercially.

commerciante, *n.m.* business man, merchant, trader.

commerciare, *vb.* trade.

commèrcio, *n.m.* commerce, trade.

commesso, *n.m.* salesman. **c. viaggiatore**, travelling salesman.

commestibile, *adj.* edible.

commèttere, *vb.* commit.

commiato, *n.m.* leave.

commilitone, *n.m.* comrade in arms.

comminare, *vb.* fix (a penalty).

commiserare, *vb.* commiserate.

commisurato, *adj.* commensurate.

commissariato, *n.m.* commissary.

commissàrio, *n.m.* commissioner.

commissione, *n.f.* commission; committee; errand.

committente, *n.m. and f.* buyer, purchaser.

commòsso, *adj.* moved; deeply felt.

commovènte, *adj.* moving; affecting; touching.

commozione, *n.f.* commotion, stir.

commuòvere, *vb.* move; affect; touch (emotionally).

commutare, *vb.* switch, commute.

commutazione, *n.f.* commutation.

comodamente, *adv.* comfortably.

comodino, *n.m.* night table.

còmodo, **1.** *n.m.* ease; leisure. **2.** *adj.* comfortable; leisurely; snug.

compaesano, *n.m.* compatriot.

compàgine, *n.f.* structure; strict union, connection.

compagna, *n.f.* companion.

compagnia, *n.f.* company, companionship.

compagno, *n.m.* companion; mate; partner.

companàtico, *n.m.* food (generic); food to eat with bread.

comparàbile, *adj.* comparable.

comparare, *vb.* compare.

comparativamente, *adv.* comparatively.

comparativo, *adj.* comparative.

compare, *n.m.* godfather; crony.

comparire, *vb.* appear.

compassione, *n.f.* compassion.

compassionévole, *adj.* compassionate.

compassionevolmente, *adv.* compassionately.

compasso, *n.m.* compass.

compatibile, *adj.* compatible.

compatriòta, *n.m.* compatriot, fellow-countryman.

compattezza, *n.f.* compactness.

compatto, *adj.* compact.

compensare, *vb.* compensate.

compensativo, *adj.* compensatory.

compensazione, *n.f.* compensation. **stanza di c.**, clearing-house.

compènso, *n.m.* compensation.

comperare, *vb.* buy, purchase.

competènte, *adj.* competent, (law) cognizant.

competentemente, *adv.* competently.

competènza, *n.f.* competence, fitness, (legal) cognizance.

compètere, *vb.* compete; be within the province of.

competitivo, *adj.* competitive.

competizione, *n.f.* competition.

compiacènza, *n.f.* complaisance, kindness.

compilare, *vb.* compile.

compilatore, *n.m.* compiler.

compimento, *n.m.* completion, achievement, accomplishment.

compire, *vb.* complete, finish, accomplish, achieve.

compito, *adj.* accomplished.

còmpito, *n.m.* task, assignment.

compleanno, *n.m.* birthday.

complemento, *n.m.* complement.

complessità, *n.f.* complexity.

complesso, *n.m. and adj.* complex, complicated.

completamente, *adv.* completely; altogether; outright; wholly; quite; throughout; utterly.

completamento, *n.m.* completion.

completare, *vb.* complete.

completezza, *n.f.* completeness.

complèto, *adj.* complete; thorough; utter.

complicare, *vb.* complicate.

complicato, *adj.* complicated, involved, intricate.

complicazione, *n.f.* complication; intricacy.

còmplice, *n.m. and f.* accomplice.

complicità, *n.f.* complicity.

complimentare, *vb.* compliment.

complimento, *n.m.* compliment.

complòtto, *n.m.* plot.

componènte, *n.m. and adj.* component.

comporre, *vb.* compose.

comportamento, *n.m.* behavior.

comportare, *vb.* entail, involve; *(refl.)* behave, act.

compòsito, *adj.* composite, compound.

compositore, *n.m.* composer.

composizione, *n.f.* composition.

compostezza, *n.f.* composure.

composto, 1. *n.m.* compound. 2. *adj.* composed; compound; composite.

compra, *n.f.* purchase.

comprare, *vb.* buy; purchase.

compratore, *n.m.* buyer, purchaser.

compravéndita, *n.f.* transaction.

comprèndere, *vb.* comprehend; comprise.

comprensìbile, *adj.* comprehensible.

comprensione, *n.f.* comprehension, understanding.

comprensivo, *adj.* comprehensive.

compreso, *adj.* comprised; including.

comprèssa, *n.f.* compress; (med.) tablet.

compressione, *n.f.* compression.

comprèsso, *adj.* compressed.

compressore, *n.m.* compressor.

comprimàrio, *n.m.* associate chief of staff.

comprimere, *vb.* compress.

compromesso, *n.m.* compromise.

comprométtere, *vb.* compromise, endanger.

compropriété, *n.f.* joint ownership.

comprovare, *vb.* prove.

compunto, *adj.* contrite, remorseful, repentant.

compunzione, *n.f.* compunction.

computare, *vb.* compute.

computazione, *n.f.* computation.

comunale, *adj.* communal.

comune, *adj.* common.

comunella, *n.f.* master-key.

comunemente, *adv.* commonly.

comunicàbile, *adj.* communicable.

comunicante, *n.m.* communicant.

comunicare, *vb.* communicate; *(refl.)* take communion.

comunicativo, *adj.* communicative.

comunicato, *n.m.* communiqué.

comunicazione, *n.f.* communication.

comunione, *n.f.* communion.

comunismo, *n.m.* communism.

comunista, *adj. and n.m. or f.* communist.

comunità, *n.f.* community.

comunque, *adv.* however; howsoever.

con, *prep.* with.

conca, *n.f.* washbowl, basin, tub.

concavo, *adj.* concave.

concèdere, *vb.* grant, concede, allow.

concentramento, *n.m.* gathering.

concentrare, *vb.* concentrate.

concentrato, 1. *adj.* concentrated. 2. *n.m.* tomato paste.

concentrazione, *n.f.* concentration.

concepìbile, *adj.* conceivable.

concepibilmente, *adv.* conceivably.

concepire, vb. conceive.
concèrnere, vb. concern.
concertare, vb. concert.
concertista, n.m. and f. concert performer.
concèrto, n.m. concert; concerto.
concessionàrio, n.m. agent, dealer.
concessione, n.f. concession; grant, bestowal.
concètto, n.m. concept.
concettuale, adj. conceptual.
concezione, n.f. conception, idea.
conchiglia, n.f. conch-shell.
conciare, vb. tan.
conciliàbolo, n.m. secret meeting.
conciliare, vb. conciliate.
conciliativo, adj. conciliatory.
conciliatore, n.m. conciliator.
conciliazione, n.f. conciliation.
concimare, vb. manure.
concime, n.m. compost, manure.
concisamente, adv. concisely.
concisione, n.f. concision, conciseness.
conciso, adj. concise.
concitare, vb. excite, rouse.
conclave, n.m. conclave.
conclùdere, vb. conclude.
conclusione, n.f. conclusion.
conclusivamente, adv. conclusively.
conclusivo, adj. conclusive.
concomitante, adj. concomitant.
concordare, vb. agree.
concordato, n.m. concordat.
concòrde, adj. concordant, agreeing.
concorrènte, n.m. or f. competitor; (sports) entrant.
concorrènza, n.f. concurrence; competition.
concòrrere, vb. compete; concur.
concorso, n.m. competition; tournament; contribution; concurrence; rush (of people).
concozione, n.f. concoction.
concretamente, adv. concretely.
concretézza, n.f. concreteness.
concrèto, adj. concrete.
concubina, n.f. concubine.
concuòcere, vb. concoct.
concupire, vb. covet.
concupiscènte, adj. lustful.
concupiscènza, n.f. lust.

concussione, n.f. concussion.
condanna, n.f. condemnation; doom; conviction; sentence.
condannàbile, adj. condemnable.
condannare, vb. condemn, doom; sentence.
condannato, n.m. convict.
condensare, vb. condense; thicken.
condensatore, n.m. condenser.
condensàzione, n.f. condensation.
condimento, n.m. condiment, seasoning; dressing, relish.
condire, vb. season, use condiments.
condividere, vb. share.
condizionale, adj. conditional.
condizionalmente, adv. conditionally.
condizionare, vb. condition.
condizione, n.f. condition; status.
condoglianza, n.f. condolence.
condolere, vb. condole.
condominio, n.m. condominium.
condonare, vb. condone.
condotta, n.f. conduct, behavior; bearing, deportment.
condotto, n.m. conduct.
conducènte, n.m. driver.
condurre, vb. conduct, lead, guide; drive (a car); (refl.) behave.
conduttività, n.f. conductivity.
conduttivo, adj. conductive.
conduttore, n.m. conductor.
conduttura, n.f. flue.
confederarsi, vb. confederate.
confederato, n.m. confederate.
confederazione, n.f. confederation, confederacy.
conferènza, n.f. conference; lecture.
conferenzière, n.m. lecturer.
conferire, vb. confer, bestow.
conferma, n.f. confirmation.
confermare, vb. confirm.
confessare, vb. confess, admit; avow.
confessionale, n.m. and confessional.
confessione, n.f. c mission, avowal.
confessore, n.m. conf

confetteria, *n.f.* confectionery, confectioner's shop.
confettière, *n.m.* confectioner.
confètto, *n.m.* candy; confection.
confettura, *n.f.* candy; confection.
confezione, *n.f.* ready-to-wear dress.
confidare, *vb.* confide, entrust; rely.
confidènte, 1. *n.m. or f.* confidant. **2.** *adj.* confident.
confidentemente, *adv.* confidently.
confidènza, *n.f.* confidence.
confidenziale, *adj.* confidential.
confinare, *vb.* abut; border; confine; verge.
confine, *n.m.* boundary, border.
confisca, *n.f.* confiscation.
confiscare, *vb.* confiscate.
conflagrazione, *n.f.* conflagration.
conflitto, *n.m.* conflict, strife.
confóndere, *vb.* confuse, confound, addle, bewilder, befuddle.
conformarsi, *vb.* conform.
conformazione, *n.f.* conformation.
conforme, *adj.* in accordance, in conformity.
conformemente, *adv.* accordingly, in conformity.
conformista, *n.m.* conformer, conformist.
conformità, *n.f.* conformity, accordance.
confortare, *vb.* comfort; encourage.
confortatore, *n.m.* comforter.
confòrto, *n.m.* comfort; encouragement.
confrontare, *vb.* compare; confront.
confronto, *n.m.* comparison; collation.
confusione, *n.f.* confusion, blur, mix-up, turmoil.
confuso, *adj.* confused, addled, bewildered.
confutare, *vb.* disprove, refute.
confutazione, *n.f.* disproof, refutation; rebuttal.
ngedare, *vb.* dismiss.
gedo, *n.m.* dismissal; leave.

congegno, *n.m.* contrivance, device, contraption, gadget; gearing.
congelamento, *n.m.* congealment; freezing; frostbite.
congelare, *vb.* congeal, freeze.
congelatore, *n.m.* freezer.
congenitamente, *adv.* congenitally.
congènito, *adj.* congenital.
congestione, *n.f.* congestion.
congettura, *n.f.* conjecture, surmise.
congetturare, *vb.* conjecture, surmise.
congiùngere, *vb.* join, splice.
congiuntamente, *adv.* conjointly.
congiuntivite, *n.f.* conjunctivitis.
congiuntivo, 1. *n.m. (gram.)* subjunctive. **2.** *adj.* (verbs) subjunctive; (pronouns) conjunctive.
congiunto, *adj.* joint.
congiunzione, *n.f.* conjunction; join.
congiura, *n.f.* conspiracy.
congiurare, *vb.* conspire.
congiurato, *n.m.* conspirator.
conglomerare, *vb.* conglomerate.
conglomerato, *n.m. and adj.* conglomerate.
conglomerazione, *n.f.* conglomeration.
congratularsi con, *vb.* congratulate.
congratulatòrio, *adj.* congratulatory.
congregarsi, *vb.* congregate.
congregazione, *n.f.* congregation.
congrèsso, *n.m.* congress; convention.
coniare, *vb.* coin, mint.
cònico, *adj.* conic.
coniglièra, *n.f.* hutch.
coniglietto, *n.m.* little rabbit, bunny.
coniglio, *n.m.* rabbit.
cònio, *n.m.* coinage.
coniugale, *adj.* conjugal.
coniugare, *vb.* conjugate.
coniugazione, *n.f.* conjugation.
connessione, *n.f.* connection.
connèsso, *adj.* related.
connèttere, *vb.* connect.
connivènte, *adj.* conniving.

connivènza, *n.f.* connivance.

connotare, *vb.* connote.

connotazione, *n.f.* connotation.

connubiale, *adj.* connubial.

còno, *n.m.* cone.

conoscènza, *n.f.* acquaintance, knowledge, cognizance.

conóscere, *vb.* know, be acquainted with.

conoscitore, *n.m.* connoisseur.

conosciuto, *adj.* known, acquainted.

conquista, *n.f.* conquest.

conquistàbile, *adj.* conquerable.

conquistare, *vb.* conquer.

conquistatore, *n.m.* conqueror.

consacrare, *vb.* consecrate.

consacrazione, *n.f.* consecration.

consapévole, *adj.* conscious, aware.

consciamente, *adv.* consciously.

cònscio, *adj.* conscious, aware.

consecutivamente, *adv.* consecutively.

consecutivo, *adv.* consecutive.

consegna, *n.f.* consignment, delivery.

consegnare, *vb.* consign, deliver.

consènso, *n.m.* concurrence, agreement, assent, consent; consensus.

consentire, *vb.* consent, accede.

consequènte, *adj.* consequent.

consequentemente, *adv.* consequently.

consequènza, *n.f.* consequence.

consequenziale, *adj.* consequential.

consèrva, *n.f.* jam, preserves; compote.

conservare, *vb.* conserve, keep, preserve, retain, store.

conservativo, *adj.* preservative.

conservatore, *n.m. and adj.* conservative.

conservatòrio, *n.m.* conservatory.

conservazione, *n.f.* conservation, preservation.

consideràbile, *adj.* considerable.

considerabilmente, *adv.* considerably.

considerare, *vb.* consider.

considerazione, *n.f.* consideration.

considerévole, *adj.* considerable.

consigliare, *vb.* advise, counsel.

consigliatamente, *adv.* advisedly.

consigliatore, *n.m.* adviser.

consiglière, *n.m.* councilor, counselor.

consiglio, *n.m.* advice, counsel; council; board.

consistènza, *n.f.* consistency.

consìstere, *vb.* consist.

consolare, *adj.* consular.

consolare, *vb.* console, comfort, solace.

consolato, *n.m.* consulate; consulship.

consolatore, *n.m.* consoler, comforter.

consolazione, *n.f.* consolation, solace.

cònsole, *n.m.* consul.

consolidare, *vb.* consolidate.

consòlida reale, *n.f.* larkspur.

consonante, *n.f. and adj.* consonant.

consòrte, *n.m. and f.* consort, mate.

consòrzio, *n.m.* syndicate; trust.

consòrzio automobilìstico, *n.m.* car pool.

constare, *vb.* consist of, be composed of.

constatare, *vb.* verify; observe; remark.

consuèto, *n.m.* customary.

consuetùdine, *n.f.* custom.

consulènte, *n.m. and f.* adviser, expert.

consulènza, *n.f.* expert advice.

consultare, *vb.* consult.

consultatore, *n.m.* consultant.

consultazione, *n.f.* consultation.

consulto, *n.m.* consultation.

consumare, *vb.* consume; expend, wear out.

consumato, *adj.* worn out; experienced; consummate.

consumatore, *n.m.* consumer.

consumazione, *n.f.* consummation.

consumismo, *n.m.* consumerism.

consumo, *n.m.* consumption; wear.

consuntivo, 1. *adj.* final, end-of-year (*e.g.,* report). **2.** *n.m.* balance sheet.

contàbile, *n.m.* bookkeeper.

contabilità, *n.f.* accounting, bookkeeping.

contachilòmetri, *n.m.* odometer; speedometer.

contadino, 1. *n.m.* peasant; countryman; farmer. **2.** *adj.* peasant; rustic.

contàgio, *n.m.* contagion.

contagioso, *adj.* contagious.

contagocce, *n.m.* dropper.

contaminare, *vb.* contaminate; pollute.

contaminazione, *n.f.* contamination; infection.

contanti, *n.m.pl.* cash.

contare, *vb.* count; **c. su** count on, rely on.

contatore, *n.m.* meter.

contattare, *vb.* contact.

contatto, *n.m.* contact.

conte, *n.m.* count, earl.

contèa, *n.f.* county.

contegno, *n.m.* reserved attitude, reserved behavior.

contemplare, *vb.* contemplate.

contemplativo, *adj.* contemplative.

contemplazione, *n.f.* contemplation.

contemporàneo, *adj.* contemporary.

contendènte, *n.m.* contender.

contèndere, *vb.* contend, quarrel.

contenere, *vb.* contain.

contentezza, *n.f.* contentment, gladness.

contènto, *adj.* glad, happy, content.

contenzione, *n.f.* contention.

contesa, *n.f.* contest.

contessa, *n.f.* countess.

contestàbile, *adj.* contestable.

contestare, *vb.* contest.

contestazione, *n.f.* dispute, disagreement; notification.

contesto, *n.m.* context.

contiguo, *adj.* contiguous.

continentale, *adj.* continental.

continènte, 1. *n.m.* continent. **2.** *adj.* continent, chaste.

continènza, *n.f.* continence.

contingènte, *adj.* contingent.

contingènza, *n.f.* contingency.

continuamente, *adv.* continually.

continuare, *vb.* continue.

continuazione, *n.f.* continuation.

continuità, *n.f.* continuity.

contìnuo, *adj.* continual, continuous. **corrènte continua,** direct current.

conto, *n.m.* account; bill; check; count. **rèndere c. di,** account for. **rèndersi c. di,** realize.

contòrcere, *vb.* contort; (*refl.*) writhe.

contorno, *n.m.* contour; side-dish.

contorsione, *n.f.* contortion.

contorsionista, *n.m.* contortionist.

contorto, *adj.* contorted, twisted.

contrabbandare, *vb.* smuggle.

contrabbandière, *n.m.* smuggler.

contrabbando, *n.m.* contraband, smuggling.

contrabasso, *n.m.* contrabass.

contraccolpo, *n.m.* rebound; repercussion; recoil.

contraddìcibile, *adj.* contradictable.

contraddire, *vb.* contradict, gainsay.

contraddistìnguere, *vb.* qualify, characterize, earmark.

contraddittòrio, *adj.* contradictory.

contraddizione, *n.f.* contradiction.

contraffare, *vb.* counterfeit; forge; imitate; impersonate.

contraffattore, *n.m.* forger; impersonator.

contraffazione, *n.f.* forgery; impersonation.

contrafffòrte, *n.m.* buttress.

contralto, *n.m.* contralto; alto.

contrappeso, *n.m.* counterbalance.

contrariare, *vb.* spite.

contràrio, *adj.* contrary; reverse.

contrarre, *vb.* contract; (*refl.*) shrink.

contrastare, *vb.* contrast.

contrasto, *n.m.* contrast.

contrattacco, *n.m.* counter-attack.

contrattatore, *n.m.* contractor.

contratto, *n.m.* contract.

contravvenire, *vb.* infringe upon, transgress.

contravventore, *n.m.* violator.

contravvenzione, *n.f.* misdemeanor, violation, summons.

contrazione, *n.f.* contraction.

contribuènte, *n.m.* taxpayer.

contribuire, *vb.* contribute.

contributivo, *adj.* contributive.

contributo, *n.m.* contribution.

contributore, *n.m.* contributor.

contributòrio, *adj.* contributory.

contribuzione, *n.f.* contribution.

contrito, *adj.* contrite.

contrizione, *n.f.* contrition.

contro, *prep.* against, versus. **c. assegno,** C.O.D.

controazione, *n.f.* counteraction.

controbàttere, *vb.* counter-attack; rebut, dispute.

controcorrènte, *adv.* upstream.

controcurva, *n.f.* reverse curve.

controffensiva, *n.f.* counteroffensive.

controfigura, *n.f.* stuntman, stand-in.

controllàbile, *adj.* controllable.

controllare, *vb.* check, inspect; audit.

contròllo, *n.m.* check; restraint; inspection; audit.

controllo delle nàscite, *n.m.* birth control, contraception.

controllore, *n.m.* controller; inspector; auditor; ticket-collector.

controluce, 1. *adv.* against the light. **2.** *n.f.* back lighting.

contromandare, *vb.* countermand.

contromano, *adv.* against traffic.

contromarca, *n.f.* check.

controparte, *n.f.* opponent.

contropartita, *n.f.* counterpart.

contropelo, *adv.* against the grain; close (shave).

Controriforma, *n.f.* Counter-Reformation.

controspionàggio, *n.m.* counterespionage.

controvèrsia, *n.f.* controversy.

controvèrso, *adj.* controversial.

contumace, *adj.* defaulting.

contumàcia, *n.f.* default.

contusione, *n.f.* contusion.

convalescènte, *adj.* convalescent.

convalescènza, *n.f.* convalescence.

conveniènte, *adj.* convenient; advisable; suitable, fitting.

convenientemente, *adv.* conveniently.

conveniènza, *n.f.* convenience; advisability; suitability; propriety.

convenire, *vb.* come together, convene; be suitable; become; befit.

convènto, *n.m.* convent; monastery.

convenzionale, *adj.* conventional.

convenzionalmente, *adv.* conventionally.

convenzione, *n.f.* convention; covenant.

convergènte, *adj.* convergent.

convergènza, *n.f.* convergence.

convèrgere, *vb.* converge.

conversare, *vb.* converse.

conversatore, *n.m.* conversationalist.

convèrso, *adj.* converse.

convertìbile, *adj.* convertible.

convertire, *vb.* convey.

convertitore, *n.m.* converter.

convertitore, *n.m.* converter.

convertitrice, *n.f.* converter.

convèsso, *adj.* convex.

convincènte, *adj.* convincing, cogent.

convìncere, *vb.* convince.

convincimento, *n.m.* persuasion, belief.

convinzione, *n.f.* conviction.

convitato, *adj. and n.m.* invited guest.

convivènte, *n.m. and f.* roommate.

conviviale, *adj.* convivial.

convocare, *vb.* convoke.

convocazione, *n.f.* convocation.

convogliare, *vb.* convoy.

convòglio, *n.m.* convoy, train, procession.

convulsione, *n.f.* convulsion.

convulsivo, *adj.* convulsive.

cooperare, vb. cooperate.

cooperativa, n.f. cooperative.

cooperativamente, adv. cooperatively.

cooperativo, adj. cooperative.

cooperazione, n.f. cooperation.

coordinare, vb. coordinate.

coordinatore, n.m. coordinator.

coordinazione, n.m. coordination.

coòrte, n.f. cohort.

copèrchio, n.m. lid.

copèrta, n.f. cover, blanket.

copertina, n.f. cover (of book).

copertone, n.m. tire casing; tarpaulin.

copertura, n.f. cover, covering.

còpia, n.f. copy; copiousness.

copiare, vb. copy.

copiativo, adj. copying; indelible.

copiatore, n.m. copier.

copiosamente, adv. copiously.

copiosità, n.f. copiousness.

copioso, adj. copious.

copista, n.m. copyist.

coppa, n.f. cup, mug, flagon, goblet.

cóppia, n.f. couple.

coprifuòco, n.m. curfew.

coprire, vb. cover.

coraggio, n.m. courage, bravery; gameness; gallantry; mettle.

coraggiosamente, adv. courageously, gamely, gallantly.

coraggioso, adj. brave, courageous; game; gallant.

corale, adj. choral.

corallino, adj. coral.

corallo, n.m. coral.

Corano, n.m. Koran.

corazza, n.f. armorplate, breastplate; shell.

còrda, n.f. string, rope, cord; chord.

cordiale, n.m. and adj. cordial, hearty.

cordialità, n.f. cordiality.

cordialmente, adv. cordially.

cordiglièra, n.f. ladder; run.

cordòglio, n.m. affliction, sorrow, grief.

cordone, n.m. cordon.

cordovano, n.m. cordovan.

Corèa, n.f. Korea.

coreggiato, n.m. flail.

coreografia, n.f. choreography.

coreògrafo, n.m. choreographer.

coriàceo, adj. coriaceous, tough.

coriàndoli, n.m.pl. confetti.

coricare, vb. lay down, bed down.

corista, n.m. chorister.

cormorano, n.m. cormorant.

cornamusa, n.f. bagpipe.

còrnea, n.f. cornea.

cornetta, n.f. cornet.

cornettista, n.m. cornetist.

cornice, n.m. frame, mantel.

cornicione, n.m. cornice.

còrno, n.m. horn.

cornucòpia, n.m. or f. cornucopia.

còro, n.m. chorus, choir; chancel.

corollàrio, n.m. corollary.

corona, n.f. crown. **c. nobiliare,** coronet.

coronàrio, adj. coronary.

còrpo, n.m. body; corps.

corporale, adj. corporal.

corporato, adj. corporate.

corporazione, n.f. corporation; guild.

corpòreo, adj. corporeal, bodily.

corpulènto, adj. corpulent, burly, portly.

corpùscolo, n.m. corpuscle.

corredare, vb. equip, outfit; provide.

corredino, n.m. layette, baby's outfits.

corrèdo, n.m. equipment, outfit.

corrèggere, vb. correct, amend, right.

correità, n.f. complicity.

correlare, vb. correlate.

correlazione, n.f. correlation.

corrènte, 1. n.f. current; stream. **c. alternata,** alternating current. **c. continua,** direct current. **c. d'ària,** draft. **2.** adj. current: (in dates) instant.

correntemente, adv. currently.

correntista, n.m. depositor.

córrere, vb. run; race.

corresponsàbile, 1. adj. jointly responsible. **2.** n.m. accomplice, co-respondent.

correttamente, adv. correctly.

correttezza, n.f. correctness.

correttivo, adj. corrective.

corrètto, adj. correct, right.

correzione, n.f. correction.

còrricòrri, *n.m.* rush.

corridoio, *n.m.* corridor, hallway; lobby.

corridore, *n.m.* runner.

corriera, *n.f.* bus.

corrière, *n.m.* courier.

corrispondènte, 1. *n.* correspondent. 2. *adj.* corresponding; correspondent.

corrispondènza, *n.f.* correspondence.

corrispóndere, *vb.* correspond.

corroborante, *adj.* corroborating.

corroborare, *vb.* corroborate.

corroborativo, *adj.* corroborative.

corroborazione, *n.f.* corroboration.

corródere, *vb.* corrode.

corrómpere, *vb.* corrupt; bribe.

corrosione, *n.f.* corrosion.

corrosivo, *adj.* corrosive.

corroso, *adj.* corroded.

corrotto, *adj.* corrupted.

corrugare, *vb.* corrugate, wrinkle.

corruttìbile, *adj.* corruptible.

corruttivo, *adj.* corruptive.

corruttore, *n.m.* corrupter; briber.

corruzione, *n.f.* corruption; bribery.

corsa, *n.f.* race; ride; trip.

corso, *n.m.* course.

còrso, *adj.* Corsican.

corte, *n.f.* court.

cortéccia, *n.f.* bark.

corteggiamento, *n.m.* courting, courtship.

corteggiare, *vb.* court, woo.

corteggiatore, *n.m.* wooer, beau, suitor.

cortèo, *n.m.* cortege, procession; pageant.

cortese, *adj.* courteous, accommodating, polite.

cortesia, *n.f.* courtesy, politeness.

cortigiana, *n.f.* courtesan, prostitute.

cortigiano, *n.m.* courtier.

cortile, *n.m.* courtyard, patio.

cortina, *n.f.* curtain.

corto, *adj.* short; stupid; (of sea) choppy.

corvetta, *n.f.* corvette.

corvino, *adj.* raven.

còrvo, *n.m.* crow; raven.

còsa, *n.f.* thing.

còscia, *n.f.* thigh.

cosciènza, *n.f.* consciousness; conscience.

coscienziosamente, *adv.* conscientiously.

coscienzioso, *adj.* conscientious, painstaking.

cosciòtto, *n.m.* leg of lamb.

coscritto, *n.m. and adj.* conscript.

coscrizione, *n.f.* conscription.

così, *adv.* so, thus.

cosiddetto, *adj.* so-called.

cosmètico, *n.m. and adj.* cosmetic.

còsmico, *adj.* cosmic.

còsmo, *n.m.* cosmos.

cosmologia, *n.f.* cosmology.

cosmonàuta, *n.m. and f.* astronaut.

cosmopolita, *adj.* cosmopolitan.

còso, *n.m.* thingumajig.

cospàrgere, *vb.* scatter, intersperse, sprinkle, strew.

cospètto, *n.m.* presence.

cospicuamente, *adv.* conspicuously.

cospicuità, *n.f.* conspicuousness.

cospìcuo, *adj.* conspicuous.

costa, *n.f.* coast.

costante, *adj.* constant, fixed, firm.

costantemente, *adv.* constantly.

costanza, *n.f.* constancy.

costare, *vb.* cost.

costata, *n.f.* rib roast, rack.

costeggiare, *vb.* flank, coast, sail alongside.

costei, *pron.dem.f.sg.* this one, this woman, she.

costellazione, *n.f.* constellation.

costernare, *vb.* dismay.

costernazione, *n.f.* consternation, dismay.

costì, *adv.* there.

costièro, *adj.* coastal.

costipazione, *n.f.* constipation.

costituènte, *adj.* constituent.

costituìre, *vb.* constitute.

costituzionale, *adj.* constitutional.

costituzione, *n.f.* constitution.

còsto, *n.m.* cost, expense.

còstola, *n.f.* rib.

costoletta, *n.f.* chop, rib.

costosamente, *adv.* expensively.

costoro, *pron. dem. m.f.pl.* these, these men, these women, they.

costoso, *adj.* costly, dear, expensive, valuable.

costringere, *vb.* force, coerce, compel, constrict, constrain.

costruire, *vb.* construct, build, erect.

costruttivamente, *adv.* constructively.

costruttivo, *adj.* constructive.

costruttore, *n.m.* builder, constructor.

costruzione, *n.f.* construction, erection.

costui, *pron. dem. m.sg.* this one, this man, he.

costume, *n.m.* costume, garb; custom; *(pl.)* mores.

còte, *n.f.* hone.

cotenna, *n.f.* pigskin, scalp.

cotiglione, *n.m.* cotillion.

cotognata, *n.f.* quince jam.

cotoletta, *n.f.* cutlet.

cotone, *n.m.* cotton.

cotonificio, *n.m.* cotton mill.

cotonina, *n.f.* cotton cloth, cretonne.

còtto, *adj.* cooked; done.

covare, *vb.* brood, hatch; smolder.

covata, *n.f.* brood.

covo, *n.m.* den, lair.

covone, *n.m.* sheaf.

crampo, *n.m.* cramp.

crànio, *n.m.* cranium, skull.

cratère, *n.m.* crater.

cravatta, *n.f.* necktie.

creare, *vb.* create.

creativo, *adj.* creative.

creatore, *n.m.* creator.

creatura, *n.f.* creature.

creazione, *n.f.* creation.

credènte, *n.m.* believer.

credènza, *n.f.* belief, credence; cupboard; dresser.

credenziali, *f.pl.* credentials.

crédere, *vb.* believe, think.

credibile, *adj.* credible, believable.

credibilità, *n.f.* credibility.

crèdito, *n.m.* credit.

creditore, *n.m.* creditor.

crèdo, *n.m.* credo, creed.

credulità, *n.f.* credulity.

crèdulo, *adj.* credulous, gullible.

credulone, *n.m.* dupe.

crèma, *n.f.* cream.

crema caramella, *n.f.* custard.

cremaglièra, *n.f.* rack.

cremare, *vb.* cremate.

crematòrio, *adj.* crematory.

cremazione, *n.f.* cremation.

cremerìa, *n.f.* creamery.

crèmisi, *adj.* crimson.

creosòto, *n.m.* creosote.

crèpa, *n.f.* crack, chink.

crepàccio, *n.m.* crevasse.

crepacuòre, *n.m.* heartbreak.

crepùscolo, *n.m.* twilight, dusk.

créscere, *vb.* grow.

créscita, *n.f.* growth.

crespo, 1. *n.m.* crepe. 2. *adj.* wavy; crisp.

cresta, *n.f.* crest, ridge; (rooster's) comb.

crèta, *n.f.* clay.

cricca, *n.f.* clique, clan.

cricco, *n.m.* jack.

criminale, *adj.* criminal.

criminologìa, *n.f.* criminology.

criminòlogo, *n.m.* criminologist.

criminoso, *adj.* criminal; incriminating.

crinale, *n.m.* edge, ridge.

crine, *n.f.* hair.

crinièra, *n.f.* mane.

criochirurgìa, *n.f.* cryosurgery.

cripta, *n.f.* crypt.

crisàlide, *n.f.* chrysalis.

crisantèmo, *n.m.* chrysanthemum.

crisi, *n.f.* crisis.

cristallerìe, *n.f.pl.* glassware.

cristallino, *adj.* crystalline.

cristallizzare, *vb.* crystalize.

cristallo, *n.m.* crystal; cut glass.

cristianésimo, *n.m.* Christianity.

cristianità, *n.f.* Christendom.

cristiano, *n. and adj.* Christian.

Cristo, *n.m.* Christ.

critèrio, *n.m.* criterion.

crìtica, *n.f.* criticism, critique, fault finding.

criticare, *vb.* criticize.

crìtico, 1. *n.* critic. 2. *adj.* critical.

crittografìa, *n.f.* cryptography.

crittogramma, *n.m.* cryptogram.

crivellare, *vb.* sift; screen.
crivèllo, *n.m.* sieve; screen.
croato, *n.m. and adj.* Croatian.
Croàzia, *n.f.* Croatia.
croccante, *adj.* crisp.
crocchetta, *n.f.* croquette.
croce, *n.f.* cross.
crocefissione, *n.f.* crucifixion.
crocefisso, *n.m.* crucifix.
crocevìa, *n.f.* crossroads.
crociata, *n.f.* crusade.
crociato, *n.m.* crusader.
crocicchio, *n.m.* crossroads.
crocièra, *n.f.* crusade.
crocifìggere, *vb.* crucify.
cròco, *n.m.* crocus.
crogiolo, *n.m.* crucible.
crollare, *vb.* collapse, crash.
cròllo, *n.m.* collapse, crash.
cromàtico, *adj.* chromatic.
cròmo, *n.m.* chrome, chromium.
cromosòma, *n.m.* chromosome.
crònaca, *n.f.* chronicle.
cronicamente, *adv.* chronically.
crònico, *adj.* chronic.
cronista, *n.m.* chronicler; (newspaper) columnist; (radio) commentator.
cronologìa, *n.f.* chronology.
cronològico, *adj.* chronological.
cronometrare, *vb.* time.
cronòmetro, *n.m.* chronometer, stopwatch.
crosta, *n.f.* crust; scab.
crostàceo, *n.m. and adj.* crustacean.
crostata, *n.f.* tart.
crostino, *n.m.* crouton; canapé.
crostoso, *adj.* crusty.
crucciato, *adj.* worried, upset.
crùccio, *n.m.* chagrin.
cruciale, *adj.* crucial.
crucivèrba, *n.m.* cross-word puzzle.
crudèle, *adj.* cruel.
crudeltà, *n.f.* cruelty.
crudezza, *n.f.* crudeness.
crudità, *n.f.* crudity.
crudo, *adj.* crude, raw.
crumiro, *n.m.* scab, strikebreaker.
cruna, *n.f.* eye (of a needle).
crusca, *n.f.* bran.
cruscòtto, *n.m.* dashboard.
Cuba, *n.f.* Cuba
cubano, *adj.* Cuban.

cubatura, *n.f.* volume.
cùbico, *adj.* cubic.
cubìcolo, *n.m.* cubicle.
cubismo, *n.m.* cubism.
cubo, *n.m.* cube.
cubo per flash, *n.m.* flashcube.
cuccetta, *n.f.* berth, bunk.
cucchiaiata, *n.f.* spoonful.
cucchiaìno, *n.m.* teaspoon.
cùccia, *n.f.* dog's bed.
cùcciolo, *n.m.* puppy.
cucchiàio, *s.m.* spoon, tablespoon; tablespoonful.
cucina, *n.f.* kitchen, cuisine; cooking. **c. econòmica,** range. **libro di c.,** cookbook.
cucinare, *vb.* cook.
cucire, *vb.* sew.
cucitura, *n.f.* sewing; seam.
cuculo, *n.m.* cuckoo.
cuffia, *n.f.* cap; hood; earphone.
cugina, *n.f.* cousin.
cugino, *n.m.* cousin.
cùi, *pron.* which; to which; whom; to whom; of which; whose.
cùlice, *n.m.* gnat.
culinàrio, *adj.* culinary.
culla, *n.f.* cradle.
cullare, *vb.* cradle, lull.
culminante, *adj.* culminating, climactic.
culminare, *vb.* culminate.
cùlmine, *n.m.* top, summit; climax.
culo, *n.m.* posterior.
culto, *n.m.* cult; worship.
cultore, *n.m.* enthusiast (of arts); expert.
cultura, *n.f.* culture.
culturale, *adj.* cultural.
cumulativo, *adj.* cumulative.
cùneo, *n.m.* wedge.
cunetta, *n.f.* gutter.
cuòco, *n.m.* cook, chef.
cuòio, *n.m.* leather.
cuòre, *n.m.* heart.
cupè, *n.m.* coupé.
cupidigia, *n.f.* greed; cupidity.
cupo, *adj.* sullen.
cùpola, *n.f.* cupola, dome.
cura, *n.f.* care; cure; worry.
curare, *vb.* care for, take care of, nurse, nurture, tend; (*refl.*) care.
curativo, *adj.* healing, curative.
curato, *n.m.* curate.

curatore, *n.m.* curator.
curia, *n.f.* curia.
curiosare, *vb.* browse; pry, snoop.
curiosità, *n.f.* curiosity, curio.
curioso, *adj.* curious.
currìcolo, *n.m.* curriculum.
curva, *n.f.* curve.
curvare, *vb.* curve, bend, warp; hunch; *(refl.)* stoop.
curvatura, *n.f.* curvature; crook.
curvo, *adj.* curved, bent; stooped.
cuscinetto, *n.m.* pad; stamp pad; (machinery) bearing. **stato c.,** buffer state. **c. a rotolamento,** roller bearing. **c. a sfere,** ball bearing.
cuscino, *n.m.* cushion.
custòde, *n.m.* custodian, guardian, keeper.
custòdia, *n.f.* custody, charge.
custodire, *vb.* guard.
cutàneo, *adj.* cutaneous.
cute, *n.f.* skin.
cutìcola, *n.f.* cuticle.

D

da, *prep.* from; by; for; fit for, suitable for; characteristic of; at . . .'s (house, shop, etc.).
dabbasso, *adv.* downstairs.
dabbène, *adj.* honest, upright.
dado, *n.m.* die (*pl.* dice).
daga, *n.f.* dagger.
dàina, *n.f.* hind.
dàino, *n.m.* buck.
dàlia, *n.f.* dahlia.
daltònico, *adj.* color blind.
dama, *n.f.* lady; checkers.
damasco, *n.m.* damask.
damerino, *n.m.* dandy, fop.
damigèlla, *n.f.* damsel. **d. d'onore,** maid of honor, bridesmaid.
damigiana, *n.f.* demijohn.
danese, *adj.* Danish.
Danimarca, *n.f.* Denmark.
dannare, *vb.* damn.
dannazione, *n.f.* damnation.
danneggiare, *vb.* harm, damage, injure; mar.
danno, *n.m.* harm, damage, detriment, hurt, injury.
dannoso, *adj.* harmful, baneful, detrimental, hurtful, injurious.
danza, *n.f.* dance.
danzare, *vb.* dance.
dappertutto, *adv.* everywhere; throughout.
dardo, *n.m.* dart.
dare, *vb.* give.
dàrsena, *n.f.* marina, dock, basin.
data, *n.f.* date.
datare, *vb.* date (administrative).
dati, *n.m.pl.* data.
datore, *n.m.* giver. **d. di lavoro,** employer.

dàttero, *n.m.* date.
dattilògrafa, *vb.* typist.
dattilografare, *vb.* type.
dattiloscritto, *n.m.* typed.
davanti, 1. *n.m.* front. **2.** *adv.* before. **d. a,** *prep.* before.
davanzale, *n.m.* sill.
davvero, *adv.* indeed, really.
dàzio, *n.m.* excise.
dèa, *n.f.* goddess.
debilitare, *vb.* debilitate.
debitamente, *adv.* duly.
dèbito, 1. *n.m.* debt, debit. **2.** *adj.* due.
debitore, *n.m.* debtor.
dèbole, *adj.* weak, feeble, faint, frail, puny.
debolezza, *n.f.* weakness, feebleness, failing, frailty.
debolmente, *adv.* weakly, faintly.
debordare, *vb.* overflow.
debuttante, *n.* debutant(e).
debutto, *n.m.* debut.
dècade, *n.f.* decade.
decadenza, *n.f.* decline, decay, decadence.
decalcomanìa, *n.f.* decalcomania.
decadènte, *adj.* decadent.
decadènza, *n.f.* decay, decadence, decline.
decadere, *vb.* decay, decline, lapse.
decaffeinizzato, *adj.* decaffeinated.
decano, *n.m.* dean.
decapitare, *vb.* behead, decapitate.
deceduto, *adj.* deceased.

decelerare, *vb.* decelerate.
decènnio, *n.m.* decade.
decènte, *adj.* decent.
decentralizzare, *vb.* decentralize.
decentramento, *n.m.* decentralization.
decentrare, *vb.* decentralize.
decènza, *n.f.* decency.
dècibel, *n.m.* decibel.
decidere, *vb.* decide; *(refl.)* decide, make up one's mind, resolve.
deciduo, *adj.* deciduous.
decifrare, *vb.* decipher, decode.
decimale, *adj.* decimal.
decimare, *vb.* decimate.
dècimo, *adj.* tenth.
decimonòno, *adj.* nineteenth.
decimosèsto, *adj.* sixteenth.
decimotèrzo, *adj.* thirteenth.
decimottavo, *adj.* eighteenth.
decisione, *n.f.* decision, resolve.
decisivo, *adj.* decisive.
declamare, *vb.* delaim.
declamazione, *n.f.* declamation.
declinare, *vb.* decline.
declinazione, *n.f.* declension.
declino, *n.m.* decline, decrease.
declivio, *n.m.* slope.
decollare, *vb.* take off.
decomporre, *vb.* decompose, decay.
decomposizione, *n.f.* decomposition, decay.
decongestionante, *adj.* decongestant.
decontaminare, *vb.* decontaminate.
decorare, *vb.* decorate.
decorativo, *adj.* decorative.
decoratore, *n.m.* decorator.
decorazione, *n.f.* decoration.
decòro, *n.m.* decorum.
decoroso, *adj.* decorous.
decorrènza, *n.f.* beginning; effective date.
decrèpito, *adj.* decrepit.
decréscere, *vb.* diminish, decrease.
decretare, *vb.* decree; enact.
decreto, *n.m.* decree; enactment.
decuplicare, *vb.* multiply tenfold.
dèdica, *n.f.* dedication.
dedicare, *vb.* dedicate, devote; *(refl.)* become addicted.
dedurre, *vb.* deduce, deduct.

deduttivo, *adj.* deductive.
deduzione, *n.f.* deduction.
deferènte, *adj.* deferent.
deferènza, *n.f.* deference.
defezione, *n.f.* defection.
deficiènte, *adj.* deficient.
deficiènza, *n.f.* deficiency.
dèficit, *n.m.* deficit.
definibile, *adj.* definable.
definire, *vb.* define, determine.
definitivamente, *adj.* definitely.
definitivo, *adj.* definitive, final.
definito, *adj.* definite; finite.
definizione, *n.f.* definition.
deflagrare, *vb.* explode, burst.
deflagrazione, *n.f.* burst, explosion.
deflazionare, *vb.* deflate.
deflazione, *n.f.* deflation.
deflèttere, *vb.* deflect.
deformare, *vb.* deform.
deforme, *adj.* deformed.
deformità, *n.f.* deformity.
defraudare, *vb.* defraud.
defunto, *adj.* defunct, deceased.
degenerare, *vb.* degenerate.
degenerato, *n.m. and adj.* degenerate.
degenerazione, *n.f.* degeneration.
degènte, *adj.* bedridden.
degènza, *n.f.* hospitalization.
degnarsi, *vb.* deign.
degno, *adj.* worthy.
degradare, *vb.* degrade, demote.
degradazione, *n.f.* degradation.
degustare, *vb.* taste.
deificare, *vb.* deify.
deità, *n.f.* deity.
delatore, *n.m.* informer, spy.
delegare, *vb.* delegate.
delegato, *n.m.* delegate.
delegazione, *n.f.* delegation.
deletèrio, *adj.* deleterious, harmful.
delfino, *n.m.* dolphin.
deliberare, *vb.* deliberate.
deliberatamente, *adv.* deliberately.
deliberativo, *adj.* deliberative.
deliberato, *adj.* deliberate.
deliberazione, *n.f.* advisement; resolution.
delicatezza, *n.f.* delicacy.
delicato, *adj.* delicate, dainty.

delimitare, *vb.* delimit, define.

delineare, *vb.* delineate.

delinquènte, *adj.* delinquent.

delinquènza, *n.f.* delinquency.

delirante, *adj.* delirious.

delirare, *vb.* be delirious, rave.

delirio, *n.m.* delirium.

delitto, *n.m.* crime.

delizia, *n.f.* delight.

delizioso, *adj.* delicious.

delucidare, *vb.* explain.

delùdere, *vb.* delude; disappoint.

delusione, *n.f.* delusion; disappointment.

demagògo, *n.m.* demagogue.

demarcazione, *n.f.* demarcation.

demènte, *adj.* demented.

demeritare, *vb.* forfeit.

demèrito, *n.m.* demerit.

democràtico, 1. *n.m.* democrat. **2.** *adj.* democratic.

democrazìa, *n.f.* democracy.

demolire, *vb.* demolish.

demolizione, *n.f.* demolition.

demonìaco, *adj.* demoniacal, fiendish.

demònio, *n.m.* demon, fiend.

demoralizzare, *vb.* demoralize.

denaro, *n.m.* money.

denaturare, *vb.* denature.

denigrare, *vb.* denigrate, blacken, slander, cast aspersions on, belittle.

denigrazione, *n.f.* slander, aspersion.

denominatore, *n.m.* denominator.

denominazione, *n.f.* denomination.

densità, *n.f.* density.

dènso, *adj.* dense, thick.

dentale, *adj.* dental.

dènte, *n.m.* tooth; cog.

dentellare, *vb.* indent.

dentellatura, *n.f.* indentation.

dentièra, *n.f.* denture; gearing. **ferrovìa a d.,** cog railway.

dentifricio, *n.m.* dentifrice.

dentista, *n.m.* dentist.

dentro, *adv. and prep.* inside, within.

denuclearizzare, *vb.* denuclearize.

denudare, *vb.* denude.

denùncia, *n.f.* denunciation.

denunciare, *vb.* denounce; report.

denutrito, *adj.* undernourished, starving.

denutrizione, *n.f.* undernourishment, starvation.

deodorante, *n.m.* deodorant.

deodorare, *vb.* deodorize.

depennare, *vb.* cross out, strike out, expunge.

deperìbile, *adj.* perishable.

deplorare, *vb.* deplore.

deplorévole, *adj.* deplorable.

deporre, *vb.* depose; put down, set down; lay.

deportare, *vb.* deport.

deportazione, *n.f.* deportation.

depositante, *n.m.* depositor.

depositare, *vb.* deposit.

depòsito, *n.m.* deposit; depot. **d. bagagli,** checkroom.

deposizione, *n.f.* deposition, statement.

depravare, *vb.* deprave.

depravazione, *n.f.* depravity.

deprecare, *vb.* deprecate, decry.

depredamento, *n.m.* depredation.

depressione, *n.f.* depression.

deprezzamento, *n.m.* depreciation.

deprezzare, *vb.* depreciate, cheapen.

deprimere, *vb.* depress.

deputato, *n.m.* deputy, representative.

deragliare, *vb.* derail.

derelitto, *adj.* derelict.

deretano, *n.m.* buttocks, behind.

derìdere, *vb.* deride, mock, laugh at, ridicule.

derisione, *n.f.* derision, mockery.

derisivo, *adj.* derisive.

deriva, *n.f.* drift. **alla d.,** adrift.

derivare, *vb.* derive.

derivativo, *adj.* derivative.

derivato, 1. *adj.* derived. **2.** *n.m.* byproduct, derivative.

derivazione, *n.f.* derivation.

dermatologìa, *n.f.* dermatology.

dermatòlogo, *n.m.* dermatologist.

dèroga, *n.f.* derogation; exception.

derogatòrio, *adj.* derogatory.

derubare, *vb.* rob.

descrittivo, *adj.* descriptive.
descrizione, *n.f.* description.
desensibilizzare, *vb.* desensitize.
desèrto, *n.m.* desert; wilderness.
desideràbile, *adj.* desirable.
desiderabilità, *n.f.* desirability.
desiderare, *vb.* desire, want, wish.
desidèrio, *n.m.* desire, wish.
desideroso, *adj.* desirous.
designare, *vb.* designate, nominate.
designato, *n.m.* nominee.
designazione, *n.f.* designation.
desinènza, *n.f.* ending.
desistere, *vb.* desist.
desolante, *adj.* desolating, distressing.
desolare, *vb.* desolate.
desolato, *adj.* desolate, afflicted, sorry.
desolazione, *n.f.* desolation, sorrow.
dèspota, *n.m.* despot.
dessèrt, *n.m.* dessert.
destare, *vb.* awaken.
destinare, *vb.* destine.
destinatàrio, *n.m.* addressee.
destinazione, *n.f.* destination.
destino, *n.m.* destiny, doom.
destituire, *vb.* dismiss, remove.
destituito, *adj.* destitute.
destituzione, *n.f.* destitution.
desto, *adj.* awake.
dèstra, *n.f.* right.
destramente, *adv.* skillfully, dexterously.
destreggiarsi, *vb.* manage shrewdly.
destrezza, *n.f.* adroitness, adeptness, dexterity, skill.
destrièro, *n.m.* steed.
dèstro, *adj.* adroit, adept, deft, skillful, dexterous, handy; right.
destròrso, *adj. and adv.* clockwise.
destròsio, *n.m.* destrose.
desùmere, *vb.* gather; infer.
detenere, *vb.* detain.
detenzione, *n.f.* detention.
detergènte, *n.m. and adj.* detergent.
deteriorare, *vb.* deteriorate.
deterioramento, *n.m.* deterioration.
determinare, *vb.* determine.

determinazione, *n.f.* determination.
determinismo, *n.m.* determinism.
detestare, *vb.* detest, abhor.
detestazione, *n.f.* detestation, abhorrence.
detonare, *vb.* detonate.
detonazione, *n.f.* detonation, report.
detrarre, *vb.* detract.
detrimento, *n.m.* detriment.
detriti, *n.m.pl.* debris.
detronizzare, *vb.* dethrone.
dettàglio, *n.m.* detail. **al d.,** at retail.
dettare, *vb.* dictate.
dettatura, *n.f.* dictation.
devastare, *vb.* devastate, ravage.
devastazione, *n.f.* devastation, havoc, ravage.
deviante, *adj.* negative; misleading.
deviare, *vb.* deviate.
deviazione, *n.f.* deviation, detour.
dèvio, *adj.* devious.
devitalizzare, *vb.* devitalize.
dev.mo, (for **devotissimo,** *adj.*): **Vostro d.,** yours truly.
devoluzione, *n.f.* transfer; charity.
devòto, *adj.* devout, devoted, godly.
devozione, *n.f.* devotion.
di, *prep.* of; than.
dì, *n.m.* day.
diabète, *n.m.* diabetes.
diabòlico, *adj.* diabolic, devilish.
diàcono, *n.m.* deacon.
diadèma, *n.m.* diadem, coronet.
diaframma, *n.m.* diaphragm; midriff.
diàgnosi, *n.f.* diagnosis.
diagnosticare, *vb.* diagnose.
diagnòstico, *adj.* diagnostic.
diagonale, *adj.* diagonal.
diagonalmente, *adv.* diagonally.
diagramma, *n.m.* diagram.
dialètto, *n.m.* dialect.
diàlogo, *n.m.* dialogue.
diamante, *n.m.* diamond.
diametrale, *adj.* diametrical.
diàmetro, *n.m.* diameter.
diàmine!, *interj.* the dickens!

diàpason, *n.m.* tuning fork.

diapositiva, *n.f.* slide.

diàrio, *n.m.* diary.

diarrèa, *n.f.* diarrhea.

diatermìa, *n.f.* diathermy.

diatrìba, *n.f.* diatribe.

diavolerìa, *n.f.* devilry, evil plot, trick.

diàvolo, *n.m.* devil.

dibàttere, *vb.* debate; *(refl.)* flounder.

dibattimento, *n.m.* debate.

dibàttito, *n.m.* debate, discussion.

di buon' ora, *adv.* early.

dicastèro, *n.m.* department, ministry.

dicèmbre, *n.m.* December.

dicerìa, *n.f.* gossip, rumor.

dichiarare, *vb.* declare, explain. **d. ricevuta di**, acknowledge receipt of.

dichiarativo, *adj.* declarative.

dichiarazione, *n.f.* declaration; explanation.

diciannòve, *num.* nineteen.

diciannovèsimo, *adj.* nineteenth.

diciassètte, *num.* seventeen.

diciassettèsimo, *adj.* seventeenth.

diciottèsimo, *adj.* eighteenth.

diciòtto, *num.* eighteen.

dicitura, *n.f.* caption, legend.

didàttico, *adj.* didactic.

didiètro, *n.m.* behind.

dièci, *num.* ten.

diecimila, *adj., n.m., num.* ten thousand.

dièsis, *n.m.* sharp (music).

dièta, *n.f.* diet.

dietètica, *n.f.* dietetics.

dietètico, *adj.* dietetic, dietary.

dietista, *n.f.* dietitian.

diètro a, *prep.* behind.

dietrofrònt, *n.m.* about face.

difatti, *adv.* indeed.

difèndere, *vb.* defend, advocate.

difensìbile, *adj.* defensible.

difensivo, *adj.* defensive.

difensore, *n.m.* defender, advocate.

difesa, *n.f.* defense, advocacy.

difettare, *vb.* be lacking.

difètto, *n.m.* defect, fault, flaw.

difettoso, *adj.* defective, faulty.

diffamare, *vb.* defame, libel, malign.

diffamatòrio, *adj.* defamatory, libelous.

diffamazione, *n.f.* defamation.

differènte, *adj.* different.

differènza, *n.f.* difference.

differenziale, *adj.* differential.

differenziare, *vb.* differentiate.

differire, *vb.* defer, put off; differ.

difficile, *adj.* difficult.

difficoltà, *n.f.* difficulty.

difficoltoso, *adj.* fussy.

diffida, *n.f.* warning; intimation.

diffidare di, *vb.* mistrust.

diffidènte, *adj.* distrustful.

diffóndere, *vb.* diffuse, spread; *(refl.)* expatiate, dwell upon.

diffórme, *adj.* different; divergent.

diffrazione, *n.f.* diffraction.

diffusione, *n.f.* diffusion.

diffuso, *adj.* diffuse, widespread.

difterite, *n.f.* diphtheria.

diga, *n.f.* dike, dam, levee.

digerìbile, *adj.* digestible.

digerire, *vb.* digest.

digestione, *n.f.* digestion.

digestivo, *adj.* digestive.

digitale, **1.** *n.f.* digitalis, foxglove. **2.** *adj.* digital.

digiunare, *vb.* fast.

digiuno, *n.m.* fast.

dignificare, *vb.* dignify.

dignità, *n.f.* dignity, respect.

dignitàrio, *n.m.* dignitary.

dignitoso, *adj.* dignified.

digradante, *adj.* sloping, dimming.

digredire, *vb.* digress.

digressione, *n.f.* digression.

digressivo, *adj.* discursive.

digrignare, *vb.* gnash.

dilapidato, *adj.* dilapidated.

dilapidazione, *n.f.* dilapidation, disrepair.

dilatare, *vb.* dilate.

dilatòrio, *adj.* dilatory.

dilemma, *n.m.* dilemma.

dilettante, *n.m.* amateur.

dilettévole, *adj.* delightful, delectable.

dilètto, **1.** *n.m.* delight. **2.** *adj.* beloved, darling.

diligènte, *adj.* diligent.

diligènza, *n.f.* diligence.

diluire, *vb.* dilute.

dilungare, *vb.* stretch; dwell.

diluviare, *vb.* rain cats and dogs.

dilùvio, *n.m.* deluge.

diluzione, *n.f.* dilution.

dimagrante, *adj.* reducing.

dimagrire, *vb.* lose weight, slim down.

dimenare, *vb.* wag; *(refl.)* toss about; flounce.

dimensione, *n.f.* dimension.

dimenticare, *vb.* forget.

diméntico, *adj.* forgetful.

dimèsso, *adj.* humble; shabby; dismissed, discharged.

dimestichezza, *n.f.* familiarity.

diméttere, *vb.* dismiss; *(refl.)* resign, quit.

dimezzare, *vb.* halve, cut in half.

diminuire, *vb.* diminish, lessen, abate, decrease, dwindle, let up, subside.

diminutivo, *n.m. and adj.* diminutive.

diminuzione, *n.f.* diminution, lessening, abatement, decrease.

dimissione, *n.f.* resignation.

dimora, *n.f.* abode, dwelling.

dimostràbile, *adj.* demonstrable.

dimostrare, *vb.* demonstrate.

dimostrativo, *adj.* demonstrative.

dimostratore, *n.m.* demonstrator.

dimostrazione, *n.f.* demonstration.

dinàmica, *n.f.* dynamics.

dinàmico, *adj.* dynamic.

dinamite, *n.f.* dynamite.

dìnamo, *n.f.* dynamo.

dinanzi, *adv. and adj.* before; in front.

dinastìa, *n.f.* dynasty.

diniègo, *n.m.* denial.

dinosàuro, *n.m.* dinosaur.

dintorni, *n.m.pl.* environs, surroundings.

dìo, *n.m.* god.

diòcesi, *n.f.* diocese, bishopric.

diottrìa, *n.f.* diopter.

dipanare, *vb.* reel off, unwind.

dipartimentale, *adj.* departmental.

dipartimento, *n.m.* department.

dipartita, *n.f.* departure; demise, death.

dipendènte, *n.m. and adj.* dependent.

dipendènza, *n.f.* dependence.

dipèndere, *vb.* depend.

dipìngere, *vb.* paint, depict.

dipinto, *n.m.* painting.

diplòma, *n.m.* diploma.

diplomàtico, 1. *n.m.* diplomat. **2.** *adj.* diplomatic.

diplomazìa, *n.f.* diplomacy.

dipòrto, *n.m.* sport.

diradare, *vb.* thin out, diminish; become less frequent.

diramazione, *n.f.* junction.

dire, *vb.* say.

direttamente, *adv.* directly.

direttìssimo, *n.m.* express train.

direttivo, *adj.* directive, directional.

dirètto, *adj.* direct; directed; bound; lineal; right; through.

direttorato, *n.m.* directorate.

direttore, *n.m.* director; conductor; editor; manager; principal.

direzione, *n.f.* direction, management.

dirigere, *vb.* manage; aim; conduct; steer; edit.

dirigìbile, *n.m. and adj.* dirigible.

dirimpètto, *adv.* **d. a,** *prep.* opposite; facing.

diritti, *n.m.pl.* civil rights. **d. d'autore,** copyright.

diritto, 1. *n.m.* right; law. **2.** *adj.,* *adv.* straight; upright.

diroccare, *vb.* knock down, demolish.

diroccato, *adj.* dilapidated, crumbling.

dirottatore, *n.m.* hijacker.

dirotto, *adv.* **a d.** excessively.

dirupo, *n.m.* cliff, ravine.

disaccòrdo, *n.m.* discord, variance.

disadatto, *adj.* unfit.

disadorno, *adj.* unadorned, bare, plain.

disagio, *n.m.* discomfort.

disapprovare, *vb.* disapprove.

disapprovazione, *n.f.* disapproval.

disarmare, *vb.* disarm.

disarmo, *n.m.* disarmament.

disastro, *n.m.* disaster, debacle.

disastroso, *adj.* disastrous.

discendènte, *n.m. and f.* descendant.

discépolo, *n.m.* disciple.

discèrnere, *vb.* discern.

discesa, *n.f.* descent.

discettare, *vb.* dispute, debate.

disciplina, *n.f.* discipline.

disciplinare, 1. *adj.* disciplinary. **2.** *vb.* discipline.

disco, 1. *n.m.* disc, record. **2.** *adj.* disco (music).

discolo, *n.m.* undisciplined child, urchin.

disconóscere, *vb.* disavow, disclaim, disown.

disconoscimento, *n.m.* disavowal, disclaimer.

discordante, *adj.* discordant.

discordare, *vb.* disagree, be discordant.

discòrdia, *n.f.* discord.

discórrere, *vb.* discourse.

discorso, *n.m.* speech, discourse, talk, address.

discotèca, *n.f.* record library; discotheque.

discrèdito, *n.m.* discredit.

discrepante, *adj.* discrepant.

discrepanza, *n.f.* discrepancy.

discreto, *adj.* discreet; moderate; fair.

discrezione, *n.f.* discretion.

discriminare, *vb.* discriminate.

discriminazione, *n.f.* discrimination.

discussione, *n.f.* discussion.

discusso, *adj.* moot.

discùtere, *vb.* discuss.

discutibile, *adj.* debatable.

disdegnare, *vb.* disdain, spurn.

disdegno, *n.m.* disdain, scorn.

disdegnoso, *adj.* disdainful, scornful.

disdétta, *n.f.* cancellation; misfortune.

disdicévole, *adj.* unbecoming.

disdire, *vb.* cancel, terminate (contract), retract.

disegnare, *vb.* design; draw.

disegnatore, *n.m.* designer; draftsman.

disegno, *n.m.* picture; cartoon; design; drawing.

diserbante, *n.m.* weed killer.

diseredare, *vb.* disinherit.

disertare, *vb.* desert.

disertore, *n.m.* deserter.

diserzione, *n.f.* desertion.

disfare, *vb.* undo.

disfatta, *n.f.* defeat.

disfattismo, *n.m.* defeatism.

disfida, *n.f.* challenge.

disfigurare, *vb.* disfigure.

disfunzione, *n.f.* malfunction, disorder.

disgèlo, *n.m.* thaw.

disgrazia, *n.f.* misfortune, mishap, accident; disgrace.

disgraziato, *adj.* unfortunate, unlucky.

disgustare, *vb.* disgust.

disgusto, *n.m.* disgust, distaste.

disgustoso, *adj.* disgusting, distasteful, nasty.

disidratare, *vb.* dehydrate.

disillùdere, *vb.* disillusion.

disillusione, *n.f.* disillusion.

disimballare, *vb.* unpack.

disimpegnare, *vb.* disengage.

disincanto, *n.m.* disenchantment.

disinfettante, *n.m.* disinfectant.

disinfettare, *vb.* disinfect.

disingannare, *vb.* undeceive, disabuse.

disintegrare, *vb.* disintegrate.

disinteressato, *adj.* disinterested, unselfish, impartial.

disinterèsse, *n.m.* indifference.

dislessia, *n.f.* dyslexia.

dislocamento, *n.m.* displacement.

disobbediènte, *adj.* disobedient.

disoccupato, *adj.* unemployed.

disonestà, *n.f.* dishonesty.

disonèsto, *adj.* dishonest; foul.

disonorante, *adj.* disgraceful.

disonorare, *vb.* dishonor, disgrace.

disonore, *n.m.* dishonor, disgrace.

disonorévole, *adj.* dishonorable, discreditable, disreputable.

disordinare, *vb.* disorder.

disordinato, *adj.* disorderly.

disórdine, *n.m.* disorder, litter.

disorganizzare, *vb.* disorganize.

disorientamento, *n.m.* confusion, disorientation.

disorientato, *adj.* confused, puzzled.

disossare, *vb.* bone.

disotto, *adv.* underneath, below; downstairs.

dispàccio, *n.m.* dispatch.

disparato, *adj.* disparate.

dìspari, *adj.* odd.

disparità, *n.f.* disparity.

disparte: in d., *adv.* apart, aloof.

dispènsa, *n.f.* pantry.

dispensàbile, *adj.* dispensable.

dispensare, *vb.* dispense.

dispensàrio, *n.m.* dispensary.

dispensazione, *n.f.* dispensation.

dispepsia, *n.f.* dyspepsia.

dispèptico, *adj.* dyspeptic.

disperare, *vb.* despair.

disperato, 1. *n.* desperado. 2. *adj.* desperate; forlorn, hopeless.

disperazione, *n.f.* desperation, despair, hopelessness.

dispèrdere, *vb.* disperse, waste.

dispersione, *n.f.* dispersal.

dispersivo, *adj.* dispersive.

disperso, 1. *n.m.* missing in action. 2. *adj.* missing, lost; scattered.

dispètto, *n.m.* spite.

dispiacènte, *adj.* sorry; displeasing.

dispiacere, 1. *n.m.* displeasure. 2. *vb.* displease.

disponìbile, *adj.* available.

disporre, *vb.* dispose, arrange; range.

dispositivo, *n.m.* device.

disposizione, *n.f.* disposition; disposal; instruction; arrangement.

dispòtico, *adj.* despotic.

dispotismo, *n.m.* despotism.

dispregiativo, *adj.* derogatory, pejorative.

disprezzare, *vb.* despise, disparage, scorn, slight.

disprèzzo, *n.m.* contempt, scorn, slight.

dìsputa, *n.f.* dispute, controversy.

disputàbile, *adj.* disputable.

disputare, *vb.* dispute.

disquisizione, *n.f.* disquisition.

dissacrare, *vb.* desecrate.

dissecare, *vb.* dissect.

disseminare, *vb.* disseminate.

dissènso, *n.m.* dissent, disagreement, dissension.

dissenterìa, *n.f.* dysentery.

dissentire, *vb.* dissent, disagree.

disserrare, *vb.* unlock.

dissertazione, *n.f.* dissertation.

disservìzio, *n.m.* disservice, bad service.

dissetare, *vb.* quench (one's) thirst.

dissezione, *n.f.* dissection.

dissidènte, *adj. and n.m.* dissident.

dissìdio, *n.m.* dispute, discord.

dissìmile, *adj.* dissimilar, unlike.

dissimulare, *vb.* dissimulate, dissemble.

dissipare, *vb.* dissipate, dispel.

dissipazione, *n.f.* dissipation.

dissociare, *vb.* dissociate.

dissolutezza, *n.f.* dissoluteness, dissipation.

dissoluto, *adj.* dissolute, dissipated.

dissoluzione, *n.f.* dissolution.

dissolvènza, *n.f.* fading, fade-out, dissolve.

dissòlvere, *vb.* dissolve.

dissonante, *adj.* dissonant.

dissonanza, *n.f.* dissonance.

dissotterrare, *vb.* unearth.

dissuadere, *vb.* dissuade.

distaccamento, *n.m.* detachment *(mil.)*.

distaccare, *vb.* detach.

distacco, *n.m.* detachment.

distante, *adj.* distant.

distanza, *n.f.* distance.

distare, *vb.* be distant.

distèndere, *vb.* distend.

distensione, *n.f.* détente.

distesa, *n.f.* expanse; extent; spread.

distéso, *adj.* spread.

distillare, *vb.* distill.

distillatore, *n.m.* distiller.

distillatòrio, *n.m.* distillery.

distillazione, *n.f.* distillation.

distìnguere, *vb.* distinguish.

distinta, *n.f.* list, note.

distintamente, *adv.* distinctly.

distintivo, 1. *n.m.* badge. 2. *adj.* distinctive.

distinto, *adj.* distinct.

distinzione, *n.f.* distinction.

distògliere, vb. deter.

distòrcere, vb. distort.

distrarre, vb. distract.

distratto, adj. absentminded.

distrazione, n.f. distraction.

distretto, n.m. district.

distribuire, vb. distribute, apportion, deal out, dole out.

distributore, n.m. distributor.

distribuzione, n.f. distribution; deal.

districare, vb. disentangle, extricate, unravel.

distrofia, n.f. dystrophy.

distrùggere, vb. destroy.

distruttìbile, adj. destructible.

distruttivo, adj. destructive.

distruzione, n.f. destruction.

disturbare, vb. disturb, trouble.

disturbo, n.m. disturbance, trouble.

disubbidiènza, n.f. disobedience.

disubbidire, vb. disobey.

disuguale, adj. uneven.

disumano, adj. inhumane, cruel.

disunire, vb. disunite.

disuso, n.m. disuse.

ditale, n.m. thimble.

dito, n.m. finger. **d. del piède,** toe.

ditta, n.f. firm.

dittàfono, n.m. dictaphone.

dittatore, n.m. dictator.

dittatoriale, adj. dictatorial.

dittatura, n.f. dictatorship.

dittòngo, n.m. dipthong.

diurètico, adj. diuretic.

diurno, adj. daytime.

diva, n.f. famous singer, diva.

divagare, vb. ramble, get off the subject.

divampare, vb. burst into flames.

divano, n.m. divan, davenport, lounge.

divàrio, n.m. difference.

divenire, vb. become; get.

diventare, vb. become; get.

divèrbio, n.m. altercation, argument.

divergènte, adj. divergent.

divergènza, n.f. divergence.

divèrgere, vb. diverge.

diversione, n.f. diversion.

diversità, n.f. diversity.

diversivo, n.m. distraction.

divèrso, adj. diverse, different.

divertènte, adj. amusing.

divertimento, n.m. amusement, hobby, recreation, entertainment, fun.

divertire, vb. amuse, divert, entertain; (refl.) have a good time.

dividèndo, n.m. dividend.

divìdere, vb. divide, split.

divièto, n.m. prohibition.

divinare, vb. divine.

divincolare, vb. wriggle.

divinità, n.f. divinity.

divinizzare, vb. deify; predict.

divino, adj. divine, godlike.

divisa, n.f. uniform.

divisìbile, adj. divisible.

divisione, n.f. division.

divismo, n.m. star system.

divisòrio, adj. dividing.

divorare, vb. devour.

divorziare, vb. divorce.

divòrzio, n.m. divorce.

divulgare, vb. divulge.

dizionàrio, n.m. dictionary.

dizione, n.f. diction.

dòccia, n.f. shower.

dòcile, adj. docile, tame, submissive, amenable.

documentare, vb. document.

documentàrio, adj. documentary.

documentazione, n.f. documentation.

documento, n.m. document.

dodicésimo, adj. twelfth.

dódici, num. twelve.

dogana, n.f. customs, customshouse.

doganière, n.m. customs officer.

dòglia, n.f. sharp pain.

dòglie, n.f.pl. labor pains.

dògma, n.m. dogma.

dogmaticità, n.f. assertiveness.

dogmàtico, adj. dogmatic, assertive.

dogmatismo, n.m. dogmatism.

dolce, 1. n.m. candy, bonbon. **2.** adj. sweet.

dolcemente, adv. sweetly, soothingly.

dolcezza, n.f. sweetness.

dolciastro, adj. sweetish; mellifluous.

dolciume, n.m. sweet.

dolènte, adj. sore.

dolere, *vb.* hurt, pain; *(refl.)* complain.

dòllaro, *n.m.* dollar.

dòlo, *n.m.* fraud, guile.

dolore, *n.m.* sorrow, pain, ache, grief.

doloroso, *adj.* dolorous, sorrowful, mournful, painful, grievous.

doloso, *adj.* fradulent, malicious.

domanda, *n.f.* question; request; application; demand; query.

domandare, *vb.* ask; demand; request; query; *(refl.)* wonder.

domani, *n.m. and adv.* tomorrow.

domare, *vb.* tame.

domattina, *adv.* tomorrow morning.

doménica, *n.f.* Sunday.

doméstica, *n.f.* housemaid.

domesticare, *vb.* domesticate.

domèstico, 1. *n.* servant. **2.** *adj.* domestic.

domicílio, *n.m.* domicile.

dominante, *adj.* dominant.

dominare, *vb.* dominate, sway.

dominazione, *n.f.* domination.

dominio, *n.m.* domain, dominion.

dòmino, *n.m.* domino.

donare, *vb.* donate.

donatore, *vb.* giver.

donazione, *n.f.* donation.

donchisciottesco, *adj.* quixotic.

donde, *adv.* whence.

dondolare, *vb.* rock, swing.

dònna, *n.f.* woman.

donnaiòlo, *n.m.* playboy.

dònnola, *n.f.* weasel.

dono, 1. *m.* gift, grant, present.

dopo, 1. *adv.* afterwards. **2.** *prep.* after. **d. che,** *conj.* after.

dopobarba, *n.m.* aftershave (lotion).

dopodomani, *adv.* the day after tomorrow.

dopoguerra, *n.m.* postwar era.

doppiamente, *adv.* doubly.

doppiare, *vb.* double.

doppiétta, *n.f.* double-barreled shotgun.

dóppio, *adj.* double; duplex.

dorare, *vb.* gild.

dorato, *adj.* gilt.

doratura, *n.f.* gilt.

dormiglione, *n.m* sleepyhead.

dormire, *vb.* sleep.

dormitòrio, *n.m.* dormitory.

dormivéglia, *n.m.* drowsiness, doze

dorsale, *adj.* dorsal, pertaining to the back.

dòrso, *n.m.* back.

dosare, *vb.* dose.

dosatura, *n.f.* dosage.

dòse, *n.f.* dose.

dòsso, *n.m.* back.

dotare, *vb.* endow.

dotato, *adj.* gifted.

dotazione, *n.f.* endowment.

dòte, *n.f.* dowry.

dòtto, 1. *n.* scholar. **2.** *adj.* learned.

dottorato, *n.m.* doctorate.

dottore, *n.m.* doctor.

dottrina, *n.f.* doctrine; learning.

dottrinàrio, *adj.* doctrinaire.

dove, *adv.* where.

dovere, 1. *n.m.* duty. **2.** *vb.* owe; be supposed to; have to; ought; must.

dovunque, *adv.* wherever.

dovuto, *adj.* due, owing.

dozzina, *n.f.* dozen.

dozzinale, *adj.* cheap second rate, ordinary.

draga, *n.f.* dredge.

dragamine, *n.m.* minesweeper.

dragare, *vb.* dredge.

dragone, *n.m.* dragon.

dramma, *n.m.* dram; drama, play.

drammàtica, *n.f.* dramatics.

drammàtico, *adj.* dramatic.

drammatizzare, *vb.* dramatize.

drammaturgìa, *n.f.* dramaturgy, play-writing.

drammaturgo, *n.m.* dramatist, playwright.

drappeggiare, *vb.* drape.

drappéggio, *n.m.* drapery, drapes.

drappèllo, *n.m.* platoon.

dràstico, *adj.* drastic.

drenàggio, *n.m.* drainage.

drizza, *n.f.* halyard.

drizzare, *vb.* straighten.

dròga, *n.f.* drug.

dromedàrio, *n.m.* dromedary.

duale, *n.m. and adj.* dual.

dualismo, *n.m.* dualism.

dùbbio, 1. *n.m.* doubt. **2.** *adj.* doubtful, dubious.

dubbioso, *adj.* doubtful.

dubitare, vb. doubt.
duca, n.m. duke.
ducato, n.m. duchy, dukedom.
duce, n.m. (Fascist) leader.
duchessa, n.f. duchess.
due, num. two.
duecènto, num. two hundred; **il D.** the thirteenth century.
duellante, n.m. duellist.
duellare, vb. duel.
duèllo, n.m. duel.
duetto, n.m. duet.
duna, n.f. dune.
dunque, adv. therefore; so; then.
duòmo, n.m. cathedral.
duplicare, vb. duplicate.

duplicato, n.m. duplicate.
duplicazione, n.f. duplication.
duplicità, n.f. duplicity, double-dealing.
duràbile, adj. durable, enduring.
durabilità, n.f. durability.
duramente, adv. hard.
durante, prep. during.
durare, vb. endure, last.
durata, n.f. duration.
duraturo, adj. lasting, enduring.
durévole, adj. lasting.
durezza, n.f. hardness.
duro, adj. hard.
durone, n.m. callosity.
dùttile, adj. ductile.

E

e, conj. and.
èbano, n.m. ebony.
ebbène, interj. well!
ebbrezza, n.f. intoxication.
ebràico, n. and adj. Hebrew, Hebraic; Jewish.
ebrèo, n. and adj. Hebrew, Jew(ish).
ebùrneo, adj. of ivory.
ecatombe, n.f. massacre, carnage.
eccèdere, vb. exceed.
eccellènte, adj. excellent.
eccellènza, n.f. excellence.
Eccellènza, n.f. Excellency.
eccèllere, vb. excel.
eccentricità, n.f. eccentricity.
eccèntrico, adj. eccentric.
eccessivo, adj. excessive.
eccèsso, n.m. excess.
eccètto, prep. except; but.
eccettuare, vb. except.
eccezionale, adj. exceptional.
eccezione, n.f. exception.
eccitàbile, adj. excitable, high-strung, hot-headed.
eccitamento, n.m. excitement.
eccitare, vb. excite.
eccitazione, n.f. excitement.
ecclesiàstico, 1. n. ecclesiastic, cleric, clergyman. **2.** adj. ecclesiastical.
ècco, vb. here is; there is; lo; behold.
echeggiare, vb. echo.
eclissare, vb. eclipse.

eclissi, n.f. eclipse.
eco, n.m. echo.
ecologìa, n.f. ecology.
ecològico, adj. ecological.
economìa, n.f. economy, thrift. **e. polìtica,** economics.
economicamente, adv. economically, cheaply.
econòmico, adj. economic, economical, cheap.
economista, n.m. economist.
economizzare, vb. economize, save.
ecosistèma, n.m ecosystem.
ecumènico, adj. ecumenical.
eczèma, n.m. eczema.
ed, conj. and.
édera, n.f. ivy.
edìcola, n.f. newsstand.
edificare, vb. edify, build.
edifìcio, n.m. edifice, building.
edile, adj. building, construction.
edilìzia, n.f. building trade.
editore, n.m. publisher.
editorìa, n.f. publishing industry.
editoriale, adj. editorial.
editto, n.m. edict.
edizione, n.f. edition, publication.
edonismo, n.m. hedonism.
edòtto, adj. aware, informed.
educare, vb. educate, train.
educativo, adj. educational.
educatore, n.m. educator.
educazione, n.f. education, breeding, manners.

effeminato, *adj.* effeminate.

effervescènza, *n.f.* effervescence.

effettivamente, *adv.* effectively; in effect.

effettivo, *adj.* effective.

effètto, *n.m.* effect.

effettuare, *vb.* effect, bring about, contrive.

efficace, *adj.* efficacious, effectual.

efficàcia, *n.f.* efficacy.

efficiènte, *adj.* efficient.

efficientemente, *adv.* efficiently.

efficiènza, *n.f.* efficiency.

effigie, *n.f.* effigy.

effimero, *adj.* ephemeral.

egemonìa, *n.f.* hegemony.

ègida, *n.f.* aegis, auspices, protection.

Egitto, *n.m.* Egypt.

egiziano, *adj.* Egyptian.

egli, *pron.* he.

egoismo, *n.m.* egoism, selfishness.

egoìstico, *adj.* selfish.

egotismo, *n.m.* egotism.

egotista, *n.m.* egotist.

egrègio, *adj.* eminent.

eguaglianza, *n.f.* equality.

éhi, *interj.* hey!

eiaculare, *vb.* ejaculate.

eiezione, *n.f.* ejection.

elaborare, *vb.* elaborate.

elaborato, *adj.* elaborate, complicated.

elaborazione, *n.f.* data processing.

elasticità, *n.f.* elasticity.

elàstico, *n.m. and adj.* elastic.

elefante, *n.m.* elephant.

elefantesco, *adj.* elephantine.

elegante, *adj.* elegant, smart.

eleganza, *n.f.* elegance.

elèggere, *vb.* elect.

eleggìbile, *adj.* eligible.

eleggibilità, *n.f.* eligibility.

elegìa, *n.f.* elegy.

elegìaco, *adj.* elegiac.

elementare, *adj.* elemental, elementary.

elemento, *n.m.* element.

elemòsina, *n.f.* charity, alms, dole.

elencare, *vb.* list, itemize.

elènco, *n.m.* list. **e. telefònico,** telephone directory.

elettivo, *adj.* elective.

elettricista, *n.m.* electrician.

elettricità, *n.f.* electricity.

elèttrico, *adj.* electric, electrical.

elettrocardiógramma, *n.m.* electrocardiogram.

elettrocuzione, *n.f.* electrocution.

elèttrodo, *n.m.* electrode.

elettrodomèstici, *n.m.pl.* electric household appliances.

elettrògeno, *adj.* generating (unit).

elettròlisi, *n.f.* electrolysis.

elettromotrice, *n.f.* electric railcar.

elettrone, *n.m.* electron.

elettrònica, *n.f.* electronics.

elettrònico, *adj.* electronic.

elettrotreno, *n.m.* express train of electric railcars.

elevare, *vb.* elevate.

elevazione, *n.f.* elevation.

elezione, *n.f.* election.

èlfo, *n.m.* elf.

èlica, *n.f.* propeller.

elicòttero, *n.m.* helicopter.

elìdere, *vb.* elide, suppress, annul.

eliminare, *vb.* eliminate.

eliminazione, *n.f.* elimination.

èlio, *n.m.* helium.

eliocèntrico, *adj.* heliocentric.

eliògrafo, *n.m.* heliograph.

eliotipìa, *n.f.* blueprint.

eliotròpio, *n.m.* heliotrope.

elisir, *n.m.* elixir.

ella, *pron.f.* she; (very formal) you.

ellènico, *adj.* Hellenic.

ellenismo, *n.m.* Hellenism.

ellisse, *n.m.* ellipse.

èlmo, *n.m.* helmet.

elocuzione, *n.f.* elocution.

elogiare, *vb.* eulogize.

elògio, *n.m.* eulogy.

eloquènte, *adj.* eloquent.

eloquentemente, *adv.* eloquently.

eloquènza, *n.f.* eloquence.

èlsa, *n.f.* hilt.

elucidare, *vb.* elucidate.

elùdere, *vb.* elude, dodge, evade.

elusivo, *adj.* elusive.

emaciato, *adj.* emaciated.

emanare, *vb.* emanate.

emancipare, *vb.* emancipate.

emancipatore, *n.m.* emancipator.

emancipazione, *n.f.* emancipation.

emarginare, *vb.* neglect; put aside.

emarginato, *n.m. and adj.* misfit, outcast.

ematite, *n.f.* hematite.

embargo, *n.m.* embargo.

emblèma, *n.m.* emblem, badge.

emblemàtico, *adj.* emblematic.

embolìa, *n.f.* embolism.

embriologìa, *n.f.* embryology.

embrionale, *n.m.* embryonic.

embrione, *n.m.* embryo.

emendamento, *n.m.* amendment.

emendare, *vb.* amend, emend.

emergènte, *adj.* emergent.

emergènza, *n.f.* emergency.

emèrgere, *vb.* emerge.

emèrito, *adj.* emeritus.

emersione, *n.f.* emersion.

emètico, *adj.* emetic.

eméttere, *vb.* emit; send forth; issue; utter.

emiciclo, *n.m.* hemicycle; legislative chamber.

emicrània, *n.f.* migraine.

emigrante, *n.m. and adj.* emigrant.

emigrare, *vb.* emigrate.

emigrazione, *n.f.* emigration.

eminènte, *adj.* eminent.

eminènza, *n.f.* eminence.

emisfèro, *n.m.* hemisphere.

emissàrio, *n.m.* emissary.

emissione, *n.f.* issue.

emittènte, 1. *adj.* issuing; transmitting; broadcasting. **2** *n.f.* issuer; transmitter; broadcast station.

emofilìa, *n.f.* hemophilia.

emoglobina, *n.f.* hemoglobin.

emolliènte, *n.m. and adj.* emollient.

emolumento, *n.m.* emolument.

emorragìa, *n.f.* hemorrhage.

emorròide, *n.f.* hemorrhoid, pile.

emotivo, *adj.* emotional.

emozionàbile, *adj.* emotional.

emozione, *n.f.* emotion.

empiastro, *n.m.* plaster.

émpio, *adj.* impious, blasphemous, godless.

empìreo, *adj.* empyreal, sublime.

empìrico, *adj.* empirical. **rimèdio e.,** nostrum.

empòrio, *n.m.* mart, emporium.

emulare, *vb.* emulate.

emulsione, *n.f.* emulsion.

encefalite, *n.f.* encephalitis.

encèfalo, *n.m.* encephalon.

enciclica, *n.f.* encyclical.

enciclopedìa, *n.f.* encyclopaedia.

endèmico, *adj.* endemic.

endòcrino, *adj.* endocrine.

endovenoso, *adj.* intravenous.

energìa, *n.f.* energy.

enèrgico, *adj.* energetic.

energùmeno, *n.m.* possessed person, madman; bully.

ènfasi, *n.f.* emphasis.

enfàtico, *adj.* emphatic.

enfisèma, *n.m.* emphysema.

enigma, *n.m.* enigma, riddle.

enigmàtico, *adj.* enigmatic.

enné, *n.f.* henna.

enòlogo, *n.m.* oenologist.

enòrme, *adj.* enormous.

enormità, *n.f.* enormity.

enteroclisma, *n.m.* enema, colonic irrigation.

entità, *n.f.* entity.

entrare, *vb.* enter.

entrata, *n.f.* entrance, entry; admission; revenue; input.

entro, *prep.* in; within.

entrotèrra, *n.f.* inland.

entusiasmo, *n.m.* enthusiasm.

entusiasta, *n.m. or f.* enthusiast, devotee.

entusiàstico, *adj.* enthusiastic.

enumerare, *vb.* enumerate.

enumerazione, *n.f.* enumeration.

enunciare, *vb.* enunciate.

enunciazione, *n.f.* enunciation.

epàtica, *n.f.* hepatica.

epàtico, *adj.* hepatic.

eperlano, *n.m.* smelt.

èpico, *adj.* epic.

epicurèo, *n.m.* epicure.

epidemìa, *n.f.* epidemic.

epidèmico, *adj.* epidemic.

epidèrmide, *n.f.* epidermis.

Epifanìa, *n.f.* Epiphany.

epigramma, *n.m.* epigram.

epilessìa, *n.f.* epilepsy.

epìlogo, *n.m.* epilogue.

episcopato, *n.m.* bishopric.

episòdio, *n.m.* episode.

epistola, *n.f.* epistle.

epitaffio, *n.m.* epitaph.

epiteto, *n.m.* epithet.

epitomare, *vb.* epitomize.

epitome, *n.f.* epitome.

época, *n.f.* epoch.

epopéa, *n.f.* epic.

epurare, *vb.* purify, cleanse, purge.

equanimità, *n.f.* equanimity.

equatore, *n.m.* equator.

equatoriale, *adj.* equatorial.

equazione, *n.f.* equation.

equèstre, *adj.* equestrian.

equidistante, *adj.* equidistant.

equilàtero, *adj.* equilateral.

equilibrare, *vb.* balance, equilibrate.

equilibrato, *adj.* balanced; level.

equilibrio, *n.m.* balance, equilibrium; poise.

equino, *adj.* equine.

equinòzio, *n.m.* equinox.

equipaggiare, *vb.* rig.

equipaggio, *n.m.* crew; equipment; rig.

equipe, *n.f.* team.

equità, *n.f.* equity.

equitazione, *n.f.* equitation, horsemanship.

equivalènte, *adj.* equivalent.

equivalere, *vb.* be equivalent.

equivoco, 1. *n.m.* mistake. 2. *adj.* equivocal.

èquo, *adj.* equable, equitable, fair, just.

èra, *n.f.* era.

eràrio, *n.m.* treasury.

èrba, *n.f.* grass; herb.

erbàccia, *n.f.* weed.

erbàceo, *n.m.* herbaceous.

erbàrio, *n.m.* herbarium.

erbicida, *n.m.* weed killer.

erbìvoro, *adj.* herbivorous.

erboso, *adj.* grassy.

ercùleo, *adj.* Herculean.

erède, *n.m.* heir.

eredità, *n.f.* heredity; heritage; inheritance.

ereditare, *vb.* inherit.

ereditàrio, *adj.* hereditary.

ereditièra, *n.f.* heiress.

eremita, *n.m.* hermit.

eremitaggio, *n.m.* hermitage.

èremo, *n.m.* hermitage, monastery.

eresia, *n.f.* heresy.

erètico, 1. *n.* heretic. 2. *adj.* heretical.

erètto, *adj.* erect, upright.

erezione, *n.f.* erection.

èrgere, *vb.* raise.

ergo, *adv.* thus, therefore.

èrica, *n.f.* heather.

erìgere, *vb.* erect, raise.

ermellino, *n.m.* ermine.

ermètico, *adj.* hermetic.

èrnia, *n.f.* hernia.

eródere, *vb.* erode.

eròe, *n.m.* hero.

eroicamente, *adv.* heroically.

eròico, *adj.* heroic.

eroina, *n.f.* heroine; heroin.

eroismo, *n.m.* heroism.

erosione, *n.f.* erosion.

erosivo, *adj.* erosive.

eròtico, *adj.* erotic.

erotismo, *n.m.* eroticism.

èrpete, *n.f.* herpes, shingles.

erpicare, *vb.* harrow.

èrpice, *n.m.* harrow.

errabondo, *adj.* vagrant, roaming.

errante, *adj.* errant.

errare, *vb.* err, make a mistake, be wrong; wander; rove.

erràtico, *adj.* erratic.

errato, *adj.* wrong, mistaken.

erròneo, *adj.* erroneous, mistaken.

errore, *n.m.* error, mistake, blunder, slip.

èrto, *adj.* steep.

erudito, 1. *n.* scholar. 2. *adj.* erudite.

erudizione, *n.f.* erudition, scholarship.

eruttare, *vb.* erupt.

eruzione, *n.f.* eruption; rash.

esacerbare, *vb.* embitter, exasperate.

esagerare, *vb.* exaggerate.

esagerazione, *n.f.* exaggeration.

esàgono, *n.m.* hexagon.

esalare, *vb.* exhale.

esalazione, *n.f.* fume.

esaltare, *vb.* exalt, elate.

esaltato, *adj.* exalted, elated.

esaltazione, *n.f.* exaltation, elation.

esame, *n.m.* examination; canvass; survey.

esaminando, *n.m.* examinee.

esaminare, *vb.* examine; canvass; survey.

esangue, *adj.* bloodless.

esànime, *adj.* exanimate, inanimate.

esasperante, *adj.* irritating.

esasperare, *vb.* exasperate.

esasperazione, *n.f.* exasperation.

esattamente, *adv.* exactly.

esatto, *adj.* exact.

esattòre, *n.m.* tax collector.

esaudire, *vb.* grant, fulfil.

esauriènte, *adj.* exhaustive; in-depth.

esaurimento, *n.m.* exhaustion.

esaurire, *vb.* exhaust, deplete.

esca, *n.f.* bait; tinder.

eschimese, *n.m.* Eskimo pie.

esclamare, *vb.* exclaim.

esclamazione, *n.f.* exclamation.

esclùdere, *vb.* exclude.

esclusione, *n.f.* exclusion.

esclusivo, *adj.* exclusive.

escogitare, *vb.* excogitate, devise.

escoriare, *vb.* excoriate.

escremento, *n.m.* excrement.

escursione, *n.f.* excursion, jaunt, junket, outing.

esecràbile, *adj.* execrable.

esecutivo, *adj.* executive.

esecutore, *n.m.* executor.

esecuzione, *n.f.* execution, enforcement; performance, rendition.

esegèsi, *n.f.* exegesis.

eseguire, *vb.* execute, enforce; perform.

esèmpio, *n.m.* example.

esemplare, **1.** *n.m.* copy. **2.** *adj.* exemplary.

esemplificare, *vb.* exemplify.

esentare, *vb.* exempt; dispense.

esènte, *adj.* exempt; immune. **e. da dogana,** duty-free.

esenzione, *n.f.* exemption.

esèquie, *n.f.pl.* funeral rites.

esercènte, *n.m.* store owner, dealer, merchant.

esercitare, *vb.* exercise; exert; drill, practice.

esercitazione, *n.f.* practice, drill.

esèrcito, *n.m.* army.

esercizio, *n.m.* exercise.

esibire, *vb.* exhibit, display.

esibizione, *n.f.* exhibition, display.

esibizionismo, *n.m.* exhibitionism.

esigènza, *n.f.* exigency; requirement.

esìgere, *vb.* exact, require, demand.

esìguo, *adj.* thin, scanty, meager.

esilarante, *adj.* exhilarating, cheering.

esilarare, *vb.* exhilarate.

èsile, *adj.* weak, slender, thin.

esiliare, *vb.* exile, banish.

esìlio, *n.m.* exile, banishment.

esìmio, *adj.* eminent.

esistènte, *adj.* existent, extant.

esistènza, *n.f.* existence, being.

esìstere, *vb.* exist.

esitante, *adj.* hesitant.

esitare, *vb.* hesitate, falter, waver.

esitazione, *n.f.* hesitation.

èsodo, *n.m.* exodus.

esòfago, *n.m.* esophagus.

esonerare, *vb.* exonerate.

esorbitante, *adj.* exorbitant.

esorcizzare, *vb.* exorcise.

esortare, *vb.* exhort; plead with.

esortativo, *adj.* exhortatory.

esortazione, *n.f.* exhortation.

esotèrico, *adj.* esoteric.

esòtico, *adj.* exotic.

espàndere, *vb.* expand.

espansione, *n.f.* expansion.

espansivo, *adj.* expansive, effusive.

espanso, **1.** *adj.* expanded, flared. **2.** *n.m.* styrofoam.

espatriato, *n.m.* expatriate.

espediènte, *n.m. and adj.* expedient; makeshift.

espèllere, *vb.* expel, drive out, eject, evict, oust.

esperiènza, *n.f.* experience.

esperimentare, *n.m.* experiment; experience.

esperimento, *n.m.* experiment.

espèrto, *n.m. and adj.* expert; experienced, practiced, proficient.

espettorare, *vb.* expectorate.

espiare, *vb.* expiate, atone for.

espiazione, *n.f.* expiation, atonement.

espirare, *vb.* expire.

espirazione, *n.f.* expiration.

espletivo, *adj.* expletive.

esplicare, *vb.* explicate; carry out; practice.

esplicativo, *adj.* explanatory.

esplicito, *adj.* explicit.

esplòdere, *vb.* explode.

esplorare, *vb.* explore.

esplorativo, *adj.* exploratory.

esploratore, *n.m.* explorer; scout.

esplorazione, *n.f.* exploration.

esplosione, *n.f.* explosion, blast.

esplosivo, *n.m. and adj.* explosive.

esponènte, *n.m.* exponent.

esporre, *vb.* expose.

esportare, *vb.* export.

esportazione, *n.f.* export, exportation.

espositivo, *adj.* expository.

esposizione, *n.f.* exposition; exposé; exposure; show.

esposto, *n.m.* exposé.

espressamente, *adv.* expressly.

espressione, *n.f.* expression.

espressivo, *adj.* expressive.

espresso, *n.m. and adj.* express; special delivery; coffee 'espresso.'

esprimere, *vb.* express.

espropriare, *vb.* expropriate.

espugnare, *vb.* conquer.

espulsione, *n.f.* expulsion, ejection, eviction, ouster.

espùngere, *vb.* expunge.

espurgare, *vb.* expurgate.

essa, *pron.f.sg.* she; it.

esse, *pron.f.pl.* they.

essènza, *n.f.* essence.

essenziale, *adj.* essential.

essenzialmente, *adv.* essentially.

èssere, 1. *n.* being. **2.** *vb.* be.

essi, *pron.m.pl.* they.

essiccatòio, *n.m.* drier.

esso, *pron.m.sg.* he; it.

essudare, *vb.* exude.

essudato, *n.m.* exudation.

èst, *n.m.* east.

èstasi, *n.f.* ecstasy, rapture.

estasiare, *vb.* send into ecstasies, enrapture.

estate, *n.f.* summer.

estemporàneo, *adj.* extemporaneous.

estèndere, *vb.* extend, enlarge, broaden.

estensione, *n.f.* extent; extension; range.

estenuante, *adj.* enervating, exhausting.

estenuare, *vb.* extenuate.

esteriore, *adj.* exterior, outer, outward.

esteriormente, *adv.* outwardly.

esternare, *vb.* manifest, express.

estèrno, *adj.* external, outside.

èstero, 1. *n.m.* foreign parts. **2.** *adj.* foreign; external.

estesamente, *adv.* extensively.

esteso, *adj.* extensive; far-flung.

estètica, *n.f.* aesthetics.

estètico, *adj.* aesthetic.

estetista, *n.m. and f.* beautician.

èstimo, *n.m.* evaluation, appraisal, quotation.

estìnguere, *vb.* extinguish, quench.

estinto, *adj.* extinct.

estintore, *n.m.* fire extinguisher.

estinzione, *n.f.* extinction.

estirpare, *vb.* extirpate.

estivo, *adj.* of summer.

estòllere, *vb.* extol.

estòrcere, *vb.* extort.

estorsione, *n.f.* extortion.

estra-, *prefix.* extra-.

estradare, *vb.* extradite.

estradizione, *n.f.* extradition.

estràneo, *adj.* extraneous.

estrapolare, *vb.* extrapolate.

estrarre, *vb.* extract.

estratto, *n.m.* extract.

estrazione, *n.f.* extraction.

estremamente, *adv.* extremely, exceedingly.

estremista, *n.m. and f.* extremist.

estremità, *n.f.* extremity; end; butt.

estrèmo, 1. *n.* fullback. **2.** *adj.* extreme, utmost.

èstro, *n.m.* whim, inspiration; fancy; immagination.

estroverso, *adj.* extrovert.

estuàrio, *n.m.* estuary.

esuberante, *adj.* exuberant; ebullient.

èsule, *n.m. and f.* exile.

esultante, *adj.* exultant.

esultare, *vb.* exult.
esumare, *vb.* exhume; resurrect.
esumazione, *n.f.* exhumation.
età, *n.f.* age.
ètere, *n.m.* ether.
etèreo, *adj.* ethereal.
eternamente, *adv.* eternally, forevermore.
eternità, *n.f.* eternity; eon.
etèrno, *adj.* eternal.
eterodossia, *n.f.* heterodoxy.
eterodòsso, *adj.* heterodox.
eterogèneo, *adj.* heterogeneous, motley.
eterosessuale, *adj.* heterosexual.
ètica, *n.f.* ethics.
etichetta, *n.f.* label; docket; sticker; tag.
ètico, *adj.* ethical; hectic.
etìlico, *adj.* ethyl.
etimologìa, *n.f.* etymology.
ètnico, *adj.* ethnic.
etnografìa, *n.f.* ethnography.
etnologìa, *n.f.* ethnology.
èttaro, *n.m.* hectare.
ètto, *n.m.* hectogram.
ettogramma, *n.m.* hectogram.
eucalìpto, *n.m.* eucalyptus.
eucarìstia, *n.f.* Eucharist.
eufemismo, *n.m.* euphemism.
eufònico, *adj.* euphonious.
euforìa, *n.f.* euphoria, elation.
eugenètica, *n.f.* eugenics.
eugènico, *adj.* eugenic.
eunuco, *n.m.* eunuch.
Europa, *n.f.* Europe.
europèo, *adj. and n.* European.
eurovisione, *n.f.* European television chain.
eutanasìa, *n.f.* euthanasia.
evacuare, *vb.* evacuate.
evanescènte, *adj.* evanescent.
evangelista, *n.m.* evangelist.
evaporare, *vb.* evaporate.
evaporazione, *n.f.* evaporation.
evasione, *n.f.* evasion; escape.
evasivo, *adj.* evasive.
eveniènza, *n.f.* eventuality, chance, circumstance.
evènto, *n.m.* outcome.
eversivo, *adj.* destructive.
evidènte, *adj.* evident.
evidentemente, *adv.* evidently.
evidènza, *n.f.* evidence.
evirare, *vb.* emasculate.
evitàbile, *adj.* avoidable.
evitare, *vb.* avoid, evade, eschew, obviate.
èvo, *n.m.* times, age, era.
evocare, *vb.* evoke.
evoluzione, *n.f.* evolution.
evoluzionista, *n.m.* evolutionist.
evòlvere, *vb.* evolve.
evviva, *interj.* hurrah (for).
extra, *adj.* extra.
ex voto, *n.m.* votive offering.

F

F (on water faucets) — **freddo,** *adj.* cold.
fa, *adv.* ago.
fàbbrica, *n.f.* factory, mill; (architecture) fabric.
fabbricante, *n.m.* manufacturer.
fabbricare, *vb.* build; manufacture, fabricate.
fabbricazione, *n.f.* manufacture; fabrication.
fabbro, *n.m.* smith. **f. ferraio,** blacksmith.
faccendière, *n.m.* busybody.
faccetta, *n.f.* facet.
facchino, *n.m.* porter.
faccia, *n.f.* face.
facciata, *n.f.* facade.
facèto, *adj.* facetious, witty, humorous.
facchino, *n.m.* porter.
facciale, *adj.* facial.
fàcile, *adj.* easy, facile.
facilità, *n.f.* facility, ease, easiness.
facilitare, *vb.* facilitate.
facilmente, *adv.* easily.
facinoroso, *adj.* violent, riotous; bullying.
facoltà, *n.f.* faculty, knack, power.
facoltativo, *adv.* optional.
facsìmile, *n.m.* facsimile.
factotum, *n.m.* handy-man; jack-of-all-trades.
fàggio, *n.m.* beech.
fagiano, *n.m.* pheasant.

fagiòlo, *n.m.* string bean.

faglia, *n.f.* faille.

fagòtto, *n.m.* bassoon.

fàida, *n.f.* feud; vengeance.

falcata, *n.f.* stride.

falce, *n.f.* scythe.

falciare, *vb.* mow.

falco, *n.m.* hawk.

falcone, *n.m.* falcon.

falconeria, *n.f.* falconry.

falegname, *n.m.* carpenter.

falla, *n.f.* leak.

fallace, *adj.* fallacious.

fallàcia, *n.f.* fallacy.

fallìbile, *adj.* fallible.

fallimento, *n.m.* bankruptcy; failure.

fallire, *vb.* fail; go bankrupt.

fallito, *adj.* bankrupt.

fallòcrate, *adj.* macho.

falò, *n.m.* bonfire.

falsetto, *n.m.* falsetto.

falsificare, *vb.* falsify, fake, counterfeit.

falsificatore, *n.f.* faker.

falsificazione, *n.f.* falsification.

falsità, *n.f.* falsity.

falso, 1. *n.m.* counterfeit, fake. 2. *adj.* false, counterfeit.

fama, *n.f.* fame.

fame, *n.f.* hunger; starvation. aver f., be hungry.

famigerato, *adj.* notorious.

famiglia, *n.f.* family; household.

familiare, *adj.* familiar, well-known; acquainted.

familiarità, *n.f.* familiarity.

familiarizzare, *vb.* familiarize.

famoso, *adj.* famous, famed.

fanale, *n.m.* lamp; light. f. anteriore, headlight.

fanàtico, *n.m. and adj.* fanatic, fanatical.

fanatismo, *n.m.* fanaticism.

fanciulla, *n.f.* maiden; girl.

fanciullescamente, *adv.* childishly; boyishly.

fanciullesco, *adj.* childish; boyish.

fanciullezza, *n.f.* childhood; boyhood; girlhood.

fanciullo, *n.m.* child; boy.

fandònia, *n.f.* fib; story, tale; *(pl.)* nonsense.

fanfara, *n.f.* fanfare.

fanfarone, *n.m.* boaster, braggart.

fanghìglia, *n.f.* slush.

fango, *n.m.* mud, mire.

fangoso, *adj.* muddy.

fannullone, *n.m.* idler, slacker; bum.

fantascienza, *n.f.* science fiction.

fantasìa, *n.f.* fantasy, imagination. di f., fancy.

fantasma, *n.m.* phantom.

fantasticheria, *n.f.* reverie, daydream.

fantàstico, *adj.* fantastic.

fante, *n.m.* infantryman.

fanterìa, *n.f.* infantry.

fantino, *n.m.* jockey.

fantòccio, *n.m.* puppet, dummy.

farabutto, *n.m.* scoundrel, rascal.

faraona, *n.f.* guinea fowl.

faraone, *n.m.* Pharaoh.

farcire, *vb.* stuff.

fardèllo, *n.m.* burden.

fare, *vb.* do; make. f. a meno di, go without. f. finta di, pretend to.

farètra, *n.f.* quiver (arrowcase).

farfalla, *n.f.* butterfly.

farfugliare, *vb.* mutter, mumble.

farina, *n.f.* flour; farina; meal.

faringe, *n.f.* pharynx.

farmacìa, *n.f.* drug store, pharmacy.

farmacista, *n.m.* druggist, pharmacist.

faro, *n.m.* beacon, lighthouse.

farsa, *n.f.* farce.

farsesco, *adj.* farcical.

fàscia, *n.f.* band; bandage.

fàscino, *n.m.* fascination; charm; glamor.

fàscio, *n.m.* bundle; sheaf; Fascist group.

fascismo, *n.m.* fascism.

fascista, *n. and adj.* fascist.

fase, *n.f.* phase, stage.

fastidio, *n.m.* annoyance, bother, trouble, unpleasantness, nuisance.

fastidioso, *adj.* fastidious; bothersome, troublesome.

fasto, *n.m.* pomp.

fastoso, *adj.* pompous.

fata, *n.f.* fairy.

fatale, *adj.* fatal; fateful.

fatalità, *n.f.* fatality.

fatalmente, vb. fatally.

fatica, n.f. fatigue; toil, hard work.

faticare, vb. toil.

fato, n.m. fate.

fattibile, adj. feasible.

fattispècie, n.f. **nella f.** in this particular case.

fatto, n.m. fact; deed, feat.

fattore, n.m. maker; factor; steward; granger.

fattoria, n.f. farm; grange; homestead; ranch; station.

fattorino, n.m. messenger, delivery boy.

fattura, n.f. invoice.

fatturare, vb. invoice.

fàtuo, adj. fatuous.

fàuci, n.f.pl. jaws.

fàuna, n.f. fauna.

fàuno, n.m. faun.

fàusto, adj. prosperous; propitious, lucky.

fava, n.f. bean.

favo, n.m. honeycomb.

fàvola, n.f. fable.

favoloso, adj. fabulous.

favore, n.m. favor; behalf. **a f. di,** in behalf of. **per f.,** please.

favorévole, adj. favorable, auspicious.

favorire, vb. favor.

favoritismo, n.m. favoritism.

favorito, n.m. and adj. favorite.

fazione, n.f. faction.

fazzoletti detergenti, n.m.pl. facial tissues.

fazzoletto, n.m. handkerchief.

febbraio, n.m. February.

fèbbre, n.f. fever.

febbrile, adj. feverish.

febbrilmente, adv. feverishly.

fèccia, n.f. dregs; lees; (pl.) faeces.

fèci, n.f.pl. feces.

fecondo, adj. fecund.

fede, n.f. faith, creed.

fededegno, adj. trustworthy, reliable.

fedele, adj. faithful, true.

fedeltà, n.f. faithfulness, allegiance, fidelity.

fèdera, n.f. pillowcase.

federale, adj. federal.

federazione, n.f. federation.

fedifrago, adj. unfaithful.

fedina, n.f. police record. **avere la f. sporca,** to have a bad record.

fégato, n.m. liver; pluck, guts.

felce, n.f. fern.

felice, adj. happy, felicitous.

felicemente, adv. happily.

felicità, n.f. felicity, happiness.

felicitare, vb. congratulate; felicitate; compliment.

felicitazione, n.f. congratulation; felicitation.

felino, adj. feline.

fellone, n.m. felon.

feltro, n.m. felt.

fémmina, n.f. female.

femminile, adj. female, feminine.

femminilità, n.f. femininity.

femminismo, n.m. feminism.

fèmore, n.m. femur, thighbone.

fèndere, vb. split, cleave, crack.

fenditura, n.f. split, cleft, crack.

fenomenale, adj. phenomenal.

fenòmeno, n.m. phenomenon.

fèretro, n.m. coffin.

feriale, adj. weekday.

fèrie, n.f.pl. holiday, vacation.

ferire, vb. wound, injure.

ferita, n.f. wound, injury.

ferito, n.m. wounded person, casualty.

feritòia, n.f. loophole.

ferma biancheria, n.m. clothespin.

fermamente, adv. firmly, fast.

fermare, vb. stop, halt, stay.

fermata, n.f. stop, halt. **f. intermèdia,** stop-over.

fermatura, n.f. fastening.

fermentare, vb. ferment.

fermentazione, n.f. fermentation.

fermento, n.m. ferment.

fermezza, n.f. firmness.

fermo, adj. firm, fixed, fast, steady. **f. pòsta,** general delivery. **mettere il f. su,** garnishee.

feroce, adj. ferocious, fierce.

ferocemente, adv. ferociously.

feròcia, n.f. ferocity.

ferragosto, n.m. Assumption; mid-August holiday.

ferramenta, n.f.pl. hardware.

ferrare, vb. shoe.

fèrreo, adj. iron.

ferrièra, *n.f.* ironworks.

fèrro, *n.m.* iron. **f. da stirare,** flat-iron. **f. di cavallo,** horseshoe.

ferrovìa, *n.f.* railroad.

ferroviàrio, *adj.* railroad.

fèrtile, *adj.* fertile.

fertilità, *n.f.* fertility.

fertilizzante, *n.m.* fertilizer.

fertilizzare, *vb.* fertilize.

fertilizzazióne, *n.f.* fertilization.

fervènte, *adj.* fervent.

ferventemente, *adv.* fervently.

fèrvido, *adj.* fervid.

fervóre, *n.m.* fervor, fervency.

fesserìa, *n.f.* nonsense, blunder, trifle.

fèsso, *adj.* cracked; crazy.

fessùra, *n.f.* split, cleavage, cranny, fissure; slit; slot.

fèsta, *n.f.* feast, festival, fête, holiday, vacation.

festeggiare, *vb.* celebrate.

festività, *n.f.* festivity.

festìvo, *adj.* festive. **giorno f.,** holiday.

festóne, *n.m.* festoon.

fetàle, *adj.* fetal.

feticcio, *n.m.* fetish.

fètido, *adj.* fetid.

fèto, *n.m.* fetus.

fetóre, *n.m.* stench.

fetta, *n.f.* slice, fillet.

feudàle, *adj.* feudal.

feudalìsmo, *n.m.* feudalism.

fèudo, *n.m.* fief, feud.

fiàba, *n.f.* fairy tale.

fiacco, *adj.* limp.

fiàccola, *n.f.* torch.

fiàla, *n.f.* vial.

fiamma, *n.f.* flame, blaze.

fiammante, *adj.* flaming, **nuovo f.,** brand new.

fiammeggiare, *vb.* flame, blaze; flare.

fiammìfero, *n.m.* match.

fiammingo, 1. *n.* Fleming; flamingo. **2.** *adj.* Flemish.

fiancheggiare, *vb.* flank.

fianco, *n.m.* flank; hip; side. **di f. a,** beside, abreast of.

fiasco, *n.m.* flask; fiasco; flop.

fiato, *n.m.* breath.

fibbia, *n.f.* buckle.

fibra, *n.f.* fiber.

fibróso, *adj.* fibrous.

ficcanàso, *n.m.* nosy person, busybody.

ficcare, *vb.* put; thrust, stick, shove.

fico, *n.m.* fig.

fidanzaménto, *n.m.* betrothal, engagement.

fidanzare, *vb.* betroth, affiance; *(refl.)* get engaged.

fidanzàta, *n.f.* fiancée.

fidanzàto, *n.m.* fiancé.

fidatézza, *n.f.* dependability.

fidènte, *adj.* reliant.

fido, *adj.* dependable.

fidùcia, *n.f.* trust.

fiduciàrio, *adj.* fiduciary.

fiducióso, *adj.* trustful, confident.

fièle, *n.m.* gall. **vescica del f.,** gallbladder.

fienile, *n.m.* hayloft.

fièno, *n.m.* hay.

fièra, *n.f.* fair. **f. campionària,** sample fair.

fifóne, *n.m.* (coll.) scaredy-cat, coward.

figlia, *n.f.* daughter.

figliare, *vb.* have a litter.

figliàstra, *n.f.* stepdaughter.

figliàstro, *n.m.* stepson, stepchild.

figliàta, *n.f.* litter.

figlio, *n.m.* son.

figliòccio, *n.m.* godchild.

figliòla, *n.f.* daughter; girl.

figliòlo, *n.m.* son; boy.

figura, *n.f.* figure.

figurare, *vb.* figure.

figurarsi, *vb.* imagine, fancy, envisage.

figuratamente, *adv.* figuratively.

figuràto, *adj.* figurative.

figurìna, *n.f.* figurine.

fila, *n.f.* file; line; row; rank; tier.

filàccia inglése, *n.f.* lint.

filaménto, *n.m.* filament.

filantropìa, *n.f.* philanthropy.

filare, *vb.* spin.

filastròcca, *n.f.* rhyme; children's song.

filatèlica, *n.f.* philately.

filàto, *n.m.* yarn.

filétto, *n.m.* fillet.

filiàle, *adj.* filial.

filigràna, *n.f.sg.* filigree.

film, *n.m.* movie.

filo, *n.m.* thread; string; clew; wire.

fìlobus, n.m. trolley-bus.
filogovernativo, adj. on the government side.
filone, n.m. vein, lode.
filosofìa, n.f. philosophy.
filosòfico, adj. philosophical.
filòsofo, n.m. philosopher.
filovìa, n.f. trolley-bus line.
filtrare, vb. filter.
filtro, n.m. filter.
filza, n.f. string; collection; file.
finale, 1. n.m. finale. 2. adj. final, eventual.
finalista, n.m. finalist.
finalità, n.f. finality; purpose.
finalmente, adv. finally.
finanza, n.f. finance.
finanziàrio, adj. financial.
finanzière, n.m. financier.
finchè, conj. till, until.
fine, n.m. purpose; f. end, finish.
finesettimana, n.m. weekend.
finèstra, n.f. window.
finezza, n.f. finesse.
fìngere, vb. pretend, feign, assume, make believe.
finimondo, n.m. disaster, fracas.
finire, vb. end, finish.
fino, adj. fine; pure.
fino a., prep. as far as; until, till. **f. dove?** how far? **f. a quando?** how long?
finòcchio, n.m. fennel; (slang) pederast.
finora, adv. up to now, so far, hereto, hitherto.
finta, n.f. pretense, make-believe.
finto, adj. pretended, fictional, mock, make-believe.
finzione, n.f. fiction; figment.
fiòcco, n.m. flake; (boat) jib. **f. da cìpria**, powder-puff.
fiòcina, n.f. harpoon.
fiocinare, vb. harpoon.
fiòco, adj. hoarse.
fionda, n.f. sling.
fioraio, n.m. florist.
fiòrdo, n.m. fjord, inlet.
fiore, n.m. flower, bloom, blossom.
fiorentino, adj. Florentine.
fioretto, n.m. foil.
fiori, n.m.pl. clubs (cards).
fiorire, vb. flower, bloom, blossom; flourish.

fiorista, n.m. florist.
fiorito, adj. flowery.
fiòtto, n.m. stream.
Firènze, n.f. Florence.
firma, n.f. signature.
firmare, vb. sign; endorse.
firmatàrio, n.m. signer, responsible party.
fisarmònica, n.f. accordion.
fiscale, adj. fiscal.
fischiare, vb. whistle.
fischietto, n.m. whistle (instrument).
fischio, n.m. whistle (sound).
Fisco, n.m. (coll.) Internal Revenue Service.
fìsica, n.f. physics.
fìsico, 1. n.m. physicist; physique. 2. adj. physical.
fìsima, n.f. caprice, whim, fancy; nonsense.
fisiologìa, n.f. physiology.
fisioterapìa, n.f. physiotherapy.
fissare, vb. fix; set; appoint; assess (a fine); fasten.
fissazione, n.f. fixation.
fissione, n.f. fission.
fisso, adj. fixed; set.
fìstola, n.f. fistula (pathology).
fittiziamente, adv. fictitiously.
fittìzio, adj. fictitious.
fitto, adj. thick.
fiume, n.m. river.
fiumicino, n.m. stream, creek.
fiutare, vb. smell.
fiuto, n.m. scent; smell; flair.
flàccido, adj. flaccid.
flacone, n.m. flacon.
flagellante, n.m. flagellant.
flagellare, vb. flagellate.
flagrante, adj. flagrant.
flagrantemente, adv. flagrantly.
flan, n.m. custard.
flanèlla, n.f. flannel.
flautista, n.m. flautist.
flàuto, n.m. flute.
flèbile, adj. feeble, weak.
flebite, n.f. phlebitis.
flèmma, n.m. phlegm.
flemmàtico, adj. phlegmatic.
flessìbile, adj. flexible; limp.
flessibilità, n.f. flexibility.
flessione, n.f. inflection.
flessuoso, adj. lithe.
flèttere, vb. flex.

flirt, *n.m.* flirtation.

flirtare, *vb.* flirt.

floreale, *adj.* floral.

flòscio, *adj.* soft; flabby.

flòtta, *n.f.* fleet.

fluènte, *adj.* glib.

fluidità, *n.f.* fluidity.

flùido, *n.m. and adj.* fluid.

fluorescènte, *adj.* fluorescent.

fluoroscòpio, *n.m.* fluoroscope.

flusso, *n.m.* flux.

fluttuare, *vb.* fluctuate.

fluttuazione, *n.f.* fluctuation.

fluviale, *adj.* fluvial, river.

fobìa, *n.f.* phobia.

fòca, *n.f.* seal.

focàccia, *n.f.* cake.

focale, *adj.* focal.

focolare, *n.m.* fireplace, hearth.

focolàio, *n.m.* focus *(pathology);* hotbed.

focoso, *adj.* fiery.

fòdera, *n.f.* lining.

fòdero, *n.m.* sheath.

foga, *n.f.* enthusiasm, ardor.

fòggia, *n.f.* shape, guise.

foggiare, *vb.* make; forge; shape.

fòglia, *n.f.* leaf; blade (of grass); foil.

fogliame, *n.m.* foliage.

fòglio, *n.m.* sheet.

fogliolina, *n.f.* leaflet.

fogliuto, *adj.* leafy.

fogna, *n.f.* drain; sewer.

folata, *n.f.* gust.

folclore, *n.m.* folklore.

folgorante, *adj.* striking.

folgorare, *vb.* strike *(lightning).*

folgore, *n.f.* thunderbolt.

fòlio, *n.m.* folio.

fòlla, *n.f.* crowd; crush; mob.

folle, *adj.* crazy; mad.

folletto, *n.m.* elf, hobgoblin.

follìa, *n.f.* folly.

follìcolo, *n.m.* follicle.

folto, *adj.* thick; bushy.

fomentare, *vb.* foment.

fonda, *n.f.* anchorage; **alla f.** at anchor.

fondale, *n.m.* backdrop; ocean floor.

fondamentale, *adj.* fundamental, basic.

fondamento, *n.m.* foundation.

fondare, *vb.* found.

fondatore, *n.m.* founder.

fondazione, *n.f.* foundation.

fondènte, *n.m.* fondant.

fóndere, *vb.* melt; (metal) cast; fuse; (ore) smelt.

fonderìa, *n.f.* foundry.

fondina, *n.f.* holster.

fonditore, *n.m.* melter; smelter; caster.

fondo, *n.m.* bottom; fund.

fonètico, *adj.* phonetic.

fontana, *n.f.* fountain.

fonte, *n.f.* spring; source.

foràggio, *n.m.* forage; fodder.

forare, *vb.* bore, pierce, puncture.

foratura, *n.f.* puncture.

fòrbici, *n.f.pl.* scissors.

forca, *n.f.* pitchfork; gallows.

forchetta, *n.f.* fork.

forcina, *n.f.* hairpin, bobby pin.

fòrcipe, *n.m.* forceps.

forènse, *adj.* forensic.

forèsta, *n.f.* forest, wood.

forestièro, 1. *n.* foreigner. **2.** *adj.* foreign.

fórfora, *n.f.* dandruff.

forgiare, *vb.* forge, shape.

forma, *n.f.* form, mold, shape; (shoe) last.

formàggio, *n.m.* cheese.

formaldèide, *n.f.* formaldehyde.

formale, *adj.* formal.

formalità, *n.f.* formality.

formalmente, *adv.* formally.

formare, *vb.* form, mold, shape; (telephone) dial (a number).

formativo, *adj.* formative.

formato, *n.m.* format.

formazione, *n.f.* formation.

formica, *n.f.* ant.

formicàio, *n.m.* anthill.

formicolare, *vb.* swarm.

formidàbile, *adj.* formidable.

formoso, *adj.* buxom, shapely.

fòrmula, *n.f.* formula.

formulare, *vb.* formulate.

formulazione, *n.f.* formulation.

fornace, *n.f.* furnace; kiln.

fornàio, *n.m.* baker.

fornèllo, *n.m.* stove.

fornire, *vb.* furnish, equip, supply.

fornitura, *n.f.* supply.

forno, *n.m.* oven; bakery.

foro, *n.m.* hole, bore, vent.

fòro, *n.m.* forum.

forse, *adv.* perhaps, maybe, possibly.

forsennato, *n.m.* frantic, mad.

forsìzia, *n.f.* forsythia.

fòrte, 1. *n.m.* forte. **2.** *adj.* strong; loud. **3.** *adv.* loud.

fortemente, *adv.* strongly; hard.

fortezza, *n.f.* fort, fortress; fortitude.

fortificare, *vb.* fortify.

fortificazione, *n.f.* fortification.

fortino, *n.m.* blockhouse, redoubt.

fortùito, *adj.* fortuitous, chance.

fortuna, *n.f.* fortune, luck.

fortunale, *n.m.* tempest, storm.

fortunato, *adj.* fortunate, lucky.

forùncolo, *n.m.* boil; pimple.

forviante, *adj.* misleading.

forviare, *vb.* mislead.

fòrza, *n.f.* force, strength.

forzare, *vb.* force.

forzato, *adj.* forced; forcible.

foschìa, *n.f.* fog.

fosco, *adj.* dark, dreary, dusky, grim, somber.

fòsforo, *n.m.* phosphorus.

fòssa, *n.f.* moat.

fossato, *n.m.* ditch.

fossetta, *n.f.* dimple.

fòssile, *n.m. and adj.* fossil.

fossilizzare, *vb.* fossilize.

fosso, *n.m.* ditch.

fotocopia, *n.f.* photocopy.

fotocopiatore, *n.m.* photocopier.

fotoelèttrico, *adj.* photoelectric.

fotogènico, *adj.* photogenic.

fotografare, *vb.* photograph.

fotografìa, *n.f.* photograph; photography.

fotògrafo, *n.m.* photographer.

fotogramma, *n.m.* frame.

fotomontaggio, *n.m.* photomontage.

fra, *prep.* between, among, amid.

f. pòco, soon, by-and-by, presently.

frac, *n.m.* tails (coat).

fracassare, *vb.* smash.

fracasso, *n.m.* uproar, fuss, ado, fracas.

fràdicio, *adj.* soaked; rotten.

fràgile, *adj.* fragile, brittle, frail.

fràgola, *n.f.* strawberry.

fragore, *n.m.* clang, crash.

fragrante, *adj.* fragrant.

fragranza, *n.f.* fragrance.

fraintèndere, *vb.* misunderstand, misconstrue.

frammentare, *vb.* fragment.

frammentàrio, *adj.* fragmentary.

frammento, *n.m.* fragment.

frana, *n.f.* landslide.

franare, *vb.* crumble; slide; collapse.

francamente, *adv.* frankly, candidly.

francese, 1. *n.m.* Frenchman; *f.* Frenchwoman. **2.** *adj.* France.

franchezza, *n.f.* frankness, candidness, directness.

franchigia, *n.f.* immunity, franchise, exemption.

Frància, *n.f.* France.

franco, *adj.* frank, candid, straightforward.

francobollo, *n.m.* postage stamp.

frangènte, *n.m.* breaker; *(pl.)* surf.

fràngere, *vb.* break, crush.

fràngia, *n.f.* fringe; (hair-do) bang.

frangi-ònde, *n.m.* breakwater.

frantumare, *vb.* shatter, smash.

frappé, *n.m.* shake, frappé.

frapporre, *vb.* interpose, insert.

frase, *n.f.* phrase; sentence.

fràssino, *n.m.* ash-tree.

frastagliare, *vb.* indent.

frastuòno, *n.m.* uproar, racket.

frate, *n.m.* friar.

fratellanza, *n.f.* brotherhood.

fratellastro, *n.m.* half-brother; step-brother.

fratèllo, *n.m.* brother.

fraternamente, *adv.* fraternally.

fraternità, *n.f.* fraternity.

fraternizzare, *vb.* fraternize.

fratèrno, *adj.* brotherly, fraternal.

fratricida, *n.m.* fratricide (person).

fratricìdio, *n.m.* fratricide (act).

fratta, *n.f.* thicket.

frattèmpo, *n.m.* meantime, meanwhile, interim.

frattura, *n.f.* fracture.

fratturare, *vb.* fracture.

fraudolentemente, *adv.* fraudulently.

fraudolento, *adj.* fraudulent.

frazione, *n.f.* fraction.

fréccia, *n.f.* arrow; directional signal.

freddamente, *adv.* coldly.

freddare, *vb.* chill; kill.

freddezza, *n.f.* coldness.

freddo, 1. *n.m.* cold; chill. **2.** *adj.* cold, chilly. **aver f.,** feel cold. **far f.,** be cold.

freddura, *n.f.* pun.

fregare, *vb.* rub.

fregata, *n.f.* rub; frigate.

fregatura, *n.f.* swindle, fraud.

fregiare, *vb.* decorate; fret.

frèmito, *n.m.* thrill.

frenare, *vb.* brake; check.

frenesia, *n.f.* frenzy.

frenètico, *adj.* frantic, frenzied.

freno, *n.m.* brake; check.

frenologìa, *n.f.* phrenology.

frequentare, *vb.* frequent, attend, haunt.

frequentatore, *n.m.* habitué.

frequènte, *adj.* frequent.

frequentemente, *adv.* frequently.

frequènza, *n.* frequency.

freschezza, *n.f.* freshness.

fresco, 1. *n.m.* coolness. **2.** *adj.* cool; fresh.

fretta, *n.f.* haste, hurry, hustle, rush.

frettolosamente, *adv.* hastily.

frettoloso, *adj.* hasty, cursory.

fricassèa, *n.f.* fricassee.

frìggere, *vb.* fry.

frìgido, *adj.* frigid.

frigorìfero, *n.m.* refrigerator; freezer.

frittata, *n.f.* omelet.

frittèlla, *n.f.* fritter, pancake.

frivolezza, *n.f.* frivolousness.

frivolità, *n.f.* frivolity.

frìvolo, *adj.* frivolous.

frizione, *n.f.* friction; rubbing; (auto) clutch.

fròde, *n.f.* fraud.

frontale, *adj.* frontal; head on.

fronte, *n.m.* forehead, brow; front.

fronteggiare, *vb.* face.

frontièra, *n.f.* frontier, border.

fròttola, *n.f.* fib, canard; *(pl.)* nonsense.

frugale, *adj.* frugal.

frugalità, *n.f.* frugality.

fruizione, *n.f.* fruition.

frumento, *n.m.* wheat.

frusciare, *vb.* rustle.

fruscìo, *n.m.* rustle.

frusta, *n.f.* lash, whip.

frustare, *vb.* lash, whip.

frustino, *n.m.* horsewhip.

frusto, *adj.* worn, threadbare.

frustrare, *vb.* frustrate, foil, thwart.

frustrazione, *n.f.* frustration.

frutta, *n.f.* fruit.

fruttare, *vb.* yield, produce.

frutteto, *n.m.* orchard.

fruttificare, *vb.* fructify.

fruttivéndolo, *n.m.* greengrocer, fruit merchant.

frutto, *n.m.* fruit.

fruttuoso, *adj.* fruitful.

fucilare, *vb.* shoot.

fucile, *n.m.* gun, rifle.

fucilerìa, *n.f.* fusillade.

fucina, *n.f.* forge, smithy.

fuco, *n.m.* drone.

fùcsia, *n.f.* fuchsia.

fuga, *n.f.* flight, escape, getaway; fugue.

fugace, *adj.* fleeting.

fugare, *vb.* dispel; put to flight.

fuggènte, *adj.* transitory, passing, fleeting.

fuggiasco, *n.m.* fugitive.

fuggifuggi, *n.m.* stampede.

fuggire, *vb.* flee; elope; run away.

fuggitivo, *n.m. and adj.* fugitive.

fulcro, *n.m.* fulcrum.

fulgore, *n.m.* radiance.

fulìggine, *n.f.* soot.

fulminare, *vb.* fulminate.

fulminazione, *n.f.* fulmination.

fùlmine, *n.m.* (bolt of) lightning; thunderbolt.

fulvo, *adj.* tawny.

fumaiòlo, *n.m.* smokestack.

fumare, *vb.* smoke.

fumetto, *n.m.* comic strip. **giornalino a fumetti,** comic book.

fumigare, *vb.* fumigate.

fumigatore, *n.m.* fumigator.

fumo, *n.m.* smoke.

fune, *n.f.* rope.

fùnebre, *adj.* funeral.

funerale, *n.m.* funeral.

funèreo, *adj.* funereal.

funèsto, *adj.* mournful, sad.

fungicida, *n.m.* fungicide.

fungo, *n.m.* fungus; mushroom.

funivia, *n.f.* cableway.

funzionale, *adj.* functional.

funzionare, *vb.* function; work; run.

funzionàrio, *n.m.* functionary, official.

funzione, *n.f.* function.

fuòchi d'artifìcio, *m.pl.* fireworks.

fuochista, *n.m.* fireman.

fuòco, *n.m.* fire, blaze; focus.

fuòri, *adv.* out; outside; forth. **f. di**, outside.

fuorilegge, *n.m* and *f.* outlaw.

fuoristrada, 1. *n.m.* four-wheel drive vehicle. 2. *adj.* off-road.

fuoriuscito, *n.m.* exile.

furbo, *adj.* crafty, tricky, sly, shrewd.

furènte, *adj.* furious.

furfante, *n.m.* blackguard, scoundrel, villain.

furgone, *n.m.* van.

fùria, *n.f.* fury.

furibondo, *adj.* wild, furious.

furioso, *adj.* furious; wild.

furore, *n.m.* furor, fury.

furtivamente, *adv.* stealthily.

furtivo, *adj.* furtive, stealthy.

furto, *n.m.* theft, burglary, larceny, robbery.

fusa, *n.f.pl.* **fare le f.**, to purr.

fusibile, 1. *n.m.* fuse. 2. *adj.* easily melted.

fusione, *n.f.* fusion, merger; (nuclear) meltdown.

fuso, *adj.* molten.

fusolièra, *n.f.* fuselage.

fustigare, *vb.* flog.

fùtile, *adj.* futile.

futilità, *n.f.* futility.

futuro, *n.m* and *adj.* future.

futurologia, *n.f.* futurology.

G

gabardina, *n.f.* gabardine.

gàbbia, *n.f.* cage.

gabbiano, *n.m.* gull.

gabinetto, *n.m.* cabinet; toilet; closet; office.

gagliardo, *adj.* sturdy.

gaiamente, *adv.* gaily.

gaiezza, *n.f.* gaiety.

gaio, *adj.* gay, cheerful, jolly, blithe, debonair.

gala, *n.f.* frill; gala.

galante, *adj.* gallant.

galàssia, *n.f.* galaxy.

galatèo, *n.m.* etiquette, good manners.

galèa, *n.f.* galley.

galeone, *n.m.* galleon.

galla, *n.f.* **a g.**, afloat.

galleggiare, *vb.* float.

gallerìa, *n.f.* gallery; tunnel; arcade.

gàllico, *adj.* Gallic.

gallina, *n.f.* hen.

gallismo, *n.m.* machismo.

gallo, *n.m.* rooster, cock.

gallone, *n.m.* stripe; chevron; gallon.

galoppare, *vb.* gallop.

galòppo, *n.m.* gallop.

galòscia, *n.f.* galosh.

galvanizzare, *vb.* galvanize.

galvanoplàstica, *n.f.* electroplating.

gamba, *n.f.* leg.

gamberetto, *n.m.* shrimp.

gambo, *n.m.* stalk.

gamma, *n.f.* scale; gamut.

ganàscia, *n.f.* jaw; brake shoe.

gancio, *n.m.* clip; clasp; hook.

gànghero, *n.m.* hinge.

gara, *n.f.* competition.

garage, *n.m.* garage.

garante, *n.m.* and *f.* guarantor.

garantire, *vb.* guarantee.

garanzìa, *n.f.* guarantee; guaranty; bail.

garbùglio, *n.m.* tangle.

gardènia, *n.f.* gardenia.

gareggiare, *vb.* vie, compete.

gargarismo, *n.m.* gargle.

gargarizzare, *vb.* gargle.

garòfano, *n.m.* carnation.

garrota, *n.f.* garrote.

gàrrulo, *adj.* garrulous.

garza, *n.f.* gauze; cheesecloth.
garzone, *n.m.* helper, shop-boy.
gas, *n.m.* gas.
gasdotto, *n.m.* gas pipeline.
gasòlio, *n.m.* diesel oil.
gassoso, *adj.* gassy, gaseous.
gàstrico, *adj.* gastric.
gastrite, *n.f.* gastritis.
gastronomìa, *n.f.* gastronomy.
gastronòmico, *adj.* gastronomic.
gatta, *n.f.* cat.
gattino, *n.m.* kitten.
gatto, *n.m.* cat, tomcat.
gavòtta, *n.f.* gavotte.
gazzèlla, *n.f.* gazelle.
gazzetta, *n.f.* gazette.
gelare, *vb.* freeze.
gelatàio, *n.m.* ice-cream dealer.
gelatina, *n.f.* gelatine; jelly.
gelatinoso, *adj.* gelatinous.
gelato, *n.m.* ice cream.
gèlido, *adj.* chilly, frosty.
gelone, *n.m.* chilblain.
gelosìa, *n.f.* jealousy.
geloso, *adj.* jealous.
gelso, *n.m.* mulberry.
gelsomino, *n.m.* jasmine.
gemèllo, *n.m.* twin.
gèmere, *vb.* groan, moan.
gèmito, *n.m.* moan, groan.
gèmma, *n.f.* gem; bud.
gemmare, *vb.* bud.
gendarme, *n.m.* policeman.
gène, *n.m.* gene.
genealogìa, *n.f.* genealogy, pedigree.
genealògico, *adj.* genealogical.
generale, *n.m.* and *adj.* general.
generalità, *n.f.* generality.
generalizzare, *vb.* generalize.
generalizzazione, *n.f.* generalization.
generalmente, *adv.* generally.
generare, *vb.* generate, beget, breed, engender.
generatore, *n.m.* generator.
generazione, *n.f.* generation.
gènere, *n.m.* kind, gender, sort, genus. **g. alimentari,** foodstuffs.
genèrico, *adj.* generic.
gènero, *n.m.* son-in-law.
generosamente, *adv.* generously.
generosità, *n.f.* generosity.
generoso, *adj.* generous.
gènesi, *n.f.* genesis.

genètica, *n.f.* genetics.
genètico, *adj.* genetic.
gengiva, *n.f.* gum.
geniale, *adj.* ingenious, clever.
gènio, *n.m.* genius; engineering.
genitale, *adj.* genital.
genitali, *n.m.pl.* genitals.
genitivo, *n.m.* and *adj.* genitive.
genitore, *n.m.* parent.
gennaio, *n.m.* January.
genocidio, *n.m.* genocide.
Gènova, *n.f.* Genoa.
genovese, *adj.* Genoese.
gentàglia, *n.f.* disreputable people, rabble.
gènte, *n.f.* people, folks.
gentile, *adj.* gentile; nice, kind.
gentilezza, *n.f.* kindness.
gentilìzio, *adj.* of noble family.
gentiluòmo, *n.m.* gentleman.
genuflèttersi, *vb.* genuflect.
genuinamente, *adv.* genuinely.
genuinità, *n.f.* genuineness.
genuino, *adj.* genuine.
genziana, *n.f.* gentian.
geografìa, *n.f.* geography.
geogràfico, *adj.* geographical.
geògrafo, *n.m.* geographer.
geometrìa, *n.f.* geometry.
geomètrico, *adj.* geometric.
geopolìtica, *n.f.* geopolitics.
gerànio, *n.m.* geranium.
gerarchìa, *n.f.* hierarchy.
geràrchico, *adj.* hierarchical.
gerente, *n.m.* manager.
gèrgo, *n.m.* jargon, slang.
geriatrìa, *n.f.* geriatrics.
Germània, *n.f.* Germany.
germànico, *adj.* Germanic.
gèrme, *n.m.* germ.
germicida, *n.m.* germicide.
germinale, *adj.* germinal.
germinare, *vb.* germinate.
germogliare, *vb.* sprout.
germòglio, *n.m.* sprout; shoot.
geroglìfico, *adj.* hieroglyphic.
Gerusalèmme, *n.f.* Jerusalem.
gesso, *n.m.* chalk; gypsum.
gessoso, *adj.* chalky.
gestante, *adj.* pregnant.
gestazione, *n.f.* gestation.
gesticolare, *vb.* gesticulate.
gesticolazione, *n.f.* gesticulation.
gèsto, *n.m.* gesture.

gestore, *n.m.* manager.
Gesù, *prop.m.* Jesus.
gesuita, *n.m.* Jesuit.
gettare, *vb.* throw, hurl; cast; dash; flip.
gèttito, *n.m.* yield.
gètto, *n.m.* throw; cast; jet.
gettone, *n.m.* token.
gherìglio, *n.m.* kernel.
ghermire, *vb.* snatch.
gherone, *n.m.* gusset.
ghette, *f. pl.* panty hose.
ghiacciaia, *n.f.* ice-box.
ghiacciaio, *n.m.* glacier.
ghiàccio, *n.m.* ice.
ghiaia, *n.f.* gravel.
ghianda, *n.f.* acorn.
ghiandaia, *n.f.* jay.
ghiàndola, *n.f.* gland.
ghigliottina, *n.f.* guillotine.
ghignare, *vb.* grin; sneer.
ghingano, *n.m.* gingham.
ghiotto, *adj.* gluttonous.
ghiottone, 1. *n.m.* gutton, gourmand. **2.** *adj.* greedy.
ghiottoneria, *n.f.* greediness.
ghirigoro, *n.m.* curlycue, doodle.
ghirlanda, *n.f.* garland, wreath.
ghiro, *n.m.* dormouse.
ghisa, *n.f.* cast iron.
già, 1. *adj.* former; sometime. **2.** *adv.* already, formerly.
giacca, *n.f.* coat, jacket.
giacchè, *conj.* since.
giacchetta, *n.f.* jacket.
giàcchio, *n.m.* dragnet.
giacere, *vb.* lie.
giaciglio, *n.m.* cot.
giacimento, *n.m.* field.
giacinto, *n.m.* hyacinth.
giada, *n.f.* jade.
giaguaro, *n.m.* jaguar.
giallo, *adj.* yellow.
giàmbico, *adj.* iambic.
giammai, *adv.* never.
Giappone, *n.m.* Japan.
giapponese, *adj.* Japanese.
giara, *n.f.* jar.
giardinetta, *n.f.* station wagon.
giardinière, *n.m.* gardener.
giardino, *n.m.* garden. **g. d'infànzia,** kindergarten.
giarrettièra, *n.f.* garter.
giavellòtto, *n.m.* javelin.
gibbone, *n.m.* gibbon.

giga, *n.f.* jig.
gigante, *n.m.* giant.
gigantesco, *adj.* gigantic; giant.
giglio, *n.m.* lily.
gilè, *n.m.* vest; waistcoat.
gimnòto, *n.m.* electric eel.
ginecologia, *n.f.* gynaecology.
ginepro, *n.m.* juniper.
Ginèvra, *n.f.* Geneva.
ginevrino, *adj.* Genevan.
ginnàsio, *n.m.* high school.
ginnasta, *n.m.* gymnast.
ginnàstica, *n.f.* gymnastics.
ginnàstico, *adj.* gymnastic.
ginòcchio, *n.m.* knee.
giocare, *vb.* play. **g. d'azzardo,** gamble.
giocatore, *n.m.* player. **g. d'azzardo,** gambler.
giocàttolo, *n.m.* toy.
giòco, *n.m.* game. **g. d'azzardo,** game of chance; gambling.
giocondo, *adj.* jocund.
giogo, *n.m.* yoke.
giòia, *n.f.* joy, glee.
gioielleria, *n.f.* jewelry.
gioiellière, *n.m.* jeweler.
gioièllo, *n.m.* jewel.
gioire, *vb.* rejoice; gloat.
gioioso, *adj.* joyful, happy, blithe, gleeful.
giornalaio, *n.m.* news-vendor.
giornale, *n.m.* newspaper; journal; daily.
giornalièro, *adj.* daily.
giornalismo, *n.m.* journalism.
giornalista, *n.m.* journalist.
giornata, *n.f.* day.
giorno, *n.m.* day. **g. feriale,** weekday; workday. **g. festivo,** holiday.
gióvane, *adj.* young.
giovanile, *adj.* youthful; juvenile.
giovedì, *n.m.* Thursday.
giovènca, *n.f.* heifer.
gioviale, *adj.* jovial.
giovinezza, *n.f.* youth.
giradischi, *n.m.* record player.
giraffa, *n.f.* giraffe.
giramondo, *n.m.* globetrotter.
girare, *vb.* turn, revolve, spin, whirl; crank; endorse.
girasole, *n.m.* sunflower.
girata, *n.f.* endorsement.
giretto, *n.m.* spin.
girino, *n.m.* tadpole.

giro, *n.m.* turn; revolution; round.
  prèndere in g., make fun of/ kid.
giroscòpio, *n.m.* gyroscope.
girotondo, *n.m.* ring-around-a-rosy.
girovago, *adj.* itinerant.
gita, *n.f.* outing; picnic.
gittata, *n.f.* range (of gun).
giù, *adv.* down.
giubbotto, *n.m.* jacket.
giubilante, *adj.* jubilant.
giubilèo, *n.m.* jubilee.
giudaismo, *n.m.* Judaism.
giudèo, *n.m.* Jew.
giudicare, *vb.* judge; deem.
giùdice, *n.m.* judge.
giudiziàrio, *adj.* judiciary; judicial.
giudìzio, *n.m.* judgment, discernment.
giudizioso, *adj.* judicious.
giugno, *n.m.* June.
giugulare, *adj.* jugular.
giulivo, *adj.* happy, joyful.
giullare, *n.m.* joker.
giuncata, *n.f.* junket.
giunchìglia, *n.f.* jonquil.
giunco, *n.m.* rush.
giùngere, *vb.* join; arrive.
giungla, *n.f.* jungle.
giuntura, *n.f.* juncture, joint.
giuramento, *n.m.* oath.
giurare, *vb.* swear.
giurato, *n.m.* juror.
giurìa, *n.f.* jury.
giurisdizione, *n.f.* jurisdiction.
giurisprudènza, *n.f.* jurisprudence.
giurista, *n.m.* jurist.
giustacuòre, *n.m.* jerkin.
giustamente, *adv.* justly, fairly.
giustezza, *n.f.* fairness.
giustificàbile, *adj.* justifiable.
giustificare, *vb.* justify.
giustificazione, *n.f.* justification.
giustìzia, *n.f.* justice; righteousness.
giustiziare, *vb.* execute.
giusto, *adj.* just, fair; even, right; righteous; sound.
glabro, *adj.* smooth, hairless.
glaciale, *adj.* glacial. **zona g.,** frigid zone.
gladiatore, *n.m.* gladiator.
gladìolo, *n.m.* gladiolus.

glassa, *n.f.* icing.
glaucòma, *n.m.* glaucoma.
gli, 1. *def. art. m.pl.* the. **2.** *pron. 3. sg.m. dative.* to him.
glicerina, *n.f.* glycerine.
glìcine, *n.m.* wisteria.
globale, *adj.* global.
glòbo, *n.m.* globe. **g. dell'òcchio,** eyeball.
globulare, *adj.* globular.
glòbulo, *n.m.* globule.
glòria, *n.f.* glory.
gloriarsi, *vb.* glory.
glorificare, *vb.* glorify.
glorificazione, *n.f.* glorification.
glorioso, *adj.* glorious.
glossàrio, *n.m.* glossary.
glucòsio, *n.m.* glucose.
glutinoso, *adj.* glutinous.
gnòcco, *n.m.* dumpling.
gobba, *n.f.* hunchback (woman); hump; hunch.
gobbo, *n.m.* humpback, hunchback.
góccia, *n.f.* drop.
gocciamento, *n.m.* dripping.
gocciolare, *vb.* drip.
godere, *vb.* enjoy; *(refl.)* bask in.
godìbile, *adj.* enjoyable.
godimento, *n.m.* enjoyment.
goffàggine, *n.f.* clumsiness.
gòffo, *adj.* awkward, clumsy, gawky, uncouth.
gola, *n.f.* throat; gorge; gullet.
golf, *n.m.* golf; sweater.
golfo, *n.m.* gulf.
goliardo, *n.m.* university student; goliard.
golosità, *n.f.* gluttony.
goloso, *adj.* gluttonous.
gòmena, *n.f.* hawser.
gomitata, *n.f.* hit with the elbow, nudge.
gómito, *n.m.* elbow.
gomma, *n.f.* gum; rubber. **g. lacca,** shellac.
gommista, *n.m.* tire dealer.
gommoso, *adj.* gummy.
góndola, *n.f.* gondola.
gondolière, *n.m.* gondolier.
gonfiamento, *n.m.* inflation; swelling up.
gonfiare, *vb.* inflate; swell; bloat; *(refl.)* bulge.

gonfio, *adj.* inflated; swollen; baggy.

gonfiore, *n.m.* swelling.

gong, *n.m.* gong.

gònna, *n.f.* skirt.

gonnèlla, *n.f.* gown; petticoat.

gonorrèa, *n.f.* gonorrhea.

gonzo, *n.m.* fool, blockhead.

gorgo, *n.m.* whirlpool.

gorgogliare, *vb.* gurgle.

gorgòglio, *n.m.* gurgle.

gorilla, *n.m.* gorilla.

gota, *n.f.* cheek.

gòtico, *adj.* Gothic.

gotta, *n.f.* gout (medical).

governante, *n.f.* governess.

governare, *vb.* govern.

governativo, *adj.* governmental.

governatorato, *n.m.* governorship.

governatore, *n.m.* governor.

governatoriale, *adj.* gubernatorial.

govèrno, *n.m.* government.

gozzo, *n.m.* goiter.

gozzovìglia, *n.f.* revel.

gozzovigliare, *vb.* revel.

gracchiare, *vb.* caw.

gràcchio, *n.m.* grackle.

gracidare, *vb.* croak.

gradale, *n.m.* grail.

gradatamente, *adv.* by degrees.

gradévole, *adj.* pleasing; acceptable; agreeable.

gradevolmente, *adv.* pleasingly; agreeably; acceptably.

gradino, *n.m.* step.

gradire, *vb.* like; appreciate.

grado, *n.m.* degree; grade; rank.

graduale, *adj.* gradual.

gradualmente, *adv.* gradually.

graduare, *vb.* graduate.

graduatòria, *n.f.* ranking.

graduazione, *n.f.* foreclosure.

graffa, *n.f.* clamp; bracket.

graffiare, *vb.* scratch.

graffiatura, *n.f.* scratch.

gràffio, *n.m.* scratch.

grafia, *n.f.* writing.

gràfico, 1. *n.m.* graph. 2. *adj.* graphic.

grafite, *n.f.* graphite.

grafologia, *n.f.* graphology.

grammàtica, *n.f.* grammar.

grammaticale, *adj.* grammatical.

grammàtico, *n.m.* grammarian.

grammo, *n.m.* gram.

grammòfono, *n.m.* gramophone, phonograph.

gramo, *adj.* miserable, sad, poor.

granaio, *n.m.* granary; barn.

granata, *n.f.* grenade.

granatina, *n.f.* grenadine.

granato, *n.m.* garnet.

Gran Bretagna, *n.f.* Great Britain.

grancassa, *n.f.* bass drum.

grànchio, *n.m.* crab.

grandangolare, *n.m* wide-angle lens.

grande, *adj.* big; large; great; grand.

grandezza, *n.f.* greatness, grandeur; size; magnitude.

grandinare, *vb.* hail.

grandinata, *n.f.* hailstorm.

gràndine, *n.f.* hail.

grandiosamente, *adv.* grandiosely, grandly.

grandioso, *adj.* grandiose.

granello, *n.m.* grain, seed.

granito, *n.m.* granite.

grano, *n.m.* grain; bead. **g. saraceno,** buckwheat.

granturco, *n.m.* corn; maize.

granulare, 1. *adj.* granular. 2. *vb.* granulate.

granulazione, *n.f.* granulation.

granèllo, *n.m.* granule.

grappa, *n.f.* clamp.

gràppolo, *n.m.* bunch, cluster.

grassatore, *n.m.* highway robber.

grassazione, *n.f.* hold-up.

grassetto, *adj.* chubby; boldface.

grasso, 1. *n.m.* fat; grease. 2. *adj.* fat; stout; fatty; greasy.

grassòccio, *adj.* plump, buxom.

grata, *n.f.* lattice.

gratìcola, *n.f.* grate; grill; grid; gridiron; griddle; broiler.

gratifica, *n.f.* bonus.

gratificare, *vb.* gratify.

gratificazione, *n.f.* gratification; bonus.

gratis, *adv.* free, without charge.

gratitùdine, *n.f.* gratitude.

grato, *adj.* grateful, thankful; pleasing.

grattacapo, *n.m.* concern, worry.

grattacièlo, *n.m.* skyscraper.

grattare, *vb.* scratch.

grattùgia, *n.f.* grater.

grattugiare, *vb.* grate.

gratuitamente, *adv.* gratis.

gratùito, *adj.* free, gratis, complimentary, gratuitous.

gravare, *vb.* burden.

grave, *adj.* grave; grievous.

gravemente, *adv.* gravely.

gràvida, *adj.f.* pregnant, big with child.

gravidanza, *n.f.* pregnancy.

gravità, *n.f.* gravity.

gravitare, *vb.* gravitate.

gravitazione, *n.f.* gravitation.

gravoso, *adj.* burdensome, oppressive.

gràzia, *n.f.* grace.

gràzie, *interj.* thanks!

graziosamente, *adv.* graciously.

grazioso, *adj.* gracious; pretty; becoming; comely.

Grècia, *n.f.* Greece.

grèco, *adj.* Greek.

gregàrio, *adj.* gregarious.

gregge, *n.m.* flock, herd.

greggio, 1. *n.m.* crude oil. **2.** *adj.* unrefined.

grembiule, *n.m.* apron.

grèmbo, *n.m.* lap.

gretto, *adj.* mean; shabby.

grezzo, *adj.* raw.

gridare, *vb.* cry; shout, yell.

grido, *n.m.* cry; shout, yell.

grigiastro, *adj.* grayish.

grìgio, *adj.* gray; drab.

grilletto, *n.m.* trigger.

grillo, *n.m.* cricket.

grisou, *n.m.* firedamp.

gròg, *n.m.* grog.

gronda, *n.f.* eaves.

grondaia, *n.f.* gutter.

grossagrana, *n.f.* grosgrain.

gròsso, *adj.* big; large; fat.

grossolanamente, *adv.* grossly.

grossolanità, *n.f.* coarseness; grossness.

grossolano, *adj.* coarse; gross.

grotta, *n.f.* grotto.

grottesco, *adj.* grotesque.

grovìglio, *n.m.* ravel, tangle, snarl.

gru, *n.f.* crane; derrick.

grùccia, *n.f.* crutch.

grugnire, *vb.* grunt.

grugnito, *n.m.* grunt.

grumo, *n.m.* clot.

gruppo, *n.m.* group, clump, cluster; gang.

gruzzolo, *n.m.* hoard, savings, stock.

guadagnare, *vb.* earn; gain.

guadagno, *n.m.* gain; profit; *(pl.)* earnings.

guadare, *vb.* wade, ford, cross.

guado, *n.m.* ford.

guaìna, *n.f.* sheath.

guaio, *n.m.* trouble, woe.

guaire, *vb.* yelp; whimper.

guància, *n.f.* cheek; jowl.

guanciale, *n.m.* pillow.

guanto, *n.m.* glove; gauntlet.

guardaboschi, *n.m.* park ranger.

guardacòste, *adj.* coast guard.

guardare, *vb.* look at; guard; gaze; regard; watch; *(refl.)* beware.

guardaròba, *n.f.* cloakroom; wardrobe.

guardaspalle, *n.m.* bodyguard.

guàrdia, *n.f.* guard; watch.

guardiano, *n.m.* guardian; caretaker; watchman.

guardina, *n.f.* guard-house.

guardingo, *adj.* wary.

guardone, *n.m.* voyeur, Peeping Tom.

guarìbile, *adj.* curable.

guarigione, *n.f.* cure, recovery.

guarire, *vb.* cure, heal.

guarnigione, *n.f.* garrison.

guarnire, *vb.* garnish.

guarnizione, *n.f.* garnishment; gasket.

guastafeste, *n.m.* spoilsport.

guastare, *vb.* spoil, mar.

guazzabùglio, *n.m.* mess; hash.

guèrra, *n.f.* war.

guerresco, *adj.* warlike.

guerrièro, *n.m.* warrior.

guerriglia, *n.f.* guerrilla.

guerrigliero, *n.m.* guerrilla fighter.

gufo, *n.m.* owl.

gùglia, *n.f.* spire.

guida, *n.f.* guide; guidance; leadership; guidebook; directory.

guidare, *vb.* guide; drive (auto).

guinzàglio, *n.m.* leash.

guisa, *n.f.* manner, way. **a g. di** under the guise of.

guizzare, *vb.* wriggle; flash.

guru, *n.m.* guru.

gùscio, *n.m.* shell.

gustare, *vb.* taste.

gustativo, *adj.* gustatory, involving taste.

gusto, *n.m.* taste; gusto; relish.

gustoso, *adj.* tasty, appetizing, palatable.

gutturale, *adj.* guttural.

H,I

hascisc, *n.m.* hashish.

hennè, *n.m.pl.* henna.

hertz, *n.m.* hertz.

holliwoodiano, *adj.* Hollywood-like.

hurrá, *interj.* Hurrah!

i, *def. art. m.pl.* the.

iarda, *n.f.* yard.

iato, *n.m.* hiatus.

iattura, *n.f.* misfortune.

ibernazione, *n.f.* hibernation.

ibisco, *n.m.* hibiscus.

ibridazione, *n.f.* cross-fertilization.

ìbrido, *adj.* hybrid.

icòne, *n.f.* icon.

iddìo, *n.m.* god.

idèa, *n.f.* idea.

ideale, *adj.* ideal.

idealismo, *n.m.* idealism.

idealista, *n.m.* idealist.

idealìstico, *adj.* idealistic.

idealizzare, *vb.* idealize.

idealmente, *adj.* ideally.

idèntico, *adj.* identical.

identificàbile, *adj.* identifiable.

identificare, *vb.* identify.

identificazione, *n.f.* identification.

identità, *n.f.* identity.

ideologìa, *n.f.* ideology.

idilliaco, *adj.* idyllic.

idìllio, *n.m.* idyll.

idiòma, *n.m.* idiom.

idiòta, 1. *n.* idiot. **2.** *adj.* idiotic.

idiozìa, *n.f.* idiocy.

idolatra, *n.m. or f.* idolater.

idolatrare, *vb.* idolize.

idolatrìa, *n.* idolatry.

ìdolo, *n.m.* idol.

idoneità, *n.f.* fitness.

idòneo, *adj.* fit; qualified.

idrante, *n.m.* hydrant.

idrato di carbone, *n.m.* carbohydrate.

idràulico, 1. *n.m.* plumber. **2.** *adj.* hydraulic.

idroclòrico, *adj.* hydrochloric.

idroelèttrico, *adj.* hydroelectric.

idrofobìa, *n.f.* hydrophobia.

idrògeno, *n.m.* hydrogen.

idropisìa, *n.f.* dropsy.

idroscalo, *n.m.* seaplane airport.

idroterapèutica, *n.f.* hydrotherapy.

idrovolante, *n.m.* seaplane; hydroplane.

ièna, *n.f.* hyena.

ièri, *n.m. and adv.* yesterday.

igiène, *n.f.* hygiene; sanitation.

igiènico, *adj.* hygienic; sanitary.

ignaro, *adj.* ignorant.

ignòbile, *adj.* ignoble.

ignominioso, *adj.* ignominious.

ignorante, *adj.* ignorant.

ignorantone, *n.m.* ignoramus.

ignoranza, *n.f.* ignorance.

ignòto, *adj.* unknown.

ignudo, *adj.* naked.

il, *def. art. m.sg.* the.

ilare, *adj.* hilarious.

ilarità, *n.f.* hilarity.

illanguidire, *vb.* languish, get weak.

illécito, *adj.* illicit.

illegale, *adj.* illegal.

illeggibile, *adj.* illegible.

illeggibilmente, *adv.* illegibly.

illegittimità, *n.f.* illegitimacy.

illegìttimo, *adj.* illegitimate.

illeso, *adj.* unhurt.

illibato, *adj.* pure, untouched.

illimitatamente, *adv.* boundlessly.

illimitato, *adj.* unlimited; boundless; limitless.

illògico, *adj.* illogical.

illuminare, *vb.* illuminate; light up; brighten; enlighten.

illuminazione, *n.f.* illumination.

illuminismo, *n.m.* Age of Enlightenment.

illusione, *n.f.* illusion.

illusòrio, *adj.* illusory; illusive.

illustrare, *vb.* illustrate.

illustrativo, *adj.* illustrative.

illustrazione, *n.f.* illustration.

illustre, *adj.* illustrious.

imam, *n.m.* imam.

imbaccuccare, *vb.* wrap up.

imbaldanzire, *vb.* embolden; animate.

imballàggio, *n.m.* packing.

imballare, *vb.* pack.

imbalsamare, *vb.* embalm.

imbambolato, *adj.* stunned; gazing; sleepy.

imbandire, *vb.* set the table; prepare lavishly.

imbarazzare, *vb.* embarrass.

imbarazzo, *n.m.* embarrassment.

imbarcare, *vb.* embark.

imbastire, *vb.* baste.

imbattìbile, *adj.* unbeatable.

imbavagliare, *vb.* gag.

imbecille, *n.m. and adj.* imbecile; half-wit; moron.

imbèrbe, *adj.* beardless.

imbiancare, *vb.* whiten; bleach.

imboccare, *vb.* feed by mouth.

imboccatura, *n.f.* mouthpiece; nozzle.

imboscata, *n.f.* ambush. **tendere un' i.,** to ambush.

imbottire, *vb.* pad; stuff.

imbottita, *n.f.* quilt.

imbottitura, *n.f.* wadding; padding; batting.

imbrattare, *vb.* soil; stain; daub.

imbrattatura, *n.f.* daub.

imbrogliare, *vb.* embroil; entangle.

imbròglio, *n.m.* trick, cheat, fraud.

imbronciato, *adj.* sulky, surly.

imbucare, *vb.* mail.

imbuto, *n.m.* funnel.

imitare, *vb.* imitate; mimic.

imitativo, *adj.* imitative.

imitatore, *n.m.* mimic; imitator.

imitazione, *n.f.* imitation.

immacolato, *adj.* immaculate.

immagazzinare, *vb.* store.

immaginàbile, *adj.* imaginable.

immaginare, *vb.* imagine; fancy.

immaginàrio, *adj.* imaginary.

immaginativo, *adj.* imaginative.

immaginazione, *n.f.* fancy, imagination.

immàgine, *n.f.* image.

immaginoso, *adj.* fanciful.

immane, *adj.* huge.

immanènte, *adj.* immanent.

immateriale, *adj.* immaterial.

immaturo, *adj.* immature.

immediatamente, *adv.* immediately, instantly; directly; forthwith; presently.

immediato, *adj.* immediate, instant.

immènso, *adj.* immense.

immèrgere, *vb.* immerse, dip.

imperitato, *adj.* undeserved.

immigrante, *n. and adj.* immigrant.

immigrare, *vb.* immigrate.

imminènte, *adj.* imminent.

immischiarsi, *vb.* interfere, meddle, tamper.

immiserire, *vb.* impoverish.

immissione, *n.m.* letting in, introduction.

immòbile, *adj.* immobile, motionless, immovable.

immobilizzare, *vb.* immobilize.

immoderato, *adj.* immoderate.

immodèstia, *n.f.* immodesty.

immodèsto, *adj.* immodest.

immorale, *adj.* immoral.

immoralità, *n.f.* immorality.

immoralmente, *adv.* immorally.

immortalare, *vb.* immortalize.

immortale, *adj.* immortal, deathless.

immortalità, *n.f.* immortality.

immune, *adj.* immune.

immunità, *n.f.* immunity.

immunizzare, *vb.* immunize.

immutàbile, *adj.* immutable.

impaginare, *vb.* arrange in pages.

impalare, *vb.* impale.

impalcatura, *n.f.* scaffolding.

impallidire, *vb.* pale; blanch; fade.

impantanarsi, *vb.* bog down.

imparare, *vb.* learn.

imparentato, *adj.* related, kindred.

impartire, *vb.* impart.

imparziale, *adj.* impartial.

impastare, *vb.* knead.

impaziènte, *adj.* impatient, eager.

impazientemente, *adv.* impatiently, eagerly.

impaziènza, *n.f.* impatience, eagerness.

impazzire, *vb.* go crazy.

impazzito, *adj.* gone crazy, deranged.

impeccàbile, *adj.* impeccable.

impedimento, *n.m.* impediment, hindrance.

impedire, *vb.* impede, hinder, hamper, avert, balk, forestall, prevent.

impegnare, *vb.* pledge; pawn.

impegno, *n.m.* undertaking, commitment.

impegolare, *vb.* entangle, get mixed up with.

impèllere, *vb.* impel.

impenetràbile, *adj.* impenetrable.

impenitènte, *adj.* impenitent.

impennarsi, *vb.* rear.

impensàbile, *adj.* unthinkable.

imperante, *adj.* prevailing.

imperativo, *adj. and adj.* imperative.

imperatore, *n.m.* emperor.

imperatrice, *n.f.* empress.

impercettìbile, *adj.* imperceptible.

imperfètto, *adj.* imperfect.

imperfezione, *n.f.* imperfection.

imperiale, *adj.* imperial.

imperialismo, *n.m.* imperialism.

imperioso, *adj.* imperious.

imperituro, *adj.* imperishable; immortal.

impermeàbile, 1. *n.m.* raincoat. **2.** *adj.* water-proof.

imperniare, *vb.* pivot.

impèro, *n.m.* empire.

imperscrutàbile, *adj.* inscrutable.

impersonale, *adj.* impersonal.

impersonare, *vb.* impersonate.

impersonatore, *n.m.* impersonator.

impertèrrito, *adj.* impassible; undaunted.

impertinènte, *adj.* impertinent.

impertinènza, *n.f.* impertinence.

impèrvio, *adj.* impervious.

impeto, *n.m.* impetus.

impettito, *adj.* puffed up with pride.

impetuosamente, *adv.* impetuously; boisterously.

impetuoso, *adj.* impetuous; boisterous; dashing; heady.

impiallacciare, *vb.* veneer.

impiantare, *vb.* implant.

impianto, *n.m.* installation; plant.

impiccagione, *n.f.* hanging.

impiccare, *vb.* hang.

impiccatore, *n.m.* hangman.

impiccio, *n.m.* jam, fix, pickle, predicament, scrape.

impiccione, *n.m.* busybody, meddler.

impiegare, *vb.* employ; use.

impiegata, *n.f.* employee.

impiegato, *n.m.* employee, clerk.

impiègo, *n.m.* employment, job.

impietrire, *vb.* petrify.

impigliare, *vb.* entangle.

impigrire, *vb.* get lazy.

impinzare, *vb.* stuff, fill.

implacàbile, *adj.* implacable.

implicare, *vb.* implicate; imply; involve.

implicazione, *n.f.* implication.

implìcito, *adj.* implicit, implied.

implorare, *vb.* implore, beg, plead with.

implume, *adj.* featherless.

impollinare, *vb.* pollinate.

imponderàbile, *adj.* imponderable.

imporre, *vb.* impose; levy.

importante, *adj.* important, momentous.

importanza, *n.f.* importance.

importare, *vb.* import; be important, matter.

importazione, *n.f.* import, importation.

importunare, *vb.* importune.

importuno, *adj.* importunate.

imposizione, *n.f.* imposition.

impossìbile, *adj.* impossible.

impossibilità, *n.f.* impossibility.

imposta, *n.f.* tax, duty, levy. **i. sul valore aggiunto,** value-added tax.

impostare, *vb.* mail, post.

impostura, *n.f.* imposture, humbug.

impotènte, *adj.* impotent, powerless, helpless.

impotènza, *n.f.* impotence.

impoverire, *vb.* impoverish.

impregnare, *vb.* impregnate.

imprenditore, *n.m.* contractor; entrepreneur. **i. di pompe fùnebri,** undertaker.

impresa, *n.f.* enterprise, undertaking; feat.

impresàrio, *n.m.* impresario, theatrical manager.

impressionante, *adj.* impressive.

impressionare, *vb.* impress.

impressione, *n.f.* impression.

imprigionare, *vb.* imprison.

imprìmere, *vb.* impress.

improbàbile, *adj.* improbable, unlikely.

impronta, *n.f.* mark; print. **i. digitale,** fingerprint.

impròprio, *adj.* improper.

improvvisare, *vb.* improvise.

improvviso, 1. *n.m.* impromptu. **2.** *adj.* unforeseen; sudden, abrupt.

impudènte, *adj.* impudent, cocky.

impudìcizia, *n.f.* immodesty, shamelessness.

impùdico, *adj.* immodest, shameless; lewd.

impugnare, *vb.* impugn.

impulsivo, *adj.* impulsive.

impulso, *n.m.* impulse.

impunità, *n.f.* impunity.

impurità, *n.f.* impurity.

impuro, *adj.* impure.

imputare, *vb.* impute; accuse; impeach.

imputato, *n.m.* defendant.

imputridire, *vb.* rot; *(refl.)* go rotten; (egg) addle.

in, *prep.* in; into.

inàbile, *adj.* ineligible; unfitted.

inabissare, *vb.* sink.

inabitàbile, *adj.* uninhabitable.

inaccessìbile, *adj.* inaccessible.

inaccettàbile, *adj.* unacceptable.

inadempiente, *adj.* defaulting.

inalare, *vb.* inhale.

inalienàbile, *adj.* inalienable.

inamidare, *vb.* starch.

inano, *adj.* inane.

inarcare, *vb.* arch, bend, curve.

inaridire, *vb.* parch.

inaspettatamente, *adv.* unexpectedly.

inaspettato, *adj.* unexpected.

inattivo, *adj.* inactive, dormant.

inaugurale, *adj.* inaugural.

inaugurare, *vb.* inaugurate.

inaugurazione, *n.f.* inauguration.

inavvertènza, *n.f.* oversight.

inavvertitamente, *adv.* inadvertently.

incandescènte, *adj.* incandescent, glowing.

incandescènza, *n.f.* incandescence, glow.

incantamento, *n.m.* incantation.

incantare, *vb.* enchant, charm.

incantatore, *n.m.* enchanter, charmer.

incantatrice, *n.f.* enchantress, charmer.

incantésimo, *n.m.* spell.

incantèvole, *adj.* enchanting.

incanto, *n.m.* enchantment, charm.

incanutire, *vb.* turn gray (hair).

incapace, *adj.* unable.

incapacità, *n.f.* incapacity; disability.

incaparbire, *vb.* turn obstinate.

incappare, *vb.* meet, run into.

incarcerare, *vb.* incarcerate.

incaricare, *vb.* charge, entrust, commission.

incàrico, *n.m.* charge; commission, task, assignment.

incarnato, *adj.* incarnate.

incarnazione, *n.f.* incarnation.

incartamento, *n.m.* dossier.

incassare, *vb.* box up; cash.

incatenare, *vb.* chain.

incatramare, *vb.* tar.

incavo, *n.m.* dent.

incendiàrio, *n.m. and adj.* incendiary.

incèndio, *n.m.* fire. **i. doloso,** arson.

incenerire, *vb.* reduce to ashes.

incènso, *n.m.* incense, frankincense.

incentivo, *n.m.* incentive.

incerare, *vb.* wax.

incertezza, *n.f.* uncertainty, suspense.

incèrto, *adj.* uncertain.

incespicare, *vb.* stumble, falter.

incessante, *adj.* incessant, ceaseless.

incèsto, *n.m.* incest.

inchièsta, *n.f.* inquiry; inquest.

inchinarsi, *vb.* bow.

inchino, *n.m.* bow.

inchiodare, *vb.* nail.

inchiòstro, *n.m.* ink.

inciampare, *vb.* stumble.

incidentale, *adv.* incidental.

incidentalmente, *adv.* incidentally.

incidènte, *n.m.* accident; incident.

incidènza, *n.f.* incidence.

incìdere, *vb.* incise, engrave; record.

incinta, *adj.f.* pregnant.

incipiènte, *adj.* incipient.

incipriare, *vb.* powder.

incirca, *adv.* about, approximately. **all'i.,** more or less.

incisione, *n.f.* incision; engraving; gravure; recording.

incisivo, *adj.* incisive. **dènte i.,** incisor.

inciso, 1. *n.m.* parenthetical clause. **per i.,** incidentally. **2.** *adj.* engraved.

incisore, *n.m.* engraver.

incitare, *vb.* incite.

incivile, *adj.* uncivilized.

inclinare, *vb.* incline; list; slant; tilt; tip.

inclinazione, *n.f.* inclination; tilt; list; penchant.

inclùdere, *vb.* include.

inclusivo, *adj.* inclusive.

incoerente, *adj.* incoherent.

incògnito, *adj.* incognito.

incollare, *vb.* glue, paste.

incollatura, *n.f.* sizing.

incolpare, *vb.* blame, accuse.

incolpato, *n.m.* accused, blamed.

incolpatore, *n.m.* blamer, accuser.

incombènte, *adj.* incumbent.

incombustibile, *adj.* fireproof, incombustible.

incominciare, *vb.* begin.

incomodare, *vb.* inconvenience.

incòmodo, *adj.* inconvenient.

incomparàbile, *adj.* incomparable.

incompatibile, *adj.* incompatible.

incompetènte, *adj.* unqualified.

incompleto, *adj.* incomplete.

incomprensibile, *adj.* incomprehensible.

inconcepibile, *adj.* inconceivable.

incondizionato, *adj.* unqualified.

inconscio, *adj.* unconscious.

inconsiderato, *adj.* rash.

inconsulto, *adj.* rash, unadvised.

incontrare, *vb.* meet, encounter.

incontro, 1. *n.m.* meeting, encounter; match. **2.** *prep.* towards; opposite.

incoraggiamento, *n.m.* encouragement, urging, abetment.

incoraggiare, *vb.* encourage, urge, abet.

incoraggiatore, *n.m.* encourager, urger, abettor.

incornare, *vb.* gore.

incorniciare, *vb.* frame.

incoronare, *vb.* crown.

incoronazione, *n.f.* coronation.

incorporare, *vb.* incorporate; embody.

incorpòreo, *adj.* incorporeal; disembodied.

incorreggibile, *adj.* incorrigible.

incórrere, *vb.* incur.

incostante, *adj.* inconstant, fickle.

incostanza, *n.f.* inconstancy, fickleness.

incredibile, *adj.* incredible.

incredulità, *n.f.* incredulity.

incrèdulo, *adj.* incredulous.

incremento, *n.m.* increment.

increspare, *vb.* ruffle.

increspatura, *n.f.* ruffle; ripple.

incriminare, *vb.* incriminate.

incriminazione, *n.f.* incrimination.

incrociare, *vb.* cross; intersect; cruise.

incrociato, *adj.* crossed; crisscross.

incrociatore, *n.m.* cruiser.

incrocio, *n.m.* crossing; cross; intersection.

incrostare, *vb.* incrust.

incubatrice, *n.f.* incubator.

incubo, *n.m.* nightmare.

incùdine, *n.f.* anvil.

inculcare, *vb.* inculcate.

incuneare, *vb.* wedge.

incuràbile, *adj.* incurable.

incurante, *adj.* not caring, nonchalant.

incùria, *n.f.* negligence, carelessness.

incursione, *n.f.* inroad, raid.

indebitato, *adj.* indebted.

indebolire, *vb.* weaken; sap.

indefinitamente, *adv.* indefinitely.

indefinito, *adj.* indefinite.

indegnità, *n.f.* indignity; unworthiness.

indegno, *adj.* unworthy.

indelèbile, *adj.* indelible.

indenne, *adj.* unharmed, undamaged, unscathed.

indennità, *n.f.* indemnity.

indennizzare, *vb.* indemnify.

inderogàbile, *adj.* inescapable, intransgressible.

indi, *adv.* thence.

India, *n.f.* India.

indiana, *n.f.* chintz.

indiano, *adj.* Indian.

indicare, *vb.* indicate, point to.

indicativo, *n.m. and adj.* indicative.

indicatore, *n.m.* indicator.

indicazione, *n.f.* indication.

indice, *n.m.* index; forefinger.

indietreggiare, *vb.* back (up); go backwards; recoil.

indiètro, *adv.* backwards; aft; behind; slow.

indifeso, *adj.* defenseless, unprotected.

indifferente, *adj.* indifferent, casual, nonchalant.

indifferentemente, *adv.* indifferently, casually.

indifferenza, *n.f.* indifference, casualness, disregard.

indìgeno, 1. *n.m.* aborigine, native. 2. *adj.* indigenous, aboriginal, native.

indigente, *adj.* indigent.

indigestione, *n.f.* indigestion.

indignato, *adj.* indignant.

indignazione, *n.f.* indignation.

indimenticàbile, *adj.* unforgettable.

indipendente, *adj.* independent.

indipendènza, *n.f.* independence.

indire, *vb.* announce; notify.

indiretto, *adj.* indirect.

indirizzare, *vb.* address.

indirizzàrio, *n.m.* mailing list.

indirizzo, *n.m.* address; direction.

indisciplina, *n.f.* lack of discipline, unruliness.

indiscreto, *adj.* indiscreet.

indiscrezione, *n.f.* indiscretion.

indiscusso, *adj.* unquestioned.

indiscutìbile, *adj.* indisputable.

indispensàbile, *adj.* indispensable.

indisposizione, *n.f.* indisposition; distemper.

indisposto, *adj.* indisposed, unwell.

indistinto, *adj.* indistinct, blurred.

individuale, *adj.* individual.

individualità, *n.f.* individuality.

individualmente, *adv.* individually.

individuo, *n.m.* individual; fellow.

indivisìbile, *adj.* indivisible.

indiziare, *vb.* cast suspicion on.

indìzio, *n.m.* indication, clue; symptom.

ìndole, *n.f.* nature, disposition, temperament.

indolènte, *adj.* indolent.

Indonèsia, *n.f.* Indonesia.

indorare, *vb.* gild.

indossare, *vb.* put on, don.

indovinare, *vb.* guess.

indovinèllo, *n.m.* riddle, conundrum, puzzle.

indùbbio, *adj.* certain, undisputed, sure.

indugiare, *vb.* delay, loiter, dally, dawdle, lag, linger.

indùgio, *n.m.* delay.

indulgente, *adj.* indulgent.

indulgènza, *n.f.* indulgence.

indùlgere, *vb.* indulge.

indurire, *vb.* harden, steel.

indurre, *vb.* induce.

indùstria, *n.f.* industry.

industriale, 1. *n.* industrialist. 2. *adj.* industrial, manufacturing.

industrioso, *adj.* industrious.

induttivo, *adj.* inductive.

induzione, *n.f.* induction.

inebriante, *adj.* intoxicating, heady.

inebriare, *vb.* inebriate, intoxicate.

ineguale, *adj.* unequal.

ineleggìbile, *adj.* ineligible.

inerènte, *adj.* inherent.

inèrte, *adj.* inert.

inèrzia, *n.f.* inertia.

inesattèzza, *n.f.* inaccuracy, mistake.

inesoràbile, *adj.* inexorable.

inespèrto, *adj.* inexperienced, callow.

inesplicàbile, *adj.* inexplicable.

inespugnàbile, *adj.* impregnable.

inestimàbile, *adj.* priceless.

inètto, *adj.* inept.

inevaso, *adj.* outstanding, unfinished.

inevitàbile, *adj.* inevitable.

infallìbile, *adj.* infallible.

infame, *adj.* infamous.

infàmia, *n.f.* infamy.

infante, *n.m.* infant.

infantìle, *adj.* infantile, childish, childlike, babyish.

infantilità, *n.f.* childishness.

infànzia, *n.f.* infancy, childhood.

infarcire, *vb.* stuff, cram.

infastidìre, *vb.* annoy, bother, irk, be troublesome.

infaticàbile, *adj.* indefatigable.

infatuare, *vb.* infatuate.

infàusto, *adj.* ill-omened, ominous.

infedèle, *n. and adj.* unfaithful, infidel.

infedeltà, *n.f.* infidelity.

infelice, *adj.* unhappy; unlucky.

inferènza, *n.f.* inference.

inferiore, *adj.* inferior, lower; under.

inferiorità, *n.f.* inferiority.

inferìre, *vb.* infer.

infermerìa, *n.f.* infirmary.

infermièra, *n.f.* nurse.

infermità, *n.f.* infirmity.

infermo, *adj.* infirm.

infernale, *adj.* infernal, hellish.

infèrno, *n.m.* hell.

inferriata, *n.f.* grating.

infervorare, *vb.* excite, animate.

infestare, *vb.* infest.

infettare, *vb.* infect.

infettìvo, *adj.* infectious.

infètto, *adj.* infected.

infezione, *n.f.* infection.

infiacchìre, *vb.* enfeeble, weaken, enervate.

infiammàbile, *adj.* inflammable.

infiammare, *vb.* inflame.

infiammatòrio, *adj.* inflammatory.

infiammazione, *n.f.* inflammation.

infido, *adj.* untrustworthy, false.

infìggere, *vb.* fix, stick.

infilare, *vb.* string, thread.

infiltrare, *vb.* infiltrate.

infiltrazione, *n.f.* infiltration; leakage.

ìnfimo, *adj.* lowest; bottom; mean.

infine, *adv.* finally.

infinità, *n.f.* infinity.

infinitesimale, *adj.* infinitesimal.

infinito, **1.** *n.m.* infinite; infinitive. **2.** *adj.* infinite.

infisso, *n.m.* fixture.

inflazione, *n.f.* inflation.

inflessione, *n.f.* inflection.

inflìggere, *vb.* inflict.

inflizione, *n.f.* infliction.

influènte, *adj.* influential.

influènza, *n.f.* influence; influenza; grippe.

influsso, *n.m.* influence.

infoltìre, *vb.* thicken.

infondato, *adj.* groundless.

infòndere, *vb.* inspire, infuse, instill.

inforcatura, *n.f.* crotch.

informare, *vb.* inform; acquaint, appraise; *(refl.)* inquire.

informàtica, *n.f.* computer science.

informatizzare, *vb.* computerize.

informazione, *n.f.* piece of information; *(pl.)* information.

informe, *adj.* formless.

infornare, *vb.* bake, broil, cook in the oven.

infornata, *n.f.* batch.

infossato, *adj.* sunken.

inframmettènte, *adj.* meddlesome, officious.

inframméttere, *vb.* interject; *(refl.)* meddle.

inframmezzare, *vb.* intersperse, interpose.

infràngere, *vb.* infringe.

infrangìbile, *adj.* unbreakable.

infranto, *adj.* crushed, smashed.

infrarosso, *n.m.* infrared.

infrazione, *n.f.* infraction, violation.

infruttuoso, *adj.* fruitless, unsuccessful.

infuòri, *adv.* all' i. di, except for, outside of.

infuriare, *vb.* become infuriated, rage.

ingabbiare, *vb.* cage.

ingannare, *vb.* deceive, trick, fool, beguile, cheat, bluff, double-cross, hoax, hoodwink, mislead.

ingannatore, **1.** *n.m.* deceiver, cheater. **2.** *adj.* deceitful.

ingannévole, *adj.* deceptive, treacherous.

inganno, *n.m.* deceit, deception, trickery, bluff, hocus-pocus.

ingarbugliare, *vb.* tangle; garble.

ingegnère, *n.m.* engineer.

ingegnerìa, *n.f.* engineering.

ingegnosamente, *adv.* cleverly, ingeniously.

ingegnosità, *n.f.* cleverness, ingeniousness.

ingegnoso, *adj.* clever, ingenious.

ingelosire, *vb.* make jealous.

ingente, *adj.* enormous, huge, vast.

ingènuo, *adj.* naïve; artless.

ingerènza, *n.f.* interference.

ingerire, *v.b.* ingest, swallow; interfere.

Inghilterra, *n.f.* England.

inghiottire, *vb.* swallow; gulp.

inginocchiarsi, *vb.* kneel.

ingiùngere, *vb.* enjoin.

ingiunzione, *n.f.* injunction.

ingiùria, *n.f.* insult, abuse.

ingiuriare, *vb.* insult, abuse.

ingiuriosamente, *adv.* insultingly.

ingiurioso, *adj.* insulting, abusive.

ingiustificato, *adj.* unwarranted.

ingiustìzia, *n.f.* injustice.

ingiusto, *adj.* unjust, unfair.

inglese, **1.** *n.m.* or *f.* Englishman; Englishwoman. **2.** *adj.* English.

ingollare, *vb.* gobble, gulp down.

ingombrante, *adj.* cumbersome.

ingombrare, *vb.* encumber, clog, clutter.

ingozzare, *vb.* guzzle.

ingranàggio, *n.m.* gear, gearing.

ingranare, *vb.* mesh.

ingrandimento, *n.m.* enlargement, aggrandizement.

ingrandire, *vb.* enlarge, aggrandize, magnify.

ingranditore, *n.m.* enlarger.

ingrassare, *vb.* fatten.

ingravidare, *vb.* render pregnant, impregnate.

ingrediènte, *n.m.* ingredient.

ingrèsso, *n.m.* entrance, entry.

ingròsso, *n.m.* all'i., wholesale.

inguine, *n.m.* groin.

inibire, *vb.* inhibit.

inibizione, *n.f.* inhibition.

iniettare, *vb.* inject.

iniezione, *n.f.* injection.

inimicìzia, *n.f.* enmity; feud.

inimitàbile, *adj.* inimitable.

ininterrotto, *adj.* continuous, uninterrupted.

iniquità, *n.f.* iniquity.

iniquo, *adj.* unrighteous.

iniziale, *n.f.* and *adj.* initial.

iniziare, *vb.* initiate, begin, start.

iniziativa, *n.f.* initiative.

iniziazione, *n.f.* initiation.

inizio, *n.m.* beginning, inception, start.

innaffiare, *vb.* water.

innalzare, *vb.* raise, hoist.

innamorare, *vb.* enamor.

innamorarsi, *vb.* fall in love.

innamorata, *n.f.* sweetheart.

innamorato, *n.m.* sweetheart.

innanzi, **1.** *adv.* forward, further. **2.** *prep.* before.

innàrio, *n.m.* hymnal.

innegàbile, *adj.* undeniable.

innervosire, *vb.* make nervous, get on one's nerves.

innescare, *vb.* prime.

innestare, *vb.* graft.

innèsto, *n.m.* graft.

inno, *n.m.* hymn. i. nazionale, national anthem.

innocènte, *adj.* innocent; harmless; blameless.

innocènza, *n.f.* innocence.

innòcuo, *adj.* innocuous, harmless.

innovare, *vb.* innovate, change, reform.

innovazione, *n.f.* innovation.
innumerévole, *adj.* innumerable, countless, myriad.
inoculare, *vb.* inoculate.
inoculazione, *n.f.* inoculation.
inodoro, *adj.* odorless.
inoffensivo, *adj.* harmless, inoffensive.
inoltre, *adv.* besides, furthermore.
inondare, *vb.* inundate, flood, swamp.
inondazione, *n.f.* inundation, flood.
inorridire, *vb.* be horrified.
inossidàbile, *adj.* rust-proof.
inquietare, *vb.* worry; *(refl.)* be concerned.
inquièto, *adj.* uneasy.
inquilino, *n.m.* occupant, tenant.
inquinamento, *n.m.* pollution.
inquinare, *vb.* pollute.
inquirente, *adj.* investigating.
inquisizione, *n.f.* inquisition.
insabbiare, *vb.* cover with sand; shelve.
insaccare, *vb.* put in a bag.
insalata, *n.f.* salad.
insalubre, *adj.* unhealthy.
insanguinato, *adj.* gory.
insània, *n.f.* insanity.
insano, *adj.* insane.
insaporire, *vb.* flavor.
insaputa, *n.f.* **all'i. di,** without the knowledge of.
insediamento, *n.m.* installation.
insediare, *vb.* install.
insegna, *n.f.* standard; signboard; coat of arms; ensign; *(pl.)* insignia.
insegnante, *n.m. or f.* teacher.
insegnare, *vb.* teach.
inseguimento, *n.m.* pursuit.
inseguire, *vb.* follow, pursue.
insenatura, *n.f.* bay, inlet, cove.
insensibile, *adj.* insensible, insensitive, unfeeling.
insensibilità, *n.f.* insensitivity, callousness.
inseparàbile, *adj.* inseparable.
inserire, *vb.* insert, put in.
inserto, *n.m.* insert; article, file.
inservibile, *adj.* unusable.
inserzione, *n.f.* insertion; advertisement.
inserzionista, *n.m.* advertiser.

insetticida, *adj.* **pólvere i.,** insecticide.
insètto, *n.m.* insect, bug.
insidioso, *adj.* insidious.
insième, 1. *n.m.* ensemble. **2.** *adv.* together.
insigne, *adj.* remarkable; famous; notable.
insignificante, *adj.* insignificant.
insignificanza, *n.f.* insignificance.
insinuare, *vb.* insinuate.
insinuazione, *n.f.* insinuation, innuendo.
insipido, *adj.* insipid, tasteless.
insistènte, *adj.* insistent.
insistènza, *n.f.* insistence.
insistere, *vb.* insist.
insito, *adj.* innate, inborn, inbred.
insoddisfazione, *n.f.* dissatisfaction.
insolazione, *n.f.* sunstroke.
insolènte, *adj.* insolent, insulting, abusive.
insolentemente, *adv.* insolently.
insolènza, *n.f.* insolence.
insòlito, *adj.* unusual.
insomma, *adv.* in conclusion.
insònnia, *n.f.* insomnia.
insopportàbile, *adj.* unbearable.
instàbile, *adj.* unsteady.
installare, *vb.* install.
installazione, *n.f.* installation.
insù, *adv.* **all'i.,** uphill; upwards.
insuccesso, *n.m.* failure.
insufficiènte, *adj.* insufficient.
insulare, *adj.* insular.
insulina, *n.f.* insulin.
insulso, *adj.* dull, insipid.
insultare, *vb.* insult, abuse.
insulto, *n.m.* insult, abuse.
insuperàbile, *adj.* insuperable.
insurrezione, *n.f.* insurrection.
intaccare, *vb.* notch, nick.
intangibile, *adj.* intangible.
intanto, *adv.* meanwhile.
intàrsio, *n.m.* inlay; inlaid work.
intascare, *vb.* pocket.
intatto, *adj.* intact.
intavolare, *vb.* start; launch.
integèrrimo, *adj.* incorruptible.
integrale, *adj.* integral.
integrare, *vb.* integrate.
integrità, *n.f.* integrity.

intellètto, *n.m.* intellect; understanding.

intellettuale, *adj.* intellectual.

intelligènte, *adj.* intelligent, smart.

intelligènza, *n.f.* intelligence; wit.

intellighènzia, *n.f.* intelligentsia.

intelligìbile, *adj.* intelligible.

intensificare, *vb.* intensify.

intensivo, *adj.* intensive.

intènso, *adj.* intense.

intènto, *n.m. and adj.* intent.

intenzionale, *adj.* intentional.

intenzionalmente, *adv.* intentionally, designedly.

intenzione, *n.f.* intention.

interamente, *adv.* entirely, wholly.

intercapedine, *n.f.* interstice.

intercèdere, *vb.* intercede.

intercettare, *vb.* intercept.

interdetto, 1. *n.m.* interdict. **2.** *adj.* speechless.

interdire, *vb.* interdict.

interessante, *adj.* interesting.

interessare, *vb.* interest, concern; affect; (*refl.*) concern oneself.

interèsse, *n.m.* interest, concern.

interfaccia, *n.f.* interface.

interferènza, *n.f.* interference.

interiezione, *n.f.* interjection.

interiora, *n.f.pl.* entrails.

interiore, *adj.* interior, inner, inside.

interlùdio, *n.m.* interlude.

intermediàrio, 1. *n.m.* intermediary, mediator, go-between. **2.** *adj.* intermediary.

intermèdio, *adj.* intermediate.

intermissione, *n.f.* intermission.

intermittènte, *adj.* intermittent.

internare, *vb.* intern.

internazionale, *adj.* international.

internazionalismo, *n.m.* internationalism.

internista, *n.m. and f.* internist.

intèrno, 1. *n.m.* inside. **2.** *adj.* internal; inner, inside; inland.

intero, *adj.* entire, whole.

interpellare, *vb.* consult, ask.

interporre, *vb.* interpose.

interpretare, *vb.* interpret, construe.

interpretazione, *n.f.* interpretation.

intèrprete, *n.m.* interpreter.

interramento, *n.m.* burial.

interrare, *vb.* bury.

interrogare, *vb.* interrogate, question.

interrogatòrio, *n.m.* cross-examination.

interrogativo, *adj.* interrogative.

interrogazione, *n.f.* interrogation.

interrómpere, *vb.* interrupt; discontinue.

interruttore, *n.m.* switch.

interruzione, *n.f.* interruption, break.

interscàmbio, *n.m.* interchange.

intersecare, *vb.* intersect.

intersezione, *n.f.* intersection.

interstizio, *n.m.* interstice.

intervallo, *n.m.* interval; headway.

intervenire, *vb.* intervene.

intervènto, *n.m.* intervention.

intervista, *n.f.* interview.

intervistare, *vb.* interview.

intesa, *n.f.* agreement.

inteso, *adj.* understood.

intestino, 1. *n.m.* intestine, bowel, gut. **2.** *adj.* intestine.

intimamente, *adv.* intimately; inwardly.

intimare, *vb.* intimate; command.

intimidazione, *n.f.* intimidation.

intimidire, *vb.* intimidate, daunt.

intimità, *n.f.* intimacy; privacy.

ìntimo, *adj.* intimate; inward. **più ì.,** innermost.

intìngere, *vb.* dip; soak.

intingolo, *n.m.* sauce, dip.

intirizzire, *vb.* benumb; stiffen.

intitolare, *vb.* entitle.

intollerante, *adj.* intolerant.

intonacare, *vb.* plaster.

intònaco, *n.m.* plaster.

intonare, *vb.* intone.

intonazione, *n.f.* intonation.

intonso, *adj.* untrimmed, uncut.

intontire, *vb.* daze.

intontito, *adj.* groggy.

intoppo, *n.m.* impediment, obstacle, hindrance.

intorbidire, *vb.* confuse, cloud.

intorno, *adv.* around; about;

round. **i. a,** *prep.* around; about; round.

intossicare, *vb.* intoxicate.
intossicazione, *n.f.* intoxication.
intralciare, *vb.* hinder.
intràlcio, *n.m.* hindrance.
intrallazzo, *n.m.* plot, swindle.
intrappolare, *vb.* trap.
intraprèndere, *vb.* undertake, start.
intravedere, *vb.* glimpse.
intrecciare, *vb.* braid.
intréccio, *n.m.* plot.
intrepidamente, *adv.* dauntlessly, fearlessly.
intrepidezza, *n.f.* intrepidity, fearlessness.
intrèpido, *adj.* intrepid, dauntless, fearless.
intricato, *adj.* intricate.
intrigante, 1. *n.m.* schemer. **2.** *adj.* intriguing.
intridere, *vb.* soak.
intrigare, *vb.* intrigue.
intrigo, *n.m.* intrigue.
intrinseco, *adj.* intrinsic.
introdotto, *adj.* introduced; well-connected.
intriso, *adj.* soaked.
introdurre, *vb.* introduce.
introduttivo, *adj.* introductory.
introduzione, *n.f.* introduction.
introspezione, *n.f.* introspection.
introvertito, *adj.* introvert.
intrùdere, *vb.* intrude, obtrude.
intruso, *n.m.* intruder.
intuire, *vb.* sense.
intuitivo, *adj.* intuitive.
intuizione, *n.f.* intuition.
inumano, *adj.* inhuman.
inumidire, *vb.* dampen, humidify, moisten, wet.
inùtile, *adj.* useless, needless.
invadente, *adj.* intrusive.
invàdere, *vb.* invade, overrun.
invàlido, 1. *n.* invalid. **2.** *adj.* disabled; invalid.
invano, *adv.* in vain.
invariàbile, *adj.* invariable.
invasione, *n.f.* invasion.
invasore, *n.m.* invader.
invecchiare, *vb.* grow old, age.
invece, *adv.* instead.
inventare, *vb.* invent.
inventàrio, *n.m.* inventory.

inventivo, *adj.* inventive.
inventore, *n.m.* inventor.
invenzione, *n.f.* invention.
invernale, *adj.* of winter, wintry.
invèrno, *n.m.* winter.
invèrso, *adj.* inverse.
invertebrato, *n.m. and adj.* invertebrate.
investigare, *vb.* investigate.
investigazione, *n.f.* investigation; inquiry.
investimento, *n.m.* investment.
investire, *vb.* invest; run into.
inveterato, *adj.* inveterate.
invettiva, *n.f.* invective.
inviare, *vb.* send.
inviato, *n.m.* envoy, messenger; (journalism) correspondent.
invìdia, *n.f.* envy.
invidiàbile, *adj.* enviable.
invidiare, *vb.* envy, begrudge.
invidioso, *adj.* envious.
invigorire, *vb.* invigorate.
inviluppare, *vb.* enmesh.
invincìbile, *adj.* invincible.
invio, *n.m.* mailing, shipment, dispatch.
invisìbile, *adj.* invisible.
invitante, *adj.* appealing, inviting.
invitare, *vb.* invite, ask.
invito, *n.m.* invitation; bid.
invitto, *adj.* undefeated.
invocare, *vb.* invoke.
invocazione, *n.f.* invocation.
involontàrio, *adj.* involuntary.
involto, *n.m.* wrapper; bundle.
invòlucro, *n.m.* wrapping.
invulneràbile, *adj.* invulnerable.
inzuppare, *vb.* drench; soak, dunk.

ìo, 1. *pron.* I. **2.** *n.* ego.
iòdio, *n.m.* iodine.
ìosa, *adj.* **a i.** in abundance.
iperacidità, *n.f.* hyperacidity.
ipèrbole, *n.f.* hyperbole.
ipercrìtico, *adj.* hypercritical.
ipersensitivo, *adj.* hypersensitive.
ipertensione, *n.f.* hypertension.
ipnòsi, *n.f.* hypnosis.
ipnòtico, *adj.* hypnotic.
ipnotismo, *n.m.* hypnotism.
ipnotizzare, *vb.* hypnotize.
ipocondria, *n.f.* hypochondria.
ipocondrìaco, *n.m. and adj.* hypochondriac.

ipocrisìa, *n.f.* hypocrisy, cant.
ipòcrita, *n.m.* hypocrite.
ipòcrito, *adj.* hypocritical.
ipodèrmico, *adj.* hypodermic.
ipotèca, *n.f.* mortgage.
ipotecare, *vb.* mortgage.
ipotenusa, *n.f.* hypotenuse.
ipòtesi, *n.f.* hypothesis.
ipotètico, *adj.* hypothetical.
ìppico, *adj.* horse; horse-racing.
ippòdromo, *n.m.* hippodrome; race-track.
ippopòtamo, *n.m.* hippopotamus.
ira, *n.f.* anger, ire, wrath.
Iràk, *n.m.* Iraq.
irato, *adj.* irate, wrathful.
ìride, *n.f.* iris.
irìdio, *n.m.* iridium.
ìris, *n.f.* iris.
Irlanda, *n.f.* Ireland.
irlandese, *adj.* Irish.
ironìa, *n.f.* irony.
irònico, *adj.* ironical.
irradiare, *vb.* beam, shine, radiate.
irradiazione, *n.f.* radiation.
irraggiungìbile, *adj.* unreachable, unobtainable.
irragionévole, *adj.* irrational, absurd.
irrazionale, *adj.* irrational.
irreale, *adj.* unreal.
irrecuperàbile, *adj.* irrecoverable.
irrefutàbile, *adj.* irrefutable.
irregolare, *adj.* irregular; fitful.
irregolarità, *n.f.* irregularity.
irremissìbile, *adj.* unpardonable.
irreprensìbile, *adj.* irreprehensible, faultless.
irreprensibilmente, *adv.* irreprehensibly, faultlessly.
irrequièto, *adj.* restless.
irresistìbile, *adj.* irresistible.
irresponsàbile, *adj.* irresponsible.
irretire, *vb.* snare, entrap, entice.
irrevocàbile, *adj.* irrevocable.
irriconoscìbile, *adj.* unrecognizable.
irrìdere, *vb.* deride, mock.
irriducìbile, *adj.* stubborn, indomitable.
irrigare, *vb.* irrigate.

irrigazione, *n.f.* irrigation.
irrigidire, *vb.* stiffen.
irrilevante, *adj.* irrelevant.
irrispettoso, *adj.* disrespectful.
irritàbile, *adj.* irritable, on edge, edgy, fretful.
irritabilità, *n.f.* irritability, fretfulness.
irritabilmente, *adv.* irritably, fretfully.
irritante, *adj.* irritant.
irritare, *vb. tr.* irritate, fret, gall, vex.
irritato, *adj.* irritated, cross.
irritazione, *n.f.* irritation.
irriverènte, *adj.* irreverent.
irrompere, *vb.* burst.
irrorare, *vb.* sprinkle; wet.
irsuto, *adj.* hirsute.
iscrìvere, *vb.* inscribe; enroll, register.
iscrizione, *n.f.* inscription; enrollment, registration.
ìsola, *n.f.* island.
isolamento, *n.m.* isolation; insulation.
isolare, *vb.* isolate; insulate.
isolatore, *n.m.* insulator.
isolazione, *n.f.* isolation.
isolazionista, *n.m.* isolationist.
isolotto salvagènte, *n.m.* safety island.
isòscele, *adj.* isosceles.
ispànico, *adj.* Hispanic.
ispettore, *n.m.* inspector.
ispezionare, *vb.* inspect.
ispezione, *n.f.* inspection.
ìspido, *adj.* shaggy.
ispirare, *vb.* inspire.
ispirazione, *n.f.* inspiration.
Israèle, *n.m.* Israel.
israeliano, *adj.* Israeli.
israelita, *n.m.* Israelite.
israelìtico, *adj.* Israelite.
issare, *vb.* hoist.
istallare, *vb.* install, set up; settle.
istantànea, *n.f.* snapshot.
istantàneo, *adj.* instantaneous.
istante, *n.m.* instant.
istanza, *n.f.* request, instance.
isterectomìa, *n.f.* hysterectomy.
istèrico, *adj.* hysterical.
isterismo, *n.m.* hysteria, hysterics.
istigare, *vb.* instigate.

istillare, *vb.* instill.
istintivo, *adj.* instinctive.
istinto, *n.m.* instinct.
istituto, *n.m.* institute.
istituzione, *n.f.* institution.
istmo, *n.m.* isthmus.
ìstrice, *n.f.* hedgehog.
istriònica, *n.f.* histrionics.
istriònico, *adj.* histrionic.
istruire, *vb.* instruct.
istruttivo, *adj.* instructive.
istruttore, *n.m.* instructor.

istruttrice, *n.f.* instructress.
istruzione, *n.f.* education, culture.
istupidito, *adj.* dulled, dazed.
Itàlia, *n.f.* Italy.
italiano, *n.m. and adj.* Italian.
itàlico, *adj.* Italic.
itineràrio, *n.m.* itinerary.
itterizia, *n.f.* jaundice.
ittiologìa, *n.f.* ichthyology.
iuta, *n.f.* jute.
ivi, *adv.* there.

J,K

jeans, *m.pl.* jeans.
Jugoslàvia, *n.f.* Yugoslavia.
jugoslavo, *adj.* Yugoslav.
kapút, *adj.* finished; damaged.
karakiri, *n.m.* harakiri.
karate, *n.m.* karate.

kg., *abbr.* kilogram.
kilohertz, *n.m.* kilohertz.
km., *abbr.* kilometer.
kohl, *n.m.* mascara.
kw., *abbr.* kilowatt.

L

l', **1.** *def. art.* the. **2.** *pron.* **3.** *sg.* him; her.
la, 1. *pron.* her; it; you. **2.** *def. art. f.* the.
là, *adv.* there.
labbro, *n.f.* lip. **l. leporino,** hairlip.
labiale, *adj.* labial.
làbile, *adj.* weak.
labirinto, *n.m.* labyrinth, maze.
laboratòrio, *n.m.* laboratory.
laborioso, *adj.* laborious, industrious.
lacca, *n.f.* lacquer.
laccare, *vb.* lacquer.
lacchè, *n.m.* lackey, flunkey.
làccio, *n.m.* string; trap; noose; lariat, lasso; loop.
lacerare, *vb.* lacerate.
lacerazione, *n.f.* laceration.
lacònico, *adj.* laconic.
làcrima, *n.f.* tear.
laddove, *conj.* while, whereas.
ladro, *n.m.* thief, burglar.
ladrone, *n.m.* robber.
laggiú, *adv.* down there.
lagnanza, *n.f.* complaint, grievance.
lagnarsi, *vb.* complain.

lago, *n.m.* lake.
laguna, *n.f.* lagoon.
laicato, *n.m.* laity.
làico, 1. *n.* layman. **2.** *adj.* lay.
lama, *n.f.* blade.
lambiccato, *adj.* overelaborate.
lambire, *vb.* lap.
lamentare, *vb.* lament, bewail.
lamentazione, *n.f.* lamentation.
lamentela, *n.f.* complaint.
lamentévole, *adj.* lamentable.
lamento, *n.m.* lament.
lametta, *n.f.* razor blade.
laminare, *vb.* laminate.
làmpada, *n.f.* lamp.
lampadàrio, *n.m.* chandelier.
lampadina, *n.f.* light bulb. **l. tascàbile,** flashlight.
lampante, *adj.* evident, manifest; shining.
lampeggiare, *vb.* lighten.
lampeggiatore, *n.m.* blinker.
lampo, *n.m.* (flash of) lightning.
lampone, *n.m.* raspberry.
lana, *n.f.* wool. **l. di acciaio** *n.f.* steel wool.
lancetta, *n.f.* pointer, hand.
lància, *n.f.* lance, spear; launch.

lanciafiamme, *n.m.* flamethrower.

lanciarazzi, *n.m.* rocket launcher.

lanciare, *vb.* hurl, cast, chuck, fling, launch, pitch, sling, throw.

lanciatore, *n.m.* pitcher.

lancinante, *adj.* excruciating.

landa, *n.f.,* moor; wasteland.

lànguido, *adj.* languid; lackadaisical.

languire, *vb.* languish, pine.

languore, *n.m.* languor.

lanificio, *n.m.* wool mill.

lanolina, *n.f.* lanolin.

lantèrna, *n.f.* lantern.

lanùgine, *n.f.* down, fuzz.

lanuginoso, *adj.* fluffy, downy; fuzzy.

lapalissiano, *adj.* obvious, evident.

lapidare, *vb.* stone.

làpis, *n.m.* pencil.

lardo, *n.m.* lard.

largamente, *adv.* broadly, widely.

largheggiare, *vb.* be lavish.

larghezza, *n.f.* breadth; width.

largire, *vb.* to give liberally.

largo, *adj.* broad, wide; (music) largo.

làrice, *n.m.* larch.

laringe, *n.f.* larynx.

laringite, *n.f.* laryngitis.

larva, *n.f.* larva; grub; ghost.

lasciare, *vb.* let; leave; quit. **l. stare,** let alone.

làscito, *n.m.* legacy.

lascivo, *adj.* lascivious, lecherous.

làser, *n.m.* laser.

lassativo, *n.m. and adj.* laxative.

lassismo, *n.m.* laxity.

lasso, *n.m.* period (of time).

lassù, *adv.* up there.

lastra, *n.f.* plate; sheet; slab.

latènte, *adj.* latent.

laterale, *adj.* lateral.

latifondo, *n.m.* large estate.

latino, *n.m. and adj.* Latin.

latitanza, *n.f.* hiding (used of criminals).

latitùdine, *n.f.* latitude.

lato, 1. *n.m.* side, standpoint. **2.** *adj.* wide.

latore, *n.m.* bearer.

latrare, *vb.* howl, bay.

latrato, *n.m.* howl, bay.

latrina, *n.f.* latrine, lavatory, toilet, privy.

latta, *n.f.* tin.

lattaia, *n.f.* milkmaid, dairymaid.

lattaio, *n.m.* milkman, dairyman.

lattante, 1. *n.m.* baby. **2.** *adj.* unweaned.

latte, *n.m.* milk.

làtteo, *adj.* milky.

latteria, *n.f.* dairy; milk-bar.

làttico, *adj.* lactic.

lattòsio, *n.m.* lactose.

lattuga, *n.f.* lettuce.

làudano, *n.m.* laudanum.

làurea, *n.f.* degree.

laurearsi, *vb.* graduate.

laureato, *adj.* laureate.

làuro, *n.m.* laurel; bay.

làuto, *adj.* magnificent, sumptuous, abundant.

lava, *n.f.* lava.

lavabiancheria, *n.m.* washing machine.

lavabo, *n.m.* wash-basin.

lavagna, *n.f.* blackboard; slate.

lavàggio, *n.m.* washing.

lavanda, *n.f.* lavender.

lavandaia, *n.f.* laundress.

lavandaio, *n.m.* laundryman.

lavanderìa, *n.f.* laundry.

lavandino, *n.m.* sink.

lavapiatti, *n.f.* dishwater.

lavare, *vb.* wash, launder.

lavata, *n.f.* washing. **l. di capo,** scolding.

lavativo, *adj.* lazy; tiresome (person).

lavatòio, *n.m.* washroom.

lavorare, *vb.* work.

lavoratore, *n.m.* worker.

lavorìo, *n.m.* bustle, activity.

lavoro, *n.m.* work.

laziale, *adj.* of Latium.

Làzio, *n.m.* Latium.

le, 1. *def. art. f.pl.* the. **2.** *pron.* 3. *sg. dative* to her; 3. *pl.f.* them.

leale, *adj.* loyal.

lealista, *n.m.* loyalist.

lealtà, *n.f.* loyalty.

lebbra, *n.f.* leprosy.

lebbroso, 1. *n.* leper. **2.** *adj.* leprous.

lécca-lécca, *n.m.* lollypop.

leccapièdi, *n.m.* bootlicker.
leccare, *vb.* lick.
leccato, *adj.* affected; polished.
lega, *n.f.* league; alloy.
legale, *adj.* legal, lawful.
legalità, *n.f.* legality.
legalizzare, *vb.* legalize.
legame, *n.m.* tie, bond, link.
legamento, *n.m.* ligament.
legare, *vb.* bequeath, leave (in will); bind, tie.
legato, *n.m.* bequest, legacy.
legatore, *n.m.* bookbinder.
legatorìa, *n.f.* bindery, bookbindery.
legatura, *n.f.* ligature; (music) slur.
legazione, *n.f.* legation.
legge, *n.f.* law.
leggènda, *n.f.* legend.
leggendàrio, *adj.* legendary.
lèggere, *vb.* read.
leggerezza, *n.f.* lightness; levity.
leggermente, *adv.* lightly.
leggero, *adj.* light.
leggiadro, *adj.* lovely.
leggìbile, *adj.* legible.
legione, *n.f.* legion.
legislatore, *n.m.* legislator.
legislazione, *n.f.* legislation.
legittimità, *n.f.* legitimacy.
legìttimo, *adj.* legitimate, lawful.
legna, *n.f.* firewood.
legnata, *n.f.* clubbing, thrashing.
legname, *n.m.* lumber, timber.
legume, *n.m.* vegetable, legume.
lèi, *pron.* she; her; you.
lembo, *n.m.* hem; flap.
lena, *n.f.* energy; enthusiasm.
lentamente, *adv.* slowly.
lènte, *n.f.* lens; eyeglass.
lentezza, *n.f.* slowness.
lentìcchia, *n.f.* lentil.
lentìggine, *n.f.* freckle.
lentigginoso, *adj.* freckled.
lento, *adj.* slow, slack, sluggish.
lenzuòla, *n.f.pl.* sheets, bedclothes.
lenzuòlo, *n.m.* sheet.
leone, *n.m.* lion.
leopardo, *n.m.* leopard.
lèpre, *n.f.* hare.
lèsbica, *n.f.* lesbian.
lèsbico, *adj.* lesbian.

lesione, *n.f.* lesion.
lèssico, *n.m.* lexicon.
lesto, *adj.* quick, nimble.
letale, *adj.* lethal.
letame, *n.m.* dung, manure, muck.
letargìa, *n.f.* lethargy.
letàrgico, *n.m.* lethargic.
letargo, *n.m.* lethargy.
letìzia, *n.f.* happiness, joy.
lèttera, *n.f.* letter.
letterale, *adj.* literal.
letteràrio, *adj.* literary.
letterato, *adj.* literate.
letteratura, *n.f.* literature.
lettièra, *n.f.* bedstead; litter; (animal's) bed.
lettiga, *n.f.* stretcher.
lettino, *n.m.* cot.
lètto, *n.m.* bed; couch. **l. ad acqua**, waterbed. **l. del mare**, seabed.
lettore, *n.m.* reader.
lettura, *n.f.* reading.
leucèmia, *n.f.* leukemia.
lèva, *n.f.* lever; levy.
levante, **1.** *n.m.* east; levant. **2.** *adj.* rising.
levare, *vb.* raise; (*refl.*) get up, arise.
levatrice, *n.f.* midwife.
levigare, *vb.* smooth.
levigato, *adj.* smooth.
levrière, *n.m.* greyhound.
lezione, *n.f.* lesson.
leziosaggire, *n.f.* affectation, simpering.
lezioso, *adj.* mincing, mannered.
lézzo, *n.m.* stench; filth.
li, *pron.* **3.** *pl.m.* them.
lì, *adv.* there.
libagione, *n.f.* libation.
libbra, *n.f.* pound.
libéccio, *n.m.* southwest wind.
liberale, *adj.* liberal, generous, bounteous.
liberalismo, *n.m.* liberalism.
liberalità, *n.f.* liberality, generosity, bounty.
liberare, *vb.* liberate, deliver, free, relieve, release, rescue.
liberazione, *n.f.* liberation, deliverance, relief, release, rescue.
liberismo, *n.m.* free trade.

líbero, *adj.* free.

libertà, *n.f.* liberty, freedom.

libertino, *n.m. and adj.* libertine.

libidinoso, *adj.* libidinous.

libraio, *n.m.* bookseller.

librería, *n.f.* bookstore.

libretto, *n.m.* booklet; (opera) libretto.

libro, *n.m.* book. **l. in brossura,** paperback.

liceale, *adj.* high school.

licènza, *n.f.* license; furlough; leave.

licenziamento, *n.m.* discharge.

licenziare, *vb.* discharge, fire, sack.

licenzioso, *adj.* licentious.

licèo, *n.m.* high school.

lichene, *n.m.* lichen.

lido, *n.m.* beach, shore, seashore.

lietamente, *adv.* gladly.

lièto, *adj.* glad, pleased.

lieve, *adj.* light; slight.

lièvito, *n.m.* leaven.

ligio, *adj.* devoted.

lignàggio, *n.m.* lineage, ancestry.

lignite, *n.f.* lignite.

ligure, *adj.* Ligurian.

ligustro, *n.m.* privet.

lillà, *n.m.* lilac.

lima, *n.f.* file.

limaccioso, *adj.* miry, muddy.

limare, *vb.* file.

limatura, *n.f.* filings.

limbo, *n.m.* limbo.

limitare, *vb.* limit.

limitazione, *n.f.* limitation.

límite, *n.m.* limit, bound.

limo, *n.m.* mud, mire.

limonare, *vb.* spoon.

limonata, *n.f.* lemonade.

limone, *n.m.* lemon.

limoso, *adj.* slimy.

límpido, *adj.* limpid.

lince, *n.f.* lynx. **l. persiana,** caracul.

linciàggio, *n.m.* lynching.

linciare, *vb.* lynch.

lindo, *adj.* neat.

línea, *n.f.* line; figure.

lineare, *adj.* linear.

linfa, *n.f.* lymph; sap.

lingua, *n.f.* tongue, language.

linguaggio, *n.m.* language.

linguista, *n.m.* linguist.

linguística, *n.f.* linguistics.

linguístico, *adj.* linguistic.

linimento, *n.m.* liniment.

lino, *n.m.* linen.

liquefare, *vb.* liquefy.

liquidare, *vb.* liquidate.

liquidazione, *n.f.* liquidation.

liquido, *n.m. and adj.* liquid.

liquirizia, *n.f.* licorice.

liquore, *n.m.* liquor; liqueur.

lira, *n.f.* lira; lyre.

liricismo, *n.m.* lyricism.

lírico, *adj.* lyric; operatic.

lisciare, *vb.* smooth.

liscio, *adj.* smooth, sleek.

lista, *n.f.* list; menu, bill of fare; stripe.

listèllo, *n.m.* lath.

litania, *n.f.* litany.

lite, *n.f.* fight, quarrel, struggle, affray, brawl, row.

litigante, *n.m.* litigant.

litigare, *vb.* quarrel, bicker, row.

litigioso, *adj.* quarrelsome, argumentative, rowdy.

litografare, *vb.* lithograph.

litografia, *n.f.* lithography, lithograph.

litro, *n.m.* liter.

liturgía, *n.f.* liturgy.

litúrgico, *adj.* liturgical.

liuto, *n.m.* lute.

livellare, *vb.* level.

livellatrice, *n.f.* bulldozer.

livèllo, *n.m.* level.

lívido, *adj.* livid.

livore, *n.m.* hatred; envy.

Livorno, *n.m.* Leghorn.

livrèa, *n.f.* livery.

lizza, *n.f.* **essere in l.** be in competition.

lo, 1. *pron.* him; it; you. **2.** *def. art.* m. the.

lòbo, *n.m.* lobe.

locale, *adj.* local.

località, *n.f.* locality, locale.

localizzare, *vb.* localize.

locanda, *n.f.* inn.

locandina, *n.f.* playbill; flyer.

locomotiva, *n.f.* locomotive, engine.

locomotore, *n.m.* locomotive.

locomozione, *n.f.* locomotion.

locusta, *n.f.* locust.

locuzione, *n.f.* expression.

lodare, *vb.* praise, commend, laud.

lòde, *n.f.* praise, commendation.

lodévole, *adj.* praiseworthy, commendable, laudable.

lodevolmente, *adv.* praiseworthily, commendably.

logaritmo, *n.m.* logarithm.

lòggia, *n.f.* loge.

loggione, *n.m.* top gallery.

lògica, *n.f.* logic.

lògico, *adj.* logical.

logorare, *vb.* wear out.

logorìo, *n.m.* wear and tear.

lògoro, *adj.* worn-out, shabby.

lombàggine, *n.f.* lumbago.

Lombardia, *n.f.* Lombardy.

lombardo, *adj.* Lombard.

lombata, *n.f.* loin.

lombo, *n.m.* loin; sirloin.

lombrico, *n.m.* earthworm.

londinese, *adj.* of London.

Londra, *n.f.* London.

longevità, *n.f.* longevity.

longèvo, *adj.* long-lived.

longitudinale, *adj.* longitudinal.

longitùdine, *n.f.* longitude.

lontananza, *n.f.* distance.

lontano, 1. *adj.* distant, far. **2.** *adv.* far away, far off, afar.

lóntra, *n.f.* otter.

lonza, *n.f.* pork loin.

lòppa, *n.f.* chaff.

loquace, *adj.* loquacious, talkative.

lordo, *adj.* soiled; (weight) gross.

lordume, *n.m.* filth.

loro, *pron.* they; their; theirs; them; to them; you; your; yours; to you.

losanga, *n.f.* lozenge.

losco, *adj.* sly; questionable, suspicious.

lòto, *n.m.* lotus; mud, mire.

lotta, *n.f.* struggle, fight.

lottare, *vb.* struggle, wrestle.

lotterìa, *n.f.* lottery, raffle.

lotto, *n.m.* lot.

lozione, *n.f.* lotion.

lùbrico, *adj.* lewd.

lubrificante, *n.m. and adj.* lubricant.

lubrificare, *vb.* lubricate, grease, oil.

lucchetto, *n.m.* padlock.

luccicare, *vb.* glitter.

lùccio, *n.m.* pike.

lùcciola, *n.f.* firefly; glowworm.

luce, *n.f.* light.

lucernàrio, *n.m.* skylight.

lucèrtola, *n.f.* lizard.

lucidare, *vb.* polish, shine.

lucidatura, *n.f.* polish.

luci di città, *n.f.pl.* parking lights.

luciditá, *n.f.* shininess, gloss.

lùcido, 1. *n.m.* polish. **2.** *adj.* shiny, glossy.

lucrare, *vb.* profit; earn.

lucrativo, *adj.* lucrative.

lucro, *n.m.* profit, gain, earning.

lucrosamente, *adv.* gainfully.

lucroso, *adj.* gainful.

lùglio, *n.m.* July.

lùi, *pron.* he; him.

lumaca, *n.f.* snail.

luminoso, *adj.* luminous, bright, light, shining.

lunare, *adj.* lunar.

lunàtico, *n.m. and adj.* lunatic.

lunedì, *n.m.* Monday.

lunga, *adj.* **di gran l.,** by far.

lungamente, *adv.* long.

lunghezza, *n.f.* length.

lungo, 1. *adj.* long. **2.** *prep.* along.

luogo, *n.m.* place. **l. comune,** cliché. **aver l.,** take place.

lupa, *n.f.* she-wolf.

lupo, *n.m.* wolf.

lùppolo, *n.m.* hop.

lusingare, *vb.* flatter, cajole.

lusingatore, *n.m.* flatterer.

lusinghe, *n.f.pl.* flattery.

lusinghièro, *adj.* flattering.

lusso, *n.m.* luxury. **di l.,** de luxe.

lussuoso, *adj.* luxurious.

lussureggiante, *adj.* luxuriant, lush.

lustrascarpe, *n.m.* bootblack.

lustro, *n.m.* luster.

luterano, *adj.* Lutheran.

lutto, *n.m.* mourning.

M

ma, *conj.* but.

màcabro, *adj.* macabre.

maccheroni, *n.m.pl.* macaroni.

màcchia, *n.f.* spot, blemish, stain, blot; underbrush, brushwood.

macchiare, *vb.* spot, blot.

macchietta, *n.f.* flock.

macchiettato, *adj.* spotted, dappled.

màcchina, *n.f.* machine; engine. **m. da scrivere,** typewriter.

macchinare, *vb.* scheme.

macchinàrio, *n.m.* machinery.

macchinista, *n.m.* engineer; machinist.

macchinoso, *adj.* complicated.

macedònia, *n.f.* fruit salad.

macellaio, *n.m.* butcher.

macellare, *vb.* butcher, slaughter.

macèllo, *n.m.* butchery, slaughter.

macerare, *vb.* soak.

macèrie, *n.f.pl.* rubble, debris.

macigno, *n.m.* boulder.

màcina, *n.f.* grindstone.

macinacaffè, *n.m.* coffee grinder.

macinare, *vb.* grind, mill.

madornale, *adv.* gross.

madre, *n.f.* mother; (cheque) stub.

madrigale, *n.m.* madrigal.

madrina, *n.f.* godmother.

maestà, *n.f.* majesty.

maestoso, *adj.* majestic.

maestra, *n.f.* teacher.

maestrìa, *n.f.* ability, skill.

maestro, *n.m.* master, teacher.

mafia, *n.f.* mafia.

magari, *adv.* perhaps even.

magazzinàggio, *n.m.* storage.

magazzino, *n.m.* storehouse; (arms) depot, armory.

maggese, *n.m.* fallow field. **a m.,** fallow.

màggio, *n.m.* May.

maggioranza, *n.f.* majority.

maggiorazione, *n.f.* increase, appreciation.

maggiordòmo, *n.m.* butler.

maggiore, 1. *n.m.* major; elder; senior. **2.** *adj.* greater; elder; greatest; eldest.

maggiorenne, 1. *adj.* over 18 years old, of age. **2.** *n.m.* adult.

maggiormente, *adv.* mostly.

Magi, *n.m.pl.* Magi, Wise Men.

magìa, *n.f.* magic.

màgico, *adj.* magic.

magione, *n.f.* mansion; dwelling.

magistrale, *adj.* masterly, magistral.

magistrato, *n.m.* magistrate.

magistratura, *n.f.* judiciary.

màglia, *n.f.* jersey; stitch.

maglietta, *n.f.* T-shirt.

màglio, *n.m.* mallet.

magnànimo, *adj.* magnanimous, high-minded.

magnate, *n.m.* magnate.

magnèsio, *n.m.* magnesium.

magnète, *n.m.* magnet.

magnètico, *adj.* magnetic.

magnetizzare, *vb.* magnetize.

magnetòfono, *n.m.* tape recorder.

magnificare, *vb.* extol, praise; magnify.

magnificènza, *n.f.* magnificence.

magnìfico, *adj.* magnificent.

magniloquènte, *adj.* grandiloquent.

mago, *n.m.* magician.

magro, *adj.* lean, gaunt, meager, spare, thin.

mai, *adv.* ever; never.

maiale, *n.m.* pig; pork.

maionese, *n.f.* mayonnaise.

malamente, *adv.* badly.

malària, *n.f.* malaria.

malato, *adj.* sick, ill, ailing.

malattìa, *n.f.* sickness, malady, illness, ailment, disease.

malaugùrio, *n.m.* ill omen, jinx.

malavita, *n.f.* underworld.

maldicènza, *n.f.* scandal.

male, 1. *n.m.* evil; pain, ache, hurt. **m. di mare,** seasickness. **2.** *adv.* badly.

maledetto, *adj.* accursed.

maledire, *vb.* curse.

maledizione, *n.f.* curse.

malevolènza, *n.f.* malice.

malèvolo, *adj.* malevolent.

malfattore, *n.m.* ruffian.

malgrado, *prep.* despite.

maligno, *adj.* malignant.

malinconìa, *n.f.* melancholy.
malincònico, *adj.* melancholy.
malìzia, *n.f.* malice.
malizióso, *adj.* mischievous.
malleàbile, *adj.* malleable.
mallevadóre, *n.m.* guarantor; sponsor.
malóre, *n.m.* illness.
malsàno, *adj.* unhealthy.
malsicuro, *adj.* uncertain; unsafe.
màlto, *n.m.* malt.
maltrattàre, *vb.* maltreat, mistreat.
malvàgio, *adj.* wicked, fell.
malvagità, *n.f.* wickedness.
malvaròsa, *n.f.* hollyhock.
malvisto, *adj.* unpopular.
mamma, *n.f.* mother.
mammèlla, *n.f.* breast; udder.
mammìfero, *n.m.* mammal.
manàta, *n.f.* handful.
mancànza, *n.f.* lack; failure; shortage. **in m. di,** failing; lacking.
mancàre, *vb.* be missing, be lacking; fail.
mància, *n.f.* tip, gratuity.
mancorrènte, *n.m.* hand-rail.
mandàre, *vb.* send.
mandàto, *n.m.* mandate; warrant.
mandìbola, *n.f.* jaw.
mandolino, *n.m.* mandolin.
màndorla, *n.f.* almond.
màndorlo, *n.m.* almond-tree.
mandria, *n.f.* herd, drove.
mandrillo, *n.m.* mandrill.
maneggiàre, *vb.* handle.
manétte, *n.f.pl.* handcuffs.
manganèllo, *n.m.* bludgeon, cudgel.
manganèse, *n.m.* manganese.
mangiàbile, *adj.* edible, eatable.
mangiapàne, *n.m.* loafer, idler.
mangiàre, *vb.* eat.
mangiatòia, *n.f.* manger.
mangime, *n.m.* fodder.
manìa, *n.f.* mania, craze, fad.
maniaco, *n.m. and adj.* maniac.
mànica, *n.f.* sleeve.
mànico, *n.m.* handle, haft.
manicòmio, *n.m.* madhouse, (insane) asylum.
manicòtto, *n.m.* muff.
manicure, *n.f.* manicure.

manièra, *n.f.* manner, way, fashion.
manierìsmo, *n.m.* mannerism.
manifestàre, *vb.* manifest, evince.
manifestazióne, *n.f.* demonstration.
manifèsto, 1. *n.m.* manifesto. **2.** *adj.* manifest.
manìglia, *n.f.* handle.
manipolàre, *vb.* manipulate.
manna, *n.f.* manna, godsend.
mannàia, *n.f.* axe, chopper, cleaver.
màno, *n.f.* hand.
manodòpera, *n.f.* labor.
manomèttere, *vb.* tamper with.
manòpola, *n.f.* knob; mitten.
manoscritto, *n.m. and adj.* manuscript.
manovàle, *n.m.* laborer, helper.
manovèlla, *n.f.* handle, crank.
manòvra, *n.f.* maneuver.
manovràre, *vb.* maneuver.
mansuèto, *adj.* tame.
mantèllo, *n.m.* cloak, mantle, wrap.
mantenére, *vb.* maintain, keep.
mantenimènto, *n.m.* maintenance.
màntice, *n.m.* bellows.
Màntova, *n.f.* Mantua.
mantovàno, *adj.* Mantuan.
manuàle, 1. *n.m.* manual, handbook. **2.** *adj.* manual.
manùbrio, *n.m.* handle-bar.
manufatto, *n.m.* manufactured article.
manzo, *n.m.* steer; beef.
mappa, *n.f.* map.
marasma, *n.m.* chaos, confusion.
màrca, *n.f.* brand.
marcàre, *vb.* mark.
marchése, *n.m.* marquis.
marchigiàno, *adj.* of the Marche.
màrchio, *n.m.* stamp, hallmark.
màrcia, *n.f.* march.
marciapiède, *n.m.* sidewalk.
marciàre, *vb.* march.
màrcio, *adj.* rotten, decayed; (egg) addled.
marcire, *vb.* rot, decay.
marciume, *n.m.* rottenness.
màre, *n.m.* sea.
marèa, *n.f.* tide.
maremòto, *n.m.* seaquake.

maresciallo, *n.m.* marshal.
margarina, *n.f.* margarine.
margherita, *n.f.* daisy.
marginale, *adj.* marginal, border-line.
màrgine, *n.m.* margin, edge.
marijuana, *n.f.* marijuana.
marina, *n.f.* navy; marine.
marinaio, *n.m.* mariner, sailor.
marinare, *vb.* marinate. **m. la scuola,** cut school.
marino, *adj.* marine.
marionetta, *n.f.* marionette.
maritale, *adj.* marital.
maritare, *vb.* marry.
marito, *n.m.* husband.
marittimo, *adj.* maritime; marine.
marmàglia, *n.f.* riffraff, rabble.
marmellata, *n.f.* marmalade; jam.
marmitta, *n.f.* muffler.
marmo, *n.m.* marble.
marmòcchio, *n.m.* brat.
marmotta, *n.f.* ground hog.
maroso, *n.m.* billow.
marrone, *n.m.* maroon; chestnut.
marrùbio, *n.m.* horehound.
Marsìglia, *n.f.* Marseilles.
martedì, *n.m.* Tuesday.
martellare, *vb.* hammer.
martèllo, *n.m.* hammer.
martinèllo, *n.m.* jack.
màrtire, *n.m.* martyr.
martìrio, *n.m.* martyrdom.
marziale, *adj.* martial.
marzo, *n.m.* March.
mascalzone, *n.m.* scoundrel, blackguard; crook.
mascèlla, *n.f.* jaw.
màschera, *n.f.* mask; usher. **m. antigas,** gas mask.
mascherare, *vb.* mask.
mascherata, *n.f.* masquerade.
maschile, *adj.* masculine.
maschio, 1. *n.* male; cock; buck. **2.** *adj.* masculine; male.
massa, *n.f.* mass; bulk; lump.
massacrare, *vb.* massacre, slaughter.
massacro, *n.m.* massacre, slaughter.
massaggiare, *vb.* massage.
massaggiatore, *n.m.* masseur.
massàggio, *n.m.* massage.
massaia, *n.f.* housekeeper; house-wife.

massìccio, *adj.* massive; solid.
màssima, *n.f.* maxim.
màssimo, *n.m. and adj.* maxi-mum.
masso, *n.m.* rock, boulder.
massone, *n.m.* Mason.
massoneria, *n.f.* Masonry.
masticare, *vb.* chew, masticate.
masticatore, *n.m.* chewer.
mastice, *n.m.* mastic; putty.
mastro, *n.m.* master. **libro m.,** ledger.
matassa, *n.f.* skein, hank.
matemàtica, *n.f.* mathematics.
matemàtico, *adj.* mathematical.
materasso, *n.m.* mattress.
matèria, *n.f.* matter; subject.
materiale, *n.m. and adj.* material.
materialismo, *n.m.* materialism.
materializzare, *vb.* materialize.
maternità, *n.f.* maternity.
matèrno, *adj.* maternal.
matita, *n.f.* pencil; crayon.
matriarcato, *n.m.* matriarchy.
matrice, *n.f.* matrix; stub.
matrìcola, *n.f.* freshman.
matrigna, *n.f.* stepmother.
matrimònio, *n.m.* matrimony, marriage; match.
matrona, *n.f.* matron.
mattacchione, *n.m.* jester, joker.
mattarello, *n.m.* rolling pin.
mattatòio, *n.m.* stockyards.
mattina, *n.f.* morning.
mattinata, *n.f.* morning; matinée.
mattino, *n.m.* morning.
mattone, *n.m.* brick.
mattutino, *adj.* morning.
maturare, *vb.* ripen; mature.
maturato, *adj.* ripened; mellow.
maturità, *n.f.* maturity.
maturo, *adj.* mature; ripe; grown.
mausolèo, *n.m.* mausoleum.
mazza, *n.f.* bludgeon, cudgel.
mazzo, *n.m.* bunch; (cards) pack.
me, *pron.* me.
meandro, *n.m.* meander(ing), winding; labyrinth.
meccànico, 1. *n.m.* mechanic. **2.** *adj.* mechanical.
meccanismo, *n.m.* mechanism, machinery.
meccanizzare, *vb.* mechanize.
mecenate, *n.m.* patron.
medàglia, *n.f.* medal.

medaglione, *n.m.* medallion; locket.

mèdia, *n.f.* average; mean.

mediano, *adj.* median.

mediante, *prep.* through, by means of.

mediatore, *n.m.* ombudsman.

medicare, *vb.* medicate.

medicina, *n.f.* medicine.

mèdico, 1. *n.* doctor, physician. **2.** *adj.* medical.

mèdio, *adj.* middle; average; medium; mean; mid-.

mediòcre, *adj.* mediocre.

mediocrità, *n.f.* mediocrity.

medioevale, *adj.* mediaeval.

medioèvo, *n.m.* Middle Ages.

Medio Oriente, *n.m.* Middle East.

meditare, *vb.* meditate, muse.

meditazione, *n.f.* meditation.

mediterràneo, *n.m. and adj.* Mediterranean.

medusa, *n.f.* jellyfish.

megàfono, *n.m.* megaphone.

megahertz, *n.m.* megahertz.

megera, *n.f.* hag, witch, vixen.

mèglio, *adv.* better. **il m.,** (the) best.

mela, *n.f.* apple.

melagrana, *n.f.* pomegranate.

melancònico, *adj.* melancholy, dismal.

melanzana, *n.f.* eggplant.

melassa, *n.f.* molasses.

melenso, *adj.* dull; silly.

melma, *n.f.* muck, mire, ooze, slime.

melo, *n.m.* apple-tree.

melodìa, *n.f.* melody, tune.

melodioso, *adj.* melodious, tuneful.

melodramma, *n.m.* melodrama.

melone, *n.m.* melon; cantaloupe.

membrana, *n.f.* membrane.

mèmbro, *n.m.* member; limb.

memoràbile, *adj.* memorable.

mèmore, *adj.* mindful.

memòria, *n.f.* memory; memoir; record.

memoriale, *n.m.* memorial.

memorizzare, *vb.* memorize.

menare, *vb.* lead.

mènda, *n.f.* fault, defect, imperfection.

mendace, *adj.* mendacious, lying.

mendicante, *n.m. and adj.* beggar, mendicant.

mendicare, *vb.* beg.

mèndico, *n.m.* mendicant.

menefreghismo, *n.m.* couldn't-care-less attitude.

menestrèllo, *n.m.* minstrel.

meno, *adv. and prep.* minus; less. **a m. di,** without. **a m. che . . . non,** unless.

menomare, *vb.* diminish, reduce; impair.

menopàusa, *n.f.* menopause.

mensile, *adj.* monthly.

mènsola, *n.f.* shelf; bracket.

menta, *n.f.* mint.

mentale, *adj.* mental.

mentalità, *n.f.* mentality.

mente, *n.f.* mind.

mentire, *vb.* lie.

mento, *n.m.* chin.

mentòlo, *n.m.* menthol.

mentre, *conj.* while.

menù, *n.m.* menu.

menzionare, *vb.* mention.

menzione, *n.f.* mention.

menzogna, *n.f.* lie, untruth.

menzognèro, *adj.* lying, untruthful.

meramente, *adv.* merely.

meraviglia, *n.f.* marvel, wonder; amazement, astonishment.

meravigliare, *bv.* amaze, astonish; *(refl.)* be amazed, marvel, wonder.

meraviglioso, *adj.* marvelous, wonderful, amazing.

mercante, *n.m.* merchant.

mercanteggiare, *vb.* bargain, haggle.

mercantile, *adj.* mercantile.

mercanzìa, *n.f.* merchandise.

mercato, *n.m.* market.

mèrce, *n.f.* commodity; ware. *(pl.)* goods; freight.

mercé, *n.f.* favor; mercy.

mercenàrio, 1. *n.* hireling; mercenary. **2.** *adj.* mercenary.

mercerìa, *n.f.* haberdashery.

merciàio, *n.m.* haberdasher.

mercoledì, *n.m.* Wednesday.

mercùrio, *n.m.* mercury.

merènda, *n.f.* light meal, collation.

meretrice, *n.f.* harlot.
meridionale, *adj.* southern.
meringa, *n.f.* meringue.
meritare, *vb.* deserve, merit, earn.
meritévole, *adj.* deserving.
mèrito, *n.m.* merit.
meritòrio, *adj.* meritorious.
merletto, *n.m.* lace.
mèrlo, *n.m.* blackbird.
merluzzo, *n.m.* cod, codfish.
mèro, *adj.* mere.
mescere, *vb.* pour.
meschino, *adj.* mean, petty; paltry, shabby, beggarly, picayune, trivial.
mescolanza, *n.f.* mixture, admixture, blend.
mescolare, *vb.* mix, blend, mingle; alloy.
mese, *n.m.* month.
messa, *n.f.* mass.
messaggèro, *n.m.* messenger.
messàggio, *n.m.* message.
Messìa, *n.m.* Messiah.
messicano, *adj.* Mexican.
Mèssico, *n.m.* Mexico.
messinscena, *n.f.* production, staging; faking.
messo, *n.m.* messenger.
mestiere, *n.m.* job, occupation.
méstola, *n.f.* ladle.
mèstolo, *n.m.* ladle, dipper.
mestruazioni, *n.f.pl.* menstruation.
mèta, *n.f.* goal.
metà, *n.f.* half.
metabolismo, *n.m.* metabolism.
metafisica, *n.f.* metaphysics.
metàllico, *adj.* metallic.
metallo, *n.m.* metal.
metallurgìa, *n.f.* metallurgy.
metamòrfosi, *n.f.* metamorphosis.
mètano, *n.m.* methane, firedamp.
metanodotto, *n.m.* natural gas pipeline.
metèora, *n.f.* meteor.
meteorologìa, *n.f.* meteorology.
meticcio, *n.m. and adj.* half-breed.
meticoloso, *adj.* meticulous.
metòdico, *adj.* methodical.
metodista, *n.m. and n.f. and adj.* Methodist.
mètodo, *n.m.* method.

metràggio, *n.m.* length in meters; footage.
mètrico, *adj.* metric.
mètro, *n.m.* meter.
metrònomo, *n.m.* metronome.
metròpoli, *n.f.* metropolis.
metropolitana, *n.f.* subway.
metropolitano, *adj.* metropolitan.
méttere, *vb.* place, put, set, lay.
mezzadrìa, *n.f.* sharecropping.
mezzaluna, *n.f.* half-moon.
mezzanino, *n.m.* mezzanine.
mezzanòtte, *n.f.* midnight.
mèzzo, 1. *n.m.* middle; medium; means. **in m. a,** amid. **2.** *adj.* half; mid-.
mezzogiorno, *n.m.* noon; south.
mezzùccio, *n.m.* ruse, expedient.
mi, *pron.* me; to me.
miccia, *n.f.* fuse.
microfilm, *n.m.* microfilm.
micròfono, *n.m.* microphone.
microforma, *n.f.* microform.
microònda, *n.f.* microwave.
microscheda, *n.f.* microfiche.
microscòpico, *adj.* microscopic.
microscòpio, *n.m.* microscope.
midollo, *n.m.* marrow.
mièle, *n.m.* honey.
mietere, *vb.* reap.
miglio, *n.m.* mile.
miglioramento, *n.m.* improvement.
migliorare, *vb.* improve, better, ameliorate, amend.
migliore, *adj.* better. **il m.,** (the) best.
migrare, *vb.* migrate.
migratòrio, *adj.* migratory.
migrazione, *n.f.* migration.
milanese, *adj.* Milanese.
Milano, *n.f.* Milan.
miliare, *adj.* **pietra m.,** milestone.
milionàrio, *n.m.* millionaire.
milione, *n.m.* million.
militante, *adj.* militant.
militare, *adj.* military.
militaresco, *adj.* military.
militarismo, *n.m.* militarism.
milite, *n.m.* soldier.
milizia, *n.f.* militia.
miliziano, *n.m.* militiaman.
millantare, *vb.* bluster, brag.

millantatore, *n.m.* braggart.

millanterìa, *n.f.* bluster, brag.

mille, *num.* thousand.

millefòglie, *n.f.* napoleon (pastry).

millenàrio, *afj.* millenial.

millìmetro, *n.m.* millimeter.

milza, *n.f.* spleen.

mimetismo, *n.m.* mimicry; camouflage.

mimetizzare, *vb.* camouflage.

mina, *n.f.* mine.

minàccia, *n.f.* menace, threat.

minacciare, *vb.* menace, threaten.

minare, *vb.* mine.

minatore, *n.m.* miner.

minatòrio, *adj.* threatening.

minerale, *n.m. and adj.* mineral, ore.

mineràrio, *adj.* mining.

minèstra, *n.f.* soup.

mingherlino, *adj.* skinny, frail, thin.

miniatura, *n.f.* miniature.

miniaturizzare, *vb.* miniaturize.

minièra, *n.f.* mine.

minimamente, *adv.* least.

mìnimo, 1. *n.m.* minimum. **2.** *adj.* least, minimum.

ministèro, *n.m.* ministry.

ministro, *n.m.* minister.

minoranza, *n.f.* minority.

minore, *adj.* minor, lesser; younger, junior.

minorènne, *n.m. and adj.* minor.

minùgia, *n.f.pl.* catgut.

minùscolo, *adj.* tiny.

minuto, *n.m. and adj.* minute. **al m.,** at retail.

mìo, *adj.* my; mine.

mìope, *adj.* short-sighted.

miopìa, *n.f.* myopia.

miosòtide, *n.f.* forget-me-not.

mira, *n.f.* aim.

miràcolo, *n.m.* miracle.

miracoloso, *adj.* miraculous.

miràggio, *n.m.* mirage.

mirare, *vb.* aim.

mirìade, *n.f.* myriad.

mirtillo, *n.m.* blueberry.

mirto, *n.m.* myrtle.

miscèla, *n.f.* blend, mixture.

miscellàneo, *adj.* miscellaneous.

misconoscere, *vb.* disregard, ignore, deny.

miscredènte, *n. and adj.* miscreant; infidel.

miscùglio, *n.m.* mixture; medley; hodge-podge.

miseràbile, *adj.* pitiful; poor.

misèria, *n.f.* poverty, want; misery.

misericòrdia, *n.f.* mercy.

misero, *adj.* miserable, wretched.

misfatto, *n.m.* misdeed; crime.

missile, *n.m.* missile.

missionàrio, *n.m. and adj.* missionary.

missione, *n.f.* mission.

missiva, *n.f.* letter.

misterioso, *adj.* mysterious.

mistèro, *n.m.* mystery.

mìstico, *adj.* mystic.

mistificare, *vb.* mystify.

misto, *adj.* mixed; coeducational.

mistura, *n.f.* mixture.

misura, *n.f.* measure; size.

misurare, *vb.* measure, gauge.

misuratore, *adj.* measuring.

misurazione, *n.f.* measurement.

misurino, *n.m.* measuring spoon or cup.

mite, *adj.* gentle; meek; mild.

mitemente, *adv.* mildly, gently.

mitezza, *n.f.* mildness, meekness.

mìtico, *adj.* mythical.

mitigare, *vb.* mitigate, soften, lessen, assuage.

mìtili, *n.m.pl.* mussels.

mito, *n.m.* myth.

mitologìa, *n.f.* mythology.

mitòmane, *n.m. and f.* compulsive liar.

mitràglia, *n.f.* grapeshot.

mitragliatrice, *n.f.* machine gun.

mòbile, 1. *n.m.* piece of furniture. **2.** *adj.* movable, mobile.

mobìlia, *n.f.* furnishings.

mobilitare, *vb.* mobilize.

mobilitazione, *n.f.* mobilization.

mòda, *n.f.* mode, fashion. **alla m.,** fashionable, modish.

modellare, *vb.* model, mold.

modèllo, *n.m.* model, pattern.

moderare, *vb.* moderate.

moderato, *adj.* moderate.

moderazione, *n.f.* moderation.

modèrno, *adj.* modern.

modèstia, *n.f.* modesty.

modèsto, *adj.* modest, demure; plain.

modificare, *vb.* modify.

modista, *n.m. or f.* milliner.

modisteria, *n.f.* millinery.

mòdo, *n.m.* manner; mode; way.
m. di vìvere, life style.

modulare, *vb.* modulate.

mòdulo, *n.m.* blank form.

moffetta, *n.f.* skunk.

mògano, *n.m.* mahogany.

mòggio, *n.m.* bushel.

mòglie, *n.f.* wife.

molare, *adj.* molar.

molècola, *n.f.* molecule.

molestare, *vb.* molest.

molla, *n.f.* spring.

molle, *adj.* soft.

mòlo, *n.m.* jetty, mole, pier.

molòsso, *n.m.* bulldog.

moltéplice, *adj.* multiple, manifold.

molteplicità, *n.f.* multiplicity.

moltiplicare, *vb.* multiply.

moltiplicazione, *n.f.* multiplication.

moltitùdine, *n.f.* multitude, host.

molto, **1.** *adj.* much; (*pl.*) many, plenty of. **2.** *adv.* very; much.

momentàneo, *adj.* momentary.

momènto, *n.m.* moment.

mònaca, *n.f.* nun.

mònaco, *n.m.* monk.

Mònaco di Bavièra, *n.m.* Munich.

monarca, *n.m.* monarch.

monarchìa, *n.f.* monarchy.

monastèro, *n.m.* monastery.

moncone, *n.m.* stump.

mondano, *adj.* worldly.

mondare, *vb.* peel; cleanse.

mondiale, *adj.* world-wide.

mondo, *n.m.* world.

monèllo, *n.m.* gamin, urchin.

moneta, *n.f.* coin.

monetàrio, *adj.* monetary.

monile, *n.m.* necklace; jewel.

monìto, *n.m.* admonition, warning.

monitore, *n.m.* monitor.

monòcolo, *n.m.* monocle.

monogamìa, *n.f.* monogamy.

monòlogo, *n.m.* monologue.

monoplano, *n.m.* monoplane.

monopolizzare, *vb.* monopolize.

monopòlio, *n.m.* monopoly.

monosìllabo, *n.m.* monosyllable.

monòssido, *n.m.* monoxide.

monotonìa, *n.f.* monotony, dullness.

monòtono, *adj.* monotonous, dull, dreary, humdrum.

monsone, *n.m.* monsoon.

montacarichi, *n.m.* freight elevator.

montàggio, *n.m.* assembly.

montagna, *n.f.* mountain.

montagnoso, *adj.* mountainous.

montanaro, *n.m.* mountaineer.

montano, *adj.* mountain.

montare, *vb.* mount; set.

montatura, *n.f.* mounting, setting; frame; (*fig.*) lie.

monte, *n.m.* mount, mountain.

montone, *n.m.* ram.

montuoso, *adj.* mountainous.

monumentale, *adj.* monumental.

monumento, *n.m.* monument, memorial.

moquette, *n.f.* carpeting.

mòra, *n.f.* blackberry.

morale, **1.** *n.m.* morale. **2.** *n.f.* and *adj.* moral.

moralista, *n.m.* moralist.

moralità, *n.f.* morality.

moralmente, *adj.* morally.

moratòria, *n.f.* moratorium.

mòrbido, *adj.* soft.

morbillo, *n.m.* measles.

morbo, *n.m.* disease; illness.

morboso, *adj.* morbid.

mordace, *adj.* scathing.

mòrdere, *vb.* bite.

morente, *adj.* dying.

morfina, *n.f.* morphine.

morìa, *n.f.* high mortality; pestilence.

mormorare, *vb.* murmur.

mormorio, *n.m.* murmur.

morosa, *n.f.* sweetheart.

moroso, *n.m.* boyfriend.

mòrso, *n.m.* bite; (harness) bit.

mortale, *adj.* mortal, deadly, deathly, fatal.

mortalità, *n.f.* mortality.

mòrte, *n.f.* death, demise.

mortificare, *vb.* mortify.

mòrto, *adj.* dead.
mortuàrio, *adj.* mortuary.
mosàico, *n.m.* mosaic.
mosca, *n.f.* fly. **m. cavallina,** horsefly.
moscerino, *n.m.* gnat.
mostarda, *n.f.* mustard.
mosto, *n.m.* must, new wine.
mostra, *n.f.* show, exhibit, exhibition.
mostrare, *vb.* show, exhibit.
mostro, *n.m.* monster.
mostruosità, *n.f.* monstrosity, freak.
mostruoso, *adj.* monstrous, freak.
motivare, *vb.* motivate.
motivazione, *n.f.* justification.
motivo, *n.m.* motive; motif; sake.
mòto, *n.m.* motion.
motocicletta, *n.f.* motorcycle.
motocultura, *n.f.* motorized farming.
motore, 1. *n.m.* motor. **2.** *adj.* motive.
motorizzare, *vb.* motorize.
motoscafo, *n.m.* motor-boat.
motto, *n.m.* motto, quip, slogan.
movimento, *n.m.* movement.
mozione, *n.f.* motion.
mozzare, *vb.* lop off.
mozzicone, *n.m.* stub.
mozzo, *n.m.* deck-hand.
mòzzo, *n.m.* hub.
mùcchio, *n.m.* heap, pile, stack.
muco, *n.m.* mucus.
mucoso, *adj.* mucous.
muffa, *n.f.* mold. **m. bianca,** mildew.
muffito, *adj.* moldy.
mugghiare, *vb.* bellow, low.
mùgghio, *n.m.* bellow.
muggire, *vb.* bellow.
muggito, *n.m.* bellow.
mughetto, *n.m.* lily of the valley.
mugnaio, *n.m.* miller.
mulatto, *n.m.* mulatto.
mulino, *n.m.* mill.
mulla(h), *n.m.* mullah.
mulo, *n.m.* mule.

multa, *n.f.* fine.
multare, *vb.* fine.
multicolore, *adj.* multicolored, motley.
multilaterale, *adj.* multilateral.
multinazionale, *adj.* multinational.
mùltiplo, *adj.* multiple.
mùmmia, *n.f.* mummy.
mùngere, *vb.* milk.
municipale, *adj.* municipal.
municìpio, *n.m.* city hall.
munifico, *adj.* munificent.
munizione, *n.f.* munition, ammunition.
muòvere, *vb.* move, stir; *(refl.)* budge.
murale, *adj.* mural.
muratore, *n.m.* bricklayer, mason.
muratura, *n.f.* masonry, bricklaying.
muro, *n.m.* wall.
musa, *n.f.* muse.
muschio, *n.m.* moss.
muscolare, *adj.* muscular.
mùscolo, *n.m.* muscle.
musèo, *n.m.* museum.
museruòla, *n.f.* muzzle.
mùsica, *n.f.* music. **m. da càmera,** chamber music.
musicale, *adj.* musical.
musicista, *n.f.* musician.
muso, *n.m.* muzzle.
mussolina, *n.f.* muslin.
musulmano, *n.m. and adj.* Moslem.
muta, *n.f.* pack (of dogs).
mutabilità, *n.f.* changeability.
mutamento, *n.m.* change.
mutande, *n.f.pl.* briefs, underwear.
mutandine, *n.f.pl.* panties.
mutare, *vb.* change.
mutazione, *n.f.* mutation.
mutévole, *adj.* changeable.
mutilare, *vb.* mutilate.
mutilato, *n.m.* amputee.
muto, *adj.* mute, dumb.
mutua, *n.f.* medical insurance.
mùtuo, *adj.* mutual.

nababbo, *n.m.* nabob; rich person.

nàcchere, *n.f.pl.* castanets.

nafta, *n.f.* naphtha.

nàia, *n.f.* military service (slang.).

nàilon, *n.m.* nylon.

nanna, *n.f.* sleep (of child), beddy-bye.

nano, *n.m.* dwarf, midget.

napoletano, *adj.* Neapolitan.

Nàpoli, *n.f.* Naples.

narciso, *n.m.* narcissus, daffodil.

narcòtico, *n.m. and adj.* narcotic.

narice, *n.f.* nostril.

narrare, *vb.* narrate, relate.

narrativo, *adj.* narrative.

narrazione, *n.f.* narration, relation.

nasale, *adj.* nasal.

nàscere, *vb.* come into being; be born; arise.

nàscita, *n.f.* birth.

nascóndere, *vb.* hide; *(refl.)* lurk.

nascondìglio, *n.m.* hide-out, cache.

nascondino, *n.m.* hide-and-seek.

naso, *n.m.* nose.

nastro, *n.m.* ribbon; tape. **n. televisivo,** videotape.

natale, *adj.* natal.

Natale, *n.m.* Christmas; Noël.

natalità, *n.f.* birth rate.

natante, 1. *n.m.* craft. **2.** *adj.* floating.

nàtica, *n.f.* buttock.

natìo, *adj.* native.

nativìtà, *n.f.* nativity.

nativo, *adj.* native.

nato, *adj.* born.

natura, *n.f.* nature. **n. mòrta,** still life.

naturale, *adj.* natural.

naturalezza, *n.f.* naturalness.

naturalista, *n.m.* naturalist.

naturalizzare, *vb.* naturalize.

naturalmente, *adv.* of course; by nature, naturally.

naufragare, *vb.* wreck.

naufràgio, *n.m.* shipwreck.

nàufrago, *n.m.* castaway.

nàusea, *n.f.* nausea.

nauseante, *adj.* nauseating.

nauseare, *vb.* nauseate, disgust.

nàutico, *adj.* nautical.

navale, *adj.* naval.

navata, *n.f.* aisle; nave.

nave, *n.f.* ship, vessel.

navigàbile, *adj.* navigable.

navigare, *vb.* navigate; sail.

navigato, *adj.* experienced.

navigatore, *n.m.* navigator.

navigazione, *n.f.* navigation.

navìglio, *n.m.* fleet; canal.

nazionale, *adj.* national.

nazionalismo, *n.m.* nationalism.

nazionalità, *n.f.* nationality.

nazionalizzare, *vb.* nationalize.

nazionalizzazione, *n.f.* nationalization.

nazione, *n.f.* nation.

nazista, *n.m. and f. and adj.* Nazi.

ne, *pro-phrase* (replaces phrases introduced by **di** and by **da** when meaning "from") some; any; thereof; of it (him, her); about it (him, her); from there.

nè, *conj.* neither; nor.

neanche, *adv.* not even; nor.

nébbia, *n.f.* fog, haze, mist.

nebbioso, *adj.* foggy, hazy, misty.

nebulizzare, *vb.* atomize (liquids); spray.

nebulosa, *n.f.* nebula.

nebulóso, *adj.* nebulous.

nécessaire, *n.m.* vanity case; small tool box.

necessàrio, *adj.* necessary, needful, requisite.

necessità, *n.f.* necessity.

necrològio, *n.m.* obituary.

necròsi, *n.f.* necrosis.

nefando, *adj.* nefarious.

negare, *vb.* deny.

negativo, *n.m. and adj.* negative.

negletto, *adj.* neglected; ignored.

negligènte, *adj.* remiss.

negligènza, *n.f.* oversight.

negoziante, *n.m.* dealer.

negoziare, *vb.* negotiate.

negoziazione, *n.f.* negotiation.

negòzio, *n.m.* store, shop.

negra, *n.f.* Black (woman).

negro, *n.m.* Black (man *or* person).

nèmesi, *n.f.* nemesis.

nemico, *n.m. and adj.* enemy, foe.

nemmeno, *adv.* not even.

nènia, *n.f.* lamentation, dirge.

nèo, *n.m.* mole; imperfection.

neòfita, *n.m.* neophyte.

nèon, *n.m.* neon.

neonato, 1. *n.m.* baby; newborn. **2.** *adj.* newborn.

nepotismo, *n.m.* nepotism.

nèrbo, *n.m.* sinew.

nero, *adj.* black.

nèrvo, *n.m.* nerve.

nervoso, *adj.* nervous, jittery.

nessuno, 1. *adj.* no; (after negative) any. **2.** *pron.* nobody, no one; none.

nettare, *vb.* clean, cleanse.

nèttare, *n.m.* nectar.

nettézza, *n.f.* cleanness. **n. urbana,** garbage collection.

netto, *adj.* clean; clear-cut; net.

netturbino, *n.m.* street cleaner.

neurologia, *n.f.* neurology.

neutralità, *n.f.* neutrality.

neutralizzare, *vb.* neutralize, counteract.

nèutro, *n.m. and adj.* neutral.

neutrone, *n.m.* neutron.

nevàio, *n.m.* snowfield; glacier.

neve, *n.f.* snow.

nevicare, *vb.* snow.

nevicata, *n.f.* snowfall, snowstorm.

nevischio, *n.m.* sleet.

nevralgìa, *n.f.* neuralgia.

nevròtico, *adj.* neurotic.

nìbbio, *n.m.* kite.

nìcchia, *n.f.* niche.

nìchel, *n.m.* nickel.

nicotina, *n.f.* nicotine.

nidiata, *n.f.* nestful.

nido, *n.m.* nest, aerie.

niènte, *pron.* nothing. **n. affatto,** *adv.* not at all.

ninfa, *n.f.* nymph.

ninna-nanna, *n.f.* lullaby.

ninnolo, *n.m.* knicknack.

nipote, *n.m. and f.* nephew; niece; grandson; granddaughter.

nitrato, *n.m.* nitrate.

nitrògeno, *n.m.* nitrogen.

nò, *interj.* no.

nòbile, *n. and adj.* noble.

nobilmente, *adv.* nobly.

nobiltà, *n.f.* nobility.

nobiluòmo, *n.m.* nobleman.

nòcca, *n.f.* knuckle; fetlock.

nocciòla, *n.f.* nut; hazelnut.

nocciolina, *n.f.* small nut. **n. americana,** peanut.

nocciòlo, *n.m.* hazel; *(fig.)* kernel.

noce, n. 1. *m.* nut-tree; walnut. **n. americano,** hickory. **2.** *f.* nut; walnut.

nocivo, *adj.* harmful, injurious.

nòdo, *n.m.* knot, gnarl, kink, node. **n. scorsòio,** slipknot; noose.

nodoso, *adj.* knotty.

noi, *pron.* we; us.

nòia, *n.f.* boredom, ennui.

noleggiare, *vb.* hire.

noléggio, *n.m.* rental.

nòlo, *n.m.* hire.

nòmade, *n.m.* nomad.

nome, *n.m.* name; given name.

nomìgnolo, *n.m.* nickname.

nòmina, *n.f.* nomimation, appointment.

nominale, *adj.* nominal.

nominare, *vb.* nominate, name, appoint.

non, *adv.* not.

non allineato, *adj.* non-aligned.

noncurante, *adj.* easy-going.

nondimeno, *adv.* nonetheless, nevertheless, all the same.

nònna, *n.f.* grandmother.

nònno, *n.m.* grandfather.

nòno, *adj.* ninth.

nonostante, *prep.* notwithstanding.

non-ti-scordar-di-mé, *n.m.* forget-me-not.

nord, *n.m.* north.

nord-èst, *n.m.* northeast.

nord-òvest, *n.m.* northwest.

nòrma, *n.f.* norm; standard.

normale, *adj.* normal; standard.

normalmente, *adv.* normally.

norvegese, *adj.* Norwegian.

Norvègia, *n.f.* Norway.

nostalgìa, *n.f.* nostalgia; homesickness.

nòstro, *adj.* our; ours.

nostròmo, *n.m.* boatswain.

nòta, *n.f.* note; footnote.

notàbile, *adj.* noteworthy.

notàio, *n.m.* notary.

notare, *vb.* note.

notazione, *n.f.* notation.

nòtes, *n.m.* notepad.

notévole, *adj.* notable, noticeable, remarkable.

notificare, *vb.* notify.

notificazione, *n.f.* notification.

notìzia, *n.f.* piece of news.

notiziàrio, *n.m.* news report.

nòto, *adj.* well-known.

notorietà, *n.f.* notoriety.

notòrio, *adj.* notorious.

notte, *n.f.* night. **buona n.,** good night.

nottetempo, *adv.* at night.

notturno, 1. *n.m.* nocturne. 2. *adj.* nocturnal.

novanta, *num.* ninety.

novantésimo, *adj.* ninetieth.

nòve, *num.* nine.

novella, *n.f.* short story; good news.

novellino, 1. *n.m.* inexperienced person, beginner. 2. *adj.* inexperienced.

novellìstica, *n.f.* novel-writting, fiction.

novello, *adj.* new, tender.

novèmbre, *n.m.* November.

novèna, *n.f.* novena.

novità, *n.f.* novelty.

novìzio, *n.m.* novice.

novocaìna, *n.f.* novocaine.

nozione, *n.f.* notion.

nòzze, *n.f. pl.* wedding.

nube, *n.f.* cloud.

nucleare, *adj.* nuclear.

nùcleo, *n.m.* nucleus.

nudità, *n.f.* nudity, bareness.

nudo, *adj.* naked, nude, bare.

nulla, *pron.* nothing.

nullità, *n.f.* nonentity.

nullo, *adj.* void.

nume, *n.m.* deity.

numerare, *vb.* number.

numèrico, *adj.* numerical.

nùmero, *n.m.* number.

numeroso, *adj.* numerous.

nùnzio, *n.m.* nuncio.

nuòcere, *vb.* harm, injure.

nuòra, *n.f.* daughter-in-law.

nuotare, *vb.* swim.

nuotata, *n.f.* swim.

nuotatore, *n.m.* swimmer.

nuòvo, *adj.* new. **di n.,** anew; again.

nutrice, *n.f.* nurse.

nutriènte, *adj.* nutritious.

nutrimento, *n.m.* nourishment; feed.

nutrire, *vb.* nourish; feed.

nutrizione, *n.f.* nutrition.

nùvola, *n.f.* cloud.

nuvolosità, *n.f.* cloudiness.

nuvoloso, *adj.* cloudy.

nuziale, *adj.* nuptial, bridal.

O

o, *conj.* or. **o . . . o,** either . . . or.

oasi, *n.f.* oasis.

obbediènte, *adj.* obedient, compliant.

obbediènza, *n.f.* obedience, compliance.

obbedire, *vb.* obey, comply.

obbiettare, *vb.* object.

obbligare, *vb.* oblige.

obbligatòrio, *adj.* obligatory, binding, compulsory, mandatory.

obbligazione, *n.f.* obligation; bond, debenture.

obbròbrio, *n.m.* opprobrium, disgrace, shame.

obelisco, *n.m.* obelisk.

obèso, *adj.* obese.

òbice, *n.m.* howitzer.

obiettare, *vb.* object, demur.

obiettivo, 1. *n.m.* objective. 2. *adj.* objective; factual.

obiezione, *n.f.* objection.

obitòrio, *n.m.* morgue.

oblazione, *n.f.* fine paid voluntarily.

oblìo, *n.m.* oblivion.

obliquo, *adj.* oblique, slant.

obliterare, *vb.* obliterate.

oblò, *n.m.* porthole.

oblungo, *adj.* oblong.

òbolo, *n.m.* obol; mite.

òca, *n.f.* goose.

occasionale, *adj.* occasional.

occasione, *n.f.* occasion, opportunity, chance; bargain.

occhiali, *n.m.pl.* eyeglasses, spectacles.

occhiata, *n.f.* glance, look.

occhiello, *n.m.* button-hole; eyelet.

òcchio, *n.m.* eye. **o. della mànica,** armhole. **o. pesto,** black eye.

occidentale, *adj.* occidental, western.

occidènte, *n.m.* Occident, west.

occulto, *adj.* occult.

occupante, *n.m.* occupant.

occupare, *vb.* occupy.

occupato, *adj.* busy.

occupazione, *n.f.* occupation, job.

ocèano, *n.m.* ocean.

oculare, *adj.* ocular. **testimone o.,** eye-witness.

oculista, *n.m.* oculist.

od, *conj.* or.

odiare, *vb.* hate.

odierno, *adj.* today's, current.

òdio, *n.m.* hate, hatred.

odioso, *adj.* hateful, invidious, odious, obnoxious.

odissea, *n.f.* odyssey.

odontoiatrìa, *f.* dentistry.

odore, *n.m.* odor, scent, smell.

offèndere, *vb.* offend.

offensiva, *n.f.* offensive.

offensivo, *adj.* offensive, objectionable.

offensore, *n.m.* offender.

offerènte, *n.m.* bidder.

offèrta, *n.f.* offer; bid.

offesa, *n.f.* offense.

officiare, *adv.* officiate.

officina, *n.f.* workshop.

offrire, *vb.* offer, tender; bid.

offuscare, *vb.* darken, obscure.

oftàlmico, *adj.* ophthalmic.

oggettività, n.f. objectivity.

oggètto, *n.m.* object.

òggi, *n.m.and adv.* today.

oggigiorno, *adv.* nowadays.

ogni, *adj.* each, every.

ogniqualvòlta, *adv.* whenever.

ognuno, *pron.* everybody, everyone.

Olanda, *n.f.* Holland.

olandese, 1. *n.m.* Dutchman. **2.** *adj.* Dutch.

oleificio, *n.m.* oil refinery.

oleoso, *adj.* oily.

olfattòrio, *n.m.* olfactory.

oligarchìa, *n.f.* oligarchy.

olimpiadi, *n.f.* pl. Olympic Games.

òlio, *n.m.* oil.

oliva, *n.f.* olive.

olivastro, *adj.* livid; olive colored.

oliveto, *n.m.* olive yard.

olivo, *n.m.* olive-tree.

olmo, *n.m.* elm.

olocàusto, *n.m.* holocaust.

olografia, *n.f.* holography.

ologramma, *n.m.* hologram.

oltràggio, *n.m.* outrage.

oltraggioso, *adj.* outrageous.

oltranza, *adv.* **a o.,** to the bitter end.

oltre, *adv. and prep.* beyond; besides, further.

oltremare, *adv.* overseas.

oltrepassare, *vb.* pass beyond; outrun.

omàggio, *n.m.* homage; gift, present.

ombellico, *n.m.* navel.

ombra, *n.f.* shade; shadow.

ombelico, *n.m.* navel.

ombreggiare, *vb.* shade.

ombrèllo, *n.m.* umbrella.

ombroso, *adj.* shady.

omelìa, *n.f.* homily.

omeopàtico, *adj.* homeopathic.

omertà, *n.f.* silence, code of silence.

ométtere, *vb.* omit, leave out; overlook.

omètto, *n.m.* little man; clothes hanger.

omicida, *n.m.* homicide (person).

omicìdio, *n.m.* homicide, manslaughter.

omissione, *n.f.* omission.

òmnibus, *n.m.* local (train).

omnisciente, *adj.* all-knowing.

omogèneo, *adj.* homogeneous.

omogenizzare, *vb.* homogenize.

omologare, *vb.* probate.

omologazione, *n.f.* probate.

omònimo, 1. *n.m.* homonym; namesake. **2.** *adj.* homonymous, of the same name.

omosessuale, *adj.* homosexual.

óncia, *n.f.* ounce.

onda, *n.f.* wave.

ondeggiare, *vb.* undulate.

ònere, *n.m.* burden, onus.

oneroso, *adj.* burdensome.

onestà, *n.f.* honesty, integrity.

onestamente, *adv.* honestly, decently.

onèsto, *adj.* honest, decent, above board.

onnipotènte, *adj.* almighty, omnipotent.

onorare, *vb.* honor.

onoràrio, **1.** *n.m.* honorarium, fee. **2.** *adj.* honorary.

onore, *n.m.* honor.

onorévole, *adj.* honorable, decent.

onorevolezza, *n.f.* honorableness, decency.

onta, *n.f.* shame; insult.

opacità, *n.f.* opacity.

opaco, *adj.* opaque.

opale, *n.m.* opal.

òpera, *n.f.* work; opera.

operaio, *n.m.* worker.

operare, *vb.* operate.

operativo, *adj.* operative.

operatore, *n.m.* operator.

operazione, *n.f.* operation; transaction.

operetta, *n.f.* operetta; musical comedy.

operoso, *adj.* industrious.

opinione, *n.f.* opinion.

opporre, *vb.* oppose; *(refl.)* object.

opportunamente, *adv.* advisably.

opportunismo, *n.m.* opportunism.

opportunità, *n.f.* desirability; suitability; advisability; expediency.

opportuno, *adv.* fitting; desirable; advisable; expedient.

opposizione, *n.f.* opposition.

oppressione, *n.f.* oppression.

oppòsto, *n.m. and adj.* opposite.

oppressivo, *adj.* oppressive.

opprèsso, *adj.* oppressed, downtrodden.

oppressore, *n.m.* oppressor.

opprimènte, *adj.* oppressive, burdensome.

opprimere, *vb.* oppress.

oppugnare, *vb.* attack, assail.

optare, *vb.* opt, choose.

optometria, *n.f.* optometry.

opulènto, *adj.* opulent, affluent.

opulènza, *n.f.* opulence, affluence.

opùscolo, *n.m.* pamphlet.

opzione, *n.f.* option.

ora, **1.** *n.f.* hour; o'clock; time. **che o. è?** what time is it? **2.** *adv.* now.

oràcolo, *n.m.* oracle.

orale, *adj.* oral.

oràrio, *n.m.* timetable, schedule.

oratore, *n.m.* orator, speaker.

oratòria, *n.f.* oratory.

orazione, *n.f.* oration.

orbare, *vb.* bereave.

òrbe, *n.f.* world.

orbene, *adv.* well.

òrbita, *n.f.* orbit; socket.

òrbo, *n.m.* (coll.) blind man.

orchèstra, *n.f.* orchestra.

orchidèa, *n.f.* orchid.

òrda, *n.f.* horde.

ordàlia, *n.f.* ordeal.

ordinamento, *n.m.* arrangement.

ordinanza, *n.f.* ordinance.

ordinare, *vb.* order, arrange, array; ordain; tidy, trim.

ordinàrio, *adj.* ordinary.

ordinato, *adj.* orderly, tidy, trim.

ordinazione, *n.f.* ordination.

òrdine, *n.m.* order, array; fiat.

ordire, *vb.* hatch (a plot); warp.

orecchino, *n.m.* ear-ring.

orécchio, *n.m.* ear.

orecchioni, *n.m.pl.* mumps.

oréfice, *n.m.* goldsmith.

òrfano, *n.m.* orphan.

orfanotròfio, *n.m.* orphanage.

orgànico, *adj.* organic.

organigramma, *n.m.* organization chart.

organismo, *n.m.* organism.

organista, *n.m.* organist.

organizzare, *vb.* organize.

organizzazione, *n.f.* organization.

òrgano, *n.m.* organ.

orgasmo, *n.m.* orgasm.

organza, *n.f.* organdy.

òrgia, *n.f.* orgy, debauch.

orgòglio, *n.m.* pride.

orgoglioso, *adj.* proud.

orientale, *adj.* Oriental; eastern.

orientamento, *n.m.* orientation; bearings.

orientare, *vb.* orient.
orientazione, *n.f.* orientation.
oriènte, *n.m.* Orient; east.
orifízio, *n.m.* orifice, opening.
originale, *adj.* original, novel.
originalità, *n.f.* originality.
orìgine, *n.f.* origin.
origliare, *vb.* eavesdrop.
orina, *n.f.* urine.
orinare, *vb.* urinate.
orinatòio, *n.m.* urinal.
oriundo, *adj.* native.
orizzontale, *adj.* horizontal; level.
orizzonte, *n.m.* horizon.
orlare, *vb.* hem; edge.
orlatura, *n.f.* edging.
orlo, *n.m.* brink, brim, edge, rim, verge; hem. **o. a giorno,** hem-stitch.
orma, *n.f.* footstep; footprint.
ormeggiare, *vb.* moor.
ormeggio, *n.m.* mooring.
ormone, *n.m.* hormone.
ornamentale, *adj.* ornamental.
ornamento, *n.m.* ornament.
ornare, *vb.* ornament, adorn.
ornato, *adj.* ornate.
ornitologia, *n.f.* ornithology.
òro, *n.m.* gold.
orologiaio, *n.m.* watchmaker.
orològio, *n.m.* clock; watch. **o. a pólvere,** hourglass.
or' ora, *adv.* just now.
oròscopo, *n.m.* horoscope.
orpello, *n.m.* Dutch gold.
orrèndo, *adj.* ghastly, gruesome.
orribile, *adj.* horrible, grisly.
òrrido, *adj.* horrid.
orripilante, *adj.* bloodcurdling.
orrore, *n.m.* horror.
orsachiotto, *n.m.* teddy bear.
orso, *n.m.* bear.
ortènsia, *n.f.* hydrangea.
ortica, *n.f.* nettle; hives.
orticària, *n.f.* nettle rash.
orticultura, *n.f.* horticulture.
òrto, *n.m.* orchard; garden.
ortodòsso, *adj.* orthodox.
ortografia, *n.f.* orthography, spelling.
ortolano, *n.m.* greengrocer.
ortopèdico, *adj.* orthopedic.
orzaiòlo, *n.m.* sty.
orzata, *n.f.* orgeat.
orzo, *n.m.* barley.

osannare, *vb.* acclaim.
osare, *vb.* dare; venture.
oscèno, *adj.* obscene.
oscillare, *vb.* oscillate, sway.
oscuramento, *n.m.* darkening; blackout.
oscurare, *vb.* darken, obscure, dim, shade.
oscurità, *n.f.* darkness, obscurity, dimness, gloom.
oscuro, *adj.* dark, obscure, dim, gloomy.
osmòsi, *n.f.* osmosis.
ospedale, *n.m.* hospital.
ospedaliere, *n.m.* hospital worker.
ospedalizzare, *vb.* hospitalize.
ospedalizzazione, *n.f.* hospitalization.
ospitale, *adj.* hospitable.
ospitalità, *n.f.* hospitality.
òspite, *n.* 1. *m.* host; guest; visitor; lodger. 2. *f.* hostess; guest; visitor.
ospízio, *n.m.* nursing home; hospice.
ossatura, *n.f.* framework.
òsseo, *adj.* bony.
ossequiare, *vb.* pay respects to.
ossequioso, *adj.* ceremonious.
osservanza, *n.f.* observance.
osservare, *vb.* observe, notice, remark.
osservatore, *n.m.* observer.
osservatòrio, *n.m.* observatory.
osservazione, *n.f.* observation, remark.
ossessionare, *vb.* obsess.
ossessione, *n.f.* obsession.
ossesso, *n.m.* possessed.
ossia, *conj.* or.
ossido, *n.m.* oxide.
ossìgeno, *n.m.* oxygen.
òsso, *n.m.* bone.
ossuto, *adj.* bony.
ostacolare, *vb.* hinder, bar, block, interfere with, obstruct.
ostàcolo, *n.m.* obstacle, bar, hindrance, block, snag.
ostàggio, *n.m.* hostage.
ostare, *vb.* hinder. **nulla osta,** no objection.
òste, *n.m.* innkeeper.
ostensibile, *adj.* ostensible.
ostentare, *vb.* show off, display, flaunt.

ostentato, *adj.* ostentatious.

ostentazione, *n.f.* ostentation, display.

osteria, *n.f.* tavern.

ostètrico, 1. *n.m.* obstetrician. **2.** *adj.* obstetrical.

òstia, *n.f.* Host.

ostile, *adj.* hostile, antagonistic.

ostilità, *n.f.* hostility.

ostinato, *adj.* obstinate, dogged, headstrong; obdurate.

ostracizzare, *vb.* ostracize.

òstrica, *n.f.* oyster.

ostruire, *vb.* obstruct.

ostruzione, *n.f.* obstruction.

otorinolaringoiatra, *n.m.* ear, nose, and throat specialist.

òtre, *n.f.* wineskin.

ottàgono, *n.m.* octagon.

ottanta, *num.* eighty, fourscore.

ottantésimo, *adj.* eightieth.

ottava, *n.f.* eight; octave.

ottavino, *n.m.* piccolo.

ottavo, *adj.* eighth.

ottemperare, *vb.* obey.

ottenebrare, *vb.* becloud.

ottenere, *vb.* obtain, get.

òttica, *n.f.* optics.

òttico, 1. *n.m.* optician. **2.** *adj.* optic.

ottimismo, *n.m.* optimism.

ottimìstico, *adj.* optimistic.

òtto, *num.* eight.

ottobre, *n.m.* October.

ottone, *n.m.* brass.

ottopode, *n.m.* octopus.

ottùndere, *vb.* dull.

otturare, *vb.* stop up; fill.

otturatore, *n.m.* shutter.

otturazione, *n.f.* filling.

ottusamente, *adv.* bluntly, obtusely.

ottusità, *n.f.* obtuseness, dullness, bluntness.

ottuso, *adj.* obtuse, dull, blunt.

ovaia, *n.f.* ovary.

ovale, *n.m. and adj.* oval.

ovatta, *n.f.* wadding.

ovazione, *n.f.* ovation.

òvest, *n.* west.

ovile, *n.m.* sheepcote, fold.

ovino, *n.m.* sheep.

ovunque, *adv.* wherever; everywhere.

ovvero, *conj.* or.

òvvio, *adj.* obvious.

oziare, *vb.* loaf.

òzio, *n.m.* idleness.

ozioso, *adj.* idle.

ozono, *n.m.* ozone.

P

pacare, *vb.* placate.

pacato, *adj.* serene.

pacca, *n.f.* smack.

pàcchia, *n.f.* well-being; godsend.

pacco, *n.m.* package, pack, parcel.

pace, *n.f.* peace.

pacificare, *vb.* pacify.

pacificatore, *n.m.* pacifier.

pacìfico, *adj.* pacific, peaceful.

pacifismo, *n.m.* pacifism.

pacifista, *n.m.* pacifist.

padèlla, *n.f.* pan, frying pan.

padiglione, *n.m.* pavilion; stand.

Pàdova, *n.f.* Padua.

padovano, *adj.* Paduan.

padre, *n.m.* father.

padrino, *n.m.* godfather.

padrona, *n.f.* mistress; landlady.

padronanza, *n.f.* mastery.

padrone, *n.m.* boss, employer; landlord; master.

paesàggio, *n.m.* landscape, scenery.

paese, *n.m.* country.

paga, *n.f.* pay.

pagamento, *n.m.* payment.

pagano, *n. and adj.* pagan, heathen.

pagare, *vb.* pay, defray.

pàggio, *n.m.* page.

pàgina, *n.f.* page.

pàgine centrali, *n.f.pl.* centerfold.

pàglia, *n.f.* straw. **p. di acciàio,** *n.f.* steel wool.

pagliaccesco, *adj.* clownish.

pagliàccio, *n.m.* clown.

pagliàio, *n.m.* haystack.

pagnòtta, *n.f.* loaf.

pago, *adj.* satisfied.

pagòda, *n.f.* pagoda.

paio, *n.m.* pair, couple.

pala, *n.f.* shovel.
palafitta, *n.f.* pile.
palafrenière, *n.m.* groom.
palata, *n.f.* shovelful. **a palate,** a lot.
pàlato, *n.m.* palate.
palazzo, *n.m.* palace; large building; mansion. **p. di giustizia,** courthouse.
palco, *n.m.* antler; box (in theater).
palcoscènico, *n.m.* stage.
palesare, *vb.* disclose, reveal.
palese, *adj.* evident, obvious.
palesemente, *adv.* openly.
palèstra, *n.f.* gymnasium.
palizzata, *n.f.* fence.
palla, *n.f.* ball.
pallacanestro, *n.f.* basketball.
pallamàglio, *n.m.* croquet.
pallavolo, *n.f.* volleyball.
palliativo, *adj.* palliative.
pàllido, *adj.* pale, pallid, wan, pasty.
pallinacci, *n.m.pl.* buckshot.
pallini, *n.m.pl.* shot.
pallino, *n.m.* craze, mania; gunshot.
pallone, *n.m.* balloon.
pallore, *n.f.* paleness.
pallòttola, *n.f.* bullet; ball.
palma, *n.f.* palm.
palo, *n.m.* pole, post, stake.
pàlpebra, *n.f* eyelid.
palpitare, *vb.* palpitate.
palude, *n.f.* swamp, bog, marsh.
panacèa, *n.f.* panacea.
pancetta, *n.f.* bacon.
pància, *n.f.* paunch, belly.
panciòtto, *n.m.* vest.
pane, *n.m.* bread, loaf. **p. abbrustolito,** toast.
pànfilo, *n.m.* yacht.
pànico, *n.m.* panic.
paniere, *n.m.* basket.
panino, *n.m.* roll.
panna, *n.f.* cream.
pannaiòlo, *n.m.* clothier; draper.
panne, *n.f.* breakdown.
pannèllo, *n.m.* panel.
pannolino, *n.m.* diaper.
panorama, *n.m.* panorama.
pantaloni, *n.m.(pl.)* trousers, pants, breeches.
pantano, *n.m.* bog.

pantèra, *n.f.* panther.
pantòfola, *n.f.* slipper.
pantomima, *n.f.* pantomime.
panzana, *n.f.* (coll.) lie, fib, humbug.
paonazzo, *adj.* purple. **divenir p.** blush.
papa, *n.m.* pope.
papà, *n.m.* papa.
papàbile, *adj.* likely to be chosen.
papale, *adj.* papal.
papavero, *n.m.* poppy.
pàpera, *n.f.* goose; slip (of the tongue).
paperetto, *n.m.* gosling.
pàpero, *n.m.* gander.
papiro, *n.m.* papyrus.
pappa, *n.f.* gruel.
pappagallo, *n.m.* parrot; parakeet.
pappare, *vb.* gulp down; gobble up while unseen.
paràbola, *n.f.* parabola.
parabrezza, *n.m.* windshield, windscreen.
paracadute, *n.m.* parachute.
paradiso, *n.m.* paradise.
paradòsso, *n.m.* paradox.
parafango, *n.m.* mudguard; fender.
paraffina, *n.f.* paraffin.
parafrasare, *vb.* paraphrase.
paràfrasi, *n.f.* paraphrase.
parafùlmine, *n.m.* lightning-rod.
parafuòco, *n.m.* firescreen.
paraggi, *n.m.pl.* environs, vicinity.
paragonàbile, *adj.* comparable.
paragonare, *vb.* compare.
paragone, *n.m.* comparison.
paràgrafo, *n.m.* paragraph.
paràlisi, *n.f.* paralysis.
paralizzare, *vb.* paralyze.
parallelo, *n.m. and adj.* parallel.
paralume, *n.m.* shade.
paramèdico, *n.m.* paramedic.
paràmetro, *n.m.* parameter.
parapiglia, *n.m.* scramble.
parare, *vb.* stop; protect; adorn, decorate.
parassita, *n.m.* parasite.
parata, *n.f.* parade.
paratìa, *n.f.* bulkhead.
paravènto, *n.m.* screen; windshield.
parchèggio, *n.m.* parking.

parco, 1. n.m. park. **2.** adj. frugal.
parécchio, adj. some; considerable; (pl.) several.
parènte, n.f. relative.
parentela, n.f. kin, kindred; relationship.
parèntesi, n.f. parenthesis. **p. quadra,** bracket.
parere, 1. n.m. opinion. **2.** vb. appear, seem.
pari, 1. n.m. peer. **2.** n.f. par. **3.** adj. even, equal.
pària, n.m. pariah, outcast.
Parigi, n.f. Paris.
parigino, adj. Parisian.
parità, n.f. parity. **p. àurea,** gold standard.
parlamentare, 1. adj. parliamentary. **2.** vb. parley.
parlamento, n.m. parliament, legislature; parley.
parlare, vb. speak, talk.
parmigiano, adj. Parmesan.
parodia, n.f. parody.
parodiare, vb. parody.
paròla, n.f. word.
parolàccia, n.f. swear word.
parolìo, n.m. chatter.
parossismo, n.m. paroxysm.
parricìdio, n.m. patricide.
parròcchia, n.f. parish.
parrocchiale, adj. parochial.
pàrroco, n.m. parish priest; parson.
parrucca, n.f. wig.
parrucchière, n.m. hairdresser; barber.
parsimònia, n.f. parsimony.
parsimonioso, adj. parsimonious.
parte, n.f. part; share. **a p.,** apart. **p. del discorso,** part of speech.
partecipante, n.m. participant.
partecipare, vb. participate, partake.
partecipazione, n.f. participation.
partecipe, adj. partaking; informed.
parteggiare, vb. to take sides.
partènza, n.f. departure.
particèlla, n.f. particle.
participio, n.m. participle.
particolare, 1. adj. particular, peculiar. **2.** n.m. detail.

particolareggiato, adj. detailed; circumstantial.
partigiano, n.m. and adj. partisan.
partire, vb. depart, leave.
partita, n.f. game.
partito, n.m. party.
partitura, n.f. score.
partizione, n.f. partition.
parto, n.m. childbirth.
partorire, vb. bear, give birth to.
parvenza, n.f. appearance.
parziale, adj. partial.
parzialità, n.f. partiality, bias.
pàscere, vb. graze.
pasciuto, adj. nourished, fed.
pàscolo, n.m. pasture; grazing.
Pasqua, n.f. Easter.
pasquinata, n.f. lampoon.
passàbile, adj. passable.
passàggio, n.m. passage; aisle; crossing. **p. a livèllo,** grade crossing.
passante, n.m. passer-by.
passapòrto, n.m. passport.
passare, vb. pass; spend.
passatèmpo, n.m. pastime.
passato, 1. n.m. past; purée. **2.** adj. past, over, bygone.
passeggiare, vb. walk, stroll.
passeggiata, n.f. walk, stroll; ride.
passeggèro, n.m. passenger.
passeggiatore, n.m. stroller.
passerèlla, n.f. gangway.
pàssero, n.m. sparrow.
passìbile, liable, adj. **p. di,** liable to.
passione, n.f. passion; fondness.
passivo, n.m. and adj. passive.
passo, n.m. pass; pace; step; tread.
pasta, n.f. paste; dough, batter. **p. asciutta,** macaroni. **p. fròlla,** frosting.
pastello, n.m. pastel; crayon.
pasteurizzare, vb. pasteurize.
pasticca, n.f. pastille, lozenge, tablet.
pasticcerìa, n.f. pastry; pastryshop.
pasticcini, n.m.pl. pastries, cookies.
pastìccio, n.f. mess; pasty.
pasticcione, n.m. bungler, muddler.
pastiglia, n.f. pastille.
pasto, n.m. meal.

pastore, *n.m.* shepherd; pastor.

pastoso, *adj.* dense; doughy; mellow.

patata, *n.f.* potato.

patènte, *n.m.* license.

paternità, *n.f.* paternity, fatherhood.

patèrno, *adj.* paternal, fatherly.

patètico, *adj.* pathetic.

patìbolo, *n.m.* scaffold.

patina, *n.f.* coating; film; shoe polish.

patinoso, *adj.* furry.

patologia, *n.f.* pathology.

pàtos, *n.m.* pathos.

pàtria, *n.f.* country; fatherland, homeland.

patriarca, *n.m.* patriarch.

patrigno, *n.m.* stepfather.

patrimònio, *n.m.* patrimony, inheritance; estate.

patriòta, *n.m.* patriot.

patriòttico, *adj.* patriotic.

patriottismo, *n.m.* patriotism.

patrocinare, *vb.* sponsor.

patronato, *n.m.* patronage.

patròno, *n.m.* patron.

pattinare, *vb.* skate.

pàttino, *n.m.* skate.

patto, *n.m.* pact; compact.

pattùglia, *n.f.* patrol.

pattuire, *vb.* strike a deal, agree.

paùra, *n.f.* fear. **aver p.,** be afraid.

pauroso, *adj.* fearful.

pàusa, *n.f.* pause.

paventare, *vb.* fear.

pavimentare, *vb.* pave.

pavimentazione, *n.f.* flooring.

pavimento, *n.m.* floor.

pavone, *n.m.* peacock.

pavoneggiarsi, *vb.* strut.

paziènte, *adj.* patient.

paziènza, *n.f.* patience.

pazzìa, *n.f.* insanity, madness, lunacy.

pazzo, *adj.* crazy, insane, mad.

peccaminoso, *adj.* sinful.

peccare, *vb.* sin.

peccato, *n.m.* sin; pity; shame. **che p.!** what a pity!

peccatore, *n.m.* sinner.

pece, *n.f.* pitch.

pècora, *n.f.* sheep, ewe.

pecorino, *n.m.* sheep-milk cheese.

peculato, *n.m.* embezzlement.

peculiare, *adj.* peculiar.

peculiarità, *n.f.* peculiarity.

pecuniàrio, *adj.* pecuniary.

pedàggio, *n.m.* toll.

pedagogia, *n.f.* pedagogy.

pedagògo, *n.m.* pedagogue.

pedale, *n.m.* pedal.

pedante, *n.m.* pedant.

pedata, *n.f.* kick.

pedèstre, *adj.* pedestrian.

pediàtra, *n.m.* pediatrician.

pedina, *n.f.* pawn.

pedonale, *adj.* pedestrian.

pedone, *n.m.* pedestrian.

pedula, *n.f.* hiking boot.

pèggio, *adv.* worse. **il p.,** worst.

peggiore, *adj.* worse. **il p.,** the worst.

pegno, *n.m.* pledge; pawn.

pelapatate, *n.m.* potato peeler.

pelare, *vb.* skin, peel.

pèlle, *n.f.* skin, hide. **p. verniciata,** patent leather.

pellegrinàggio, *n.m.* pilgrimage.

pellegrino, *n.m.* pilgrim.

pellerossa, *n.m.* native American.

pelliccia, *n.f.* fur.

pellicciaio, *n.m.* furrier.

pellìcola, *n.f.* film, movie.

pelo, *n.m.* hair.

peloso, *adj.* hairy.

pelùria, *n.f.* down.

pèlvi, *n.f.* pelvis.

pena, *n.f.* pain; penalty.

penalista, *n.m.* criminalist.

penare, *vb.* suffer.

pendènte, 1. *n.m.* pendant. **2.** *adj.* pending; hanging.

pendènza, *n.f.* slope.

pèndere, *vb.* hang.

pendio, *n.m.* slope, slant, incline.

pendolare, *n.m.* commuter.

pèndolo, *n.m.* pendulum.

penetrante, *adj.* penetrating, discerning.

penetrare, *vb.* penetrate.

penetrazione, *n.f.* penetration, insight.

penicillina, *n.f.* penicillin.

penìsola, *n.f.* peninsula.

penitènte, *n.m. and adj.* penitent.

penitènza, *n.f.* penitence.

penitenziàrio, *n.m.* prison.

penna, *n.f.* feather, plume; pen. **p. stilogràfica,** fountain pen.

pennarello, n.m. felt-tip pen.
pennèllo, n.m. brush.
pennuto, adj. feathered.
penómbra, n.f. twilight, half-light.
penoso, adj. painful.
pensare, vb. think.
pensatore, n.m. thinker.
pensièro, n.m. thought.
pensilina, n.f. marquee.
pensionante, n.m. boarder.
pensionato, 1. n.m. retired person. **2.** adj. retired.
pensione, n.f. pension, boarding house.
pensoso, adj. pensive, thoughtful.
pentimento, n.m. repentance.
pentirsi, vb. repent, rue.
péntola, n.f. kettle, pot. **p. a pressione,** pressure cooker.
penùria, n.f. penury.
penzolare, vb. dangle.
penzoloni, adv. dangling, hanging.
pepe, n.m. pepper.
peperoncino, n.m. hot pepper.
peperone, n.m. bell pepper.
pepita, n.f. nugget.
per, prep. for; through; by; per.
pera, n.f. pear.
per cènto, adv. per cent.
percentuale, n.m. percentage.
percettìbile, adj. perceptible.
percezione, n.f. perception.
perché, 1. adv. why. **2.** conj. because; for.
perciò, adv. therefore.
percome, n.m. and conj. wherefore.
percorrènza, n.f. distance travelled.
percorso, n.m. passage (of time); lapse; route.
percòssa, n.f. blow; (pl.) beating.
percuòtere, vb. hit, strike; maul; tap.
percussione, n.f. percussion.
pèrdere, vb. lose; miss; forfeit; leak.
pèrdita, n.f. loss; bereavement; forfeiture; leakage.
perdizione, n.f. perdition.
perdonare, vb. pardon, forgive.
perdono, n.m. pardon, forgiveness.

perènne, adj. perennial.
perentòrio, adj. peremptory.
perfettamente, adv. perfectly.
perfètto, adj. perfect, flawless.
perfezionare, vb. perfect.
perfezione, n.f. perfection.
perfino, adv. even.
perforare, vb. punch.
perforazione, n.f. perforation.
pergamena, n.f. parchment.
pergolato, n.m. arbor, bower.
perìcolo, n.m. danger, peril, jeopardy.
pericoloso, adj. dangerous, perilous.
periferìa, n.f. periphery, outskirts.
perìmetro, n.m. perimeter.
periòdico, 1. n.m. periodical, magazine. **2.** adj. periodical; periodic; serial.
perìodo, n.m. period, term.
perire, vb. perish.
perito, 1. n.m. specialist, expert. **2.** adj. dead.
perizia, n.f. survey (by an expert).
pèrla, n.f. pearl.
perlaceo, adj. pearly.
perlomeno, adv. at least.
perlopiù, adv. in general, mostly.
permanènte, adj. permanent.
permanènza, n.f. stay.
permeare, vb. permeate.
permesso, n.m. permission, leave, license.
permèttere, vb. permit, let, allow.
permissìbile, adj. permissible.
permuta, n.f. exchange.
pernàcchia, n.f. Bronx cheer.
pernice, n.f. partridge.
pernicioso, adj. pernicious.
pèrnio, n.m. pivot.
pernottare, vb. stay overnight.
pero, n.m. pear-tree.
però, adv. however; though.
perpendicolare, n.m. and adj. perpendicular.
perpetrare, vb. perpetrate.
perpètuo, adj. perpetual.
perplessità, n.f. perplexity, bafflement, bewilderment, quandary.
perplèsso, adj. perplexed, baffled, bewildered.
persecuzione, n.f. persecution.
perseguire, vb. pursue.

perseguitare, *vb.* persecute.
perseveranza, *n.f.* perseverance.
perseverare, *vb.* persevere.
pèrsico, *adj.* **pesce p.,** bass (fish); perch.
persistènte, *adj.* persistent.
persistere, *vb.* persist.
persona, *n.f.* person. **p. anziana,** senior citizen.
personàggio, *n.m.* personage.
personale, 1. *n.m.* personnel, staff. **2.** *adj.* personal.
personalità, *n.f.* personality.
personalmente, *adv.* personally.
perspicare, *adj.* farsighted, shrewd, sagacious.
persuadere, *vb.* persuade.
persuasivo, *adj.* persuasive.
pèrtica, *n.f.* perch; pole.
pertinènte, *adj.* pertinent, relevant.
pertùgio, *n.m.* hole, perforation.
perturbare, *vb.* perturb.
pervàdere, *vb.* pervade.
perversione, *n.f.* perversion.
pervèrso, *adj.* perverse.
pervertire, *vb.* pervert, debauch.
pesante, *adj.* heavy.
pesare, *vb.* weigh; balance.
pesca, *n.f.* fishing.
pèsca, *n.f.* peach.
pescàggio, *n.m.* draft.
pescare, *vb.* fish; angle.
pescatore, *n.m.* fisherman.
pesce, *n.m.* fish. **p. rosso,** goldfish. **p. spada,** swordfish.
pescecane, *n.m.* shark; profiteer.
pescheréccio, *n.m.* fishing boat.
peschièra, *n.f.* fishery.
pesciolino, *n.m.* minnow.
pescivéndola, *n.f.* fishwife.
pescivéndolo, *n.m.* fishmonger.
pèsco, *n.m.* peach-tree.
peso, *n.m.* weight. **p. màssimo,** heavyweight. **p. lordo,** gross weight.
pessimismo, *n.m.* pessimism.
pestare, *vb.* pound.
pèste, *n.f.* plague.
pestífero, *adj.* (*col.*) troublemaking; pestiferous.
pestilènza, *n.f.* pestilence.
pesto, *adj.* pounded, crushed. **òcchio p.,** black eye.
pètalo, *n.m.* petal.

petardo, *n.m.* firecracker.
petizione, *n.f.* petition.
pèto, *n.m.* fart.
petròlio, *n.m.* petroleum. **p. raffinato,** kerosene.
pettégola, *n.f.* gossip.
pettegolare, *vb.* gossip.
pettegolezzo, *n.m.* gossip.
pettégolo, 1. *n.m.* gossip. **2.** *adj.* gossipy.
pettinare, *vb.* comb.
pettinatura, *n.f.* coiffure, hair-do.
pèttine, *n.m.* comb.
pettirosso, *n.m.* robin.
pètto, *n.m.* chest, bosom; (meat) brisket.
pettorale, *n.m.* pectoral.
petulante, *adj.* petulant.
petulanza, *n.f.* petulance, huff.
pèzza, *n.f.* patch.
pezzènte, *n.m.* beggar.
pezzettino, *n.m.* little bit, mite.
pezzetto, *n.m.* scrap.
pèzzo, *n.m.* piece, bit, chunk. **p. di ricàmbio,** spare part. **p. gròsso,** big shot.
piacere, 1. *n.m.* pleasure. **2.** *vb.* please.
piacévole, *adj.* pleasing, pleasant, agreeable, genial.
piacevolezza, *n.f.* pleasing quality, geniality.
piacevolmente, *adv.* pleasingly, agreeably, genially.
piacimento, *n.m.* liking, taste.
piaga, *n.f.* sore; wound.
piagnisteo, *n.m.* moaning.
piagnucolare, *vb.* whimper, snivel, blubber.
piagnucolone, *n.m.* whiner, whimperer, sniveler, complainer.
piagnucoloso, *adj.* maudlin.
pialla, *n.f.* plane.
piallàccio, *n.m.* veneer.
piallare, *vb.* plane.
pianeggiante, *adj.* flat, level.
pianeta, *n.m.* planet.
piàngere, *vb.* weep, cry, bewail, mourn.
pianista, *n.m.* pianist.
piano, 1. *n.m.* plan; story, floor; plane. **2.** *adj.* level, flat.
pianofòrte, *n.m.* piano.
pianta, *n.f.* plant; plan, plot; map.
piantagione, *n.f.* plantation.

piantare, *vb.* plant.

piantonare, *vb.* guard.

piantatore, *n.m.* planter.

pianto, *n.m.* crying, weeping.

pianura, *n.f.* plain.

pianuzza, *n.f.* halibut.

piastra, *n.f.* plate.

piastrella, *n.f.* tile.

pietire, *vb.* beg.

piattaforma, *n.f.* platform, dais.

piattino, *n.m.* saucer.

piatto, 1. *n.m.* dish, plate; cymbal. **2.** *adj.* flat.

piàttola, *n.f.* roach, crab louse, bore.

piazza, *n.f.* square.

piazzale, *n.m.* large square.

piazzare, *vb.* place; sell.

piazzista, *n.m.* salesman.

piccante, *adj.* piquant.

picchetto, *n.m.* picket.

picchiare, *vb.* hit, smack, sock, clout, cuff, rap.

picchiata, *n.f.* nose dive.

picchiatore, *n.m.* divebomber.

picchio, *n.m.* blow, rap.

piccino, 1. *adj.* little. **2.** *n.m.* child.

piccione, *n.m.* pigeon. **p. viaggiatore,** homing pigeon, carrier pigeon.

picco, *n.m.* peak, crag.

piccolo, *adj.* little, small, petty.

piccone, *n.m.* pick.

pidòcchio, *n.m.* louse.

piède, *n.m.* foot. **p. stòrto,** clubfoot.

piedestallo, *n.m.* pedestal.

pièga, *n.f.* fold, crease, pleat, tuck.

piegare, *vb.* fold, bend, crease.

piegatura, *n.f.* bending, folding.

pieghettato, *adj.* pleated.

pieghévole, *adj.* pliable, pliant; folding.

Piemonte, *n.m.* Piedmont.

piemontese, *adj.* Piedmontese.

pienamente, *adv.* fully.

pienezza, *n.f.* fullness.

pieno, *adj.* full.

pietà, *n.f.* mercy, pity, piety.

pietanza, *n.f.* entree (meal).

pietoso, *adj.* merciful, pitiful.

piètra, *n.f.* stone. **p. angolare,** cornerstone. **p. focaia,** flint.

pietrificare, *vb.* petrify.

piffero, *n.m.* fife, fifer, piper.

pìgia pìgia, *n.m.* crowd, crush.

pigiama, *n.m.pl.* pajamas.

pigiare, *vb.* press, crush, squeeze.

pigione, *n.f.* rent.

pigmènto, *n.m.* pigment.

pignolo, *adj.* fussy, pernickety.

pignoramento, *n.m.* seizure (law).

pignorare, *vb.* attach, distrain, seize.

pigrìzia, *n.f.* laziness.

pigro, *adj.* lazy.

pila, *n.f.* battery. **p. a secco,** dry cell.

pilastro, *n.m.* pillar.

pillola, *n.f.* pill.

pilone, *n.m.* pier; pillar.

pilòta, *n.m.* pilot.

piluccare, *vb.* nibble, pick at; pluck.

pinacoteca, *n.f.* picture gallery.

pineta, *n.f.* pine grove.

pingue, *adj.* corpulent; big; rich.

pinna, *n.f.* fin.

pinnàcolo, *n.m.* pinnacle.

pino, *n.m.* pine.

pinta, *n.f.* pint.

pinze, *n.f.pl.* pincers, pliers.

pinzette, *n.f.pl.* tweezers.

pio, *adj.* pious.

pioggerèlla, *n.f.* drizzle.

piòggia, *n.f.* rain.

piombo, *n.m.* lead.

pionière, *n.m.* pioneer.

piòta, *n.f.* turf, sod.

piòvere, *vb.* rain.

piovigginare, *vb.* drizzle.

piovoso, *adj.* rainy.

piovra, *n.f.* octopus.

pipa, *n.f.* pipe.

pipistrèllo, *n.m.* bat.

pira, *n.f.* pyre.

piràmide, *n.f.* pyramid.

pirata, *n.m.* pirate.

piròscafo, *n.m.* steamship.

piscina, *n.f.* swimming pool.

pisèllo, *n.m.* pea.

pisolino, *n.m.* doze, snooze, nap.

pista, *n.f.* (race) track; (race) course; (cinder) path. **p. d'atteràggio,** landing strip, runway.

pistola, *n.f.* pistol.

pistone, *n.m.* piston.

pittore, *n.m.* painter.

pittoresco, *adj.* picturesque.

pittura, *n.f.* painting.
più, 1. *adv.* more; **per di p.**, moreover; **per lo p.**, mostly. 2. *prep.* plus.
piuma, *n.f.* plume, feather.
piumàggio, *n.m.* plumage.
piumato, *adj.* plumed, feathered.
piumino, *n.m.* feathers.
piumoso, *adj.* feathery.
piuttosto, *adv.* rather.
pizza, *n.f.* pizza.
pizzicòtto, *n.m.* nip, pinch.
pizzo, *n.m.* lace.
placare, *vb.* appease, placate.
placatore, *n.m.* appeaser.
plàcido, *adj.* placid.
plagiare, *vb.* plagiarize.
plàgio, *n.m.* plagiarism.
planetàrio, 1. *n.m.* planetarium. 2. *adj.* planetary.
plasma, *n.m.* plasma.
plàstica, *n.f.* plastic.
plàstico, *adj.* plastic.
plàtino, *n.m.* platinum.
plausìbile, *adj.* plausible.
plebe, *n.f.* populace, humble people.
plebàglia, *n.f.* mob, rabble.
plebiscito, *n.m.* plebiscite.
plenàrio, *adj.* plenary.
plenilùnio, *n.m.* full moon.
pleurite, *n.f.* pleurisy.
plico, *n.m.* stack (of paper); file.
plotone, *n.m.* platoon.
plùmbeo, *adj.* leaden.
plurale, *n.m.* and *adj.* plural.
plutòcrate, *n.m.* plutocrat.
pneumàtico, 1. *n.m.* tire. 2. *adj.* pneumatic.
po', *n.m.* un **p.**, a little, somewhat.
pòchi, *adj.* and *pron. pl.* few.
pòco, *n.* and *adv.* little. **fra p.**, in a short time, presently, soon.
podére, *n.m.* farm; property.
poderoso, *adj.* strong, powerful.
podismo, *n.m.* running; walking.
poèma, *n.m.* poem.
poesìa, *n.f.* poem; poetry.
poèta, *n.m.* poet.
poetéssa, *n.f.* woman poet.
poètico, *adj.* poetic.
pòi, *adv.* then.
poiana, *n.f.* buzzard.
poichè, *conj.* since.
polacca, *n.f.* polonaise.

polacco, *adj.* Polish.
polare, *adj.* polar.
polarizzare, *vb.* polarize.
polèmica, *n.f.* polemic; controversial subject.
polèmico, *adj.* polemical, controversial.
poligamìa, *n.f.* polygamy.
poliglòtto, *adj.* polyglot.
poligono, *n.m.* polygon.
polipo, *n.m.* polyp.
polistirolo, *n.m.* polystyrene, styrofoam.
polìtica, *n.f.* politics; policy.
polìtico, 1. *n.m.* politician. 2. *adj.* politic, political.
polizìa, *n.f.* police.
poliziòtto, *n.m.* policeman, cop.
pòlizza, *n.f.* policy.
pollàio, *n.m.* chicken coop.
pollame, *n.m.* poultry.
pòllice, *n.m.* thumb; big toe; inch.
pòlline, *n.m.* pollen.
pollo, *n.m.* chicken, fowl.
polmonare, *adj.* pulmonary.
polmone, *n.m.* lung.
polmonite, *n.f.* pneumonia.
pòlo, *n.m.* pole.
Polònia, *n.f.* Poland.
polpa, *n.f.* pulp.
polpetta, *n.f.* meat-ball; croquette.
polpettone, *n.m.* meat loaf.
polsino, *n.m.* cuff.
polso, *n.m.* wrist; pulse.
poltrona, *n.f.* armchair, easy-chair.
pólvere, *n.m.* dust; powder.
polverizzare, *vb.* pulverize; powder.
polveroso, *adj.* dusty.
pomeriggio, *n.m.* afternoon.
pomiciare, *vb.* spoon (slang).
pomo, *n.m.* apple.
pomodoro, *n.m.* tomato.
pompa, *n.f.* pump; pomp. **p. da incèndio**, fire engine.
pompare, *vb.* pump.
pompèlmo, *n.m.* grapefruit.
pompière, *n.m.* fireman.
pomposo, *adj.* pompous.
pònce, *n.m.* punch.
ponderare, *vb.* ponder.
ponderoso, *adj.* ponderous.
ponente, *n.m.* west.

ponte, *n.m.* bridge; deck; span. **p. levatòio,** drawbridge. **p. sospeso,** suspension bridge.

pontéfice, *n.m.* pontiff.

pontile, *n.m.* gangplank.

pontone, *n.m.* pontoon.

popelina, *n.f.* broadcloth.

popolare, *adj.* popular.

popolarità, *n.f.* popularity.

popolazione, *n.f.* population.

pòpolo, *n.m.* people, folk.

poppa, *n.f.* stern; breast.

pòrca, *n.f.* sow; ridge.

porcellana, *n.f.* porcelain, china.

porcellino, *n.m.* piglet. **p. d'India,** guinea pig.

porcile, *n.m.* sty.

pòrco, *n.m.* hog, pig, swine.

pornografia, *n.f.* pornography.

pòro, *n.m.* pore.

poroso, *adj.* porous.

pórpora, *n.f.* purple.

porre, *vb.* put, place, set, lay.

pòrro, *n.m.* leek.

pòrta, *n.f.* door; gate; gateway; goal.

portabagagli, *n.m.* porter.

portacéneri, *n.m.* ash-tray.

portaèrei, *n.m.* aircraft carrier, flat-top.

portafògli, *n.m.* billfold, wallet; pocketbook.

portafòglio, *n.m.* wallet, portfolio.

portafortuna, *n.m.* good-luck charm; mascot.

portale, *n.m.* portal.

portamento, *n.m.* bearing, posture, conduct.

portare, *vb.* carry, bear, bring; wear.

portamonete, *n.m.* wallet, purse.

portasigarette, *n.m.* cigarette-holder.

portata, *n.f.* reach; range; scope.

portàtile, *adj.* portable.

portatore, *n.m.* carrier, bearer.

portavoce, *n.m.* spokesman, mouthpiece.

portento, *n.m.* prodigy, marvel.

pòrtico, *n.m.* portico, porch.

portièra, *n.f.* door.

portière, *n.m.* goal-keeper; porter.

portinàio, *n.m.* doorman, concierge.

portinería, *n.f.* concierge's office.

pòrto, *n.m.* port, harbor, haven, inlet.

Portogallo, *n.m.* Portugal.

portoghese, *adj.* Portuguese.

portone, *n.m.* gate.

porzione, *n.f.* portion, helping, share.

pòsa, *n.f.* pose; exposure.

posare, *vb.* pose.

posarsi, *vb.* perch.

posata, *n.f.* silverware.

posatería, *n.f.* cutlery.

posato, *adj.* quiet, well behaved.

posatòio, *n.m.* perch.

poscritto, *n.m.* postscript.

positivo, *adj.* positive.

posizione, *n.f.* position.

posporre, *vb.* postpone.

possedere, *vb.* possess, own.

possènte, *adj.* powerful.

possessivo, *adj.* possessive.

possèsso, *n.m.* possession, belonging.

possessore, *n.m.* possessor, owner.

possibile, *adj.* possible.

possibilità, *n.f.* possibility.

possibilmente, *adv.* possibly.

possidente, *n.m. and f.* proprietor; wealthy person.

pòsta, *n.f.* mail, post.

postale, *adj.* postal.

postbèllico, *adj.* postwar.

postdatare, *vb.* postdate.

posteggiare, *vb.* park.

postèggio, *n.m.* parking.

pòsteri, *n.m.pl.* posterity.

posteriore, *adj.* posterior, rear, back, hind.

posterità, *n.f.* posterity.

posticipare, *vb.* postpone, defer, reschedule.

postino, *n.m.* mailman, postman.

posto, *n.m.* place; post; room; spout.

postulante, *n.m. and f.* petitioner.

postulare, *vb.* solicit, petition, postulate.

potàssio, *n.m.* potassium.

potatura, *n.f.* pruning.

potènte, *adj.* powerful, potent, forcible, mighty.

potènza, *n.f.* power, might.

potenziale, *n.m. and adj.* potential.

potere, 1. *n.m.* power. **2.** *vb.* be able, can, may.

poveràccio, *n.m.* poor fellow.

pòvero, 1. *n.m.* poor man, pauper. **2.** *adj.* poor.

povertà, *n.f.* poverty.

pozione, *n.f.* potion.

pozzànghera, *n.f.* puddle.

pozzo, *n.m.* well; shaft. **p. nero,** cesspool.

prammàtico, *adj.* pragmatic.

pranzare, *vb.* dine.

pranzo, *n.m.* dinner.

prassi, *n.f.* praxis, practice.

prateria, *n.f.* prairie.

pràtica, 1. *n.f.* practice. **2.** *n.f.* file, dossier.

praticàbile, *adj.* passable; practicable.

praticamente, *adv.* practically.

praticante, 1. *adj.* practicing; **2.** *n.m.* apprentice; observant.

praticare, *vb.* practice.

pràtico, *adj.* practical, business-like. **p. di,** skilled in; acquainted with, familiar with.

praticone, *n.m.* old hand (pejorative).

prato, *n.m.* meadow, field; lawn.

preàmbolo, *n.m.* preamble.

preavvertire, *vb.* forewarn.

precàrio, *adj.* precarious.

precauzione, *n.f.* precaution.

precedènte, 1. *n.m.* precedent. **2.** *adj.* preceding, former, previous.

precedènza, *n.f.* precedence, right of way.

precédere, *vb.* precede, go before, (in time) antedate.

precètto, *n.m.* precept.

precipitare, *vb.* precipitate; (*refl.*) rush.

precipizio, *n.m.* precipice.

precisione, *n.f.* precision.

preciso, *adj.* precise.

preclùdere, *vb.* preclude.

precòce, *adj.* precocious.

precursore, *n.m.* precursor, fore-runner, harbinger.

prèda, *n.f.* prey.

predare, *vb.* plunder, forage.

predatòrio, *adj.* predatory.

predecessore, *n.m.* predecessor.

predestinazione, *n.f.* predestination.

predicare, *vb.* preach.

predicato, *n.m.* predicate.

predicatore, *n.m.* preacher.

predilètto, *n. and adj.* favorite, darling.

predilezione, *n.f.* predilection.

predire, *vb.* predict, foretell.

predisporre, *vb.* predispose, bias.

predominante, *adj.* predominant.

predomìnio, *n.m.* dominance.

predone, *n.m.* marauder, robber.

prefabbricato, *adj.* prefabricated.

prefazione, *n.f.* preface, foreword.

preferènza, *n.f.* preference.

preferìbile, *adj.* preferable.

preferire, *vb.* prefer.

prefètto, *n.m.* prefect.

prefisso, 1. *n.m.* prefix. **p. teleselettivo,** area code.

pregare, *vb.* pray, beg.

preghièra, *n.f.* prayer, request, plea.

prègio, *n.m.* virtue, value, worth.

pregiudicare, *vb.* prejudice.

pregiudicato, *n.m.* criminal; previous offender.

pregiudìzio, *n.m.* prejudice, bias.

prègna, *adj.f.* pregnant.

prego, *interj.* Please!; You're welcome.; Come in!

pregustare, *vb.* foretaste.

pregustazione, *n.f.* foretaste.

preistòrico, *adj.* prehistoric.

prelato, *n.m.* priest.

prelazione, *n.f.* privilege; preemption.

prelevare, *v.b.* draw, withdraw; take away.

preliminare, *adj.* preliminary.

prelùdio, *n.m.* prelude.

prematuro, *adj.* premature.

premeditare, *vb.* premeditate.

prèmere, *vb.* press.

premessa, *n.f.* premise.

premiare, *vb.* award (a prize to); reward.

prèmio, *n.m.* prize, award, premium.

premonizione, *n.f.* premonition.

premunirsi, vb. (refl.) forearm, protect.

premurosamente, adv. considerately.

premuroso, adj. considerate.

prenatale, adj. prenatal.

préndere, vb. take; get; catch.

prenotare, vb. reserve.

prenotazione, n.f. reservation.

preoccupante, adj. worrisome.

preoccupare, vb. worry.

preoccupazione, n.f. worry.

preparare, vb. prepare.

preparatòrio, adj. preparatory.

preparazione, n.f. preparation.

preponderante, adj. preponderant.

preposizione, n.f. preposition.

preposto, adj. responsible for.

prepotènte, 1. adj. overbearing, tyrannical. **2.** n. bully.

prerogativa, n.f. prerogative.

presa, n.f. grasp, grip, hold; (electrical) outlet; socket. **p. di tèrra,** (electrical) ground.

presàgio, n.m. omen, portent.

presagire, vb. presage, predict, forebode, foreshadow, portend.

presbite, adj. farsighted.

prescritto, adj. prescribed, fixed; compulsory.

prescrivere, vb. prescribe.

prescrizione, n.f. prescription.

presentàbile, adj. presentable.

presentare, vb. present, introduce.

presentatore, n.m. announcer.

presentazione, n.f. presentation, introduction.

presènte, adj. present.

presentimento, n.m. presentiment, foreboding.

presentire, vb. forebode.

presènza, n.f. presence.

presenziare, vb. attend; be present.

preservare, vb. preserve.

preservativo, n.m. condom.

presidènte, n.m. president, chairman.

presidentessa, n.f. chairwoman.

presidènza, n.f. presidency, chairmanship.

presìdio, n.m. defense garrison.

presièdere, vb. preside.

prèssa, n.f. press.

pressappòco, adv. about, approximately.

pressione, n.f. pressure.

prèsso a, prep. near; by.

prestare, vb. lend, loan.

prestìgio, n.m. prestige.

prèstito, n.m. loan.

prèsto, adv. soon, quickly; early.

presùmere, vb. presume.

presuntuosità, n.f. presumptuousness, forwardness.

presuntuoso, adj. presumptuous.

presunzione, n.f. presumption.

presupporre, vb. presuppose.

prète, n.m. priest.

pretèndere, vb. pretend; claim.

pretenzioso, adj. pretentious.

pretesa, n.f. pretense.

pretèsto, n.m. pretext.

prevalènte, adj. prevalent.

prevalere, vb. prevail.

prevedere, vb. foresee, forecast.

prevedìbile, adj. foreseeable.

preventivo, 1. n.m. estimate; budget; deterrent. **2.** adj. preventive.

prevenzione, n.f. prevention.

previdènza, n.f. foresight.

previsione, n.f. forecast.

prezioso, adj. precious, valuable.

prezzémolo, n.m. parsley.

prèzzo, n.m. price, charge; fare; rate.

prigione, n.f. prison, jail.

prigionìa, n.f. imprisonment, captivity.

prigionièro, n.m. and adj. prisoner, captive.

prima, 1. n. première. **2.** adv. first; before; beforehand. **p. che,** conj. before. **p. di,** prep. before.

primario, 1. adj. primary. **2.** n.m. head physician.

primato, n.m. record.

primavera, n.f. spring.

primaverile, adj. spring-like.

primitivo, adj. primitive; original.

primo, adj. first; foremost; prime.

primordiale, adj. primeval.

principale, adj. principal, chief, main, prime.

principalmente, adv. principally, chiefly, mainly.

principato, n.m. principality, princedom.

prìncipe, *n.m.* prince.

principesco, *adj.* princely, luxurious.

principessa, *n.f.* princess.

principiante, *n.m.* beginner.

principiare, *vb.* begin.

principio, *n.m.* beginning; principle.

priorità, *n.f.* priority.

prisma, *n.m.* prism.

privare, *vb.* deprive, bereave.

privato, *adj.* private.

privazione, *n.f.* deprivation.

privilègio, *n.m.* privilege.

privo, *adj.* devoid, void, lacking (in); destitute.

probàbile, *adj.* probable.

probabilità, *n.f.* probability, likelihood.

probante, *adj.* probatory, constituting evidence.

probità, *n.f.* probity.

problèma, *n.m.* problem.

probo, *adj.* upright.

procace, *adj.* forward; provoking.

procèdere, *vb.* proceed.

procedimento, *n.m.* proceeding; procedure.

procedura, *n.f.* procedure.

processare, *vb.* prosecute.

processione, *n.f.* procession.

procèsso, *n.m.* process; trial.

procione, *n.m.* racoon.

proclamare, *vb.* proclaim.

proclamazione, *n.f.* proclamation.

procrastinare, *vb.* procrastinate.

procreare, *vb.* procreate, generate.

procura, *n.f.* proxy.

procurare, *vb.* procure.

procuratore, *n.m.* attorney; proxy.

prode, *adj.* brave, gallant.

prodezza, *n.f.* prowess.

prodigalità, *n.f.* prodigality, extravagance.

prodigare, *vb.* lavish.

prodigio, *n.m.* prodigy.

pròdigo, *adj.* prodigal, extravagant, lavish.

proditòrio, *adj.* treacherous.

prodotto, *n.m.* product.

produrre, *vb.* produce.

produttivo, *adj.* productive.

produzione, *n.f.* production, output, yield.

profanare, *vb.* profane, defile.

profano, *adj.* profane.

proferire, *vb.* utter.

professare, *vb.* profess.

professionale, *adj.* professional.

professione, *n.f.* profession, calling, occupation.

professionista, *n.m.* professional; practitioner.

professore, *n.m.* professor.

profèta, *n.m.* prophet.

profètico, *adj.* prophetic.

profetizzare, *vb.* prophesy.

profezìa, *n.f.* prophecy.

profìcuo, *adj.* profitable.

profilassi, *n.f.* prophylaxis; prescribed cure.

profilàttico, *n.m.* condom.

profilo, *n.m.* profile.

profitto, *n.m.* profit.

proflùvio, *n.m.* overflow, flood; superabundance; *(pathology)* discharge.

profondamente, *adv.* deeply, profoundly.

profondità, *n.f.* profundity, depth.

profondo, *adj.* deep, profound; in-depth.

profumare, *vb.* perfume.

profumo, *n.m.* perfume, scent.

profuso, *adj.* profuse.

progettare, *vb.* project, plan.

progètto, *n.m.* project, plan, scheme. **p. di legge,** (legislative) bill.

prògnosi, *n.f.* prognosis.

programma, *n.m.* program.

progredire, *vb.* progress, advance.

progredito, *adj.* progressed; advanced.

progressione, *n.f.* progression.

progressivo, *adj.* progressive.

progrèsso, *n.m.* progress, headway.

proibire, *vb.* prohibit, forbid, ban.

proibitivo, *adj.* prohibitive.

proibizione, *n.f.* prohibition, band.

proiettare, *vb.* project.

proièttile, *n.m.* projectile.

proiettore, *n.m.* projector.

proiezione, *n.f.* projection.

pròle, *n.f.* offspring, issue.

proliferazione, *n.f.* proliferation.

prolìfico, *adj.* prolific.

pròlogo, *n.m.* prologue.

prolungamento, *n.m.* prolongation, extension.

prolungare, *vb.* prolong, extend.

promessa, *n.f.* promise.

prométtere, *vb.* promise.

prominènte, *adj.* prominent.

promìscuo, *adj.* promiscuous.

promontòrio, *n.m.* promontory.

promotore, *n.m.* promoter.

promozione, *n.f.* promotion.

promulgare, *vb.* promulgate.

promuòvere, *vb.* promote.

pronipote, *n.m.* great-grandchild; descendant.

prono, *adj.* prone; with the habit of.

pronome, *n.m.* pronoun.

pronosticare, *vb.* forecast.

prontamente, *adv.* readily.

pronto, 1. *adj.* ready; prompt; quick; willing. **2.** *interj.* (telephone) hello.

prontuàrio, *n.m.* handbook, reference book, manual.

pronùncia, *n.f.* pronunciation.

pronunciare, *vb.* pronounce.

propaganda, *n.f.* propaganda.

propagare, *vb.* propagate.

propaggine, *n.f.* ramification, physical appendix.

propèndere, *vb.* incline.

propensione, *n.f.* propensity.

propènso, *adj.* inclined.

propinare, *vb.* administer, give.

propìzio, *adj.* propitious, favorable.

proponènte, *n.m.* proponent.

proporre, *vb.* propose.

proporzionato, *adj.* proportionate.

proporzione, *n.f.* proportion.

propòsito, *n.m.* purpose. **a p.,** apropos. **di p.,** on purpose.

proposizione, *n.f.* sentence.

propòsta, *n.f.* proposal; proposition.

proprietà, *n.f.* property, belongings.

proprietàrio, *n.m.* proprietor.

pròprio, 1. *adj.* proper; own. **2.** *adv.* just; right; quite.

propugnare, *vb.* advocate.

propugnatore, *n.m.* advocate.

propugnazione, *n.f.* advocacy.

propulsione, *n.f.* propulsion.

pròra, *n.f.* prow, bow.

pròroga, *n.f.* delay; extension.

prorogare, *vb.* delay; extend.

prorómpere, *vb.* burst forth.

pròsa, *n.f.* prose.

prosàico, *adj.* prosaic.

prosciògliere, *vb.* set free; acquit, absolve.

prosciugare, *vb.* drain, dry up.

prosciutto, *n.m.* ham.

proscrivere, *vb.* proscribe.

prosecuzione, *n.f.* prosecution; continuation.

proseguimento, *n.m.* continuation.

proseguire, *vb.* continue, follow, carry on.

prosèlito, *n.m.* proselyte.

prosperare, *vb.* prosper, thrive.

prosperità, *n.f.* prosperity, boom.

pròspero, *adj.* prosperous.

prospettiva, *n.f.* perspective.

prospettivo, *adj.* prospective.

prospètto, *n.m.* prospect.

prossimità, *n.f.* proximity, nearness, closeness.

pròssimo, 1. *n.* neighbor. **2.** *adj.* next; nearest; forthcoming.

prostituta, *n.f.* prostitute.

prostrare, *vb.* prostrate.

prostrato, *adj.* prostrate.

protagonista, *n.m. and f.* protagonist.

protèggere, *vb.* protect, shield.

proteìna, *n.f.* protein.

protèndere, *vb.* stretch.

protèsta, *n.f.* protest.

protestante, *n.m. and adj.* Protestant.

protestantésimo, *n.m.* Protestantism.

protestare, *vb.* protest.

protettivo, *adj.* protective.

protettore, *n.m.* protector.

protezione, *n.f.* protection.

protocòllo, *n.m.* protocol.

protone, *n.m.* proton.

protòtipo, *n.m.* prototype.

protrarre, *vb.* protract.

protuberanza, *n.f.* protuberance, swelling, bulge, lump.

pròva, *n.f.* proof; test; ordeal; rehearsal; probation; trial. **p. conclusiva,** acid test. **p. generale,** dress rehearsal.

provare, *vb.* try; essay; rehearse; test.

proverbiale, *adj.* proverbial.

provèrbio, *n.m.* proverb, adage.

provìncia, *n.f.* province.

provinciale, *adj.* provincial.

provocante, *adj.* defiant.

provocare, *vb.* provoke.

provocazione, *n.f.* provocation.

provvedere, *vb.* provide, supply.

provvidènza, *n.f.* providence.

provvisòrio, *adj.* temporary, acting, interim.

provvista, *n.f.* provision; supply, store, stock.

prudènte, *adj.* prudent.

prudènza, *n.f.* prudence.

prùdere, *vb.* itch.

prudore, *n.m.* itch.

prugna, *n.f.* plum.

prurire, *vb.* itch.

prurito, *n.m.* itch.

pseudònimo, *n.m.* pseudonym.

psichedèlico, *adj.* psychedelic.

psichiatra, *n.m.* psychiatrist.

psichiatrìa, *n.f.* psychiatry.

psicoanàlisi, *n.f.* psychoanalysis.

psicologìa, *n.f.* psychology.

psicològico, *adj.* psychological.

psicòsi, *n.f.* psychosis.

ptomaìna, *n.f.* ptomaine.

pubblicare, *vb.* publish.

pubblicazione, *n.f.* publication.

pubblicità, *n.f.* publicity; advertising.

pubblicizzare, *v.b.* advertise.

pùbblico, *n. and adj.* public.

pubertà, *n.f.* puberty.

pudico, *adj.* reserved, demure; bashful.

pudore, *n.m.* decency; shame.

pugilato, *n.m.* boxing.

pugilatore, *n.m.* boxer.

pugilìstico, *adj.* pugilistic, fistic.

Pùglie, *n.f.pl.* Apulia.

pugliese, *adj.* Apulian.

pugnace, *adj.* pugnacious.

pugnalare, *vb.* stab.

pugnalata, *n.f.* stab.

pugnale, *n.m.* dagger.

pugno, *n.m.* fist; punch.

pula, *n.f.* chaff.

pulce, *n.f.* flea.

pulcino, *n.m.* chick.

puledro, *n.m.* colt.

puléggia, *n.f.* pulley.

pulire, *vb.* clean; polish. **p. a secco,** dry-clean.

pulito, *adj.* clean; polished.

pulitore, *n.m.* cleaner.

pulitura, *n.f.* cleaning. **p. a secco,** dry-cleaning.

pulizia, *n.f.* cleanliness.

pullman, *n.m.* de luxe bus.

pùlpito, *n.m.* pulpit.

pulsante, *n.m.* push button.

pùlsar, *n.m.* pulsar.

pulsare, *vb.* pulsate.

puma, *n.m.* cougar.

pungènte, *adj.* pungent, sharp, biting.

pùngere, *vb.* prick, sting.

pungiglione, *n.m.* sting.

pùngolo, *n.m.* goad.

punire, *vb.* punish, chastise.

punitivo, *adj.* punitive.

punizione, *n.f.* punishment, chastisement.

punta, *n.f.* tip.

puntare, *vb.* point; aim; wager, stake.

puntata, *n.f.* installment.

punteggiare, *vb.* punctuate.

punteggiatura, *n.f.* punctuation.

puntellare, *vb.* prop.

puntèllo, *n.m.* prop.

puntìglio, *n.m.* stubbornness, obstinacy.

puntina, *n.f.* needle.

punto, *n.m.* point; period; dot; stitch. **p. di vista,** viewpoint; standpoint. **due punti,** colon. **p. mòrto,** stalemate, deadlock. **p. esclamativo,** exclamation point. **p. e vìrgola,** semicolon.

puntuale, *adj.* punctual.

puntura, *n.f.* puncture; sting.

pupàttola, *n.f.* doll.
pupazzo, *n.m.* puppet.
pupillo, *n.m.* ward.
pupo, *n.m.* baby.
purchè, *conj.* provided that.
pure, 1. *too, also; even* **2.** *conj.* though.
purè, *n.m.* puree.
purezza, *n.f.* purity.
purga, *n.f.* purge.
purgante, *n.m. and adj.* purgative, laxative.
purgare, *vb.* purge.
purgativo, *adj.* cathartic.
purgatòrio, *n.m.* purgatory.

purificare, *vb.* purify.
purità, *n.f.* purity.
puritano, *adj.* puritan.
puro, *adj.* pure.
purpùreo, *adj.* purple.
putrefatto, *adj.* rotten, decayed.
putrefazione, *n.f.* rot.
pùtrido, *adj.* decayed, putrid, rotten; (egg) addled.
puttana, *n.f.* whore, tart.
puzzare, *vb.* stink, smell.
puzzo, *n.m.* stench, smell.
puzzolènte, *adj.* stinking, noisome.
puzzone, *n.m.* skunk.

Q

qua, *adv.* hither.
quadràngolo, *n.m.* quadrangle.
quadrante, *n.m.* quadrant; dial.
quadrare, *vb.* square.
quadrato, 1. *n.m.* square; ring. **2.** *adj.* square.
quadrifònico, *adj.* quadraphonic.
quadro, *n.m.* picture; table; cadre.
quadro generale, *n.m.* overview.
quadrùpede, *n.m.* quadruped.
quàglia, *n.f.* quail.
quagliare, *vb.* curdle.
quagliata, *n.f.* curd, clabber.
qualche, *adj.* some.
qualcosa, *pron.* something; anything.
qualcuno, *pron.* somebody; anybody.
quale, *adj.* which. **il q.,** which; who.
qualifica, *n.f.* qualification.
qualificare, *vb.* qualify.
qualificazione, *n.f.* qualification.
qualità, *n.f.* quality.
qualunque, *adj.* whatever; whichever.
quando, *adv.* when. **di q. in q.,** from time to time, occasionally.
quantità, *n.f.* quantity, amount.
quanto, *adj. and adv.* how much; how many. **in q. che,** in so far as.
quantunque, *conj.* although.
quaranta, *num.* forty.
quarantésimo, *adj.* fortieth.
quarantena, *n.f.* quarantine.

quarantotto, 1. *uproar, mess.* **2.** *num.* forty-eight.
quarésima, *n.f.* Lent.
quartetto, *n.m.* quartet.
quartière, *n.m.* quarter. **q. generale,** headquarters.
quarto, 1. *n.m.* quarter. **2.** *adj.* fourth.
quarzo, *n.m.* quartz.
quàsar, *n.m.* quasar.
quasi, 1. *adv.* almost, nearly. **2.** *conj.* as if.
quassù, *adv.* up here.
quatto, *adj.* crouching.
quatto quatto, *adv.* stealthily, silently.
quattòrdici, *num.* fourteen.
quattrini, *n.m.pl.* money.
quattro, *num.* four.
quegli, *adj.m.pl.* those.
quei, *adj.m.pl.* those.
quel, *adj.m.sg.* that.
quella, *adj. and pron. f.sg.* that.
quelle, *adj. and pron. f.pl.* those.
quelli, *pron.m.pl.* those.
quello, 1. *adj.* that. **2.** *pron.* that one; the former.
quèrcia, *n.f.* oak.
querela, *n.f.* lawsuit, complaint.
querelare, *vb.* sue.
quesito, *n.m.* question; query; problem.
questa, *adj. and pron. f.sg.* this.
queste, *adj. and pron. f.pl.* these.
questi, *adj. and pron. m.pl.* these.

quésti, *pron. m.sg.* this man.
questionàrio, *n.m.* questionnaire.
questióne, *n.f.* question.
quésto, 1. *adj.* this. **2.** *pron.* this one; the latter.
questóre, *n.m.* police commissioner.
quèstua, *n.f.* (church) collection.
questùra, *n.f.* police headquarters.
qui, *adv.* here.
quietànza, *n.f.* receipt.
quiète, *n.f.* quiet, stillness.
quièto, *adj.* quiet.
quìndi, *adv.* hence, therefore.
quindicésimo, *adj.* fifteenth.

quìndici, *num.* fifteen.
quindicinàle, *adj.* fortnightly, bimonthly.
quìnte, *n.f.pl.* **dietro le q.** backstage.
quintàle, *n.m.* 100 kilograms.
quintétto, *n.m.* quintet.
quìnto, *adj.* fifth.
quisquìlia, *n.f.* trifle.
quòta, *n.f.* quota; dues; fee.
quotazióne, *n.f.* quotation (of prices).
quotidianamènte, *adv.* daily.
quotidiàno, *n.m. and adj.* daily, everyday.
quoziènte, *n.m.* quotient.

R

rabàrbaro, *n.m.* rhubarb.
rabberciàre, *vb.* botch.
ràbbia, *n.f.* anger, rage; rabies.
rabbìno, *n.m.* rabbi.
rabbióso, *adj.* rabid.
rabbrividìre, *vb.* shudder; shiver.
raccapricciànte, *adj.* horryfying, bloodcurdling.
raccattàre, *vb.* pick up.
racchétta, *n.f.* racket.
raccògliere, *vb.* collect; gather; harvest, reap.
raccòlta, *n.f.* collection, gathering; harvest, crop.
raccòlto, *n.m.* crop, harvest.
raccomandàre, *vb.* recommend; commend.
raccomandazióne, *n.f.* recommendation.
raccontàre, *vb.* tell, narrate.
raccónto, *n.m.* story, tale, account, narrative.
raccorciaménto, *n.m.* abbreviation; shortening.
raccorciàre, *vb.* abbreviate; shorten.
raddrizzàre, *vb.* straighten.
ràdere, *vb.* shave.
radiatóre, *n.m.* radiator.
radicàle, *n.m. and adj.* radical.
radicchièlla, *n.f.* dandelion.
radìce, *n.f.* root.
ràdio, n. 1. *m.* radium. **2.** *f.* radio, wireless.
radioattìvo, *adj.* radio-active.

radiocorrière, *n.m.* radio news.
radiofònico, *adj.* radio.
radiotelemetrìa, *n.f.* radar.
radiotelèmetro, *n.m.* radar.
rado, *adj.* sparse.
radunàre, *vb.* gather; muster.
radùno, *n.m.* rally.
radùra, *n.f.* glade, clearing.
ràfano, *n.m.* horse-radish.
raffazzonaménto, *n.m.* reworking; patchwork.
raffèrmo, *adj.* stale.
ràffica, *n.f.* gust; squall; blast.
raffinàre, *vb.* refine.
raffinatézza, *n.f.* refinement.
ràffio, *n.m.* claw.
rafforzàre, *vb.* strengthen.
raffreddàre, *vb.* chill.
raffreddóre, *n.m.* cold.
raffrenàre, *vb.* restrain, curb.
ragàzza, *n.f.* girl, lass.
ragàzzo, *n.m.* boy, lad.
raggiànte, *adj.* radiant, beaming.
ràggio, *n.m.* spoke; ray, beam; shaft; radius.
raggiùngere, *vb.* arrive at, achieve, attain; reach; overtake.
raggiungìbile, *adj.* attainable.
raggiungiménto, *n.m.* achievement, attainment.
raggrumàrsi, *vb.* clot.
raggruppaménto, *n.m.* grouping.
raggruppàre, *vb.* group.
ragguàglio, *n.m.* report; information.

ragionamento, *n.m.* reasoning, argument.

ragionare, *vb.* reason; talk.

ragione, *n.f.* reason. **aver r.,** be right.

ragioneria, *n.f.* accounting.

ragionévole, *adj.* reasonable.

ragionière, *n.m.* accountant.

ragliare, *vb.* bray.

raglio, *n.m.* bray.

ragnatela, *n.f.* cobweb.

ragno, *n.m.* spider.

ragù, *n.m.* meat sauce.

ràion, *n.m.* rayon.

rallegrare, *vb.* cheer up, rejoice.

rallentare, *vb.* slow down, slacken.

ramaiuòlo, *n.m.* ladle, scoop.

ramanzina, *n.f.* scolding.

rame, *n.m.* copper.

rammendare, *vb.* mend, darn.

rammendo, *n.m.* mend, darn.

rammentare, *vb.* remind; *(refl.)* recollect.

ramingo, *adj.* wandering, roving.

rammaricare, *vb. (refl.)* regret, be sorry.

rammollito, *adj.* soft-headed, imbecile.

ramo, *n.m.* branch, bough, limb.

ramolàccio, *n.m.* radish.

ramoscèllo, *n.m.* twig; sprig.

rana, *n.f.* frog.

ràncido, *adj.* rancid.

ràncio, *n.m.* mess.

rancore, *n.m.* rancor.

randellare, *vb.* bludgeon, cudgel, club.

randello, *n.m.* bludgeon, cudgel.

rango, *n.m.* rank.

rannicchiarsi, *vb.* huddle.

rannuvolarsi, *vb.* cloud over.

ranòcchio, *n.m.* frog.

ràntolo, *n.m.* rattle.

ranùncolo, *n.m.* buttercup.

rapa, *n.f.* turnip.

rapare, *vb.* shave.

rapidamente, *vb.* rapidly, quickly, fast.

ràpido, 1. *n.m.* limited (train). **2.** *adj.* rapid, fast, quick, speedy.

rapimento, *n.m.* abduction, kidnapping.

rapina, *n.f.* rapine, plunder. **uccèllo di r.,** *n.m.* bird of prey.

rapire, *vb.* abduct, kidnap.

rapitore, *n.m.* abductor, kidnapper.

rappacificare, *vb.* reconcile; pacify.

rappezzare, *vb.* patch.

rappòrto, *n.m.* relation; report; rapport; ratio; intercourse.

rapprendere, *vb.* congeal.

rappresàglia, *n.f.* reprisal, retaliation.

rappresentare, *vb.* represent; perform.

rappresentativo, *adj.* representative.

rappresentazione, *n.f.* representation; performance.

raramente, *adv.* rarely, seldom.

rarità, *n.f.* rarity, scarcity.

raro, *adj.* rare.

raschiare, *vb.* scrape; scratch out; erase.

raschino, *n.m.* eraser.

rasente, *adv.* close, near.

rasentare, *vb.* skirt, skim.

raso, *n.m.* satin.

rasòio, *n.m.* razor.

rassegna, *n.f.* review; exhibition.

rassegnarsi, *vb.* resign oneself.

rassegnazione, *n.f.* resignation.

rassicurare, *vb.* reassure.

rassomigliare, *vb.* resemble.

rastrellare, *vb.* rake.

rastrellièra, *n.f.* rack.

rastrèllo, *n.m.* rake.

rata, *n.f.* installment.

ratificare, *vb.* ratify.

ratto, *n.m.* rat; abduction.

rattoppare, *vb.* patch.

rattristare, *vb.* sadden.

ràuco, *adj.* hoarse, raucous.

ravanèllo, *n.m.* radish.

ravvivamento, *n.m.* revival.

ravvivare, *vb.* enliven; revive.

razionale, *adj.* rational.

razionare, *vb.* ration.

razione, *n.f.* ration.

razza, *n.f.* race, breed, kind.

razzo, *n.m.* rocket.

re, *n.m.* king.

reagire, *vb.* react.

reale, *adj.* real; royal.

realista, *n.m.* realist.

realizzare, *vb.* realize; fulfill.

realizzazione, *n.f.* realization; fulfillment.

realmente, *adv.* really.

realtà, *n.f.* reality.

reame, *n.m.* realm.

reattore, *n.m.* reactor; jet.

reazionàrio, *adj.* reactionary.

reazione, *n.f.* reaction.

recare, *vb.* reach; hand (over); *(refl.)* go, betake oneself.

recèdere, *vb.* recede.

recensione, *n.f.* review.

recensire, *vb.* review.

recènte, *adj.* recent; latter.

recentemente, *adv.* recently, lately.

recinto, *n.m.* enclosure, fence.

recipiènte, *n.m.* vessel; beaker; bin; container; holder.

recitare, *vb.* act; play; recite.

recitazione, *n.f.* recitation; acting.

reclamante, *n.m.* claimant.

reclamare, *vb.* claim.

réclame, *n.f.* advertising.

reclamizzare, *vb.* advertise.

reclamo, *n.m.* claim.

reclinare, *vb.* recline.

reclusione, *n.f.* seclusion; confinement; imprisonment.

recluso, 1. *adj.* secluded. **2.** *n.m.* recluse, prisoner.

rècluta, *n.f.* recruit.

reclutare, *vb.* recruit.

recòndito, *adj.* concealed, hidden.

recriminare, *vb.* recriminate; complain.

redditìzio, *adj.* lucrative, profitable.

rèddito, *n.m.* income.

redentore, *n.m.* redeemer.

redenzione, *n.f.* redemption.

redìgere, *vb.* draw up, draft; edit.

redìmere, *vb.* redeem, reclaim.

rèdina, *n.f.* rein.

regalare, *vb.* present.

regale, *adj.* regal.

regalità, *n.f.* royalty.

regalo, *n.m.* present.

reggènte, *n.m.* regent.

règgere, *vb.* hold up; wield.

reggimento, *n.m.* regiment.

reggipètto, *n.m.* brassière.

reggiseno, *n.m.* brassière.

regime, *n.m.* regime, rule; diet.

regina, *n.f.* queen.

règio, *adj.* royal.

regione, *n.f.* region.

registrare, *vb.* register; record; (luggage) check.

registratore a filo, *n.m.* wire recorder.

registratore magnètico, *n.m.* tape recorder.

registrazione, *n.f.* registration.

registro, *n.m.* register; record.

regnare, *vb.* reign, rule.

regno, *n.m.* kingdom, realm, reign.

régola, *n.f.* rule; *(pl.)* menstruation.

regolamento, *n.m.* regulation.

regolare, 1. *adj.* regular. **2.** *vb.* regulate, rule; set.

regolarità, *n.f.* regularity.

regolatore, *n.m.* regulator.

régolo, *n.m.* ruler. **r. calcolatore,** slide-rule.

regredire, *vb.* regress.

reiètto, *n.m.* outcast.

reincarnare, *vb.* reincarnate.

reintegrare, *vb.* restore, reinstate.

reiterare, *vb.* reiterate.

relatività, *n.f.* relativity.

relativo, *adj.* relative.

relazione, *n.f.* relation; liaison.

relè, *n.m.* relay.

relegare, *vb.* banish; relegate.

religione, *n.f.* religion.

religioso, *adj.* religious.

relìquia, *n.f.* relic.

remare, *vb.* row.

remata, *n.f.* row.

reminiscènza, *n.f.* reminiscence.

remissivo, *adj.* submissive.

remo, *n.m.* oar, paddle.

rèmora, *n.f.* hindrance; impediment.

remòto, *adj.* remote.

rena, *n.f.* sand.

rèndere, *vb.* render; give back. **r. conto di,** account for.

rendiconto, *n.m.* statement.

rendimento, *n.m.* output.

rène, *n.f.* kidney.

reniforme, *adj.* kidney-shaped.

renitente, *adj.* reluctant, unwilling. **r. alla leva,** draft dodger.

rènna, *n.f.* reindeer.

renoso, *adj.* sandy.
repellènte, *adj.* repulsive.
reperto, *n.m.* finding, evidence.
repentino, *adj.* sudden, unexpected.
reperìbile, *adj.* to be found; available; recoverable.
repertòrio, *n.m.* repertoire.
rèplica, *n.f.* reply, rejoinder; repeat performance.
replicare, *vb.* reply, rejoin; repeat.
repressione, *n.f.* repression.
reprìmere, *vb.* repress.
repùbblica, *n.f.* republic; commonwealth.
repubblicano, *adj.* republican.
repulsivo, *adj.* repulsive; forbidding.
reputare, *vb.* consider, deem.
requisire, *vb.* requisition, commandeer.
requisito, *n.m.* requirement, qualification.
requisizione, *n.f.* requisition.
rescìndere, *vb.* rescind.
residènte, *adj.* resident.
residènza, *n.f.* residence.
residuo, *n.m.* residue.
rèsina, *n.f.* rosin.
resistènza, *n.f.* resistance.
resìstere, *vb.* resist.
respingènte, *n.m.* bumper, buffer.
respìngere, *vb.* reject, repel, repulse.
respirare, *vb.* breathe.
respirazione, *n.f.* respiration.
respiro, *n.m.* breath, breathing.
responsàbile, *adj.* responsible, accountable, answerable, liable; amenable.
responsabilità, *n.f.* responsibility, liability.
responsivo, *adj.* responsive.
restare, *vb.* remain, stay.
restaurare, *vb.* restore.
restaurazione, *n.f.* restoration.
restituìre, *vb.* restore; refund.
restituzione, *n.f.* restitution.
rèsto, *n.m.* remainder, remnant; change.
restrìngere, *vb.* restrict.
restrizione, *n.f.* restriction.
retàggio, *n.m.* inheritance.
retata, *n.f.* roundup.

rete, *n.f.* net; netting; network.
reticèlla, *n.f.* luggage rack.
reticènte, *adj.* reticent.
reticènza, *n.f.* reticence.
reticolato, *n.m.* grid; barbed wire.
rètina, *n.f.* retina.
retràttile, *adj.* retractable.
retribuzione, *n.f.* retribution.
retroattivo, *adj.* retroactive.
retrocèdere, *vb.* recede, retreat.
retroguàrdia, *n.f.* rear-guard.
retroscèna, *n.m.* backstage.
retrospettivo, *adj.* retrospective.
retrotèrra, *n.f.* hinterland.
retrovisore, *adj.* **specchio r.,** rear-view mirror.
rettàngolo, *n.m.* rectangle.
rettificare, *vb.* rectify.
rettificatrice, *n.f.* rectifier.
rèttile, *n.m.* reptile.
rettilìneo, *n.m.* straightaway.
rètto, *adj.* straight.
retorica, *n.f.* rhetoric.
retorico, *adj.* rhetorical.
reumàtico, *adj.* rheumatic.
reumatismo, *n.m.* rheumatism.
reverèndo, *adj.* reverend.
revisione, *n.f.* revision.
revisore, *n.m.* (accounts) auditor; (proof) proof-reader.
rèvoca, *n.f.* revocation.
revocare, *vb.* revoke.
riabilitare, *vb.* rehabilitate.
rialzo, *n.m.* rise; raise.
rianimare, *vb.* revive; cheer up.
riarmo, *n.m.* rearmament.
riassùmere, *vb.* make a résumé of, summarize.
riassunto, *n.m.* abstract, résumé.
ribadire, *vb.* rivet.
ribalta, *n.f.* footlights.
ribàttere, *vb.* retort.
ribellarsi, *vb.* rebel, revolt.
ribèlle, 1. *n.m.* rebel, insurgent. **2.** *adj.* rebellious, insurgent; refractory.
ribellione, *n.f.* rebellion.
ribes, *n.m.* gooseberry; currant.
ribrezzo, *n.m.* disgust.
ricadere, *vb.* relapse.
ricaduta, *n.f.* relapse.
ricamare, *vb.* embroider.
ricambiare, *vb.* reciprocate, retaliate.

ricàmbio, *n.m.* exchange. **di r.,** spare.

ricamo, *n.m.* embroidery.

ricapitolare, *vb.* recapitulate, sum up.

ricaricare, *vb.* reload.

ricattare, *vb.* blackmail.

ricattatore, *n.m.* blackmailer, extortioner.

ricatto, *n.m.* blackmail.

ricavato, *n.m.* proceeds; yield.

ricchezza, *n.f.* riches, wealth.

riccio, *n.m.* hedgehog.

ricciolo, *n.m.* curl.

ricciuto, *adj.* curly.

ricco, *adj.* rich, wealthy.

ricerca, *n.f.* search, quest; research.

ricercare, *vb.* search.

ricercato, *adj.* recherché; far-fetched.

ricètta, *n.f.* recipe.

ricettàcolo, *n.m.* receptacle.

ricettivo, *adj.* receptive.

ricevènte, *n.m.* recipient.

ricévere, *vb.* receive, get.

ricevimento, *n.m.* reception; party.

ricevitore, *n.m.* receiver.

ricevitorìa, *n.f.* collection office.

ricevuta, *n.f.* receipt.

richiamare, *vb.* recall.

richiedènte, *n.m.* applicant.

richièdere, *vb.* request, ask for; demand; entail; require.

richièsta, *n.f.* request; demand.

riciclare, *vb.* recycle.

rìcino, *n.m.* castor oil.

recognitore, *n.m.* scout.

ricognizione, *n.f.* reconnaissance; acknowledgment.

ricolmo, *adj.* full (of liquid).

ricompènsa, *n.f.* recompense, reward.

ricompensare, *vb.* recompense, reward.

riconciliare, *vb.* reconcile.

ricondurre, *vb.* bring back; take back; lead back.

ricongiùngersi, *vb.* rejoin.

riconoscenza, *n.f.* gratitude.

riconóscere, *vb.* recognize; acknowledge.

riconoscimento, *n.m.* recognition.

ricordare, *vb.* remember, recollect.

ricòrdo, *n.m.* remembrance, souvenir, keepsake, memento; record.

ricórrere, *vb.* recur; resort; have recourse.

ricorso, *n.m.* recourse; resort.

ricostruire, *vb.* reconstruct, rebuild.

ricoverare, *vb.* shelter; hospitalize.

ricòvero, *n.m.* shelter; hospitalization.

ricuperare, *vb.* recover, recuperate; retrieve.

ricùpero, *n.m.* recovery.

ridacchiare, *vb.* giggle, chortle.

rìdere, *vb.* laugh.

ridìcolo, **1.** *n.* ridicule. **2.** *adj.* ridiculous, laughable, ludicrous.

ridire, *vb.* say again.

ridòsso, **1.** *n.m.* shelter. **2.** *adv.* **a r.** adjacent to a bigger object or thing.

ridotto, *n.m.* redoubt; foyer.

ridurre, *vb.* reduce, curtail; (music) arrange.

riduttore, *n.m.* adapter.

riduzione, *n.f.* reduction; (music) arrangement.

rielezione, *n.f.* reelection.

riempire, *vb.* fill.

rientranza, *n.f.* recess.

rièntro, *n.m.* reentry; recess.

riepilogo, *n.m.* recapitulation, summary.

riesame, *n.m.* review.

riesaminare, *vb.* re-examine, review.

riesumare, *vb.* exhume; bring back.

rievocare, *vb.* recall, reminisce.

riferimento, *n.m.* reference.

riferire, *vb.* refer; *(refl.)* relate.

riffa, *n.f.* raffle.

rifiutare, *vb.* refuse, decline.

rifiuto, *n.m.* refusal.

rifiuti, *n.m.pl.* refuse, garbage. **r. nucleari,** nuclear waste.

riflessione, *n.f.* reflection.

riflèsso, *n.m.* reflection, glint; reflex.

riflèttere, *vb.* reflect.

rifluire, vb. ebb.
riflusso, n.m. ebb.
riforma, n.f. reform, reformation.
riformare, vb. reform.
rifuggire, vb. shrink.
rifugiarsi, vb. take refuge.
rifugiato, n.m. refugee.
rifùgio, n.m. refuge, shelter, asylum, haven.
riga, n.f. line, file, row.
rigàglie, n.f.pl. giblets.
rigettare, vb. reject.
righello, n.m. ruler.
rigidezza, n.f. rigidity, stiffness.
rìgido, adj. rigid, stiff.
rigo, n.m. line; staff.
rigoglioso, adj. luxuriant.
rigore, n.m. rigor.
rigoroso, adj. rigorous, stringent.
riguardare, vb. regard, concern.
riguardo, n.m. regard. **r. a,** regarding.
rilanciare, vb. toss back; throw again; raise (poker).
rilasciare, vb. release.
rilassamento, n.m. relaxation, laxity.
rilassato, adj. relaxed, lax.
rilegare, vb. bind.
rilegatura, n.f. binding.
rilevamento, n.m. survey.
rilevante, adj. relevant, germane.
rilièvo, n.m. relief; remark; prominence.
rilucènte, adj. shiny, lustrous.
riluttante, adj. reluctant, loath.
riluttanza, n.f. reluctance.
rima, n.f. rhyme.
rimandare, vb. postpone, put off.
rimando, n.m. reference.
rimanènte, n.m. remainder, rest.
rimanere, vb. remain, stay, abide.
rimarchévole, adj. noteworthy, remarkable.
rimasùglio, n.m. residues, leftovers.
rimare, vb. rhyme.
rimbalzare, vb. bounce, rebound.
rimbalzo, n.m. bounce, rebound.
rimbambimento, n.m. dotage.
rimbambirsi, vb. grow childish (in old age).
rimbeccare, vb. retort.
rimboccare, vb. tuck.
rimbombo, n.m. loud noise; echo.

rimborsare, vb. reimburse, repay.
rimborso, n.m. repayment, reimbursement.
rimediare, vb. remedy.
rimèdio, n.m. remedy.
rimestare, vb. stir.
rìmmel, n.m. mascara.
rimèttere, vb. put back; remit; reinstate; (refl.) get back.
rimodernare, vb. modernize, renovate.
rimorchiare, vb. tow.
rimorchiatore, n.m. tugboat.
rimòrchio, n.m. trailer.
rimorso, n.m. remorse.
rimozione, n.f. removal.
rimpatriare, vb. repatriate.
rimpiàngere, vb. regret.
rimpianto, n.m. regret.
rimpiazzare, vb. replace.
rimpinzare, vb. cram, stuff.
rimproverare, vb. reprove, chide, rebuke, reproach, reprimand, upbraid.
rimpròvero, n.m. rebuke, reproof, reproach, reprimand.
rimuòvere, vb. remove.
rinàscere, vb. be reborn.
rinascimento, n.m. renaissance.
rinàscita, n.f. rebirth.
rinato, adj. born-again.
rinchiùdere, vb. enclose.
rincréscere, vb. cause regret.
rincrescimento, n.m. regret.
rinforzare, vb. reinforce.
rinfòrzo, n.m. reinforcement.
rinfrescare, vb. cool; refresh; freshen.
ringhiare, vb. snarl.
ringhièra, n.f. railing, banister.
rìnghio, n.m. snarl.
ringiovanire, vb. rejuvenate.
ringraziare, vb. thank.
rinnovamento, n.m. renewal.
rinnovare, vb. renew.
rinoceronte, n.m. rhinoceros.
rinomanza, n.f. renown.
rinomato, adj. renowned.
rintocco, n.m. knell.
rintanare, vb. (refl.) hide.
rintontire, vb. stun, daze.
rintracciare, vb. trace.
rinùncia, n.f. waiver.
rinunciare, vb. renounce, forego; waive.

rinviare, vb. postpone; send back.

rinvio, n.m. postponement.

rione, n.m. ward.

ripagare, vb. repay.

riparare, vb. repair, recondition.

riparazione, n.f. repair, reparation, redress.

ripètere, vb. repeat.

ripetizione, n.f. repetition.

ripetutamente, adv. repeatedly, again and again.

ripiano, n.m. ledge.

rìpido, adj. steep; abrupt.

ripièno, 1. n.m. stuffing. **2.** adj. stuffed.

riposante, adj. restful.

riposare, vb. rest, repose.

ripòso, n.m. repose, rest, leisure.

ripostiglio, n.m. closet.

riprèndere, vb. retake; resume; reprehend.

ripresa, n.f. revival; (music) repeat.

ripristinare, vb. reestablish; restore.

riprodurre, vb. reproduce.

riproduzione, n.f. reproduction.

riproduzione esatta, n.f. clone.

ripudiare, vb. repudiate.

ripùdio, n.m. repudiation.

ripugnante, adj. repugnant, abhorrent.

ripugnanza, n.f. repugnance, abhorrence, loathing.

ripulsa, n.f. rebuff, repulse.

risàia, n.f. rice field.

risanare, vb. heal.

risata, n.f. burst of laughter.

risatina, n.f. snicker.

riscaldare, vb. warm up, heat; (refl.) warm oneself; bask.

riscattare, vb. ransom.

riscatto, n.m. ransom.

rischiare, vb. risk, hazard; stake; venture.

rìschio, n.m. risk, hazard, venture.

rischioso, adj. risky, hazardous.

risciacquare, vb. rinse.

riscossa, n.f. insurrection; recovery; counterattack.

riscossione, n.f. collection.

riscuòtere, vb. shake; collect; cash.

riserbo, n.m. discretion.

risèrva, n.f. reserve.

riservare, vb. reserve.

riservato, adj. reserved, aloof.

risièdere, vb. reside.

riso, n.m. laughter; rice.

risolino, n.m. giggle.

risoluto, adj. resolute, determined.

risoluzione, n.f. resolution.

risòlvere, vb. resolve, solve.

resolvibile, adj. solvable.

risonante, adj. resonant.

risonanza, n.f. resonance.

risonare, vb. resound, ring out.

risorgènte, adj. resurgent.

risorsa, n.f. resource.

risparmiare, vb. save.

rispàrmio, n.m. saving(s).

rispettàbile, adj. respectable.

rispettare, vb. respect.

rispettivo, adj. respective.

rispètto, n.m. respect, regard.

rispettoso, adj. respectful.

risplendènte, adj. resplendent, beaming, effulgent.

risplèndere, vb. be resplendent, shine, beam, glitter.

rispóndere, vb. answer, respond, reply.

risposta, n.f. answer, response, reply.

rissa, n.f. brawl, fight, affray.

rissoso, adj. quarrelsome.

ristagnare, vb. stagnate.

ristorante, n.m. restaurant.

ristorare, vb. restore, refresh.

ristoratore, n.m. restaurant.

ristòro, n.m. refreshment.

risultare, vb. result; appear; be evident.

risultato, n.m. result, outgrowth.

risurrezione, n.f. resurrection.

risvegliare, vb. rouse.

risvòlta, n.f. lapel.

ritaglio, n.m. clipping, cutting.

ritardare, vb. delay, retard.

ritardo, n.m. delay, lag. **in r.,** delayed, late.

ritenere, vb. retain.

ritenzione, n.f. retention.

ritirare, vb. retire, withdraw; (refl.) retreat, pull back, back out; flinch.

ritirata, n.f. retreat; toilet.

rìtmico, *adj.* rhythmical.
ritmo, *n.m.* rhythm.
rito, *n.m.* rite.
ritornare, *vb.* return; revert.
ritorno, *n.m.* return.
ritrarre, *vb.* retract, pull back.
ritrasméttere, *vb.* relay.
ritrattare, *vb.* portray; retract.
ritratto, *n.m.* portrait.
ritroso, *adj.* unwilling, balky.
ritrovare, *vb.* find, discover; regain.
ritrovato, *n.m.* finding.
ritròvo, *n.m.* meeting-place, hangout. **r. notturno,** cabaret.
rituale, *n.m.* and *adj.* ritual.
riunione, *n.f.* reunion; meeting, assembly.
riunire, *vb.* reunite; join; assemble; *(refl.)* meet, foregather.
riuscire, *vb.* succeed; turn out.
riuscita, *n.f.* success.
riuscito, *adj.* successful.
riva, *n.f.* bank; strand.
rivale, *n.* and *adj.* rival.
rivaleggiare, *vb.* rival.
rivalità, *n.f.* rivalry.
rivalsa, *n.f.* revenge.
rivangare, *vb.* dig up; mull over.
rivedere, *vb.* see again; review.
rivelare, *vb.* reveal, disclose.
rivelazione, *n.f.* revelation, disclosure, exposure.
rivendicare, *vb.* claim; demand.
riverberare, *vb.* reverberate.
riverbero, *n.m.* glare.
riverènte, *adj.* reverent.
riverènza, *n.f.* reverence; bow, curtsy, obeisance.
riverire, *vb.* revere.
rivestitura, *n.f.* facing.
rivista, *n.f.* magazine; review; revue; musical comedy; muster.
rivòlgere, *vb.* turn to; address; turn around.
rivòlta, *n.f.* revolt.
rivoltare, *vb.* revolt.
rivoltèlla, *n.f.* revolver.
rivoluzionàrio, *adj.* revolutionary.
rivoluzione, *n.f.* revolution.
ròba, *n.f.* stuff. **r. da chiòdi,** junk; nonsense.
robustezza, *n.f.* hardiness.

robusto, *adj.* robust, strong, hardy, hale, stalwart, sturdy.
ròcca, *n.f.* fortress; rock.
roccafòrte, *n.f.* stronghold.
rocchetto, *n.m.* reel; spool.
ròccia, *n.f.* rock.
roccioso, *adj.* rocky.
rock, *n.m.* and *adj.* rock (music).
rodàggio, *n.m.* breaking in (period).
ródere, *vb.* gnaw, champ.
roditore, *n.m.* rodent.
rollìo, *n.m.* roll (of ship).
Roma, *n.f.* Rome.
romano, *adj.* Roman.
romàntico, *adj.* romantic.
romanzière, *n.m.* novelist.
romanzo, *n.m.* novel; romance.
rombo, *n.m.* roar.
romitàggio, *n.m.* hermitage.
rómpere, *vb.* break.
rompìbile, *adj.* breakable.
rompicapo, *n.m.* puzzle.
rompicollo, *adv.* **a r.,** breakneck.
rompistàcole, *n.m.* pest.
róndine, *n.f.* swallow.
ronzare, *vb.* buzz, drone; hum.
ronzino, *n.m.* nag.
ronzìo, *n.m.* buzz, drone, hum.
ròsa, 1. *n.f.* rose. **2.** *adj.* pink.
rosàrio, *n.m.* rosary.
ròseo, *adj.* rosy.
roseto, *n.m.* rose garden.
rosicchiare, *vb.* nibble, gnaw.
rosolare, *vb.* brown, sauté.
rosolìa, *n.f.* German measles.
rospo, *n.m.* toad.
rossetto, *n.m.* lipstick; rouge.
rosso, *adj.* red.
rossore, *n.m.* blush.
rosticceria, *n.f.* grillroom.
rotàia, *n.f.* rail.
rotatòrio, *adj.* rotatory.
rotazione, *n.f.* rotation.
rotèlla, *n.f.* roller. **r. del ginòcchio,** knee-cap.
rotolare, *vb.* roll.
ròtolo, *n.m.* roll; scroll.
rotondo, *adj.* round.
rotta, *n.f.* rout.
rottame, *n.m.* scrap, wreck.
rotto, *adj.* broken.
rottura, *n.f.* break, breakage; rupture.

ròtula, *n.f.* kneecap.

rovesciare, *vb.* reverse; spill.

rovèscio, *n.m.* reverse; downpour. **a r.**, backhand.

rovina, *n.f.* ruin, downfall, wreck.

rovinare, *vb.* ruin, wreck.

rovinoso, *adj.* ruinous.

rovente, *adj.* red-hot.

ròvo, *n.m.* briar.

rozzo, *adj.* rough.

rubacchiare, *vb.* pilfer.

rubare, *vb.* rob, steal, burglarize, filch.

rubicondo, *adj.* rubicund, ruddy, florid.

rubinetto, *n.m.* faucet, tap; cock.

rubino, *n.m.* ruby.

rude, *adj.* rude, rough, curt, abrupt, blunt.

rùdere, *n.m.* ruin.

rudezza, *n.f.* roughness, curtness, abruptness.

rudimento, *n.m.* rudiment.

ruga, *n.f.* wrinkle.

rùggine, *n.f.* rust.

rugginoso, *adj.* rusty.

ruggire, *vb.* roar.

ruggito, *n.m.* roar.

rugiada, *n.f.* dew.

rugiadoso, *adj.* dewy.

rullare, *vb.* roll.

rullìo, *n.m.* roll.

rullo, *n.m.* roller.

ruminare, *vb.* chew the cud.

rumore, *n.m.* noise, clatter, din.

rumoroso, *adj.* noisy, blatant.

ruòlo, *n.m.* list, roll; rôle.

ruòta, *n.f.* wheel.

ruotare, *vb.* rotate.

rupe, *n.f.* cliff, rock.

rurale, *adj.* rural.

ruscèllo, *n.m.* brook.

ruspa, *n.f.* excavator.

ruspante, *adj.* scratching about. **pollo r.**, barnyard chicken.

russare, *vb.* snore.

Rùssia, *n.f.* Russia.

russo, *adj.* Russian.

rùstico, *n.m. and adj.* rustic.

ruttare, *vb.* belch.

rutto, *n.m.* belch.

rùvido, *adj.* rough.

S

sàbato, *n.m.* Saturday.

sàbbia, *n.f.* sand; grit.

sabbiature, *n.f.pl.* sand baths.

sabbioso, *adj.* sandy.

sabotàggio, *n.m.* sabotage.

sabotare, *vb.* sabotage.

sabotatore, *n.m.* saboteur.

saccarina, *n.f.* saccharine.

saccarino, *adj.* saccharine.

saccheggiare, *vb.* sack, pillage, plunder.

sacchèggio, *n.m.* sack, pillage.

sacco, *n.m.* sack, bag. **s. ad aria**, (automobile) airbag. **s. da montagna**, backpack.

sacerdote, *n.m.* clergyman.

sacramento, *n.m.* sacrament.

sacrificare, *vb.* sacrifice.

sacrificio, *n.m.* sacrifice.

sacrilègio, *n.m.* sacrilege.

sacrìlego, *adj.* sacrilegious.

sacro, *adj.* sacred.

sadismo, *n.m.* sadism.

saétta, *n.f.* stroke of lightning.

sagace, *adj.* sagacious.

saggezza, *n.f.* wisdom.

saggiare, *vb.* sample, try, assay, test.

sàggio, 1. *n.m.* essay; sample, specimen; assay, test. 2. *adj.* wise, sage.

saggista, *n.m.* essayist.

sàgoma, *n.f.* loading gauge.

sagrestano, *n.m.* sacristan, sexton.

sagrestìa, *n.f.* sacristy, vestry.

sàio, *n.m.* habit (of monk), frock.

saia, *n.f.* denim.

sala, *n.f.* hall; room.

salame, *n.m.* salami; bologna.

salamòia, *n.f.* pickle.

salare, *vb.* salt.

salàrio, *n.m.* wages.

salato, *adj.* salty; briny.

saldare, *vb.* solder; (comm.) settle; balance.

saldatura, *n.f.* solder.

saldo, 1. *n.m.* (comm.) balance. 2. *adj.* steady, steadfast.

sale, *n.m.* salt.

sàlice, *n.m.* willow.
saliente, *adj.* salient.
salire, *vb.* go up, ascend, mount.
saliscendi, *n.m.* latch.
salita, *n.f.* ascent.
saliva, *n.f.* saliva.
salma, *n.f.* corpse, body.
salmastro, *adj.* briny, salty.
salmì, *n.m.* **in s.,** in a stew.
salmo, *n.m.* psalm.
salmone, *n.m.* salmon.
salone, *n.m.* salon; lounge.
salottino, *n.m.* boudoir.
salòtto, *n.m.* parlor.
salpare, *vb.* set sail.
salsa, *n.f.* sauce.
salsedine, *n.f.* airborne saltiness.
salsiccia, *n.f.* sausage.
salsiera, *n.f.* gravy boat.
salso, *adj.* salt, salty.
saltare, *vb.* jump, leap, bound, hop, gambol, skip, spring, vault.
saltimbanco, *n.m.* acrobat, tumbler; street performer.
salto, *n.m.* jump, leap, bound, hop, gambol, spring, vault. **s. mortale,** somersault.
saltuàrio, *adj.* desultory.
salubre, *adj.* salubrious, healthful.
salumeria, *n.f.* pork butcher shop; delicatessen.
salutare, 1. *adj.* salutary, beneficial. **2.** *vb.* greet, salute, hail.
salutazione, *n.f.* salutation.
salute, *n.f.* health.
saluto, *n.m.* greeting, salute, salutation.
salvagente, *n.m.* life-buoy; lifepreserver. **isolòtto s.,** safety island.
salvare, *vb.* save, salvage.
salvaguardare, *vb.* safeguard.
salvaguàrdia, *n.f.* safeguard.
salvatàggio, *n.m.* salvage.
salvatore, *n.m.* savior.
salvezza, *n.f.* salvation.
sàlvia, *n.f.* sage.
salvo, 1. *adj.* safe. **2.** *prep.* except, but, save.
sambuco, *n.m.* elder tree.
sanatòrio, *n.m.* sanatorium.
sàndalo, *n.m.* sandal.
sangue, *n.m.* blood; gore.
sanguinare, *vb.* bleed.

sanguinàrio, *adj.* bloodthirsty, sanguinary.
sanguinoso, *adj.* bloody.
sanguisuga, *n.f.* leech.
sanità, *n.f.* sanity.
sanitàrio, *adj.* sanitary.
sano, *adj.* healthy, sound, sane, wholesome.
santificare, *vb.* sanctify, hallow.
santità, *n.f.* holiness, sanctity.
santo, 1. *n.* saint. **2.** *adj.* holy, sainted.
santuàrio, *vb.* sanctuary, shrine.
sanzionare, *vb.* sanction.
sanzione, *n.f.* sanction.
sapere, *vb.* know; know how to; savor, taste.
sapiente, 1. *adj.* sage; wise. **2.** *n.m.* wise man.
sapone, *n.m.* soap.
sapore, *n.m.* taste, flavor, savor.
saporito, *adj.* savory, tasty.
saporoso, *adj.* tasty, luscious.
sarcasmo, *n.m.* sarcasm.
sarcàstico, *adj.* sarcastic.
sarcòfago, *n.m.* sarcophagus.
Sardegna, *n.f.* Sardinia.
sardèlla, sardina, *n.f.* sardine.
sardo, *adj.* Sardinian.
sarta, *n.f.* dressmaker.
sarto, *n.m.* tailor.
sassata, *n.f.* throwing of a stone; pelt of a stone.
sasso, *n.m.* rock, boulder, stone.
sassoso, *adj.* stony.
Satana, *n.m.* Satan.
satanasso, *n.m.* devil.
satèllite, *n.m.* satellite.
sàtira, *n.f.* satire.
satireggiare, *vb.* satirize.
satollo, *adj.* sated, full.
saturare, *vb.* saturate.
saturazione, *n.f.* saturation, glut.
saziare, *vb.* satiate, sate, cloy.
sbadato, *adj.* careless, heedless.
sbadigliare, *vb.* yawn.
sbadiglio, *n.m.* yawn.
sbagliare, *vb.* err, blunder, make a mistake, slip.
sbàglio, *n.m.* mistake.
sbalordire, *vb.* astound, dumbfound.
sballottare, *vb.* toss.
sbalzo, *n.m.* leap; climb; relief; sudden change.

sbandare, *vb.* disband.
sbandato, *adj.* stray; alienated; skidding.
sbarazzare, *vb.* rid.
sbarcare, *vb.* disembark, land.
sbarco, *n.m.* disembarkation, landing.
sbarra, *n.f.* bar, rail.
sbarramento, *n.m.* **fuòco di s.,** barrage.
sbarrare, *vb.* bar.
sbàttere, *vb.* slam, bang.
sbavare, *vb.* drivel.
sbirciare, *vb.* peek, look sideways.
sbirro, *n.m.* cop.
sbloccare, *vb.* unblock.
sbocco, *n.m.* outlet.
sborsare, *vb.* disburse, pay out.
sbraitare, *vb.* squall.
sbranare, *vb.* eat by tearing to pieces.
sbriciolare, *vb.* crumble.
sbrigare, *vb.* expedite.
sbrinamento, *n.m.* defrosting (refrigerator).
sbrinare, *vb.* defrost (refrigerator).
sbronzare, *vb. refl.* get drunk.
sbucciare, *vb.* peel, pare.
sbuffare, *vb.* puff, chug.
sbuffo, *n.m.* puff, chug.
scabroso, *adj.* rugged.
scacchi, *n.m.pl.* chess.
scacchièra, *n.f.* chessboard, checkerboard.
scacco, *n.m.* chessman. **s. matto,** checkmate.
scadènza, *n.f.* maturity.
scadere, *vb.* fall due.
scaffale, *n.m.* shelf; bookcase.
scafo, *n.m.* hull.
scagliare, *vb.* hurl, sling.
scaglione, *n.m.* echelon.
scala, *n.f.* staircase; scale. **s. a piòli,** ladder.
scalare, *vb.* scale, climb.
scalèo, *n.m.* stepladder.
scalo, *n.m.* station. **s. mèrci,** freight station. **s. di smistamento,** marshalling yards, freight yard.
scalzo, *adj.* barefoot.
scambiàbile, *adj.* exchangeable.
scambiare, *vb.* exchange.
scàmbio, *n.m.* exchange; (railroad) switch; points.

scampanare, *vb.* chime, peal.
scampanellata, *n.f.* ring.
scampanìo, *n.m.* chime, peal.
scampo, *n.m.* escape.
scandagliare, *vb.* take soundings, sound out, fathom.
scàndalo, *n.m.* scandal.
scandaloso, *adj.* scandalous.
scandire, *vb.* scan (poetry).
scanso, *n.m.* avoidance. **a s. di,** so as to avoid.
scapaccione, *n.m.* cuff.
scappare, *vb.* escape.
scappata, *n.f.* escapade.
scappatòia, *n.f.* means of escape, loophole.
scarafàggio, *n.m.* beetle.
scaramùccia, *n.f.* skirmish.
scaramucciare, *vb.* skirmish.
scàrica, *n.f.* discharge.
scaricare, *vb.* unload, discharge, dump.
scàrico, *n.m.* discharge; spillway.
scarlattina, *n.f.* scarlet fever.
scarlatto, *n.m. and adj.* scarlet.
scarpa, *n.f.* shoe.
scarponi, *n.m.pl.* heavy boots.
scarseggiare, *vb.* be scarce.
scarsezza, *n.f.* scarcity, dearth.
scarsità, *n.f.* scarcity, dearth.
scarso, *adj.* scarce, meager, scant.
scartamento, *n.m.* gauge.
scartare, *vb.* discard, scrap.
scarti, *n.m.pl.* rubbish.
scartòffie, *n.f.pl.* papers.
scassare, *vb.* break.
scassinare, *vb.* burglarize; break open; pick the lock.
scatenare, *vb.* unleash; excite; trigger, provoke.
scàtola, *n.f.* box; can.
scattare, *vb.* spring up; burst forth; spurt; dash.
scatto, *n.m.* spring; spurt; dash.
scavare, *vb.* excavate, dig out; burrow, delve.
scavezzacollo, *n.m.* daredevil.
scavo, *n.m.* excavation.
scégliere, *vb.* choose, pick, select.
scelta, *n.f.* choice, selection; triage.
scelto, *adj.* select, choice.
scémpio, *n.m.* ruin; slaughter.
scèna, *n.f.* scene.
scenàrio, *n.m.* scenario.

scéndere, vb. descend, go down, get down, alight.

scervellato, adj. harebrained, madcap.

scèttico, 1. n. skeptic. 2. adj. skeptical.

scèttro, n.m. scepter.

scevro, adj. free, exempt.

scheda, n.f. card; form; ballot.

schedàrio, n.m. card-file.

schedina, n.f. (filing) card.

scheggia, n.f. chip, splinter.

scheggiare, vb. chip, splinter.

schèletro, n.m. skeleton.

schema, n.m. diagram; draft; plan.

scherma, n.f. fencing.

schermidore, n.m. fencer.

schermire, vb. fence.

schermo, n.m. screen.

schernire, vb. mock, scoff at, taunt.

scherno, n.m. mockery.

scherzare, vb. joke, jest, banter.

scherzo, n.m. joke, jest, banter; play; (music) scherzo.

scherzoso, adj. joking, playful.

schiaccianoci, n.m. nutcracker.

schiacciare, vb. crush, mash.

schiaffeggiare, vb. slap, buffet, smack.

schiaffo, n.m. slap, buffet.

schiappa, n.m. bungler.

schiarire, vb. clear up.

schiavitù, n.f. slavery.

schiavo, n.m. slave.

schièna, n.f. back.

schifoso, adj. loathsome.

schioccare, vb. snap.

schiuma, n.f. foam, froth, lather, suds. **s. per capelli**, hairspray.

schivare, vb. avoid, dodge, shun.

schizzare, vb. sketch; squirt.

schizzinoso, adj. squeamish.

schizzo, n.m. splash, splotch, dab; sketch, outline.

sci, n.m. ski.

scia, n.f. wake.

sciàbola, n.f. saber.

sciacallo, n.m. jackal.

sciagura, n.f. calamity.

scialacquare, vb. squander.

scialle, n.m. shawl.

sciamare, vb. swarm.

sciame, n.m. swarm.

sciampo, n.m. shampoo.

sciancato, 1. n. cripple. 2. adj. crippled.

sciare, vb. ski.

sciarpa, n.f. scarf, muffler.

sciàtica, n.f. sciatica.

sciatto, adj. sloppy; dowdy.

scìbile, n.m. knowledge.

scientìfico, adj. scientific.

sciènza, n.f. science.

scienziato, n.f. scientist.

scìmmia, n.f. ape; monkey.

scimpanzè, n.m. chimpanzee.

scìndere, vb. split.

scintilla, n.f. spark.

scintillare, vb. sparkle, glitter, glisten.

scintillìo, n.m. sparkle, glitter.

sciòcco, adj. stupid, foolish, dumb, silly.

sciògliere, vb. untie; loosen; resolve; dissolve; melt.

scioglimento, n.m. dénouement.

sciolina, n.f. ski wax.

sciòlto, adj. loose.

scioperante, n.m. and f. striker.

scioperare, vb. strike.

scioperato, adj. lazy, idle.

sciòpero, n.m. strike.

sciròppo, n.m. syrup.

scissione, n.f. division; cleavage; split.

sciupare, vb. spoil; waste; fritter away.

sciupone, n.m. spendthrift.

scivolare, vb. slip; slide; glide.

scivolone, n.m. slip.

scodèlla, n.f. bowl.

scòglio, n.m. reef.

scoiàttolo, n.m. squirrel.

scolare, vb. drain.

scolaro, n.m. pupil.

scollato, adj. décolleté.

scolorimento, n.m. discoloration.

scolorire, vb. discolor.

scolpire, vb. carve.

scommessa, n.f. bet, wager.

scomméttere, vb. bet, wager.

scomodare, vb. inconvenience, disturb.

scomodità, n.f. inconvenience.

scompagnato, adj. odd.

scomparire, vb. disappear.

scomparsa, n.f. disappearance.

scompartimento, *n.m.* compartment.

scompigliare, *vb.* disarrange.

scompiglio, *n.m.* disarray.

scomposto, *adj.* unseemly. **stare s.,** slouch.

scomùnica, *n.f.* excommunication.

scomunicare, *vb.* excommunicate.

sconcertante, *adj.* disconcerting, upsetting, bewildering.

sconcertare, *vb.* disconcert, upset, faze, abash.

sconfiggere, *vb.* defeat.

sconfinato, *adj.* unbounded.

sconfitta, *n.f.* defeat, discomfiture.

scongiurare, *vb.* conjure.

sconnèsso, *adj.* disconnected, disjointed.

sconnèttere, *vb.* disconnect.

sconosciuto, *adj.* unknown.

sconsolato, *adj.* disconsolate, comfortless.

scontare, *vb.* discount.

scontentare, *vb.* discontent.

scontènto, 1. *n.m.* discontent. 2. *adj.* discontented, disgruntled.

sconto, *n.m.* discount, rebate.

scontrarsi, *vb.* collide.

scontrino, *n.m.* check.

scontro, *n.m.* collision.

sconveniènte, *adj.* unbecoming, improper, unseemly.

sconvòlgere, *vb.* upset, overturn; overthrow; derange; unsettle.

sconvolgimento, *n.m.* upset, overturn; overthrow; derangement.

scopa, *n.f.* broom.

scopare, *vb.* sweep; (coll.) to have sexual intercourse.

scopèrta, *n.f.* discovery.

scopèrto, *adj.* uncovered, bare.

scopetta, *n.f.* whisk-broom.

scòpo, *n.m.* purpose, aim.

scoppiare, *vb.* burst, explode.

scoppiettare, *vb.* pop.

scòppio, *n.m.* outbreak; explosion.

scoprimento, *n.m.* uncovering.

scoprire, *vb.* discover, uncover, bare, detect.

scopritore, *n.m.* discoverer.

scoraggiamento, *n.m.* discouragement, dejection.

scoraggiare, *vb.* discourage, dishearten.

scoraggiato, *adj.* discouraged, dejected, downhearted.

scorato, *adj.* broken-hearted.

scorciatòia, *n.f.* shortcut.

scordare, *vb.* forget.

scòrgere, *vb.* perceive, discern.

scorpacciata, *n.f.* gorge; gluttonous eating. **fare una s.,** pig out (coll.).

scórrere, *vb.* flow; peruse.

scorrerìa, *n.f.* foray.

scorrettezza, *n.f.* impropriety.

scorrévole, *adj.* fluent.

scorrevolezza, *n.f.* fluency.

scorso, *adj.* past, last.

scorsòio, *adj.* running.

scòrta, *n.f.* escort.

scortare, *vb.* escort.

scortese, *adj.* discourteous, impolite.

scortesìa, *n.f.* discourtesy.

scorticare, *vb.* flay.

scorza, *n.f.* bark.

scosceso, *adj.* steep.

scòssa, *n.f.* jolt; shake; shock.

scossone, *n.m.* jerk, jolt.

scostare, *vb.* shift, move away.

scostumato, *adj.* bad-mannered; dissolute.

scotennare, *vb.* scalp; skin.

scottare, *vb.* scald.

scottatura, *n.f.* scald.

scovare, *vb.* find, discover.

Scòzia, *n.f.* Scotland.

scozzese, *adj.* Scotch.

screditare, *vb.* discredit, debunk.

scremare, *vb.* skim.

screpolare, *vb.* chap.

screpolatura, *n.f.* chapping; crevice.

scrèzio, *n.m.* tiff, disagreement.

scriba, *n.m.* scribe.

scribacchiare, *vb.* scribble.

scricchiolare, *vb.* creak.

scrigno, *n.m.* strong-box, safe, coffer.

scritto, *n.m.* writing.

scrittòio, *n.m.* writing desk.

scrittore, *n.m.* writer.

scrittura, *n.f.* writing; scripture.

scritturare, *vb.* engage.

scrivanìa, *n.f.* desk.
scrìvere, *vb.* write.
scrofa, *n.f.* sow.
scròscio, *n.m.* gust.
scrostare, *vb.* scale.
scrùpolo, *n.m.* scruple.
scrupoloso, *adj.* scrupulous.
scrutare, *vb.* scrutinize, scan.
scudo, *n.m.* shield, escutcheon.
sculacciare, *vb.* spank.
sculacciata, *n.f.* spanking.
scultore, *n.m.* sculptor, carver.
scultura, *n.f.* sculpture, carving.
scuòla, *n.f.* school.
scuòtere, *vb.* shake, jog, jar; wag; (*refl.*) bestir oneself.
scuretto, *n.m.* shutter.
scusa, *n.f.* excuse, apology.
scusàbile, *adj.* excusable.
scusare, *vb.* excuse; (*refl.*) apologize.
sdegno, *n.m.* indignation.
sdentato, *adj.* toothless.
sdraiarsi, *vb.* stretch out, sprawl.
sdrucciolare, *vb.* slide, slip.
sdrucciolévole, *adj.* slippery.
sdrucire, *vb.* tear, rip, rend.
se, *conj.* if; whether.
sè, *pron.* himself; herself; itself; themselves.
sebbène, *conj.* although.
sebo, *n.m.* sebum, tallow.
secca, *n.f.* sandbank.
seccare, *vb.* dry; bore; hassle.
seccatura, *n.f.* bore, nuisance; hassle.
secchezza, *n.f.* dryness.
sécchia, *n.f.* bucket, pail, hod.
secco, *adj.* dry.
secolare, *adj.* secular; century-long.
sècolo, *n.m.* century.
secondàrio, *adj.* secondary.
secondo, 1. *n.* second; halfback; mate. **2.** *adj.* second. **3.** *prep.* according to.
secrezione, *n.f.* secretion.
sèdano, *n.m.* celery.
sedativo, *n.m. and adj.* sedative.
sede, *n.f.* seat. **Santa S.,** Holy See.
sedere, *vb.* sit.
sèdia, *n.f.* chair, seat. **s. a dòndolo,** rocker.
sedicésimo, *adj.* sixteenth.

sédici, *num.* sixteen.
seducènte, *adj.* seductive, alluring.
sedurre, *vb.* seduce.
seduta, *n.f.* sitting.
seduzione, *n.f.* seduction.
sega, *n.f.* saw.
ségale, *n.f.* rye.
segare, *vb.* saw.
sèggio, *n.m.* seat. **s. elettorale,** voting polls.
seggiovia, *n.f.* ski-lift.
seghettato, *adj.* jagged.
segmento, *n.m.* segment.
segnalare, *vb.* signal.
segnale, *n.m.* signal.
segnalibro, *n.m.* bookmark.
segnare, *vb.* mark; score.
segno, *n.m.* sign, cue, mark, token.
sego, *n.m.* tallow.
segregare, *vb.* segregate.
segretària, *n.f.* secretary.
segretàrio, *n.m.* secretary.
segreto, *n.m. and adj.* secret.
seguace, *n.m.* follower, hanger-on.
seguènte, *adj.* next.
segùgio, *n.m.* bloodhound.
seguire, *vb.* follow.
sèguito, *n.m.* retinue, suite.
sèi, *num.* six.
selce, *n.f.* flint.
selciato, *n.m.* pavement.
selettivo, *adj.* selective.
selezione, *n.f.* selection.
sèlla, *n.f.* saddle.
sellare, *vb.* saddle.
selva, *n.f.* forest.
selvaggina, *n.f.* game.
selvàggio, *n.m. and adj.* savage, wild.
selvàtico, *adj.* wild.
selvaticume, *n.m.* wildlife.
semàforo, *n.m.* traffic light.
semàntica, *n.f.* semantics.
semàntico, *adj.* semantic.
sembrare, *vb.* seem.
seme, *n.m.* seed.
semèstre, *n.m.* semester.
semicérchio, *n.m.* semicircle.
semidìo, *n.m.* demigod.
seminare, *vb.* sow.
seminàrio, *n.m.* seminary.
seminterrato, *n.m.* basement.

semmài, *conj.* if ever.
semolino, *n.m.* semolina.
sempitèrno, *adj.* everlasting.
sémplice, *adj.* simple, plain; no-frills.
semplicemente, *adv.* simply.
semplicità, *n.f.* simplicity.
semplificare, *vb.* simplify.
sèmpre, *adv.* always, ever; still, yet.
sempreverde, *adj.* evergreen.
sènape, *n.f.* mustard.
senato, *n.m.* senate.
senatore, *n.m.* senator.
senile, *adj.* senile.
senno, *n.m.* sense.
seno, *n.m.* breast, bosom. **s. frontale,** sinus.
senonché, *conj.* except that, but.
sensale, *n.m.* broker.
sensato, *adj.* reasonable, sensible.
sensazionale, *adj.* sensational, lurid.
sensazione, *n.f.* sensation.
senserìa, *n.f.* brokerage.
sensibile, *adj.* sensitive, sympathetic.
sensitivo, *adj.* sensitive.
sènso, *n.m.* sense; direction. **s. unico,** one-way (street).
sensuale, *adj.* sensual.
sentièro, *n.m.* path, trail.
sentimentale, *adj.* sentimental.
sentimento, *n.m.* feeling, sentiment.
sentire, *vb.* feel; hear.
sènza, *prep.* without. **s. piombo,** unleaded (gasoline).
separare, *vb.* separate, part.
separato, *adj.* separate.
separazione, *n.f.* separation, parting.
sepolcro, *n.m.* grave.
sepoltura, *n.f.* burial, interment.
seppellire, *vb.* bury, entomb, inter.
séppia, *n.f.* cuttlefish.
sequela, *n.f.* series, succession.
sequenza, *n.f.* sequence, succession.
sequèstro, *n.m.* lien.
sera, *n.f.* evening.
serbare, *vb.* keep, preserve.
serbatòio, *n.m.* reservoir; cistern; tank.

serenata, *n.f.* serenade.
serenità, *n.f.* serenity.
sereno, 1. *n.f.* clear sky. **2.** *adj.* serene; clear; cloudless.
sergènte, *n.m.* sergeant.
seriamente, *adv.* seriously.
sèrie, *n.f.* series; row; array; set; suite; succession.
serietà, *n.f.* seriousness, earnestness.
sèrio, *adj.* serious, earnest. **sul s.,** earnestly.
sermone, *n.m.* sermon.
sèrpe, *n.m.* snake.
serpènte, *n.m.* serpent.
sèrra, *n.f.* greenhouse, hothouse.
serràglio, *n.m.* menagerie.
serranda, *n.f.* shutter, gate.
serrata, *n.f.* lockout.
serrato, *adj.* locked; compact; quick.
serratura, *n.f.* lock.
servile, *adj.* servile, menial, subservient.
servitù, *n.f.* servitude, bondage; servants.
servizièvole, *adj.* helpful, obliging.
servìzio, *n.m.* service; employ.
sèrvo, *n.m.* servant.
servosterzo, *n.m.* power steering.
sessanta, *num.* sixty.
sessantésimo, *adj.* sixtieth.
sessione, *n.f.* session.
sessismo, *n.m.* sexism.
sessista, *adj.* sexist.
sèsso, *n.m.* sex.
sessuale, *adj.* sexual.
sèsto, *adj.* sixth.
seta, *n.f.* silk.
setàceo, *adj.* silken.
sete, *n.f.* thirsty.
sétola, *n.f.* bristle.
setoloso, *adj.* bristly.
sètta, *n.f.* sect, denomination.
settanta, *num.* seventy.
settantésimo, *adj.* seventieth.
sètte, *num.* seven.
settèmbre, *n.m.* September.
settentrionale, *adj.* northern.
settimana, *n.f.* week.
settimanale, *n.m. and adj.* weekly.
sèttimo, *adj.* seventh.
severità, *n.f.* severity.

sevèro, *adj.* severe, dour, stern, strict.

seviziare, *vb.* torture, torment.

sezionale, *adj.* sectional.

sezione, *n.f.* section.

sfaccendato, *n.m.* loafer.

sfacèlo, *n.m.* breakdown, ruin, debacle.

sfamare, *vb.* feed, nourish; *(refl.)* feed.

sfarzo, *n.m.* pomp, ostentation; magnificence, luxury.

sfarzoso, *adj.* magnificent, gorgeous.

sfavore, *n.m.* disfavor, disgrace.

sfavorévole, *adj.* unfavorable.

sfèra, *n.f.* sphere.

sfèrza, *n.f.* whip, scourge, lash.

sferzare, *vb.* lash, whip, scourge.

sfida, *n.f.* challenge, dare, defiance.

sfidante, *n.m.* defier, challenger.

sfidare, *vb.* defy, challenge, dare.

sfidùcia, *n.f.* distrust.

sfilare, *vb.* defile; file off.

sfinito, *adj.* tired out; jaded.

sfiorare, *vb.* touch lightly, brush against, dab at, skim.

sfitto, *adj.* untenanted.

sfociare, *vb.* flow; lead to.

sfogare, *vb.* vent.

sfògo, *n.m.* expression; outlet; scope; vent.

sfondo, *n.m.* background.

sfortuna, *n.f.* misfortune, bad luck.

sfortunato, *adj.* unfortunate.

sforzare, *vb.* strain.

sforzarsi, *vb.* make an effort, endeavor, strive.

sforzo, *n.m.* effort, endeavor, exertion; stress.

sfòttere, *vb.* tease, harass.

sfracellare, *vb.* smash, crash.

sfregiare, *vb.* deface.

sfrontatezza, *n.f.* effrontery.

sfruttamento, *n.m.* exploitation.

sfruttare, *vb.* exploit.

sfuggire, *vb.* escape.

sfumatura, *n.f.* nuance.

sgabèllo, *n.m.* stool; footstool.

sgarberia, *n.f.* indignity.

sgargiante, *adj.* flamboyant, garish.

sghignazzare, *vb.* guffaw.

sghignazzata, *n.f.* guffaw.

sgomberare, *vb.* clear.

sgombro, *n.m.* mackerel.

sgonfiare, *vb.* deflate.

sgòrbio, *n.m.* blotch; daub; scrawl.

sgorgare, *vb.* empty, disgorge; gush, well forth.

sgradévole, *adj.* disagreeable.

sgranocchiare, *vb.* munch.

sgravare, *vb.* relieve, ease; lessen.

sgraziato, *adj.* graceless.

sgretolare, *vb.* crumble.

sgridare, *vb.* scold, bawl out, berate, chide.

sguardo, *n.m.* look, glance.

sguattero, *n.m.* servant, busboy.

si, *pron.* himself; herself; itself; themselves; yourself; yourselves.

sì, *interj.* yes.

sìa, *conj.* either; or.

sibilare, *vb.* hiss.

sìbilo, *n.m.* hiss.

sicàrio, *n.m.* hired killer.

siccità, *n.f.* dryness, drought.

Sicìlia, *n.f.* Sicily.

siciliano, *adj.* Sicilian.

sicura, *n.f.* safety lock.

sicuramente, *adv.* surely; securely; assuredly.

sicurezza, *n.f.* safety, security, surety.

sicuro, *adj.* sure; secure; assured; safe.

sidro, *n.m.* cider.

sièpe, *n.f.* hedge.

sièro, *n.m.* buttermilk; whey; serum.

sifilide, *n.f.* syphilis.

sifilìtico, *adj.* syphilitic.

sifone, *n.m.* syphon.

Sig., *n.m.* (abbr. for Signore) Mr.

sigaretta, *n.f.* cigarette.

sìgaro, *n.m.* cigar.

sigillare, *vb.* seal.

sigillo, *n.m.* seal; cachet.

significare, *vb.* signify, mean, betoken, purport.

significativo, *adj.* significant.

significato, *n.m.* significance, meaning, import, purport.

signora, *n.f.* lady; Mrs.; madam.

signore, *n.f.pl.* (on toilets) ladies.

signore, *n.m.* gentleman; lord; Mr.; sir.

signorìa, *n.f.* lordship.

silenziatore, *n.m.* silencer, muffler.

silènzio, *n.m.* silence.

silenzioso, *adj.* silent, quiet, noiseless.

sillaba, *n.f.* syllable.

silo, *n.m.* silo.

silòfono, *n.m.* xylophone.

silurare, *vb.* undermine.

siluro, *n.m.* torpedo.

silvicultore, *n.m.* forester.

silvicultura, *n.f.* forestry.

simbòlico, *adj.* symbolic.

simbolo, *n.m.* symbol.

similcuòio, *n.m.* artificial leather.

sìmile, *adj.* similar, alike, like.

similmente, *adv.* similarly, alike, likewise.

simmetrìa, *n.f.* symmetry.

simpatìa, *n.f.* sympathy.

simpàtico, *adj.* likeable, aggreable, pleasant, congenial.

simpatizzare, *vb.* sympathize.

simpòsio, *n.m.* symposium.

simulare, *vb.* simulate.

simultàneo, *adj.* simultaneous.

sinagoga, *n.f.* synagogue.

sinceramente, *adv.* sincerely.

sincerità, *n.f.* sincerity.

sincèro, *adj.* sincere, heartfelt.

sincronizzare, *vb.* synchronize.

sìncrono, *adj.* synchronous.

sindacato, *n.m.* union.

sindaco, *n.m.* mayor.

sindrome, *n.f.* syndrome.

sinfonìa, *n.f.* symphony; overture.

sinfònico, *adj.* symphonic.

singhiozzare, *vb.* sob.

singhiozzo, *n.m.* sob.

singolare, *adj.* singular.

sìngolo, *adj.* single; unique.

singulto, *n.m.* hiccup.

sinistra, *n.f.* left.

sinistro, 1. *n.m.* accident. **2.** *adj.* left; sinister.

sinistròrso, *adj. and adv.* counterclockwise.

sino, *prep.* as far as, up to, till. **s. da,** since.

sinònimo, 1. *n.m.* synonym. **2.** *adj.* synonymous.

sintassi, *n.f.* syntax.

sìntesi, *n.f.* synthesis.

sintètico, *adj.* synthetic.

sìntomo, *n.m.* symptom.

sintonìa, *n.f.* harmony, accord; tuning (radio).

sintonizzare, *vb.* tune in.

sinuoso, *adj.* sinuous.

sipàrio, *n.m.* curtain.

sirèna, *n.f.* siren; mermaid.

siringa, *n.f.* syringe.

sisma, *n.m.* earthquake.

sistèma, *n.m.* system.

sistemare, *vb.* put in order, arrange, settle, fix up.

sistemàtico, *adj.* systematic.

sistemazione, *n.f.* arrangement; settlement; solution.

sito, *n.m.* site.

situare, *vb.* situate.

situazione, *n.f.* situation, location.

slacciare, *vb.* unlace, untie, unfasten, unbutton, undo.

slanciarsi, *vb.* rush, dash.

slancio, *n.m.* rush, dash; impetus; élan.

slavo, *adj.* Slavic.

sleale, *adj.* disloyal.

slealtà, *n.f.* disloyalty.

slitta, *n.f.* sleigh, sled.

slittamento, *n.m.* skid.

slittare, *vb.* slide, skid.

slogare, *vb.* dislocate.

sloggiare, *vb.* dislodge.

smacchiatore, *n.m.* stain remover.

smagliante, *adj.* bright, dazzling, resplendent.

smagliatura, *n.f.* run (in stockings); imperfection; stretch mark.

smagrire, *vb.* become thin or lean, lose weight.

smaltare, *vb.* enamel, glaze.

smalto, *n.m.* enamel, glaze.

smantellare, *vb.* dismantle.

smarrire, *vb.* mislay, misplace, lose.

smarrito, *adj.* stray.

smascherare, *vb.* unmask.

smembrare, *vb.* dismember.

smemorato, *adj.* forgetful, absent-minded.

smentire, *vb.* give the lie to, belie.

smeraldo, *n.m.* emerald.

smeriglio, *n.m.* emery.

sméttere, *vb.* stop, quit.

smilitarizzare, *vb.* demilitarize.

smilzo, *adj.* gangling.

smobilitare, *vb.* demobilize.

smobilitazione, *n.f.* demobilization.

smontare, *vb.* dismount, alight, disassemble.

smòrfia, *n.f.* grimace.

smorzare, *vb.* attenuate, extinguish; diminish, lessen; tone down, taper.

snaturare, *vb.* denaturalize.

snervamento, *n.m.* enervation.

snervare, *vb.* enervate.

sobbalzare, *vb.* jounce, jolt; throb.

sobbalzo, *n.m.* jounce, jolt.

sobborgo, *n.m.* suburb, *(pl.)* outskirts.

sòbrio, *adj.* sober, somber.

socchiuso, *adj.* half-closed, ajar.

soccómbere, *vb.* succumb.

soccórrere, *vb.* succor, relieve.

soccorso, *n.m.* succor, relief.

sociale, *adj.* social.

socialismo, *n.m.* socialism.

socialista, *n. and adj.* socialist.

società, *n.f.* society; company. **S. delle Nazioni,** League of Nations.

sociévole, *adj.* sociable, companionable.

sòcio, *n.m.* member; fellow; partner.

sociologìa, *n.f.* sociology.

sòda, *n.f.* soda.

soddisfacènte, *adj.* satisfactory.

soddisfare, *vb.* satisfy.

soddisfazione, *n.f.* satisfaction.

sòdio, *n.m.* sodium.

sòdo, *adj.* hard-boiled.

sofà, *n.m.* sofa.

sofaletto, *n.m.* davenport.

soffiare, *vb.* blow.

soffietto, *n.m.* bellows.

soffitta, *n.f.* attic, garret.

soffitto, *n.m.* ceiling.

soffocare, *vb.* suffocate, choke, smother, stifle.

soffrigere, *vb.* sauté, fry lightly.

soffrire, *vb.* suffer, tolerate, put up with.

sofisma, *n.m.* chicanery.

sofisticato, *adj.* sophisticated.

soggètto, 1. *n.m.* subject. 2. *adj.* subject, liable.

soggezione, *n.f.* awe; uneasiness.

sogghignare, *vb.* sneer.

sogghigno, *n.m.* sneer.

soggiogare, *vb.* subjugate, subdue.

soggiornare, *vb.* sojourn, stay.

soggiorno, *n.m.* sojourn, stay.

sòglia, *n.f.* doorsill; threshhold, entrance.

sògliola, *n.f.* sole.

sognare, *vb.* dream.

sognatore, *n.m.* dreamer.

sogno, *n.m.* dream.

sòia, *n.f.* soy.

solaio, *n.m.* loft.

solamente, *vb.* only, alone.

solare, *adj.* solar.

solatìo, *adj.* sunny.

solcare, *vb.* furrow, groove; plow.

solco, *n.m.* furrow; groove; rut.

soldato, *n.m.* soldier. **s. sémplice,** private.

sòldo, *n.m.* penny.

sole, *n.m.* sun; sunshine.

solènne, *adj.* solemn.

solennità, *n.f.* solemnity.

solere, *vb.* be in the habit of, be accustomed to.

solerte, *adj.* diligent, zealous, industrious.

solidarietà, *n.f.* solidarity.

solidificare, *vb.* solidify.

solidità, *n.f.* solidity.

sòlido, *n.m. and adj.* solid.

solista, *n.m. or f.* soloist.

solitàrio, *adj.* solitary, lone, lonely, lonesome.

sòlito, *adj.* usual, habitual, accustomed.

solitùdine, *n.f.* solitude, privacy.

sollazzo, *n.m.* amusement, pastime.

sollecitare, *vb.* solicit; urge.

sollecitazione, *n.f.* urging, solicitation.

sollécito, *adj.* solicitous.

solleticare, *vb.* ticklish.

sollevamento, *n.m.* lifting, raising.

sollevare, *vb.* raise, lift, heave; relieve, ease.

sollevazione, *n.f.* uprising.

sollièvo, *n.m.* relief.

solo, *adj.* alone, sole, only, single.

soltanto, *adv.* only.

solùbile, *adj.* soluble.

soluzione, *n.f.* solution.
solvènte, *n.m. and adj.* solvent.
somaro, *n.m.* donkey.
somiglianza, *n.f.* likeness, similarity.
somma, *n.f.* sum, amount, quantity.
sommare, *vb.* sum up, add.
sommàrio, *n.m. and adj.* summary.
sommèrgere, *vb.* submerge.
sommergibile, *n.m.* submarine.
sommesso, *adj.* subdued, submissive.
sommità, *n.f.* summit, top.
sondare, *vb.* probe; sound.
sonnecchiare, *vb.* doze, nap, drowse.
sonnellino, *n.m.* nap, doze.
sonno, *n.m.* sleep, slumber.
sonnolènto, *adj.* somnolent, drowsy, sleepy.
sonnolènza, *n.f.* somnolence, drowsiness.
sontuoso, *adj.* sumptuous.
sopire, *vb.* appease, pacify; make drowsy.
sopore, *n.m.* drowsiness, stupor.
soporìfero, *adj.* soporific, sedative.
soppiantare, *vb.* supplant, supersede.
soppiatto, *adj.* **di s.**, stealthily.
sopportàbile, *adj.* bearable.
sopportare, *vb.* support, bear; abide, endure.
sopportazione, *n.f.* endurance.
soppressione, *n.f.* suppression.
sopprìmere, *vb.* suppress, put down, quell.
sopra, *adv. and prep.* over, above; upon.
sopràbito, *n.m.* overcoat, topcoat.
sopraccìglio, *n.m.* eyebrow.
sopraffare, *vb.* overcome, overwhelm.
sopraindicato, *adj.* aforementioned.
soprammòbile, *n.m.* knicknack.
soprannaturale, *adj.* supernatural.
soprannome, *n.m.* nickname.
soprappensiero, *adv.* absent minded, distracted.

sopratutto, *adv.* above all.
sopravvivènza, *n.f.* survival.
sopravvivère, *vb.* survive, outlive.
sorbetto, *n.m.* sherry.
sórcio, *n.m.* mouse.
sòrdido, *adj.* sordid.
sordità, *n.f.* deafness.
sordo, *adj.* deaf.
sordomuto, *n.m.* deaf-mute.
sorèlla, *n.f.* sister.
sorellastra, *n.f.* stepsister.
sorgènte, *n.f.* source; spring; headwater(s).
sórgere, *vb.* rise, spring.
sormontare, *vb.* surmount.
sornione, *adj.* sneaky, cunning, sly.
sorpassare, *vb.* pass; surpass; cross over.
sorpasso, *n.m.* passing.
sorprèndere, *vb.* surprise.
sorpresa, *n.f.* surprise, astonishment.
sorrèggere, *vb.* sustain, support.
sorrìdere, *vb.* smile.
sorriso, *n.m.* smile.
sorsata, *n.f.* sip; gulp down.
sorseggiare, *vb.* sip.
sorso, *n.m.* swallow; sip.
sòrta, *n.f.* sort.
sòrte, *n.f.* luck; lot.
sortèggio, *n.m.* drawing.
sortilègio, *n.m.* sorcery magic; spell.
sorveglianza, *n.f.* surveillance, supervision.
sorvegliare, *vb.* oversee, supervise.
sorvolare, *vb.* flyover.
sòsia, *adj.* look alike.
sospèndere, *vb.* suspend, discontinue.
sospensione, *n.f.* suspension; abeyance; stay.
sospettare, *vb.* suspect.
sospètto, **1.** *n.m.* suspicion, hunch. **2.** *adj.* suspicious, suspect.
sospettosamente, *adv.* suspiciously, askance.
sospettoso, *adj.* suspicious, distrustful.
sospìngere, *vb.* push, drive.
sospirare, *vb.* sigh.
sospiro, *n.m.* sigh.

sòsta, *n.f.* stopping.

sostantivo, *n.m.* noun.

sostanza, *n.f.* substance.

sostanziale, *adj.* substantial.

sostare, *vb.* stop.

sostegno, *n.m.* backing, support; foothold.

sostenere, *vb.* uphold, sustain; maintain; support, back (up).

sostenitore, *n.m.* upholder, backer, sponsor.

sostituire, *vb.* substitute, replace.

sostituto, *n.m.* substitute, alternate.

sostrato, *n.m.* substratum.

sostituzione, *n.f.* substitution.

sottana, *n.f.* petticoat; skirt.

sotterfùgio, *n.m.* subterfuge.

sotterràneo, *adj.* underground.

sottile, *adj.* subtle; thin, slim.

sotto, *adv. and prep.* under, underneath, below, beneath.

sottolineare, *vb.* underline.

sottomarino, *adj.* submarine.

sottométtere, *vb.* submit.

sottomissione, *n.f.* submission.

sottopassàggio, *n.m.* underpass.

sottoporre, *vb.* subject.

sottoposto, 1. *adj.* subject to. 2. *n.m.* subordinate.

sottoprodotto, *n.m.* by-product.

sottoscritto, *adj.* undersigned.

sottoscrivere, *vb.* subscribe; sign.

sottosopra, *adv.* upside down, topsy-turvy.

sottotenènte, *n.m.* second lieutenant.

sottovalutare, *vb.* underestimate.

sottovènto, 1. *n.m.* lee. 2. *adv.* leeward.

sottovèste, *n.f.* slip; (*pl.*) underwear.

sottrarre, *vb.* subtract, deduct; (*refl.*) get out of, shirk.

sottufficiale, *n.m.* non-commissioned officer.

sovente, *adv.* often.

soviètico, *adj.* soviet.

sovraccàrico, *adj.* overloaded.

sovranità, *n.f.* sovereignty.

sovrano, *n.m. and adj.* sovereign, ruler.

sovrintendènte, *n.m.* superintendent.

sovrumano, *adj.* superhuman.

sovenzionare, *vb.* subsidize.

sovvenzione, *n.f.* subvention.

sovversivo, *adj.* subversive.

sovvertire, *vb.* subvert; overthrow.

sozzo, *adj.* dirty, filthy.

spaccare, *vb.* split.

spacciare, *vb.* sell (dope), deal; pretend to be (*refl.*).

spàccio, *n.m.* sale; shop.

spacconata, *n.f.* brag.

spada, *n.f.* sword.

spadroneggiare, *vb.* act as if one owned the place; be bossy, domineer.

spaghetti, *n.m.pl.* spaghetti.

Spagna, *n.f.* Spain.

spagnuòlo, 1. *n.m.* Spaniard. 2. *adj.* Spanish.

spago, *n.m.* twine.

spalancare, *vb.* open wide.

spalla, *n.f.* shoulder.

spalleggiare, *vb.* back (up).

spalmare, *vb.* smear.

spanna, *n.f.* span.

sparare, *vb.* fire, shoot.

spàrgere, *vb.* scatter.

sparire, *vb.* disappear.

sparlare, *vb.* speak ill.

sparo, *n.m.* shot.

sparpagliare, *vb.* scatter, disseminate.

sparuto, *adj.* haggard.

spasimare, *vb.* long for; suffer; writhe.

spàsimo, *n.m.* spasm, pang.

spasmòdico, *adj.* spasmodic.

spassionato, *adj.* dispassionate.

spassoso, *adj.* amusing, funny.

spauràcchio, *n.m.* scarecrow.

spavaldo, *adj.* bold, audacious.

spaventare, *vb.* frighten, alarm, appal, scare.

spavènto, *n.m.* fright, scare.

spaventoso, *adj.* fearful, frightful.

spàzio, *n.m.* space.

spazioso, *adj.* spacious, capacious; roomy, commodious.

spazzacamino, *n.m.* chimneysweep.

spazzamine, *n.m.* **nave s.,** minesweeper.

spazzaneve, *n.m.* snowplow.

spazzare, *vb.* sweep.

spazzatura, *n.f.* sweepings, dust.

spazzino, *n.m.* street-cleaner; scavenger.

spàzzola, *n.f.* brush.

spazzolare, *vb.* brush.

spècchio, *n.m.* mirror, looking-glass.

speciale, *adj.* special, especial.

specialista, *n.m.* specialist.

specialità, *n.f.* specialty.

specialmente, *adv.* specially, especially.

spècie, *n.f.* species.

specificare, *vb.* specify.

specífico, *adj.* specific.

speculare, *vb.* speculate.

speculazione, *n.f.* speculation.

spedire, *vb.* send, despatch, ship; remit.

speditore, *n.m.* sender, shipper, dispatcher.

spedizione, *n.f.* expedition; despatch; shipment; remittance.

spedizionière, *n.m.* shipping agent.

spègnere, *vb.* put out; douse; switch off.

spellare, *vb.* skin, flay.

spèndere, *vb.* spend; expend.

spennare, *vb.* pluck.

spennellare, *vb.* dab, smear.

spensieratamente, *adv.* thoughtlessly, heedlessly, carelessly.

spensieratezza, *n.f.* thoughtlessness, heedlessness, carelessness.

spensierato, *adj.* thoughtless, heedless, careless, happy-go-lucky.

speranza, *n.f.* hope.

sperare, *vb.* hope.

spergiurare, *vb.* perjure oneself.

spergiuro, *n.m.* perjury.

sperimentale, *adj.* experimental; tentative.

sperimentare, *vb.* experiment.

sperone, *n.m.* spur.

spesa, *n.f.* expense, expenditure.

spesso, 1. *adj.* thick. **2.** *adv.* often.

spessore, *n.m.* thickness.

spettacolare, *adj.* spectacular.

spettàcolo, *n.m.* spectacle, show.

spettatore, *n.m.* spectator, onlooker, bystander.

spettegolare, *vb.* gossip.

spettinare, *vb.* muss (hair).

spettinato, *adj.* uncombed, ungroomed.

spèttro, *n.m.* specter, ghost; spectrum.

spèzie, *n.f.pl.* spice.

spezzare, *vb.* break, fracture.

spezzatino, *n.m.* stew.

spiaccicare, *vb.* squash.

spiacévole, *adj.* unpleasant.

spiàggia, *n.f.* beach, shore.

spia, *n.f.* spy.

spiano, *n.m.* levelling, smoothing. **a tutto s.,** at full blast; profusely.

spiare, *vb.* spy.

spiccàgnolo, *adj.* freestone.

spidocchiare, *vb.* delouse.

spiedino, *n.m.* skewer, kebab.

spiedo, *n.m.* spit, skewer. **allo s.,** barbecued.

spiegare, *vb.* explain; spread; unfold; unfurl.

spiegazione, *n.f.* explanation.

spiegazzare, *vb.* crinkle, crease, crumple.

spietato, *adj.* pitiless, merciless, ruthless.

spiga, *n.f.* ear (of grain).

spilla, *n.f.* brooch.

spillo, *n.m.* pin. **s. di sicurezza,** safety-pin.

spina, *n.f.* thorn; spine; (electric) plug. **s. dorsale,** backbone.

spinaci, *n.m.pl.* spinach.

spinetta, *n.f.* spinet.

spìngere, *vb.* push, jostle, shove; thrust; urge.

spinta, *n.f.* push, shove; thrust.

spionàggio, *n.m.* espionage.

spione, *n.m.* spy.

spira, *n.f.* spire, coil.

spiràglio, *n.m.* opening, aperture.

spirale, *n.f. and adj.* spiral.

spiritismo, *n.m.* spiritualism.

spírito, *n.m.* spirit; wit.

spiritoso, *adj.* witty.

spirituale, *adj.* spiritual.

splèndere, *vb.* shine.

splèndido, *adj.* splendid, gorgeous.

splendore, *n.m.* splendor, brilliance.

spodestare, *vb.* dispossess.

spogliare, *vb.* unclothe; divest, despoil, strip; harry.

spoletta, *n.f.* fuse.

sponda, *n.f.* shore.

spontaneità, *n.f.* spontaneity.

spontàneo, *adj.* spontaneous.

spopolare, *vb.* depopulate.

spòra, *n.f.* spore.

sporàdico, *adj.* sporadic.

sporcare, *vb.* foul, soil.

spòrco, *adj.* dirty, foul, soiled.

spòrgere, *vb.* put out; project.

sporta, *n.f.* shopping bag.

sportello, *n.m.* door; window (bank, station, post office).

sportivo, 1. *n.* sportsman. **2.** *adj.* sport.

sposa, *n.f.* bride, spouse.

sposalizio, *n.m.* wedding, espousal.

sposare, *vb.* marry, espouse.

sposi, *n.m.pl.* bride and groom; newlyweds.

sposo, *n.m.* bridegroom, spouse.

spostamento, *n.m.* displacement.

spostare, *vb.* displace.

sprecare, *vb.* waste.

sprèco, *n.m.* waste.

spregévole, *adj.* contemptible, despicable, mean.

spregiare, *vb.* despise.

sprègio, *n.m.* scorn, contempt, disdain.

spregiudicato, *adj.* broadminded.

sprèmere, *vb.* squeeze.

spremuta, *n.f.* squash.

sprezzante, *adj.* contemptuous, despising, scornful.

sprezzantemente, *adv.* contemptuously.

sprezzo, *n.m.* disdain.

sprigionare, *vb.* release.

sprizzare, *vb.* spray.

sprofondarsi, *vb.* subside; sink.

sprolòquio, long, rambling speech.

spronare, *vb.* spur.

sprone, *n.m.* spur.

sproporzionato, *adj.* disproportionate.

sproporzione, *n.f.* disproportion.

spropòsito, *n.m.* mistaken, slip. **a s.** *adv.* out of place.

spruzzare, *vb.* spout; spurt; splash; spatter.

spruzzo, *n.m.* splash, spatter.

spudorato, *adj.* shameless, brazen.

spugna, *n.f.* sponge.

spugnoso, *adj.* spongy.

spuma, *n.f.* foam, froth.

spuntare, *vb.* appear; dawn.

spuntino, *n.m.* snack.

spùrio, *adj.* spurious.

sputacchièra, *n.f.* spittoon, cuspidor.

sputare, *vb.* spit.

squadra, *n.f.* squad, gang; team.

squadrone, *n.m.* squadron.

squalìfica, *n.f.* disqualification.

squalificare, *vb.* disqualify.

squàllido, *adj.* squalid, bleak.

squallore, *n.m.* squalor, bleakness.

squama, *n.f.* scale.

squarciare, *vb.* gash, slash.

squàrcio, *n.m.* gash, slash.

squillare, *vb.* blare.

squillo, *n.m.* blare.

squisitezza, *n.f.* exquisiteness, daintiness, delicacy.

squisito, *adj.* exquisite, dainty, delicate.

Sra., *n.f.* (abbr. for Signora) Mrs.

sradicare, *vb.* eradicate; uproot.

sradicatore, *n.m.* eradicator.

sregolatezza, *n.f.* dissipation, debauchery.

stàbile, *adj.* stable.

stabilimento, *n.m.* establishment.

stabilire, *vb.* establish; set; appoint; settle.

stabilità, *n.f.* stability.

stabilizzare, *vb.* stabilize.

staccare, *vb.* detach, sever.

stacciare, *vb.* sift.

stàccio, *n.m.* sieve.

stàdio, *n.m.* stadium; stage.

staffétta, *n.f.* courier; relay race.

staffière, *n.m.* footman; groom.

staffilata, *n.f.* lash, whip.

stagione, *n.f.* season.

stagliare, *vb.* mangle; *(refl.)* stand out.

stagnante, *adj.* stagnant.

stagnare, *vb.* stagnate.

stagnino, *n.m.* tinsmith; plumber.

stagno, *n.m.* pond; pool; tin.

stalla, *n.f.* stable.

stallo, *n.m.* stall.

stallone, *n.m.* stallion.

stame, *n.m.* stamen.

stamigna, *n.f.* bunting.

stampa, *n.f.* press; printing.

stampare, *vb.* print.

stampatello, *n.m.* block letters.

stampella, *n.f.* crutch.

stampino, *n.m.* stencil.

stampo, *n.m.* stamp; mold; die.

stancare, *vb.* tire.

stanco, *adj.* tired, fagged, weary.

standardizzare, *vb.* standardize.

stanga, *n.f.* shaft.

stangata, *n.f.* blow, strike.

stanghetta, *n.f.* hang-over.

stantuffo, *n.m.* piston.

stanza, *n.f.* room. **s. da bagno,** bathroom. **s. da letto,** bedroom.

stanziamento, *n.m.* appropriation.

stanziare, *vb.* appropriate.

stappare, *vb.* uncork.

stare, *vb.* stand; be.

starnutire, *vb.* sneeze.

starnuto, *n.m.* sneeze.

stasera, *adv.* tonight.

stasi, *n.f.* standstill, stasis.

statico, *adj.* static.

statistica, *n.f.* statistics.

stato, *n.m.* state; estate.

statua, *n.f.* statue.

statura, *n.f.* stature.

statuto, *n.m.* statute.

stazionario, *adj.* stationary.

stazione, *n.f.* station; resort. **s. balneare,** bathing resort.

stecca, *n.f.* stick; cue; slat; splint.

stella, *n.f.* star.

stellare, *adj.* stellar.

stelo, *n.m.* stem.

stemma, *n.m.* coat of arms.

stendere, *vb.* extend; spread; draw up; *(refl.)* span.

stenografa, *n.f.* stenographer.

stenografia, *n.f.* stenography, shorthand.

stentatamente, *adv.* with difficulty.

stento, *n.m.* hardship; difficulty; privation. **a s.,** hardly.

sterco, *n.m.* dung.

stereofonico, *adj.* stereophonic.

stereotipia, *n.f.* stereotype.

sterile, *adj.* sterile, barren.

sterilità, *n.f.* sterility, barrenness.

sterilizzare, *vb.* sterilize.

sterlina, *n.f.* pound sterling.

sterminare, *vb.* exterminate.

sterminio, *n.m.* extermination.

sterno, *n.m.* breastbone, sternum.

sterzata, *n.f.* swerve, veer.

sterzo, *n.m.* steering wheel.

stesso, *adj.* same; self.

stetoscopio, *n.m.* stethoscope.

stia, *n.f.* hen-coop.

stigma, *n.m.* stigma.

stile, *n.m.* style.

stiletto, *n.m.* dagger.

stillare, *vb.* ooze, exude, drip.

stima, *n.f.* esteem, estimate, appraisal.

stimabile, *adj.* estimable.

stimare, *vb.* esteem, estimate, appraise, deem, value.

stimmate, *n.f.pl.* stigmata.

stimolante, *n.m. and adj.* stimulant.

stimolare, *vb.* stimulate, goad.

stimolo, *n.m.* stimulus, goad.

stinco, *n.m.* shin.

stingere, *vb.* discolor, fade.

stipendio, *n.m.* salary.

stipettaio, *n.m.* cabinetmaker.

stipite, *n.m.* jamb.

stipo, *n.m.* cabinet.

stipulare, *vb.* stipulate.

stirare, *vb.* iron.

stirpe, *f.* lineage; stock.

stitichezza, *n.f.* constipation.

stitico, *adj.* constipated.

stiva, *n.f.* hold (of boat).

stivale, *n.m.* boot.

stivare, *vb.* stow.

stivatore, *n.m.* stevedore.

stizza, *n.f.* upset, annoyance, anger.

stizzoso, *adj.* peevish.

Stoccarda, *n.f.* Stuttgart.

Stoccolma, *n.f.* Stockholm.

stoffa, *n.f.* cloth, stuff, material, fabric.

stoico, **1.** *n.* stoic, **2.** *adj.* stoical.

stola, *n.f.* stole.

stolido, *adj.* stolid.

stolto, **1.** *n.* fool, dunce. **2.** *adj.* foolish.

stomachevole, *adj.* sickening.

stomaco, *n.m.* stomach.

storcere, *vb.* sprain.

stordimento, *n.m.* dizziness.

stordire, *vb.* stun.

stordito, *adj.* stunned, dizzy.

stòria, *n.f.* history; story, yarn.

stòrico, 1. *n.* historian. **2.** *adj.* historic, historical.

storione, *n.m.* sturgeon.

stormo, *n.m.* swarm, flock.

stornare, *vb.* turn away; divert.

storpiare, *vb.* maim.

stòrta, *n.f.* sprain.

stòrto, *adj.* crooked.

stoviglie, *n.f.pl.* earthenware, pottery.

stra-, *prefix,* extra-.

stràbico, *adj.* cross-eyed.

stràccio, *n.m.* rag; clout.

straccione, *n.m.* ragamuffin.

stracotto, *adj.* overcooked; stew.

strada, *n.f.* road, street. **s. maestra,** highway.

stradale, *adj.* pertaining to roads.

strafalcione, *n.m* blunder, blooper.

strafare, *vb.* overdo.

strafottènte, *adj.* inconsiderate.

strale, *n.m.* arrow; shaft.

stralunato, *adj.* upset; wild-eyed; troubled.

stranezza, *n.f.* strangeness, oddity.

strangolare, *vb.* strangle, choke.

stranièro, 1. *n.* stranger; foreigner. **2.** *adj.* foreign.

strano, *adj.* strange, odd, peculiar, queer, quaint, weird.

straordinàrio, *adj.* extraordinary; extra.

strappare, *vb.* tear, rip, rend; snatch, wrench.

strapazzate, *adj.* **uòva s.,** scrambled eggs.

straripare, *vb.* overflow.

stratagèmma, *n.m.* stratagem.

strategìa, *n.f.* strategy.

stratègico, *adj.* strategic.

strato, *n.m.* stratum, layer; coating.

stratosfèra, *n.f.* stratosphere.

strattone, *n.m.* jerk.

stravagante, *adj.* extravagant.

stravaganza, *n.f.* extravagance.

straziante, *adj.* heart-rending.

straziato, *adj.* heartbroken.

strega, *n.f.* witch, hag.

stregare, *vb.* bewitch.

stregone, *n.m.* wizard.

stregonerìa, *n.f.* sorcery.

strènuo, *adj.* strenuous.

streptocòcco, *n.m.* streptococcus.

stretta, *n.f.* clasp; squeeze. **s. di mano,** hand-shake.

stretto, 1. *n.m.* strait. **2.** *adj.* narrow, tight.

stria, *n.f.* streak.

stridore, *n.m.* shriek; squeak.

stridulo, *adj.* shrill, strident.

strigliare, *vb.* curry.

strillare, *vb.* scream, shriek.

strillo, *n.m.* scream, shriek.

striminzito, *adj.* small; shrunken; skinny.

strinare, *vb.* singe.

stringere, *vb.* hold tight; clasp; clench; squeeze; press; tighten. **s. la mano a,** shake hands with.

striscia, *n.f.* strip; stripe; band; slip.

strisciare, *vb.* creep.

striscione, *n.m.* banner, festoon.

stritolare, *vb.* crush, mash.

strofinàccio, *n.m.* wiper; dustcloth; dishcloth.

strofinare, *vb.* rub; wipe.

stroncare, *vb.* break down; repress; slash.

strozzare, *vb.* strangle.

strozzino, *n.m.* loan shark.

strumentale, *adj.* instrumental.

strumento, *n.m.* instrument; implement.

strutto, *n.m.* lard.

struttura, *n.f.* structure.

struzzo, *n.m.* ostrich.

stucco, *n.m.* stucco.

studènte, *n.m.* student.

studentessa, *n.f.* student.

studiare, *vb.* study.

stùdio, *n.m.* study; studio.

studioso, *adj.* studious.

stufa, *n.f.* stove.

stufare, *vb.* stew.

stufato, *n.m.* stew.

stufo, *adj.* fed up, sick and tired.

stuòia, *n.f.* mat.

stuoìno, *n.m.* door-mat.

stuòlo, *n.m.* group, throng, crowd; company.

stupèndo, *adj.* stupendous.

stupidità, *n.f.* stupidity, dumbness, backwardness.

stùpido, *adj.* stupid, dumb, backward.

stupire, *vb.* amaze, astonish, astound, surprise, daze.

stupirsi, *vb.* be amazed, be astonished, be surprised.

stupore, *n.m.* daze, stupor; astonishment, amazement, wonder.

sturare, *vb.* uncork.

su, *prep. and adv.* on; upon; up.

subcosciènte, *adj.* subconscious.

subire, *vb.* undergo.

sùbito, *adv.* immediately.

sublimare, *vb.* sublimate.

sublimato, *n.m. and adj.* sublimate.

sublime, *adj.* sublime.

subnormale, *adj.* subnormal.

subodorare, *vb.* sense, suspect.

subordinato, *n.m. and adj.* subordinate.

succèdere, *vb.* succeed; happen, occur.

successione, *n.f.* succession.

successivo, *adj.* successive; subsequent.

successo, *n.m.* success.

successore, *n.m.* successor.

succhiare, *vb.* suck.

succhièllo, *n.m.* auger, gimlet.

succinto, *adj.* concise; scarce.

succo, *n.m.* juice.

succoso, *adj.* juicy.

succursale, *n.f.* branch.

sud, *n.m.* south. **polo s.,** South Pole.

sudare, *vb.* sweat, perspire, swelter.

sudàrio, *n.m.* shroud.

suddetto, *adj.* aforesaid.

suddividere, *vb.* subdivide.

sùddito, *n.m.* subject.

sud-èst, *n.m.* southeast.

sùdicio, *adj.* dirty, dingy, filthy, grimy.

sudiciume, *n.m.* dirt, filth, grime.

sudore, *n.m.* sweat, perspiration.

sud-òvest, *n.m.* southwest.

sufficiènte, *adj.* sufficient, adequate, enough.

sufficientemente, *adv.* sufficiently, adequately.

sufficiènza, *n.f.* sufficiency, adequacy.

suffisso, *n.m.* suffix.

suffragare, *vb.* substantiate, corroborate.

suffràgio, *n.m.* suffrage.

suggellare, *vb.* seal.

suggèllo, *n.m.* seal.

suggerimento, *n.m.* suggestion.

suggerire, *vb.* suggest.

suggeritore, *n.m.* prompter.

sùghero, *n.m.* cork.

sugo, *n.m.* sauce. **s. di carne,** gravy.

sugoso, *adj.* juicy.

suicidarsi, *vb.* commit suicide.

suicìdio, *n.m.* suicide.

suindicato, *adj.* aforementioned.

suìno, 1. *n.m.* swine. **2.** *adj.* of pork, swinish.

sultanina, *adj.* **uva s.,** sultana raisin.

sunto, *n.m.* abstract, résumé.

suo, *adj.* his; her; hers; its; your; yours.

suòcera, *n.f.* mother-in-law.

suòcero, *n.m.* father-in-law.

suòla, *n.f.* sole.

suòlo, *n.m.* soil.

suonare, *vb.* sound; ring; play.

suonatore, *n.m.* player.

suòno, *n.m.* sound; ring.

suòra, *n.f.* nun, sister.

superare, *vb.* overcome; surpass, exceed; excel; top; pass (exam.).

supèrbia, *n.f.* haughtiness, pride.

supèrbo, *adj.* haughty, proud; superb.

superficiale, *adj.* superficial.

superficie, *n.f.* surface.

supèrfluo, *adj.* superfluous.

superiore, *adj.* superior; upper.

superiorità, *n.f.* superiority.

superlativo, *n.m. and adj.* superlative.

supermercato, *n.m.* supermarket.

supèrstite, 1. *adj.* surviving. **2.** *n.m. and f.* survivor.

superstizione, *n.f.* superstition.

superstizioso, *adj.* superstitious.

superuòmo, *n.m.* superman.

supino, *adj.* supine, lying down.

supplemento, *n.m.* supplement.

sùpplica, *n.f.* supplication, entreaty.

supplicare, *vb.* supplicate, beseech, entreat.

supplichévole, *adj.* beseeching.

supplichevolmente, *adv.* beseechingly.

supplire, *vb.* replace; make up for; eke out.

supplízio, *n.m.* torture, torment, agony.

supporre, *vb.* suppose.

supposizione, *n.f.* supposition, assumption.

suppurare, *vb.* suppurate, fester.

supremazia, *n.f.* supremacy, ascendancy.

suprèmo, *adj.* supreme, paramount.

surclassare, *vb.* outclass.

surgelamento, *n.m.* deep freeze.

surrenale, *adj.* adrenal.

surriscaldare, *vb.* overheat.

surrogato, *n.m.* surrogate, substitute; makeshift.

susina, *n.f.* plum.

susino, *n.m.* plum-tree.

sussidiare, *vb.* subsidize.

sussídio, *n.m.* subsidy.

sussultare, *vb.* start.

sussulto, *n.m.* start.

svaligiare, *vb.* rob completely.

svalutare, *vb.* devalue.

svanire, *vb.* vanish.

svantàggio, *n.m.* disadvantage, drawback, handicap.

svariato, *adj.* varied.

svedese, 1. *n.* Swede. **2.** *adj.* Swedish.

svegliare, *vb.* awaken, wake up, arouse; *(refl.)* awake.

svéglio, *adj.* awake.

svelto, *adj.* quick; slender.

svenimento, *n.m.* faint, swoon.

svenire, *vb.* faint, swoon.

sventolare, *vb.* wave; fan.

sventura, *n.f.* misfortune, bad luck.

sventurato, *adj.* unfortunate, unlucky, miserable.

svergognato, *adj.* shameless, impudent.

svernare, *vb.* winter; hibernate.

svestire, *vb.* undress; *(refl.)* disrobe.

Svèzia, *n.f.* Sweden.

svignàrsela, *vb. (fam.)* abscond.

sviluppare, *vb.* develop.

sviluppatore, *n.m.* developer.

sviluppo, *n.m.* development, growth.

sviscerare, *vb.* eviscerate; dissect.

svista, *n.f.* blunder.

Svizzera, *n.f.* Switzerland.

svizzero, *n. and adj.* Swiss.

svogliato, *adj.* listless.

svolazzare, *vb.* flutter.

svòlgere, *vb.* unfold; develop; occur, happen.

svòlta, *n.f.* turn.

T

tabacco, *n.m.* tobacco.

tabellone, *n.m.* (bulletin) board.

tabernàcolo, *n.m.* tabernacle.

tacca, *n.f.* nick, notch.

taccagno, *adj.* niggardly.

tacchino, *n.m.* turkey, gobbler.

tacco, *n.m.* heel.

taccuino, *n.m.* note-book.

tacere, *vb.* be quiet, keep quiet.

tachímetro, *n.m.* speedometer.

taciturno, *adj.* taciturn, silent.

tafano, *n.m.* gadfly.

tafferùglio, *n.m.* scuffle, scrap.

tàglia, *n.f.* size, measure; ransom, reward.

tagliando, *n.m.* coupon.

tagliare, *vb.* cut; carve; chop; clip; hack; hew.

tagliatèlle, *n.f.pl.* noodles.

tagliatore, *n.m.* cutter.

tàglio, *n.m.* cut.

tale, *adj.* such.

talènto, *n.m.* talent.

talloncino, *n.m.* stub, coupon.

tallone, *n.m.* heel.

talpa, *n.f.* mole.

tamburo, *n.m.* drum; drummer. **t. maggiore,** drum major.

tamponare, *vb.* tampon; hit from rear.

tana, *n.f.* burrow, den, lair.

tànghero, *n.m.* boor, cold.

tangìbile, *adj.* tangible.

tantíno, *n.m.* a bit, a little.

tanto, 1. *adj.* much. **2.** *adv.* very; very much, a lot.

tappare, vb. plug, stop up.

tappeto, n.m. carpet, rug.

tappezzare, vb. upholster.

tappezzeria, n.f. tapestry, hanging; wallcovering.

tappezzière, n.m. upholsterer.

tappo, m. cork, stopper, plug.

tarchiato, adj. squat, stocky.

tardi, adv. late.

tardivo, adj. tardy, late.

tardo, adj. late.

targa, n.f. plate.

tariffa, n.f. tariff; fare.

tarma, n.f. moth.

tarpare, vb. clip, cut.

tartagliare, vb. stutter.

tartaruga, n.f. turtle.

tasca, n.f. pocket.

tascàbile, adj. pocket size.

tassa, n.f. tax; fee. **t. di scambio,** sales tax.

tassèllo, n.m. dowel.

tassì, n.m. taxicab.

tasso, n.m. badger.

tastièra, n.f. keyboard.

tasto, n.m. key.

tastoni, adv. **andare a t.,** grope.

tatto, n.m. tact; feel.

tàvola, n.f. table; board; plank.

tavoletta, n.f. tablet.

tavolòzza, n.f. palette.

tazza, n.f. cup.

te, pron. 2. sg. thee; you.

tè, n.m. tea.

teatro, n.m. theater.

tèca, n.f. case.

tècnica, n.f. technique.

tècnico, adj. technical.

tedesco, n. and adj. German.

tediare, vb. bore.

tèdio, n.m. tedium.

tedioso, adj. tedious.

tegame, n.m. pan, casserole dish.

tègola, n.f. tile.

teièra, n.f. tea-pot.

tela, n.f. cloth; web. **t. cerata,** oilcloth. **t. da fusto,** buckram.

telaio, n.m. loom; frame; chassis.

telefonare, vb. telephone.

telefonata, n.f. telephone call.

telèfono, n.m. telephone.

telegrafare, vb. telegraph.

telègrafo, n.m. telegraph.

telegramma, n.m. telegram.

teleschermo, n.m. television screen.

telescòpio, n.m. telescope.

telescrivènte, n.f. teletype.

televisione, n.f. television.

televisore, n.m. television set.

tèma, n.m. theme.

temerarietà, n.f. rashness, foolhardiness.

temeràrio, 1. n.m. daredevil. **2.** adj. rash, foolhardy.

temere, vb. fear, dread.

temperamento, n.m. temperament.

temperanza, n.f. temperance.

temperare, vb. temper.

temperato, adj. temperate.

temperatura, n.f. temperature.

temperino, n.m. pen-knife.

tempèsta, n.f. tempest, storm; gale.

tempestare, vb. pound, storm; harass, assail.

tempestivo, adj. timely, opportune.

tempestoso, adj. tempestuous, stormy, gusty.

tèmpia, n.f. temple.

tèmpio, n.m. temple.

tèmpo, n.m. time; weather.

temporàneo, adj. temporary.

temprare, vb. harden.

tenace, adj. tenacious, dogged.

tènda, n.f. tent; awning; booth.

tendènte, adj. tending, conducive.

tendènza, n.f. tendency, trend.

tèndere, vb. tend, conduce; stretch.

tèndine, n.m. tendon.

tendòpoli, n.f.pl. tent city, encampment.

tènebre, n.f.pl. darkness.

tenebroso, adj. dark.

tenènte, n.m. lieutenant.

teneramente, adv. tenderly, fondly.

tenere, vb. hold; keep.

tenerezza, n.f. tenderness, fondness.

tènero, adj. tender, fond.

tènia, n.f. tapeworm.

tenore, n.m. tenor.

tensione, n.f. tension, strain, stress.

tentàcolo, *n.m.* tentacle.

tentare, *vb.* attempt, try; tempt.

tentativo, 1. *n.m.* attempt. **2.** *adj.* tentative.

tentazione, *n.f.* temptation.

tènue, *adj.* tenuous, flimsy.

teologìa, *n.f.* theology.

teòlogo, *n.m.* theologian.

teorema, *n.m.* theorem.

teorìa, *n.f.* theory.

teòrico, *adj.* theoretical.

tepore, *n.m.* warmth.

teppista, *n.m.* hoodlum.

terapìa, *n.f.* therapy.

tergicristallo, *n.m.* windshield-wiper.

terminale, *adj.* terminal.

terminare, *vb.* terminate, end, finish.

tèrmine, *n.m.* end; terminus; term; deadline; abutment.

termòmetro, *n.m.* thermometer.

termosifone, *n.m.* heating system.

tèrra, *n.f.* earth, ground, land.

terrazza, *n.f.* terrace.

terremòto, *n.m.* earthquake.

terreno, 1. *n.m.* soil, terrain; lot. **2.** *adj.* earthy, earthly.

terrìbile, *adj.* terrible, awful, frightful, dire, dreadful.

terribilmente, *adv.* terribly, awfully, dreadfully.

terrìccio, *n.m.* loam.

terrificare, *vb.* horrify.

territòrio, *n.m.* territory.

terrore, *n.m.* terror, fear, awe.

terrorismo, *n.m.* terrorism.

terso, *adj.* terse, clear.

tèrzo, *adj.* third.

Terzo Mondo, *n.m.* Third World.

tesa, *n.f.* (hat) brim.

teso, *adj.* tight, taut, tense, up-tight.

tesorière, *n.m.* treasurer.

tesòro, *n.m.* treasure; treasury.

tèssera, *n.f.* card; ticket.

tèssere, *vb.* weave.

tèssile, *adj.* textile.

tessitore, *n.m.* weaver.

tessitura, *n.f.* texture; weaving.

tessuto, *n.m.* tissue; textile.

tèsta, *n.f.* head. **t. di sbarco,** bridgehead. **tener t. a,** cope with.

testamento, *n.m.* testament, will.

testardo, *adj.* stubborn, head-strong, self-willed.

testata càrica, *n.f.* warhead.

testàtico, *n.m.* poll-tax.

testé, *adv.* just now, just; soon.

testimòne, *n.m.* witness. **t. oculare,** eyewitness.

testimonianza, *n.f.* testimony.

testimoniare, *vb.* testify.

tèsto, *n.m.* text.

testone, *n.m.* headstrong person; dolt.

testuale, *adj.* verbatim, precise.

tètano, *n.m.* tetanus, lockjaw.

tetraone, *n.m.* grouse.

tètto, *n.m.* roof.

tettòia, *n.f.* shed.

thè, *n.m.* tea.

ti, *pron.* 2. *sg.* thee; you.

tièpido, *adj.* tepid, lukewarm.

tifo, *n.m.* typhus.

tifoidèo, *adj.* typhoid.

tifoso, *n.m.* fan, enthusiast.

tiglio, *n.m.* lime-tree; linden.

tiglioso, *adj.* tough, leathery.

tigre, *n.m.* tiger.

timbrare, *vb.* stamp.

timbro, *n.m.* stamp.

timidamente, *adv.* timidly, shyly, bashfully.

timidezza, *n.f.* timidity, shyness, bashfulness.

tìmido, *adj.* timid, shy, bashful, coy; chicken-hearted; diffident.

timone, *n.m.* helm; rudder; (wagon) pole.

timonière, *n.m.* steersman, helmsman; coxswain.

timore, *n.m.* fear, apprehension, dread.

timoroso, *adj.* timorous, fearful, apprehensive.

tìmpano, *n.m.* ear-drum; kettledrum.

tingere, *vb.* dye.

tino, *n.m.* vat.

tinca, *n.f.* tench.

tinello, *n.m.* pantry.

tinta, *n.f.* tint, shade.

tintinnare, *vb.* tinkle, jingle.

tintore, *n.m.* dyer; dry-cleaner.

tintura, *n.f.* dye.

tìpico, *adj.* typical.

tipo, *n.m.* type.

tirabaci, *n.m.* spitcurl.

tirannìa, *n.f.* tyranny.

tiranno, *n.m.* tyrant.

tirante, *n.m.* rod; tightening; brace.

tirare, *vb.* draw, pull, tag.

tirata, *n.f.* pull.

tiratura, *n.f.* printing.

tìrchio, *adj.* stingy.

tiro, *n.m.* trick.

tirocìnio, *n.m.* internship.

tìsi, *n.f.* consumption, tuberculosis.

tìsico, *adj.* consumptive.

titolare, 1. *n.* incumbent. **2.** *adj.* titular.

tìtolo, *n.m.* title, headline, heading, caption.

tìzio, *n.m.* chap, fellow, guy.

toccante, *adj.* touching, moving, poignant.

toccare, *vb.* touch.

toccasana, *n.m.* cure, panacea.

tocco, *n.m.* touch.

toga, *n.f.* gown.

tògliere, *vb.* take away, remove.

tollerante, *adj.* tolerant.

tolleranza, *n.f.* tolerance.

tollerare, *vb.* tolerate, stand.

tomba, *n.f.* tomb, grave.

tombale, *adj.* pertaining to a tomb or grave.

tombino, *n.m.* sewer cap, manhole.

tondo, *adj.* round.

tonfo, *n.m.* splash; thud.

tònica, *n.f.* (music) tonic.

tònico, *n.m. and adj.* tonic.

tonnellata, *n.f.* ton.

tonno, *n.m.* tuna.

tòno, *n.m.* tone, pitch.

tonsilla, *n.f.* tonsil.

tonto, *adj.* dumb, dull.

topo, *n.m.* mouse.

torace, *n.m.* thorax.

tòrcere, *vb.* twist, wring.

torinese, *n.f.* Turinese.

Torino, *n.f.* Turin.

tormenta, *n.f.* snowstorm, blizzard.

tormentare, *vb.* torment; fret; nag; tease.

tormento, *n.m.* torment.

tormentoso, *adj.* excruciating.

tornaconto, *n.m.* profit, advantage.

tornare, *vb.* return.

tornasole, *n.m.* litmus.

tórnio, *n.m.* lathe.

tòro, *n.m.* bull.

torre, *n.f.* tower.

torrefazione, *n.f.* roasting (of coffee).

torrènte, *n.m.* torrent; mountain stream.

torretta, *n.f.* turret.

tórsolo, *n.m.* core.

torta, *n.f.* cake, tart, pie.

tòrto, *n.m.* wrong. **aver t.,** be wrong.

tortuóso, *adj.* tortuous, winding, twisted; ambiguous.

tortura, *n.f.* torture.

torturare, *vb.* torture.

tosare, *vb.* clip, shear.

tosatore, *n.m.* clipper.

tosatura, *n.f.* clipping.

Toscana, *n.f.* Tuscany.

toscano, *adj.* Tuscan.

tosse, *n.f.* cough.

tòssico, 1. *n.m. (coll.)* drug addict. **2.** *adj.* toxic.

tossicòmane, *n.m.* drug addict.

tossire, *vb.* cough.

tot, *n.m.* so much; a specific amount.

totale, *n.m. and adj.* total.

totalità, *n.f.* totality, entirety.

totalitàrio, *adj.* totalitarian.

tovàglia, *n.f.* tablecloth.

tovagliolino, *n.m.* little napkin; doily.

tovagliòlo, *n.m.* napkin.

tòzzo, *adj.* stocky, chunky.

tra, *prep.* between, among, amid.

traballare, *vb.* reel, stagger, lurch.

traboccare, *vb.* overflow.

tràccia, *n.f.* trace.

tradimento, *n.m.* betrayal, treason.

tradire, *vb.* betray.

traditore, *n.m.* traitor.

tradizionale, *adj.* traditional.

tradizione, *n.f.* tradition.

tradurre, *vb.* translate.

traduzione, *n.f.* translation.

tràffico, *n.m.* traffic.

trafìggere, *vb.* transfix, spear.

traforare, *vb.* pierce; tunnel.

traforo, *n.m.* tunnel.

tragèdia, *n.f.* tragedy.

traghetto, *n.m.* ferry.

tràgico, *adj.* tragic.

traguardo di puntamento, *n.m.* bombsight.

tram, *n.m.* street-car, trolley-car.

trambusto, *n.m.* flurry.

tramestìo, *n.m.* bustle.

tramezzino, *n.m.* sandwich.

trampolino, *n.m.* springboard.

tramutare, *vb.* transform, change.

trangugiare, *vb.* gulp.

tranne, *prep.* except.

tranquillità, *n.f.* tranquillity.

tranquillo, *adj.* tranquil, quiet, peaceful.

transatlàntico, 1. *n.m.* liner. **2.** *adj.* transatlantic.

transizione, *n.f.* transition.

transvestito, *adj.* transvestite.

trantran, *n.m.* routine.

tranvia, *n.f.* tramway, streetcar line.

tranviàrio, *adj.* tramway.

trapanare, *vb.* drill.

tràpano, *n.m.* drill.

trapassare, *vb.* pierce through; pass through; pass away.

trapasso, *n.m.* death, passage; (property) conveyance.

trapelare, *vb.* ooze, leak through.

tràppola, *n.f.* pitfall, snare, trap.

trapunta, *n.f.* quilt.

trarre, *vb.* get; take; pull, drag; draw; lead; heave.

trasalire, *vb.* give a start.

trasandato, *adj.* sloppy.

trascinare, *vb.* drag, haul, lug.

trascinarsi, *vb.* crawl.

trascórrere, *vb.* elapse, pass.

trascuràbile, *adj.* negligible.

trascurare, *vb.* neglect, disregard, ignore, overlook.

trascuratamente, *adv.* negligently, carelessly.

trascuratezza, *n.f.* negligence, carelessness.

trascurato, *adj.* negligent, careless, frowzy, sloppy, slovenly.

trasferimento, *n.m.* transfer.

trasferire, *vb.* transfer.

trasferta, *n.f.* transfer; business trip.

trasformare, *vb.* transform.

trasfusione, *n.f.* transfusion.

traslòco, *n.m.* move; (household goods) moving.

trasméttere, *vb.* transmit, broadcast, convey.

trasmettitore, *n.m.* transmitter, broadcaster.

trasmissione, *n.f.* transmission. **t. radiofònica,** broadcast.

trasparènte, *adj.* transparent.

trasportare, *vb.* transport, carry, haul, convey.

trasportatore, *n.m.* conveyor.

traspòrto, *n.m.* transport; transportation; carriage; cartage; haulage.

trastullare, *vb.* amuse; *(refl.)* toy.

trastullo, *n.m.* toy.

trasudare, *vb.* ooze, seep.

tratta, *n.f.* draft.

trattàbile, *adj.* negotiable; tractable, manageable, friendly.

trattamento, *n.m.* treatment.

trattare, *vb.* treat; deal.

trattativa, *n.f.* negotiation.

trattato, *n.m.* treaty; treatise.

trattenere, *vb.* entertain; refrain; restrain; withhold; *(refl.)* forbear.

trattenuta, *n.f.* withholding.

trattino, *n.m.* hyphen; dash.

tratto, *n.m.* trait; feature; dash; stretch; tract. **t. d'unione,** hyphen.

trattore, *n.m.* restaurant-keeper.

trattoria, *n.f.* restaurant.

trattrice, *n.f.* tractor.

traumatizzare, *vb.* traumatize.

travaglio, *n.m.* labor.

travasare, *vb.* scoop; pour off.

trave, *n.f.* beam, girder.

travèrso, *adv.* **di travèrso,** awry.

travestimento, *n.m.* disguise; travesty.

travestire, *vb.* disguise; travesty.

travicèllo, *n.m.* joist, rafter.

travisare, *vb.* distort, misunderstand.

travòlgere, *vb.* overwhelm; sweep away; knock over; overturn.

tre, *num.* three.

tréccia, *n.f.* braid.

tredicésimo, *adj.* thirteenth.

trédici, *num.* thirteen.

trégua, *n.f.* truce; respite.

tremare, *vb.* tremble, quake, shake.

tremèndo, *adj.* tremendous; awesome.

trèmito, *n.m.* trembling, quake.

tremolare, *vb.* tremble, flicker, quaver.

tremolìo, *n.m.* trembling, flicker.

treno, *n.m.* train.

trenta, *num.* thirty.

trentésimo, *adj.* thirtieth.

trepidare, *vb.* fear; fret, worry.

tresca, *n.f.* intrigue; (illicit) love affair.

trescone, *n.m.* reel (dance).

triàngolo, *n.m.* triangle.

tribade, *n.f.* Lesbian.

tribolare, *vb.* trouble, suffer; worry.

tribolazione, *n.f.* tribulation.

tribòrdo, *n.m.* starboard.

tribù, *n.f.* tribe, clan.

tribuna, *n.f.* stand, grandstand.

tributàrio, *n.m. and adj.* tributary.

tributo, *n.m.* tribute.

trichèco, *n.m.* walrus.

trifòglio, *n.m.* clover.

trimestrale, *adj.* every three months, quarterly.

trimèstre, *n.m.* three-month period, quarter; (school) term.

trincèa, *n.f.* trench; cutting.

trincerare, *vb.* entrench.

trinciante, *n.m.* carving-knife.

trinciare, *vb.* carve, cut up.

trionfale, *adj.* triumphal.

trionfante, *adj.* triumphal.

trionfare, *vb.* triumph.

trionfo, *n.m.* triumph

triplicare, *vb.* triple.

trìplice, *adj.* triple.

trippa, *n.f.* tripe; (coll.) fat.

tripudiare, *vb.* exult.

tripùdio, *n.m.* exultation, happiness.

triste, *adj.* sad, gloomy, depressed, doleful, glum.

tristezza, *n.f.* sadness, gloom, glumness.

tritacarne, *n.m.* meat grinder.

tritare, *vb.* pound, mangle.

trito, *adj.* trite.

tritòlo, *n.m.* T.N.T.

triturare, *vb.* mince.

trivèllo, *n.m.* auger, borer.

trofèo, *n.m.* trophy.

trògolo, *n.m.* trough.

tròia, *n.f.* sow.

tromba, *n.f.* trumpet.

trombettière, *n.m.* trumpeter.

tronco, *n.m.* trunk; log.

trónfio, *adj.* haughty, conceited.

tròno, *n.m.* throne.

tròpico, **1.** *n.m.* tropic. **2.** *adj.* tropical.

troppo, **1.** *adj.* too many; too much. **2.** *adv.* too.

tròta, *n.f.* trout.

trottare, *vb.* trot.

tròtto, *n.m.* trot.

trovare, *vb.* find, locate; (*refl.*) be; be located; happen to be.

trovata, *n.f.* find; invention; idea; trick.

trovatèllo, *n.m.* foundling.

trucco, *n.m.* trick.

trucidare, *vb.* slay.

truffare, *vb.* cheat, swindle.

truffatore, *n.m.* cheater, swindler.

truppa, *n.f.* troop.

tu, *pron.* **2.** *sg.* thou; you.

tubercolosi, *n.f.* tuberculosis.

tubo, *n.m.* tube, pipe.

tuffare, *vb.* plunge; dip; dunk; (*refl.*) dive.

tuffatore, *n.m.* diver; divebomber.

tuffo, *n.m.* dive, plunge.

tugùrio, *n.m.* hovel.

tulipano, *n.m.* tulip.

tumefazione, *n.m.* tumefaction, swelling.

tumore, *n.m.* tumor.

tùmulo, *n.m.* mound.

tumulto, *n.m.* tumult, uproar, hubbub, riot.

tùnica, *n.f.* tunic, gown.

tuo, *adj.* thy; your.

tuonare, *vb.* thunder.

tuòno, *n.m.* thunder.

tuórlo, *n.m.* yolk.

turbante, *n.m.* turban.

turbare, *vb.* upset; disturb; trouble, perturb.

turbina, *n.f.* turbine.

turbinare, *vb.* whirl, gyrate, swirl.

tùrbine, *n.m.* whirlwind.

turbo-èlica, *n.f.* turbo-prop.
turbolènto, *adj.* turbulent; boisterous.
turboreattore, *n.m.* turbojet.
Turchia, *n.f.* Turkey.
turco, 1. *n.m.* Turk. **2.** *adj.* Turkish.
tùrgido, *adj.* turgid.
turismo, *n.m.* sightseeing, tourism.
turista, *n.m.* tourist.

turìstico, *adj.* tourist.
turno, *n.m.* turn, shift.
turpe, *adj.* abject; ugly; vile.
tuta, *n.f.* overalls; dungarees.
tutèla, *n.f.* guardianship.
tutore, *n.m.* guardian.
tuttavìa, *adv.* however; yet.
tutto, 1. *adj.* all; whole. **t. a un tratto,** all of a sudden. **2.** *pron.* everything.
tuttóra, *adv.* yet, still, even now.

U

ubbidire, *vb.* obey.
ubriachezza, *n.f.* drunkenness, intoxication.
ubriaco, *adj.* drunk, drunken.
ubriacone, *n.m.* drunkard, inebriate.
uccellièra, *n.f.* bird-house, aviary.
uccellino, *n.m.* fledgling.
uccèllo, *n.m.* bird. **u. di rapina,** bird of prey.
uccidere, *vb.* kill.
uccisore, *n.m.* killer.
udìbile, *adj.* audible.
udiènza, *n.f.* audience, interview, hearing.
udire, *vb.* hearing.
uditìvo, *adj.* auditory.
udito, *n.m.* hearing.
uditore, *n.m.* hearer, auditor.
uditòrio, *n.m.* audience.
uditrice, *n.f.* hearer, auditor.
ufficiale, 1. *n.m.* officer, official. **2.** *adj.* official.
ufficio, *n.m.* office, bureau.
ufficioso, *adj.* unofficial.
ufo, a u., *adv.* free; parasitically.
ùgola, *n.f.* uvula.
uguaglianza, *n.f.* equality.
uguagliare, *vb.* equal, equalize, equate, match.
uguale, *adj.* equal.
ùlcera, *n.f.* ulcer.
ulivo, *n.m.* olive tree.
ulteriore, *adj.* ulterior, further.
ùltimo, *adj.* last, end, hindmost, ultimate.
ultraterreno, *adj.* unearthly.
ultraviolétto, *n.m.* ultraviolet.
ululare, *vb.* howl.
umanamente, *adv.* humanly.

umanésimo, *n.m.* humanism.
umanista, *n.m.* humanist.
umanità, *n.f.* humanity, mankind.
umanitàrio, *adj.* humanitarian, humane.
umano, *adj.* human.
umbro, *adj.* Umbrian.
umidità, *n.f.* dampness, humidity, moisture.
ùmido, *adj.* damp, humid, moist, wet.
ùmile, *adj.* humble, lowly.
umiliare, *vb.* humiliate, humble; *(refl.)* grovel.
umiliazione, *n.f.* humiliation.
umiltà, *n.f.* humility.
umore, *n.m.* humor.
umorismo, *n.m.* humor.
umorista, *n.m.* humorist.
umorìstico, *adj.* humorous, jocular.
un, *art.* a, an.
unànime, *adj.* unanimous.
uncinare, *vb.* hook.
uncino, *n.m.* hook, grapple.
undicésimo, *adj.* eleventh.
ùndici, *num.* eleven.
ùngere, *vb.* grease; smear; anoint; oil.
ungherese, *adj.* Hungarian.
Ungherìa, *n.f.* Hungary.
ùnghia, *n.f.* fingernail.
unguènto, *n.m.* unguent, salve, ointment.
ùnico, *adj.* only; unique; single; sole.
unificare, *vb.* unify.
uniforme, 1. *n.m.* uniform. **2.** *adj.* uniform, even.

uniformità, *n.f.* uniformity, evenness.

unilaterale, *adj.* unilateral, onesided.

unione, *n.f.* union.

unire, *vb.* unite.

unisessuale, *adj.* unisex.

unità, *n.f.* unity; unit.

universale, *adj.* universal.

università, *n.f.* university, college.

universitàrio, *adj.* pertaining to a university, collegiate.

univèrso, *n.m.* universe.

uno, *m.,* **una** *f.* **1.** *art.* a, an. **2.** *num.* one.

unto, *adj.* oily, greasy.

untuoso, *adj.* greasy.

uòmo, *n.m.* man.

uòpo, *n.m.* purpose.

uòvo, *n.m.* egg. **u. affogato,** poached egg.

uragano, *n.m.* hurricane.

uraninite, *n.f.* pitchblende.

urbano, *adj.* urban.

urgènte, *adj.* urgent, pressing.

urgènza, *n.f.* urgency.

urina, *n.f.* urine.

urlare, *vb.* yell, holler, bawl, shout, cry, howl.

urlo, *n.m.* yell, shout, howl.

urna, *n.f.* urn.

urtare, *vb.* bump; shock; clash.

urto, *n.m.* bump; shock; impact; clash.

usanza, *n.f.* usage.

usare, *vb.* use.

usato, 1. *adj.* used. **2.** *n.m.* secondhand, vintage.

uscènte, *adj.* ending, closing, terminating.

uscière, *n.m.* usher; bailiff.

ùscio, *n.m.* door.

uscita, *n.f.* exit; airport gate.

usignuòlo, *n.m.* nightingale.

uso, *n.m.* use; custom.

ustione, *n.f.* burn.

usuale, *adj.* usual.

usufruire, *vb.* have the use of; use; benefit.

usura, *n.f.* usury.

usurpare, *vb.* usurp, encroach upon.

utènsile, *n.m.* utensil, tool.

utènte, *n.m.* user.

ùtero, *n.m.* uterus, womb.

ùtile, *adj.* useful, helpful.

utilità, *n.f.* utility, usefulness, helpfulness.

utilitària, *n.f.* economy car.

utilizzare, *vb.* utilize.

utopìa, *n.f.* utopia.

uva, *n.f.* grape.

ùzzolo, *n.m.* whim; impulse.

V

va bene, *interj.* O.K.

vacante, *adj.* vacant.

vacanza, *n.f.* holiday, *(pl.)* vacation.

vacca, *n.f.* cow.

vaccaro, *n.m.* cowboy, cowhand.

vacchetta, *n.f.* cowhide.

vaccinare, *vb.* vaccinate.

vaccinazione, *n.f.* vaccination.

vaccìnio, *n.m.* huckleberry.

vaccìno, *n.m.* vaccine.

vacillante, *adj.* vacillating, flickening, unstable.

vacillare, *vb.* vacillate, waver.

vacuità, *n.f.* vacuity, emptiness.

vàcuo, *adj.* vacuous.

vademecum, *n.m.* handbook.

vagabondo, *n.m.* vagabond, hobo, bum, tramp.

vagare, *vb.* wander around, gallivant, ramble, roam.

vàglia, *n.m.* money-order.

vàglio, *n.m.* sieve.

vago, *adj.* vague, dreamy, hazy; (poetical) charming.

vagone, *n.m.* car; coach. **v. ristorante,** dining car. **v. lètti,** sleeper.

vaiòlo, *n.m.* smallpox.

valanga, *n.f.* avalanche.

valere, *vb.* be worth.

valico, *n.m.* mountain pass.

vàlido, *adj.* valid.

valigetta, *n.f.* little suitcase; handbag.

valìgia, *n.f.* suitcase, valise.

valle, *n.f.* valley.

valletta, *n.f.* vale, dale, glen.

valore, *n.m.* valor; value, worth.
valorizzare, *vb.* value; exploit.
valoroso, *adj.* valiant.
valuta, *n.f.* currency.
valutare, *vb.* evaluate, estimate, value.
valutazione, *n.f.* evaluation, estimate.
vàlvola, *n.f.* valve; (radio) tube.
vàlzer, *n.m.* waltz.
vampiro, *n.m.* vampire.
vanaglorioso, *adj.* vainglorious, boastful.
vàndalo, *n.m.* vandal.
vanga, *n.f.* spade.
vangèlo, *n.m.* gospel.
vaniglia, *n.f.* vanilla.
vanità, *n.f.* vanity, conceit.
vanitoso, *adj.* vain, conceited.
vano, 1. *n.m.* room. **2.** *adj.* vain.
vantàggio, *n.m.* advantage, benefit, profit. **trarre v. da,** benefit by.
vantaggiosamente, *adv.* advantageously.
vantaggioso, *adj.* advantageous, beneficial, profitable.
vantare, *vb.* boast.
vanteria, *n.f.* boast, boasting, boastfulness.
vanto, *n.m.* boast.
vànvera, *adv. at random.* **parlare a v.,** ramble.
vapore, *n.m.* vapor, steam.
varare, *vb.* launch.
variàbile, *n.f. and adj.* variable.
variare, *vb.* vary.
variazione, *n.f.* variation.
varicèlla, *n.f.* chicken-pox.
variegato, *adj.* variegated.
varietà, *n.f.* variety.
vàrio, *adj.* various.
variopinto, *adj.* multicolored.
varo, *n.m.* launching.
vasca, *n.f.* tub.
vascello, *n.m.* vessel, ship.
vasellame, *n.m.* crockery, earthenware.
vasectomia, *n.f.* vasectomy.
vaso, *n.m.* vase. **v. da nòtte,** chamber-pot.
vassallo, *n.m.* vassal.
vassòio, *n.m.* tray.
vasto, *adj.* vast.
vècchia, *n.f.* old woman, crone.
vècchio, *adj.* old, aged, elderly.

vece, *n.m.* behalf. **in v. di,** on behalf of.
vedere, *vb.* see, behold.
védova, *n.f.* widow.
vedovo, *n.m.* widower.
veduta, *n.f.* view.
veemènte, *adj.* vehement.
veemènza, *n.f.* vehemence.
vegetale, *adj.* vegetable.
vegetariano, *adj.* vegetarian.
vegetazione, *n.f.* vegetation.
vègeto, *adj.* vigorous, strong.
vèggente, *n.m. and f.* seer; prophet.
véglia, *n.f.* vigil; wake.
vegliare, *vb.* be awake.
vegliardo, *n.m.* old man.
veicolo, *n.m.* vehicle.
vela, *n.f.* sail.
velato, *adj.* veiled, filmy.
veleno, *n.m.* poison, venom.
velenoso, *adj.* poisonous, venomous.
vèllo, *n.m.* fleece.
velluto, *n.m.* velvet.
velo, *n.m.* veil.
veloce, *adj.* swift, fleet, speedy.
velocista, *n.m.* sprinter.
velocità, *n.f.* velocity, speed.
velòdromo, *n.m.* bicycle ring.
vena, *n.f.* vein.
venale, *adj.* venal.
venato, *adj.* veined; streaked, variegated.
vendèmmia, *n.f.* vintage.
véndere, *vb.* sell.
vendetta, *n.f.* revenge, vengeance.
vendicare, *vb.* avenge, revenge.
vendicativo, *adj.* vindictive, vengeful.
vendicatore, *n.m.* avenger.
véndita, *n.f.* sale. **v. all'asta,** auction.
venerdì, *n.m.* Friday. **v. santo,** Good Friday.
venèreo, *adj.* venereal.
Venèzia, *n.f.* Venice.
veneziano, *adj.* Venetian.
venire, *vb.* come.
ventàglio, *n.m.* fan.
ventèsimo, *adj.* twentieth.
venti, *num.* twenty.
ventilare, *vb.* ventilate.
ventilazione, *n.f.* ventilation.
ventina, *n.f.* score.

vènto, *n.m.* wind.

ventoso, *adj.* windy, breezy.

vèntre, *n.m.* belly.

ventriglio, *n.m.* gizzard.

ventura, *n.f.* venture.

venuta, *n.f.* coming.

veramente, *adv.* truly, really, actually.

veranda, *n.f.* porch.

verbale, 1. *n.m.* minutes. **2.** *adj.* verbal.

vèrbo, *n.m.* verb.

verboso, *adj.* verbose, wordy.

verde, *adj.* green. **al v.,** broke, penniless.

verdetto, *n.m.* verdict.

verdura, *n.f.* vegetables.

verga, *n.f.* rod, switch.

vérgine, *n.f.* virgin.

vergogna, *n.f.* shame.

vergognarsi di, *vb.* be ashamed of.

vergognoso, *adj.* ashamed; shameful.

verídico, *adj.* truthful.

verifica, *n.f.* verification, check, audit.

verificare, *vb.* verify, check, audit.

verità, *n.f.* truth, reality, actuality.

veritiero, *adj.* truthful, earnest.

vèrme, *n.m.* worm.

vermiglio, *adj.* vermilion.

vernàcolo, *n.m.* and *adj.* vernacular.

vernice, *n.f.* varnish, glaze.

verniciare, *vb.* varnish, glaze.

vero, *adj.* true, real, actual; very.

verosìmile, *adj.* likely, probable.

vèrro, *n.m.* boar.

verruca, *n.f.* wart.

versamento, *n.m.* payment.

versare, *vb.* pour; pay in; shed.

versàtile, *adj.* versatile.

versato, *adj.* versed, conversant.

versificare, *vb.* versify.

versione, *n.f.* version.

vèrso, 1. *n.m.* verse; song; (hen, goose) cackle. **2.** *prep.* toward.

versucci, *n.m.pl.* doggerel.

vèrtebra, *n.f.* vertebra.

vertebrato, *n.m.* and *adj.* vertebrate.

vèrtenza, *n.f.* quarrel, dispute, controversy.

verticale, *adj.* vergical.

vèrtice, *n.m.* vertex, top; summit.

vertìgine, *n.f.* vertigo, dizziness.

vertiginoso, *adj.* vertiginous, dizzy.

verza, *n.f.* cabbage.

verzura, *n.f.* greenery.

vescica, *n.f.* bladder; blister.

vescovado, *n.m.* bishopric.

véscovo, *n.m.* bishop.

vèspa, *n.f.* wasp.

vespasiano, *n.m.* public urinal.

vèspri, *n.m.pl.* vespers.

vessillo, *n.m.* flag, emblem.

vestàglia, *n.f.* dressing-gown, bathrobe, negligée.

vèste, *n.f.* dress, garb, apparel, robe.

vestìbolo, *n.m.* vestibule, hallway.

vestigia, *n.f.pl.* vestiges.

vestire, *vb.* dress, clothe, garb, apparel.

vestito, 1. *n.m.* dress, suit, garment; *(pl.)* clothes, clothing. **2.** *adj.* clad, clothed.

Vesùvio, *n.m.* Vesuvius.

veterano, *n.m.* veteran.

veterinàrio, *n.m.* and *adj.* veterinary.

vèto, *n.m.* veto.

vetràio, *n.m.* glazier.

vetrina, *n.f.* shop window; showcase.

vetro, *n.m.* glass, pane.

vetroresina, *n.m.* fiberglass.

vetroso, *adj.* glassy.

vetta, *n.f.* summit.

vettovàglie, *n.f.pl.* victuals.

vettura, *n.f.* carriage; car.

vezzeggiare, *vb.* fondle, coddle, pet.

vèzzo, *n.m.* habit, quirk.

vi, *pron.* 2. *pl.* you.

vi, *pro-phrase* (replaces phrases introduced by prepositions of place) there; to it; at it.

vìa, 1. *n.f.* way, road, street. **2.** *adv.* away; off. **3.** *prep.* via.

viadotto, *n.m.* viaduct.

viaggiare, *vb.* journey, travel, tour, voyage.

viaggiatore, *n.m.* traveller.

viàggio, *n.m.* journey, trip, travel, tour, voyage.

viale, *n.m.* avenue, boulevard; drive(way); (in garden) alley.

viandante, *n.m.* wayfarer, wonderer.

viavài, *n.m.* bustle, coming and going.

vibrare, *vb.* vibrate.

vibrazione, *n.f.* vibration.

vicàrio, *n.m.* vicar.

vicenda, 1. *n.f.* story, vicissitude. 2. *adv.* av., alternatively, reciprocally.

vicinanza, *n.f.* neighborhood, vicinity.

vicinato, *n.m.* neighborhood.

vicino, 1. *n.m.* neighbor. 2. *adj.* nearby, neighboring, close. **vicino a,** *prep.* near, about. 3. *adv.* near, close.

vico, *n.m.* hamlet.

vicolo, *n.m.* alley. **v. cièco,** blind alley, dead end.

videocassetta, *n.f.* videotape.

videodisco, *n.m.* videodisc.

vidimare, *vb.* validate, authenticate.

vietare, *vb.* forbid, veto.

vietato, *adj.* forbidden.

vigilante, *adj.* vigilant, alert, watchful.

vigilare, *vb.* watch, look out.

vìgile, *n.m.* policeman.

vigília, *n.f.* vigil; eve.

vigliaccheria, *n.f.* cowardice.

vigliacco, *n.m.* cad.

vigna, *n.f.* vineyard.

vigneto, *n.m.* vineyard.

vignetta, *n.f.* cartoon.

vigore, *n.m.* vigor, force.

vigoroso, *adj.* vigorous, forceful, lusty.

vile, *adj.* vile.

vilipèndere, *vb.* scorn, despise, insult.

villàggio, *n.m.* village.

villano, *adj.* inconsiderate.

villetta, *n.f.* cottage.

villoso, *adj.* fleecy, hairy.

vincere, *vb.* conquer, overcome, overpower, beat, vanquish, win.

vincìbile, *adj.* conquerable.

vincitore, *n.m.* victor, conqueror, winner.

vincolare, *vb.* bind.

vìncolo, *n.m.* bind, link.

vinile, *n.m.* vinyl.

vino, *n.m.* wine. **v. di Xeres,** sherry.

viòla, *n.f.* viola; viol; violet.

violare, *vb.* violate; rape.

violatore, *n.m.* violator.

violazione, *n.f.* violation, breach.

violènto, *adj.* violent.

violènza, *n.f.* violence.

violino, *n.m.* violin, fiddle.

violoncellista, *n.m.* cellist.

violoncèllo, *n.m.* cello.

viòttolo, *n.m.* byway, lane.

vìpera, *n.f.* adder, viper.

virare, *vb.* tack, veer.

vìrgola, *n.f.* comma.

virile, *adj.* virile, manly.

virilità, *n.f.* virility, manhood.

virtù, *n.f.* virtue.

virtuale, *adj.* virtual.

virtuosìsmo, *n.m.* virtuosity.

virtuoso, *adj.* virtuous.

virulento, *adj.* virulent, deadly.

vìscere, *n.f.pl.* viscera, guts, bowels.

vischio, *n.m.* bird-lime; mistletoe.

viscoso, *adj.* viscous, sticky.

visìbile, *adj.* visible.

visiera, *n.f.* visor.

visione, *n.f.* vision.

vìsita, *n.f.* visit.

visitare, *vb.* visit.

visivo, *adj.* of vision.

viso, *n.m.* face, countenance.

visone, *n.m.* mink.

vispo, *adj.* brisk, lively; attentive.

vista, *n.f.* sight; eyesight; view.

vistare, *vb.* visa.

visto, *n.m.* visa.

vistosamente, *adv.* gaudily.

vistosità, *n.f.* flashiness, gaudiness.

vistoso, *adj.* flashy, gaudy.

visuale, *adj.* visual.

vita, *n.f.* life; livelihood; living; waist.

vitale, *adj.* vital.

vitalità, *n.f.* vitality.

vitalìzio, *adj.* for life.

vitamina, *n.f.* vitamin.

vite, *n.f.* vine; grapevine; screw.

vitèllo, *n.m.* calf; veal.

vitìccio, *n.m.* tendril.

vìtreo, *adj.* glassy, of glass.

vìttima, *n.f.* victim.

vitto, *n.m.* food, victuals, board.

vittòria, *n.f.* victory.

vittorioso, *adj.* victorious.

viuzza, *n.f.* narrow street.

viva, *interj.* hurrah (for).

vivace, *adj.* vivacious, lively, brisk.

vivacemente, *adv.* vivaciously, briskly.

vivacità, *n.f.* vivacity, liveliness, briskness.

vivàio, *n.m.* hatchery, nursery.

vivanda, *n.f.* food, dish.

vivènte, *adj.* living, alive.

vivere, *vb.* live, be alive.

vìvido, *adj.* vivid.

vivo, *adj.* live.

viziare, *vb.* vitiate.

vìzio, *n.m.* vice.

vizioso, *adj.* vicious.

vizzo, *adj.* withered; flabby.

vocabolàrio, *n.m.* vocabulary.

vocale, 1. *n.f.* vowel. **2.** *adj.* vocal.

vocazione, *n.f.* vocation, calling.

voce, *n.f.* voice; word, rumor, report.

vociare, *vb.* vociferate.

voga, *n.f.* vogue.

vòglia, *n.f.* wish, desire; birthmark.

voi, *pron.* 2. *pl.* you.

volante, *n.m.* steering-wheel; flounce.

volantino, *n.m.* flier.

volare, *vb.* fly.

volerci, *vb.* be necessary.

volgare, *adj.* vulgar; common; vernacular.

volgarità, *n.f.* vulgarity, commonness.

volgo, *n.m.* rabble.

volo, *n.m.* flight. **v. noleggiato,** charter flight.

volontà, *n.f.* will.

volontàrio, 1. *n.m.* volunteer. **2.** *adj.* voluntary.

volpe, *n.f.* fox.

volpino, *adj.* foxy.

vòlta, *n.f.* time; vault.

voltafàccia, *n.m.* about-face.

voltagabbana, *n.m.* turncoat, traitor.

voltàggio, *n.m.* voltage.

voltastòmaco, *n.m.* revulsion, nausea.

volteggiare, *vb.* hover; turn; vault.

volume, *n.m.* volume, bulk.

voluminoso, *adj.* voluminous, bulky.

voluttà, *n.f.* pleasure, delight.

vòmere, *n.m.* coulter; plowshare.

vomitare, *vb.* vomit, disgorge.

vòmito, *n.m.* vomit.

vorace, *adj.* voracious.

vòrtice, *n.m.* vortex, whirlpool, eddy.

vòstro, *adj.* your; yours.

votante, *n.m.* voter.

votare, *vb.* vote.

votazione, *n.f.* voting, ballot.

voto, *n.m.* vow; wish; mark; grade.

vulcano, *n.m.* volcano.

vulneràbile, *adj.* vulnerable.

vuotare, *vb.* empty.

vuòto, 1. *n.m.* emptiness; vacuum. **2.** *adj.* empty, blank, vacant.

W, X, Z

W., abbr. for **evviva** hurrah for.

W.C., abbr. for water-closet (toilet).

xenòfobo, *adj.* xenophobe.

zabaióne, *n.m.* eggnog.

zaffiro, *n.m.* sapphire.

zàino, *n.m.* knapsack.

zampa, *n.f.* paw.

zampillare, *vb.* gush; squirt.

zampogna, *n.f.* bagpipe.

zàngola, *n.f.* churn.

zanna, *n.f.* fang.

zanzara, *n.f.* mosquito.

zanzarièra, *n.f.* mosquito-net.

zappa, *n.f.* hoe.

zappare, *vb.* hoe.

zar, *n.m.* czar.

zàttera, *n.f.* raft.

zavorra, *n.f.* ballast.

zèbra, *n.f.* zebra.

zecca, *n.f.* mint.

zecchino, *n.m.* first-quality gold, pure gold; sequin.

zèffiro, *n.m.* zephyr.

zelante, *n.m.* zealous.

zèlo, *n.m.* zeal.

zènzero, *n.m.* ginger.

zeppo, *adj.* chock full.

zèro, *n.m.* zero; cipher.

zìa, *n.f.* aunt.

zibellino, *n.m.* sable.

zigrinare, *vb.* grain, groove; mill, knurl.

zimbello, *n.m.* laughing stock.

zinco, *n.m.* zinc.

zìngara, *n.f.* gypsy woman.

zìngaro, *n.m.* gypsy.

zìo, *n.m.* uncle.

zitèlla, *n.f.* old maid, spinster.

zittire, *fb.* shut up, silence; hiss.

zitto, *adj.* silent.

zòccolo, *n.m.* hoof; wooden shoe; baseboard.

zòlla, *n.f.* clod, sod.

zòna, *n.f.* zone.

zoològico, *adj.* zoological.

zoologìa, *n.f.* zoology.

zoppicamento, *n.m.* limp.

zoppicare, *vb.* limp, hobble.

zòppo, *adj.* lame.

zòtico, 1. *n.* boor. 2. *adj.* boorish.

zoticone, *n.m.* lout.

zucca, *n.f.* gourd, pumpkin, squash.

zùcchero, *n.m.* sugar.

zuppa, *n.f.* soup.

Zurigo, *n.m.* Zurich.

zuzzerellone, *n.m.* hobblede-hoy.

a, *art.* un *m.*, una *f.*

aback, *adv.* all'indietro.

abacus, *n.* àbaco *m.*

abandon, 1. *n.* abbandono *m.* **2.** *vb.* abbandonare.

abandoned, *adj.* abbandonato.

abandonment, *n.* abbandono *m.*

abase, *vb.* abbassare, avvilire.

abasement, *n.* abbassamento *m.*, avvilimento *m.*

abash, *vb.* sconcertare.

abate, *vb.* diminuire.

abatement, *n.* diminuzione *f.*

abbacy, *n.* abbazia *f.*

abbess, *n.* badessa *f.*

abbey, *n.* badía *f.*, abbazía *f.*

abbot, *n.* abate *m.*

abbreviate, *vb.* abbreviare, raccorciare.

abbreviation, *n.* abbreviatura *f.*, raccorciamento *m.*

abdicate, *vb.* abdicare.

abdication, *n.* abdicazione *f.*

abdomen, *n.* addòme *m.*

abdominal, *adj.* addominale.

abduct, *vb.* rapire.

abduction, *n.* rapimento *m.*, ratto *m.*

abductor, *n.* rapitore *m.*

abed, *adv.* a letto.

aberrant, *adj.* aberrante.

aberration, *n.* aberrazione *f.*

abet, *vb.* incoraggiare.

abetment, *n.* incoraggiamento *m.*

abettor, *n.* incoraggiatore *m.*

abeyance, *n.* sospensione *f.*

abhor, *vb.* aborrire, detestare.

abhorrence, *n.* aborrimento *m.*, ripugnanza *f.*

abhorrent, *adj.* ripugnante.

abide, *vb.* (dwell) abitare; (remain) rimanere; (tolerate) sopportare.

abiding, *adj.* permanènte, costante.

ability, *n.* abilità *f.*, capacità *f.*

abject, *adj.* abiètto.

abjuration, *n.* abiura *f.*

abjure, *vb.* abiurare.

abjurer, *n.* chi abiura.

ablative, *adj. and n.* ablativo (*m.*).

ablaze, *adj.* in fiamme.

able, *adj.* àbile, capace (di); **(be a.)** potere.

able-bodied, *adj.* forte, robusto.

abloom, *adj.* in fiore.

ablution, *n.* abluzione *f.*

ably, *adv.* abilmente.

abnegate, *vb.* abnegare.

abnegation, *n.* abnegazione *f.*

abnormal, *adj.* anormale.

abnormality, *n.* anormalità *f.*

abnormally, *adv.* anormalmente.

aboard, **1.** *adv.* (naut.) a bordo; **(all a.)** in carrozza. **2.** *prep.* a bordo di.

abode, *n.* dimora *f.*

abolish, *vb.* abolire.

abolishment, *n.* abolimento *m.*

abolition, *n.* abolizione *f.*

A-bomb, *n.* bomba atòmica *f.*

abominable, *adj.* abominévole.

abominate, *vb.* abominare.

abomination, *n.* abominazione *f.*

aboriginal, *adj.* indigeno, aborigeno.

aborigine, *n.* indigeno *m.*, aborigeno *m.*

aborning, *adj.* nascente.

abort, *vb.* abortire.

abortion, *n.* aborto *m.*

abortive, *adj.* abortivo.

abound, *vb.* abbondare.

about, 1. *adv.* (approximately) pressappòco, all'incirca; (around) intorno; **(be a. to)** stare per. **2.** *prep.* (concerning; around) intorno a; (near) vicino a.

about-face, *n.* voltafàccia *m.*

above, *adv. and prep.* sopra.

aboveboard, 1. *adj.* sincèro, onèsto. **2.** *adv.* apertamente, onestamente.

above-mentioned, *adj.* summenzionato.

abrasion, *n.* abrasione *f.*

abrasive, *n. and adj.* abrasivo (*m.*).

abreast, *adv. and prep.* di fianco (a).

abridge, *vb.* abbreviare.

abridgment, *n.* abbreviamento *m.*

abroad, *adv.* all'èstero.

abrogate, *vb.* abrogare.
abrogation, *n.* abrogazione *f.*
abrupt, *adj.* (sudden) improviso; (steep) rípido; (curt) rude.
abruptly, *adv.* (suddenly) all'improvviso, improvvisamente; (curtly) rudemente.
abruptness, *n.* rudezza *f.*
abscess, *n.* ascèsso *m.*
abscissa, *n.* ascissa *f.*
abscond, *vb.* sparire; *(fam.)* svignàrsela.
absence, *n.* assènza *f.*
absent, *adj.* assènte.
absentee, *n.* assènte *m.*
absenteeism, *n.* assenteismo *m.*
absent-minded, *adj.* distratto.
absinthe, *n.* assènzio *m.*
absolute, *adj.* assoluto.
absolutely, *adv.* assolutamente.
absoluteness, *n.* assolutezza *f.*
absolution, *n.* assoluzione *f.*
absolutism, *n.* assolutismo *m.*
absolve, *vb.* assòlvere.
absorb, *vb.* assorbire.
absorbed, *adj.* *(lit.)* assorbito; *(fig.)* assorto.
absorbent, *n. and adj.* assorbènte *m.*
absorbing, *adj.* assorbènte.
absorption, *n.* assorbimento *m.*
abstain, *vb.* astenersi.
abstemious, *adj.* astèmio.
abstinence, *n.* astinènza *f.*
abstract, 1. *n.* (book, article) riassunto *m.,* sunto *m.* **2.** *adj.* astratto. **3.** *vb.* astrarre, riassùmere.
abstracted, *adj.* astratto.
abstraction, *n.* astrazione *f.*
abstruse, *adj.* astruso.
absurd, *adj.* assurdo.
absurdity, *n.* assurdità *f.,* assurdo *m.*
absurdly, *adv.* assurdamente.
abundance, *n.* abbondanza *f.*
abundant, *adj.* abbondante.
abundantly, *adv.* abbondantemente.
abuse, 1. *n.* (misuse) abuso *m.;* (insult) insulto *m.,* ingiùria *f.* **2.** *vb.* abusare (di), insultare, ingiuriare.
abusive, *adj.* (misusing) abusivo; (insulting) insolente, ingiurioso.
abusively, *adv.* abusivamente, insolentemente, ingiuriosamente.

abut, *vb.* confinare con.
abutment, *n.* tèrmine *m.*
abysmal, *adj.* abissale.
abyss, *n.* abisso *m.*
Abyssinia, *n.* Abissínia *f.*
Abyssinian, *n. and adj.* abissino.
acacia, *n.* acàcia *f.*
academic, *adj.* accadèmico.
academic freedom, *n.* libertà d'insegnamento *f.*
academic year, *n.* anno accademico *m.*
academy, *n.* accadèmia *f.*
acanthus, *n.* acanto *m.*
accede, *vb.* consentire.
accelerate, *vb.* accelerare.
acceleration, *n.* accelerazione *f.*
accelerator, *n.* acceleratore *m.*
accent, *n.* accènto *m.*
accentuate, *vb.* *(lit.)* accentare; *(fig.)* accentuare.
accept, *vb.* accettare.
acceptability, *n.* accettabilità.
acceptable, *adj.* accètto, accettàbile, gradévole.
acceptably, *adv.* accettabilmente.
acceptance, *n.* accettazione *f.*
access, *n.* accèsso *m.*
accessible, *adj.* accessíbile.
accessory, *n. and adj.* accessòrio *(m.).*
accident, *n.* incidènte *m.,* sinistro *m.;* (by a.) per caso.
accidental, *adj.* accidentale.
accidentally, *adv.* accidentalmente.
acclaim, *vb.* acclamare.
acclamation, *n.* acclamazione *f.*
acclimate, *vb.* acclimare, acclimatare.
acclivity, *n.* acclività *f.*
accolade, *n.* accollata *f.*
accommodate, *vb.* accomodare; (lodge) alloggiare.
accommodating, *adj.* accomodante, cortese.
accommodation, *n.* accomodazione *f;* (lodging) allòggio *m.*
accompaniment, *n.* accompagnamento *m.*
accompanist, *n.* accompagnatore *m.*
accompany, *vb.* accompagnare.
accomplice, *n.* còmplice *m. and f.*
accomplish, *vb.* compire.

accomplished, *adj.* compito.

accomplishment, *n.* compimento *m.*

accord, *n.* accòrdo *m.*

accordance, *n.* conformità *f.*; **(in a. with)** conforme a.

accordingly, *adv.* (correspondingly) conformemente; (therefore) dunque.

according to, *prep.* secondo.

accordion, *n.* fisarmònica *f.*

accost, *vb.* abbordare.

account, *n. (comm.)* conto *m.*; (narrative) racconto *m.*

accountable for, *adj.* responsàbile di.

accountant, *n.* ragioniere.

account for, *vb.* rèndere conto di.

accounting, *n.* (occupation) ragioneria *f.*; (procedure) contabilità *f.*

accouter, *vb.* abbigliare.

accouterments, *n.* abbigliatura *f.sg.*

accredit, *vb.* accreditare.

accretion, *n.* accrescimento *m.*

accrual, *n.* accrescimento *m.*

accrue, *vb.* accréscere.

accumulate, *vb.* accumulare.

accumulation, *n.* accumulazione *f.*

accumulative, *adj.* accumulativo.

accumulator, *n.* accumulatore *m.*

accuracy, *n.* accuratezza *f.*

accurate, *adj.* accurato.

accursed, *adj.* maledetto.

accusation, *n.* accusa *f.*

accusative, *n. and adj.* accusativo *(m.).*

accuse, *vb.* accusare, incolpare, imputare.

accused, *n.* accusato *m.*, incolpato *m.*

accuser, *n.* accusatore *m.*, incolpatore *m.*

accustom, *vb.* abituare.

accustomed, *adj.* sòlito, abituale; (be accustomed to) solere; (become accustomed to) abituarsi a.

ace, *n.* asso *m.* **(a. in the hole)** asso nella manica

acerbity, *n.* acerbità *f.*

acetate, *n.* acetato *m.*

acetic, *adj.* acètico.

acetify, *vb.* acidificare.

acetone, *n.* acetone *m.*

acetylene, *n.* acetilène *m.*

ache, *n.* dolore *m.*, male *m.*

achieve, *vb.* compire, raggiùngere.

achievement, *n.* compimento *m.*, raggiungimento *m.*

Achilles' heel, *n.* tallone d'Achille *m.*

acid, *n. and adj.* àcido *(m.).*

acidify, *vb.* acidificare.

acidity, *n.* acidità *f.*

acid test, *n.* prova del fuoco *f.*

acidosis, *n.* acidòsi *f.*

acidulous, *adj.* acìdulo.

acknowledge, *vb.* (recognize) riconóscere; **(a. receipt of)** accusare, dichiarare ricevuta di.

acme, *n.* acme *f.*, punto culminante *m.*

acne, *n.* acne *f.*

acolyte, *n.* accòlito *m.*

acorn, *n.* ghianda *f.*

acoustics, *n.* acùstica *f.sg.*

acquaint, *vb.* informare, far sapere; (be acquainted with) conóscere.

acquaintance, *n.* conoscènza *f.*

acquainted, *adj.* conosciuto, familiare.

acquiesce, *vb.* acquietarsi, consentire tacitamente.

acquiescence, *n.* acquiescenza *f.*

acquire, *vb.* acquistare.

acquisition, *n.* acquisto *m.*

acquisitive, *adj.* acquisitivo.

acquit, *v.* assòlvere.

acquittal, *n.* assoluzione *f.*

acre, *n.* acro *m.*

acreage, *n.* estensione di terra *f.*

acrid, *adj.* acre.

acrimonious, *adj.* acre.

acrimony, *n.* acrèdine *f.*, acrimònia *f.*

acrobat, *n.* acròbata *m. and f.*

acrobatics, *n.* acrobàtica *f.*

acronym, *n.* acrònimo *m.*

acropolis, *n.* acròpoli, *f.*

across, *adv. and prep.* attraverso. **(a. the board)** generalizzato.

acrostic, *n.* acròstico *m.*

act, **1.** *n.* atto *m.* **2.** *vb.* agire; (stage) recitare; (behave) comportarsi.

acting, 1. *n.* recitazione *f.* **2.** *adj.* provvisòrio.

actinium, *n.* attínio *m.*

action, *n.* azione *f.*

activate, *vb.* attivare.

activation, *n.* attivazione *f.*

activator, *n.* attivatore *m.*

active, *adj.* attivo.

activism, *n.* attivismo *m.*

activity, *n.* attività *f.*

actor, *n.* attore *m.*

actress, *n.* attrice *f.*

actual, *adj.* vero.

actuality, *n.* verità *f.*

actually, *adv.* veramente.

actuary, *n.* attuàrio *m.*

actuate, *vb.* attuare.

acumen, *n.* acume *m.*

acupuncture, *n.* agopuntura *f.*

acute, *adj.* acuto.

acutely, *adv.* acutamente.

acuteness, *n.* acutezza *f.*

adage, *n.* adàgio *m.*, màssima *f.*, provèrbio *m.*

Adam, Adamo.

adamant, *adj.* adamantino.

Adam's apple, *n.* pomo d'Adamo *m.*

adapt, *vb.* addattare.

adaptability, *n.* adattabilità *f.*

adaptable, *adj.* adattàbile.

adaptation, *n.* adattamento *m.*

adapter, *n.* riduttore *m.*

adaptive, *adj.* adattévole.

add, *vb.* (join) aggiùngere; *(arith.)* sommare, addizionare.

addendum, *n.* addendo *m.*

adder, *n.* vipera *f.*

addict, *n.* dipendente *m.; (drug a.)* tossicòmane *m.*

addict oneself to, *vb.* dedicarsi a.

adding machine, *n.* calcolatrice *f.*

addition, *n.* addizione *f.*

additional, *adj.* addizionale.

additive, *n.* additivo *m.*

addle, *vb.* confondere; (egg) imputridirsi.

addled, *adj.* confuso; (egg) màrcio, pùtrido.

address, 1. *n.* (on letters, etc.) indirizzo *m.;* (speech) discorso *m.* **2.** *vb.* (a letter) indirizzare; (a person) indirizzarsi a.

addressee, *n.* destinatàrio *m.*

adduce, *vb.* addurre.

adenoid, 1. *n.* vegetazione adenòide *f.* **2.** *adj.* adenòide.

adept, *adj.* dèstro, àbile.

adeptly, *adv.* destramente, abilmente.

adeptness, *n.* destrezza *f.*, abilità *f.*

adequacy, *n.* sufficiènza *f.*

adequate, *adj.* adeguato, sufficiènte.

adequately, *adv.* adeguatamente, sufficientemente.

adhere, *vb.* aderire.

adherence, *n.* aderènza *f.*

adherent, *n.* aderènte *m.*

adhesion, *n.* adesione *f.*

adhesive, *n.* and *adj.* adesivo *(m.).*

adhesiveness, *n.* adesività *f.*

adieu, *interj.* addìo.

adjacent, *adj.* adiacènte.

adjustable, *adj.* regolàbile.

adjective, *n.* aggettivo *m.*

adjoin, *vb.* essere adiacènte a.

adjoining, *adj.* adiacènte.

adjourn, *vb.* aggiornare.

adjournment, *n.* aggiornamento *m.*

adjunct, *n.* and *adj.* aggiunto, accessòrio.

adjust, *vb.* aggiustare.

adjuster, *n.* aggiustatore *m.*

adjustment, *n.* (action) aggiustamento *m.;* (money) aggiustatura *f.*

adjutant, *n.* aiutante *m.*, assistènte *m.*

ad-lib, *vb.* improvvisare.

administer, *vb.* amministrare.

administration, *n.* amministrazione *f.*

administrative, *adj.* amministrativo.

administrator, *n.* amministratore *m.*

admirable, *adj.* ammirévole, ammiràbile.

admirably, *adv.* ammirabilmente.

admiral, *n.* ammiràglio *m.*

admiralty, *n.* ammiragliato *m.*, ministero della marina *m.*

admiration, *n.* ammirazione *f.*

admire, *vb.* ammirare.

admirer, *n.* ammiratore *m.*

admiringly, *adv.* con ammirazione.

admissible, *adj.* ammissíbile.

admission, *n.* (entrance) ammissione *f.;* (entry) entrata *f.;* (confession) confessione *f.*

admit, *vb.* amméttere.

admittance, *n.* ammissione *f.;* (entry) entrata *f.*

admittedly, *adv.* ammettendo.

admixture, *n.* mescolanza *f.*

admonish, *vb.* ammonire.

admonition, *n.* ammonizione *f.*

ado, *n.* fracasso *m.*

adobe, *n.* mattone crudo *m.*

adolescence, *n.* adolescènza *f.*

adolescent, *n. and adj.* adolescènte (*m.*).

adopt, *vb.* adottare.

adoption, *n.* adozione *f.*

adorable, *adj.* adoràbile.

adoration, *n.* adorazione *f.*

adore, *vb.* adorare.

adorn, *vb.* adornare, ornare.

adorned, *adj.* adorno.

adornment, *n.* adornamento *m.*

adrenal glands, *n.* ghiàndole surrenali *f.pl.*

adrenalin, *n.* adrenalina *f.*

Adriatic, *adj.* Adriatico.

adrift, *adv.* alla deriva.

adroit, *adj.* destro, àbile.

adulate, *vb.* adulare.

adulation, *n.* adulazione *f.*

adult, *n. and adj.* adulto.

adulterant, *n. and adj.* adulterante.

adulterate, *vb.* adulterare.

adulterer, *n.* adùltero *m.*

adulteress, *n.* adùltera *f.*

adultery, *n.* adultèrio *m.*

advance, 1. *n.* progresso *m.;* (pay) antìcipo *m.;* **(in a.)** in antìcipo. **2.** *vb.* avanzare, progredire; (pay) anticipare.

advanced, *adj.* avanzato, progredito.

advancement, *n.* avanzamento *m.*

advantage, *n.* vantàggio *m.*

advantageous, *adj.* vantaggioso.

advantageously, *adv.* vantaggiosamente.

advent, *n.* avvènto *m.*

adventitious, *adj.* avventízio.

adventure, 1. *n.* avventura *f.* **2.** *vb.* avventurare, rischiare.

adventurer, *n.* avventurière *m.*

adventurous, *adj.* avventuroso.

adventurously, *adv.* avventurosamente.

adverb, *n.* avvèrbio *m.*

adverbial, *adj.* avverbiale.

adversary, *n.* avversàrio *m.*

adverse, *adj.* avvèrso.

adversely, *adv.* avversamente.

adversity, *n.* avversità *f.*

advert, *vb.* avvertire.

advertise, *vb.* far réclame per, reclamizzare.

advertisement, *n.* réclame *f.,* pubblicità *f.;* (newspaper) annunzio *m.,* inserzione *f.*

advertiser, *n.* inserzionista *m.*

advertising, *n.* réclame *f.,* pubblicità *f.* **(a. agent)** *n.* pubblicista *m. and f.;* **(a. campaign)** *n.* campagna pubblicitaria *f.*

advice, *n.* consiglio *m.;* (news) avviso *m.*

advisability, *n.* convenienza *f.,* opportunità *f.*

advisable, *adj.* conveniente, opportuno.

advisably, *adv.* opportunamente.

advise, *adv.* consigliare; (inform) avvisare.

advisedly, *adv.* consigliatamente, apposta.

advisement, *n.* deliberazione *f.*

adviser, *n.* consigliere *m.*

advisory, *adj.* consultivo.

advocacy, *n.* difesa *f.,* propugnazione *f.*

advocate, 1. *n.* (law) avvocato *m.;* (defender) difensore *m.,* propugnatore *m.* **2.** *vb.* propugnare, difèndere.

aegis, *n.* égida *f.*

aerate, *vb.* aerare.

aeration, *n.* aerazione *f.*

aerial, *adj.* aèreo.

aerially, *adv.* per ària.

aerie, *n.* nido *m.*

aerodynamic, *adj.* aerodinàmico.

aeronautics, *n.* aeronàutica *f.*

aerosol bomb, *n.* bomboletta nebulizzante *f.*

aesthete, *n.* esteta *m. and f.*

aesthetic, *adj.* estètico.

aesthetics, *n.* estètica *f.*

afar, *adv.* lontano.

affability, *n.* affabilità *f.*

affable, *adj.* affàbile.

affably, *adv.* affabilmente.

affair, *n.* affare *m.*

affect, *vb.* (move) commuovere; (concern) interessare; (pretend) affettare.

affectation, *n.* affettazione *f.*

affected, *adj.* affettato.

affecting, *adj.* commovènte.

affection, *n.* affezione *f.*

affectionate, *adj.* affettuoso.

affectionately, *adv.* affettosamente.

afferent, *adj.* afferènte.

affiance, *vb.* fidanzare.

affidavit, *n.* dichiarazione giurata *f.*

affiliate, *vb.* affiliare, associare.

affiliation, *n.* affiliazione *f.*, associazione *f.*

affinity, *n.* affinità *f.*

affirm, *vb.* affermare.

affirmation, *n.* affermazione *f.*

affirmative, *adj.* affermativo.

affirmatively, *adv.* affermativamente.

affix, 1. *n.* affisso *m.* 2. *vb.* affissare.

afflict, *vb.* affliggere.

affliction, *n.* afflizione *f.*

affluence, *n.* opulènza *f.*

affluent, *adj.* opulènto.

afford, *vb.* (have the means to) avere i mezzi di.

affray, *n.* lite *f.*, rissa *f.*

affront, 1. *n.* affronto *m.* 2. *vb.* affrontare.

afield, *adv.* (far a.) lontano.

afire, *adv.* in fiamme.

aflame, *adv.* in fiamme.

afloat, *adj.* a galla.

afoot, *adj.* a piedi.

aforementioned, *adj.* sopraindicato, suindicato.

aforesaid, *adj.* sopraddetto, suddetto.

afraid, *pred.adj.* (be a.) aver paùra.

afresh, *adv.* di nuovo, da capo, daccapo.

Africa, *n.* Àfrica *f.*

African, *n. and adj.* africano (*m.*)

aft, *adv.* indiètro.

after, 1. *prep.* dopo. 2. *conj.* dopo che.

aftereffect, *n.* effètto *m.*

afterlife, *n.* al-di-là *m.*

aftermath, *n.* conseguènze *f. (pl.)*

afternoon, *n.* pomeriggio *m.*

aftershave, *n.* dopobarba *m.*

afterthought, *n.* (as an a.) ripensàndoci.

afterward, *adv.* dopo.

afterwards, *adv.* dopo.

again, *adv.* di nuòvo; (again and again) ripetutamente.

against, *prep.* contro.

agape, *adv.* a bocca aperta.

agate, *n.* àgata *f.*

age, 1. *n.* età *f.* 2. *vb.* invecchiare.

aged, *adj.* vècchio.

ageism, *n.* discriminazione basata sull'età *f.*

ageless, *adj.* che non invècchia.

agency, *n.* agenzia *f.*

agenda, *n.* òrdine del giorno *m.*

agent, *n.* agènte *m.*

agglutinate, *vb.* agglutinare.

agglutination, *n.* agglutinazione *f.*

aggrandize, *vb.* ingrandire.

aggrandizement, *n.* ingrandimento *m.*

aggravate, *vb.* aggravare.

aggravation, *n.* aggravamento *m.*

aggregate, 1. *n.* aggregato *m.* 2. *vb.* aggregare.

aggregation, *n.* aggregazione *f.*

aggression, *n.* aggressione *f.*

aggressive, *adj.* aggressivo.

aggressively, *adv.* aggressivamente.

aggressiveness, *n.* aggressività *f.*

aggressor, *n.* aggressore *m.*

aghast, *adj.* sbalordito.

agile, *adj.* àgile.

agility, *n.* agilità *f.*

agitate, *vb.* agitare.

agitation, *n.* agitazione *f.*

agitator, *n.* agitatore *m.*

agnostic, *n. and adj.* agnòstico (*m.*)

ago, *adv.* fa (*always follows*).

agonize, *vb.* agonizzare; (*refl.*) angosciarsi.

agonized, *adj.* agonizzante.

agony, n. agonía f.; **(be in a.)** agonizzare.

agrarian, adj. agràrio.

agree, vb. concordare, èssere d'accordo.

agreeable, adj. piacévole, gradévole; (of persons) simpàtico.

agreeably, adv. piacevolmente, gradevolmente.

agreeing, adj. concòrde.

agreement, n. accòrdo m.

agribusiness, n. agricultura, orticultura f.

agriculture, n. agricultura f.

agronomy, n. agronomia f.

ahead, adv. avanti; **(straight a.)** sèmpre diritto.

aid, 1. n. aiuto m. 2. vb. aiutare.

aide, n. aiutante m.

AIDS, n. aids. f. (sindrome di immunodeficenza aggravata).

ail, vb. èssere malato.

ailing, adj. malato.

ailment, n. malattía f.

aim, 1. n. mira; (purpose) scòpo m. 2. vb. (point) puntare; (direct) dirígere; (look toward) mirare.

aimless, adj. senza scòpo.

aimlessly, adv. senza scòpo.

air, 1. n. ària f. 2. vb. aerare.

airbag, n. (in automobiles) sacco ad aria m.

air base, n. base aèrea f.

airborne, adj. aviotrasportato.

air-condition, vb. istallare un impianto di condizionamento d'ària in.

air-conditioned, adj. ad ària condizionata.

air-conditioning, n. aria condizionata f.

aircraft, n. aèreo m.

aircraft-carrier, n. portaèrei m.

air fleet, n. flotta aèrea f.

air gun, n. fucile ad ària compressa m.

airing, n. (walk) passeggiata f.

airline, n. aviolínea f.

air liner, n. aeroplano m.

air mail, n. posta aèrea f.

airplane, n. aeroplano m.

air pollution, n. inquinamento dell'aria m.

airport, n. aeropòrto m., aeroscalo m.; (for seaplanes) idroscalo m.

air pressure, n. pressione dell'ària f.

air raid, n. attacco aèreo m.

air-sick, adj. **(be a.),** sentir nàusea (in un aeroplano) f.

airtight, adj. impermeàbile all'aria.

airy, adj. arioso.

aisle, n. passaggio m.; (church) navata f.

ajar, adj. socchiuso.

akin, adj. affine.

alacrity, n. alacrità f.

alarm, 1. n. allarme m. 2. vb. allarmare, spaventare.

alarmist, n. allarmista m.

albino, n. and adj. albino (m.).

album, n. album m.

albumen, n. albume m.

alchemy, n. alchimia f.

alcohol, n. àlcool m.

alcoholic, adj. alc(o)òlico.

alcove, n. alcòva f.

ale, n. birra f.

alert, 1. n. allarme m. 2. adj. vigilante; (keen) acuto. 3. vb. avvertire.

alfalfa, n. alfalfa f.

algae, n. alghe f.pl.

algebra, n. àlgebra f.

alias, adv. àlias.

alibi, n. àlibi m.

alien, n. and adj. alièno (m.); (foreign) straniero (m.), forestiero (m.).

alienate, vb. alienare.

alight, 1. vb. (dismount) smontare; (get down) scéndere. 2. adj. acceso.

align, vb. allineare.

alike, 1. adj. símile. 2. adv. similmente.

alimentary, adj. alimentare.

alimentary canal, n. canale alimentàrio m.

alimony, n. alimenti m.pl.

alive, adj. vivente; **(be a.)** vívere.

alkali, n. àlcali m.

alkaline, adj. alcalino.

all, adj. tutto; **(a. at once)** sopratutto; **(a. at once)** tutt'a un tratto; **(a. the same)** nondimeno;

(a. of you) voi tutti; **(not at a.)** niente affatto.

allay, *vb.* alleviare; (lessen) diminuire.

allegation, *n.* accusa *f.*

allege, *vb.* accusare.

allegiance, *n.* fedeltà *f.*

allegory, *n.* allegoría *f.*

allergy, *n.* allergia *f.*

alleviate, *vb.* alleviare.

alley, *n.* vícolo *m.;* (in garden) viale *m.*

alliance, *n.* alleanza *f.*

allied, *adj.* alleato *m.;* (related) affine.

alligator, *n.* alligatore *m.*

allocate, *vb.* assegnare.

allot, *vb.* assegnare, dividere.

allotment, *n.* assegnazione *f.*

allow, *vb.* (permit) perméttere; (admit) amméttere; (grant) concédere; **(a. for)** far débito conto di.

allowance, *n.* (money) assegno *m.;* (permission) permesso *m.;* (reduction) riduzione *f.*

alloy, 1. *n.* lega *f.* 2. *vb.* mescolare.

all right, *interj.* va bène.

all-time, *adj.* senza precedenti.

allude, *vb.* allùdere.

allure, *vb.* affascinare, adescare.

alluring, *adj.* adescatore, seducènte.

allusion, *n.* allusione *f.*

ally, 1. *n.* alleato *m.* 2. *vb.* alleare.

almanac, *n.* almanacco *m.*

almighty, *adj.* onnipotente.

almond, *n.* màndorla *f.*

almond-tree, *n.* màndorlo *m.*

almost, *adv.* quasi.

alms, *n.* elemòsina *f.* (*sg.*)

aloft, *adv.* in alto.

alone, 1. *adj.* solo; **(let a.)** lasciare in pace. 2. *adv.* solamente.

along, *prep.* lungo; **(come a.!)** venite dunque!

alongside, 1. *adv.* accanto. 2. *prep.* accanto a.

aloof, 1. *adj.* riservato. 2. *adv.* in disparte.

aloud, *adv.* ad alta voce.

alpaca, *n.* alpaca *m.*

alphabet, *n.* alfabèto *m.*

alphabetical, *adj.* alfabètico.

alphabetize, *vb.* méttere in órdine alfabètico.

alpine, *adj.* alpino.

Alps, *n.* Alpi *f.pl.*

already, *adv.* già, di già.

also, *adv.* anche.

also-ran, *adj.* non-piazzato, perdente.

altar, *n.* altare *m.*

alter, *vb.* alterare.

alteration, *n.* alterazione *f.*

alternate, 1. *n.* sostituto *m.* 2. *adj.* alternativo. 3. *vb.* alternare.

alternating current, *n.* corrente alternata *f.*

alternative, 1. *n.* alternativa *f.* 2. *adj.* alternativo.

although, *conj.* benchè, quantunque, sebbene.

altitude, *n.* altitùdine *f.*

alto, *n.* contralto *m.*

altogether, *adv.* completamente.

altruism, *n.* altruismo *m.*

alum, *n.* allume *m.*

aluminum, *n.* allumínio *m.*

altruism, *n.* altruismo *m.*

always, *adv.* sèmpre.

amalgam, *n.* amàlgama *m.*

amalgamate, *vb.* amalgamare.

amass, *vb.* ammassare.

amateur, *n.* dilettante *m. and f.*

amaze, *vb.* meravigliare, stupire; **(be a.d.)** meravigliarsi, stupirsi.

amazement, *n.* meravíglia *f.,* stupore *m.*

amazing, *adj.* meraviglioso.

ambassador, *n.* ambasciatore *m.*

amber, *n.* ambra *f.*

ambidextrous, *adj.* ambidèstro.

ambiguity, *n.* ambiguità *f.*

ambiguous, *adj.* ambíguo.

ambition, *n.* ambizione *f.*

ambitious, *adj.* ambizioso.

amble, *vb.* camminare senza fretta.

ambulance, *n.* ambulanza *f.*

ambulatory, *n. and adj.* ambulatòrio (*m.*).

ambush, 1. *n.* imboscata *f.* 2. *vb.* tendere un'imboscata a.

ameliorate, *vb.* migliorare.

amen, *interj.* amen, cosí sia.

amenable, *adj.* responsàbile, governàbile, dòcile.

amend, *vb.* emendare, corrèggere, migliorare.

amendment, *n.* emendamento *m.*

amenity, *n.* amenità *f.*
America, *n.* Amèrica *f.*
American, *n. and adj.* americano (*m*).
amethyst, *n.* ametista *f.*
amiable, *adj.* amàbile.
amicable, *adj.* amichévole.
amid, *prep.* fra, tra, in mèzzo a.
amidships, *adv.* nel mezzo della nave.
amiss, *adv.* che non va bene; **(be a.)** non andar bene.
amity, *n.* amicízia *f.*
ammonia, *n.* ammoníaca *f.*
ammunition, *n.* munizione *f.*
amnesia, *n.* amnesía *f.*
amnesty, *n.* amnistía *f.*
amniocentesis, *n.* amniocèntesi *f.*
amoeba, *n.* amèba *f.*
among, *prep.* fra, tra.
amoral, *adj.* amorale.
amorous, *adj.* amoroso.
amorphous, *adj.* amorfo.
amortize, *vb.* ammortizzare.
amount, **1.** *n.* somma *f.*, quantità *f.* **2.** *vb.* ammontare.
ampere, *n.* ampère *m.*
amphibian, *n.* anfibio *m.*
amphibious, *adj.* anfíbio.
amphitheater, *n.* anfiteatro *m.*
ample, *adj.* àmpio.
amplify, *vb.* ampliare, amplificare.
amputate, *vb.* amputare.
amputee, *n.* amputato *m.*, mutilato *m.*
amuse, *vb.* divertire.
amusement, *n.* divertimento *m.*
an, *art.* un *m.*, una *f.*
anachronism, *n.* anacronismo *m.*
anagram, *n.* anagramma *m.*
analogous, *adj.* anàlogo.
analogy, *n.* analogía *f.*
analysis, *n.* anàlisi *f.*
analyst, *n.* analista *m.*
analytic, *adj.* analítico.
analyze, *vb.* analizzare.
anarchy, *n.* anarchía *f.*
anathema, *n.* anatema *m.*
anatomy, *n.* anatomía *f.*
ancestor, *n.* antenato *m.*
ancestral, *adj.* degli antenati.
ancestry, *n.* lignàggio *m.*

anchor, **1.** *n.* àncora *f.* **2.** *vb.* ancorare.
anchorage, *n.* ancoràggio *m.*
anchovy, *n.* acciuga *f.*
ancient, *adj.* antico.
and, *conj.* e; (before vowels) ed.
anecdote, *n.* anèddoto *m.*
anemia, *n.* anemía *f.*
anesthesia, *n.* anestesía *f.*
anesthetic, *n. and adj.* anestètico (*m.*).
anesthetist, *n.* anestesista *m.*
anew, *adv.* di nuòvo.
angel, *n.* àngelo *m.*
anger, *n.* ira *f.*, ràbbia *f.*
angle, **1.** *n.* àngolo *m.* **2.** *vb.* (fish) pescare.
angry, *adj.* adirato, arrabiato; **(get a.)** adirarsi, arrabbiarsi.
anguish, *n.* angóscia *f.*
angular, *adj.* angolare.
aniline, *n.* anilina *f.*
animal, *n. and adj.* animale (*m.*).
animate, *vb.* animare.
animated, *adj.* animato.
animated cartoon, *n.* disegno animato *m.*
animation, *n.* animazione *f.*
animosity, *n.* animosità *f.*
animus, *n.* ànimo *m.*
anise, *n.* ànice *m.*
ankle, *n.* cavíglia *f.*
annals, *n.* annali *m.* (*pl.*)
annex, **1.** *n.* annèsso *m.* **2.** *vb.* annèttere.
annexation, *n.* annessione *f.*
annihilate, *vb.* annichilire.
anniversary, *n.* anniversàrio *m.*
annotate, *vb.* annotare.
annotation, *n.* annotazione *f.*
announce, *vb.* annunziare, annunciare.
announcement, *n.* annùncio *m.*
announcer, *n.* annunciatore *m.*, annunciatrice *f.*
annoy, *vb.* infastidire.
annoyance, *n.* fastídio *m.*
annual, *n. and adj.* ànnuo (*m.*), annuale (*m.*).
annuity, *n.* annualità *f.*
annul, *vb.* annullare.
annunciate, *vb.* annunciare.
anode, *n.* ànodo *m.*
anoint, *vb.* ùngere.
anomalous, *adj.* anòmalo.

anomaly, *n.* anomalìa *f.*

anonymity, *n.* anonimità *f.*

anonymous, *adj.* anònimo.

anorexia, *n.* anoressìa *f.*

anorexic, *adj.* anorèssico.

another, *adj.* un altro *m.,* un'altra *f.;* (one a.) l'un l'altro.

answer, 1. *n.* risposta *f.* **2.** *vb.* rispóndere.

answerable, *adj.* responsàbile.

ant, *n.* formìca *f.*

antacid, 1. *n.* antàcido *m.* **2.** *adj.* antiàcido.

antagonism, *n.* antagonismo *m.*

antagonist, *n.* antagonista *m.*

antagonistic, *adj.* ostile.

antagonize, *vb.* rèndere ostile.

antarctic, *n. and adj.* antàrtico (*m.*).

antecede, *vb.* precèdere.

antecedent, *adj.* antecedènte.

antedate, *vb.* precèdere.

antelope, *n.* antìlope *f.*

antenna, *n.* antenna *f.*

anterior, *adj.* anteriore.

anteroom, *n.* anticàmera *f.*

anthem, *n.* (church music) antìfona *f.;* (national a.) inno nazionale *m.*

anthill, *n.* formicaio *m.*

anthology, *n.* antologìa *f.*

anthracite, *n.* antracite *f.*

anthropological, *adj.* antropològico.

anthropology, *n.* antropologìa *f.*

antiaircraft, *adj.* antiaèreo.

antibody, *n.* anticòrpo *m.*

antic, *n.* buffonàta *f.*

anticipate, *vb.* anticipare.

anticipation, *n.* anticipazione *f.*

anticlerical, *adj.* anticlericale.

anticlimax, *n.* delusione *f.*

Antichrist, *n.* Anticristo *m.*

antidote, *n.* antìdoto *m.*

antimony, *n.* antimònio *m.*

antinuclear, *adj.* antinucleare.

antipathy, *n.* antipatìa *f.*

antiquated, *adj.* antiquato.

antique, 1. *n.* oggetto antico *m.* **2.** *adj.* antico.

antiquity, *n.* antichità *f.*

antiseptic, *n. and adj.* antisèttico (*m.*).

antisocial, *adj.* antisociale.

antitoxin, *n.* antitossina *f.*

antler, *n.* palco *m.*

anvil, *n.* incùdine *f.*

anxiety, *n.* ànsia *f.,* ansietà *f.*

anxious, *adj.* ansioso.

any, 1. *adj.* (in questions, for "some") del, dello, dell' *m.sg.,* della, dell' *f.sg.,* dei, degli *m.pl.,* delle *f.pl;* (not . . . any) non . . . nessun; (no matter which) non impòrta quale; (every) ogni. **2.** *pron.* (any of it, any of them, with verb) ne.

anybody, *pron.* qualcuno; (after negative) nessuno; (no matter who) non importa chi.

anyhow, *adv.* in qualche manièra, a ogni modo.

anyone, *pron. see* **anybody.**

anything, *pron.* qualcosa, qualche còsa; (after negation) nìente; (no matter) non impòrta che còsa.

anyway, *adv. see* **anyhow.**

anywhere, *adv.* non impòrta dove.

apart, *adv.* a parte.

apartheid, *n.* segregazione razziale *f.*

apartment, *n.* appartamento *m.*

apathetic, *adj.* apàtico.

apathy, *n.* apatìa *f.*

ape, *n.* scimmia *f.*

aperture, *n.* apertura *f.*

apex, *n.* àpice *m.*

aphorism, *n.* aforismo *m.*

apiary, *n.* apiàrio *f.*

apiece, *adj.* l'uno, cadaùno.

apogee, *n.* apogèo *m.*

apologetic, *adj.* (be a.) scusarsi.

apologize for, *vb.* scusarsi di.

apology, *n.* (defense) apologìa *f.;* (excuse) scusa *f.*

apoplectic, *adj.* apoplèttico.

apoplexy, *n.* apoplessìa *f.*

apostasy, *n.* apòstasi *f.*

apostate, *n.* apòstata *m.*

apostle, *n.* apòstolo *m.*

apostolic, *adj.* apostòlico.

apostrophe, *n.* apòstrofo *m.*

apotheosis, *n.* apoteòsi *f.*

Appalachians, *n.* Appalacchi *m.pl.*

appall, *vb.* spaventare.

apparatus, *n.* apparato *m.,* apparècchio *m.*

apparel, 1. *n.* vèste *f.,* vestimento *m.* 2. *vb.* vestire.

apparent, *adj.* apparènte.

apparition, *n.* apparizione *f.*

appeal, 1. *n.* appèllo *m.* 2. *vb.* appellare.

appear, *vb.* parere; (become visible) apparire; (seem) sembrare; (be evident) risultare.

appearance, *n.* apparènza *f.;* (looks) aspètto *m.*

appease, *vb.* placare, acquetare.

appeasement, *n.* rappacificazione *f.*

appeaser, *n.* pacificatore *m.*

appellant, *n.* appellante *m.*

appellate, *adj.* d'appèllo.

appendage, *n.* appendice *f.*

appendectomy, *n.* appendectomía *f.*

appendicitis, *n.* appendicite *f.*

appendix, *n.* appendice *f.*

appetite, *n.* appetito *m.*

appetizer, *n.* antipasto *m.*

appetizing, *adj.* gustoso.

applaud, *vb.* applaudire.

applause, *n.* applàuso *m.*

apple, *n.* pomo *m.,* mela *f.*

apple pie, *n.* torta di mele *f.*

applesauce, *n.* (*lit.*) consèrva di mele *f.;* (nonsense) fròttola *f.*

apple-tree, *n.* melo *m.*

appliance, *n.* apparècchio *m.*

appliances, *n.* (electric) eletrodomèstici *m.pl.*

applicable, *adj.* applicàbile.

applicant, *n.* richiedènte *m.*

application, *n.* (putting on) applicazione *f.;* (request) domanda *f.*

appliqué, *adj.* applicato; (a. work) ricamo applicato *m.*

apply, *vb.* (put on) applicare; (request) richièdere, fare una domanda.

appoint, *vb.* (a person) nominare; (time, place) fissare, stabilire.

appointment, *n.* (nomination) nòmina *f.;* (date) appuntamento *m.*

apportion, *vb.* distribuire.

appose, *vb.* giustapporre.

apposite, *adj.* appòsito.

apposition, *n.* apposizione *f.*

appraisal, *n.* stima *f.*

appraise, *vb.* stimare.

appreciable, *adj.* apprezzàbile.

appreciate, *vb.* apprezzare, tenere in giusto conto.

appreciation, *n.* apprezzamento *m.*

apprehend, *vb.* (fear) temere; (catch) arrestare.

apprehension, *n.* timore *m.*

apprehensive, *adj.* timoroso.

apprentice, *n.* apprendista *m.*

apprise, *vb.* informare.

approach, 1. *n.* accèsso *m.* 2. *vb.* avvicinarsi a.

approachable, *adj.* avvicinàbile.

approbation, *n.* approvazione *f.*

appropriate, 1. *adj.* appropriato. 2. *vb.* (take for oneself) appropriarsi; (set aside funds) stanziare.

appropriation, *n.* stanziamento *m.*

approval, *n.* approvazione *f.*

approve, *vb.* approvare.

approximate, 1. *vb.* approssimare. 2. *adj.* approssimativo.

approximately, *adv.* approssimativamente.

approximation, *n.* approssimazione *f.*

appurtenance, *n.* appartenènza *f.*

apricot, *n.* albicòcca *f.*

April, *n.* aprile *m.*

apron, *n.* grembiule *m.*

apropos, *adv.* a propòsito.

apse, *n.* àbside *f.*

apt, *adj.* atto; (quick at) pronto a.

aptitude, *n.* attitùdine *f.*

Apulia, *n.* le Pùglie *f.pl.*

Apulian, *adj.* pugliese.

aquarium, *n.* acquàrio *m.*

aquatic, *adj.* acquàtico.

aqueduct, *n.* acquedotto *m.*

aqueous, *adj.* àcqueo.

aquiline, *adj.* aquilino.

Arab, *n.* àrabo *m.*

Arabic, *adj.* àrabo.

arable, *adj.* aràbile.

arbiter, *n.* àrbitro *m.*

arbitrary, *adj.* arbitràrio.

arbitrate, *vb.* arbitrare.

arbitration, *n.* arbitrato *m.*

arbitrator, *n.* àrbitro *m.*

arbor, *n.* pergolato *m.*

arboreal, *adj.* arbòreo.

arc, *n.* arco *m.*

arcade, *n.* galleria *f.*

arch, *n.* arco *m.*

archaeology, *n.* archeologia *f.*

archaic, *adj.* arcàico.

archbishop, *n.* arcivéscovo *m.*

archdiocese, *n.* arcidiòcesi *f.*

archduke, *n.* arciduca *m.*

archer, *n.* arcière *f.*

archery, *n.* tiro dell'arco *m.*

archetype, *n.* archètipo *m.*

archipelago, *n.* arcipèlago *m.*

architect, *n.* architetto *m.*

architectural, *adj.* architettònico.

architecture, *n.* architettura *f.*

archives, *n.* archívio *m.* (*sg.*)

archway, *n.* pòrtico *m.*

arctic, *adj.* àrtico.

Arctic Circle, *n.* circolo polare.

ardent, *adj.* ardènte.

ardor, *n.* ardore *m.*

arduous, *adj.* àrduo.

area, *n.* àrea *f.*

area code, *n.* prefisso teleselettivo *m.*

arena, *n.* arena *f.*

Argentine, 1. *n.* Argentina *f.* 2. *adj.* argentino.

argue, *vb.* (draw a conclusion) arguire; (quarrel) bisticciarsi.

argument, *n.* (in debate) argomento *m.*; (quarrel) bistíccio *m.*

argumentative, *adj.* litigioso.

aria, *n.* ària *f.*

arid, *adj.* àrido.

aridity, *n.* aridità *f.*

arise, *vb.* (get up) levarsi; (come into being) nàscere.

aristocracy, *n.* aristocrazìa *f.*

aristocrat, *n.* aristocràtico *m.*

aristocratic, *adj.* aristocràtico.

Aristotelian, *adj.* aristotèlico.

arithmetic, *n.* aritmètica *f.*

arithmetician, *n.* aritmetico *m.*

ark, *n.* arca *f.*

arm, 1. *n.* (body part) bràccio *m.*; (weapon) arma *f.* 2. *vb.* armare.

armament, *n.* armamento *m.*

armature, *n.* armatura *f.*

armchair, *n.* poltrona *f.*

armful, *n.* bracciata *f.*

armhole, *n.* òcchio della mànica *m.*

armistice, *n.* armistízio *m.*

armlet, *n.* bracciale *m.*

armor, *n.* armatura *f.*

armored, *adj.* blindato.

armory, *n.* armería *f.*; magazzino *m.*

armpit, *n.* ascèlla *f.*

arms, *n.* (weapons) armi *f.pl.*

army, *n.* esèrcito *m.*

arnica, *n.* àrnica *f.*

aroma, *n.* aròma *m.*

aromatic, *adj.* aromàtico.

around, 1. *adv.* intorno. 2. *prep.* intorno a.

arouse, *vb.* svegliare.

arraign, *vb.* accusare.

arrange, *vb.* ordinare, disporre, sistemare; (music) ridurre.

arrangement, *n.* ordinamento *m.*; (music) riduzione *f.*

array, 1. *n.* òrdine *m.*, sèrie *f.* 2. *vb.* ordinare.

arrears, *n.* arretrati *m.pl.*

arrest, 1. *n.* arrèsto *m.* 2. *vb.* arrestare.

arrival, *n.* arrivo *m.*

arrive, *vb.* arrivare, giùngere.

arrogance, *n.* arroganza *f.*

arrogant, *adj.* arrogante.

arrogate, *vb.* arrogarsi.

arrow, *n.* fréccia *f.*, strale *m.*

arrowhead, *n.* punta di fréccia *f.*

arsenal, *n.* arsenale *m.*

arsenic, *n.* arsènico *m.*

arson, *n.* incèndio doloso *m.*

art, *n.* arte *f.*; (fine arts) bèlle arti *f.pl.*

arterial, *adj.* arteriale.

arteriosclerosis, *n.* arterioscleròsi *f.*

artery, *n.* artèria *f.*

artesian well, *n.* pozzo artesiano *m.*

artful, *adj.* astuto.

arthritic, *adj. and n.* artritico *m.*

arthritis, *n.* artrite *f.*

artichoke, *n.* carciòfo *m.*

article, *n.* artícolo *m.*

articulate, 1. *adj.* articolato. 2. *vb.* articolare.

articulation, *n.* articolazione *f.*

artifice, *n.* artifício *f.*

artificial, *adj.* artificiale.

artificiality, *n.* artificialità *f.*

artillery, *n.* artiglierìa *f.*

artisan, *n.* artigiano *m.*

artist, *n.* artista *m., f.*

artistic, *adj.* artístico.

artistry, n. arte f.

artless, adj. ingènuo, senz'arte.

as, prep. and conj. come; **(as if)** quasi.

asbestos, n. asbèsto m.

ascend, vb. salire.

ascendancy, n. supremazia f.

ascendant, adj. suprèmo.

ascent, n. salita f.

ascertain, vb. accertarsi.

ascetic, n. and adj. ascètico (m.).

ascribe, vb. ascrivere.

ash, n. (tree) fràssino m.

ashamed, adj. vergognoso; **(be a. of)** vergognarsi di.

ashen, adj. di cénere.

ashes, n. cénere f. (sg.).

ashore, adv. a tèrra.

ash-tray, n. portacénere m.

Ash Wednesday, n. Mercoledì delle Ceneri m.

Asia, n. Àsia f.

Asian, adj. asiàtico.

aside, adv. a parte.

asinine, adj. asinino.

ask, vb. (question) domandare; (request) chièdere; (invite) invitare.

askance, adv. sospettosamente.

asleep, adj. addormentato; **(fall a.)** addormentarsi.

asparagus, n. aspàrago m., spàragi m.pl.

aspect, n. aspètto m.

asperity, n. asperità f.

aspersion, n. denigrazione f.

asphalt, n. asfalto m.

asphyxia, n. asfissìa f.

asphyxiate, vb. asfissiare.

aspirant, n. aspirante m.

aspirate, 1. n. aspirata f. 2. adj. aspirato. 3. vb. aspirare.

aspiration, n. aspirazione f.

aspirator, n. aspiratore m.

aspire, vb. aspirare.

aspirin, n. aspirina f.

ass, n. àsino m.; sedere m.

assail, vb. assalire, attaccare.

assailable, adj. attaccàbile.

assailant, n. assalitore m.

assassin, n. assassino m.

assassinate, vb. assassinare.

assassination, n. assassìnio m.

assault, 1. n. assalto m. 2. vb. assaltare.

assay, 1. n. sàggio m. 2. vb. saggiare, assaggiare.

assemblage, n. riunione f.

assemble, vb. (bring together) riunire; (come together) riunirsi.

assembler, n. montatore m.

assembly, n. riunione f., assemblèa f.; (autos, etc.) montàggio m.

assembly line, n. catena di montaggio f.

assent, 1. n. assènso m. 2. vb. assentire.

assert, vb. asserire.

assertion, n. asserzione f.

assertive, adj. dogmàtico.

assertiveness, n. dogmaticità f.

assess, vb. (a fine) fissare (una multa); (property) stimare.

assessment, n. valutazione f., giudìzio m.

assessor, n. assessore m.

asset, n. (possession) bène m.; (in accounting) attivo m.

asseverate, vb. asseverare.

asseveration, n. asseverazione f.

assiduity, n. assiduità f., frequenza f.

assiduous, adj. assìduo.

assiduously, adv. assiduamente.

assign, vb. assegnare.

assignable, adj. assegnàbile.

assignation, n. assegnazione f.; (date) appuntamento m.

assigned, adj. addetto.

assignee, n. ricevitore m., incaricato m.

assignment, n. assegnamento m., assegnazione f., incàrico m.; (school) cómpito m.

assimilable, adj. assimilabile.

assimilate, vb. assimilare.

assimilation, n. assimilazione f.

assimilative, adj. assimilativo.

assist, vb. aiutare.

assistance, n. aiuto m.

assistant, n. and adj. assistènte (m.).

assistantship, n. (academic) incarico di assistente m.

associate, vb. associare, tr.; associarsi, intr.

association, n. associazione f.

assonance, n. assonanza f.

assort, vb. assortire.

assorted, adj. assortito.

assortment, n. assortimento m.

assuage, vb. assùmere; (appropriate) arrogarsi; (feign) fìngere; (suppose) supporre.

assume, vb. assùmere; (appropriate) arrogarsi; (feign) fìngere; (suppose) supporre.

assuming, adj. arrogante, presuntuoso.

assumption, n. supposizione f.; (eccles.) Ascensione f.

assurance, n. assicurazione f.

assure, vb. assicurare.

assured, adj. assicurato, sicuro.

assuredly, adv. sicuramente.

aster, n. astro m.

asterisk, n. asterisco m.

astern, adv. a poppa.

asteroid, n. asteròide m.

asthma, n. asma m.

astigmatism, n. astigmatismo m.

astir, adv. in mòto.

astonish, vb. sorprèndere, meravigliare.

astonishment, n. sorpresa f., meravìglia f.

astound, vb. stupire; **(be a.ed)** stupirsi.

astral, adj. astrale.

astray, 1. adj. sviato. **2.** vb. **(go a.)** sviarsi.

astride, adv. a cavalcioni; prep. a cavalcioni di.

astringent, adj. astringènte.

astrology, n. astrologia f.

astronaut, n. astronàuta m. and f.

astronautical, adj. astronautico.

astronomical, adj. astronòmico.

astronomy, n. astronomìa f.

astrophysics, n. astrofìsica f.

astute, adj. astuto.

asunder, adv. (in twain) in due; (in pieces) a pèzzi.

aswarm, adj. pieno di.

asylum, n. (refuge) rifùgio m.; (madhouse) manicòmio m.

asymmetry, n. asimmetria f.

at, prep. (time, place, price) ad (before vowels), a (before vowels or consonants); (at someone's house, shop, etc.) da.

ataxia, n. atassìa f.

atheist, n. ateista m.

athlete, n. atlèta m.

athletic, adj. atlètico.

athletics, n. atletismo m.

athwart, adv. attravèrso.

Atlantic, adj. atlàntico.

Atlantic Ocean, n. Ocèano atlàntico m.

atlas, n. atlante m.

atmosphere, n. atmosfèra f.

atmospheric, adj. atmosfèrico.

atoll, n. atòllo m.

atom, n. àtomo m.

atomic, adj. atòmico.

atomic age, n. era atòmica f.

atomic bomb, n. bomba atòmica f.

atomic energy, n. energia atòmica f.

atomize, vb. (liquids) nebulizzare.

atonal, adj. atonale.

atone for, vb. espiare.

atonement, n. espiazione f.

atonic, adj. atònico.

atrium, n. atrio m.

atrocious, adj. atroce.

atrocity, n. atrocità f.

atrophy, n. atrofìa f.

atropine, n. atropìna f.

attach, vb. attaccare.

attaché, n. addetto m.

attachment, n. (lit.) attaccamento m.; (liking) affezione f.; (equipment) accessòrio m.

attack, 1. n. attacco m. **2.** vb. attaccare.

attacker, n. assalitore m.

attain, vb. raggiùngere.

attainable, adj. raggiungìbile.

attainment, n. raggiungimento m.

attempt, 1. n. tentativo m. **2.** vb. tentare.

attend, vb. (give heed to) prestare attenzione a; (medical) curarsi di; (serve) servire; (meeting) assistere a; (lectures) frequentare; (see to) occuparsi di.

attendance, n. assistènza f.

attendant, n. and adj. assistènte (m.).

attendee, n. assistito m.

attention, n. attenzione f.; **(pay a.)** fare attenzione.

attentive, adj. attènto.

attentively, adv. attentamente.

attenuate, vb. attenuare.

attenuation, *n.* attenuazione *m.*

attest, *vb.* attestare.

attic, *n.* soffitta *f.*

attire, 1. *n.* abbigliamento *m.* **2.** *vb.* abbigliare.

attitude, *n.* atteggiamento *m.;* **(take an a.)** atteggiarsi.

attorney, *n.* procuratore *m.*

attract, *vb.* attrarre.

attraction, *n.* attrazione *f.*

attractive, *adj.* attraènte.

attributable, *adj.* attribuíbile.

attribute, *vb.* attribuire.

attribution, *n.* attribuzione *f.*

attrition, *n.* attrito *m.*

attune, *vb.* armonizzare; **(an instrument)** accordare.

auction, *n.* véndita all'asta *f.*

auctioneer, *n.* banditore *m.*

audacious, *adj.* audace.

audacity, *n.* audàcia *f.*

audible, *adj.* udíbile.

audience, *n.* (listeners) uditòrio *m.;* (interview) udiènza *f.*

audiovisual, *adj.* audiovisivo.

audit, 1. *n.* verífica *f.,* contròllo *m.* **2.** *vb.* verificare, controllare.

audition, *n.* audizione *f.*

auditor, *n.* uditore *m.,* uditrice *f.;* (accounts) revisore *m.,* controllore *m.*

auditorium, *n.* auditòrio *m.*

auditory, *adj.* uditivo.

auger, *n.* succhièllo *m.,* trivèllo *m.*

augment, *vb.* aumentare.

augur, *vb.* augurare.

august, *adj.* augusto.

August, *n.* agosto *m.*

aunt, *n.* zía *f.*

auricular, *adj.* auricolare.

auspice, *n.* auspício *m.*

auspicious, *adj.* favorévole.

austere, *adj.* austèro.

austerity, *n.* austerità *f.*

Austria, *n.* Àustria *f.*

Austrian, *adj.* austríaco.

authentic, *adj.* autèntico.

authenticate, *vb.* autenticare.

authenticity, *n.* autenticità *f.*

author, *n.* autore *m.*

authoritarian, *adj.* autoritário.

authoritative, *adj.* autorévole.

authoritatively, *adv.* autorevolmente.

authority, *n.* autorità *f.*

authorization, *n.* autorizzazione *f.*

authorize, *vb.* autorizzare.

autism, *n.* autismo *m.*

auto, *n.* àuto *f.*

autobiographical, *adj.* autobiogràfico.

autobiography, *n.* autobiografia *f.*

autocracy, *n.* autocrazía *f.*

autocrat, *n.* autòcrate *m.*

autograph, *n.* autògrafo *m.*

automatic, *adj.* automàtico.

automatically, *adv.* automaticamente.

automaton, *n.* autòma *m.*

automobile, *n.* automòbile *f.*

automotive, *adj.* automobilístico.

autonomous, *adj.* autònomo.

autonomy, *n.* autonomía *f.*

autopsy, *n.* autopsía *f.*

autumn, *n.* autunno *m.*

auxiliary, *n.* and *adj.* ausiliare (*m.*).

avail, *vb.* servire; **(be of no a.)** non servire a nulla.

available, *adj.* disponíbile.

avalanche, *n.* valanga *f.*

avarice, *n.* avarízia *f.*

avaricious, *adj.* avaro.

avenge, *vb.* vendicare.

avenger, *n.* vendicatore *m.*

avenue, *n.* viale *m.*

average, 1. *n.* mèdia *f.* **2.** *adj.* mèdio. **3.** *vb.* fare la mèdia di.

averse, *adj.* avvèrso.

aversion, *n.* avversione *f.*

avert, *vb.* impedire.

aviary, *n.* aviàrio *m.,* uccellièra *f.*

aviation, *n.* aviazione *f.*

aviator, *n.* aviatore *m.*

aviatrix, *n.* aviatrice *f.*

avid, *adj.* àvido.

avocation, *n.* divertimento *m.*

avoid, *vb.* evitare, scansare; **(so as to a.)** a scanso di.

avoidable, *adj.* evitàbile.

avoidance, *n.* scanso *m.*

avow, *vb.* confessare.

avowal, *n.* confessione *f.*

avowedly, *adv.* lo confèsso.
await, *vb.* aspettare.
awake, 1. *adj.* svéglio. **2.** *vb.* svegliare, *tr.;* svegliarsi, *intr.*
awaken, *vb.* see awake.
award, 1. *n.* prèmio *m.* **2.** *vb.* conferire; **(a. a prize to)** premiare.
aware, *adj.* consapévole, cònscio.
awash, *adv.* al livèllo dell'acqua.
away, *adv.* via, lontano; **(go a.)** andàrsene.
awe, 1. *n.* terrore *m.,* soggezióne *f.* **2.** *vb.* ispirare terrore a.

awesome, *adj.* tremèndo.
awful, *adj.* terribile.
awhile, *adv.* per un momento.
awkward, *adj.* gòffo; **(difficult)** difficile.
awning, *n.* tènda *f.*
awry, *adv.* di travèrso.
axe, *n.* àscia *f.*
axiom, *n.* assiòma *m.*
axis, *n.* asse *m.*
axle, *n.* asse *m.*
ayatollah, *n.* ayatollah *m.*
azure, *adj.* azzurro.

B

babble, 1. *n.* balbettío *m.* **2.** *vb.* balbettare.
babbler, *n.* balbuziènte *m.*
babe, *n.* bimbo *m.;* **(girl)** ragazza *f.*
baboon, *n.* babbuino *m.*
baby, *n.* bambino *m.,* bimbo *m.;* **(b.-carriage)** carrozzèlla *f.*
babyish, *adj.* bambinesco, infantile.
bachelor, *n.* scàpolo *m.;* **(degree)** baccellière *m.*
bacillus, *n.* bacillo *m.*
back, 1. *n.* dòsso *m.,* dòrso *m.,* schièna *f.* **2.** *adj.* posterióre. **3.** *vb.* **(go backwards)** indietreggiare; **(support)** appoggiare, sostenere, spalleggiare; **(b. down)** cèdere. **4.** *adv.* indiètro.
backbone, *n.* spina dorsale *f.*
backer, *n.* sostenitore *m.*
backfire, *vb.* scoppiare.
background, *n.* sfondo *m.*
backhand, *n.* rovèscio *m.*
backing, *n.* appòggio *m.,* sostegno *m.*
backlash, *n.* reazione conservatrice *f.*
backlog, *n.* risèrve *f.pl.*
back out, *vb.* ritirarsi.
backpack, *n.* sacco da montagna *m.*
backstage, *n.* retroscèna *f.*
backward, 1. *adj.* stùpido. **2.** *adv.* indiètro.
backwardness, *n.* stupidità *f.*
backwards, *adv.* indiètro.
backwater, *n.* acqua stagnante *f.*
backwoods, *n.* retrotèrra *f.*

backyard, *n.* giardino privato *m.*
bacon, *n.* pancetta *f.*
bacteria, *n.* battèri *m.pl.*
bactericide, *adj. and n.* battericida *(m.)*
bacteriologist, *n.* batteriòlogo *m.*
bacteriology, *n.* batteriologia *f.*
bacterium, *n.* battèrio *m.*
bad, *adj.* cattivo.
badge, *n.* emblèma *f.,* distintivo *m.*
badger, *n.* tasso *m.*
badly, *adv.* male, malamente.
badmouth, *vb.* criticare, diffamare.
badness, *n.* cattivèria *f.*
bad-tempered, *adj.* di cattivo umore.
baffle, *vb.* **(hinder)** impedire; **(perplex)** rèndere perplèsso.
bafflement, *n.* perplessità *f.*
bag, 1. *n.* sacco *m.,* borsa *f.;* **(woman's purse)** borsetta *f.* **2.** *vb.* **(get)** ottenere; **(put in a b.)** insaccare.
baggage, *n.* bagàglio *m.;* **(b. check)** scontrino per bagagli *m.*
baggage cart, *n.* **(airport)** carretta per bagagli *f.*
baggy, *adj.* gónfio.
bagpipe, *n.* cornamusa *f.,* zampogna *f.*
baguette, *n.* baguette *f.,* ciabatta *f.*
bail, *n.* cauzione *f.,* garanzia *f.*
bailiff, *n.* usciere *m.*
bail out, *vb.* **(set free)** fornire garanzia per; **(water)** vuotare.

bait, *n.* esca *f.*

bake, *vb.* cuócere al forno.

baker, *n.* fornaio *m.*

bakery, *n.* forno *m.*

baking, *n.* cottura al forno *m.*

baking powder, *n.* polvere di amido e diossido di carbonio *f.*

baking soda, *n.* bicarbonato di sodio *m.*

balance, 1. *n.* (equilibrium) equilíbrio *m.; (comm.)* saldo *m.;* (scales) bilància *f.* **2.** *vb.* bilanciare; (weigh) pesare; (make of equal weight) equilibrare; *(comm.)* saldare.

balance sheet, *n.* bilancio *m.*

balcony, *n.* balcone *m.*

bald, *adj.* calvo.

baldness, *n.* calvízie *f.sg.*

bale, *n.* balla *f.*

baleful, *adj.* minacciante.

balk, *vb.* (hinder) impedire; (refuse to move) essere ritroso.

Balkans, *n.* i Balcani *m.pl.*

balky, *adj.* ritroso.

ball, *n.* palla *f.;* (bullet) pallòttola *f.;* (dance) ballo *m.*

ballad, *n.* ballata *f.*

ballade, *n.* ballata *f.*

ballast, *n.* zavorra *f.*

ball bearing, *n.* cuscinetto a sfere *m.*

ballerina, *n.* ballerina *f.*

ballet, *n.* ballo *m.*

ballistics, *n.* balistica *f.*

balloon, *n.* pallone *m.*

ballot, *n.* (voting) votazione *f;* (paper) scheda *f.*

ballot box, *n.* urna *f.*

ballpoint, *n.* penna a sfera *f.*

ballroom, *n.* sala da ballo *f.*

balm, *n.* bàlsamo *m.*

balmy, *adj.* balsàmico.

balsam, *n.* bàlsamo *m.*

baluster, *n.* balaustra *f.*

balustrade, *n.* balaùstra *f.,* balaustrata *f.*

bamboo, *n.* bambù *m.*

bamboozle, *vb.* truffare.

ban, 1. *n.* proibizione *f.* **2.** *vb.* proibire.

banal, *adj.* banale.

banana, *n.* banana *f.*

band, *n.* (group, including musical band) banda *f.;* (headband) benda *f.;* (ribbon) striscia *f.*

bandage, *n.* benda *f.*

bandanna, *n.* fazzoletto multicolore *m.*

bandbox, *n.* cappellièra *f.*

bandit, *n.* bandito *m.*

bandmaster, *n.* capobanda *m.,* maestro di banda *m.*

bandsaw, *n.* sega a nastro *f.*

bandsman, *n.* bandista *m.*

bandstand, *n.* palco della banda musicale *f.*

baneful, *adj.* dannoso.

bang, 1. *n.* (hair-do) frància *f.;* (blow) colpo *m.* **2.** *vb.* sbàttere. **3.** *interj.* pum!

banish, *vb.* bandire, esiliare.

banishment, *n.* bando, esílio *m.*

banister, *n.* ringhièra *, f.*

bank, 1. *n.* (institution) banca *f.,* banco *m.;* (edge of water) riva *f.* **2.** *vb.* (rely on) contare su; (airplane) inclinare.

bankbook, *n.* libretto di depòsito *m.*

banker, *n.* banchière *m.*

banking, 1. *n.* operazioni bancàrie *f.pl.* **2.** *adj.* bancário.

bank note, *n.* banconota *f.*

bankrupt, 1. *adj.* fallito. **2.** *vb.* far fallire; **(go b.)** fallire.

bankruptcy, *n.* fallimento *m.,* bancarotta *f.*

banner, *n.* bandièra *f.*

banns, *n.* bandi matrimoniali *m.pl.*

banquet, *n.* banchetto *m.*

banter, *n.* scherzo *m.,* cèlia *f.* **2.** *vb.* scherzare, celiare.

baptism, *n.* battésimo *m.*

baptismal, *adj.* battesimale.

Baptist, *n.* battista *m.*

baptistery, *n.* battistèro *m.*

baptize, *vb.* battezzare.

bar, *n.* **1.** sbarra *f.;* (obstacle) ostàcolo *m.;* (for drinks) bar *m.* **2.** *vb.* sbarrare; ostacolare.

bar association, *n.* ordine degli avvocati *m.*

barb, *n.* punta ricurva *f.*

barbarian, *n.* bàrbaro *m.*

barbaric, *adj.* barbarico.

barbarism, n. barbàrie f.; (gram.) barbarismo m.

barbarous, adj. bàrbaro m.

barbecue, vb. cucinare alla brace.

barbed, adj. pungente, spinoso.

barbed wire, n. filo spinato m.

barber, n. barbière m., parrucchière m.

barbiturate, n. barbitùrico m.

bare, 1. adj. nudo, scopèrto. **2.** vb. scoprire.

bareback, adv. sènza sèlla.

barefoot, adj. scalzo.

barely, adv. appena.

bareness, n. nudità f.

bargain, 1. n. affare m.; (cheap purchase) occasione f. **2.** vb. mercanteggiare.

barge, n. chiatta f.

baritone, n. and adj. barítono (m.).

barium, n. bàrio m.

bark, 1. n. (of tree) scorza f., corteccia f.; (of dog) abbaiamento m. **2.** vb. abbaiare.

barley, n. orzo m.

barn, n. granaio m.

barnacle, n. cirrìpede m.

barnyard, n. cortile m.

barometer, n. baròmetro m.

barometric, adj. baròmetrico.

baron, n. barone m.

baroness, n. baronessa f.

baronial, adj. baronale.

baroque, adj. baròcco.

barracks, n. casèrma f.sg.

barrage, n. fuoco di sbarramento m.

barred, adj. sbarrato; (excluded) escluso; (forbidden) vietato.

barrel, n. barile m.

barren, adj. stèrile.

barrenness, n. sterilità f.

barricade, n. barricata f.

barrier, n. barrièra f.

barroom, n. bèttola f., bar m.

barter, 1. n. baratto m. **2.** vb. barattare.

base, 1. n. base f. **2.** adj. basso. **3.** vb. basare.

baseball, n. baseball m.

baseboard, n. zòccolo m.

Basel, n. Basilèa f.

basement, n. cantina f.

baseness, n. bassezza f.

bashful, adj. tímido.

bashfully, adv. timidamente.

bashfulness, n. timidezza f.

basic, adj. fondamentale.

basin, n. catino m.

basis, n. base f.

bask, vb. riscaldarsi, godersi.

basket, n. cesta f.

basketball, n. pallacanestro m.

bass, n. (voice) basso m.; (fish) pesce pèrsico m.

bassinet, n. culla f.

bassoon, n. fagòtto m.

bastard, n. and adj. bastardo (m.).

baste, vb. (sewing) imbastire; (cooking) ammorbidire.

bat, n. (animal) pipistrèllo m.; (baseball) bastone m.

batch, n. infornata f.

bate, vb. diminuire.

bath, n. bagno m.

bathe, vb. (tr.) bagnare; (intr.) fare il bagno.

bather, n. bagnante m. or f.

bathing resort, n. stazione balneare f.

bathing suit, n. costume da bagno m.

bathrobe, n. vestàglia f.

bathroom, n. stanza da bagno f.

bathtub, n. vasca da bagno f.

baton, n. (military) bastone m.; (conductor's) bacchetta f.

battalion, n. battaglione m.

batter, 1. n. (cooking) pasta f. **2.** vb. bàttere.

battery, n. batterìa f., pila f.

batting, n. imbottitura f.

battle, 1. n. battàglia f. **2.** vb. combàttere.

battlefield, n. campo di battàglia m.

battleship, n. nave da guèrra f.

bauxite, n. bauxite m.

bawl, vb. urlare; (b. out) sgridare.

bay, 1. n. (geography) bàia f.; (plant) làuro m.; (howl) latrato m.; (at b.) a bada. **2.** adj. (color) baio. **3.** vb. latrare; abbaiare.

bayonet, n. baionetta f.

bazaar, n. bazàr m.

be, vb. èssere; (health) stare.

beach, n. spiàggia f., lido m.

beachhead, *n.* tèsta di ponte *f.*
beach robe, *n.* accappatòio *m.*
beach umbrella, *n.* ombrellone *m.*
beacon, *n.* faro *m.*
bead, **1.** *n.* grano *m.* **2.** *vb.* ornare di grani.
beading, *n.* ornamento di grani *m.*
beady, *adj.* a forma di grano.
beagle, *n.* segugio *m.*
beak, *n.* becco *m.*
beaker, *n.* recipiènte *m.*
beam, **1.** *n.* (construction) trave *f.*; (light) ràggio *m.* **2.** *vb.* irradiare, risplèndere.
beaming, *adj.* raggiante, risplendènte.
bean, *n.* fagiòlo *m.*, fava *f.*
bear, **1.** *n.* (animal) orso *m.* **2.** *vb.* (carry) portare; (endure) sopportare; (give birth to) partorire.
bearable, *adj.* sopportàbile.
beard, *n.* barba *f.*
bearded, *adj.* barbuto.
beardless, *adj.* imbèrbe.
bearer, *n.* portatore *m.*
bearing, *n.* (behavior) condotta *f.*; (position) orientaménto *m.*; (machinery) cuscinetto *m.*
bearish, *adj.* orsesco; al ribasso (financial).
bearskin, *n.* pèlle d'orso *f.*
beast, *n.* bèstia *f.*
beastly, *adj.* bestiale.
beat, **1.** *n.* bàttito *m.* **2.** *vb.* bàttere; (conquer) vìncere.
beaten, *adj.* battuto.
beaten path, *n.* la via nota *f.*; sentiero marcato *m.*
beater, *n.* frullatore *m.*
beatify, *vb.* beatificare.
beating, *n.* percosse *f.pl.*; (defeat) disfatta *f.*
beatitude, *n.* beatitùdine *f.*
beau, *n.* (fop) damerino *m.*; (wooer) corteggiatore *m.*
beautician, *n.* estetista *m. and f.*
beautiful, *adj.* bèllo; (excellent) eccellènte.
beautifully, *adv.* in bel modo, bène, eccellentemente.
beautify, *vb.* abbellire.
beauty, *n.* bellezza *f.*; **(b. parlor)** salone di bellezza *f.*
beaver, *n.* castòro *m.*

becalm, *vb.* abbonacciare.
because, *conj.* perché; **(b. of)** a causa di.
beckon, *vb.* far cenno, accennare.
becloud, *vb.* annebbiare; confondere.
become, *vb.* divenire, diventare; (be suitable for) convenire a; (be attractive on) stare bène a.
becoming, *adj.* grazioso.
bed, *n.* lètto *m.*; (for animals) lettièra *f.*
bed and board, *n.* vitto e allòggio *m.*
bedbug, *n.* cìmice *f.*
bedclothes, *n.* lenzuòla *f.pl.*
bedding, *n.* letterecci *m.pl.*
bedevil, *vb.* tormentare; confondere.
bedfellow, *n.* compagno di lètto *m.*
bedizen, *vb.* ornare.
bedridden, *adj.* degènte.
bedroom, *n.* stanza da lètto *f.*
bedside, *n.* **(at the b. of)** al capezzale di.
bedsore, *n.* piaga *f.*
bedspread, *n.* copèrta da lètto *f.*
bedstead, *n.* lettièra *f.*
bedtime, *n.* ora d'andare a lètto *m.*
bee, *n.* ape *f.*
beech, *n.* faggio *m.*
beef, *n.* bue *m.*
beefsteak, *n.* bistecca *f.*
beef stew, *n.* stufato di manzo *m.*
beehive, *n.* alveare *m.*
beer, *n.* birra *f.*
beeswax, *n.* cera *f.*
beet, *n.* barbabiètola *f.*
beetle, *n.* scarafàggio *m.*
befall, *vb.* accadere, capitare.
befit, *vb.* convenire a.
befitting, *adj.* conveniènte.
before, **1.** *adv.* (in front) avanti, davanti; (earlier) prima. **2.** *prep.* avanti, davanti a, prima di. **3.** *conj.* prima che.
beforehand, *adv.* prima, in antìcipo.
befriend, *vb.* aiutare.
befuddle, *vb.* confóndere.
beg, *vb.* (ask alms) mendicare; (request) chièdere; (implore) implorare; implorare.

beget, vb. generare.

beggar, n. mendicante m.

beggarly, adj. meschino.

begin, vb. cominciare, incominciare, iniziare.

beginner, n. principiante m.

beginning, n. princípio m., cominciamento m., inízio m.

begrudge, vb. invidiare.

beguile, vb. ingannare.

behalf, n. favore m.; **(on b. of)** da parte di; **(in b. of)** a favore di.

behave, vb. comportarsi, condursi.

behavior, n. comportamento m., condotta f.

behead, vb. decapitare.

behest, n. ordine m., comando m.

behind, 1. adv. indiètro. **2.** prep. diètro a.

behold, vb. vedere.

beige, adj. beige, avana.

being, n. èssere m.; (existence) esistènza f.

bejewel, vb. ornare di gioièlli.

belated, adj. tardivo.

belch, 1. n. rutto m. **2.** vb. ruttare.

belfry, n. campanile m.

Belgian, n. and adj. bèlga.

Belgium, n. il Bèlgio m.

belie, vb. smentire.

belief, n. credènza f., opinione f., fede f.

believable, adj. credíbile.

believe, vb. crédere; (make believe) fingere.

believer, n. credènte m.

belittle, vb. denigrare.

bell, n. (house) campanèllo m.; (church) campana f.

bellboy, n. camerière m.

bell buoy, n. bòa a campana f.

bellglass, n. campana di vetro f.

bellicose, adj. bellicoso, battaglièro.

belligerence, n. belligeranza f.

belligerent, adj. belligerante, bellicoso.

belligerently, adv. bellicosamente.

bellringer, n. campanaro m.

bellow, 1. n. mùggio m., muggito m. **2.** vb. muggire, mugghiare.

bellows, n. (large) màntice m.; (small) soffietto m.

bell-tower, n. campanile m.

belly, n. vèntre m., pància f.

belong, vb. appartenere.

belongings, n. possessi m.pl. proprietà f.sg.

beloved, adj. amato, dilètto.

below, adv. and prep. sotto.

belt, n. cintura f.

bench, n. banco m.

bend, vb. piegare; (curve) curvare.

beneath, adv. and prep. sotto.

benediction, n. benedizione f.

benefactor, n. benefattore m.

benefactress, n. benefattrice f.

beneficent, adj. benèfico.

beneficial, adj. vantaggioso, salutare.

beneficiary, n. beneficiàrio m.

benefit, 1. n. benefício m., vantaggio m. **2.** vb. beneficare, trarre vantaggio da (intr.).

benevolence, n. benevolènza f.

benevolent, adj. benèvolo, caritatévole.

benevolently, adv. benevolmente, caritatevolmente.

benign, adj. benigno.

benignity, n. benignità f.

bent, adj. piegato, curvo.

benzine, n. benzina f.

bequeath, vb. legare.

bequest, n. legato m.

berate, vb. sgridare.

bereave, vb. orbare, privare.

bereavement, n. pèrdita f.

beriberi, n. beri-bèri m.

Bern, n. Berna f.

berry, n. bacca f.

berth, n. cuccetta f.

beseech, vb. supplicare.

beseeching, adj. supplichévole.

beseechingly, adv. supplichevolmente.

beset, vb. assalire, assediare.

beside, prep. accanto a.

besides, 1. adv. inoltre. **2.** prep. oltre.

besiege, vb. assediare.

besieger, n. assediante m.

besmirch, vb. insudiciare; (dishonor) disonorare.

best, 1. adj. il migliore. **2.** adv. il mèglio. **3.** vb. vincere.

bestial, adj. bestiale.

bestir oneself, vb. scuòtersi.

best man, *n.* testimone dello sposo *m.*

bestow, *vb.* conferire.

bestowal, *n.* concessione *f.*

bet, 1. *n.* scommessa *f.* **2.** *vb.* scométtere.

betake (oneself), *vb.* recarsi, andare.

betoken, *vb.* significare.

betray, *vb.* tradire.

betrayal, *n.* tradimento *m.*

betroth, *vb.* fidanzare.

betrothal, *n.* fidanzamento *m.*

better, 1. *adj.* migliore. **2.** *adv.* méglio. **3.** *vb.* migliorare.

between, *prep.* fra, tra.

bevel, *n.* inclinazione *f.*

beverage, *n.* bevanda *f.*

bewail, *vb.* lamentare, piàngere.

beware, *vb.* guardarsi.

bewilder, *vb.* confóndere, rèndere perplèsso.

bewildered, *adj.* confuso, perplèsso.

bewildering, *adj.* sconcertante.

bewilderment, *n.* confusione *f.,* perplessità *f.*

bewitch, *vb.* ammaliare, stregare.

beyond, 1. *adv.* al di là, oltre. **2.** *prep.* al di là di, oltre.

biannual, *adj.* biennale.

bias, 1. *n.* parzialità *f.,* pregiudizio *m.;* **(on the b.)** disbieco. **2.** *vb.* predisporre.

bib, *n.* bavaglino *m.*

Bible, *n.* Bìbbia *f.*

Biblical, *adj.* bíblico.

bibliography, *n.* bibliografia *f.*

bibliophile, *n.* bibliòfilo *m.*

bicarbonate, *n.* bicarbonato *m.*

bicentennial, *adj.* bicentennale.

biceps, *n.* bicipite *m.*

bicker, *vb.* litigare, bisticciarsi.

bicycle, *n.* bicicletta *f.*

bicyclist, *n.* ciclista *m. or f.*

bid, 1. *n.* (offer) offèrta *f.;* (invitation) invito *m.* **2.** *vb.* (offer) offrire; (command) comandare.

bidder, *n.* offerènte *m.*

bidding, *n.* ordine *m.;* offerte *f.pl.*

bide, *vb.* aspettare.

biennial, *adj.* biennale.

bier, *n.* bara *f.*

bifocal, *adj.* bifocale.

big, *adj.* grande, gròsso; (preg-

nant) gràvida *f.;* **(b. shot)** pèzzo gròsso *m.*

bigamist, *n.* bígamo *m.*

bigamous, *adj.* bígamo.

bigamy, *n.* bigamía *f.*

big game, *n.* caccia grossa *f.*

big-hearted, *adj.* buono; magnanimo.

bigmouthed, *adj.* sbraitante.

bigot, *n.* bigòtto *m.*

bigoted, *adj.* bigòtto.

bigotry, *n.* bigotteria *f.,* bigottismo *m.*

big shot, *n.* pezzo grosso *m.,* alto papavero *m.*

big toe, *n.* alluce *m.*

bike, *n.* bicicletta *f.*

bilateral, *adj.* bilaterale.

bile, *n.* bile *f.*

bilingual, *adj.* bilingue.

bilious, *adj.* (pertaining to bile) biliare; (temperament) bilioso.

bilk, *vb.* defraudare.

bill, *n.* (bird) becco *m.;* biglietto *m.;* (sum owed) conto *m.;* (legislative) progètto di legge *m.;* **(b. of fare)** lista *f.*

billboard, *n.* cartèllo pubblicitàrio *m.*

billet, 1. *n.* allòggio *m.* **2.** *vb.* alloggiare.

billfold, *n.* portafògli *m.*

billiard ball, *n.* palla da biliardo *f.*

billiards, *n.* biliardo *m.sg.*

billion, *n.* bilione *m.*

bill of health, *n.* certificato mèdico *m.*

bill of lading, *n.* polizza di càrico *f.*

bill of rights, *n.* dichiarazione dei diritti.

bill of sale, *n.* manifèsto di véndita *m.*

billow, *n.* maroso *m.*

bimetallic, *adj.* bimetàllico.

bimonthly, *adj.* (twice a month) bimensile, quindicinale; (every two months) bimestrale.

bin, *n.* recipiènte *m.*

bind, *vb.* legare; (oblige) obbligare; (a book) rilegare.

binder, *n.* rilegatore *m.*

bindery, *n.* legatoria *f.*

binding, 1. *n.* (book) rilegatura *f.* **2.** *adj.* obbligatòrio.

bingo, n. tombola f.

binocular, 1. n. binòcolo m. **2.** adj. binoculare.

biochemical, adj. biochímico.

biochemistry, n. biochímica f.

biodegradable, adj. biodegradàbile.

biofeedback, n. feedback biològico m. biofeedback m.

biographer, n. biògrafo m.

biographical, adj. biogràfico.

biography, n. biografía f.

biological, adj. biològico.

biologically, adv. biologicamente.

biology, n. biología f.

bipartisan, adj. di tutti e due i partiti.

biped, n. and adj. bípede (m.).

bird, n. uccèllo m.

birdlike, adj. come un uccèllo, uccellescamente.

bird of prey, n. uccèllo di rapina m.; repace m.

birth, n. nàscita f.

birth control, n. controllo delle nàscite m.

birthday, n. compleanno m.

birthmark, n. vòglia f.

birthplace, n. luògo di nàscita m.

birth rate, n. natalità f.

birthright, n. diritto di primogenitura m.

biscuit, n. (roll) panino m.; (cracker) biscòtto m.

bisect, vb. bisecare.

bishop, n. véscovo m.

bishopric, n. vescovato m., diòcesi f.

bismuth, n. bismuto m.

bison, n. bisonte m.

bisulfate, n. bisolfato m.

bit, n. (piece) pèzzo m.; (a b. of) un po' di; (harness) mòrso m.; (computer) síngola unità d'informazione f.

bitch, n. cagna f.; donnaccia f.

bite, 1. n. mòrso m. **2.** vb. mòrdere.

biting, adj. pungènte.

bitter, adj. amaro.

bitterly, adv. amaramente.

bitterness, n. amarezza f.

bittersweet, adj. agrodolce, dolceamaro.

bivouac, n. bivacco m.

biweekly, adj. (twice a week) bisettimanale; (every two weeks) quindicinale.

biyearly, adj. biennale; semestrale.

bizzare, adj. bizzarro.

black, adj. nero.

Black, (n. and adj.) (person) negro m.; negra f.

blackberry, n. mòra f.

blackbird, n. mèrlo m.

blackboard, n. lavagna f.

Black Death, n. peste bubbònica f.

blacken, vb. annerire.

black eye, n. òcchio pesto m.

blackguard, n. mascalzone m.; furfante m.

blackish, adj. nerastro.

black magic, n. magia nera f.

blackmail, 1. n. ricatto m. **2.** vb. ricattare.

blackmailer, n. ricattatore m.

black market, n. mercato nero m.

blackout, n. oscuramento m.

blacksmith, n. fabbro ferraio m.

bladder, n. vescica f.

blade, n. (of cutting tool) lama f.; (grass) fòglia f.

blame, 1. n. biàsimo m. **2.** vb. biasimare.

blameless, adj. innocènte.

blanch, vb. impallidire.

bland, adj. blando.

blandish, vb. blandire.

blank, 1. n. (empty space) spàzio bianco m.; (form) mòdulo m. **2.** adj. (page) bianco; (empty) vuòto.

blank check, n. assegno in bianco m.

blanket, n. copèrta f.

blank verse, n. verso sciolto m.

blare, 1. n. squillo m. **2.** vb. squillare.

blaspheme, vb. bestemmiare.

blasphemer, n. bestemmiatore m.

blasphemous, adj. émpio.

blasphemy, n. bestémmia f.

blast, 1. n. (of wind) ràffica f.; (explosion) esplosione f. **2.** vb. far saltare.

blast furnace, n. altoforno m.

blastoff, n. lancio (of rocket) m.

blatant, adj. clamoroso, rumoroso.

blaze, 1. *n.* fiamma *f.;* (fire) fuòco *m.* **2.** *vb.* fiammeggiare.
bleach, *vb.* imbiancare.
bleachers, *n.* tribune *f.pl.*
bleak, *adj.* squàllido.
bleakness, *n.* squallore *m.*
bleary, *adj.* cisposo; poco chiaro.
bleed, *vb.* sanguinare.
blemish, *n.* màcchia *f.*
blend, 1. *n.* mescolanza *f.* **2.** *vb.* mescolare.
bless, *vb.* benedire.
blessed, *adj.* benedetto, beato.
blessing, *n.* benedizione *f.*
blight, 1. *n.* malattia *f.* **2.** *vb.* (be b.ed) ammalare.
blind, 1. *adj.* cièco. **2.** *vb.* accecare.
blindfold, 1. *n.* benda *f.* **2.** *adj.* bendato. **3.** *vb.* bendare.
blindly, *adv.* ciecamente.
blindness, *n.* cecità *f.*
blink, *vb.* sbàttere le pàlpebre.
blinker, *n.* (signal) lampeggiatore *m.*
bliss, *n.* beatitùdine *f.*
blissful, *adj.* beato.
blissfully, *adv.* beatamente.
blister, *n.* vescica *f.*
blithe, *adj.* gaio, gioioso.
blizzard, *n.* tempèsta di neve *f.*
bloat, *vb.* gonfiare.
bloc, *n.* blòcco *m.*
block, 1. *n.* blòcco *m.,* ostàcolo *m.* **2.** *vb.* bloccare, ostacolare.
blockade, *n.* blòcco *m.*
blond, *adj.* biondo.
blood, *n.* sangue *m.*
bloodhound, *n.* cane poliziòtto *m.*
bloodless, *adj.* esangue, senza sangue.
blood plasma, *n.* plasma *m.*
blood poisoning, *n.* avvelenamento del sangue *m.*
blood pressure, *n.* pressione del sangue *f.*
bloodshed, *n.* spargimento di sangue *m.*
bloodshot, *adj.* infiammato.
bloodthirsty, *adj.* sanguinàrio.
bloody, *adj.* sanguinoso.
bloom, 1. *n.* fiore *m.* **2.** *vb.* fiorire.
blossom, 1. *n.* fiore *m.* **2.** *vb.* fiorire.

blot, 1. *n.* màcchia *f.* **2.** *vb.* macchiare; (dry ink) asciugare.
blotch, *n.* (spot) màcchia *f.;* sgòrbio *m.*
blotchy, *adj.* macchiato.
blotter, *n.* carta assorbente *f.*
blouse, *n.* blusa *f.*
blow, 1. *n.* colpo *m.* **2.** *vb.* soffiare.
blowout, *n.* scòppio d'un pneumàtico *m.*
blubber, 1. *n.* (whale) grasso di balena *f.* **2.** *vb.* piagnucolare.
bludgeon, *n.* mazza *f.*
blue, *adj.* azzurro, blu; (gloomy) triste.
blueberry, *n.* mirtillo *m.*
bluebird, *n.* uccèllo azzurro *m.*
blue cheese, *n.* gorgonzola *m.*
blue chip, *n.* azioni leader (financial).
blue jeans, *n.* blue jeans *m.pl.*
blueprint, *n.* eliotipìa *f.;* (plan) piano *m.*
bluff, 1. *n.* (cliff) rupe scoscesa *f.;* (cards) bluff *m.;* (trickery) inganno *m.* **2.** *adj.* franco. **3.** *vb.* bluffare, ingannare.
bluffer, *n.* bluffatore *m.*
bluing, *n.* anile *m.*
bluish, *adj.* bluastro.
blunder, 1. *n.* errore *m.;* svista *f.* **2.** *vb.* sbagliare.
blunderer, *n.* stordito *m.*
blunt, *adj.* (dull) ottuso; (curt) rude.
bluntly, *adv.* ottusamente.
bluntness, *n.* ottusità *f.*
blur, 1. *n.* confusione *f.* **2.** *vb.* rèndere indistinto.
blush, 1. *n.* rossore *m.* **2.** *vb.* arrossire.
bluster, 1. *n.* millanteria *f.* **2.** *vb.* millantare.
boar, *n.* vèrro *m.*
board, 1. *n.* (plank) asse *f.,* tàvola *f.;* (food) vitto *m.;* (committee) comitato *m.;* (council) consiglio *m.;* (of ship) bordo *m.* **2.** *vb.* **(go on b.)** andare a bordo.
boarder, *n.* pensionante *m.*
boarding house, *n.* pensione *f.*
boarding pass, *n.* carta d'imbarco *f.*
boarding school, *n.* collegio *m.*

board of directors, *n.* consíglio d'amministrazione *m.*

board of health, *n.* ufficio d'igiene *m.*

board of trade, *n.* càmera di commèrcio *f.*

boast, **1.** *n.* vanto *m.,* vantería *f.* **2.** *vb.* vantare, *tr.*

boaster, *n.* vantatore *m.*

boastful, *adj.* vanaglorioso.

boastfulness, *n.* vantería *f.*

boat, *n.* barca *f.,* battèllo *m.*

boathouse, *n.* tettòia per barche.

boatswain, *n.* nostròmo *m.*

bob, *vb.* tagliare corto.

bobbin, *n.* bobina *f.*

bobby pin, *n.* forcina *f.*

bode, *vb.* presagire.

bodice, *n.* busto *m.*

bodily, *adj.* corpòreo.

body, *n.* còrpo *m.*

bodyguard, *n.* guàrdia del còrpo *f.*

bog, **1.** *n.* pantano *m.,* palude *f.* **2.** *vb.* **(b. down)** impantanarsi.

Bohemian, *n.* and *adj.* boemo (*m.*).

boil, **1.** *n.* (med.) forùncolo *m.* **2.** *vb.* bollire.

boiler, *n.* caldaia *f.*

boisterous, *adj.* impetuoso, turbolènto.

boisterously, *adv.* impetuosamente.

bold, *adj.* ardito; **(be b.)** ardire.

boldface, *n.* (type) caràtteri grassi *m.pl.*

boldly, *adv.* arditamente.

boldness, *n.* ardimento *m.*

Bolivian, *adj.* boliviano.

bologna, *n.* salsíccia *f.,* salame *m.*

bolster, *vb.* appoggiare.

bolster up, *vb.* tenere su.

bolt, **1.** *n.* catenàccio *m.* **2.** *vb.* (shut) chiùdere a catenàccio; (run away) fuggire.

bomb, *n.* bomba *f.*

bombard, *vb.* bombardare.

bombardier, *n.* bombardière *m.*

bombardment, *n.* bombardamento *m.*

bomber, *n.* bombardière *m.*

bombproof, *adj.* a pròva di bomba.

bombshell, *n.* bomba *f.*

bombsight, *n.* traguardo di puntamento *m.*

bonbon, *n.* dolce *m.*

bond, *n.* legame *m.,* obbligazione *f.,* víncolo *m.,* buòno *m.*

bondage, *n.* servitù *f.*

bonded, *adj.* vincolato.

bone, *n.* òsso *m.*

boneless, *adj.* sènza òssa.

bonfire, *n.* falò *m.*

bonnet, *n.* (headdress) cappèllo *m.;* (motor-car) còfano *m.*

bonus, *n.* gratificazione *f.*

bony, *adj.* ossuto.

book, *n.* libro *m.*

bookbinder, *n.* legatore *m.*

bookbindery, *n.* legatoría *f.*

bookcase, *n.* scaffale *m.*

bookkeeper, *n.* contàbile *m.*

bookkeeping, *n.* contabilità *f.*

booklet, *n.* libretto *m.*

bookmaker, *n.* (bets) allibratore *m.*

bookmark, *n.* segnalibro *m.*

bookseller, *n.* libraio *m.*

bookshelf, *n.* scaffale *m.*

bookstore, *n.* librería *f.*

boom, *n.* prosperità *f.*

boon, *n.* dono *m.*

boor, *n.* zòtico *m.*

boorish, *adj.* zòtico.

boost, **1.** *n.* (increase) accrescimento *m.;* (push) spinta *f.* **2.** *vb.* (increase) accréscere; (push) spíngere; (praise) lodare.

booster, *n.* (telephone) amplificatore *m.;* (person) entusiasta *m.*

boot, *n.* stivale *m.*

bootblack, *n.* lustrascarpe *m.*

booth, *n.* tènda *f.*

booty, *n.* bottino *m.*

booze, *vb.* ubriacarsi.

border, **1.** *n.* confine *m.,* frontièra *f.* **2.** *vb.* confinare.

borderline, **1.** *n.* línea di confine *f.* **2.** *adj.* marginale.

bore, **1.** *n.* (hole) foro *m.;* (annoyance) seccatura *f.* **2.** *vb.* (make a hole) forare; (annoy) seccare.

boredom, *n.* nòia *f.*

boric, *adj.* bòrico.

boring, **1.** *n.* (hole) foro *m.* **2.** *adj.* seccante.

born, *adj.* nato; **(be b.)** nàscere.

born-again, *adj.* rinato.

borough, *n.* borgo *m.*

borrow, *vb.* prendere in prèstito.

borrower, *n.* chi prende a prèstito.

bosom, *n.* pètto *m.*, seno *m.*

boss, *n.* padrone *m.*

bossy, *adj.* spadroneggiante.

botanical, *adj.* botànico.

botany, *n.* botànica *f.*

botch, *vb.* rabberciare.

both, *adj. and pron.* ambedue.

bother, 1. *n.* fastídio *m.* 2. *vb.* infastidire.

bothersome, *adj.* fastidioso.

bottle, *n.* bottiglia *f.*

bottom, *n.* fondo *m.*

bottomless, *adj.* sènza fondo.

boudoir, *n.* salottino *m.*

bough, *n.* ramo *m.*

bouillon, *n.* bròdo *m.*

boulder, *n.* sasso *m.*

boulevard, *n.* viale *m.*

bounce, 1. *n.* rimbalzo *m.* 2. *vb.* rimbalzare.

bound, 1. *n.* límite *m.*; (jump) balzo *m.*, salto *m.* 2. *vb.* balzare, saltare.

boundary, *n.* confine *m.*

bound for, *adj.* diretto a.

boundless, *adj.* illimitato.

boundlessly, *adv.* illimitatamente.

bounteous, *adj.* liberale.

bounty, *n.* liberalità *f.*

bouquet, *n.* mazzo di fiori *m.*

bourgeois, *adj.* borghese.

bout, *n.* (boxing) assalto *m.*

bovine, *adj.* bovino.

bow, 1. *n.* (for arrows, violin) arco *m.*; (greeting) inchino *m.*; (of boat) pròra *f.* 2. *vb.* inchinarsi.

bowels, *n.* budella *f.pl.*, intestini *m.pl.*

bower, *n.* pergolato *m.*

bowl, 1. *n.* (vessel) scodèlla *f.* 2. *vb.* giocare alle bocce.

bowlegged, *adj.* colle gambe ad archetto.

bowler, *n.* giocatore di bocce *m.*

bowling, *n.* giòco delle bocce *f.*

box, 1. *n.* scàtola *f.*, cassetta *f.*; (theater) palco *m.*; (P.O.) casèlla postale *f.* 2. *vb.* fare del pugilato.

boxcar, *n.* vagone mèrci *m.*

boxer, *n.* pugilatore *m.*

boxing, *n.* pugilato *m.*

box office, *n.* botteghino *m.*

boy, *n.* ragazzo *m.*, fanciullo *m.*

boycott, 1. *n.* boicottàggio *m.* 2. *vb.* boicottare.

boyhood, *n.* fanciullezza *f.*

boyish, *adj.* fanciullesco.

boyishly, *adv.* fanciullescamente.

brace, 1. *n.* sostegno *m.* 2. *vb.* sostenere.

bracelet, *n.* braccialetto *m.*

bracket, *n.* mènsola *f.*; (group) gruppo *m.*; (typography) parèntesi quadra *f.*

brag, *vb.* millantare.

braggart, *n.* millantatore *m.*

braid, 1. *n.* tréccia *f.* 2. *vb.* intrecciare.

brain, *n.* cervèllo *m.*

brainy, *adj.* intelligènte.

brake, 1. *n.* freno *m.* 2. *vb.* frenare.

bran, *n.* crusca *f.*

branch, *n.* ramo *m.*; (comm.) succursale *f.*

brand, *n.* marca *f.*

brandish, *vb.* brandire.

brand-new, *adj.* nuovíssimo.

brandy, *n.* acquavite *f.*

brash, *adj.* impertinènte.

brass, *n.* ottone *m.*

brassiere, *n.* reggipètto *m.*, reggiseno *m.*

brassy, *adj.* d'ottone; sfacciato.

brat, *n.* marmòcchio *m.*

bravado, *n.* bravata *f.*

brave, *adj.* coraggioso.

bravery, *n.* coràggio *m.*

brawl, *n.* lite *f.*, rissa *f.*

brawn, *n.* fòrza muscolare *f.*

bray, 1. *n.* ràglio *m.* 2. *vb.* ragliare.

braze, *vb.* brasare.

brazen, *adj.* di ottone; (insolent) insolènte.

Brazil, *n.* il Brasile *m.*

Brazilian, *adj.* brasiliano.

breach, *n.* bréccia *f.*; (of law) violazione *f.*

bread, *n.* pane *m.*; (b. crumbs) pangrattato *m.*; (b. stick) grissino *m.*

breaded, *adj.* impanato.

breadth, *n.* larghezza *f.*, ampiezza *f.*

bread winner, *n.* sostegno della famiglia *m.*

break, 1. *n.* rottura *f.;* interruzione *f.* **2.** *vb.* rómpere.

breakable, *adj.* rompíbile.

breakage, *n.* rottura *f.*

breaker, *n.* frangente *m.*

breakfast, *n.* prima colazione *f.*

breakneck, *adv.* a rompicollo.

breakwater, *n.* frangi-onde *m.*

breast, *n.* seno *m.,* mammèlla *f.,* poppa *f.;* (chest) pètto *m.*

breath, *n.* fiato *m.,* respiro *m.*

breathe, *vb.* respirare.

breathing, *n.* respiro *m.*

breathless, *adj.* sènza fiato; ansante.

breathlessly, *adv.* ansando.

breeches, *n.* brache *f.pl.,* pantaloni *m.pl.*

breed, 1. *n.* razza *f.* **2.** *vb.* (beget) generare; (train) educare; (raise) allevare.

breeder, *n.* generatore *m.,* allevatore *m.*

breeding, *n.* educazione *f.*

breeze, *n.* brezza *f.*

breezy, *adj.* (windy) ventoso; (cool) fresco.

brevity, *n.* brevità *f.*

brew, *vb.* fabbricare la birra.

brewer, *n.* birràio *m.,* fabbricante di birra *m.*

brewery, *n.* fàbbrica di birra *f.*

briar, *n.* rovo *m.*

bribe, *vb.* corrómpere.

briber, *n.* corruttore *m.*

bribery, *n.* corruzione *f.*

brick, *n.* mattone *m.*

bricklayer, *n.* muratore *m.*

bricklaying, *n.* muratura *f.*

bricklike, *adj.* come un mattone.

bridal, *adj.* nuziale.

bride, *n.* sposa *f.*

bridegroom, *n.* sposo *m.*

bridesmaid, *n.* damigèlla d'onore *f.*

bridge, *n.* ponte *m.*

bridged, *adj.* connèsso.

bridgehead, *n.* tèsta di ponte *f.*

bridle, *n.* briglia *f.*

brief, *adj.* brève.

brief case, *n.* borsa *f.*

briefly, *adv.* brevemente.

briefness, *n.* brevità *f.*

brier, *n.* rovo *m.*

brig, *n.* brigantino *m.*

brigade, *n.* brigata *f.*

bright, *adj.* chiaro; luminoso.

brighten, *vb.* illuminare.

brightness, *n.* chiarore *m.*

brilliance, *n.* splendore *m.*

brilliant, *adj.* brillante.

brim, *n.* (cup) orlo *m.;* (hat) tesa *f.*

brimstone, *n.* zolfo *m.*

brine, *n.* acqua salata *f.*

bring, *vb.* portare; apportare; **(b. about)** causare.

brink, *n.* orlo *m.;* bordo *m.*

briny, *adj.* salato.

brisk, *adj.* vivace.

brisket, *n.* (meat) pètto *m.*

briskly, *adv.* vivacemente.

briskness, *n.* vivacità *f.*

bristle, 1. *n.* sétola *f.* **2.** *vb.* arruffare.

bristly, *adj.* setoloso.

Britain, *n.* **(Great B.)** la Gran Bretagna *f.*

British, *adj.* britànnico.

Briton, *n.* Brètone *m.*

brittle, *adj.* fràgile.

broad, *adj.* largo, àmpio.

broadcast, 1. *n.* trasmissione radiofònica *f.* **2.** *vb.* trasméttere.

broadcaster, *n.* trasmettitore *m.*

broadcloth, *n.* popelina *f.*

broaden, *vb.* allargare.

broadly, *adv.* largamente.

broadminded, *adv.* spregiudicato.

broadside, *n.* bordata *f.*

brocade, *n.* broccato *f.*

brocaded, *adj.* di broccato.

broil, *adv.* mettere alla graticola.

broiler, *n.* graticola *f.*

broke, *adj.* al verde.

broken, *adj.* rotto.

broken-down, *adj.* avvilito; rovinato.

broken-hearted, *adj.* scorato.

broker, *n.* sensale *m.*

brokerage, *n.* senseria *f.*

bronchial, *adj.* bronchiale.

bronchitis, *n.* bronchite *f.*

bronco, *n.* puledro brado *m.*

bronze, *n.* bronzo *m.*

brooch, *n.* spilla *f.*

brood, 1. *n.* covata *f.,* famiglia *f.* **2.** *vb.* covare.

brook, *n.* ruscèllo *m.*

broom, *n.* scopa *f.*

broomstick, *n.* mànico della scopa *f.*

broth, *n.* bròdo *m.*

brothel, *n.* bordèllo *m.*

brother, *n.* fratèllo *m.*

brotherhood, *n.* fratellanza *f.*

brother-in-law, *n.* cognato *m.*

brotherly, *adj.* fratèrno.

brow, *n.* frónte *f.*

browbeat, *vb.* intimorire.

brown, *adj.* bruno.

browse, *vb.* brucare.

bruise, 1. *n.* ammaccatura *f.* **2.** *vb.* ammaccare.

brunette, *n.* bruna *f.*

brunt, *n.* urto *m.*

brush, 1. *n.* spàzzola *f.;* (artist's) pennèllo *m.* **2.** *vb.* spazzolare; **(b. against)** sfiorare.

brush-off, *n.* scortesia *f.*

brushwood, *n.* màcchia *f.*

brusque, *adj.* brusco.

brusquely, *adv.* bruscamente.

brutal, *adj.* brutale.

brutality, *n.* brutalità *f.*

brutalize, *vb.* maltrattare.

brute, *n. and adj.* bruto (*m.*).

bubble, *n.* bolla *f.*

buck, *n.* dàino *m.;* (male) màschio *m.*

bucket, *n.* sécchia *f.*

buckle, 1. *n.* fìbbia *f.* **2.** *vb.* affibbiare.

buckram, *n.* tela di fusto *f.*

bucksaw, *n.* sega intelaiata *f.*

buckshot, *n.* pallinacci *m.pl.*

buckwheat, *n.* grano saraceno *m.*

bud, 1. *n.* gèmma *f.* **2.** *vb.* gemmare.

Buddhism, *n.* buddismo *m.*

buddy, *n.* amico *m.,* compagno *m.*

budge, *vb.* muòversi.

budget, *n.* preventivo *m.*

buff, *adj.* bruno-giallàstro.

buffalo, *n.* bùfalo *m.*

buffer, *n.* respingènte *m.;* **(b. state)** stato cuscinetto *m.*

buffet, 1. *n.* (slap) schiaffo *m.;* (eating place) caffè *m.* **2.** *vb.* schiaffeggiare.

buffoon, *n.* buffone *m.*

bug, *n.* insètto *m.*

bugle, *n.* bùccina *f.*

build, *vb.* costruire, fabbricare.

builder, *n.* costruttore *m.*

building, *n.* edificio *m.*

buildup, *n.* concentrazione *f.;* sviluppo *m.;* preparazione *f.*

built-in, *adj.* incorporato.

bulb, 1. *n.* (of plant) bulbo *m.;* (electric light) lampadina *f.*

bulge, 1. *n.* protuberanza *f.* **2.** *vb.* gonfiarsi.

bulk, *n.* volume *m.,* massa *f.*

bulkhead, *n.* paratìa *f.*

bulky, *adj.* voluminoso.

bull, *n.* tòro *m.*

bulldog, *n.* molòsso *m.*

bulldozer, *n.* livellatrice *f.*

bullet, *n.* pallòttola *f.*

bulletin, *n.* bollettino *m.*

bulletproof, *adj.* a pròva di fucile.

bullfight, *n.* corrida *f.*

bullfinch, *n.* ciuffolòtto *m.*

bullion, *n.* (gold) oro in lingotti *m.*

bullock, *n.* manzo *m.*

bullring, *n.* arèna *f.*

bully, *n.* prepotènte *m.*

bulwark, *n.* baluardo *m.*

bum, *n.* vagabondo *m.*

bumblebee, *n.* calabrone *m.*

bump, 1. *n.* urto *m.* **2.** *vb.* urtare.

bumper, *n.* respingènte *m.*

bun, *n.* panino *m.*

bunch, *n.* mazzo *m.,* gràppolo *m.*

bundle, *n.* fàscio *m.*

bungle, *vb.* abborracciare.

bunion, *n.* infiammazione del pòllice del piède *f.*

bunk, *n.* (bed) cuccetta *f.;* (nonsense) fròttole *f.pl.*

bunny, *n.* coniglietto *m.*

bunting, *n.* stamigna *f.*

buoy, *n.* bòa *f.*

buoyant, *adj.* che può galleggiare; (cheerful) allegro.

burden, *n.* fardèllo *m.;* **(b. of proof)** ònere della pròva *m.*

burdensome, *adj.* opprimènte, oneroso.

bureau, *n.* ufficio *m.*

burglar, *n.* ladro *m.*

burglarize, *vb.* rubare.

burglary, *n.* furto *m.*

burial, *n.* sepoltura *f.*

burlap, *n.* canovàccio rozzo *m.*

burly, *adj.* corpulènto.

burn, 1. *n.* bruciatura *f.* **2.** *vb.* bruciare, àrdere.

burner, *n.* bècco *m.*

burning, *adj.* bruciante, ardènte.

burnish, *vb.* brunire.

burrow, 1. *n.* tana *f.* **2.** *vb.* scavare.

burst, 1. *n.* scatto *m.* **2.** *vb.* scoppiare; (dash) scattare; **(b. forth)** prorómpere.

bury, *vb.* seppellire.

bus, *n.* àutobus *m.;* **(trolley b.)** filobus *m.;* **(de luxe b.)** pullman *m.;* **(b. line)** autolínea *f.*

bus driver, *n.* conducente d'autobus *m.*

bush, *n.* cespùglio *m.*

bushel, *n.* mòggio *m.*

bushy, *adj.* cespuglioso; (thick) folto.

busily, *adv.* attivamente.

business, *n.* affare *m.; affari m.pl.*

businesslike, *adj.* pràtico.

businessman, *n.* uòmo d'affari *m.*

businesswoman, *n.* dònna d'affari *f.*

buss, *n.* bacio con schiocco *m.*

bus stop, *n.* fermata d'autobus *f.*

bust, *n.* busto *m.*

bustle, *n.* tramestío *m.*

busy, *adj.* occupato, affaccendato, attivo.

busybody, *n.* faccendière *m.*

but, 1. *prep.* eccètto, salvo. **2.** *conj.* ma.

butcher, 1. *n.* macellaio *m.* **2.** *vb.* macellare.

butchery, *n.* macèllo *m.*

butler, *n.* maggiordòmo *m.*

butt, *n.* estremità *f.;* (of gun) càlcio *m.*

butter, *n.* burro *m.*

buttercup, *n.* ranùncolo *m.*

butterfat, *n.* grasso del latte *m.*

butterfly, *n.* farfalla *f.*

buttermilk, *n.* sièro *m.*

buttock, *n.* nàtica *f.*

button, *n.* bottone *m.*

buttonhole, *n.* occhièllo *m.*

buttress, *n.* contrafforte *m.*

buxom, *adj.* grassòccio.

buy, *vb.* comprare.

buyer, *n.* compratore *m.*

buzz, 1. *n.* ronzio *m.* **2.** *vb.* ronzare.

buzzard, *n.* poiana *f.*

buzzer, *n.* campanèllo *m.*

buzz saw, *n.* sega circolare *f.*

by, *prep.* (through) per; (near) prèsso a; (at) a; (indicating agent) da.

by-and-by, *adv.* fra pòco.

bygone, *adj.* passato.

by-law, *n.* legge particolare *f.*

by-pass, *vb.* evitare.

by-path, *n.* sentiero secondario *m.;* strada privata *f.*

by-product, *n.* prodotto secondàrio *m.*

bystander, *n.* spettatore *m.*

byte, *n.* byte *m.*

byway, *n.* viòttolo *m.*

C

cab, *n.* tassi *m.*

cabaret, *n.* ritròvo notturno *m.*

cabbage, *n.* càvolo *m.*

cabin, *n.* capanna *f.;* (on boat) cabina *f.*

cabin boy, *n.* mozzo *m.*

cabinet, *n.* (furniture) stipo *m.;* (politics) gabinetto *m.*

cabinetmaker, *n.* stipettaio *m.*

cable, *n.* cavo *m.*

cable car, *n.* teleferica *f.*

cablegram, *n.* cablogramma *m.*

cableway, *n.* funivia *f.*

cache, *n.* nascondìglio *m.*

cachet, *n.* sigillo *m.*

cackle, 1. *n.* vèrso *m.* **2.** *vb.* cantare.

cacophony, *n.* cacofonía *f.*

cactus, *n.* cactus *m.*

cad, *n.* vigliacco *m.*

cadaver, *n.* cadàvero *m.*

cadaverous, *adj.* cadavèrico.

cadet, *n.* cadetto *m.*

cadence, *n.* cadènza *f.*

caddie, *n.* portamazze *m.*

cadmium, *n.* càdmio *m.*

cadre, *n.* quadro *m.*

café, *n.* caffè *m.*

café society, *n.* bel mondo *m.*

caffeine, *n.* caffeína *f.*

cage, 1. *n.* gàbbia *f.* **2.** *vb.* ingabbiare.

caisson, *n.* cassone *m.*

cajole, *vb.* lusingare.

cake, n. tòrta f., focàccia f.

calamitous, adj. calamitoso.

calcify, vb. calcificare.

calcium, n. càlcio m.

calculable, adj. calcolàbile.

calculate, vb. calcolare.

calculating, adj. calcolatore; (c. machine) màcchina calcolatrice f.

calculation, n. càlcolo m.

calculus, n. càlcolo m.

caldron, n. caldaia f.

calendar, n. calendàrio m.

calf, n. vitèllo m.

calfskin, n. pèlle di vitèllo f.

caliber, n. càlibro m.

calibrate, vb. calibrare.

calico, n. càlcolo m.

caliper, n. càlibro m.

caliph, n. califfo m.

calisthenic, adj. ginnàstico.

calisthenics, n. ginnàstica f.

calk, vb. calafatare.

calker, n. calafato m.

call, n. chiamata f., appèllo m. 2. vb. chiamare.

caller, n. chiamante m.; visitatore m.

calligraphy, n. calligrafìa f.

calling, n. vocazione f., professione f.

calling card, n. biglietto da visita m.; carta telefonica f.

callous, adj. calloso; (unfeeling) insensìbile.

callousness, n. callosità f., insensibilità f.

callow, adj. inespèrto.

call to arms, n. chiamata alle armi f.

callus, n. callo m.

calm, 1. n. calma f. 2. adj. calmo. 3. vb. calmare.

calmly, adv. con calmo.

calmness, n. calma f.

caloric, adj. calòrico.

calorie, n. calorìa f.

calorimeter, n. calorímetro m.

calumniate, vb. calunniare.

calumny, n. calùnnia f.

Calvary, n. Calvàrio m.

calve, vb. partorire.

calyx, n. càlice m.

camaraderie, n. cameratismo m.

camber, n. curvatura f.

cambric, n. cambrì m.

camel, n. cammèllo m.

camelia, n. camèlia f.

camel's hair, n. peli di cammèllo m.pl.

cameo, n. cammèo m.

camera, n. màcchina fotogràfica f.

camomile, n. camomilla f.

camouflage, 1. n. camuffamento m., mimetismo m. 2. vb. camuffare, mimetizzare.

camp, 1. n. accampamento m. 2. vb. accamparsi; (sport) campeggiare.

campaign, n. campagna f.

camper, n. campeggiatore m.

camphor, n. cànfora f.

camping, n. campèggio m.

campus, n. città universitària f.

camshaft, n. albero a camme m.; distribuzione f.

can, 1. n. (tin) scàtola f.; (large) bidone m. 2. vb. (be able) potere.

Canada, n. il Canadà m.

Canadian, adj. canadese.

canal, n. canale m.

canalize, vb. canalizzare.

canapé, n. crostino m.

canard, n. fròttola f.

canary, n. canarino m.

Canary Islands, n. Canàrie f.pl.

cancel, vb. annullare, cancellare, disdire.

cancellation, n. annullamento m.

cancer, n. cancro m.

candelabrum, n. candelabro m.

candid, adj. càndido, franco.

candidacy, n. candidatura f.

candidate, n. candidato m.

candidly, adv. candidamente, francamente.

candidness, n. franchezza f., candore m.

candied, adj. candito.

candle, n. candela f.

candlestick, n. candelière f.

candor, n. candore m.

candy, n. dolciumi m.pl.; caramella f.

cane, n. bastone m.; (plants) canna f.

cane seat, n. sedia impagliata f.

cane sugar, n. zucchero di canna f.

canine, adj. canino.

canister, n. scàtola f.

canker, n. cancro m.

cankerworm, n. bruco m.

canned, adj. in scàtola.

canner, n. fabbricante di consèrve alimentari m.

cannery, n. stabilimento dí consèrve alimentari m.

cannibal, n. cannibale m.

canning, n. preparazione di consèrve alimentari f.

cannon, n. cannone m.

cannonade, n. cannoneggiamento m.

cannoneer, n. cannonière m.

cannot, vb. non potere.

canny, adj. astuto.

canoe, n. canòa f.

canon, n. (rule, law) cànone m.; (person) canònico m.

canonical, adj. canònico.

canonize, vb. canonizzare.

canon law, n. diritto canonico m.

can-opener, n. apriscàtole m.

canopy, n. baldacchino m.

cant, n. ipocrisía f.

can't, vb. non potere.

cantaloupe, n. melone m.

canteen, n. cantina f.

canter, vb. andare al piccolo galòppo.

cantonment, n. accantonamento m.

canvas, n. canovàccio m.

canvass, 1. n. esame m. 2. vb. esaminare.

canyon, n. burrone m.

cap, n. berretto m.

capability, n. capacità f.

capable, adj. capace, àbile.

capably, adv. abilmente.

capacious, adj. spazioso.

capacity, n. capacità f.

caparison, 1. n. bardatura f. 2. vb. bardare.

cape, n. cappa f.

caper, 1. n. capriòla f. 2. vb. far capriòle.

capillary, adj. capillare.

capital, 1. n. (money) capitale m.; (city) capitale f. 2. adj. capitale.

capital punishment, n. pena capitale f.; pena di morte f.

capitalism, n. capitalismo m.

capitalist, n. capitalista m.

capitalistic, adj. capitalístico.

capitalization, n. capitalizzazione f.

capitalize, vb. capitalizzare.

capitulate, vb. capitolare.

capon, n. cappone m.

caprice, n. capríccio m.

capricious, adj. capriccioso.

capriciously, adv. capricciosamente.

capriciousness, n. capricciosità f.

capsize, vb. capovólgere.

capsule, n. càpsula f.

captain, n. capitano m.

caption, n. títolo m.

captious, adj. capzioso.

captivate, vb. affascinare.

captive, n. and adj. prigionièro (m.).

captivity, n. prigionía f.

captor, n. catturatore m.

capture, 1. n. cattura f. 2. vb. catturare.

car, n. carro m., vettura f.; (auto) automòbile f.; (railroad) vagone m.

caracul, n. lince persiana f.

carafe, n. caraffa f.

caramel, n. caramèlla f.

carat, n. carato m.

caravan, n. carovana f.

caraway, n. cumino m.

carbide, n. carburo m.

carbine, n. carabina f.

carbohydrate, n. idrato di carbònio m.

carbon, n. carbònio m.

carbon dioxide, n. biòssido di carbònio m.

carbon monoxide, n. monòssido di carbònio m.

carbon paper, n. carta carbone m.

carbuncle, n. carbónchio m.

carburetor, n. carburatore m.

carcass, n. carcassa f.

carcinogenic, adj. carcinògeno.

card, n. carta f., biglietto m.; (filing) schedina f.

cardboard, n. cartone m.; (thin) cartoncino m.

card-carrying, adj. tesserato, socio.

card holder, n. tesserato m., socio m.

cardiac, adj. cardíaco.

cardigan, *n.* golf *m.*

cardinal, *adj. and n.* cardinale *(m).*

cardsharp, *n.* baro *m.*

care, 1. *n.* cura *f.* **2.** *vb.* curarsi; **(take c. of)** curare.

careen, *vb.* carenare.

career, *n.* carriera *f.*

carefree, *adj.* senza preoccupazioni.

careful, *adj.* accurato, attento.

carefully, *adv.* accuratamente, attentamente.

carefulness, *n.* accuratezza *f.,* attenzione *f.*

careless, *adj.* spensierato, trascurato.

carelessly, *adv.* spensieratamente, trascuratamente.

carelessness, *n.* spensieratezza *f.,* trascuratezza *f.*

caress, 1. *n.* carezza *f.* **2.** *vb.* accarezzare.

caretaker, *n.* guardiano *m.*

carfare, *n.* spiccioli per il tram *m.pl.*

cargo, *n.* càrico *m.*

caricature, *n.* caricatura *f.*

caries, *n.* càrie *f.*

carillon, *n.* carillón *m.*

carload, *n.* carrettata *f.*

carnage, *n.* carneficina *f.*

carnal, *adj.* carnale.

carnation, *n.* garòfano *m.*

carnival, *n.* carnevale *m.*

carnivorous, *adj.* carnivoro.

carol, 1. *n.* canto di Natale *m.* **2.** *vb.* cantare.

carouse, *vb.* far baldòria.

carousel, *n.* carosèllo *m.*

carpenter, *n.* falegname *m.*

carpet, *n.* tappeto *m.*

carpeting, *n.* stoffa per tappeti *f.*

car pool, *n.* consòrzio automobilìstico *m.*

carriage, *n.* (vehicle) vettura *f.;* (transportation) trasporto *m.*

carrier, *n.* portatore *m.*

carrier pigeon, *n.* piccione viaggiatore *m.*

carrot, *n.* caròta *f.*

carry, *vb.* portare; **(c. on)** continuare; **(c. out)** eseguire; **(c. through)** condurre a buon fine.

cart, *n.* carro *m.*

cartage, *n.* trasporto *m.*

carte blanche, *n.* carta bianca *f.*

cartel, *n.* cartèllo *m.*

carter, *n.* carrettière *m.*

cart horse, *n.* cavallo da tiro *m.*

cartilage, *n.* cartilàgine *f.*

carton, *n.* scàtola di cartone *f.*

cartoon, *n.* (sketch) cartone *m.;* (picture) disegno *m.*

cartoonist, *n.* disegnatore *m.,* vignettista *m.*

cartridge, *n.* cartùccia *f.*

carve, *vb.* (art) scolpire; (meat) tagliare, trinciare.

carver, *n.* scultore *m.*

carving, *n.* scultura *f.*

carving-knife, *n.* trinciante *m.*

cascade, *n.* cascata *f.*

case, *n.* (instance; state of things) caso *m.;* (law) càusa *f.;* (packing) cassa *f.;* (holder) astùccio *m.;* **(in any c.)** in ogni caso.

case study, *n.* casistica *f.*

cash, 1. *n.* contanti *m.pl.* **2.** *vb.* (cheque) riscuòtere.

cashew, *n.* anacardio *m.;* mandorla indiana *f.*

cashier, *n.* cassière *m.;* (cashier's desk) cassa *f.*

cashmere, *n.* casimiro *f.*

casing, *n.* copertura *f.*

casino, *n.* casino *m.*

cask, *n.* barile *m.*

casket, *n.* cassettina *f.*

casserole, *n.* casseruòla *f.*

cassette, *n.* cassetta *f.*

cast, 1. *n.* (throw) gètto *m.* **2.** *vb.* gettare; (metal) fóndere.

castanets, *n.* nàcchere *f.pl.*

castaway, *n.* nàufrago *m.*

caste, *n.* casta *f.*

caster, *n.* fonditore *m.*

castigate, *vb.* castigare.

cast iron, *n.* ghisa *f.*

castle, *n.* castèllo *m.*

castoff, *adj.* abbandonato.

castrate, *vb.* castrare.

casual, *adj.* (accidental) casuale; (nonchalant) indifferente.

casually, *adv.* casualmente, indifferentemente.

casualness, *n.* indifferenza *f.*

casualty, *n.* (accident) disgràzia *f.;* (injured person) ferito *m.*

cat, *n.* gatto *m.,* gatta *f.*

cataclysm, n. cataclisma m.

catacomb, n. catacomba f.

catalogue, n. catàlogo m.

catapult, n. catapulta f.

cataract, n. cateratta f.

catarrh, n. catarro m.

catastrophe, n. catàstrofe f.

catch, vb. afferràre; (sickness) préndere.

catcher, n. chi affèrra, chi prende.

catchword, n. parola di richiamo f.

catchy, adj. melodioso.

catechism, n. catechismo m.

catechize, vb. catechizzare.

categorical, adj. categórico.

category, n. categoria f.

cater, vb. provvedere a.

caterpillar, n. bruco m.

catgut, n. minùgia f.pl.

catharsis, n. catarsi f.

cathartic, adj. purgativo.

cathedral, n. cattedrale f.

catheter, n. catètere m.

cathode, n. càtodo m.

Catholic, adj. cattòlico.

Catholicism, n. cattolicismo m.

cat nap, n. pisolino m.

catsup, n. salsa di pomodoro f.

cattle, n. bestiame m.

cattleman, n. bovaro m.

catwalk, n. ballatòio m.

cauliflower, n. cavolfiore m.

causation, n. causalità f.

cause, 1. n. càusa f. 2. vb. causare, cagionare.

causeway, n. strada selciata f.

caustic, adj. càustico, sarcàstico.

cauterize, vb. cauterizzare.

cautery, n. cautèrio m.

caution, 1. n. cautèla f. 2. vb. ammonire.

cautious, adj. càuto.

cavalcade, n. cavalcata f.

cavalier, n. cavalière m.

cavalry, n. cavalleria f.

cave, n. cavèrna f.

cave-in, n. crollo m.

cavern, n. cavèrna f.

caviar, n. caviale m.

cavity, n. cavità f.

caw, vb. gracchiare.

cayman, n. caimano m.

cease, vb. cessare.

ceasefire, n. cessate il fuoco m.

ceaseless, adj. incessante.

cedar, n. cedro m.

cede, vb. cédere.

ceiling, n. soffitto m.

celebrant, n. celebrante m.

celebrate, vb. celebrare.

celebrated, adj. (famous) cèlebre.

celebration, n. celebrazione f.

celebrity, n. celebrità f.

celerity, n. celerità f.

celery, n. sèdano m.

celestial, adj. celèste.

celibacy, n. celibato m.

celibate, adj. cèlibe.

cell, n. (room) cèlla f.; (biology) cèllula f.

cellar, n. cantina f.

cellist, n. violoncellista m.

cello, n. violoncèllo m.

cellophane, n. cellofane m.

cellular, adj. cellulare.

celluloid, n. cellulòide f.

cellulose, n. cellulosa f.

Celtic, adj. cèltico.

cement, 1. n. cemento m. 2. vb. cementare.

cemetery, n. cimitèro m., camposanto m.

censor, 1. n. censore m. 2. vb. censurare.

censorious, adj. censòrio.

censorship, n. censura f.

censure, n. censura f.

census, n. censimento m.

cent, n. centèsimo m.

centaur, n. centàuro m.

centenary, adj. and n. centenàrio (m.)

centennial, adj. and n. centennale (m.)

center, n. cèntro m.

centerfold, n. pàgine centrali f.pl.

centerpiece, n. centro da tàvola m; centrino m.

centigrade, adj. centígrado.

central, adj. centrale.

centralize, vb. centralizzare.

century, n. sècolo m.

century plant, n. àgave f.

ceramic, adj. ceràmico.

ceramics, n. ceràmica f.

cereal, n. and adj. cereale (m.)

cerebral, adj. cerebrale.

ceremonial, adj. cerimoniale.

ceremonious, adj. cerimonioso.

ceremony, n. cerimònia f.

certain, adj. cèrto.

certainly, adv. certamente.

certainty, n. certezza f.

certificate, n. certificato m.

certification, n. certificazione f.

certified, adj. garantito; **(c. check)** assegno a copertura garantita m.; **(c. copy)** còpia conforme f.

certify, vb. certificare.

certitude, n. certezza f.

cervical, adj. cervicale.

cervix, n. cervice f.

cesarean section, n. taglio cesàreo m.

cessation, n. cessazione f.

cession, n. cessione f.

cesspool, n. pozzo nero m.

chafe, vb. (warm) riscaldare; (irritate) irritare.

chaff, 1. n. pula f., lòppa f.; (banter) cèlia f. 2. vb. celiare.

chagrin, n. crùccio m.

chain, 1. n. catena f. 2. vb. incatenare.

chain reaction, n. reazione a catena f.

chain saw, n. motosega f.

chain smoke, vb. fumarne una via l'altra.

chair, n. sèdia f.

chairman, n. presidènte m.

chairmanship, n. presidènza f.

chairperson, n. presidènte m.; presidèntessa f.

chairwoman, n. presidentessa f.

chalice, n. càlice f.

chalk, n. gesso m.

chalky, adj. gessoso.

challenge, 1. n. sfida f. 2. vb. sfidare.

challenger, n. sfidante m.

chamber, n. càmera f.; **(c.-pot)** vaso da nòtte m.

chamber of commerce, n. camera di commercio f.

chamberlain, n. ciambellano m.

chambermaid, n. camerièra f.

chamber music, n. mùsica da càmera f.

chameleon, n. camaleonte m.

chamois, n. camòscio m.

champ, vb. ròdere.

champagne, n. champagne f.

champion, n. campione m.

championship, n. campionato m.

chance, 1. n. caso m.; (opportunity) occasione f.; **(by c.)** per caso. 2. adj. fortùito.

chancel, n. còro m.

chancellery, n. cancellería f.

chancellor, n. cancellière m.

chandelier, n. lampadàrio m.

change, 1. n. cambio m., cambiamento m., mutamento m.; (small coins) moneta spícciola f.; (money due) rèsto m. 2. vb. cambiare, mutare.

changeability, n. mutabilità f.

changeable, adj. mutévole.

change of heart, n. pentimento m.; conversione f.

change of life, n. menopausa f.

changer, n. (money-changer) cambiavalute m.

channel, n. canale m.

chant, 1. n. canto m. 2. vb. cantare.

chaos, n. càos m.

chaotic, adj. caòtico.

chap, 1. n. (on skin) screpolatura f.; (fellow) tizio m. 2. vb. screpolare.

chapel, n. cappèlla f.

chaplain, n. cappellano m.

chapter, n. capítolo m.

char, vb. carbonizzare.

character, n. caràttere m.

characteristic, 1. n. caratterística f. 2. adj. caratterístico.

chracteristically, adv. caratteristicamente.

characterization, n. caratterizzazione f.

characterize, vb. caratterizzare.

charcoal, n. carbone di legna m.

charge, 1. n. (load) càrico m.; (attack; gun) càrica f. (price) prèzzo m.; (custody) custòdia f. 2. vb. (load) caricare; (set a price) far pagare.

charger, n. cavallo da guerra m.

chariot, n. carro m.

charioteer, n. auriga m.

charisma, n. carisma m.

charitable, adj. caritatévole.

charitableness, n. carità f.

charitably, adv. caritatevolmente.

charity, n. carità f.

charlatan, n. ciarlatano m.

charlatanism, n. ciarlatanismo m.

charm, 1. n. incanto m.; **(good-luck c.)** portafortuna m. **2.** vb. incantare, affascinare.

charmer, n. incantatore m., incantatrice f.

charming, adj. affascinante

chart, n. (map) carta f.; (graph) gràfico m.

charter, n. carta f.

charter flight, n. volo noleggiato m.

charter member, n. sòcio fondatore m.

charwoman, n. domèstica f.

chase, 1. n. càccia f. **2.** vb. cacciare.

chaser, n. cacciatore m.

chasm, n. abisso m.

chassis, n. telaio m.

chaste, adj. casto.

chasten, vb. castigare.

chasteness, n. castità f.

chastise, vb. castigare, punire.

chastisement, n. castigo m., punizione f.

chastity, n. castità f.

chat, 1. n. chiàcchiera f. **2.** vb. chiacchierare.

château, n. castèllo m.

chattel, n. bène mòbile m.

chatter, 1. n. chiàcchiera f. **2.** vb. chiacchierare.

chatterbox, n. chiacchierone m.

chauffeur, n. autista m.

cheap, adj. a buòn mercato, econòmico.

cheapen, vb. (prices) calare; (depreciate) deprezzare.

cheaply, adv. a buòn mercato, economicamente.

cheapness, n. buòn mercato m.

cheat, vb. ingannare, truffare.

cheater, n. ingannatore m., truffatore m.

check, 1. n. (restraint) freno m.; (verification) contròllo m.; (theater) contromarca f.; (clothes, luggage) scontrino m.; (bill) conto m.; (bank) assegno m. **2.** vb. (restrain) frenare; (verify) controllare; (luggage) registrare.

checkbook, n. libretto per gli assegni m.

checker, n. scacco m.

checkerboard, n. scacchièra f.

checkered, adj. (career) vissuta; (color) variegato

checkers, n. dama f.

checking account, n. conto corrente m., c.c. m.

checkmate, n. scacco matto m.

checkout, n. (hotel) partenza f.

checkpoint, n. posto d'ispezione m.

checkroom, n. guardaroba m.

checkup, n. ispezione m.; visita mèdica f.

cheek, n. guància f.

cheekbone, n. zigomo m.

cheer, 1. n. applàuso m. **2.** vb. applaudire; **(c. up)** rallegrare, tr.

cheerful, adj. allegro.

cheerfulness, n. allegría f.

cheerless, adj. triste.

cheery, adj. allegro.

cheese, n. càcio m., formàggio m.

cheesecloth, n. garza f.

cheesy, adj. di qualità inferiore.

chef, n. cuòco m.

chemical, adj. chímico.

chemically, adv. chimicamente.

chemist, n. chímico m.

chemistry, n. chímica f.

chemotherapy, n. chemioterapía f.

chenille, n. ciniglia f.

cheque, n. assegno m.

cherish, vb. tener caro.

cherry, n. ciliègia f.

cherry-tree, n. ciliègio m.

cherub, n. cherubino m.

chess, n. scacchi m.pl.

chessboard, n. scacchièra f.

chessman, scacco m.

chest, n. (box) cassa f.; (body) pètto m.

chestnut, n. (nut) castagna f.; (tree) castagno m.

chevron, n. gallone m.

chew, vb. masticare.

chewer, n. masticatore m.

chewing gum, n. gomma da masticare f.

chic, adj. alla mòda.

chicanery, n. sofisma m.

chick, n. pulcino m.

chicken, *n.* pollo *m.*

chicken-hearted, *adj.* tímido.

chicken-pox, *n.* varicèlla *f.*

chickpea, *n.* cece *m.*

chicory, *n.* cicòria *f.*

chide, *vb.* rimproverare, sgridare.

chief, 1. *n.* capo *m.* **2.** *adj.* principale.

chief executive, *n.* capo del governo *m.*

chief justice, *n.* presidente della corte suprema *m.*

chiefly, *adv.* principalmente.

chief of staff, *n.* capo di stato maggiore *m.*

chieftain, *n.* capo *m.*

chiffon, *n.* mussolina leggeríssima *f.*

chilblain, *n.* gelone *m.*

child, *n.* bambino *m.*, bambina *f.*

childbirth, *n.* parto *m.*

childhood, *n.* infànzia *f.*

childish, *adj.* infantile.

childishness, *n.* infantilità *f.*

childless, *adj.* sènza figli.

childlessness, *n.* mancanza di prole *f.*

childlike, *adj.* infantile.

chill, 1. *n.* freddo *m.;* (shiver) brívido *m.* **2.** *vb.* raffreddare.

chilliness, *n.* freddo *m.*

chilly, *adj.* freddo, glaciale.

chime, 1. *n.* scampanío *m.* **2.** *vb.* scampanare.

chimney, *n.* camino *m.*

chimney-sweep, *n.* spazzacamino *m.*

chimpanzee, *n.* scimpanzè *m.*

chin, *n.* mento *m.*

China, *n.* (la) Cina *f.*

china, *n.* porcellana *f.*

chinaware, *n.* porcellane *f.pl.*

chinchilla, *n.* cincillà *f.*

Chinese, *adj.* cinese.

chink, *n.* crèpa *f.*

chintz, *n.* indiana *f.*

chip, 1. *n.* schèggia *f.* **2.** *vb.* scheggiare.

chiropodist, *n.* callista *m.*

chiropractor, *n.* callista *m.*

chirp, 1. *n.* cinguettío *m.* **2.** *vb.* cinguettare.

chisel, 1. *n.* cesèllo *m.* **2.** *vb.* cesellare.

chivalrous, *adj.* cavalleresco.

chivalry, *n.* cavalleria *f.*

chive, *n.* cipolla *f.*

chloride, *n.* cloruro *m.*

chlorine, *n.* clòro *m.*

chloroform, *n.* clorofòrmio *m.*

chlorophyll, *n.* clorofilla *f.*

chock full, *adj.* pieno zeppo.

chocolate, *n.* cioccolato *m.*

choice, 1. *n.* scelta *f.* **2.** *adj.* scelto.

choir, *n.* còro *m.*

choke, *vb.* soffocare, strangolare.

choker, *n.* cravatta *f.*

choler, *n.* còllera *f.*

cholera, *n.* colèra *f.*

choleric, *adj.* collèrico.

choose, *vb.* scégliere.

chop, 1. *n.* (meat) costoletta *f.* **2.** *vb.* tagliare.

chopper, *n.* (knife) mannaia *f.*

choppy, *adj.* (of sea) corto.

chopstick, *n.* bacchetta *f.*

choral, *adj.* corale.

chord, *n.* (string) còrda *f.;* (harmony) accòrdo *m.*

chore, *n.* lavoro di casa *m.;* corvè *f.*

choreographer, *n.* coreògrafo *m.*

choreography, *n.* coreografia *f.*

chorister, *n.* corista *m.*

chortle, *vb.* ridacchiare.

chorus, *n.* còro *m.*

chowder, *n.* minestra di pesce *f.*

Christ, *n.* Cristo *m.*

christen, *vb.* battezzare.

Christendom, *n.* cristianità *f.*

christening, *n.* battésimo *m.*

Christian, *n. and adj.* cristiano.

Christianity, *n.* cristianésimo *m.*

Christmas, *n.* Natale *m.*

chromatic, *adj.* cromàtico.

chrome, chromium, *n.* cròmo *m.*

chromosome, *n.* cromosòma *m.*

chronic, *adj.* crònico.

chronically, *adv.* cronicamente.

chronological, *adj.* cronològico.

chronology, *n.* cronologia *f.*

chrysalis, *n.* crisàlide *f.*

chrysanthemum, *n.* crisantèmo *m.*

chubby, *adj.* grassetto.

chuck, *vb.* (cluck) chiocciare; (throw) lanciare.

chuckle, *vb.* ridere sotto voce.

chug, 1. n. sbuffo m. **2.** vb. sbuffare.

chum, n. compagno m.

chummy, adj. intimo.

chump, n. ciocco m., ceppo, m.

chunk, n. pèzzo m.

chunky, adj. tozzo.

church, n. chièsa f.

churchman, n. prète m.

churchyard, n. cimitèro m., camposanto m.

churlish, adj. villano.

churn, n. zàngola f.

chute, n. canale di scolo m.

cicada, n. cicala f.

cider, n. sidro m.

cigar, n. sigaro m.

cigarette, n. sigaretta f.; **(c. butt)** cicca f.

cigar store, n. tabaccheria f.

cilia, n. ciglio m.

ciliary, adj. ciliare.

cinch, n. còsa cèrta f.

cinchona, n. cincona f.

cinder, n. brùscolo m.

cinema, n. cinema m., cinematògrafo m.

cinematic, adj. cinematogràfico.

cinnamon, n. (tree) cinnamòmo m.; (spice) cannèlla f.

cipher, n. (zero) zèro m.; (figure, secret writing) cifra f.

circle, n. (figure) cérchio m.; (group) circolo m.

circuit, n. circùito m.; **(short c.)** corto circùito m.

circuitous, adj. indirètto.

circuitously, adv. indirettamente.

circuitry, n. schema di montaggio m.; circuitazione f.

circular, n. and adj. circolare (m.).

circularize, vb. mandare dei circolari a.

circulate, vb. circolare.

circulation, n. circolazione f.

circulatory, adj. circolatòrio.

circumcise, vb. circoncìdere.

circumcision, n. circoncisione f.

circumference, n. circonferènza f.

circumflex, adj. circonflèsso.

circumlocution, n. circonlocuzione f.

circumscribe, vb. circonscrìvere.

circumspect, adj. circospètto.

circumstance, n. circostanza f.

circumstantial, adj. circostanziale; (detailed) particolareggiato.

circumstantially, adv. circostanziatamente.

circumvent, vb. circonvenire, impedire.

circumvention, n. circonvenzione f.

circus, n. circo m.

cirrhosis, n. cirròsi f.

cistern, n. cistèrna f., serbatòio m.

citadel, n. cittadèlla f.

citation, n. citazione f.

cite, vb. citare.

citizen, n. cittadino m., cittadina f.

citizenry, n. cittadinanza f.

citizenship, n. cittadinanza f.

citric, adj. cìtrico.

citron, n. cedro m.

city, n. città f.; **(small c.)** cittadina f.

city council, n. consiglio municipale m.

city editor, n. capo cronista m.

city hall, n. municipio m.

city planning, n. urbanistica f.

city room, n. redazione f.

civic, adj. cìvico.

civil, adj. civile.

civilian, n. and adj. civile.

civility, n. civiltà f.

civilization, n. civiltà f.

civilize, vb. civilizzare.

civilized, adj. civile.

clabber, n. quagliata f.

clad, adj. vestito.

claim, 1. n. reclamo m. **2.** vb. reclamare.

claimant, n. reclamante m.

clairvoyance, n. chiaroveggènza f.

clairvoyant, n. and adj. chiaroveggènte m. and f.

clamber, vb. arrampicarsi.

clammy, adj. freddo e ùmido.

clamor, n. clamore m.

clamorous, adj. clamoroso.

clamp, n. grappa f.

clan, n. clan m., tribù f.; (clique) cricca f.

clandestine, adj. clandestino.

clandestinely, *adv.* clandestinamente.

clang, *n.* fragore *m.*

clangor, *n.* clangore *m.*

clap, *vb.* (applaud) applaudire; (hands) bàttere le mani.

clapboard, *n.* tégola di legno *f.*

clapper, *n.* battàglio *m.*

claret, *n.* claretto *m.*

clarification, *n.* chiarificazione *f.*

clarify, *vb.* chiarificare.

clarinet, *n.* clarinetto *m.*

clarinetist, *n.* clarinettista *m.*

clarion, *n.* chiarina *f.*

clarity, *n.* chiarità *f.*

clash, 1. *n.* urto *m.* 2. *vb.* urtarsi.

clasp, 1. *n.* gàncio *m.*; (hand) stretta di mano *f.*; (embrace) abbràccio *m.* 2. *vb.* agganciare, stríngere, abbracciare.

class, 1. *n.* classe *f.*; (social) cèto *m.* 2. *vb.* classificare.

classic, classical, *adj.* clàssico.

classicism, *n.* classicismo *m.*

classifiable, *adj.* classificàbile; (secret) segreto.

classification, *n.* classificazione *f.*

classified, *adj.* segreto.

classify, *vb.* classificare.

classmate, *n.* compagno di classe *m.*

classroom, *n.* àula *f.*

classy, *adj.* di classe.

clatter, *n.* rumore *m.*

clause, *n.* clàusola *f.*

claustrophobia, *n.* claustrofobía *f.*

clavicle, *n.* clavícola *f.*

claw, *n.* artíglio *m.*, ràffio *m.*

claw-hammer, *n.* martello a ràffio *m.*

clay, *n.* argilla *f.*, creta *f.*

clayey, *adj.* argilloso.

clean, 1. *adj.* pulito, netto. 2. *vb.* pulire.

clean-cut, *adj.* netto.

cleaner, *n.* pulitore *m.*

cleanliness, cleanness, *n.* pulizia *f.*

cleanse, *vb.* pulire.

clean-shaven, *adj.* appenarasato.

cleanup, *n.* pulizía *f.*

clear, 1. *n.* chiaro. 2. *vb.* (clear up) chiarire; (profit) guadagnare; (pass beyond) sorpassare;

(weather, *refl.*) schiarirsi; (leave free) sgomberare.

clearance, *n.* permesso di partire *m.*

clear-cut, *adj.* netto.

clearing, *n.* radura *f.*

clearing house, *n.* stanza di compensazione *f.*

clearly, *adv.* chiaramente.

clearness, *n.* chiarezza *f.*

cleat, *n.* bietta *f.*

cleavage, *n.* fessura *f.*, scissione *f.*

cleave, *vb.* fèndere.

cleaver, *n.* mannaia *f.*

clef, *n.* chiave *f.*

cleft, *n.* fenditura *f.*

clemency, *n.* clemènza *f.*

clement, *adj.* clemente.

clench, *vb.* stríngere.

clergy, *n.* clèro *m.*

clergyman, *n.* ecclesiàstico *m.*

clerical, *adj.* clericale.

clericalism, *n.* clericalismo *m.*

clerk, *n.* (clergyman) ecclesiàstico *m.*; (employee) impiegato *m.*

clerkship, *n.* posto d'impiegato *m.*

clever, *adj.* àbile, ingegnoso.

cleverly, *adv.* abilmente, ingegnosamente.

cleverness, *n.* abilità *f.*, ingegnosità *f.*

clew, *n.* filo *m.*

cliché, *n.* luògo comune *m.*

click, *n.* rumore secco *m.*

client, *n.* cliènte *m.*

clientele, *n.* clientèla *f.*

cliff, *n.* rupe *f.*

climactic, *adj.* culminante.

climate, *n.* clíma *f.*

climatic, *adj.* climàtico.

climax, *n.* cúlmine *m.*

climb, *vb.* scalare, arrampicarsi su.

climber, *n.* arrampicatore *m.*; (social) arrivísta *m.* ó *f.*

clinch, *vb.* (grasp) afferrare; (confirm) confermare; (conclude) conclùdere.

cling, *vb.* aderire.

clinic, *n.* clínica *f.*

clinical, *adj.* clínico.

clinically, *adv.* clinicamente.

clinician, *n.* clínico *m.*

clip, 1. *n.* gàncio *m.* 2. *vb.* (hair) tagliare; (wool) tosare; (plants) cimare.

clipper, n. tosatore m.

clipping, n. tosatura f.

clique, n. cricca f.

cloak, n. mantèllo m.; (cloak-room) guardaròba f.

clock, n. orològio m.; (two o'c.) le due.

clockwise, adj. and adv. destròrso.

clockwork, n. meccanismo d'orología m.

clod, n. zòlla f.; (person) tànghero m.

clog, 1. n. (wooden shoe) zòccolo m. 2. vb. ingombrare.

cloister, n. chiòstro m.

clone, n. riproduzione esatta f.

close, 1. adj. (closed) chiuso m.; (narrow) stretto; (near) vicino; (secret) riservato; 2. vb. chiùdere. 3. adv. vicino. 4. prep. (c. to) vicino a.

close call, n. rischio scampato appena m.

closed chapter, n. affare chiuso m.

close-lipped, adj. riservato.

closely, adv. da vicino.

closeness, n. prossimità f; (weather) pesantezza f.; (secrecy) riservatezza f.

closet, n. (toilet) gabinetto m.; (clothes) armàdio m.

close-up, n. primo piano m.

closing, n. fine f.

closure, n. chiusura f.

clot, 1. n. grumo m. 2. vb. raggrumarsi.

cloth, n. stòffa f., tela f.

clothe, vb. vestire.

clothes, n. vestiti m.pl.

clothespin, n. ferma biancheria f.

clothes tree, n. attaccapanni m.

clothier, n. pannaiòlo m.

clothing, n. vestiti m.pl.

cloud, 1. n. nùvola f., nube f. 2. vb. (c. over) rannuvolarsi.

cloudburst, n. acquazzone m.

cloud-capped, adj. coperto.

cloudiness, n. nuvolosità f.

cloudless, adj. senza nùvole, sereno.

cloudy, adj. nuvoloso.

clout, 1. n. (blow) colpo m.; (rag) stràccio m. 2. vb. picchiare.

clove, n. chiodo di garófano m.

cloven-hoofed, adj. satanico.

clover, n. trifòglio m.

clown, n. pagliàccio m.

clownish, adv. pagliaccesco.

cloy, vb. saziare.

club, 1. n. (group) círcolo m.; (stick) bastone m. 2. vb. bastonare.

clubfoot, n. piede stòrto m.

clubs, n. (cards) fiori m.pl.

clue, n. filo m.

clump, n. gruppo m.

clumsiness, n. goffàggine f.

clumsy, adj. goffo.

cluster, 1. n. gràppolo m.; (people) gruppo m. 2. vb. raggruppare.

clutch, 1. n. (claw) artiglio m.; (automobile) frizione f. 2. vb. afferrare.

clutter, vb. ingombrare.

coach, 1. n. (carriage) carrozza f.; (horse-drawn) còcchio m.; (train) vagone m.; (sports) allenatore m. 2. vb. (sports) allenare; (school) dare lezioni private a.

coach house, n. rimessa f.

coachman, n. cocchiere m.

coagulate, vb. coagulare.

coagulation, n. coagulazione f.

coal, n. carbone fòssile m.

coalesce, vb. coalizzarsi.

coalition, n. coalizione f.

coal oil, n. petròlio m.

coal tar, n. catrame m.

coarse, adj. grossolano.

coarsen, vb. rèndere grossolano.

coarseness, n. grossolanità f.

coast, n. còsta f.

coastal, adj. costièro.

coaster, n. (ship) nave costièra f.

coast guard, n. milízia guardacòste f.

coat, n. (of suit) giacca f.; (overcoat) sopràbito m.

coating, n. strato m.

coat of arms, n. insegna f., stèmma m.

coax, vb. blandire.

cobalt, n. cobalto m.

cobbler, n. ciabattino m., calzolàio m.

cobblestone, n. ciòttolo m.

cobra, *n.* còbra *m.*

cobweb, *n.* ragnatela *f.*

cocaine, *n.* cocaína *f.*

cock, 1. *n.* (rooster) gallo *m.*; (male) maschio *m.*; (of gun) cane *m.*; (tap) rubinetto *m.*

cocker spaniel, *n.* cocker *m.*

cockeyed, *adj.* (*lit.*) stràbico *f.*; (crazy) matto, pazzo.

cockhorse, *n.* cavallo a dóndolo *m.*

cockpit, *n.* carlinga *f.*

cockroach, *n.* blatta *f.*

cocksure, *adj.* presuntuoso.

cocktail, *n.* còctail *m.*

cocky, *adj.* impudènte.

cocoa, *n.* cacao *m.*

coconut, *n.* noce di còcco *f.*

cocoon, *n.* bòzzolo *m.*

cod, *n.* merluzzo *m.*

C.O.D., *adv.* contro assegno.

coddle, *vb.* vezzeggiare.

code, *n.* (law) còdice *m.*; (secret) cifràrio *m.*

codeine, *n.* codeína *f.*

codfish, *n.* merluzzo *m.*

codger, *n.* (old c.) vecchietto *m.*

codify, *vb.* codificare.

cod-liver oil, *n.* òlio di fégato di merluzzo *m.*

coed, *adj.* misto.

coeducation, *n.* insegnamento misto *m.*

coeducational, *adj.* misto.

coequal, *adj.* coeguale.

coerce, *vb.* costringere.

coercion, *n.* coercizíone *f.*

coercive, *adj.* coercitivo.

coexist, *vb.* coesístere.

coffee, *n.* caffè *m.*; (c. shop) caffè *m.*

coffee maker, *n.* macchina per il caffè *f.*

coffee pot, *n.* caffettiera *f.*

coffer, *n.* còfano *m.*, scrigno *m.*

coffin, *n.* cassa da mòrto *f.*

cog, *n.* dente *m.*; (c. railway) fer-rovia a cremagliera *f.*

cogent, *adj.* convincente.

cogitate, *vb.* cogitare.

cognac, *n.* cognac *m.*

cognizance, *n.* conoscènza *f.*; (legal) competènza *f.*

cognizant, *adj.* competènte.

cogwheel, *n.* ruòta dentata *f.*

cohabit, *vb.* coabitare.

cohere, *vb.* èssere coerènte.

coherent, *adj.* coerènte.

cohesion, *n.* coesíone *f.*

cohesive, *adj.* coesivo.

cohort, *n.* coòrte *f.*

coiffeur, *n.* parrucchiere per sig-nora *m.*

coiffure, *n.* pettinatura *f.*

coil, 1. *n.* spira *f.*; (electr.) bobina *f.*; (induction c.) bobina d'induz-ione *f.* **2.** *vb.* arrotolare.

coil spring, *n.* molla a spirale *f.*

coin, 1. *n.* moneta *f.* **2.** *vb.* coniare.

coinage, *n.* cònio *m.*

coincide, *vb.* coincídere.

coincidence, *n.* coincidènza *f.*

coincident, *adj.* coincidènte.

coincidental, *adj.* coincidènte.

coincidentally, *adv.* per coin-cidènza.

coke, *n.* coca *f.*

colander, *n.* colatóio *m.*

cold, 1. *n.* (temperature) freddo *m.*; (med.) raffreddore *m.* **2.** *adj.* freddo; (it is c.) fa freddo; (feel c.) aver freddo.

cold-blooded, *adj.* a sangue freddo.

cold comfort, *n.* magra consolaz-ione *f.*

cold cuts, *n.* affettati *m.pl.*

coldly, *adv.* freddamente.

coldness, *n.* freddezza *f.*

collaborate, *vb.* collaborare.

collaboration, *n.* collaborazione *f.*

collaborator, *n.* collaboratore *m.*

collapse, 1. *n.* cròllo *m.*; (med.) collasso *m.* **2.** *vb.* crollare.

collar, *n.* colletto *m.*; (dog's, priest's) collare *m.*

collarbone, *n.* clavícola *f.*

collate, *vb.* collezionare.

collateral, *n.* and *adj.* collaterale *m.*

collation, *n.* (comparison) con-fronto *m.*; (meal) merènda *f.*

colleague, *n.* collèga *m.*

collect, *vb.* raccògliere; (money) riscuòtere.

collection, *n.* raccòlta *f.*, collez-ione *f.*; (church) quèstua *f.*

collective, *adj.* collettivo.

collectively, *adv.* collettivamente.

collector, n. (art) collezionista m.; (tickets) controllore m.

college, n. università f.

collegiate, adj. universitàrio.

collide, vb. scontrarsi.

colliery, n. minièra di carbone f.

collision, n. scontro m.

colloquial, adj. colloquiale.

colloquialism, n. colloquialismo m.

colloquially, adv. colloquialmente.

colloquy, n. collòquio m.

collusion, n. collusione f.

Cologne, n. Colònia f.

colon, n. (writing) due punti m.pl.

colonel, n. colonnèllo m.

colonial, adj. coloniale.

colonist, n. colòno m.

colonization, n. colonizzazione f.

colonize, vb. colonizzare.

colony, n. colònia f.

color, 1. n. colore m. 2. vb. colorire.

coloration, n. colorazione f.

colored, adj. di colore.

colorful, adj. pittoresco.

coloring, n. coloritura f.

colorless, adj. sènza colore.

colossal, adj. colossale.

colt, n. puledro m.

column, n. colonna f.

columnist, n. cronista m.

coma, n. còma m.

comb, 1. n. pèttine m.; (rooster) cresta f. 2. vb. pettinare.

combat, 1. n. combattimento m. 2. vb. combàttere.

combatant, n. combattènte m.

combative, adj. battaglièro.

combination, n. combinazione f.

combination lock, n. serratura a combinazioni f.

combine, vb. combinare.

combustible, adj. combustibile.

combustion, n. combustione f.

come, vb. venire; (c. about) accadere; (c. across) incontrare, trovare; (c. away) andàrsene; (c. back) tornare; (c. down) scéndere; (c. in) entrare; (c. out) uscire; (c. up) salire.

comedian, n. còmico m.

comedienne, n. attrice còmica f.

comedy, n. commèdia f.

come in!, interj. avanti!

comely, adj. grazioso.

comet, n. cometa f.

comfort, 1. n. confòrto m. 2. vb. confortare, consolare.

comfortable, adj. còmodo.

comfortably, adv. comodamente.

comforter, n. confortatore m., consolatore m.; coperta f.

comfortingly, adv. in modo consolatore.

comfortless, adj. sconsolato.

comic, comical, adj. còmico.

comic book, n. giornalino a fumetti m.

comic strip, n. fumetto m.

coming, n. venuta f.

comma, n. virgola f.

command, 1. n. comando m. 2. vb. comandare.

commandeer, vb. requisire.

commander, n. comandante m.

commander in chief, n. comandante in capo m.

commandment, n. comandamento m.

commemorate, vb. commemorare.

commemoration, n. commemorazione f.

commemorative, adj. commemorativo.

commence, vb. cominciare.

commencement, n. esòrdio m.

commend, vb. raccomandare, lodare.

commendable, adj. lodévole.

commendably, adv. lodevolmente.

commendation, n. lòde f.

commensurate, adj. commisurato.

comment, 1. n. commento m. 2. vb. commentare.

commentary, n. commento m.

commentator, n. (radio) cronista m.

commerce, n. commèrcio m.

commercial, adj. commerciale.

commercialism, n. commercialismo m.

commercialize, vb. commercializzare.

commercially, adv. commercialmente.

commiserate, *vb.* commiserare.

commissary, *n.* commissariato *m.*

commission, 1. *n.* (committee, percentage) commissione *f.*; (assignment) incàrico *m.*; mandato *m.* **2.** *vb.* incaricare.

commissioner, *n.* commissàrio *m.*

commit, *vb.* commèttere.

commitment, *n.* impegno *m.*

committee, *n.* comitato *m.*, commissione *f.*

commodious, *adj.* spazioso.

commodity, *n.* mèrce *f.*

common, *adj.* comune; (vulgar) volgare.

common law, *n.* diritto consuetudinario *m.*

commonly, *adv.* comunemente.

commonness, *n.* volgarità *f.*

commonplace, 1. *n.* luògo comune *m.* **2.** *adj.* banale.

common sense, *n.* senso comune *m.*

common-sense, *adj.* giudizioso.

commonwealth, *n.* repùbblica *f.*

commotion, *n.* commozione *f.*

communal, *adj.* comunale.

commune, *vb.* comunicare.

communicable, *adj.* comunicàbile.

communicant, *n.* comunicante *m.*

communicate, *vb.* comunicare.

communication, *n.* comunicazione *f.*

communicative, *adj.* comunicativo.

communion, *n.* comunione *f.*; **(take c.)** comunicarsi.

communiqué, *n.* comunicato *m.*

communism, *n.* comunismo *m.*

communist, *n.* comunista *m.* or *f.*

communistic, *adj.* comunìstico.

community, *n.* comunità *f.*

community center, *n.* centro sociale *m.*

community chest, *n.* fondo di beneficenza *f.*

commutation, *n.* commutazione *f.*; **(c. ticket)** biglietto d'abbonamento *m.*

commute, *vb.* pendolare; (travel) viaggiare regolarmente, fare il pendolare.

commuter, *n.* pendolare *m.* or *f.*

compact, 1. *n.* accòrdo *m.*, patto *m.* **2.** *adj.* compatto.

compactness, *n.* compattezza *f.*

companion, *n.* compagno *m.*, compagna *f.*

companionable, *adj.* sociévole.

companionship, *n.* compagnìa *f.*

company, *n.* compagnìa *f.*, società *f.*

comparable, *adj.* paragonàbile, comparàbile.

comparative, *adj.* comparativo.

comparatively, *adv.* comparativamente.

compare, *vb.* paragonare, confrontare, comparare.

comparison, *n.* paragone *m.*, confronto *m.*

compartment, *n.* scompartimento *m.*

compass, *n.* (naut.) bùssola *f.*; (geom.) compasso *m.*

compass card, *n.* rosa dei venti *f.*

compassion, *n.* compassione *f.*

compassionate, *adj.* compassionévole.

compassionately, *adv.* compassionevolmente.

compatible, *adj.* compatìbile.

compatriot, *n.* compatriòta *m.*, compaesano *m.*

compel, *vb.* costrìngere.

compelling, *adj.* imperioso; inevitàbile; necessario.

compensate, *vb.* compensare.

compensation, *n.* compènso *m.*

compensatory, *adj.* compensativo.

compete, *vb.* compètere, concórrere, gareggiare.

competence, *n.* competènza *f.*

competent, *adj.* competènte.

competently, *adv.* competentemente.

competition, *n.* concorso *m.*, gara *f.*; (comm.) concorrènza *f.*

competitive, *adj.* di concorso, di concorrènza.

competitor, *n.* concorrènte *m.*

compilation, *n.* compilazione *f.*; collezione *f.*

compile, *vb.* compilare.

complacency, *n.* contentezza di sè stesso *f.*

complacent, *adj.* contento di sè stesso.

complain, *vb.* lagnarsi, dolersi.

complainant, *n.* querelante *m.*

complainer, *n.* piagnucolone *m.*

complainingly, *adv.* lagnandosi.

complaint, *n.* lagnanza *f.;* (sickness) malattìa *f.*

complaisance, *n.* compiacenza *f.*

complement, *n.* complemento *m.*

complete, 1. *adj.* complèto. **2.** *vb.* completare.

completely, *adv.* completamento.

completeness, *n.* completezza *f.*

completion, *n.* completamento *m.*

complex, *n. and adj.* complèsso *(m.).*

complexion, *n.* colorito *m.*

complexity, *n.* complessità *f.*

compliance, *n.* obbediènza *f.*

compliant, *adj.* obbediènte.

complicate, *vb.* complicare.

complicated, *adj.* complicato.

complication, *n.* complicazione *f.*

complicity, *n.* complicità *f.*

compliment, 1. *n.* complimento *m.* **2.** *vb.* complimentare, felicitare.

complimentary, *adj.* gratùito.

comply, *vb.* obbedire.

component, *n. and adj.* componènte *(m.).*

comport oneself, *vb.* comportarsi.

compose, *vb.* comporre.

composed, *adj.* (made of) composto di; (calm) calmo.

composer, *n.* compositore *m.*

composite, *adj.* composto.

composition, *n.* composizione *f.*

compositor, *n.* compositore *m.*

compost, *n.* concime *m.*

composure, *n.* compostezza *f.;* calma *f.*

compote, *n.* consèrva *f.*

compound, *n. and adj.* composto *(m.)*

comprehend, *vb.* comprèndere.

comprehensible, *adj.* comprensìbile.

comprehension, *n.* comprensione *f.*

comprehensive, *adj.* comprensivo.

compress, *vb.* comprímere.

compressed, *adj.* comprèsso.

compression, *n.* compressione *f.*

compressor, *n.* compressore *m.*

comprise, *vb.* comprèndere.

compromise, 1. *n.* compromesso *m.* **2.** *vb.* accomodarsi; (endanger) comprométtere.

compromiser, *n.* chi fa un compromesso *m.*

comptroller, *n.* economo *m.;* amministratore *m.;* controllore *m.*

compulsion, *n.* costrizione *f.*

compulsive, *adj.* coercitivo; (involuntary) involontàrio.

compulsory, *adj.* obbligatòrio.

compunction, *n.* compunzione *f.*

computation, *n.* computazione *f.*

compute, *vb.* computare.

computer, *n.* calcolatrice elettrònica *f.;* calcolatore *m.*

computer science, *n.* informàtica *f.*

computerize, *v.* informatizzare.

comrade, *n.* camerata *m.*

comradeship, *n.* cameratismo *m.*

concave, *adj.* còncavo.

conceal, *vb.* celare.

concealment, *n.* occultamento *m.*

concede, *vb.* concèdere.

conceit, *n.* vanità *f.*

conceited, *adj.* vanitoso.

conceivable, *adj.* concepibile.

conceivably, *adv.* concepibilmente.

conceive, *vb.* concepire.

concentrate, *vb.* concentrare.

concentration, *n.* concentrazione *f.,* concentramento *m.*

concentration camp, *n.* campo di concentramento *m.*

concept, *n.* concètto *m.*

conception, *n.* concezione *f.*

concern, 1. *n.* (affair) affare *m.;* (interest) interèsse *m.;* (firm) aziènda *f.;* (worry) ansietà *f.* **2.** *vb.* concèrnere, interessare, riguardare; **(c. oneself with)** interessarsi di; **(be c.ed over)** inquietarsi di.

concerning, *prep.* riguardo a, concernente.

concert, 1. *n.* concèrto *m.* **2.** *vb.* concertare.

concertmaster, *n.* primo violino *m.*

concession, *n.* concessione *f.*

conch-shell, *n.* conchíglia *f.*

concierge, *n.* portinaio *m.*; (c.'s office) portinería *f.*

conciliate, *vb.* conciliare.

conciliation, *n.* conciliazione *f.*

conciliator, *n.* conciliatore *m.*

conciliatory, *adj.* conciliativo.

concise, *adj.* conciso.

concisely, *adv.* concisamente.

conciseness, concision, *n.* concisione *f.*

conclave, *n.* conclave *m.*

conclude, *vb.* conclùdere.

conclusion, *n.* conclusione *f.*

conclusive, *adj.* conclusivo.

conclusively, *adv.* conclusivamente.

concoct, *vb.* concuòcere.

concoction, *n.* concozione *f.*

concomitant, *n.* concomitante.

concord, *n.* accòrdo *m.*

concordant, *adv.* concòrde.

concordat, *n.* concordato *m.*

concourse, *n.* concorso *m.*

concrete, **1.** *n.* cemento *m.* **2.** *adj.* concrèto.

concretely, *adv.* concretamente.

concrete mixer, *n.* betoniera *m.*

concreteness, *n.* concretezza *f.*

concubine, *n.* concubina *f.*

concur, *vb.* (events) concórrere; (persons) essere d'accòrdo.

concurrence, *n.* concorrènza *f.*; (agreement) consènso *m.*

concurrent, *adj.* concorrènte.

concussion, *n.* concussione *f.*

condemn, *vb.* condannare.

condemnable, *adj.* condannàbile.

condemnation, *n.* condanna *f.*

condensation, *n.* condensazione *f.*

condense, *vb.* condensare.

condenser, *n.* condensatore *m.*

condescend, *vb.* accondiscéndere.

condescending, *adj.* condiscendente.

condescendingly, *adv.* con accondiscendènza.

condescension, *n.* accondiscendènza *f.*

condiment, **1.** *n.* condimento *m.* **2.** *vb.* condire.

condition, **1.** *n.* condizione *f.* **2.** *vb.* condizionare.

conditional, *adj.* condizionale.

conditionally, *adv.* condizionalmente.

condole, *vb.* condolersi.

condolence, *n.* condoglianza *f.*

condom, *n.* preservativo *m.*

condominium, *n.* condomínio *m.*

condone, *vb.* condonare.

conduce, *vb.* condurre, tèndere.

conducive, *adj.* tendènte.

conduct, **1.** *n.* condotta *f.* **2.** *vb.* condurre.

conductive, *adj.* conduttivo.

conductivity, *n.* conduttività *f.*

conductor, *n.* conduttore *m.*; (orchestra) direttore *m.*; (train) capotreno *m.*; (tram, bus) bigliettaio *m.*

conduit, *n.* condotto *m.*

cone, *n.* còno *m.*

confection, *n.* (dress) confezione *f.*; (candy) confetto *m.*; confettura *f.*

confectioner, *n.* confettière *m.*; (c. shop) confetteria *f.*

confectionery, *n.* (store) confetteria *f.*

confederacy, *n.* confederazione *f.*

confederate, **1.** *n.* confederato *m.* **2.** *vb.* confederarsi.

confederation, *n.* confederazione *f.*

confer, *vb.* conferire.

conference, *n.* conferènza *f.*

confess, *vb.* confessare.

confession, *n.* confessione *f.*

confessional, *n. and adj.* confessionale *f.*

confession of faith, *n.* professione di fede *f.*

confessor, *n.* confessore *m.*

confetti, *n.* coriàndoli *m.pl.*

confidant, *n.* confidènte *m.*

confidante, *n.* confidènte *f.*

confide, *vb.* confidare.

confidence, *n.* confidènza *f.*

confident, *adj.* confidènte.

confidential, *adj.* confidenziale.

confidentially, *adv.* in confidènza.

confidently, *adv.* confidentemente.

confine, *vb.* confinare.

confirm, *vb.* confermare.

confirmation, n. conferma f.
confirmed, adj. confermato.
confiscate, vb. confiscare.
confiscation, n. confisca f.
conflagration, n. conflagrazione f.
conflict, 1. n. conflitto m. 2. vb. venire a conflitto.
conflicting, adj. contrastante, contraddittorio.
confluence, n. confluenza f.
conform, vb. conformarsi.
conformation, n. conformazione f.
conformer, conformist, n. conformista m.
conformity, n. conformità f.
confound, vb. confóndere.
confounded, adj. maledetto, odioso.
confront, vb. confrontare.
confrontation, n. contestazione f.
confuse, vb. confóndere.
confusion, n. confusione f.
congeal, vb. congelare.
congealment, n. congelamento m.
congenial, adj. simpàtico.
congenital, adj. congènito.
congenitally, adv. congenitamente.
congest, vb. congestionare.
congestion, n. congestione f.
conglomerate, 1. n. and adj. conglomerato (m.). 2. vb. conglomerare.
conglomeration, n. conglomerazione f.
congratulate, vb. felicitare, congratularsi con.
congratulation, n. felicitazione f., congratulazione f.
congratulatory, adj. congratulatòrio.
congregate, vb. congregarsi.
congregation, n. congregazione f.
congress, n. congrèsso m., parlamento m.
congressional, adj. parlamentare.
congressman, n. parlamentare al congresso degli S.U. m.

congresswoman, n. parlamentare al congresso degli S.U. f..
conic, adj. cònico.
conjecture, 1. n. congettura f. 2. vb. congetturare.
conjugal, adj. coniugale.
conjugate, vb. coniugare.
conjugation, n. coniugazione f.
conjunction, n. congiunzione f.
conjunctive, adj. congiuntivo.
conjunctivitis, n. congiuntivite f.
conjure, vb. scongiurare.
connect, vb. collegare, connèttere; (transport) coincídere.
connecting rod, n. biella f.
connection, n. collegamento m., connessione f.; (transport) coincidènza f.
connivance, n. connivènza f.
connive, vb. essere connivènte.
connoisseur, n. conoscitore m.
connotation, n. connotazione f.
connote, vb. connotare.
connubial, adj. connubiale.
conquer, vb. vincere, conquistare.
conquerable, adj. vincíbile, conquistàbile.
conqueror, n. vincitore m., conquistatore m.
conquest, n. conquista f.
conscience, n. cosciènza f.
conscientious, adj. coscienzioso.
conscientiously, adv. coscienziosamente.
conscientious objector, n. obiettore di coscienza m.
conscious, adj. cònscio, consapévole.
consciously, adv. consciamente.
consciousness, n. coscienza f.
conscript, n. coscritto m.
conscription, n. coscrizione f.
consecrate, vb. consacrare.
consecration, n. consacrazione f.
consecutive, adj. consecutivo.
consecutively, adv. consecutivamente.
consensus, n. consènso m.
consent, 1. n. consènso m. 2. vb. consentire, acconsentire.
consequence, n. conseguènza f.
consequent, adj. conseguènte.
consequential, adj. conseguenziale.

consequently, adv. conseguentemente, per conseguènza.

conservation, n. conservazione f.

conservative, n. and adj. conservatore (m.).

conservatism, n. conservatorismo m.

conservatory, n. conservatòrio m.

conserve, vb. conservare.

consider, vb. considerare.

considerable, adj. considerévole, consideràbile; (a fair amount) parécchio.

considerably, adv. considerabilmente.

considerate, vb. premuroso.

considerately, adv. premurosamente.

consideration, n. considerazione f.

considering, adv. considerando.

consign, vb. consegnare.

consignment, n. consegna f.

consist, vb. consistere.

consistency, n. consistènza f.

consistent, adj. coerènte.

consolation, n. consolazione f.

console, vb. consolare.

consolidate, vb. consolidare.

consommé, n. bròdo ristretto m.

consonant, n. and adj. consonante (f.).

consort, n. consòrte m. and f.

conspicuous, adj. cospícuo.

conspicuously, adv. cospicuamente.

conspicuousness, n. cospicuità f.

conspiracy, n. congiura f.

conspirator, n. congiurato m.

conspire, vb. congiurare.

constancy, n. costanza f.

constant, adj. costante.

constantly, adv. costantemente.

constellation, n. costellazione f.

consternation, n. costernazione f.

constipate, vb. costipare.

constipated, adj. stítico.

constipation, n. stitichezza f.

constituency, n. votanti m.pl.

constituent, adj. costituènte.

constitute, vb. costituire.

constitution, n. costituzione f.

constitutional, adj. costituzionale.

constrain, vb. costringere.

constraint, n. costrizione f.

constrict, vb. costríngere.

construct, vb. costruire.

construction, n. costruzione f.; (interpretation) interpretazione f.

constructive, adj. costruttivo.

constructively, adv. costruttivamente.

constructor, n. costruttore m.

construe, vb. interpretare.

consul, n. cònsole m.

consular, adj. consolare.

consulate, n. consolato m.

consulship, n. consolato m.

consult, vb. consultare.

consultant, n. consultatore m.

consultation, n. consultazione f., consulto m.

consume, vb. consumare.

consumer, n. consumatore m.

consumer goods, n. merci di consumo f.pl.

consumerism, n. consumismo m.

consummate, adj. consumato.

consummation, n. consumazione f.

consumption, n. consumo m.; (tuberculosis) tísi f.; tubercolosi f.

consumptive, adj. tísico.

contact, 1. n. contatto m. 2. vb. venire in contatto con.

contact lenses, n. lenti a contatto f.pl.

contagion, n. contàgio m.

contagious, adj. contagioso.

contain, vb. contenere.

container, n. recipiènte m.

contaminate, vb. contaminare.

contamination, n. contaminazione f.

contemplate, vb. contemplare.

contemplation, n. contemplaziane f.

contemplative, n. contemplativo.

contemporaneous, adj. contemporaneo.

contemporary, adj. contemporàneo.

contempt, n. disprèzzo m.

contemptible, adj. spregévole.

contempt of court, n. oltraggio alla giuria m.

contemptuous, adj. sprezzante.

contemptuously, adv. sprezzantemente.

contend, vb. contèndere; (affirm) sostenere.

contender, n. contendènte m.

content, 1. n. contento m. **2.** vb. accontentare.

contented, adj. contento.

contention, n. contenzione f.

contentment, n. accontentamento m.

contest, 1. n. contesa f., gara f. **2.** vb. contestare.

contestable, adj. contestàbile.

contestant, n. gareggiante m.

context, n. contèsto m.

contiguous, adj. contíguo.

continence, n. continènza f.

continent, n. and adj. continènte (m.).

continental, adj. continentale.

contingency, n. contingènza f.

contingent, adj. contingènte.

continual, adj. contínuo.

continuance, n. (law) rinvìo m.

continuation, n. continuazione f.

continue, vb. continuare.

continuity, n. continuità f.

continuous, adj. contínuo.

continuous showing, n. spettacolo permanente m.

continuously, adv. continuamente.

contort, vb. contòrcere.

contortion, n. contorsione f.

contortionist, n. contorsionista m.

contour, n. contorno m.

contraband, n. contrabbando m.

contrabass, n. contrabbasso m.

contraception, n. controllo delle nàscite m.

contraceptive, n. and adj. contraccettivo (m.)

contract, 1. n. contratto m. **2.** vb. contrarre; (agree) contrattare.

contraction, n. contrazione f.

contractor, n. contrattatore m., imprenditore m.

contradict, vb. contraddire.

contradictable, adj. contraddicìbile.

contradiction, n. contraddizione f.

contradictory, adj. contraddittòrio.

contralto, n. contralto m.

contraption, n. congegno m.

contrary, adj. contràrio.

contrast, 1. n. contrasto m. **2.** vb. contrastare, intr.

contravene, vb. contravvenire.

contribute, vb. contribuire; (newspaper) collaborare.

contribution, n. contributo m., contribuzione f.

contributive, adj. contributivo.

contributor, n. contributore m.; (newspaper) collaboratore m.

contributory, adj. contributòrio.

contrite, adj. contrito.

contrition, n. contrizione f.

contrivance, n. congegno m.

contrive, vb. (invent) inventare; (bring about) effettuare.

control, 1. n. controllo m. **2.** vb. controllare.

controllable, adj. controllàbile.

controller, n. controllore m.

controlling interest, n. maggioranza delle azioni f.

control stick, n. leva di comando f.

controversial, adj. controvèrso.

controversy, n. controvèrsia f.

contumacious, adj. ribelle, contumace.

contumacy, n. contumàcia f.

contusion, n. contusione f.

conundrum, n. indovinèllo m.

convalesce, vb. riméttersi in salute.

convalescence, n. convalescènza f.

convalescent, adj. convalescènte.

convene, vb. convenire.

convenience, n. conveniènza f.

convenient, adj. conveniènte.

conveniently, adv. convenientemente.

convent, n. convènto m.

convention, n. convenzione f.; (meeting) congrèsso m.

conventional, adj. convenzionale.

conventionally, adv. convenzionalmente.

converge, *vb.* convèrgere.

convergence, *n.* convergènza *f.*

convergent, *adj.* convergènte.

conversant with, *adj.* versato in, pràtico di.

conversation, *n.* conversazione *f.*

conversational, *adj.* di conversazione.

conversationalist, *n.* conversatore *m.*

converse, 1. *adj.* convèrso. **2.** *vb.* conversare.

conversely, *adv.* per convèrso.

conversion, *n.* conversione *f.*

convert, *vb.* convertire.

converter, *n.* convertitrice *f.*

convertible, *adj.* convertíbile.

convex, *adj.* convèsso.

convey, *vb.* trasméttere, trasportare.

conveyance, *n.* traspòrto *m.;* (property) trapasso di proprietà *m.*

conveyor, *n.* trasportatore *m.*

conveyor belt, *n.* nastro trasportatore *m.*

convict, 1. *n.* condannato *m.* **2.** *vb.* dichiarare colpévole.

conviction, *n.* (belief) convinzione *f.;* (law) condanna *f.*

convince, *vb.* convíncere.

convincing, *adj.* convincènte.

convincingly, *adv.* in modo convincènte.

convivial, *adj.* conviviale.

convocation, *n.* convocazione *f.*

convoke, *vb.* convocare.

convoy, 1. *n.* convòglio *m.* **2.** *vb.* convogliare.

convulse, *vb.* méttere in convulsioni.

convulsion, *n.* convulsione *f.*

convulsive, *adj.* convulsivo.

coo, *vb.* túbare, gèmere.

cook, 1. *n.* cuòco *m.* **2.** *vb.* cucinare.

cookbook, *n.* libro di cucina *m.*

cookie, *n.* biscòtto *m.*

cookout, *n.* picnic *m.*

cool, 1. *adj.* fresco *m.* **2.** *vb.* rinfrescare.

coolant, *n.* antigelo *m.*

cooler, *n.* frigorífero *m.*

cool-headed, *adj.* calmo, imperturbábile.

coolish, *adj.* freschetto.

coolness, *n.* fresco *m.; (fig.)* indifferènza *f.*

coop, *n.* stía *f.*

cooper, *n.* bottaio *m.*

cooperate, *vb.* cooperare.

cooperation, *n.* cooperazione *f.*

cooperative, 1. *n.* cooperativa *f.* **2.** *adj.* cooperativo.

cooperatively, *adv.* cooperativamente.

coordinate, *vb.* coordinare.

coordination, *n.* coordinazione *f.*

coordinator, *n.* coordinatore *m.*

coot, *n.* fòlaga *f.;* vècchio pazzo *m.*

cop, *n.* poliziòtto *m.*

copartner, *n.* sòcio *m.*

cope, *vb.* lottare; **(c. with)** tener tèsta a.

copier, *n.* macchina copiatrice *f.;* fotocopiatrice *f.*

copilot, *n.* copilota *m.*

copious, *adj.* copioso.

copiously, *adv.* copiosamente.

copiousness, *n.* copiosità *f.,* còpia *f.*

copper, *n.* rame *m.*

copperplate, *n.* calligrafía *f.*

copulate, *vb.* copulare.

copy, 1. *n.* còpia *f.;* (of book) esemplare *m.* **2.** *vb.* copiare.

copyist, *n.* copista *m.*

copyright, *n.* diritti d'autore *m.pl.*

copywriter, *n.* redattore *m.*

coquetry, *n.* civetterìa *f.*

coquette, 1. *n.* civetta *f.* **2.** *vb.* civettare.

coquettish, *adj.* civettuolo.

coral, *n.* corallo *m.*

coral reef, *n.* barriera corallina *f.*

cord, *n.* còrda *f.*

cordial, *n. and adj.* cordiale *(m.).*

cordiality, *n.* cordialità *f.*

cordially, *adv.* cordialmente.

cordon, *n.* cordone *m.*

cordovan, *n.* cordovano *m.*

core, *n.* (fruit) tórsolo *m.;* (heart) cuòre *m.*

cork, *n.* súghero *m.;* (of bottle) tappo *m.*

corkscrew, *n.* cavatappi *m. (sg.).*

corn, *n.* (grain) granturco *m.;* (on foot) callo *m.*

corn bread, *n.* pane di farina gialla *m.*

cornea, *n.* còrnea *f.*

corner, 1. *n.* àngolo *m.*, canto *m.* **2.** *vb.* *(comm.)* accaparrare.

cornerstone, *n.* piètra angolare *f.*

cornet, *n.* cornetta *f.*

cornetist, *n.* cornettista *m.*

corn exchange, *n.* borsa dei cereali *f.*

cornflakes, *n.* fiocchi di granturco *m.pl.*

corn flour, *n.* farina di granturco *f.*

cornice, *n.* cornicione *m.*

corn-plaster, *n.* callifugo *m.*

cornstarch, *n.* farina di granturco *f.*

cornucopia, *n.* cornucòpia *m.* or *f.*

corollary, *n.* corollàrio *m.*

coronary, *adj.* coronàrio *m.*

coronation, *n.* incoronazione *f.*

coronet, *n.* (noble's) corna nobiliare *f.*; (headdress) diadèma *m.*

corporal, 1. *n.* caporale *m.* **2.** *adj.* corporale.

corporate, *adj.* corporato.

corporation, *n.* corporazione *f.*

corps, *n.* còrpo *m.*

corpse, *n.* cadàvere *m.*

corpulent, *adj.* corpulènto.

corpuscle, *n.* corpùscolo *m.*

correct, 1. *adj.* corrètto. **2.** *vb.* corrèggere.

correction, *n.* correzione *f.*

corrective, *adj.* correttivo.

correctly, *adv.* correttamente.

correctness, *n.* correttezza *f.*

correlate, *vb.* méttere in correlazione.

correlation, *n.* correlazione *f.*

correspond, *vb.* corrispóndere.

correspondence, *n.* corrispondènza *f.*

correspondent, *n. and adj.* corrispondènte *(m.).*

corridor, *n.* corridòio *m.*

corroborate, *vb.* corroborare.

corroboration, *n.* corroborazione *f.*

corroborative, *adj.* corroborativo.

corrode, *vb.* corródere.

corrosion, *n.* corrosione *f.*

corrugate, *vb.* corrugare.

corrupt, *vb.* corrómpere.

corrupter, *n.* corrutore *m.*

corruptible, *adj.* corruttìbile.

corruption, *n.* corruzione *f.*

corruptive, *adj.* corruttivo.

corsage, *n.* fiori *m.pl.*

corset, *n.* busto *m.*

Corsican, *adj.* còrso.

cortège, *n.* cortèo *m.*

corvette, *n.* corvetta *f.*

cosmetic, *n. and adj.* cosmètico *(m.).*

cosmic, *adj.* còsmico.

cosmopolitan, *adj.* cosmopolita.

cosmos, *n.* còsmo *m.*

cost, 1. *n.* costo *m.* **2.** *vb.* costare.

costliness, *n.* costosità *f.*

costly, *adj.* costoso.

costume, *n.* costume *m.*

costumer, *n.* vestiarista *m.*

cot, *n.* lettino *m.*

coterie, *n.* combrìccola *f.*, cenàcolo *m.*

cotillion, *n.* cotiglione *m.*

cottage, *n.* villetta *f.*, casetta *f.*

cotton, *n.* cotone *m.*

cottonseed, *n.* seme di cotone *m.*

couch, *n.* lètto *m.*

cough, 1. *n.* tosse *f.* **2.** *vb.* tossire.

could, *vb.* use past or conditional of potere.

coulter, *n.* vòmere *m.*

council, *n.* consìglio *m.*

councilman, *n.* consiglière *m.*

counsel, 1. *n.* consìglio *m.* **2.** *vb.* consigliare.

counselor, *n.* consiglière *m.*

count, 1. *n.* conto *m.;* (noble) conte *m.* **2.** *vb.* contare.

countenance, 1. *n.* viso *m.* **2.** *vb.* approvare.

counter, *n.* banco *m.*

counteract, *vb.* neutralizzare.

counteraction, *n.* controazione *f.*

counterattack, *n.* contrattacco *m.*

counterbalance, *n.* contrappeso *m.*

counter-clockwise, *adj. and adv.* sinistròrso.

counterfeit, 1. *n. and adj.* falso *(m.).* **2.** *vb.* contraffare, falsificare.

countermand, *vb.* contromandare.

counteroffensive, *n.* controffensiva *f.*

counterpart, *n.* contropartita *f.*

Counter-Reformation, *n.* Controriforma *f.*

countess, *n.* contessa *f.*

countless, *adj.* innumerévole.

country, *n.* (nation) paese *m.;* (opposed to city) campagna *f.;* (native land) pàtria *f.*

countryman, *n.* (of same country) compatriòta *m.;* (rustic) contadino *m.*

countryside, *n.* campagna *f.*

county, *n.* contèa *f.*

coupé, *n.* cupè *m.*

couple, 1. *n.* cóppia *f.*, paio *m.* 2. *vb.* accoppiare.

coupon, *n.* tagliando *m.*, cèdola *f.*

courage, *n.* coràggio *m.*

courageous, *adj.* coraggioso.

courier, *n.* corrière *m.*

course, *n.* corso *m.;* (for races) pista *f.*

court, 1. *n.* corte *f.* 2. *vb.* corteggiare, far la corte a.

courteous, *adj.* cortese.

courtesan, *n.* cortigiana *f.*

courtesy, *n.* cortesia *f.*

courthouse, *n.* palazzo di giustízia *m.*

courtier, *n.* cortigiano *m.*

courtly, *adj.* cerimonioso.

courtmartial, *n.* corte marziale *f.*

courtroom, *n.* aula di udiènza *f.*

courtship, *n.* corteggiamento *m.*

courtyard, *n.* cortile *m.*

cousin, *n.* cugino *m.*, cugina *f.*

covenant, *n.* convenzione *f.*

cover, 1. *n.* copertura *f.,* (book) copertina *f.* 2. *vb.* coprire.

covering, *n.* copertura *f.*

covet, *vb.* bramare.

covetous, *adj.* bramoso.

cow, 1. *n.* vacca *f.*, mucca *f.* 2. *vb.* intimidire.

coward, *n.* codardo *m.*

cowardice, *n.* codardía *f.*

cowardly, *adj.* codardo.

cowboy, *n.* vaccaro *m.;* cowboy *m.*

cower, *vb.* rannicchiarsi.

cow hand, *n.* vaccaro *m.*

cowhide, *n.* vacchetta *f.*

coxswain, *n.* timonière *m.*

coy, *adj.* tímido.

crab, *n.* grànchio *m.*

crack, 1. *n.* fenditura *f.* 2. *vb.* fèndere.

cracked, *adj.* fesso.

cracker, *n.* biscòtto *m.*

crackup, *n.* incidènte *m.*

cradle, 1. *n.* culla *f.* 2. *vb.* cullare.

craft, *n.* arte *f.*

craftsman, *n.* artigiano *m.*

craftsmanship, *n.* arte *f.*

crafty, *adj.* furbo.

crag, *n.* picco *m.*

cram, *vb.* rimpinzare, infarcire.

cramp, *n.* crampo *m.*

crane, *n.* gru *f.*

cranium, *n.* crànio *m.*

crank, 1. *n.* (handle) manovella *f.;* (crackpot) pazzo *m.* 2. *vb.* girare.

cranky, *adj.* capriccioso.

cranny, *n.* fessura *f.*

crapshooter, *n.* giocatore di dadi *m.*

craps, *n.* giòco dei dadi *m.*

crash, 1. *n.* cròllo *m.* 2. *vb.* crollare.

crate, *n.* gabbietta da imballàggio *f.*

crater, *n.* cratère *m.*

crave, *vb.* bramare.

craven, *adj.* codardo.

craving, *n.* brama *f.*

craw, *n.* gozzo *m.*

crawl, *vb.* trascinarsi.

crayfish, *n.* aragosta *f.;* gambero *m.*

crayon, *n.* pastello *m.*

crazed, *adj.* pazzo.

craze, *n.* mania *f.;* moda *f.*

crazy, *adj.* pazzo, fòlle.

creak, *vb.* cigolare, scricchiolare.

creaky, *adj.* cigolante, scricchiolante.

cream, *n.* crèma *f.*, panna *f.*

creamery, *n.* cremería *f.*

cream puff, *n.* bignè *m.*

creamy, *adj.* ricco di panna.

crease, 1. *n.* pièga *f.* 2. *vb.* (fold) piegare; (crinkle) spiegazzare.

create, *vb.* creare.

creation, *n.* creazione *f.*

creative, *adj.* creativo.

creator, *n.* creatore *m.*

creature, *n.* creatura *f.*
credence, *n.* credènza *f.*
credentials, *n.* credenziali *f.pl.*
credibility, *n.* credibilità *f.*
credible, *adj.* credìbile.
credit, *n.* crèdito *m.*
creditable, *adj.* soddisfacènte.
creditably, *adv.* in modo soddisfacènte.
credit card, *n.* carta di crèdito *f.*
creditor, *n.* creditore *m.*
credo, *n.* crèdo *m.*
credulity, *n.* credulità *f.*
credulous, *adj.* crèdulo.
creed, *n.* crèdo *m.;* fede *f.*
creek, *n.* ruscello *m.;* **(mountain c.)** torrènte *m.*
creep, *vb.* strisciare, arrampicarsi.
cremate, *vb.* cremare.
cremation, *n.* cremazione *f.*
crematory, 1. *adj.* crematòrio. **2.** *n.* forno crematòrio *m.*
creosote, *n.* creosòto *m.*
crepe, *n.* crespo *m.*
crescent, *n.* mezzaluna *f.*
cress, *n.* crescione *m.*
crest, *n.* cresta *f.*
crestfallen, *adj.* a cresta bassa, scoraggiato.
cretonne, *n.* cotonina *f.*
crevasse, *n.* crepàccio *m.*
crevice, *n.* screpolatura *f.*
crew, *n.* equipàggio *m.*
crew cut, *n.* capelli a spazzola *m.pl.*
crib, *n.* lettino da bimbo *m.*
cricket, *n.* grillo *m.*
crier, *n.* banditore *m.*
crime, *n.* delitto *m.*
criminal, *n.* and *adj.* criminale *(m.).*
criminologist, *n.* criminòlogo *m.*
criminology, *n.* criminologìa *f.*
crimp, *n.* pièga *f.*
crimson, *adj.* crèmisi.
cringe, *vb.* piegarsi.
crinkle, *vb.* spiegazzare.
cripple, 1. *n.* sciancato *f.* **2.** *vb.* rèndere sciancato.
crippled, *adj.* sciancato.
crisis, *n.* crisi *f.*
crisp, *adj.* crespo; (bread, etc.) croccante.
crisscross, *adj.* incrociato.
criterion, *n.* critèrio *m.*

critic, *n.* crìtico *m.*
critical, *adj.* crìtico.
criticism, *n.* crìtica *f.*
criticize, *vb.* criticare.
critique, *n.* crìtica *f.*
croak, *vb.* gracidare.
crochet, *vb.* lavorare all'uncinetto.
crock, *n.* vaso di terracotta *m.*
crockery, *n.* vasellame *m.*
crocodile, *n.* coccodrillo *m.*
crocodile tears, *n.* làcrime di coccodrillo *f.pl.*
crocus, *n.* croco *m.*
crone, *n.* vècchia *f.*
crony, *n.* compare *m.*
crook, *n.* (bend) curvatura *f.;* (scoundrel) mascalzone *m.*
crooked, *adj.* stòrto.
croon, *vb.* canticchiare.
crop, *n.* raccòlta *f.,* raccòlto *m.*
croquet, *n.* pallamàglio *m.*
croquette, *n.* crocchetta *f.,* polpetta *f.*
cross, 1. *n.* croce *f.;* (mixture) incròcio *m.* **2.** *adj.* irritato, adirato. **3.** *vb.* attraversare; (mix) incrociare.
crossbones, *n.* tèschio con tìbie incrociate *m.;* il sìmbolo dei pirati *m.*
crossbow, *n.* balestra *f.*
crossbreed, 1. *n.* incròcio di razze *m.* **2.** *adj.* di razza incrociata.
cross-country, *adj.* campestre.
cross-examine, *vb.* esaminare in contradditòrio.
cross-eyed, *adj.* stràbico.
cross-fertilization, *n.* ibridazione *f.*
crossing, *n.* incròcio *m.;* (grade c.) passàggio a livèllo *m.*
cross-purposes, be at, *vb.* fraintèndersi.
cross-reference, *n.* richiamo *m.;* rimando *m.*
crossroads, *n.* crocìcchio *m.,* crocevìa *f.*
cross section, *n.* sezione *f.*
crossword puzzle, *n.* crucivèrba *m.*
crotch, *n.* (tree) biforcazione *f.;* (human body) inforcatura *f.*
crouch, *vb.* accucciarsi.
croup, *n.* crup *m.*

crouton, n. crostino m.

crow, 1. n. còrvo m. 2. vb. cantare.

crowd, 1. n. fòlla f. 2. vb. affollare; (push) spingere.

crowded, adj. affollato.

crown, 1. n. corona f. 2. vb. incoronare.

crown prince, n. principe ereditàrio m.

crow's-foot, n. zampa di gallina f.

crow's-nest, n. còffa f.

crucial, adj. cruciale.

crucible, n. crogiòlo m.

crucifix, n. crocefisso m.

crucifixion, n. crocefissione f.

crucify, vb. crocifiggere.

crude, adj. crudo.

crudeness, n. crudezza f.

crudity, n. crudezza f.

cruel, adj. crudèle.

cruelty, n. crudeltà f.

cruet, n. olièra f.

cruise, 1. n. crocièra f. 2. vb. incrociare.

cruiser, n. incrociatore m.

crumb, n. briciola f.

crumble, vb. sbriciolare.

crummy, adj. sporco; pòvero.

crumple, vb. spiegazzare.

crunch, vb. schiacciare rumorosamente.

crusade, n. crociata f.

crusader, n. crociato m.

crush, 1. n. fòlla f. 2. vb. schiacciare.

crust, n. crosta f.

crustacean, n. and adj. crostàceo (m.).

crusty, adj. crostoso; (manners) irritàbile.

crutch, n. grùccia f., stampèlla f.

cry, 1. n. grido m. 2. vb. (shout) gridare, urlare; (weep) piàngere.

crybaby, n. piagnone m.; lamentoso m.

crying, n. pianto m.

cryosurgery, n. criochirurgìa f.

crypt, n. cripta f.

cryptic, adj. breve ed oscuro.

cryptography, n. crittografìa f.

crystal, n. cristallo m.

crystalline, adj. cristallino.

crystallize, vb. cristallizzare.

cub, n. piccolo m.

cubbyhole, n. nascondìglio m.

cube, n. cubo m.

cubic, adj. cùbico.

cubicle, n. cubìcolo m.

cubism, n. cubismo m.

cuckold, 1. adj. cornuto becco. 2. n. cornuto m.

cuckoo, 1. n. cùculo m. 2. adj. pazzo.

cucumber, n. cetriòlo m.

cud, n. bòlo m.; **(chew the c.)** ruminare.

cuddle, vb. accarezzare.

cudgel, n. clava f., mazza f.

cue, n. segno m.; (billiards) stecca f.

cuff, 1. n. (shirt) polsino m.; (blow) scapaccione m. 2. vb. picchiare.

cuisine, n. cucina f.

culinary, adj. culinàrio.

cull, vb. cògliere.

culminate, vb. culminare.

culmination, n. culminazione f.

culpable, adj. colpévole.

culprit, n. colpévole m.

cult, n. culto m.

cultivate, vb. coltivare.

cultivated, adj. colto.

cultivation, n. coltivazione f.

cultivator, n. coltivatore m.

cultural, adj. culturale.

culture, n. cultura f.

cultured, adj. colto.

cumbersome, adj. ingombrante.

cumulative, adj. cumulativo.

cunning, 1. n. abilità f. 2. adj. astuto, àbile; (attractive) attraènte, bellino.

cup, n. tazza f.

cupboard, n. credènza f.

cupidity, n. cupidìgia f.

cupola, n. cùpola f.

curable, adj. guarìbile.

curator, n. curatore m.

curb, 1. n. (sidewalk) cordone m.; 2. vb. raffrenare.

curbstone, n. bordo di piètre f.

curd, n. quagliata f.

curdle, vb. quagliare.

cure, 1. n. cura f., guarigione f. 2. vb. guarire.

curfew, n. coprifuòco m.

curio, n. curiosità f.

curiosity, n. curiosità f.

curious, *adj.* curioso; (queer) strano.

curl, 1. *n.* ricciolo *m.* **2.** *vb.* arricciare.

curly, *adj.* ricciuto.

currant, *n.* ribes *m.*

currency, *n.* circolazione *f.;* (money) valuta *f.*

current, *n. and adj.* corrènte *(f.).*

currently, *adv.* correntemente.

curriculum, *n.* currícolo *m.*

curry, *vb.* (horse) strigliare.

curse, 1. *n.* maledizione *f.* **2.** *vb.* maledire.

cursed, *adj.* maledetto.

curse-word, *n.* bestémmia *f.*

cursive, *n. and adj.* corsivo *m.*

cursory, *adj.* frettoloso.

curt, *adj.* asciutto, breve.

curtail, *vb.* accorciare, ridurre.

curtain, *n.* cortina *f.;* (theater) sipàrio *m.*

curtain raiser, *n.* avanspettàcolo *m.*

curtsy, *n.* riverènza *f.*

curvature, *n.* curvatura *f.*

curve, 1. *n.* curva *f.* **2.** *vb.* curvare.

curved, *adj.* curvo, ricurvo; curvato.

cushion, *n.* cuscino *m.*

cuspidor, *n.* sputacchièra *f.*

cuss, *vb.* maledire; bestemmiare.

custard, *n.* crema caramella *f.*

custodian, *n.* custòde *m.*

custody, *n.* custòdia *f.*

custom, *n.* costume *m.,* consuetùdine *f.,* uso *m.*

customary, *adj.* consuèto.

custom-built, *adj.* fatto su misura.

customer, *n.* cliènte *m.;* **(regular c.)** avventore *m.*

customs-house, customs, *n.* dogana *f.*

customs-officer, *n.* doganière *m.*

cut, 1. *n.* tàglio *m.* **2.** *vb.* tagliare.

cut-and-dried, *adj.* monòtono; preparato in anticipo.

cutaneous, *adj.* cutàneo.

cutback, *n.* tàglio *m.;* riduzione *f.*

cute, *adj.* attraènte, bellino.

cut glass, *n.* cristallo *m.*

cuticle, *n.* cutícola *f.*

cutlass, *n.* sciàbola *f.*

cutlet, *n.* costoletta *f.*

cutlery, *n.* posatería *f.*

cutoff, *n.* tàglio *m.;* scorciatòia *f.*

cutout, *n.* interruttore *m.*

cut-rate, *adj.* scontato.

cutter, *n.* tagliatore *m.;* (boat) cottro *m.*

cutthroat, *n.* assassino *m.*

cutting, *n.* (railway) trincèa *f.;* (newspaper) ritàglio *m.*

cuttlefish, *n.* sèppia *f.*

cyclamate, *n.* ciclamato *m.*

cycle, 1. *n.* ciclo *m.;* (bicycle) bicicletta *f.* **2.** *vb.* andare in bicicletta.

cyclist, *n.* ciclista *m.*

cyclone, *n.* ciclone *m.*

cyclotron, *n.* ciclotrone *m.*

cylinder, *n.* cilindro *m.*

cylindrical, *adj.* cilíndrico.

cymbal, *n.* piatto *m.,* cimbali *m.pl.*

cynic, *n.* cínico *m.*

cynical, *adj.* cínico.

cynicism, *n.* cinismo *f.*

cypress, *n.* ciprèsso *m.*

cyst, *n.* ciste *f.*

czar, *n.* zar *m.*

D

dab, 1. *n.* schizzo *m.* **2.** *vb.* sfiorare.

dabble, *vb.* essere un dilettante.

dad, *n.* babbo *m.*

daddy, *n.* papà *m.;* babbo *m.*

daffodil, *n.* narciso *m.*

daffy, *adj.* pazzo.

dagger, *n.* daga *f.,* pugnale *m.*

dahlia, *n.* dàlia *f.*

daily, 1. *n.* (newspaper) giornale *m.* **2.** *adj.* giornalièro, quotidiano. **3.** *adv.* quotidianamente.

daintiness, *n.* squisitezza *f.*

dainty, *adj.* squisito, delicato.

dairy, *n.* latteria *f.*

dairymaid, *n.* lattàia *f.*

dairyman, *n.* lattàio *m.*

dais, *n.* piattaforma *f.*

daisy, *n.* margherita *f.*

dale, *n.* valle *f.*

dally, *vb.* indugiare.

dam, *n.* diga *f.*

damage, 1. n. danno m.; avaria f. **2.** vb. danneggiare, avariare.

damask, n. damasco m.

damn, vb. dannare; (curse) maledire.

damnation, n. dannazione f.

damned, adj. dannato; maledetto.

damp, 1. n. umidità f. **2.** adj. ùmido.

dampen, vb. inumidire.

dampness, n. umidità f.

damsel, n. damigèlla f.

dance, 1. n. ballo m., danza f.; (d. tune) ballàbile m. **2.** vb. ballare, danzare.

dance floor, n. pista da ballo f.

dancer, n. ballerino m., ballerina f.

dancing, n. ballo m.

dandelion, n. radicchièlla f.

dandruff, n. fórfora f.

dandy, 1. n. damerino m., bellimbusto m. **2.** adj. òttimo.

danger, n. pericolo m.

dangerous, adj. pericoloso.

dangle, vb. penzolare.

Danish, adj. danese.

dapper, adj. piccolo e vivace.

dappled, adj. macchiettato.

dare, 1. n. sfida f. **2.** vb. osare; (challenge) sfidare.

daredevil, n. temeràrio m.

daring, 1. n. audàcia f. **2.** adj. audace.

dark, 1. n. oscurità f. **2.** adj. oscuro, bùio, tenebroso.

darken, vb. oscurare.

dark horse, n. candidato sconosciuto m.

darkly, adv. oscuramente; segretamente.

darkness, n. oscurità f., bùio m., tènebre f.pl.

darkroom, n. càmera oscura f.

darling, n. and adj. prediletto.

darn, 1. n. rammendatura f. **2.** vb. rammendare. **3.** interj. accidenti!

darning needle, n. ago da rammendo m.

dart, 1. n. dardo m.; (movement) balzo m. **2.** balzare.

dash, 1. n. (energy) slàncio m.;

scatto m.; (pen) tratto m. **2.** vb. (throw) gettare; (destroy) distrùggere; (rush) slanciarsi; (spurt) scattare.

dashboard, n. cruscòtto m.

dashing, adj. impetuoso.

dastardly, adj. vile; codardo.

data, n. dati m.pl.

data processing, n. elaborazione dati f.

date, 1. n. data f.; (appointment) appuntamento m.; (fruit) dàttero m. **2.** vb. datare.

date line, n. línea del cambiamento di data f.

daub, 1. n. imbrattatura f. **2.** vb. imbrattare.

daughter, n. figlia f.

daughter-in-law, n. nuòra f.

daunt, vb. intimidire.

dauntless, adj. intrèpido.

dauntlessly, adv. intrepidamente.

davenport, n. divano m., sofaletto m.

daw, n. cornàcchia f.

dawdle, vb. indugiare.

dawn, 1. n. alba f. **2.** vb. spuntare.

day, n. giorno m.; (span of day) giornata f.

daybreak, n. alba f.

daydream, n. fantasticheria f.

daylight, n. luce del giorno f.

daylight-saving time, n. ora d'estate f.

daze, 1. n. stupore m. **2.** vb. stupire.

dazzle, vb. abbagliare.

deacon, n. diàcono m.

dead, n. and adj. mòrto (m.).

deaden, vb. ammortire.

dead end, n. vícolo cièco m.

dead letter, n. lèttera mòrta f.

deadline, n. límite m.

deadlock, n. punto mòrto m.

deadly, adj. mortale.

deadwood, n. legno mòrto m.

deaf, adj. sordo.

deafen, vb. assordare.

deaf-mute, n. and adj. sordomuto (m.).

deafness, n. sordità f.

deal, 1. n. (amount) quantità f.; (business) affare m.; (cards) distribuzione f. 2. vb. (d. with) trattare con; (d. out) distribuire.

dealer, n. negoziante m.

dean, n. decano m.

dear, adj. caro.

dearly, adv. caramente.

dearth, n. scarsezza f., scarsità f.

death, n. mòrte f.

deathless, adj. immortale, imperituro.

deathly, adj. mortale.

débâcle, n. sfacèlo m., disastro m.

debase, vb. abbassare, avvilire.

debatable, adj. discutibile.

debate, 1. n. dibattimento m. 2. vb. dibàttere.

debater, n. dibattènte m.

debauch, 1. n. òrgia f., sregolatezza f. 2. vb. pervertire.

debenture, n. obbligazione f.

debilitate, vb. debilitare.

debit, n. dèbito m.

debonair, adj. gaio.

debris, n. detriti m.pl.

debt, n. dèbito m.

debtor, n. debitore m.

debunk, vb. screditare.

debut, n. debutto m.

debutante, n. debuttante f.

decade, n. decènnio m.

decadence, n. decadènza f.

decadent, adj. decadènte.

decaffeinated, adj. decaffeinizzato.

decalcomania, n. decalcomanía f.

decanter, n. caraffa f.

decapitate, vb. decapitare.

decay, 1. n. decadènza f., decomposizione f.; (teeth) càrie f. 2. vb. decadere, decomporre, marcire; (teeth) cariarsi.

deceased, n. and adj. deceduto (m.), defunto (m.)

deceit, n. inganno m.

deceitful, adj. ingannatore.

deceive, vb. ingannare.

deceiver, n. ingannatore m.

decelerate, vb. decelerare.

December, n. dicèmbre m.

decency, n. (modesty) decènza f.; (honorable behavior) onorevolezza f.

decent, adj. (modest) decènte; (honorable) onorévole.

decentralization, n. decentramento m.

decentralize, vb. decentrare.

deception, n. inganno m.

deceptive, adj. ingannévole.

decibel, n. dècibel m.

decide, vb. decidere.

deciduous, adj. decíduo.

decimal, adj. decimale.

decimal point, n. vírgola dei decimali f.

decimate, vb. decimare.

decipher, vb. decifrare.

decision, n. decisione f.

decisive, adj. decisivo.

deck, n. ponte m.

deck chair, n. sèdia a sdràio f.

deck-hand, n. mozzo m.

declaim, vb. declamare.

declamation, n. declamazione f.

declaration, n. dichiarazione f.

declarative, adj. dichiarativo.

declare, vb. dichiarare.

declension, n. declinazione f.

declination, n. declinazione f.

decline, 1. n. decadènza f. 2. vb. declinare; (refuse) rifiutare; (decay) decadere.

declivity, n. declivio m.; pendice f.

decode, vb. decifrare.

décolleté, adj. scollato.

decompose, vb. decomporre.

decomposition, n. decomposizione f.

decongestant, adj. decongestionante.

décor, n. messa in scena f.

decorate, vb. decorare.

decoration, n. decorazione f.

decorative, adj. decorativo.

decorator, n. decoratore m.

decorous, adj. decoroso.

decorum, n. decòro m.

decoy, vb. attirare.

decrease, 1. n. diminuzione f. 2. vb. diminuire.

decree, 1. n. decreto m. 2. vb. decretare.

decrepit, adj. decrèpito.

decry, vb. deprecare.

dedicate, vb. dedicare.

dedication, n. dèdica f.

deduce, vb. dedurre.

deduct, vb. dedurre, sottrarre.

deductible, adj. (tax) deducibile.

deduction, n. deduzione f.
deductive, adj. deduttivo.
deed, n. atto m., fatto m.
deem, vb. giudicare, stimare.
deep, adj. profondo.
deepen, vb. approfondire.
deep freeze, n. surgelamento m.
deeply, adv. profondamente.
deep-rooted, adj. profondamente radicato.
deep-seated, adj. profondo, connaturato.
deer, n. cèrvo m.
deerskin, n. pèlle di dàino f.
deface, vb. sfregiare.
defamation, n. diffamazione f.
defame, vb. diffamare.
default, 1. n. contumàcia f. 2. vb. rèndersi contumace; (comm.) mancar di pagare.
defaulting, adj. contumace.
defeat, 1. n. sconfitta f., disfatta f. 2. vb. sconfiggere.
defeatism, n. disfattismo m.
defect, n. difètto m., mènda f.
defection, n. defezione f.
defective, adj. difettoso.
defend, vb. difèndere.
defendant, n. imputato m.
defender, n. difensore m.
defense, n. difesa f.
defenseless, adj. sènza difesa.
defensible, adj. difensíbile.
defensive, adj. difensivo.
defer, vb. (put off) differire; (conform) conformarsi.
deference, n. deferènza f.
deferential, adj. deferènte.
defiance, n. sfida f.
defiant, adj. provocante.
deficiency, n. deficiènza f.
deficient, adj. deficiènte.
deficit, n. dèficit m.
defile, vb. (march) sfilare; (foul) profanare.
define, vb. definire.
definite, adj. definito.
definitely, adj. definitivamente.
definition, n. definizione f.
definitive, adj. definitivo.
deflate, vb. sgonfiare; (econ.) deflazionare.
deflation, n. deflazione f.
deflect, vb. deflèttere.
deflower, vb. deflorare.

deforest, vb. disboscare.
deform, vb. deformare.
deformed, adj. deforme.
deformity, n. deformità f.
defraud, vb. defraudare.
defray, vb. pagare.
defrost, vb. scongelare.
defroster, n. (auto) cruscotto tèrmico m.
defrosting, n. (refrigerator) sbrinamento m.
deft, adj. dèstro, àbile.
defunct, adj. defunto.
defy, vb. sfidare.
degenerate, 1. n. and adj. degenerato (m.). 2. vb. degenerare.
degeneration, n. degenerazione f.
degradation, n. degradazione f.
degrade, vb. degradare.
degrading, adj. degradante.
degree, n. grado m.; (university) làurea f.
dehydrate, vb. disidratare.
deice, vb. sgelare; sghiacciare.
deify, vb. deificare.
deign, vb. degnarsi.
deity, n. deità f.
dejected, adj. scoraggiato.
dejection, n. scoraggiamento m., abbattimento m.
delay, 1. n. indùgio m., ritardo m. 2. vb. indugiare, ritardare.
delectable, adj. dilettévole.
delegate, 1. n. delegato m. 2. vb. delegare.
delegation, n. delegazione f.
delete, vb. cancellare.
deliberate, 1. adj. deliberato. 2. vb. deliberare.
deliberately, adv. deliberatamente, appòsta.
deliberation, n. deliberazione f.
deliberative, adj. deliberativo.
delicacy, n. delicatezza f.
delicate, adj. delicato.
delicious, adj. delizioso.
delight, n. dilètto m.
delightful, adj. dilettévole.
delineate, vb. delineare.
delinquency, n. delinquènza f.
delinquent, n. and adj. delinquènte (m.).
delirious, 1. adj. delirante. 2. vb. (be d.) delirare.

delirium, n. delírio m.

deliver, vb. (set free) liberare; (hand over) consegnare.

deliverance, n. liberazione f.

delivery, n. consegna f.

deliveryman, n. fattorino m.

delivery room, n. sala parto f.

delivery truck, n. furgoncino m.

delouse, vb. spidocchiare.

delude, vb. delúdere.

deluge, n. dilúvio m.

delusion, n. delusione f.

de luxe, adj. di lusso.

delve, vb. scavare.

demagnetize, vb. smagnetizzare.

demagogue, n. demagògo m.

demand, 1. n. domanda f., richièsta f. **2.** vb. domandare, richièdere, esigere.

demanding, adj. esigente; impregnativo.

demarcate, vb. demarcare, marcare.

demarcation, n. demarcazione f.

demean (oneself), vb. abbassarsi.

demeanor, n. condotta f.

demented, adj. demènte.

demerit, n. demèrito m.

demigod, n. semidio m.

demilitarize, vb. smilitarizzare.

demise, n. mòrte f.

demobilization, n. smobilitazione f.

demobilize, vb. smobilitare.

democracy, n. democrazia f.

democrat, n. democràtico m.

democratic, adj. democràtico.

demolish, vb. demolire.

demolition, n. demolizione f.

demon, n. demònio m.

demonstrable, adj. dimostràbile.

demonstrate, vb. dimostrare.

demonstration, n. dimostrazione f.

demonstrative, adj. dimostrativo.

demonstrator, n. dimostratore m.

demoralize, vb. demoralizzare.

demote, vb. degradare.

demotion, n. retrocessione f.

demur, vb. obiettare.

demure, adj. modesto.

den, n. tana f., covo m.

denaturalize, vb. snaturare.

denature, vb. denaturare.

denial, n. diniègo m.

denim, n. saia f.

denizen, n. abitante m. and f.

Denmark, n. Danimarca f.

denomination, n. denominazione f.; (church) sètta f.

denominator, n. denominatore m.

denote, vb. denotare.

dénouement, n. scioglimento m.

denounce, vb. denunciare.

dense, adj. dènso.

density, n. densità f.

dent, n. incavo m.

dental, adj. dentale.

dentifrice, n. dentifrício m.

dentist, n. dentista m.

dentistry, n. odontoiatría f.

denture, n. dentièra f.

denude, vb. denudare.

denunciation, n. denúncia f.

deny, vb. negare.

deodorant, n. and adj. deodorante (m.).

deodorize, vb. deodorare.

depart, vb. partire.

department, n. dipartimento m.

departmental, adj. dipartimentale.

department store, n. grande magazzino m.

departure, n. partènza f.

depend, vb. dipèndere.

dependability, n. dipendibilità f., fidúcia f.

dependable, adj. fidato.

dependence, n. dipendènza f.

dependency, n. dipendenza f.; possessione f.

dependent, n. and adj. dipendènte (m.).

depict, vb. dipíngere.

depiction, n. rappresentazione f.

deplete, vb. esaurire.

deplorable, adj. deplorévole.

deplore, vb. deplorare.

deploy, vb. (military) spiegare, disporre.

deployment, n. spiegamento m.

depolarize, vb. depolarizzare.

depopulate, vb. spopolare.

deport, vb. deportare.

deportation, n. deportazione f.

deportee, *n.* deportato *m.*

deportment, *n.* condotta *f.*

depose, *vb.* deporre.

deposit, 1. *n.* depòsito. **2.** *vb.* depositare.

deposition, *n.* deposizione *f.*

depositor, *n.* depositante *m.*, correntista *m.*

depository, *n.* depòsito *m.*

depot, *(n.* (military) depòsito *m.*; (railroad) stazione *f.*

deprave, *vb.* depravare.

depravity, *n.* depravazione *f.*

deprecate, *vb.* deprecare.

depreciate, *vb.* deprezzare.

depreciation, *n.* deprezzamento *m.*

depredation, *n.* depredamento *m.*

depress, *vb.* deprìmere.

depression, *n.* depressione *f.*

deprivation, *n.* privazione *f.*

deprive, *vb.* privare.

depth, *n.* profondità *f.*

depth charge, *n.* bomba di profondità *f.*

deputy, *n.* deputato *m.*

derail, *vb.* deragliare.

derailment, *n.* deragliamento *m.*

derange, *vb.* far impazzire.

deranged, *adj.* impazzito.

derangement, *n.* disordine *m.*; pazzìa *f.*

derelict, *adj.* derelitto.

dereliction, *n.* negligènza del dovere *f.*

deride, *vb.* derìdere.

derision, *n.* derisione *f.*

derisive, *adj.* ridicolizzante.

derivation, *n.* derivazione *f.*

derivative, *adj.* derivato.

derive, *vb.* derivare.

dermatology, *n.* dermatologìa *f.*

derogatory, *adj.* dispregiativo.

derrick, *n.* gru *f.*

desalinization, *n.* desalinizzazione *f.*

descend, *vb.* scéndere.

descendant, *n.* discendènte *m.*

descendent, *adj.* discendente.

descent, *n.* discesa *f.*

describe, *vb.* descrìvere.

description, *n.* descrizione *f.*

descriptive, *adj.* descrittivo.

desecrate, *vb.* profanare, dissacrare.

desegregate, *vb.* desegregare.

desensitize, *vb.* desensibilizzare.

desert, 1. *n.* desèrto *m.*; (merit) mèrito *m.* **2.** *vb.* disertare.

deserter, *n.* disertore *m.*

desertion, *n.* diserzione *f.*

deserve, *vb.* meritare.

deserving, *adj.* meritévole.

design, 1. *n.* disegno *m.* **2.** *vb.* disegnare.

designate, *vb.* designare.

designation, *n.* designazione *f.*

designedly, *adv.* intenzionalmente.

designer, *n.* disegnatore *m.*

designing, *adj.* astuto.

desirability, *n.* desiderabilità *f.*

desirable, *adj.* desideràbile.

desire, 1. *n.* desidèrio *m.* **2.** *vb.* desiderare.

desirous, *adj.* desideroso.

desist, *vb.* desistere.

desk, *n.* scrivanìa *f.*

desolate, 1. *adj.* desolato. **2.** *vb.* desolare.

desolation, *n.* desolazione *f.*

despair, 1. *n.* disperazione *f.* **2.** *vb.* disperare.

despatch, dispatch, 1. *n.* spedizione *f.*; (speed) prontezza *f.* **2.** *vb.* spedire.

desperado, *n.* disperato *m.*

desperate, *adj.* disperato.

desperation, *n.* disperazione *f.*

despicable, *adj.* spregévole.

despise, *vb.* disprezzare, spregiare.

despite, *prep.* malgrado.

despondent, *adj.* abbattuto.

despot, *n.* dèspota *m.*

despotic, *adj.* dispòtico.

despotism, *n.* dispotismo *m.*

dessert, *n.* dessèrt *m.* (French pronunciation).

destination, *n.* destinazione *f.*

destine, *vb.* destinare.

destiny, *n.* destino *m.*

destitute, *adj.* destituito.

destitution, *n.* destituzione *f.*

destroy, *vb.* distrùggere.

destroyer, *n.* cacciatorpedinière *m.*

destructible, *adj.* distruttìbile.

destruction, *n.* distruzione *f.*

destructive, *adj.* distruttivo.

desultory, adj. saltuàrio.

detach, vb. staccare, distaccare.

detachable, adj. staccàbile, separàbile.

detachment, n. distacco m.; (mil.) distaccamento m.

detail, 1. n. dettaglio m. 2. vb. dettagliare.

detain, vb. detenere.

detect, vb. scoprire.

detection, n. scoprimento m.

detective, n. detective m. (English pron.).

detective story, n. giallo m.

detente, n. distensione f.

detention, n. detenzione f.

deter, vb. distògliere.

detergent, n. and adj. detergènte (m.)

deteriorate, vb. deteriorare.

deterioration, n. deteriorazione f.

determination, n. determinazione f.

determine, vb. determinare.

determined, adj. risoluto.

determinism, n. determinismo m.

deterrence, n. preventivo m.

detest, vb. detestare.

detestation, n. fastidio m., odio m.

dethrone, vb. detronizzare.

detonate, vb. detonare.

detonation, n. detonazione f.

detonator, n. detonatore m.

detour, n. deviazione f.

detract, vb. detrarre.

detractor, n. detrattore m.

detriment, n. detrimento m., danno m.

detrimental, adj. dannoso.

devaluate, vb. svalutare.

devaluation, n. svalutazione f.

devastate, vb. devastare.

devastating, adj. devastante.

devastation, n. devastazione f.

develop, vb. sviluppare.

developer, n. sviluppatore m.

developing nation, n. nazione in via di sviluppo f.

development, n. sviluppo m.

deviate, vb. deviare.

deviation, n. deviazione f.

device, n. congegno m.

devil, n. diàvolo m.

devilish, adj. diabòlico.

devious, adj. deviato, tortuoso, traverso.

devise, vb. escogitare.

devitalize, vb. devitalizzare.

devoid, adj. privo.

devote, vb. dedicare.

devoted, adj. devòto.

devotee, n. entusiasta m. or f.

devotion, n. devozione f.

devour, vb. divorare.

devout, adj. devòto.

dew, n. rugiada f.

dewy, adj. rugiadoso.

dexterity, n. destrezza f.

dexterous, adj. dèstro.

diabetes, n. diabète m.

diabolical, adj. diabòlico.

diadem, n. diadèma m.

diagnose, vb. diagnosticare.

diagnosis, n. diàgnosi f.

diagnostic, adj. diagnòstico.

diagonal, adj. diagonale.

diagonally, adv. diagonalmente.

diagram, n. diagramma m.

dial, 1. n. quadrante m.; (telephone) disco combinatore m. 2. vb. (telephone) formare (un nùmero).

dialect, n. dialètto m.

dialogue, n. diàlogo m.

dial tone, n. segnale di via libera m.

diameter, n. diàmetro m.

diametrical, adj. diametrale.

diamond, n. diamante m.

diaper, n. pannilino m., pannolino m.

diaphragm, n. diaframma m.

diarrhea, n. diarrèa f.

diary, n. diàrio m.

diathermy, n. diatermía f.

diatribe, n. diatriba f.

dice, n. dadi m pl.

dickens (the), interj. diàmine!

dicker, vb. mercanteggiare.

dictaphone, n. dittàfono m.

dictate, vb. dettare.

dictation, n. dettatura f.

dictator, n. dittatore m.

dictatorial, adj. dittatoriale.

dictatorship, n. dittatura f.

diction, n. dizione f.

dictionary, n. dizionàrio m.

didactic, adj. didàttico.

die, 1. *n.* (gaming cube) dado *m.*; (stamper) stampo *m.* **2.** *vb.* morire.

die-hard, *adj.* intransigente.

diet, *n.* dièta *f.*, regime *m.*

dietary, *adj.* dietètico.

dietetic, *adj.* dietètico.

dietetics, *n.* dietètica *f.*

dietitian, *n.* dietista *m.*

differ, *vb.* differire.

difference, *n.* differènza *f.*

different, *adj.* differènte, divèrso.

differential, *adj.* differenziale.

differentiate, *vb.* differenziare.

difficult, *adj.* difficile.

difficulty, *n.* difficoltà *f.*

diffident, *adj.* tímido.

diffuse, 1. *adj.* diffuso. **2.** *vb.* diffóndere.

diffusion, *n.* diffusione *f.*

dig, *vb.* scavare.

digest, *vb.* digerire.

digestible, *adj.* digeríbile.

digestion, *n.* digestione *f.*

digestive, *adj.* digestivo.

digital, *adj.* digitale.

digitalis, *n.* digitale *f.*

dignified, *adj.* dignitoso.

dignify, *vb.* nobilitare.

dignitary, *n.* dignitàrio *m.*

dignity, *n.* dignità *f.*

digress, *vb.* digredire.

digression, *n.* digressione *f.*

dike, *n.* diga *f.*

dilapidated, *adj.* dilapidato.

dilapidation, *n.* dilapidazione *f.*

dilate, *vb.* dilatare.

dilatory, *adj.* dilatòrio.

dilemma, *n.* dilemma *m.*

dilettante, *n.* dilettante *m.*

diligence, *n.* diligènza *f.*

diligent, *adj.* diligènte.

dill, *n.* anèto *m.*

dilute, *vb.* diluire.

dilution, *n.* diluizione *f.*

dim, 1. *adj.* oscuro. **2.** *vb.* oscurare.

dime, *n.* moneta da dieci centesimi *f.*

dimension, *n.* dimensione *f.*

diminish, *vb.* diminuire, menomare.

diminution, *n.* diminuzione *f.*

diminutive, *n.* *and* *adj.* diminutivo (*m.*)

dimly, *adv.* indistintamente.

dimmer, *n.* smorzatore *m.*

dimness, *n.* oscurità *f.*

dimple, *n.* fossetta *f.*

din, *n.* rumore *m.*

dine, *vb.* pranzare.

diner, *n.* vettura ristorante *f.*

dining-car, *n.* vagone ristorante *m.*

dining room, *n.* sala da pranzo *f.*

dingy, *adj.* sùdicio.

dinner, *n.* pranzo *m.*

dinner set, *n.* servizio da tàvola *m.*

dinosaur, *n.* dinosàuro *m.*

dint, *n.* tacca *f.*; ammaccatura *f.*

diocese, *n.* diòcesi *f.*

diode, *n.* diodo *m.*

dip, *vb.* immèrgere, tuffare.

diphtheria, *n.* difterite *f.*

diphthong, *n.* dittongo *m.*

diploma, *n.* diplòma *m.*

diplomacy, *n.* diplomazìa *f.*

diplomat, *n.* diplomàtico *m.*

diplomatic, *adj.* diplomàtico.

dipper, *n.* mèstolo *m.*

dire, *adj.* terríbile.

direct, 1. *adj.* dirètto. **2.** *vb.* dirígere.

direct current, *n.* corrènte contínua *f.*

direction, *n.* direzione *f.*, sènso *m.*

directional, *adj.* direttivo.

directive, *adj.* direttivo.

directly, *adv.* direttamente, immediatamente.

directness, *n.* franchezza *f.*

direct object, *n.* complemento oggetto *m.*

director, *n.* direttore *m.*

directorate, *n.* direttorato *m.*

directory, *n.* guida *f.*; (telephone d.) elènco telefònico *m.*

dirge, *n.* canto funebre *m.*

dirigible, *n. and adj.* dirigíbile (*m.*)

dirt, *n.* sudiciume *m.*

dirt road, *n.* strada in terra battuta *f.*

dirty, *adj.* sùdicio, sporco.

dirty trick, *n.* tiro mancino *m.*

disability, *n.* incapacità *f.*

disable, *vb.* rèndere incapace.

disabled, *adj.* invàlido.

disabuse, *vb.* disingannare.

disadvantage, n. svantàggio m.

disagree, vb. discordare, dissentire.

disagreeable, adj. sgradévole, antipàtico.

disagreement, n. dissènso m.

disallow, vb. rifiutare; non consentire.

disappear, vb. sparire, scomparire.

disappearance, n. scomparsa f.

disappoint, vb. delùdere.

disappointment, n. delusione f.

disapproval, n. disapprovazione f.

disapprove, vb. disapprovare.

disarm, vb. disarmare.

disarmament, n. disarmo m.

disarming, adj. simpatico; accattivante.

disarrange, vb. scompigliare.

disarray, n. scompíglio m.

disassemble, vb. smontare.

disaster, n. disastro m.

disastrous, adj. disastroso.

disavow, vb. disconóscere.

disavowal, n. disconoscimento m.

disband, vb. sbandare.

disbar, vb. cancellare dall'albo dell'avvocatura.

disbelieve, vb. non credere.

disburse, vb. sborsare.

discard, vb. scartare.

discern, vb. discèrnere, scòrgere.

discernible, adj. discernibile.

discerning, adj. penetrante.

discernment, n. giudízio m.

discharge, 1. n. scàrico m.; (gun) scàrica f.; (mil., job) licenziamento m. **2.** vb. scaricare; (mil., job) licenziare.

disciple, n. discépolo m.

disciplinary, adj. disciplinare.

discipline, 1. n. disciplina f. **2.** vb. disciplinare.

disclaim, vb. disconóscere.

disclaimer, n. disconoscimento m.

disclose, vb. rivelare.

disclosure, n. rivelazione f.

disco, n. (musicaccia) disco f.

discolor, vb. scolorire.

discoloration, n. scolorimento m.

discomfit, vb. sconcertare; frustrare.

discomfiture, n. sconfitta f.

discomfort, n. disàgio m.

disconcert, vb. sconcertare.

disconnect, vb. sconnèttere.

disconsolate, adj. sconsolato.

discontent, 1. n. scontènto m. **2.** vb. scontentare.

discontented, adj. scontènto.

discontinue, vb. interrómpere, sospèndere.

discord, n. discòrdia f.; (music) disaccòrdo m.

discordant, adj. discordante.

discothèque, n. discotèca f.

discount, 1. n. sconto m. **2.** vb. scontare.

discourage, vb. scoraggiare.

discouragement, n. scoraggiamento m.

discourse, 1. n. discorso m. **2.** vb. discórrere.

discourteous, adj. scortese.

discourtesy, n. scortesia f.

discover, vb. scoprire.

discoverer, n. scopritore m.

discovery, n. scopèrta f.

discredit, 1. n. discrédito m. **2.** vb. screditare.

discreditable, adj. disonorévole.

discreet, adj. discreto.

discrepancy, n. discrepanza f.

discrepant, adj. discrepante.

discretion, n. discrezione f.

discriminate, vb. discriminare.

discrimination, n. discriminazione f.

discriminatory, adj. discriminante.

discursive, adj. digressivo.

discuss, vb. discùtere.

discussion, n. discussione f.

disdain, 1. n. disdegno m. **2.** vb. disdegnare; sdegnare.

disdainful, adj. sdegnoso.

disease, n. malattía f.

disembark, vb. sbarcare.

disembarkation, n. sbarco m.

disembodied, adj. incorpòreo.

disembowel, vb. sventrare; sbudellare.

disenchantment, n. disincanto m.

disengage, vb. disimpegnare.

disentangle, vb. districare.

disfavor, n. sfavore m.

disfigure, vb. sfigurare, deturpare.

disfranchise, vb. privare della franchígia.

disgorge, vb. vomitare; (intr.) sgorgare.

disgrace, 1. n. disgràzia f., sfavore m., disonore m. **2.** vb. disonorare.

disgraceful, adj. disonorante.

disgruntle, vb. seccare, irritare.

disgruntled, adj. scontento.

disguise, 1. n. travestimento m. **2.** vb. travestire.

disgust, 1. n. disgusto m. **2.** vb. disgustare.

disgusting, adj. disgustante, disgustoso.

dish, n. piatto m.

dishcloth, n. strofinàccio (per piatti) m.

dishearten, vb. scoraggiare.

dishonest, adj. disonèsto.

dishonesty, n. disonestà f.

dishonor, 1. n. disonore m. **2.** vb. disonorare.

dishonorable, adj. disonorèvole.

dish-towel, n. asciugapiatti m.

disillusion, 1. n. disillusione f. **2.** vb. disillùdere.

disinfect, vb. disinfettare.

disinfectant, n. disinfettante m.

disinherit, vb. diseredare.

disintegrate, vb. disintegrare.

disinterested, adj. disinteressato.

disjointed, adj. sconnèsso.

disk, n. disco m.

dislike, 1. n. antipatía f. **2.** vb. non piacere (with English subject as indirect object).

dislocate, vb. slogare.

dislodge, vb. sloggiare.

disloyal, adj. sleale.

disloyalty, n. slealtà f.

dismal, adj. melancònico.

dismantle, vb. smantellare.

dismay, 1. n. costernazione f. **2.** vb. costernare.

dismember, vb. smembrare.

dismiss, vb. congedare, dimèttere.

dismissal, n. congedo m.

dismount, vb. smontare.

disobedience, n. disubbidiènza f.

disobedient, adj. disobbediènte.

disobey, vb. disubbidire.

disorder, 1. n. disòrdine m. **2.** vb. disordinare.

disorderly, adj. disordinato.

disorganize, vb. disorganizzare.

disoriented, adj. disorientato.

disown, vb. disconóscere.

disparage, vb. disprezzare.

disparagement, n. discrédito m.

disparate, adj. disparato.

disparity, n. disparità f.

dispassionate, adj. spassionato.

dispatch, see **despatch.**

dispatcher, n. spedizioniere m.

dispel, vb. dissipare.

dispensable, adj. dispensàbile.

dispensary, n. dispensàrio m.

dispensation, n. dispensa f.

dispense, vb. dispensare; **(d. from)** esentare da.

dispenser, n. distributore m.

dispersal, n. dispersione f.

disperse, vb. dispèrdere.

dispersion, n. dispersione f.

dispersive, adj. dispersivo.

dispirit, vb. scoraggiare.

displace, vb. spostare.

displaced person, n. rifugiato m.

displacement, n. spostamento m.; (ship) dislocamento m.

display, 1. n. esibizione f.; (showing off) ostentazione f. **2.** vb. esibire, ostentare.

displease, vb. dispiacere (a).

displeasing, adj. spiacevole.

displeasure, n. dispiacere m.

disposable, adj. disponíbile.

disposal, n. disposizione f.

dispose, vb. disporre.

disposition, n. disposizione f.

dispossess, vb. spodestare.

disproof, n. confutazione f.

disproportion, n. sproporzione f.

disproportionate, adj. sproporzionato.

disprove, vb. confutare.

disputable, adj. disputàbile.

dispute, 1. n. disputa f. **2.** vb. disputare.

disqualification, n. squalifica f.

disqualify, vb. squalificare.

disquiet, 1. n. inquietùdine f. **2.** vb. turbare, inquietare.

disquisition, n. disquisizione f.

disregard, 1. n. indifferènza f. **2.** vb. trascurare.

disrepair, n. dilapidazione f.

disreputable, adj. disonorévole.

disrespect, n. mancanza di rispètto f.

disrespectful, adj. irrispetoso.

disrobe, vb. svestirsi.

disrupt, vb. interròmpere, mandare a monte.

disruption, n. interruzione f.; disarticolazione f.

dissatisfaction, n. insoddisfazione f.

dissatisfy, vb. non soddisfare.

dissect, vb. sezionare.

dissection, n. dissezione f.

dissemble, vb. dissimulare.

disseminate, vb. disseminare.

dissension, n. dissènso m.

dissent, 1. n. dissènso m. 2. vb. dissentire.

dissertation, n. dissertazione f.; tesi f.

disservice, n. disservízio m.

dissidence, n. dissidenza f.

dissimilar, adj. dissimile.

dissimulate, vb. dissimulare.

dissipate, vb. dissipare.

dissipated, adj. dissoluto.

dissipation, n. dissipazione f., dissolutezza f.

dissociate, vb. dissociare.

dissolute, adj. dissoluto.

dissoluteness, n. dissolutezza f.

dissolution, n. dissoluzione f.

dissolve, vb. dissòlvere, sciògliere.

dissonance, n. dissonanza f.

dissonant, adj. dissonante.

dissuade, vb. dissuadere.

distance, n. distanza f.

distant, adj. distante, lontano; (be d.) distare.

distaste, n. disgusto m.

distasteful, adj. disgustoso.

distemper, n. indisposizione f.

distend, vb. distèndere.

distill, vb. distillare.

distillation, n. distillazione f.

distiller, n. distillatore m.

distillery, n. distilleria f.

distinct, adj. distinto.

distinction, n. distinzione f.

distinctive, adj. distintivo.

distinctly, adv. distintamente.

distinguish, vb. distinguere.

distinguished, adj. distinto.

distort, vb. distòrcere.

distract, vb. distrarre.

distraction, n. distrazione f.

distraught, adj. pazzo.

distress, 1. n. afflizione f. 2. vb. affliggere.

distribute, vb. distribuire.

distribution, n. distribuzione f.

distributor, n. distributore m.

district, n. distretto m.

distrust, 1. n. sfidúcia f. 2. vb. non fidarsi di.

distrustful, adj. sospettoso.

disturb, vb. disturbare.

disturbance, n. disturbo m.

disunite, vb. disunire.

disuse, n. disuso m.

ditch, n. fosso m., fossato m.

dither, n. agitazione f.

ditto, n. lo stesso m.

diva, n. diva f.

divan, n. divano m.

dive, 1. n. tuffo m. 2. vb. tuffarsi.

dive-bomber, n. picchiatore m., tuffatore m.

diver, n. tuffatore m.

diverge, vb. divèrgere.

divergence, n. divergènza f.

divergent, adj. divergènte.

diverse, adj. divèrso.

diversify, vb. diversificare.

diversion, n. diversione f.

diversity, n. diversità f.

divert, vb. (turn away) stornare; (amuse) divertire.

divest, vb. spogliare.

divide, vb. dividere.

dividend, n. dividèndo m.

divine, 1. adj. divino. 2. vb. divinare.

diving board, n. trampolino m.

divinity, n. divinità f.

divisible, adj. divisíbile.

division, n. divisione f., scissione f.

divorce, 1. n. divòrzio m. 2. vb. divorziare.

divorcée, n. divorziata f.

divulge, vb. divulgare.

dizziness, n. vertigine f., stordimento m.

dizzy, adj. vertiginoso, stordito.

do, vb. fare; (how do you do?) come sta?

docile, adj. dòcile.

dock, *n.* bacino *m.*

dockage, *n.* attracco *m.*

docket, *n.* etichetta *f.;* (legal) elenco *m.*

dockyard, *n.* arsenale *m.*

doctor, *n.* dottore *m.,* mèdico *m.*

doctorate, *n.* dottorato *m.*

doctrinaire, *adj.* dottrinàrio.

doctrine, *n.* dottrina *f.*

document, 1. *n.* documento *m.* **2.** *vb.* documentare.

documentary, *adj.* documentàrio.

documentation, *n.* documentazione *f.*

doddering, *adj.* tremante; rimbambito.

dodge, *vb.* elùdere, schivare.

doe, *n.* cèrva *f.*

doeskin, *n.* pelle di cèrva *f.*

dog, *n.* cane *m.*

dogged, *adj.* ostinato, tenace.

doggerel, *n.* versucci *m.pl.*

doghouse, *n.* canile *m.*

dogma, *n.* dògma *m.*

dogmatic, *adj.* dogmàtico.

dogmatism, *n.* dogmatismo *m.*

doily, *n.* tovagliolino *m.*

doldrum, *n.* **(in the d.s)** *adj.* calmo.

dole, 1. *n.* elemòsina *f.* **2.** *vb.* **(d. out)** distribuire.

doleful, *adj.* triste.

doll, *n.* bàmbola *f.,* pupàttola *f.*

dollar, *n.* dòllaro *m.*

dolorous, *adj.* doloroso.

dolphin, *n.* delfino *m.*

domain, *n.* domínio *m.*

dome, *n.* cùpola *f.*

domestic, *adj.* domèstico.

domesticate, *vb.* domesticare.

domicile, *n.* domicílio *m.*

dominance, *n.* predomínio *m.*

dominant, *adj.* dominante.

dominate, *vb.* dominare.

domination, *n.* dominazione *f.*

domineer, *vb.* spadroneggiare.

dominion, *n.* domínio *m.*

don, *vb.* indossare.

donate, *vb.* donare.

donation, *n.* donazione *f.*

done, *adj.* fatto; (food) còtto.

donkey, *n.* àsino *m.,* somaro *m.*

don't, *vb.* non fare.

doom, 1. *n.* (condemnation) condanna *f.;* (fate) destino *m.* **2.** *vb.* condannare.

doomsday, *n.* giorno del giudízio universale *m.*

door, *n.* pòrta *f.;* (auto) portièra *f.*

doorman, *n.* portinaio *m.*

door-mat, *n.* stuoino *m.*

doorstep, *n.* gradino della pòrta *m.*

doorway, *n.* vano della pòrta *m.*

dope, *n.* (drug) narcòtico *m.;* (fool) imbecille *m.*

dormant, *adj.* inattivo.

dormer, *n.* abbaíno *m.*

dormitory, *n.* dormitòrio *m.*

dosage, *n.* dosatura *f.*

dose, 1. *n.* dòse *f.* **2.** *vb.* dosare.

dossier, *n.* incartamento *m.*

dot, *n.* punto *m.*

dotage, *n.* rimbambimento *m.*

dotard, *n.* vecchio rimbambito *m.*

dote, *vb.* esser rimbambito; **(d. upon)** adorare.

double, 1. *n. and adj.* dóppio (*m.*). **2.** *vb.* doppiare.

double bass, *n.* contrabbasso *m.*

double-breasted, *adj.* a dóppio pètto.

double-cross, *vb.* ingannare.

double-dealing, *n.* duplicità *f.*

double-decker, *n.* àutobus a due piani *m.*

double-jointed, *adj.* snodato.

double-park, *vb.* parcheggiare in dóppia fila.

double standard, *n.* due pesi e due misure *m.pl.*

double time, *n.* passo di càrica *m.*

doubly, *adv.* doppiamente.

doubt, 1. *n.* dùbbio *m.* **2.** *vb.* dubitare.

doubter, *n.* scèttico *m.*

doubtful, *adj.* dùbbio, dubbioso.

doubtless, *adv.* senza dùbbio.

dough, *n.* pasta *f.*

doughnut, *n.* ciambella *f.*

doughy, *adj.* pastoso, molle.

dour, *adj.* sevèro.

douse, *vb.* spègnere.

dove, *n.* colombo *m.*

dowager, *n.* vècchia ricca e tirànnica *f.*

dowdy, *adj.* sciatto.

dowel, *n.* tassèllo *m.*

down, 1. *n.* (on face; bird) pelùria

f.; (feathers) piumino *m.* **2.** *adv.* giù. **3.** *prep.* giù per.

downcast, *adj.* abbassato.

downfall, *n.* rovina *f.*

downhearted, *adj.* scoraggiato.

downhill, *adv.* in discesa.

down payment, *n.* anticipo *m.*

downpour, *n.* rovèscio di piòggia *m.*

downright, *adj.* chiaro, completo.

downstairs, *adv.* giù per le scale.

downstream, *adv.* a valle.

downtown, *n.* centro della città *m.*

downtrend, *n.* tendenza al ribasso *f.*

downtrodden, *adj.* opprèsso.

downward, *adv.* in giù.

downy, *adj.* copèrto di pelùria *f.*

dowry, *n.* dòte *f.*

doze, 1. *n.* sonnellino *m.*, pisolino *m.* **2.** *vb.* sonnecchiare.

dozen, *n.* dozzina *f.*

drab, *adj.* grigio.

draft, 1. *n.* (plan) abbozzo *m.*; (money) tratta *f.*; (ship) pescàggio *m.*; (air) corrènte d'ària *f.*; (military service) servizio militare *m.* **2.** *vb.* (draw up) redìgere.

draft beer, *n.* birra alla spina *f.*

draft dodger, *n.* renitente alla leva *m.*; imboscato *m.*

draftee, *n.* rècluta *f.*

draftsman, *n.* disegnatore *m.*

drafty, *adj.* pièno di corrènti d'ària.

drag, *vb.* trascinare.

dragnet, *n.* giàcchio *m.*

dragon, *n.* dragone *m.*

drain, 1. *n.* fogna *f.* **2.** *vb.* scolare.

drainage, *n.* drenàggio *m.*

dram, *n.* dramma *m.*

drama, *n.* dramma *m.*

dramatic, *adj.* drammàtico.

dramatics, *n.* drammàtica *f.*

dramatist, *n.* drammaturgo *m.*

dramatize, *vb.* drammatizzare.

dramaturgy, *n.* drammaturgìa *f.*

drape, 1. *n.* drappéggio *m.* **2.** *vb.* drappeggiare.

drapery, *n.* drappéggio *m.*

drastic, *adj.* dràstico.

draught, see **draft.**

draw, *vb.* (pull) tirare; (picture) disegnare; **(d. back)** ritirarsi; **(d. up)** stèndere.

drawback, *n.* svantàggio *m.*

drawbridge, *n.* ponte levatòio *m.*

drawer, *n.* cassetto *m.*

drawing, *n.* (picture) disegno *m.*; (lottery) sortéggio *m.*

drawl, *vb.* parlare lentamente.

dray, *n.* carro *m.*

drayhorse, *n.* cavallo da tiro *m.*

drayman, *n.* carrettière *m.*

dread, 1. *n.* timore *m.* **2.** *vb.* temere.

dreadful, *adj.* terribile.

dreadfully, *adv.* terribilmente.

dream, 1. *n.* sogno *m.* **2.** *vb.* sognare.

dreamer, *n.* sognatore *m.*

dreamy, *adj.* vago.

dreary, *adj.* fosco.

dredge, 1. *n.* draga *f.* **2.** *vb.* dragare.

dregs, *n.* fèccia *f.sg.*

drench, *vb.* inzuppare.

dress, 1. *n.* vestito *m.*, àbito *m.* **2.** *vb.* vestire.

dresser, *n.* credènza *f.*

dressing, *n.* (food) condimento *m.*, (medical) bende *f.pl.*

dressing gown, *n.* vestàglia *f.*

dressmaker, *n.* sarta da dònna *f.*

dress rehearsal, *n.* pròva generale *f.*

drier, *n.* essiccatòio *m.*

drift, 1. *n.* deriva *f.* **2.** *vb.* andare alla deriva.

driftwood, *n.* legno flottante *m.*

drill, 1. *n.* (tool) tràpano *m.*; (practice) esercitazione *f.* **2.** *vb.* trapanare; esercitare.

drink, 1. *n.* bevanda *f.*, bíbita *f.* **2.** *vb.* bere.

drinkable, *adj.* bevìbile.

drinker, *n.* bevitore *m.*

drinking water, *n.* àcqua potàbile *f.*

drip, 1. *n.* gocciolio *m.* **2.** *vb.* gocciolare.

drive, 1. *n.* (ride) passeggiata in carrozza *f.*; (avenue) viale *m.* **2.** *vb.* costrìngere; (auto) guidare.

drivel, 1. *n.* bava *f.* **2.** *vb.* sbavare.

driver, *n.* conducènte *m.*, autista *m.*

driver's license, n. patente di guida f.

driveway, n. passo carràbile m.

drizzle, 1. n. pioggerèlla f. **2.** vb. piovigginare.

droll, adj. buffo, spassoso.

dromedary, n. dromedàrio m.

drone, 1. n. (bee) fuco m.; (hum) ronzìo m. **2.** vb. ronzare.

drool, vb. sbavare.

droop, vb. abbattersi.

drop, 1. n. góccia f. **2.** vb. (fall) cadere; (let fall) lasciar cadere.

dropout, n. studente che lascia definitivamente la scuola m.

dropper, n. contagócce m.

dropsy, n. idropisìa f.

dross, n. scòria f.

drought, n. siccità f.

drove, n. màndria f.

drown, vb. annegare.

drowse, vb. sonnecchiare, assopirsi.

drowsiness, n. sonnolènza f.

drowsy, adj. sonnolènto.

drub, vb. battere.

drudge, vb. lavorare duramente.

drudgery, n. lavoro monòtono m.

drug, n. dròga f.

drug addict, n. tòssico dipendente m.

druggist, n. farmacista m.

drug store, n. farmacìa f.

drug traffic, n. narcotràffico m.

drum, n. tamburo m.

drum major, n. tamburo maggiore m.

drummer, n. tamburo m.

drumstick, n. (lit.) bacchetta del tamburo m.; (chicken) gamba di pollo f.

drunk, adj. ubriaco.

drunkard, n. ubriacóne. m.

drunken, adj. ubriaco.

drunkenness, n. ubriachezza f.

dry, 1. adj. secco, asciutto. **2.** vb. seccare, asciugare.

dry cell, n. pila a secco f.

dry-clean, vb. lavare a secco.

dry-cleaner, n. tintore m.

dry-cleaning, n. lavàggio a secco m.

dry dock, n. bacino di carenàggio m.

dry goods, n. stoffe f.pl.; tessuti m.pl.

dry law, n. legge proibizionista f.

dryness, n. secchezza f.

dry run, n. esercitazione f.

dual, n. and adj. duale (m.).

dualism, n. dualismo m.

dubbing, n. doppiàggio m.

dubious, adj. dùbbio.

duchess, n. duchessa f.

duchy, n. ducato f.

duck, 1. n. ànitra f. **2.** vb. tuffare.

duct, n. canale m.

ductile, adj. dùttile.

dud, n. bomba inesplòsa f.; (failure) fiasco m.

due, adj. dèbito, dovuto; **(fall d.)** scadere.

duel, 1. n. duèllo m. **2.** vb. duellare.

duelist, n. duellante m.

dues, n. quòta f.; (tax) diritti m.

duet, n. duetto m.

duffle bag, n. zàino m.

dugout, n. trincèa f.

duke, n. duca m.

dukedom, n. ducato m.

dulcet, adj. armonioso.

dull, 1. adj. monòtono, ottuso, insulso. **2.** vb. ottùndere.

dullard, n. stùpido m.

dullness, n. monotonìa f., ottusità f.

duly, adv. debitamente.

dumb, adj. muto; (stupid) sciocco.

dumbfound, vb. sbalordire.

dumbwaiter, n. calapranzi m., calapiatti m.

dummy, n. fantòccio m.

dump, vb. scaricare.

dumpling, n. gnòcco m.

dun, adj. grigio fosco.

dunce, n. stolto m.

dune, n. duna f.

dung, n. stèrco m., letame m.

dungarees, n. tuta f.sg.

dungeon, n. prigione sotterrànea f.

dunk, vb. tuffare, inzuppare.

dupe, n. credulone m.

duplex, n. dóppio.

duplicate, vb. duplicare.

duplication, n. duplicazione f.

duplicity, n. duplicità f.

durable, adj. duràbile.

durability, n. durabilità f.

duration, n. durata f.

duress, n. coercizione f.

during, prep. durante.

dusk, n. crepúscolo m.

dusky, adj. fosco.

dust, n. pólvere m.; (sweepings) spazzatura f.

dustpan, n. paletta per spazzature f.

dusty, adj. polveroso.

Dutch, adj. olandese.

Dutchman, n. olandese m.

dutiful, adj. obbediènte.

dutifully, adv. con ubbidiènza.

duty, n. dovere m.; (tax) imposta f.

duty-free, adj. esente da dogana.

dwarf, n. nano m.

dwell, vb. abitare; **(d. upon)** diffóndersi su.

dweller, n. abitante m.

dwelling, n. abitazione f., dimora f.

dwindle, vb. diminuire.

dye, 1. n. tintura f. **2.** vb. tíngere.

dyer, n. tintore m.

dyestuff, n. matèria colorante f.

dynamic, adj. dinàmico.

dynamics, n. dinàmica f.

dynamite, n. dinamite f.

dynamo, n. dínamo f.

dynasty, n. dinastía f.

dysentery, n. dissentería f.

dyslexia, n. dislessia f.

dyspepsia, n. dispepsía f.

dyspeptic, adj. dispèptico.

E

each, adj. ogni.

each one, pron. ciascuno, cadaùno.

each other, pron. l'un l'altro; or use reflexive.

eager, adj. bramoso, impaziènte.

eagerly, adv. bramosamente, impazientemente.

eagerness, n. brama f., impaziènza f.

eagle, n. àquila f.

eaglet, n. aquilòtto m.

ear, n. orécchio m.; (grain) spiga f.

earache, n. mal d'orecchi (m.)

eardrum, n. tímpano m.

earflap, n. paraorecchi m.

earl, n. conte m.

early, adv. di buon'ora, prèsto.

early bird, n. persona mattiniera f.

earmark, vb. riservare.

earn, vb. guadagnare; (deserve) meritare.

earnest, adj. sèrio; **(in e.)** sul sèrio.

earnestly, adv. seriamente.

earnestness, n. serietà f.

earnings, n. guadagni m.pl.

earphone, n. cùffia f.

earring, n. orecchino m.

earshot, n. portata di voce f.

earsplitting, adj. assordante.

earth, n. tèrra f.

earthenware, n. stovíglie f.pl.

earthling, n. terrestre m.

earthly, adj. terreno.

earthmover, n. ruspa f.

earthquake, n. terremòto m.

earthworm, n. lombrico m.

earthy, adj. terreno.

earwax, n. cerume m.

ease, 1. n. àgio m., còmodo m. **2.** vb. sollevare.

easel, n. cavalletto m.

easily, adv. facilmente.

easiness, n. facilità f.

east, n. èst m., oriènte m.

Easter, n. Pasqua f.

easterly, adj. ad est, da est.

eastern, adj. orientale.

eastward, adv. vèrso èst.

easy, adj. fàcile.

easygoing, adj. noncurante.

eat, vb. mangiare.

eatable, adj. mangiàbile.

eaves, n. gronda f.sg.

eavesdrop, vb. origliare.

ebb, 1. n. riflusso m.; **(ebb-tide)** bassa marèa f. **2.** vb. rifluire.

ebony, n. èbano m.

ebullient, adj. esuberante.

eccentric, adj. eccèntrico.

eccentricity, n. eccentricità f.

ecclesiastic, n. and adj. ecclesiàstico (m.)

ecclesiastical, adj. ecclesiàstico.

echelon, n. scaglione m.
echo, 1. n. èco m. 2. vb. echeggiare.
eclipse, 1. n. eclissi f. 2. vb. eclissare.
ecology, n. ecología f.
ecological, adj. ecológico.
economic, adj. econòmico.
economical, adj. econòmico.
economics, n. economía política f.
economist, n. economista m.
economize, vb. economizzare.
economy, n. economía f.
ecru, adj. (colore di) seta cruda.
ecumenical, adj. ecumènico.
ecstasy, n. èstasi f.
eczema, n. eczèma m.
eddy, n. vòrtice m.
edge, n. bordo m.; màrgine m.; orlo m.
edging, n. orlatura f.
edgy, adj. irritàbile.
edible, adj. mangiàbile.
edict, n. editto m.
edifice, n. edificio m.
edify, vb. edificare.
edifying, adj. edificante.
edit, vb. (journal) dirígere; (book) curare l'edizione di.
edition, n. edizione f.
editor, n. (journal) direttore m.
editorial, 1. n. artícolo di fondo m. 2. adj. editoriale.
educate, vb. educare.
education, n. educazione f.
educational, adj. educativo.
educator, n. educatore m.
eel, n. anguilla f.
eerie, adj. spettrale.
efface, vb. cancellare.
effect, 1. n. effètto m.; (in e.) effettivamente. 2. vb. effettuare.
effective, adj. effettivo.
effectively, adv. effettivamente.
effectiveness, n. effettività f.
effectual, adj. efficace.
effeminate, adj. effeminato.
effervescence, n. effervescènza f.
effete, adj. effeminato.
efficacious, adj. efficace.
efficacy, n. efficàcia f.
efficiency, n. efficiènza f.
efficient, adj. efficiènte.
efficiently, adv. efficientemente.

effigy, n. effigie f.
effort, n. sforzo m.; (make an e.) sforzarsi.
effortless, adj. sènza sforzo.
effrontery, n. sfrontatezza f.
effulgent, adj. risplendènte.
effusive, adj. espansivo.
egg, n. uòvo m.
eggplant, n. melanzana f.
ego, n. ío m.
egoism, n. egoismo m.
egotism, n. egotismo m.
egotist, n. egotista m.
Egypt, n. l'Egitto m.
Egyptian, adj. egiziano.
eight, num. òtto.
eighteen, num. diciòtto.
eighteenth, adj. diciottésimo, decimottavo.
eighth, adj. ottavo.
eightieth, adj. ottantésimo.
eighty, num. ottanta.
either, 1. pron. l'uno o l'altro. 2. conj. o; od; sia; (either . . . or) o . . . o; sia . . . che.
ejaculate, vb. (med.) eiaculare; (fig.) esclamare.
eject, vb. espèllere.
ejection, n. espulsione f.
eke out, vb. supplire a.
elaborate, 1. adj. elaborato. 2. vb. elaborare.
elapse, vb. trascórrere.
elastic, n. and adj. elàstico (m.)
elasticity, n. elasticità f.
elate, vb. esaltare.
elated, adj. esaltato.
elation, n. esaltazione f.
elbow, n. gómito m.
elbowroom, n. spàzio líbero m.
elder, 1. n. (older person) maggiore m.; (tree) sambuco m. 2. adj. maggiore.
elderberry, n. frutto del sambuco m.
elderly, adj. vècchio.
eldest, adj. (il) maggiore.
elect, vb. elèggere.
election, n. elezione f.
electioneer, vb. cercare voti.
elective, adj. elettivo.
electorate, n. votanti m.pl.
electric, electrical, adj. elèttrico.
electric eel, n. anguilla elèttrica f.; gimnòto m.

electrician, n. elettricista m.
electricity, n. elettricità f.
electrocardiogram, n. elettrocardiogramma m.
electrocution, n. elettrocuzione f.
electrode, n. elèttrodo m.
electrolysis, n. elettròlisi f.
electron, n. elettrone m.
electronic, adj. elettrònico.
electronics, n. elettrònica f.
electroplating, n. galvanoplàstica f.
elegance, n. eleganza f.
elegant, adj. elegante.
elegiac, adj. elegíaco.
elegy, n. elegia f.
element, n. elemento m.
elemental, elementary, adj. elementare.
elephant, n. elefante m.
elephantine, adj. elefantesco.
elevate, vb. elevare.
elevation, n. elevazione f.
elevator, n. ascensore m.
eleven, num. ùndici.
eleventh, adj. undicésimo.
eleventh hour, n. ultimo momento m., zona cesarini f.
elf, n. folletto m.
elfin, adj. di folletto.
elicit, vb. cavar fuòri.
elide, vb. elidere.
eligibility, n. eleggibilità f.
eligible, adj. eleggibile.
eliminate, vb. eliminare.
elimination, n. eliminazione f.
elision, n. elisione f.
elite, adj. eletto; d'elite.
elixir, n. elisír m.
elk, n. alce m.
ellipse, n. elissi f.
elliptic, adj. elittico.
elm, n. olmo m.
elocution, n. elocuzione f.
elongate, vb. allungare.
elope, vb. fuggire.
eloquence, n. eloquènza f.
eloquent, adj. eloquènte.
eloquently, adv. eloquentemente.
else, 1. adj. altro. **2.** adv. altrimenti.
elsewhere, adv. altrove.
elucidate, vb. elucidare.
elude, vb. elùdere.

elusive, adv. elusivo.
emaciated, adj. emaciato.
emanate, vb. emanare.
emancipate, vb. emancipare.
emancipation, n. emancipazione f.
emancipator, n. emancipatore m.
emasculate, vb. castrare.
embalm, vb. imbalsamare.
embankment, n. àrgine m.
embargo, n. embargo m.
embark, vb. imbarcare.
embarrass, vb. imbarazzare.
embarrassing, adj. imbarazzante.
embarrassment, n. imbarazzo m.
embassy, n. ambasciata f.
embed, vb. incassare.
embellish, vb. abbellire.
embellishment, n. abbellimento m.
embers, n. brace f.sg.
embezzle, vb. appropriarsi fraudolentemente.
embezzlement, n. malversazione f., peculato m.
embitter, vb. amareggiare.
emblazon, vb. adornare, illustrare.
emblem, n. emblèma m.
emblematic, adj. emblemàtico.
embody, vb. incorporare.
embolden, vb. imbaldanzire.
emboss, vb. stampare in rilièvo.
embrace, 1. n. abbràccio m.; (sexual) amplèsso m. **2.** vb. abbracciare.
embroider, vb. ricamare.
embroidery, n. ricamo m.
embroil, vb. imbrogliare.
embryo, n. embrione m.
embryology, n. embriologia f.
embryonic, adj. embrionale.
emend, vb. emendare.
emerald, n. smeraldo m.
emerge, vb. emèrgere.
emergency, n. emergènza f.
emergent, adj. emergènte.
emery, n. smeríglio m.
emetic, n. and adj. emètico (m.)
emigrant, n. and adj. emigrante (m.)
emigrate, vb. emigrare.
emigration, n. emigrazione f.
eminence, n. eminènza f.

eminent, *adj.* eminènte.

emissary, *n.* emissàrio *m.*

emission controls, *n.pl.* apparécchio per limitare l'emissione di fumi nocivi *m.*

emit, *vb.* eméttere.

emollient, *n. and adj.* emolliènte *(m.)*

emolument, *n.* emolumento *m.*

emotion, *n.* emozione *f.*

emotional, *adj.* emotivo; (easily moved) emozionàbile.

emperor, *n.* imperatore *m.*

emphasis, *n.* ènfasi *f.*

emphasize, *vb.* méttere in rilièvo.

emphatic, *adj.* enfàtico.

empire, *n.* impèro *m.*

empirical, *adj.* empírico.

employ, **1.** *n.* impiègo *m.,* servízio *m.* **2.** *vb.* impiegare.

employed, *n.* addetto.

employee, *n.* impiegato *m.,* impiegata *f.*

employer, *n.* datore di lavoro *m.;* (boss) padrone *m.*

employment, *n.* impiègo *m.*

empower, *vb.* autorizzare.

empress, *n.* imperatrice *f.*

emptiness, *n.* vuòto *m.*

empty, **1.** *adj.* vuòto. **2.** *vb.* vuotare.

emulate, *vb.* emulare.

emulsion, *n.* emulsione *f.*

enable, *vb.* méttere in grado di.

enact, *vb.* decretare.

enactment, *n.* decreto *m.*

enamel, **1.** *n.* smalto *m.* **2.** *vb.* smaltare.

enamor, *vb.* innamorare.

encamp, *vb.* accamparsi.

encampment, *n.* accampamento *m.*

encephalitis, *n.* encefalite *f.*

encephalon, *n.* encèfalo *m.*

enchant, *vb.* incantare.

enchanting, *adj.* incantévole.

enchantment, *n.* incanto *m.*

encircle, *vb.* accerchiare.

enclose, *vb.* rinchiùdere; (with letter) acclùdere.

enclosure, *n.* recinto *m.*

encompass, *vb.* (surround) circondare; (cause) causare.

encore, *n.* bis *m.*

encounter, **1.** *n.* incontro *m.* **2.** *vb.* incontrare.

encourage, *vb.* incoraggiare, confortare.

encouragement, *n.* incoraggiamento *m.*

encroach upon, *vb.* usurpare.

encumber, *vb.* ingombrare.

encyclical, *n.* encíclica *f.*

encyclopaedia, *n.* enciclopedía *f.*

end, **1.** *n.* fine *f.,* tèrmine *m.;* (aim) scòpo *m.* **2.** *adj.* última. **3.** *vb.* finire, terminare.

endanger, *vb.* méttere in perícolo.

endear, *vb.* rèndere caro.

endearment, *n.* carezza *f.*

endeavor, **1.** *n.* sforzo *m.* **2.** *vb.* sforzarsi.

endemic, *adj.* endèmico.

ending, *n.* fine *f.;* (gram.) desinènza *f.*

endive, *n.* indívia *f.*

endless, *adj.* sènza fine.

endocrine, *adj.* endòcrino.

endorse, *vb.* firmare; (cheques, etc.) girare.

endorsee, *n.* giratàrio *m.*

endorsement, *n.* girata *f.*

endorser, *n.* girante *m.;* responsabile *m.*

endow, *vb.* dotare.

endowment, *n.* dotazione *f.*

endurance, *n.* sopportazione *f.*

endure, *vb.* sopportare; (last) durare.

enduring, *adj.* durévole.

enema, *n.* clistère *m.;* (colonic irrigation) enteroclisma *m.*

enemy, *n. and adj.* nemico *(m.)*

energetic, *adj.* enèrgico.

energy, *n.* energía *f.*

enervate, *vb.* snervare.

enervation, *n.* snervamento *m.*

enfeeble, *vb.* indebolire.

enfold, *vb.* avvòlgere.

enforce, *vb.* eseguire.

enforcement, *n.* esecuzione *f.*

enfranchise, *vb.* affrancare.

engage, *vb.* (hire) prèndere a nolo; (attention) attrarre; (to get married) fidanzare.

engaged, *adj.* (to get married) fidanzato.

engagement, n. (to get married) fidanzamento m.; (date) appuntamento m.

engaging, adj. attraènte.

engender, vb. generare.

engine, n. màcchina f.; (locomotive) locomotiva f.

engineer, n. ingegnère m.; (train driver) macchinista m.

engineering, n. ingegnería f., gènio m.

England, n. Inghilterra f.

English, adj. inglese.

Englishman, n. inglese m.

Englishwoman, n. inglese f.

engrave, vb. incidere.

engraver, n. incisore m.

engraving, n. incisione f.

engross, vb. (absorb) assorbire; (copy) copiare.

engrossing, adj. assorbente.

engulf, vb. sommergere.

enhance, vb. aumentare, accréscere.

enigma, n. enigma m.

enigmatic, adj. enigmàtico.

enjoin, vb. (command) ingiùngere; (forbid) vietare.

enjoy, vb. godere.

enjoyable, adj. godìbile, piacévole.

enjoyment, n. godimento m.

enlace, vb. allacciare.

enlarge, vb. aumentare; ingrandire.

enlargement, n. ingrandimento m.

enlarger, n. ingranditore m.

enlighten, vb. illuminare.

enlightenment, n. chiarimento m.

enlist, vb. arruolare.

enlisted man, n. uòmo di truppa m.

enlistment, n. arruolamento m.

enliven, vb. ravvivare.

enmesh, vb. inviluppare.

enmity, n. inimicìzia f.

ennoble, vb. innobilire; nobilitare.

ennui, n. nòia f.

enormity, n. enormità f.

enormous, adj. enòrme.

enormously, adv. enormemente.

enough, 1. adj. sufficiènte. **2.** adv. abbastanza. **3.** vb. (be e.) bastare.

enrage, vb. far arrabbiare.

enrapture, vb. estasiare.

enrich, vb. arricchire.

enroll, vb. iscrìvere, registrare; (mil.) arruolare.

enrollment, n. iscrizione f., registrazione f.

en route, adv. in cammino.

ensemble, n. insième m.

enshrine, vb. méttere in un reliquàrio.

ensign, n. (flag) bandièra f., insegna f.; (rank) alfière m.

enslave, vb. asservire.

enslavement, n. asservimento m.

ensnare, vb. prèndere in tràppola.

ensue, vb. (follow) seguire; (happen) accadere.

ensuing, adj. risultante, conseguente.

ensure, vb. garantire.

entail, vb. comportare, richièdere.

entailment, n. conseguènza f., deduzione f.

entangle, vb. aggrovigliare.

entanglement, n. groviglio m.

enter, vb. entrare.

enterprise, n. impresa f.

enterprising, adj. avventuroso.

entertain, vb. trattenere; (guests) accògliere; (amuse) divertire.

entertainment, n. trattenimento m.; (amusement) divertimento m.

enthrall, vb. incantare.

enthusiasm, n. entusiasmo m.

enthusiast, n. entusiasta m.

enthusiastic, adj. entusiàstico.

entice, vb. adescare.

entire, adj. intero.

entirely, adj. interamente.

entirety, n. totalità f.

entitle, vb. intitolare; (authorize) autorizzare.

entity, n. entità f.

entomb, vb. seppellire.

entombment, n. sepoltura f.

entrails, n. interiora f.pl.

entrain, vb. prèndere il treno.

entrance, n. entrata f., ingròsso m.

entrant, n. concorrènte m.

entrap, vb. intrappolare.

entreat, vb. supplicare.

entreaty, n. sùpplica f.

entree, n. entrata f.; portata f.

entrench, *vb.* trincerare.
entrepreneur, *n.* imprenditore *m.*
entrust, *vb.* affidare.
entry, *n.* entrata *f.*, ingresso *m.*
enumerate, *vb.* enumerare.
enumeration, *n.* enumerazione *f.*
enunciate, *vb.* enunciare.
enunciation, *n.* enunciazione *f.*
envelop, *vb.* avviluppare.
envelope, *n.* busta *f.*
enviable, *adj.* invidiàbile.
envious, *adj.* invidioso.
environment, *n.* ambiènte *m.*
environmentalist, *n.* fautore della preservazione dell'ambiente *m.*
environmental protection, *n.* protezione dell'ambiente *f.*
environs, *n.* dintorni *m.pl.*
envisage, *vb.* figurarsi.
envoy, *n.* inviato *m.*
envy, 1. *n.* invidia *f.* **2.** *vb.* invidiare.
eon, *n.* eternità *f.*
ephemeral, *adj.* effìmero.
epic, 1. *n.* epopèa *f.* **2.** *adj.* èpico.
epicure, *n.* epicurèo *m.*
epidemic, 1. *n.* epidemìa *f.* **2.** *adj.* epidèmico.
epidermis, *n.* epidèrmide *f.*
epigram, *n.* epigramma *m.*
epilepsy, *n.* epilessìa *f.*
epilogue, *n.* epìlogo *m.*
episode, *n.* episòdio *m.*
epistle, *n.* epìstola *f.*
epitaph, *n.* epitàffio *m.*
epithet, *n.* epìteto *m.*
epitome, *n.* epìtome *f.*
epitomize, *vb.* epitomare.
epoch, *n.* època *f.*
equable, *adj.* èquo.
equal, 1. *adj.* uguale, pari. **2.** *vb.* uguagliare.
equality, *n.* uguaglianza *f.*
equalize, *vb.* uguagliare.
equanimity, *n.* equanimità *f.*
equate, *vb.* uguagliare.
equation, *n.* equazione *f.*
equator, *n.* equatore *m.*
equatorial, *adj.* equatoriale.
equestrian, *adj.* equèstre.
equidistant, *adj.* equidistante.
equilateral, *adj.* equilaterale.
equilibrate, *vb.* equilibrare.
equilibrium, *n.* equilìbrio *m.*

equinox, *n.* equinòzio *m.*
equip, *vb.* corredare, fornire.
equipment, *n.* equipàggio *m.*, corrèdo *m.*
equitable, *adj.* èquo.
equity, *n.* equità *f.*
equivalent, *adj.* equivalente; **(be e.)** equivalere.
equivocal, *adj.* equìvoco.
equivocate, *vb.* giocare sull'equìvoco.
era, *n.* èra *f.*
eradicate, *vb.* sradicare.
eradicator, *n.* sradicatore *m.*
erase, *vb.* cancellare, raschiare.
eraser, *n.* raschino *m.*, cancellino *m.*
erasure, *n.* cancellatura *f.*
erect, 1. *adj.* erètto. **2.** *vb.* erìgere, costruire.
erection, *n.* erezione *f.*, costruzione *f.*
erectness, *n.* posizione erètta *f.*
ermine, *n.* ermellino *m.*
erode, *vb.* eródere.
erosion, *n.* erosione *f.*
erosive, *adj.* erosivo.
erotic, *adj.* eròtico.
err, *vb.* errare.
errand, *n.* commissione *f.*
errand boy, *n.* fattorino *m.*; messo *m.*
errant, *adj.* errante.
erratic, *adj.* erràtico.
erroneous, *adj.* erròneo.
error, *n.* errore *m.*
erudite, *adj.* erudito.
erudition, *n.* erudizione *f.*
erupt, *vb.* eruttare.
eruption, *n.* eruzione *f.*
escalate, *vb.* aumentare.
escalator, *n.* scala mòbile *f.*
escapade, *n.* scappatella *f.*
escape, 1. *n.* fuga *f.*, scampo *m.* **2.** *vb.* sfuggire, scappare.
escapism, *n.* desidèrio di sfuggire alla realtà *m.*
escarpment, *n.* scarpata *f.*
eschew, *vb.* evitare.
escort, 1. *n.* scòrta *f.* **2.** *vb.* scortare.
esculent, *adj.* esculènto.
escutcheon, *n.* scudo *m.*
esophagus, *n.* esòfago *m.*
esoteric, *adj.* esotèrico.

espalier, n. spalliera f.

especial, adj. speciale.

especially, adv. specialmente.

espionage, n. spionàggio m.

esplanade, n. spianata f.; piazzale m.

espousal, n. sposalízio m.

espouse, vb. sposare.

essay, 1. n. sàggio m. **2.** vb. provare.

essayist, n. saggista m.

essence, n. essènza f.

essential, adj. essenziale.

essentially, adv. essenzialmente.

establish, vb. stabilire.

establishment, n. stabilimento m.

estate, n. (inheritance) patrimònio m.; (possessions) bèni m.pl.; (condition) condizione f., stato m.

esteem, 1. n. stima f.

esthete, n. esteta m.

esthetic, adj. estètico.

estimable, adj. stimàbile.

estimate, 1. n. valutazione f., stima f. **2.** vb. valutare, stimare.

estimation, n. stima f., valutazione f.

estrange, vb. alienare.

estrangement, n. disaffezione m.

estuary, n. estuàrio m.

etching, n. acquafòrte f.

eternal, adj. etèrno.

eternity, n. eternità f.

ether, n. ètere m.

ethereal, adj. etèreo.

ethical, adj. ètico.

ethics, n. ètica f.

ethnic, adj. ètnico.

etiquette, n. galatèo m.

etymology, n. etimologia f.

eucalyptus, n. eucalipto m.

eugenic, adj. eugènico.

eugenics, n. eugenètica f.

eulogize, vb. elogiare.

eulogy, n. elògio m.

eunuch, n. eunuco m.

euphonious, adj. eufònico.

Europe, n. Europa f.

European, n. and adj. europèo (m.)

euthanasia, n. eutanasia f.

evacuate, vb. evacuare.

evade, vb. evitare, elùdere.

evaluate, vb. valutare.

evaluation, n. valutazione f.

evanescent, adj. evanescènte.

evangelist, n. evangelista m.

evaporate, vb. evaporare.

evaporation, n. evaporazione f.

evasion, n. evasione f.

evasive, adj. evasivo.

eve, n. vigília f.

even, 1. adj. pari, giusto, uniforme. **2.** adv. anche, perfino.

evening, n. sera f.

evenness, n. uniformità f.

event, n. avvenimento m.

eventful, adj. pièno di avvenimenti.

eventual, adj. finale.

ever, adv. sèmpre, mai.

everglade, n. palude f.

evergreen, adj. sempreverde.

everlasting, adj. sempitèrno.

every, adj. ogni.

everybody, pron. ognuno.

everyday, adj. quotidiano.

everyone, pron. ognuno.

everything, pron. tutto.

everywhere, adv. dappertutto.

evict, vb. espèllere.

eviction, n. espulsione f.

evidence, n. evidènza f.

evident, adj. evidènte; (be e.) risultare.

evidently, adv. evidentemente.

evil, 1. n. male m. **2.** adj. cattivo.

evildoer, n. malvagio m.

evil eye, n. malòcchio m.

evil-minded, adj. malintenzionato.

evince, vb. manifestare.

eviscerate, vb. sviscerare.

evoke, vb. evocare.

evolution, n. evoluzione f.

evolutionist, n. evoluzionista m.

evolve, vb. evòlvere.

ewe, n. pècora f.

exacerbate, vb. esacerbare.

exact, 1. adj. esatto. **2.** vb. esigere.

exacting, adj. esigente.

exaction, n. esazione f.

exactly, adv. esattamente.

exaggerate, vb. esagerare.

exaggeration, n. esagerazione f.

exalt, vb. esaltare.

exaltation, n. esaltazione f.

examination, n. esame m.

examine, vb. esaminare.

example, n. esèmpio m.

exasperate, vb. esasperare.

exasperation, n. esasperazione f.

excavate, vb. scavare.

excavation, n. scavo m.

exceed, vb. eccèdere, superare.

exceedingly, adv. estremamente.

excel, vb. eccèllere, superare.

excellence, n. eccellènza f.

Excellency, n. Eccellènza f.

excellent, adj. eccellènte.

except, 1. vb. eccettuare. **2.** prep. eccètto, salvo, tranne; **(e. for)** all'infuòri di.

exception, n. eccezione f.

exceptional, adj. eccezionale.

excerpt, n. brano m.

excess, n. eccèsso m.

excess fare, n. supplemento m.

excessive, adj. eccessivo.

exchange, 1. n. scàmbio m. **2.** vb. scambiare.

exchangeable, adj. scambiàbile.

excise, n. dàzio m.

excitable, adj. eccitàbile.

excite, vb. eccitare.

excitement, n. eccitamento m., eccitazione f.

exclaim, vb. esclamare.

exclamation, n. esclamazione f.

exclamation point or mark, n. punto esclamativo m.

exclude, vb. esclùdere.

exclusion, n. esclusione f.

exclusive, adj. esclusivo.

excogitate, vb. escogitare.

excommunicate, vb. scomunicare.

excommunication, n. scomùnica f.

excoriate, vb. escoriare.

excrement, n. escremento m.

excruciating, adj. tormentoso.

exculpate, vb. discolpare.

excursion, n. escursione f.

excusable, adj. scusàbile.

excuse, 1. n. scusa f. **2.** vb. scusare.

execrable, adj. esecràbile.

execute, vb. eseguire; (kill legally) giustiziare.

execution, n. esecuzione f.; (legal killing) esecuzione capitale f.

executioner, n. bòia m., carnéfice m.

executive, 1. n. amministratore m. **2.** adj. esecutivo.

executor, n. esecutore m.

exemplary, adj. esemplare.

exemplify, vb. esemplificare.

exempt, 1. adj. esènte. **2.** vb. esentare.

exercise, 1. n. esercízio m. **2.** vb. esercitare.

exert, vb. esercitare.

exertion, n. sforzo m.

exhale, vb. esalare.

exhaust, vb. esaurire.

exhaustion, n. esaurimento m.

exhaustive, adj. esauriénte.

exhibit, 1. n. mostra f. **2.** vb. esibire, mostrare.

exhibition, n. esibizione f., mostra f.

exhibitionism, n. esibizionismo m.

exhibitor, n. espositore m.

exhilarating, adj. esilarante.

exhilarate, vb. esilarare.

exhort, vb. esortare.

exhortation, n. esortazione f.

exhume, vb. esumare.

exigency, n. esigénza f.

exile, 1. n. esílio m.; (person) fuoruscito m. **2.** vb. esiliare.

exist, vb. esístere.

existence, n. esistènza f.

existent, adj. esistènte.

existing, adj. esistente.

exit, n. uscita f.

exodus, n. èsodo m.

exonerate, vb. esonerare.

exorbitant, adj. esorbitante.

exorcise, vb. esorcizzare; (chase away) scacciare.

exotic, adj. esòtico.

expand, vb. espàndere.

expanse, n. distesa f.

expansion, n. espansione f.

expansive, adj. espansivo.

expatiate, vb. diffóndersi.

expatriate, n. espatriato m.

expect, vb. aspettarsi.

expectancy, n. aspettativa f.

expectation, n. aspettativa f.

expectorate, vb. espettorare.

expediency, n. opportunità f.

expedient, 1. *n.* espediènte *m.* **2.** *adj.* espediènte, opportuno.

expedite, *vb.* sbrigare.

expedition, *n.* spedizione *f.*

expeditious, *adj.* sbrigativo, spiccio.

expel, *vb.* espèllere.

expend, *vb.* spèndere, consumare.

expendable, *adj.* spendìbile; sacrificàbile.

expenditure, *n.* spesa *f.*

expense, *n.* spesa *f.*

expensive, *adj.* costoso.

expensively, *adv.* costosamente.

experience, 1. *n.* esperiènza *f.* **2.** *vb.* sperimentare.

experienced, *adj.* espèrto.

experiment, 1. *n.* esperimento *m.* **2.** *vb.* sperimentare.

experimental, *adj.* sperimentale.

expert, *n. and adj.* espèrto (*m.*).

expertise, *n.* maestrìa .

expiate, *vb.* espiare.

expiation, *n.* espiazione. *f.*

expiration, *n.* espirazione *f.*

expire, *vb.* espirare, morire.

explain, *vb.* spiegare.

explainable, *adj.* spiegàbile.

explanation, *n.* spiegazione *f.*

explanatory, *adj.* esplicativo.

expletive, 1. *n.* bestémmia *f.* **2.** *adj.* espletivo.

explicit, *adj.* esplìcito.

explode, *vb.* esplòdere, scoppiare.

exploit, *vb.* sfruttare.

exploitation, *n.* sfruttaménto *m.*

exploration, *n.* esplorazione *f.*

exploratory, *adj.* esplorativo.

explore, *vb.* esplorare.

explorer, *n.* esploratore.

explosion, *n.* esplosione *f.*, scòppio *m.*

explosive, *n. and adj.* esplosivo (*m.*)

exponent, *n.* esponènte *m.*

export, 1. *n.* esportazione *f.* **2.** *vb.* esportare.

exportation, *n.* esportazione *f.*

exporter, *n.* esportatore *m.*

expose, *vb.* esporre.

exposé, *n.* esposto *m.*, esposizione *f.*

exposition, *n.* esposizione *f.*

expository, *adj.* espositivo.

expostulate, *vb.* far rimostranze.

exposure, *n.* esposizione *f.*, rivelazione *f.*; (photography) pòsa *f.*

expound, *vb.* esporre.

express, 1. *n.* esprèsso *m.*; (train) direttìssimo *m.* **2.** *adj.* esprèsso. **3.** *vb.* esprìmere.

expressage, *n.* spese di traspòrto *f.pl.*

expression, *n.* espressione *f.*; (outlet) sfògo *m.*

expressive, *adj.* espressivo.

expressly, *adv.* espressamente.

expressman, *n.* impiegato della compagnìa di traspòrti *m.*

expressway, *n.* autostrada *f.*

expropriate, *vb.* espropriare.

expulsion, *n.* espulsione *f.*

expunge, *vb.* espùngere.

expurgate, *vb.* espurgare.

exquisite, *adj.* squisito.

extant, *adj.* esistènte.

extemporaneous, *adj.* estemporàneo.

extemporize, *vb.* improvvisare.

extend, *vb.* estèndere; (in time) prolungare; prorogare.

extended, *adj.* esteso; allungato.

extension, *n.* estensione *f.*; (in time) prolungamento *m.*; pròroga *f.*

extensive, *adj.* esteso.

extensively, *adv.* estesamente.

extent, *n.* estensione *f.*, distesa *f.*

extenuate, *vb.* estenuare.

exterior, *adj.* esteriore.

exterminate, *vb.* sterminare.

extermination, *n.* stermìnio *m.*

external, *adj.* estèrno; (foreign) èstero.

extinct, *adj.* estinto.

extinction, *n.* estinzione *f.*

extinguish, *vb.* estinguere.

extinguisher, *n.* estintore *f.*

extirpate, *vb.* estirpare.

extol, *vb.* elogiare.

extort, *vb.* estòrcere.

extortion, *n.* estorsione *f.*

extortioner, *n.* ricattatore *m.*

extra, *adj.* extra, aggiunto, straordinàrio.

extra-, *prefix.* estra-, stra-.

extract, 1. *n.* estratto. **2.** *vb.* estrarre.

extraction, *n.* estrazione *f.*; (race) stirpe *f.*

extracurricular, *adj.* fuoriprogramma.

extradite, *vb.* estradare.

extradition, *n.* estradizione *f.*

extramarital, *adj.* extraconiugale.

extraneous, *adj.* estràneo.

extraordinary, *adj.* straordinàrio.

extrapolate, *vb.* estrapolare.

extravaganza, *n.* stravaganza *f.*, prodigalità *f.*

extravagant, *adj.* stravagante, pròdigo.

extravaganza, *n.* rivista frivola *f.*

extreme, *adj.* estrèmo.

extremely, *adv.* estremamente.

extremist, *n. and adj.* estremista *m. and f.*

extremity, *n.* estremità *f.*

extricate, *vb.* districare.

extrinsic, *adj.* estrinseco.

extrovert, *n.* estroverso.

exuberant, *adj.* esuberante.

exudation, *n.* trasudazione *f.*

exude, *vb.* trasudare.

exult, *vb.* esultare.

exultant, *adj.* esultante.

eye, *n.* òcchio *m.*

eyeball, *n.* glòbo dell'òcchio *m.*

eyebrow, *n.* sopracciglio *m.*

eyedropper, *n.* contagòccie *m.*

eyeful, *n.* vista *f.*; colpo d'òcchio *m.*

eyeglass, *n.* lènte *f.*

eyeglasses, *n.* occhiali *m.pl.*

eyelash, *n.* ciglio *m.*

eyelet, *n.* occhièllo *m.*

eyelid, *n.* pàlpebra *f.*

eyeshade, *n.* visiera *f.*

eyeshadow, *n.* rimmel *m.*

eyesight, *n.* vista *f.*

eyesore, *n.* cosa brutta o spiacevole *f.*; (coll.) pugno nell'òcchio *m.*

eyetooth, *n.* dente canino *m.*

eyewitness, *n.* testimòne oculare *m.*

F

fable, *n.* fàvola *f.*

fabric, *n.* (cloth) stòffa *f.*; (architecture) fàbbrica *f.*

fabricate, *vb.* fabbricare.

fabrication, *n.* fabbricazione *f.*; (lie) bugìa *f.*

fabulous, *adj.* favoloso.

façade, *n.* facciata *f.*

face, 1. *n.* faccia *f.*, viso *m.* 2. *vb.* fronteggiare, affrontare.

face-lift, *n.* plàstica facciale *m.*

face powder, *n.* cìpria *f.*

facet, *n.* faccetta *f.*

facetious, *adj.* facèto.

face value, *n.* valore nominale *m.*

facial, *adj.* del viso, facciale.

facile, *adj.* fàcile.

facilitate, *vb.* facilitare.

facility, *n.* facilità *f.*

facing, 1. *n.* rivestimento *f.* 2. *adv.* dirimpètto. 3. *prep.* dirimpètto a.

facsimile, *n.* facsimile *f.*

fact, *n.* fatto *m.*

faction, *n.* fazione *f.*

factor, *n.* fattore *m.*

factory, *n.* fàbbrica *f.*

factual, *adj.* obiettivo.

faculty, *n.* facoltà *f.*

fad, *n.* manìa *f.*

fade, *vb.* appassire; (lose color) impallidire.

faeces, *n.* fèccie *f.pl.*

fagged, *adj.* stanco.

fail, *vb.* fallire, mancare; (in examination) èsser bocciato.

failing, 1. *n.* debolezza *f.* 2. *prep.* in mancanza di.

faille, *n.* fàglia *f.*

failure, *n.* fiasco *m.*, mancanza *f.*; (bankruptcy) fallimento *m.*

faint, 1. *n.* svenimento *m.* 2. *adj.* dèbole. 3. *vb.* svenire.

faintly, *adv.* debolmente.

fair, 1. *n.* fièra *f.* 2. *adj.* bèllo; (blond) biondo; (just) giusto, èquo.

fairly, *adv.* giustamente; (moderately) abbastanza.

fairness, *n.* giustezza *f.*

fairy, *n.* fata *f.*

fairyland, *n.* paese delle fate *m.*

faith, *n.* fede *f.*

faithful, *adj.* fedele.

faithfulness, *n.* fedeltà *f.*

faithless, *adj.* sènza fede.

fake, 1. *n.* falso *m.* **2.** *vb.* falsificare.

faker, *n.* falsificatore *m.*

falcon, *n.* falcone *m.*

falconry, *n.* falconeria *f.*

fall, 1. *n.* caduta *f.;* (autumn) autunno *m.* **2.** *vb.* cadere; **(f. asleep)** addormentarsi; **(f. due)** scadere; **(f. in love)** innamorarsi; **(f. upon)** attaccare.

fallacious, *adj.* fallace.

fallacy, *n.* fallàcia *f.*

fallible, *adj.* fallibile.

fallout, *n.* pioggia radioattiva *f.*

fallow, *adj.* a maggese; **(f. field)** maggese *n.m.*

false, *adj.* falso.

false-hearted, *adj.* pèrfido.

falsehood, *n.* bugìa *f.*

falseness, *n.* falsità *f.*

falsetto, *n.* falsetto *m.*

falsification, *n.* falsificazione *f.*

falsify, *vb.* falsificare.

falter, *vb.* esitare, incespicare.

fame, *n.* fama *f.*

famed, *adj.* famoso.

familiar, *adj.* familiare; **(f. with)** pràtico di.

familiarity, *n.* familiarità *f.*

familiarize, *vb.* familiarizzare.

family, *n.* famiglia *f.;* **(f. tree)** àlbero genealògico *m.*

famine, *n.* carestìa *f.*

famished, *adj.* affamato.

famous, *adj.* famoso.

fan, 1. *n.* ventàglio *m.;* (enthusiast) tifoso *m.* **2.** *vb.* sventolare.

fanatic, *n. and adj.* fanàtico *(m.).*

fanatical, *adj.* fanàtico.

fanaticism, *n.* fanatismo *m.*

fancied, *adj.* immaginàrio.

fanciful, *adj.* immaginoso, capriccioso.

fancy, 1. *n.* immaginazione *f.* **2.** *adj.* di fantasìa. **3.** *vb.* immaginare.

fanfare, *n.* fanfara *f.*

fang, *n.* zanna *f.*

fantastic, *adj.* fantàstico.

fantasy, *n.* fantasìa *f.*

far, *adj. and adv.* lontano; **(as far as)** fino a; **(by far)** di gran lunga; **(how far?)** fino dove?; **(in so far as)** in quanto che; **(so far)** finora.

faraway, *adj. and adv.* lontano.

farce, *n.* farsa *f.*

farcical, *adj.* farsesco.

fare, 1. *n.* (price) tariffa *f.;* (passenger) passeggièro *m.;* (food) cibo *m.* **2.** *vb.* andare.

farewell, *n. and interj.* addìo *(m.)*

far-fetched, *adj.* ricercato.

far-flung, *adj.* esteso.

farina, *n.* farina *f.*

farm, *n.* fattorìa *f.*

farmer, *n.* agricoltore *m.,* colòno *m.*

farmhouse, *n.* casa colònica *f.*

farming, *n.* agricultura *f.*

farmyard, *adj.* cortile *f.*

far-reaching, *adj.* esteso.

far-sighted, be, *vb.* aver vista lunga.

farther, *adv.* più lontano.

farthest, *adv.* il più lontano.

fascinate, *vb.* affascinare.

fascination, *n.* fàscino *m.*

fascism, *n.* fascismo *m.*

fascist, *n. and adj.* fascista *(m. and f.)*

fashion, *n.* mòda *f.;* (manner) manièra *f.*

fashionable, *adj.* alla mòda.

fast, 1. *n.* digiuno *m.* **2.** *adj.* (speedy) ràpido; (firm) fermo; (of clock) avanti. **3.** *vb.* digiunare. **4.** *adv.* (quickly) rapidamente; (firmly) fermamente.

fasten, *vb.* attaccare, fissare.

fastener, fastening, *n.* chiusura *f.,* fermatura *f.*

fastidious, *adj.* fastidioso.

fat, *n. and adj.* grasso *(m.)*

fatal, *adj.* fatale; (deadly) mortale.

fatality, *n.* fatalità *f.*

fatally, *adv.* fatalmente.

fate, *n.* fato *m.*

fateful, *adj.* fatale.

father, *n.* padre *m.*

fatherhood, *n.* paternità *f.*

father-in-law, *n.* suòcero *m.*

fatherland, *n.* pàtria *f.*

fatherless, *adj.* òrfano di padre.

fatherly, *adj.* patèrno.

fathom, 1. *n.* bràccio *m.* **2.** *vb.* scandagliare.

fatigue, 1. *n.* fatica *f.* **2.** *vb.* affaticare.

fatten, *vb.* ingrassare.

fatty, *adj.* grasso.

fatuous, *adj.* fàtuo.

faucet, *n.* rubinetto *m.*

fault, *n.* colpa *f.;* (defect) difètto *m.,* mènda *f.*

faultfinding, *n.* critica *f.*

faultless, *adj.* irreprensíbile.

faultlessly, *adv.* irreprensibilmente.

faulty, *adj.* difettoso.

favor, 1. *n.* favore *m.* **2.** *vb.* favorire.

favorable, *adj.* favorévole, propízio.

favorite, *n. and adj.* favorito (*m.*).

favoritism, *n.* favoritismo *m.*

fawn, 1. *n.* cerbiàtto *m.* **2.** *vb.* (f. upon) adulare.

faze, *vb.* sconcertare.

fear, 1. *n.* paùra *f.,* timore *m.* **2.** *vb.* temere, aver paùra di.

fearful, *adj.* (person) pauroso, timoroso; (thing) spaventoso.

fearless, *adj.* intrèpido.

fearlessness, *n.* intrepidezza *f.*

feasible, *adj.* fattíbile.

feast, *n.* fèsta *f.;* (banquet) banchetto *m.*

feat, *n.* fatto *m.;* impresa *f.*

feather, *n.* penna *f.,* piuma *f.*

feather, *n.* penna *f.,* piuma *f.*

feathered, *adj.* pennuto, piumato.

feathery, *adj.* piumoso.

feature, *n.* tratto *m.*

February, *n.* febbraio *m.*

fecund, *adj.* fecondo.

federal, *adj.* federale.

federation, *n.* federazione *f.*

fedora, *n.* cappèllo flòscio *m.*

fee, *n.* (for professional services) onorário *m.;* (membership) quòta *f.;* (school) tassa *f.*

feeble, *adj.* débole.

feeble-minded, *adj.* débole di cervèllo.

feebleness, *n.* debolezza *f.*

feed, 1. *n.* nutrimento *m.* **2.** *vb.* nutrire, alimentare.

feedback, *n.* feedback *m.*

feed pump, *n.* pompa d'alimentazione *f.*

feel, 1. *n.* tatto *m.* **2.** *vb.* sentire.

feeler, *n.* sondàggio *m.*

feeling, *n.* sentimento *m.*

feign, *vb.* fingere.

feint, 1. *n.* finta *f.* **2.** *vb.* fare una finta.

felicitate, *vb.* felicitare.

felicitous, *adj.* felice.

felicity, *n.* felicità *f.*

feline, *adj.* felino.

fell, 1. *adj.* malvàgio. **2.** *vb.* abbàttere.

fellow, *n.* indivíduo *m.;* (associate) sòcio *m.*

fellowship, *n.* borsa *f.*

felon, *n.* fellone *m.*

felony, *n.* fellonía *f.*

felt, *n.* feltro *m.*

felt-tip pen, *n.* pennarello *m.*

female, 1. *n.* fémmina *f.* **2.** *adj.* femminile.

feminine, *adj.* femminile.

femininity, *n.* femminilità *f.*

fence, 1. *n.* recinto *m.* **2.** *vb.* chiùdere con un recinto; (sword, foil) schermire.

fencer, *n.* schermidore *m.*

fencing, *n.* scherma *f.*

fend, *vb.* (f. off) parare; (f. for oneself) badare a se stesso.

fender, *n.* (auto) parafango *m.*

fennel, *n.* finòcchio *m.*

ferment, 1. *n.* fermento *m.* **2.** *vb.* fermentare.

fermentation, *n.* fermentazione *f.*

fern, *n.* felce *f.*

ferocious, *adj.* feroce.

ferociously, *adv.* ferocemente.

ferocity, *n.* feròcia *f.*

ferry, *n.* traghetto *m.*

fertile, *adj.* fèrtile.

fertility, *n.* fertilità *f.*

fertilization, *n.* fertilizzazione *f.*

fertilize, *vb.* fertilizzare.

fertilizer, *n.* fertilizzante *m.*

fervency, *n.* fervore *m.*

fervent, *adj.* fervènte.

fervently, *adv.* ferventemente.

fervid, *adj.* fèrvido.

fervor, *n.* fervore *m.*

fester, *vb.* suppurare.

festival, *n.* fèsta *f.*

festive, *adj.* festivo.

festivity, *n.* festività *f.*

festoon, *n.* festone *m.*

fetal, *adj.* fetale.

fetch, *vb.* (go and get) andare a cercare; (bring) apportare.

fetching, *adj.* attraènte.

fête, n. fèsta f.

fetid, adj. fètido.

fetish, n. feticcio m.

fetlock, n. nòcca f.

fetters, n. ceppi m.pl.

fetus, n. fèto m.

feud, n. inimicízia f.; (historical) fèudo m.

feudal, adj. feudale.

feudalism, n. feudalismo m.

fever, n. fèbbre f.

feverish, adj. febbrile.

feverishly, adv. febbrilmente.

few, adj. and pron. pòchi pl.

fiancé, n. fidanzato m.

fiancée, n. fidanzata f.

fiasco, n. fiasco m.

fiat, n. órdine m.

fib, n. fandónia f.

fiber, n. fibra f.

fiberglass, n. vetrorèsina f.

fibrous, adj. fibroso.

fickle, adj. incostante.

fickleness, n. incostanza f.

fiction, n. finzione f.; (novel-writing) novellística f.

fictional, adj. finto.

fictitious, adj. fittízio.

fictitiously, adv. fittiziamente.

fiddle, 1. n. violino m. **2.** vb. suonare il violino.

fiddler, n. violinista m.

fiddlesticks, interj. fandònie!

fidelity, n. fedeltà f.

fidget, vb. agitarsi.

fief, n. fèudo m.

field, n. campo m.

fiend, n. demònio m.

fiendish, adj. demoníaco.

fierce, adj. feroce.

fiery, adj. focoso.

fife, n. píffero m.

fifteen, num. quíndici.

fifteenth, n. quindicésimo.

fifth, adj. quinto.

fifty, num. cinquanta.

fig, n. fico m.

fight, 1. n. combattimento m.; (struggle) lotta f.; (quarrel) lite f. **2.** vb. combàttere.

fighter, n. combattènte m.; (plane) càccia m.

figment, n. finzione f.

figurative, adj. figurato.

figuratively, adv. figuratamente.

figure, 1. n. figura f.; (of body) linea f.; (math.) cifra f. **2.** vb. figurare, calcolare.

figurehead, n. prestanome m., fantòccio m.

figure of speech, n. figura retòrica f.

figurine, n. figurina f.

figure skating, n. pattinàggio artístico m.

filament, n. filamento m.

filch, vb. rubare.

file, 1. n. (tool) lima f.; (row) fila f.; riga f.; (papers, etc.) filza f.; archívio m.; (cards) schedàrio m. **2.** vb. (tool) limare; (papers) archiviare; **(f. off)** sfilare.

filet, n. filetto m.

filial, adj. filiale.

filiation, n. filiazione f.; (business) filiale f.

filibuster, n. (politics) ostruzionismo m.; filibustiere m.

filigree, n. filigrana f.

filing cabinet, n. schedàrio m.

filings, n. limatura f.sg.

fill, vb. riempire; (tooth) otturare.

fillet, n. (band) banda f.; (meat) filetto m.; (fish) fetta f.

filling, n. (of tooth) otturazione f.

filling station, n. stazione di servízio f.

fillip, n. stimolo m.; colpetto m.

film, n. pellícola f.

filmy, adj. velato.

filter, 1. n. filtro m. **2.** vb. filtrare.

filtering, n. filtràggio m.

filth, n. sudiciume m.

filthy, adj. súdicio.

fin, n. pinna f.

final, adj. finale.

finale, n. finale m.

finalist, n. finalista m.

finality, n. finalità f.

finally, adv. finalmente.

finance, n. finanza f.

financial, adj. finanziàrio.

financier, n. finanzière m.

financing, n. finanziamento m.

find, vb. trovare.

finding, n. ritrovato m.

fine, 1. n. multa f. ammènda f.; (voluntary) oblazione f. **2.** adj. (beautiful) bèllo; (pure) fino; (excellent) bravo. **3.** vb. multare.

fine arts, n. bèlle arti f.pl.

fine-print, n. (business) dettagli contrattuàli m.pl.

finery, n. vestiti eleganti m.pl.

finesse, n. finezza f.

finger, n. dito m.

fingernail, n. ùnghia f.

fingerprint, n. impronta digitale f.

finicky, adj. affettato.

finish, 1. n. fine f. 2. vb. finire, terminare.

finite, adj. definito.

fir, n. abete m.

fire, 1. n. fuòco m.; (burning of house, etc.) incèndio m. 2. vb. (weapon) sparare; (deprive of job) licenziare.

fire alarm, n. allarme d'incendio m.

firearm, n. arma da fuòco f.

firecracker, n. petardo m.

firedamp, n. grisou m., mètano m.

fire engine, n. pompa da incèndio f.

fire escape, n. uscita di sicurezza f.

fire extinguisher, n. estintore m.

firefly, n. lùcciola f.

fireman, n. pompière m.; (locomotive) fuochista m.

fireplace, n. focolare m.

fireproof, adj. ignifugo.

firescreen, n. parafuòco m.

fireside, n. cantùccio del focolare m.

firewood, n. legna f.

fireworks, n. fuòchi d'artificio m.pl.

firm, 1. n. ditta f. 2. adj. fermo.

firmness, n. fermezza f.

first, adj. primo.

first aid, n. pronto soccorso m.

first-class, adj. di prima classe.

first-hand, adj. di prima mano.

first-rate, adj. di prima qualità.

fiscal, adj. fiscale.

fish, 1. n. pesce m. 2. vb. pescare.

fisherman, n. pescatore m.

fishery, n. peschièra f.

fishhook, n. amo m.

fishing, n. pesca f.

fishmonger, n. pescivéndolo m.

fishwife, n. pescivéndola f.

fishy, adj. di pesce; (strange) strano.

fission, n. fissione f.

fissure, n. fessura f.

fist, n. pugno m.

fistic, adj. pugilistico.

fit, 1. n. accèsso m. 2. adj. adatto, idòneo. 3. vb. (befit) convenire a; (clothes) andar bène; (adapt) adattare.

fitful, adj. irregolare; spasmodico.

fitness, n. idoneità f.; (health) salute f.

fitting, 1. n. adattamento m. 2. adj. conveniènte.

five, num. cinque.

fix, 1. n. impiccio m. 2. vb. acconciare; (repair) riparare; (set) fissare; (**f. up**) sistemare.

fixation, n. fissazione f.

fixed, adj. fisso.

fixing, adj. fissante.

fixture, n. infisso m.

fizz, n. effervescenza f.

flabbergast, vb. sbalordire.

flabby, adj. flòscio.

flaccid, adj. flàccido.

flag, n. bandièra f.; (stone) lastra di ròccia f.

flagellant, n. flagellante m.

flagellate, vb. flagellare.

flagging, n. indebolito.

flagman, n. manovratore m.

flagon, n. coppa f.

flagpole, n. asta di bandièra f.

flagrant, adj. flagrante.

flagrantly, adv. flagrantemente.

flagship, n. nave ammiràglia f.

flagstone, n. lastra di ròccia f.

flail, n. coreggiato m.

flair, n. fiuto m.; (ability) abilità f.

flake, n. fiòcco m.

flaky, adj. a falde.

flamboyant, adj. sgargiante.

flame, 1. n. fiamma f.; (**burst into f.s**) divampare. 2. vb. fiammeggiare.

flame thrower, n. lanciafiamme m.

flaming, adj. fiammante.

flamingo, n. fiammingo m., fenicòttero m.

flammable, adj. infiammabile.

flank, 1. n. fianco m. 2. vb. fiancheggiare.

flannel, *n.* flanèlla *f.*

flap, *n.* (wing) colpo *m.;* (envelope) lembo di chiusura *m.*

flare, *vb.* fiammeggiare.

flare-up, *n.* scòppio d'ira *m.*

flash, 1. *n.* baleno *m.* **2.** *vb.* balenare.

flashback, *n.* flashback *m.*

flashcube, *n.* cubo per flash *m.*

flashiness, *n.* vistosità *f.*

flashlight, *n.* lampadina tascàbile *f.*

flashy, *adj.* vistoso.

flask, *n.* fiasco *m.*

flat, 1. *n.* appartamento *m.;* (music) bemòlle *m.* **2.** *adj.* piatto, piano; *(f. tire)* gomma a terra *f.*

flatboat, *n.* chiatta *f.*

flatcar, *n.* carro piatto *m.*

flatness, *n.* monotonìa *f.*

flatten, *vb.* appiattire.

flatter, *vb.* adulare, lusingare.

flatterer, *n.* adulatore *f.,* iusingatore *m.*

flattering, *adj.* lusinghièro.

flattery, *n.* adulazione *f.,* lusinghe *f.pl.*

flat-top, *n.* portaèrei *m.*

flatware, *n.* argenteria *f.*

flaunt, *vb.* ostentare.

flavor, 1. *n.* (taste) sapore *m.;* (odor) aròma *m.* **2.** *vb.* insaporire.

flavoring, *n.* aròma artificiale *m.*

flavorless, *adj.* sènza sapore.

flaw, *n.* difètto *m.*

flawless, *adj.* perfètto.

flawlessly, *adv.* perfettamente.

flax, *n.* lino *m.*

flay, *vb.* scorticare.

flea, *n.* pulce *f.*

fleck, *n.* macchietta *f.*

fledgling, *n.* uccellino *m.*

flee, *vb.* fuggire.

fleece, *n.* vèllo *m.*

fleecy, *adj.* velloso.

fleet, 1. *n.* fiòtta *f.* **2.** *adj.* veloce.

fleeting, *adj.* fugace.

Fleming, *n.* fiammingo *m.*

Flemish, *adj.* fiammingo *m.*

flesh, *n.* carne *f.*

fleshy, *adj.* carnoso.

flex, *vb.* flèttere.

flexibility, *n.* flessibilità *f.*

flexible, *adj.* flessìbile.

flicker, 1. *n.* tremolìo *m.* **2.** *vb.* tremolare.

flier, *n.* aviatore *m.*

flight, *n.* volo *m.*

flight attendant, *n.* camerière *m.;* camerièra *f.* assistente di volo *m. and f.*

flighty, *adj.* capriccioso.

flimsy, *adj.* tènue.

flinch, *vb.* ritirarsi.

fling, *vb.* lanciare.

flint, *n.* (lighter) piètra focaia *f.;* (stone) selce *f.*

flip, *vb.* gettare.

flippant, *adj.* leggero.

flippantly, *adv.* leggermente.

flirt, 1. *n.* civetta *f.* **2.** *vb.* civettare, flirtare.

flirtation, *n.* flirt *m.*

float, *vb.* galleggiare.

flock, 1. *n.* gregge *m.* **2.** *vb.* affollarsi.

flog, *vb.* fustigare.

flood, 1. *n.* inondazione *f.* **2.** *vb.* inondare.

floodgate, *n.* cateratta *f.*

floodlight, *n.* riflettore elèttrico *m.*

floor, *n.* pavimento *m.;* (story) piano *m.;* **(take the f.)** prèndere la paròla.

flooring, *n.* pavimentazione *f.*

floorwalker, *n.* ispettore di magazzino *m.*

flop, 1. *n.* (failure) fiasco *m.;* (thud) tonfo *m.* **2.** *vb.* muòversi goffamente; (fail) far fiasco.

floral, *adj.* floreale.

Florence, *n.* Firènze *f.*

Florentine, *adj.* fiorentino.

florescence, *n.* infiorescenza *f.*

florid, *adj.* rubicondo.

florist, *n.* fioraio *m.*

floss, *n.* lanugine *f.*

flounce, 1. *n.* volante *m.* **2.** *vb.* dimenarsi.

flounder, *vb.* dibàttersi.

flour, *n.* farina *f.*

flourish, *vb.* fiorire; (wave around) agitare.

floury, *adj.* farinoso.

flow, *vb.* scórrere.

flower, 1. *n.* fiore *m.* **2.** *vb.* fiorire.

flowerpot, *n.* vaso per fiori *m.*

flowery, *adj.* fiorito.

flu, *n.* influenza *f.*

fluctuate, *vb.* fluttuare.

fluctuation, *n.* fluttuazione *f.*

flue, *n.* conduttura *f.*

fluency, *n.* scorrevolezza *f.*

fluent, *adj.* scorrévole.

fluently, *adv.* scorrevolmente.

fluid, *n. and adj.* flùido *(m.)*

fluidity, *n.* fluidità *f.*

flunk, *vb.* bocciare.

flunkey, *n.* lacchè *m.*

fluorescent, *adj.* fluorescènte.

fluoroscope, *n.* fluoroscòpio *m.*

flurry, *n.* trambusto *m.*

flush, 1. *adj.* a livèllo di. **2.** *vb.* **(f. the toilet)** tirare lo sciacquone.

flute, *n.* flàuto *m.*

flutist, *n.* flautista *m. and f.*

flutter, *vb.* svolazzare.

flux, *n.* flusso *m.*

fly, 1. *n.* mosca *f.* **2.** *vb.* volare.

flycatcher, *n.* pigliamosche *m.*

flywheel, *n.* volano *m.*

foam, 1. *n.* schiuma *f.*, spuma *f.* **2.** *vb.* spumare.

foamy, *adj.* schiumoso.

focal, *adj.* focale.

focus, *n.* fuòco *m.*

fodder, *n.* foràggio *m.*

foe, *n.* nemico *m.*

fog, *n.* foschìa *f.*

foggy, *adj.* nebbioso.

foil, 1. *n.* **(fencing)** fioretto *m.;* **(metal)** fòglia *f.* **2.** *vb.* frustrare.

foist, *vb.* far accettare.

fold, 1. *n.* pièga *f.* **2.** *vb.* piegare.

folder, *n.* cartèlla *f.*

foliage, *n.* fogliame *m.*

folio, *n.* fòglio *m.*

folk, *n.* pòpolo *m.*

folklore, *n.* folclore *m.*

folks, *n.* la gènte *f.*

follicle, *n.* follìcolo *m.*

follow, *vb.* seguire; (pursue) inseguire.

follower, *n.* seguace *m.*

folly, *n.* follìa *f.*

foment, *vb.* fomentare.

fond, *adj.* amante, tènero.

fondant, *n.* fondant *m.*

fondle, *vb.* accarezzare.

fondly, *adv.* teneramente.

fondness, *n.* tenerezza *f.*, passione *f.*

food, *n.* cibo *m.*, alimento *m.*, vitto *m.*

foodstuffs, *n.* gèneri alimentari *m.pl.*

fool, 1. *n.* citrullo *m.*, sciòcco *m.*, stolto *m.* **2.** *vb.* ingannare.

foolhardiness, *n.* temerarietà *f.*

foolhardy, *adj.* temeràrio.

foolish, *adj.* sciòcco, stolto.

foolproof, *adj.* assolutamente sicuro.

foolscap, *n.* carta formato protocòllo *f.*

foot, *n.* piède *m.*

footage, *n.* metràggio *m.*

football, *n.* (soccer) càlcio *m.*

foothill, *n.* collina bassa *f.*

foothold, *n.* appòggio *m.*, sostegno *m.*

footing, *n.* appòggio *m.*, base *f.*

footlights, *n.* ribalta *f.sg.*

footman, *n.* staffière *m.*

footnote, *n.* nòta *f.*

footprint, *n.* orma *f.*

footsore, be, *vb.* aver male ai pièdi.

footstep, *n.* orma *f.*

footstool, *n.* sgabèllo *m.*

fop, *n.* damerino *m.*

for, 1. *prep.* per. **2.** *conj.* perchè, chè.

forage, 1. *n.* foràggio *m.* **2.** *vb.* predare.

foray, *n.* scorrerìa *f.*

forbear, *vb.* trattenersi.

forbearance, *n.* paziènza *f.*

forbid, *vb.* proibire, vietare.

forbidding, *adj.* repulsivo.

force, 1. *n.* fòrza *f.*, vigore *m.* **2.** *vb.* forzare.

forceful, *adj.* vigoroso.

forcefulness, *n.* vigore *m.*

forceps, *n.* fòrcipe *m. (sg.)*

forcible, *adj.* forzato; (powerful) potènte.

ford, *n.* guado *m.*

fore, *adj.* anteriore.

fore and aft, *adv.* a pròra e a poppa.

forearm, *n.* avambràccio *m.*

forebears, *n.* antenati *m.pl.*

forebode, *vb.* presentire.

foreboding, *n.* presentimento *m.*

forecast, 1. *n.* previsione *f.* **2.** *vb.* prevedere, pronosticare.

forecaster, *n.* pronosticatore *m.*

forecastle, *n.* castèllo di prua *m.*

foreclose, *vb.* preclùdere.

foreclosure, *n.* graduazione *f.*

foredoom, *vb.* condannare all'insuccesso.

forefather, *n.* antenato *m.*

forefinger, *n.* índice *m.*

forefront, *n.* primo piano *m.*

forego, *vb.* rinunciare a.

foregoing, *adj.* anteriore.

foregone, *adj.* anticipato.

foreground, *n.* primo piano *m.*

forehanded, *adj.* previdente.

forehead, *n.* fronte *f.*

foreign, *adj.* stranièro, èstero.

foreign aid, *n.* aiuto ai paesi èsteri *m.*

foreigner, *n.* stranièro *m.*

foreleg, *n.* gamba anteriore *f.*

foreman, *n.* capo operaio *m.*

foremost, 1. *adj.* primo. **2.** *adv.* in avanti.

forenoon, *n.* mattina *f.*

forensic, *adj.* forènse.

forerunner, *n.* precursore *m.*

foresee, *vb.* prevedere.

foreseeable, *adj.* prevedìbile.

foreshadow, *vb.* presagire.

foreshorten, *vb.* scorciare.

foresight, *n.* previdènza *f.*

foresighted, *adj.* previdente.

foreskin, *n.* prepùzio *m.*

forest, *n.* forèsta *f.*

forestall, *vb.* impedire.

forester, *n.* silvicultore *m.;* (guard) guàrdia forestale *f.*

forestry, *n.* silvicultura *f.*

foretaste, 1. *n.* pregustazione *f.* **2.** *vb.* pregustare.

foretell, *vb.* predire.

forethought, *n.* premeditazione *f.*

forever, *adv.* per sèmpre.

forevermore, *adv.* eternamente.

forewarn, *vb.* preavvertire.

foreword, *n.* prefazione *f.*

forfeit, *vb.* demeritare, pèrdere.

forfeiture, *n.* pèrdita *f.*

forgather, *vb.* riunirsi.

forge, 1. *n.* fucina *f.* **2.** *vb.* (make) foggiare; (falsify) contraffare.

forger, *n.* contraffattore *m.*

forgery, *n.* contraffazione *f.*

forget, *vb.* dimenticare.

forgetful, *adj.* diméntico.

forget-me-not, *n.* miosòtide *f.,* non ti scordar di me *m.*

forgive, *vb.* perdonare.

forgiveness, *n.* perdono *m.*

forgo, *vb.* rinunziare a.

fork, *n.* forchetta *f.;* (in road) bívio *m.*

forlorn, *adj.* disperato.

form, 1. *n.* forma *f.;* (blank) mòdulo *m.* **2.** *vb.* formare.

formal, *adj.* formale.

formaldehyde, *n.* formaldèide *f.*

formality, *n.* formalità *f.*

formally, *adv.* formalmente.

format, *n.* formato *m.*

formation, *n.* formazione *f.*

formative, *adj.* formativo.

former, 1. *adj.* precedènte. **2.** *pron.* quello.

formerly, *adv.* anticamente, già.

formidable, *adj.* formidàbile.

formless, *adj.* informe.

formula, *n.* fòrmula *f.*

formulate, *vb.* formulare.

formulation, *n.* formulazione *f.*

forsake, *vb.* abbandonare.

forsythia, *n.* forsízia *f.*

fort, *n.* fortezza *f.*

forte, *n.* fòrte *m.*

forth, *adv.* (out) fuòri; (onward) via; **(and so f.)** e così via.

forthcoming, *adj.* pròssimo.

forthright, *adj.* onèsto.

forthwith, *adv.* immediatamente.

fortieth, *adj.* quarantésimo.

fortification, *n.* fortificazione *f.*

fortify, *vb.* fortificare.

fortissimo, *adj.* fortíssimo.

fortitude, *n.* fortezza *f.*

fortnight, *n.* quíndici giorni *m.pl.*

fortress, *n.* fortezza *f.,* ròcca *f.*

fortuitous, *adj.* fortùito.

fortunate, *adj.* fortunato.

fortune, *n.* fortuna *f.*

fortune-teller, *n.* chiaroveggènte *m.*

forty, *num.* quaranta.

forum, *n.* fòro *m.*

forward, *adv.* avanti.

forwardness, *n.* presuntuosità *f.*

fossil, *n. and adj.* fòssile (*m.*)

fossilize, *vb.* fossilizzare, *tr.*

foster, *vb.* (raise) allevare; (nourish) nutrire.

foul, 1. *adj.* spòrco; (unfair) disonèsto. 2. *vb.* sporcare.

foulmouthed, *adj.* osceno.

foul play, *n.* reàto *m.*

found, *vb.* fondare.

foundation, *n.* (building) fondamento *m.;* (fund) fondazione *f.*

founder, *n.* fondatore *m.*

foundling, *n.* trovatèllo *m.;* (f. hospital) brefotròfio *m.*

foundry, *n.* fonderìa *f.*

fount, *n.* fonte *f.*

fountain, *n.* fontana *f.*

fountainhead, *n.* sorgente *f.*

fountain pen, *n.* penna stilogràfica *f.*

four, *num.* quattro.

four-cylinder, *adj.* a quattro cilindri.

four-flush, *vb.* millantare crèdito.

four-flusher, *n.* millantatore *m.*

four-footed, *adj.* quadrùpede.

four-in-hand, *n.* cravatta *f.*

fourscore, *num.* ottanta.

foursome, *n.* gruppo di quattro persone *m.*

fourteen, *num.* quattòrdici.

fourth, *adj.* quarto.

fowl, *n.* pollo *m.*

fox, *n.* volpe *f.*

foxglove, *n.* digitale *f.*

foxhole, *n.* trincèa *f.*

foxy, *adj.* volpino.

foyer, *n.* ingresso *m.;* (theater) ridotto *m.*

fracas, *n.* fracasso *m.*

fraction, *n.* frazione *f.*

fracture, 1. *n.* frattura *f.* 2. *vb.* fratturare.

fragile, *adj.* fràgile.

fragment, *n.* frammento *m.*

fragmentary, *adj.* frammentàrio.

fragrance, *n.* fragranza *f.*

fragrant, *adj.* fragrante.

frail, *adj.* fràgile; (morally) dèbole.

frailty, *n.* debolezza *f.*

frame, 1. *n.* cornice *m.* 2. *vb.* incorniciare.

framework, *n.* ossatura *f.*

France, *n.* Frància *f.*

franchise, *n.* diritto di voto *m.*

frank, *adj.* franco.

frankfurter, *n.* salsìccia *f.*

frankincense, *n.* incènso *m.*

frankly, *adv.* francamente.

frankness, *n.* franchezza *f.*

frantic, *adj.* frenètico.

fraternal, *adj.* fratèrno.

fraternally, *adv.* fraternamente.

fraternity, *n.* fraternità *f.*

fraternize, *vb.* fraternizzare.

fratricide, *n.* (act) fratricìdio *m.;* (person) fratricìda *m.*

fraud, *n.* fròde *f.*

fraudulent, *adj.* fraudolento.

fraudulently, *adv.* fraudolentemente.

fraught, *adj.* càrico.

fray, *n.* combattimento *m.*

freak, 1. *n.* mostruosità *f.* 2. *adj.* mostruoso.

freckle, *n.* lentìggine *f.*

freckled, *adj.* lentigginoso.

free, 1. *adj.* lìbero; (without cost) gratùito. 2. *vb.* liberare.

freedom, *n.* libertà *f.*

free lance, *n.* giornalista o politicante indipendènte *m.*

freestone, *adj.* spiccàgnolo.

freeze, *vb.* gelare.

freezer, *n.* frigorìfero *m.;* congelatore *m.*

freezing, *n.* congelamento *m.;* (f. point) punto di congelamento *m.*

freight, *n.* càrico *m.;* (f. train) treno mèrci *m.;* (f. station) scalo mèrci *m.*

freightage, *n.* spese di trasporto *f.pl.*

freighter, *n.* nave mercantile *f.*

French, *adj.* francese.

Frenchman, *n.* francese *m.* or *f.*

frenzied, *adj.* frenètico.

frenzy, *n.* frenesìa *f.*

frequency, *n.* frequènza *f.*

frequency modulation, *n.* modulazione di frequènza *f.*

frequent, 1. *adj.* frequènte. 2. *vb.* frequentare.

frequently, *adv.* frequentemente.

fresco, *n.* affresco *m.*

fresh, *adj.* fresco; (impudent) impudènte.

freshen, *vb.* rinfrescare.

freshman, *n.* matrìcola *f.*

freshness, *n.* freschezza *f.*

fresh-water, *adj.* d'acqua dolce.

fret, *vb.* tormentare, *tr.,* irritare, *tr.*

fretful, *adj.* irritàbile.

fretfully, *adv.* irritabilmente.

fretfulness, *n.* irritabilità *f.*

friar, *n.* frate *m.*

fricassee, *n.* fricassèa *f.*

friction, *n.* frizione *f.*

Friday, *n.* venerdì *m.*

friend, *n.* amico *m.,* amica *f.*

friendless, *adj.* sènza amici.

friendliness, *n.* amichevolezza *f.*

friendly, *adj.* amichévole, amico.

friendship, *n.* amicízia *f.*

frieze, *n.* frègio *m.*

frigate, *n.* fregata *f.*

fright, *n.* spavento *m.*

frighten, *vb.* spaventare.

frightful, *adj.* spaventoso.

frigid, *adj.* frígido.

frigidity, *n.* frigidità *f.*

Frigid Zone, *n.* zona glaciale *f.*

frill, *n.* gala *f.,* affettazione *f.*

frilly, *adj.* increspato.

fringe, *n.* frángia *f.*

fringe benefits, *n.* incentivi *m.pl.*

frippery, *n.* fronzoli *m.pl.*

frisky, *adj.* allegro.

fritter, 1. *n.* frittèlla *f.* **2.** *vb.* **(f. away)** sciupare.

frivolity, *n.* frivolezza *f.*

frivolous, *adj.* frívolo.

frivolousness, *n.* frivolezza *f.*

frizzle, *n.* ricciolo *m.*

frizzly, *adj.* crespo, riccio.

frock, *n.* àbito da donna *m.*

frog, *n.* ranòcchio *m.,* rana *f.*

frogman, *n.* sommozzatore *m.*

frolic, *vb.* far capriòle.

frolicsome, *adj.* scherzoso.

from, *prep.* da.

front, *n.* fronte *m.;* parte anteriore *f.;* davanti *m.;* **(in f.)** davanti; **(in f. of)** davanti a.

frontage, *n.* facciata *f.*

frontal, *adj.* frontale.

frontier, *n.* frontièra *f.*

frost, *n.* brina *f.*

frostbite, *n.* congelamento *m.*

frosting, *n.* glassa *f.*

frosty, *adj.* gèlido.

froth, *n.* schiuma *f.,* spuma *f.*

froward, *adj.* indòcile.

frown, *vb.* aggrottare le ciglia.

frowzy, *adj.* trascurato.

frozen foods, *n.* cibi surgelati *m.pl.*

fructify, *vb.* fruttificare.

frugal, *adj.* frugale.

frugality, *n.* frugalità *f.*

fruit, *n.* frutto *m.*

fruitful, *adj.* fruttuoso.

fruition, *n.* fruizione *f.*

fruitless, *adj.* infruttuoso.

fruit salad, *n.* macedònia *f.*

fruit stand, *n.* fruttivèndolo *m.*

frustrate, *vb.* frustrare.

frustration, *n.* frustrazione *f.*

fry, *vb.* frìggere.

fryer, *n.* (chicken) pollo gióvane *m.*

frying-pan, *n.* padèlla *f.*

fuchsia, *n.* fùcsia *f.*

fudge, 1. *n.* fondènte *m.* **2.** *interj.* sciocchezze!

fuel, *n.* combustíbile *m.;* **(motor f.)** carburante *m.*

fuel cell, *n.* unità elettrògena *f.*

fugitive, *n. and adj.* fuggitivo (*m.*)

fugue, *n.* fuga *f.*

fulcrum, *n.* fulcro *m.*

fulfill, *vb.* realizzare.

fulfillment, *n.* realizzazione *f.*

full, *adj.* pieno.

fullback, *n.* estrèmo *m.*

full dress, *n.* àbito da cerimònia *m.*

fullness, *n.* pienezza *f.*

fully, *adv.* pienamente.

fulminate, *vb.* fulminare.

fulmination, *n.* folgorazione *f.*

fumble, *vb.* lasciar cadere.

fume, *n.* esalazione *f.*

fumigate, *vb.* fumigare.

fumigator, *n.* fumigatore *m.*

fun, *n.* divertimento *m.*

function, 1. *n.* funzione *f.* **2.** *vb.* funzionare.

functional, *adj.* funzionale.

functionary, *n.* funzionàrio *m.*

fund, *n.* fondo *m.*

fundamental, *adj.* fondamentale.

funeral, 1. *n.* funerale *m.* **2.** *adj.* fùnebre.

funereal, *adj.* funèreo.

fungicide, *n.* fungicida *m.*

fungus, *n.* fungo *m.*

funnel, *n.* imbuto *m.;* **(smoke-stack)** ciminièra *f.*

funny, *adj.* còmico.

fur, *n.* pelliccia *f.*

furious, *adj.* furioso.

furlough, *n.* licènza *f.*

furnace, *n.* fornace *m.*, caldaia *f.*

furnish, *vb.* fornire; (house) ammobiliare.

furnishings, *n.* mobilia *f.*

furniture, *n.* mòbili *m.pl.*

furor, *n.* furore *m.*

furred, *adj.* copèrto di pellíccia.

furrier, *n.* pellicciaio *m.*

furrow, *n.* solco *m.*

furry, *adj.* copèrto di pellíccia; (tongue) patinoso.

further, **1.** *adj.* ulteriore. **2.** *adv.* oltre, più avanti.

furtherance, *n.* appòggio *m.*

furthermore, *adv.* inoltre.

fury, *n.* fùria *f.*, furore *m.*

fuse, **1.** *n.* (electricity) fusíbile *m.*; (explosives) spoletta *f.* **2.** *vb.* fóndere.

fuselage, *n.* fusolièra *f.*

fusillade, *n.* fucileria *f.*

fusion, *n.* fusione *f.*

fuss, *n.* chiasso *m.*

fussy, *adj.* difficoltoso.

futile, *adj.* fùtile.

futility, *n.* futilità *f.*

future, **1.** *n.* futuro *m.*, avvenire *m.* **2.** *adj.* futuro.

futurity, *n.* avvenire *m.*

futurology, *n.* futurología *f.*

fuzz, *n.* lanùgine *f.*

fuzzy, *adj.* lanuginoso; (confused) confuso.

G

gab, *vb.* chiacchierare.

gabardine, *n.* gabardina *f.*

gable, *n.* (architecture) timpano *m.*

gadabout, *n.* bighellone *m.*

gadfly, *n.* tafano *m.*

gadget, *n.* congegno *m.*

gaff, *n.* arpione *m.*

gag, **1.** *n.* bavàglio *m.*; (joke) trovata còmica *f.* **2.** *vb.* imbavagliare.

gage, *n.* pegno *m.*; sfida *f.*

gaiety, *n.* gaiezza *f.*

gaily, *vb.* gaiamente.

gain, **1.** *n.* guadagno *m.* **2.** *vb.* guadagnare.

gainful, *adj.* lucroso.

gainfully, *adv.* lucrosamente.

gainsay, *vb.* contraddire.

gait, *n.* andatura *f.*

gaiter, *n.* ghetta *f.*

gala, **1.** *n.* gala *f.* **2.** *adj.* di gala.

galaxy, *n.* galàssia *f.*

gale, *n.* tempèsta *f.*

gall, **1.** *n.* (bile) fièle *m.*; (insolence) sfacciatàggine *f.* **2.** *vb.* irritare.

gallant, *adj.* galante, coraggioso.

gallantly, *adv.* coraggiosamente.

gallantry, *n.* coràggio *m.*

gall bladder, *n.* vescica del fièle *m.*

gall bladder attack, *n.* travaso di bile *m.*

galleon, *n.* galeone *m.*

gallery, *n.* galleria *f.*; (top g., theater) loggione *m.*

galley, *n.* (ship) galèa *f.*; (kitchen) cucina *f.*; (typogr.) colonna *f.*

galley proof, *n.* bòzze in colonna *f.pl.*

Gallic, *adj.* gàllico.

gallivant, *vb.* vagare.

gallon, *n.* gallone *m.*

gallop, **1.** *n.* galòppo *m.* **2.** *vb.* galoppare.

gallows, *n.* forca *f.*

gallstone, *n.* càlcolo biliare *m.*

galore, *adv.* a bizzèffe.

galosh, *n.* galòscia *f.*

galvanize, *vb.* galvanizzare.

gamble, *vb.* giocare d'azzardo.

gambler, *n.* giocatore d'azzardo *m.*

gambling, *n.* giòco d'azzardo *m.*

gambol, **1.** *n.* salto *m.* **2.** *vb.* saltare.

game, **1.** *n.* giòco *m.*; (sports encounter) partita *f.*; (hunting) selvaggina *f.* **2.** *adj.* coraggioso.

gamely, *adv.* coraggiosamente.

gameness, *n.* coràggio *m.*

gamin, *n.* monèllo *m.*

gamut, *n.* gamma *f.*

gamy, *adj.* alquanto putrefatto.

gander, *n.* pàpero *m.*

gang, *n.* gruppo *m.*, squadra *f.*

gangling, *adj.* smilzo.

gangplank, *n.* pontile *m.*

gangrene, n. cancrena f.
gangrenous, adj. cancrenoso.
gangster, n. gangster m.
gangway, n. passerèlla f.
gap, n. apertura f.
gape, vb. spalancare la bocca.
garage, n. autorimessa f.
garb, n. costume m.
garbage, n. rifiuti f.pl.
garble, vb. ingarbugliare.
garden, n. giardino m.
gardener, n. giardinière m.
gardenia, n. gardènia f.
gargle, 1. n. gargarismo m. 2. vb. gargarizzare.
gargoyle, n. grondàia a forma di testa grottesca f.
garish, adj. sgargiante.
garland, n. ghirlanda f.
garlic, n. àglio m.
garment, n. vestito m.
garner, vb. cògliere.
garnet, n. granato m.
garnish, vb. guarnire.
garnishee, vb. méttere il fermo su.
garnishment, n. guarnizione f.
garret, n. soffitta f.
garrison, n. guarnigione f.
garrote, n. garrota f.
garrulous, adj. gàrrulo.
garter, n. giarrettièra f.
gas, n. gas m.; (gasoline) benzina f.
gaseous, adj. gassoso.
gash, 1. n. squàrcio m. 2. vb. squarciare.
gasket, n. guarnizione f.
gasless, adj. sènza gas, sènza benzina.
gas mask, n. màschera antigas f.
gas meter, n. contatore del gas m.
gasohol, n. benzina ricavata da prodotti alcòlici f.
gasoline, n. benzina f.
gasoline dealer, n. benzinàio m.
gasp, 1. n. boccheggiamento m. 2. vb. boccheggiare.
gas stove, n. cucina a gas f.
gassy, adj. gassoso.
gastric, adj. gàstrico.
gastric juice, n. succo gàstrico m.
gastritis, n. gastrite f.
gastronomical, adj. gastronòmico.
gastronomy, n. gastronomía f.

gate, n. (city) pòrta f.; (apartment house) portone m.; (fence) cancèllo m.; (airport) uscita f.
gatekeeper, n. portière m.; guardiano m.
gateway, n. pòrta m., entrata f.
gather, vb. raccògliere, radunare; (infer) desùmere.
gathering, n. adunata f., assemblèa f.
gaudily, adv. vistosamente.
gaudiness, n. vistosità f.
gaudy, adj. vistoso.
gauge, 1. n. apparécchio misuratore m.; (track) scartamento m.; (loading gun) sàgoma f. 2. vb. misurare, stimare.
gaunt, adj. magro.
gauntlet, n. guanto m.
gauze, vb. garza f.
gavel, n. martellino m.
gavotte, n. gavòtta f.
gawk, vb. guardare fissamente.
gawky, adj. goffo.
gay, n. adj. gaio; (homosexual) omosessuale. 2. n. finòcchio m.
gaze, vb. guardare.
gazelle, n. gazzèlla f.
gazette, n. gazzetta f.
gazetteer, n. dizionàrio geogràfico m.
gear, n. ingranàggio m.; (harness) finimenti m.pl.; (g. lever) lèva del cambio f.
gear box, n. scatola del cambio-màrcia f.
gearing, n. ingranàggio m.
gearshift, n. càmbio di velocità m.
gelatine, n. gelatina f.
gelatinous, adj. gelatinoso.
geld, vb. castrare.
gelding, n. castrato m.
gem, n. gèmma f.
gender, n. gènere m.
gene, n. gène m.
genealogical, adj. genealògico.
genealogy, n. genealogía f.
general, n. and adj. generale (m.)
generality, n. generalità f.
generalization, n. generalizzazione f.
generalize, vb. generalizzare.
generally, adv. generalmente.

generalship, *n.* qualità da generale *f.pl.*

general staff, *n.* stato maggiore *m.*

generate, *vb.* generare.

generation, *n.* generazione *f.*

generator, *n.* generatore *m.*

generic, *adj.* genèrico.

generosity, *n.* generosità *f.*

generous, *adj.* generoso.

generously, *adv.* generosamente.

genesis, *n.* gènesi *f.*

genetic, *adj.* genètico.

genetics, *n.* genètica *f.*

Geneva, *n.* Ginèvra *f.*

Genevan, *adj.* ginevrino.

genial, *adj.* piacèvole, cordiale.

geniality, *n.* piacevolezza *f.*, cordialità *f.*

genially, *adv.* piacevolmente, cordialmente.

genital, *adj.* genitale.

genitals, *n.* genitali *m.pl.*

genitive, *n. and adj.* genitivo (*m.*)

genius, *n.* gènio *m.*

Genoa, *n.* Gènova *f.*

Genoese, *adj.* genovese.

genocide, *n.* genocidio *m.*

genre, *n.* gènere *m.*

genteel, *adj.* eccessivamente raffinato.

gentian, *n.* genziana *f.*

gentile, *n. and adj.* gentile (*m.*); non israelítico.

gentility, *n.* raffinatezza eccessiva *f.*

gentle, *adj.* mite.

gentleman, *n.* signore *m.*, gentiluòmo *m.*

gentlemanly, *adj.* da gentiluòmo.

gentlemen's agreement, *n.* impegno d'onore *m.*

gentleness, *n.* mitezza *f.*

gently, *adv.* mitemente, adagio.

gentry, *n.* piccola nobiltà *f.*; (ironical) gènte *f.*

genuflect, *vb.* genuflèttersi.

genuine, *adj.* genuíno.

genuinely, *adv.* genuinamente.

genuineness, *n.* genuinità *f.*

genus, *n.* gènere *m.*

geographer, *n.* geògrafo *m.*

geographical, *adj.* geogràfico.

geography, *n.* geografía *f.*

geometric, *adj.* geomètrico.

geometry, *n.* geometría *f.*

geopolitics, *n.* geopolítica *f.*

geranium, *n.* gerànio *m.*

geriatrics, *n.* geriatría *f.*

germ, *n.* gèrme *m.*

German, *n. and adj.* tedesco (*m.*)

germane, *adj.* rilevante.

Germanic, *adj.* germànico.

German measles, *n.* rosolía *f.*

Germany, *n.* Germània *f.*

germicidal, *adj.* germicida.

germicide, *n.* germicida *m.*

germinal, *adj.* germinale.

germinate, *vb.* germinare.

germ warfare, *n.* guerra batteriològica *f.*

gerontology, *n.* gerontología *f.*

gerund, *n.* gerùndio *m.*

gestate, *vb.* portare nell'ùtero.

gestation, *n.* gestazione *f.*

gesticulate, *vb.* gesticolare.

gesticulation, *n.* gesticolazione *f.*

gesture, *n.* gèsto *m.*

get, *vb.* (obtain) ottenere; (receive) ricévere; (take) prèndere; (become) divenire, diventare; (arrive) arrivare; **(g. in)** entrare; **(g. off)** scéndere; **(g. on, agree)** intèndersi; **(g. on, go up)** montare; **(g. out)** uscire; **(g. up)** alzarsi.

getaway, *n.* fuga *f.*

get-together, *n.* riunione *f.*

geyser, *n.* geyser *m.*

ghastly, *adj.* orrèndo.

ghetto, *n.* ghetto *m.*

ghost, *n.* spèttro *m.*, larva *f.*

ghost writer, *n.* collaboratore anònimo *m.*

giant, *n. and adj.* gigante (*m.*)

gibberish, *n.* borbottamento *m.*

gibbon, *n.* gibbone *m.*

gibe at, *vb.* beffarsi di.

giblets, *n.* rigàglie *f.pl.*

giddiness, *n.* vertigine *f.*

giddy, *adj.* stordito.

gift, *n.* dono *m.*

gifted, *adj.* dotato.

gigantic, *adj.* gigantesco.

giggle, *vb.* rídere scioccamente.

gigolo, *n.* cicisbèo *m.*

gild, *vb.* dorare, indorare.

gill, *n.* brànchia *f.*

gilt, *n.* 1. doratura *f.* 2. *adj.* dorato.

gilt-edged, *adj.* sicuro.

gimcrack, *n.* cianfrusàglia *f.*

gimlet, *n.* succhièllo *m.*

gin, *n.* gin *m.*

ginger, *n.* zènzero *m.*

gingerly, *adj.* càuto.

gingham, *n.* ghingano *m.*

giraffe, *n.* giraffa *f.*

gird, *vb.* cíngere, *tr.*

girder, *n.* trave *f.*

girdle, *n.* cintura *f.*

girl, *n.* ragazza *f.,* fanciulla *f.*

girlish, *adj.* da ragazza.

girth, *n.* circonferènza *f.*

gist, *n.* contenuto essenziale *m.*

give, *vb.* dare; **(g. back)** rèndere; **(g. in)** cédere; **(g. out)** distribuire; **(g. up)** rinunziare a.

give-and-take, *n.* scàmbio *m.*

given name, *n.* nome di battésimo *m.*

giver, *n.* datore *m.,* donatore *m.*

gizzard, *n.* ventríglio *m.*

glacé, *adj.* lùcido.

glacial, *adj.* glaciale.

glacier, *n.* ghiacciaio *m.*

glad, *adj.* contènto, lièto.

gladden, *vb.* allietare.

glade, *n.* radura *f.*

gladiolus, *n.* gladiòlo *m.*

gladly, *adv.* lietamente, con piacere.

gladness, *n.* contentezza *f.*

glamor, *n.* fàscino *m.*

glamorous, *adj.* affascinante.

glance, *n.* sguardo *m.,* occhiata *f.*

gland, *n.* ghiàndola *f.*

glandular, *adj.* ghiandolare.

glare, *n.* bagliore *m.*

glaring, *adj.* abbagliante.

glass, *n.* vetro *m.;* **(drinking-g.)** bicchière *m.*

glass-blowing, *n.* soffiatura del vetro *f.*

glasses, *n.* occhiali *m.*

glassful, *n.* bicchière *m.*

glassware, *n.* cristallerìe *f.pl.*

glassy, *adj.* vetroso, vítreo.

glaucoma, *n.* glaucòma *f.*

glaze, 1. *n.* (enamel) smalto *m.;* (varnish) vernice *f.* 2. *vb.* smaltare, verniciare.

glazier, *n.* vetràio *m.*

gleam, *n.* barlume *m.*

glee, *n.* gìoia *f.*

glee club, *n.* còro maschile *m.*

gleeful, *adj.* gioioso.

glen, *n.* valletta *f.*

glib, *adj.* fluènte.

glide, *vb.* scivolare.

glider, *n.* aliante *m.*

glimmer, 1. *n.* barlume *m.* 2. *vb.* mandare una luce incèrta.

glimmering, 1. *n.* barlume *m.* 2. *adj.* incèrto.

glimpse, *vb.* intravedere.

glint, *n.* riflèsso *m.*

glisten, *vb.* scintillare.

glitter, 1. *n.* scintillìo *m.* 2. *vb.* scintillare, risplèndere.

gloaming, *n.* crepuscolo *m.*

gloat, *vb.* gioire.

global, *adj.* globale.

globe, *n.* glòbo *m.*

globe-trotter, *n.* giramondo *m.*

globular, *adj.* globulare.

globule, *n.* glòbulo *m.*

glockenspiel, *n.* campanette *f.pl.*

gloom, *n.* (darkness) oscurità *f.;* (sadness) tristezza *f.*

gloomy, *adj.* oscuro, triste.

glorification, *n.* glorificazióne *f.*

glorify, *vb.* glorificare.

glorious, *adj.* glorioso.

glory, 1. *n.* glòria *f.* 2. *vb.* gloriarsi.

gloss, 1. *n.* lucidità *f.;* (explanation) chiòsa *f.* 2. *vb.* lucidare; chiosare.

glossary, *n.* glossàrio *m.*

glossy, *adj.* lùcido.

glottis, *n.* glòttide *f.*

glove, *n.* guanto *m.*

glow, 1. *n.* incandescènza *f.* 2. *vb.* èssere incandescènte.

glowing, *adj.* incandescènte.

glowworm, *n.* lùcciola *f.*

glucose, *n.* glucòsio *m.*

glue, 1. *n.* còlla *f.* 2. *vb.* incollare.

gluey, *adj.* appiccicaticcio, attaccaticcio.

glum, *adj.* (frowning) accigliato; (sad) triste.

glumness, *n.* tristezza *f.*

glut, *n.* saturazione *f.*

glutinous, *adj.* glutinoso.

glutton, *n.* ghiottone *m.*

gluttonous, *adj.* ghiotto.

glycerine, *n.* glicerina *f.*

gnarl, *n.* nodo *m.*

gnash, *vb.* digrignare.

gnat, *n.* moscerino *m.*

gnaw, *vb.* ródere.

gnome, *n.* gnomo *m.*

go, *vb.* andare; (become) diventare; **(g. away)** andàrsene; **(g. back)** tornare; **(g. by)** passare; **(g. down)** scèndere; **(g. in)** entrare; **(g. on)** continuare; **(g. out)** uscire; **(g. up)** salire; **(g. without)** fare a meno di.

goad, 1. *n.* pùngolo *m.*, stímolo *m.* 2. *vb.* stimolare.

goal, *n.* mèta *f.*; (soccer) pòrta *f.*

goalie, *n.* portiere *m.*

goal-keeper, *n.* portière *m.*

goat, *n.* capra *f.*

goatee, *n.* barbetta *f.*

goatherd, *n.* capraio *m.*

goatskin, *n.* pèlle di capra *f.*

gob, *n.* massa informe *f.*

gobble, *vb.* ingollare.

gobbler, *n.* tacchino *m.*

go-between, *n.* intermediàrio *m.*

goblet, *n.* coppa *f.*

goblin, *n.* folletto *m.*

go-cart, *n.* carrettino *m.*

god, *n.* dio *m.*, iddìo *m.*

godchild, *n.* figliòccio *m.*

goddess, *n.* dèa *f.*

godfather, *n.* padrino *m.*, compare *m.*

God-fearing, *adj.* timorato di Dio.

Godforsaken, *adj.* miseràbile.

godless, *adj.* àteo; (impious) émpio.

godlike, *n.* divino.

godly, *adj.* devòto, pío.

godmother, *n.* madrina *f.*, comare *f.*

godsend, *n.* dòno del cièlo *m.*

Godspeed, *n.* buona sorte *f.*

go-getter, *n.* arrivista *m.*

goiter, *n.* gozzo *m.*

gold, *n.* òro *m.*

golden, *adj.* d'òro, àureo.

gold-filled, *adj.* (tooth) otturato d'òro.

goldfinch, *n.* cardellino *m.*

goldfish, *n.* pesce rosso *m.*

goldilocks, *n.* bionda *f.*

goldleaf, *n.* fòglia d'òro *f.*

goldsmith, *n.* oréfice *m.*

gold-plate, *vb.* dorare.

gold standard, *n.* parità àurea *f.*

golf, *n.* golf *m.*

gondola, *n.* góndola *f.*

gondolier, *n.* gondolière *m.*

gone, *adj.* (vanished) sparito; (departed) partito.

gong, *n.* gong *m.*

gonorrhea, *n.* gonorrèa *f.*

good, 1. *n.* bène *m.*; (g.s) mèrci *f.pl.* 2. *adj.* buòno.

good-by, *n. and interj.* addìo *(m.)*

Good Friday, *n.* venerdì santo *m.*

good-hearted, *adj.* di buòn cuòre.

good-humored, *adj.* di buòn umore.

good-looking, *adj.* bellino.

good-natured, *adj.* di buòn temperamento.

goodness, *n.* bontà *f.*

good will, *n.* buona volontà *f.*

goose, *n.* òca *f.*, pàpera *f.*

gooseberry, *n.* ribes *m.*

gooseneck, *n.* collo di cigna *m.*

goose step, *n.* passo d'òca *m.*

gore, *n.* sangue *m.*

gorge, *n.* gola *f.*

gorgeous, *adj.* splèndido.

gorilla, *n.* gorilla *m.*

gory, *adj.* insanguinato.

gosling, *n.* paperetto *m.*

gospel, *n.* vangèlo *m.*

gossamer, *n.* garza sottile *f.*

gossip, 1. *n.* (talk) dicerìa *f.*, pettegolezzo *m.*; (person) pettégolo *m.*, pettégola *f.* 2. *vb.* pettegolare.

gossipy, *adj.* pettégolo.

Gothic, *adj.* gòtico.

gouge, *n.* sgòrbia *f.*

gourd, *n.* zucca *f.*

gourmand, *n.* ghiottone *m.*

gourmet, *n.* buongustaio *m.*

govern, *vb.* governare.

governess, *n.* governante *f.*

government, *vb.* govèrno *m.*

governmental, *adj.* governativo.

governor, *n.* governatore *m.*

governorship, *n.* governatorato *m.*

gown, *n.* gonnèlla *f.*

grab, *vb.* arraffare, carpire.

grace, *n.* gràzia *f.*

graceful, *adj.* grazioso.

gracefully, *adv.* graziosamente.

graceless, *adj.* sgraziato.

grace note, *n.* *(music)* appoggiatura *f.*

gracious, *adj.* grazioso.

grackel, *n.* gràcchio *m.*

grade, 1. *n.* grado *m.*; (quality) qualità *f.*; (mark) voto *m.* **2.** *vb.* classificare.

grade crossing, *n.* passàggio a livèllo *m.*

gradual, *adj.* graduale.

gradually, *adv.* gradualmente.

graduate, *vb.* graduare; (university) laurearsi.

graduate school, *n.* scuòla di studi superiori *f.*

graft, 1. *n.* innèsto *m.*; (fraud) corruzióne *f.* **2.** *vb.* innestare.

graham flour, *n.* farina integrale *f.*

grail, *n.* gradale *m.*

grain, *n.* grano *m.*; (single) chicco *m.*

grain alcohol, *n.* àlcol etilico *m.*

graining, *n.* venatura *f.*

gram, *n.* grammo *m.*

grammar, *n.* grammàtica *f.*

grammarian, *n.* grammàtico *m.*

grammar school, *n.* scuòla elementare *f.*

grammatical, *adj.* grammaticale.

gramophone, *n.* grammòfono *m.*

granary, *n.* granàio *m.*

grand, *adj.* grande, grandioso.

grandchild, *n.* nipote *m. or f.*

granddaughter, *n.* nipote *f.*

grandeur, *n.* grandezza *f.*

grandfather, *n.* nònno *m.*

grandiloquent, *adj.* magniloquente.

grandiose, *adj.* grandioso.

grandly, *adv.* grandiosamente.

grandmother, *n.* nònna *f.*

grandparents, *n.* nònni *m.pl.*

grandson, *n.* nipote *m.*

grandstand, *n.* tribuna *f.*

grange, *n.* fattoria *f.*

granger, *n.* fattore *m.*

granite, *n.* granito *m.*

granny, *n.* vècchia *f.*

grant, 1. *n.* concessióne *f.*; (gift) dono *m.* **2.** *vb.* concèdere.

grantee, *n.* beneficiàrio *m.*

granular, *adj.* granulare.

granulate, *vb.* granulare.

granulation, *n.* granulazióne *f.*

granule, *n.* granèllo *m.*

grape, *n.* uva *f.*; **(g. juice)** spremuta d'uva *f.*

grapefruit, *n.* pompèlmo *m.*

grapeshot, *n.* mitràglia *f.*

grapevine, *n.* vite *f.*

graph, *n.* gràfico *m.*

graphic, *adj.* gràfico, vìvido.

graphite, *n.* grafite *m.*

graphology, *n.* grafología *f.*

grapple, 1. *n.* uncino *m.*, lotta *f.* **2.** *vb.* venire alle prese.

grasp, 1. *n.* presa *f.* **2.** *vb.* afferrare.

grasping, *adj.* avaro.

grass, *n.* èrba *f.*; (marijuana) marijuana *f.*

grasshopper, *n.* cavalletta *f.*

grassy, *adj.* erboso.

grate, 1. *n.* graticola *f.* **2.** *vb.* (cheese, etc.) grattugiare; (irritate) irritare.

grateful, *adj.* grato.

grater, *n.* grattùgia *f.*

gratify, *vb.* gratificare.

grating, *n.* inferriata *f.*

gratis, 1. *adj.* gratùito. **2.** *adv.* gratuitamente.

gratitude, *n.* gratitùdine *f.*

gratuitous, *adj.* gratùito.

gratuity, *n.* mància *f.*

grave, 1. *n.* tomba *f.* **2.** *adj.* grave.

gravel, *n.* ghiaia *f.*

gravely, *adv.* gravemente.

gravestone, *n.* piètra tombale *f.*

graveyard, *n.* camposanto *m.*

gravitate, *vb.* gravitare.

gravitation, *n.* gravitazióne *f.*

gravity, *n.* gravità *f.*

gravure, *n.* incisione *f.*

gravy, *n.* sugo di carne *m.*

gravy boat, *n.* salsiera *f.*

gray, *adj.* grigio.

gray-haired, *adj.* canuto.

grayhound, *n.* levriere *m.*

grayish, *adj.* grigiastro.

gray matter, *n.* cervèllo *m.*

graze, *vb.* pàscere.

grazing, *n.* pàscolo *m.*

grease, 1. *n.* grasso *m.* **2.** *vb.* ùngere, lubrificare.

greasy, *adj.* grasso; untuoso.
great, *adj.* grande.
greatness, *n.* grandezza *f.*
Greece, *n.* Grècia *f.*
greed, *n.* cupidigia *f.*
greediness, *n.* ghiottoneria *f.*
greedy, *adj.* ghiottone.
Greek, *adj.* grèco.
green, *adj.* verde.
greenery, *n.* verzura *f.*
greenhouse, *n.* sèrra *f.*
green thumb, *n.* pòllice verde *m.*
greet, *vb.* salutare.
greeting, *n.* saluto *m.*
greeting card, *n.* biglietto d'auguri *m.*
gregarious, *adj.* gregàrio.
grenade, *n.* granata *f.*
grenadine, *n.* granatina *f.*
greyhound, *n.* levrière *m.*
grid, *n.* graticola *f.;* (electric power) rete *f.*
griddle, *n.* graticola *f.*
gridiron, *n.* graticola *f.*
grief, *n.* dolore *m.*
grievance, *n.* lagnanza *f.*
grieve, *vb.* addolorare, *tr.*
grievous, *adj.* doloroso, grave.
griffin, *n.* grifo *m.,* grifone *m.*
grill, *n.* graticola *f.*
grillroom, *n.* rosticceria *f.*
grim, *adj.* fosco.
grimace, *n.* smòrfia *f.*
grime, *n.* sudiciume *m.*
grimy, *adj.* sùdicio.
grin, *vb.* sorrìdere da un orécchio all'altro.
grind, *vb.* macinare.
grinder, *n.* macinino *m.*
grindstone, *n.* màcina *f.*
grip, **1.** *n.* presa *f.;* (suitcase) valigia *f.* **2.** *vb.* afferrare.
gripe, **1.** *n.* lagnanza *f.* **2.** *vb.* lagnarsi.
grippe, *n.* influènza *f.*
gripping, *adj.* molto intrigante, affascinante.
grisly, *adj.* orribile.
grist, *n.* grano da macinare *m.*
gristle, *n.* cartilàgine *f.*
grit, *n.* sàbbia *f.*
grizzled, *adj.* grigio.
groan, **1.** *n.* gèmito *m.* **2.** *vb.* gèmere.

grocer, *n.* negoziante di gèneri alimentari *m.*
grocery, *n.* negòzio di gèneri alimentari *m.*
grog, *n.* gròg *m.*
groggy, *adj.* intontito.
groin, *n.* inguine *m.*
groom, *n.* palafrenière *m.;* (footman) staffière *m.;* (bridegroom) sposo *m.*
groove, *n.* solco *m.*
grope, *vb.* andare a tastoni.
gropingly, *adv.* a tastoni.
grosgrain, *n.* grana grossa *f.*
gross, *adj.* grossolano; (blunder) madornale; (weight) lordo.
grossly, *adv.* grossolanamente; (wholly) totalmente.
grossness, *n.* grossolanità *f.*
grotesque, *adj.* grottesco.
grotto, *n.* grotta *f.*
grouch, **1.** *n.* (person) brontolone *m.* **2.** *vb.* brontolare.
ground, **1.** *n.* tèrra *f.;* (reason) motivo *m.;* (basis) base *f.;* (electrical) presa a tèrra *f.* **2.** *vb.* basare.
ground hog, *n.* marmotta *f.*
groundless, *adj.* sènza base.
ground swell, *n.* mareggiata *f.*
groundwork, *n.* fondamento *m.*
group, **1.** *n.* gruppo *m.* **2.** *vb.* raggruppare, *tr.*
groupie, *n.* membro di un gruppo di ragazze *m.*
grouse, *n.* gallo cedrone *m.*
grove, *n.* boschetto *m.*
grovel, *vb.* umiliarsi.
grow, *vb.* créscere; (raise) coltivare.
growl, **1.** *n.* brontolio *m.* **2.** *vb.* brontolare.
grown, *adj.* maturo.
grown-up, *n. and adj.* adulto *(m.)*
growth, *n.* créscita *f.,* sviluppo *m.*
grub, **1.** *n.* larva *f.;* (food) cibo *m.* **2.** *vb.* scavare.
grubby, *adj.* sporco.
grudge, *n.* àstio *m.*
grudgingly, *adv.* controvoglia.
gruel, *n.* pappa *f.*
gruesome, *adj.* orrèndo.
gruff, *adj.* bùrbero.
grumble, *vb.* brontolare.
grumpy, *adj.* scontènto.

grunt, 1. n. grugnito m. **2.** vb. grugnire.

guarantee, 1. n. garanzia f. **2.** vb. garantire.

guarantor, n. mallevadore m.

guaranty, n. garanzia f.

guard, 1. n. guàrdia f. **2.** vb. custodire, guardarsi.

guarded, adj. guardingo.

guardhouse, n. guardina f.

guardian, n. guardiano m.; (legal) tutore m.

guardian angel, n. àngelo custode m.

guardianship, n. tutèla f.

guardrail, n. parapetto m.

guardsman, n. guàrdia f.

gubernatorial, adj. governatoriale.

guerilla, n. (war) guerriglia f.; (fighter) guerrigliere m.

guess, vb. indovinare.

guesswork, n. congettura f.

guest, n. òspite m.; (hotel, etc.) cliènte m.

guffaw, 1. n. sghignazzata f. **2.** vb. sghignazzare.

guidance, n. guida f.

guide, 1. n. guida f. **2.** vb. guidare.

guidebook, n. guida f.

guide dog, n. caneguida per ciechi m.

guideline, n. direttiva f.; linea di condotta f.; linea.

guidepost, n. palo indicatore m.

guild, n. arte f., corporazione f.

guile, n. astùzia f.

guileful, adj. astuto.

guileless, adj. sincero.

guillotine, n. ghigliottina f.

guilt, n. colpa f.

guiltily, adv. colpevolmente.

guiltless, adj. sènza colpa.

guilty, adj. colpévole.

guinea fowl, n. faraona f.

guinea pig, n. porcellino d'India m.

guise, n. apparènza f.; (shape) fòggia f.

guitar, n. chitarra f.

guitarist, n. chitarrista m.

gulch, n. burrone m.

gulf, n. golfo m.

gull, n. gabbiano m.

gullet, n. gola f.

gullible, adj. crèdulo.

gully, n. burrone m.

gulp, vb. inghiottire; (g. down) ingollare.

gum, n. gomma f.; (chewing-g.) gomma da masticare f.

gummy, adj. gommoso.

gun, n. pistola f.; fucile m.; (cannon) cannone m.

gunboat, n. cannonièra f.

guncotton, n. fulmicotone m.

gunman, n. bandito armato m.

gunner, n. artiglière m.

gunpowder, n. pólvere da sparo m.

gunshot, n. portata di un fucile f.

gunwale, n. parapètto m.

gurgle, 1. n. gorgoglio m. **2.** vb. gorgogliare.

guru, n. guru m.

gush, vb. sgorgare, zampillare.

gusher, n. sorgènte di petròlio f.

gushing, adj. zampillante, sgorgante.

gusset, n. gherone m.

gust, n. ràffica f.; (rain) scròscio m.

gustatory, adj. gustativo.

gusto, n. gusto m.

gusty, adj. tempestoso.

guts, n. intestino m., minùgia f.; (courage) fégato m.

gutter, n. (street) cunetta f.; (house) grondaia f.

guttural, adj. gutturale.

guy, n. tizio m.

guzzle, vb. ingozzare.

gym, n. palèstra f.

gymnasium, n. palèstra f.; (school) ginnàsio m.

gymnast, n. ginnasta m.

gymnastic, adj. di ginnàstica.

gymnastics, n. ginnàstica f.

gynaecology, n. ginecologia f.

gypsum, n. gesso m.

gypsy, n. zìngaro m., zìngara f.

gyrate, vb. turbinare.

gyroscope, n. giroscòpio m.

haberdasher, n. merciàio m.

haberdashery, n. merceria f.

habiliments, n. vestimenta f.pl.

habit, n. abitùdine f.; (dress) àbito m.

habitable, adj. abitàbile.

habitat, n. ambiènte f.

habitation, n. abitazione f.

habitual, adj. abituale.

habituate, vb. abituare.

habitué, n. frequentatore m.

hack, 1. n. cavallo da dipòrto m. **2.** vb. tagliare.

hackneyed, adj. banale.

hacksaw, n. sega per metalli f.

haft, n. mànico m.

hag, n. strega f.

haggard, adj. sparuto.

haggle, vb. mercanteggiare.

hag-ridden, adj. tormentato da streghe.

Hague, The, n. l'Aia f.

hail, 1. n. gràndine f. **2.** vb. grandinare; (call to) salutare.

Hail Mary, n. avemaria f.

hailstone, n. chicco di gràndine m.

hailstorm, n. grandinata f.

hair, n. capelli m.pl., crine, f.; (single, on head) capello m.; (body, animals) pelo m.

hairbrush, n. spàzzola per capelli f.

haircut, n. tàglio di capelli m.

hairdo, n. pettinatura f., acconciatura f.

hairdresser, n. parrucchière f.

hair dryer, n. asciuga-capelli m., phon m.

hair dye, n. tintura per capelli f.

hairless, adj. pelato; calvo; rasato.

hairline, n. linea sottilissima f.

hairpin, n. forcina f.

hair-raising, adj. orrèndo.

hair remover, n. depilatore m.

hair restorer, n. rigeneratore del pelo m.

hair's-breadth, n. grossezza di un capello f.

hairsplitting, adj. pignolo.

hairspray, n. schiuma per capelli f.

hairy, n. peloso.

halcyon, adj. felice.

hale, adj. robusto.

half, 1. n. metà f. **2.** adj. mèzzo. **3.** adv. a metà.

half-and-half, adv. metà e metà.

halfback, n. secondo m.

half-baked, adj. immaturo, imperfètto.

half-breed, n. meticcio m.

half-brother, n. fratellastro m.

half-dollar, n. mèzzo dòllaro m.

half-hearted, adj. sènza entusiasmo.

half-mast, adv. a mezz'asta.

half-staff, (at h.), adv. a mezz'asta.

halfway, adv. a mèzza via.

half-wit, n. imbecille m.

halibut, n. pianuzza f.

hall, n. sala f., àula f.; (hallway) vestìbolo m., corridoio m.

hallmark, n. màrchio m.

hallow, vb. santificare.

Halloween, n. la véglia di Ognissanti f.

hallucination, n. allucinazione f.

hallway, n. vestìbolo m., corridoio m.

halo, n. aurèola f.

halt, 1. n. fermata f. **2.** vb. fermare, tr. **3.** interj. alt!

halter, n. cavezza f., capestro m.

halve, vb. dimezzare.

halyard, n. drizza f.

ham, n. prosciutto m.

Hamburg, n. Amburgo m.

hamlet, n. frazione f.; paesino m.

hammer, 1. n. martèllo m. **2.** vb. martellare.

hammock, n. amaca f.

hamper, 1. n. cesta f. **2.** vb. impedire.

hamster, n. criceto m.

hamstring, vb. ostacolare.

hand, n. mano f.

handbag, n. (lady's) borsetta f.; (suitcase) valigetta f.

hand baggage, n. bagaglio a mano m.

handbook, n. manuale m.

handcuffs, n. manette f.pl.

handful, n. manciata f.

handicap, n. svantàggio m.

handicraft, n. lavoro manuale f.

handiwork, n. òpera f.

handkerchief, n. fazzoletto m.

handle, 1. n. mànico m., maniglia f., manovèlla f. **2.** vb. maneggiare.

handle bar, n. manùbrio m.

hand-made, adj. fatto a mano.

handmaid, n. ancella f.

handorgan, n. organetto a mano-vèlla m.

handout, n. (alms) elemosina f.; sintesi di articolo f.

hand-pick, vb. scègliere con cura.

hand-rail, n. passomano m.

handsome, adj. bèllo.

hand-to-hand, adj. còrpo a còrpo.

handwriting, n. calligrafia f.

handy, adj. (person) dèstro; (thing) còmodo; (at hand) a portata di mano.

handy-man, n. factotum m.

hang, vb. pèndere; (execute) impiccare.

hangar, n. angar m.

hangdog, adj. con una fàccia patibolare.

hanger, n. gàncio m.; **(coat-h.)** attaccapanni m.

hanger-on, n. seguace m.

hang glider, n. deltaplano m.

hanging, n. (execution) impiccagione f.; (tapestry) tappezzeria f.

hangman, n. impiccatore m.

hangnail, n. pipita f.

hangout, n. ritròvo m.

hang-over, n. stanghetta f.

hangup, n. difficoltà psicològica f.

hank, n. matassa f.

hanker, vb. bramare.

haphazard, adv. a casàccio.

hapless, adj. sfortunato.

happen, vb. (take place) accadere, succèdere; (chance to be) trovarsi.

happening, n. avvenimento m.

happily, adv. felicemente.

happiness, n. felicità f.

happy, adj. felice.

happy-go-lucky, adj. spensierato.

harakiri, n. karakiri m.

harangue, 1. n. arringa f. **2.** vb. arringare.

harass, vb. annoiare.

harbinger, n. precursore m.

harbor, n. (refuge) rifùgio m.; (port) pòrto m.

hard, 1. adj. duro; (difficult) diffìcile. **2.** adv. fortemente, duramente.

hard-and-fast, adj. inflessìbile.

hard-bitten, adj. tenace.

hard-boiled, adj. sòdo.

hard cash, n. denaro contante m.

hard coal, n. antracite f.

harden, vb. indurire.

hard-fought, adj. accanito.

hard-headed, adj. pràtico.

hard-hearted, adj. di cuòre duro.

hardiness, n. robustezza f.

hard labor, n. lavori forzati m.pl.

hardly, adv. (with difficulty) stentatamente; (scarely) appena; **(h. ever)** quasi mai.

hardness, n. durezza f.

hard-of-hearing, adj. duro d'orecchi.

hardship, n. avversità f.

hardware, n. ferramenta f.pl.

hard-won, adj. conquistato con fatica.

hardwood, n. legno duro m.

hardy, adj. robusto.

hare, n. lèpre f.

hare-brained, adj. scervellato.

hare-lip, n. labbro leporino m.

harem, n. àrem m.

hark, vb. ascoltare.

Harlequin, n. Arlecchino m.

harlot, n. meretrice f.

harm, 1. n. danno m. **2.** vb. danneggiare, nuòcere.

harmful, adj. dannoso, nocivo.

harmless, adj. innòcuo, innocènte.

harmonic, adj. armònico.

harmonica, n. armònica f.

harmonious, adj. armonioso.

harmonize, vb. armonizzare.

harmony, n. armonia f.

harness, 1. n. bardatura f. **2.** vb. bardare.

harp, n. arpa f.

harpoon, 1. n. fiòcina f. **2.** vb. fiocinare.

harpsichord, n. clavicémbalo m.

harridan, n. vecchiàccia f.

harrow, 1. n. èrpice m. **2.** vb. erpicare.

harry, vb. spogliare.

harsh, adj. aspro.

harshness, n. asprezza f.

harvest, 1. n. raccòlta f. 2. vb. raccògliere.

hash, n. guazzabùglio m.

hashish, n. hascisc m.

hasn't, vb. non à.

hassle, vb. seccare n., seccatura f.

hassock, n. cuscino m.

haste, 1. n. fretta m. 2. vb. affrettarsi.

hasten, vb. affrettare tr.

hastily, adv. affrettatamente, frettolosamente.

hasty, adj. affrettato, frettoloso.

hat, n. cappèllo m.

hatch, 1. n. (boat) boccapòrto m. 2. vb. (hen) covare; (egg) schiudersi; aprirsi.

hatchery, n. vivaio m.

hatchet, n. accetta f.

hate, 1. n. òdio m. 2. vb. odiare.

hateful, adj. odioso.

hatred, n. òdio m.

haughtiness, n. supèrbia f.

haughty, adj. supèrbo.

haul, vb. trascinare, trasportare.

haunch, n. anca f.

haunt, vb. frequentare.

have, vb. avere; **(h. to,** necessity) dovere.

haven, n. pòrto m.; (refuge) rifùgio m.

haven't, vb. non ho, etc.

havoc, n. devastazione f.

hawk, n. falco m.

hawker, n. venditore ambulante m.

hawser, n. alzaia f., gòmena f.

hawthorn, n. biancospino m.

hay, n. fièno m.

hay fever, n. asma del fièno m.

hayfield, n. campo da fièno m.

hayloft, n. fienile m.

haystack, n. covone m.

hazard, 1. n. rischio m. 2. vb. rischiare.

hazardous, adj. rischioso.

haze, n. nébbia f.

hazel, n. (plant) nocciòlo m.; (nut) nocciòla m.

hazy, adj. nebbioso, vago.

he, pron. egli, lùi.

head, n. tèsta f., capo m.

headache, n. mal di tèsta m.

headband, n. bènda f., diadèma f.

headfirst, adv. colla tèsta in avanti; di testa.

headgear, n. acconciatura del capo f.

head-hunting, n. càccia alle tèste f.

heading, n. título m.

headland, n. promontòrio m.

headless, adj. acefalo; senza testa.

headlight, n. fanale anteriore m.

headline, n. título m.

headlong, adv. a capofitto.

head-man, n. capo m.

headmaster, n. direttore m.

head-on, adj. frontale.

headquarters, n. quartière generale m.

headset, n. cùffia f.

headstone, n. piètra tombale f.

headstrong, adj. ostinato, testardo.

headwaters, n. sorgènti f.pl.

headway, n. progrèsso m.; (trains, etc.) intervallo m.

head-work, n. lavoro intellettuale m.

heady, adj. impetuoso, inebriante.

heal, vb. guarire, risanare.

healer, n. guaritore m.

health, n. salute f.; (skoal) bríndisi m.

healthful, adj. salubre.

health insurance, n. assicurazione malattia f.

healthy, adj. sano.

heap, 1. n. mùcchio m. 2. vb. ammucchiare.

hear, vb. sentire, udire.

hearer, n. ascoltatore m.

hearing, n. (sense) udito m.; (audience) udiènza f.

hearken to, vb. ascoltare.

hearsay, n. (by h.) per sentito dire.

hearse, n. carro fùnebre m.

heart, n. cuòre m.

heartache, n. angóscia f.

heart attack, n. attacco cardíaco, m., infarto m.

heart-break, n. crepacuòre m.

heartbreaker, n. rubacuori m.

heartbroken, *adj.* straziato.

heartburn, *n.* bruciore di stòmaco *m.*

hearten, *vb.* rincuorare.

heartfelt, *adj.* sincèro.

hearth, *n.* focolare *m.*

heartily, *adv.* di cuore.

heartless, *adj.* sènza cuòre.

heart-rending, *adj.* straziante.

heart-sick, *adj.* scoraggiato.

heart-stricken, *adj.* colpito al cuòre.

heart-to-heart, *adj.* íntimo.

hearty, *adj.* cordiale.

heat, 1. *n.* calore *m.*, caldo *m.* 2. *vb.* riscaldare.

heated, *adj.* (dwelling-place) riscaldato; (discussion) infiammato.

heater, *n.* calorífero *m.*

heath, *n.* brughièra *f.*

heathen, *n.* and *adj.* pagano (*m.*)

heather, *n.* èrica *f.*

heating, *n.* riscaldamento *m.*

heat-stroke, *n.* colpo di calore *m.*

heat wave, *n.* ondata di caldo *f.*

heave, *vb.* sollevare; (utter) eméttere.

heaven, *n.* cièlo *m.*

heavenly, *adj.* celèste.

heavy, *adj.* pesante.

heavyweight, *n.* and *adj.* peso màssimo (*m.*)

Hebrew, *n.* and *adj.* ebrèo (*m.*); ebràico (*m.*)

heckle, *vb.* fare domande imbarazzanti.

hectare, *n.* èttaro *m.*

hectic, *adj.* febbrile.

hectogram, *n.* ètto *m.*, ettogramma *m.*

hedge, *n.* sièpe *f.*

hedgehog, *n.* ríccio *m.*

hedge-hop, *vb.* volare rasentando la tèrra.

hedgerow, *n.* sièpe di cespùgli o di àlberi.

hedonism, *n.* edonismo *m.*

heed, *vb.* badare a, prestare attenzione a.

heedless, *adj.* spensierato.

heel, *n.* calcagno *m.*, tallone *m.*; (shoes) tacco *m.*

hefty, *adj.* pesante, vigoroso.

hegemony, *n.* egemonía *f.*

heifer, *n.* giovènca *f.*

height, *n.* altezza *f.*; (high place) altura *f.*

heighten, *vb.* (raise) innalzare; (increase) accréscere.

heinous, *adj.* atroce.

heir, *n.* erède *m.*

heir apparent, *n.* erède legíttimo *m.*

heirloom, *n.* oggètto antico di famíglia *m.*

heir presumptive, *n.* presunto erède *m.*

helicopter, *n.* elicòttero *m.*

heliocentric, *adj.* eliocèntrico.

heliograph, *n.* eliògrafo *m.*

heliotrope, *n.* eliotròpio *m.*

helium, *n.* èlio *m.*

hell, *n.* inférno *m.*

Hellenic, *adj.* ellènico.

Hellenism, *n.* ellenismo *m.*

hellish, *adj.* infernale.

hello, *interj.* buòn giorno, buòna sera; (telephone) pronto.

helm, *n.* timone *m.*

helmet, *n.* èlmo *m.*

helmsman, *n.* timonière *m.*

help, 1. *n.* aiuto *m.* 2. *vb.* aiutare; (at table) servire.

helper, *n.* aiutante *m.*

helpful, *adj.* (person) servizièvole; (thing) útile.

helpfulness, *n.* utilità *f.*

helping, *n.* porzione *f.*

helpless, *adj.* impotènte.

helter-skelter, *adv.* a casàccio.

hem, 1. *n.* orlo *m.* 2. *vb.* orlare.

hematite, *n.* ematite *f.*

hemisphere, *n.* emisfero *m.*

hemline, *n.* orlo della gonna *m.*

hemlock, *n.* cicuta *f.*

hemoglobin, *n.* emoglobina *f.*

hemophilia, *n.* emofilía *f.*

hemorrhage, *n.* emorragía *f.*

hemorrhoid, *n.* emorròide *f.*

hemp, *n.* cànapa *f.*

hemstitch, *n.* orlo a giorno *m.*

hen, *n.* gallina *f.*

hence, *adv.* (time, place) di qui; (therefore) quindi.

henceforth, *adv.* d'ora in pòi.

henchman, *n.* bravo *m.*

henhouse, *n.* pollàio *m.*

henna, *n.* ennè *m.*

henpecked, *adj.* dominato dalla móglie.

hepatic, *adj.* epàtico.

hepatica, *n.* epàtica *f.*

her, 1. *adj.* suo, di lèi. **2.** *pron.* (direct) la; (indirect) le; (alone, stressed, or with prep.) lèi.

herald, *n.* araldo *m.*

heraldic, *adj.* aràldico.

heraldry, *n.* aràldica *f.*

herb, *n.* èrba *f.*

herbaceous, *adj.* erbàceo.

herbarium, *n.* erbàrio *m.*

herculean, *adj.* ercùleo.

herd, *n.* gregge *m.,* màndria *f.*

here, *adv.* qui; **(h. is)** ècco.

hereabout, *adv.* qui vicino.

hereafter, *adv.* d'ora in pòi.

hereby, *adv.* con questo.

hereditary, *adj.* ereditàrio.

heredity, *n.* eredità *f.*

herein, *adv.* qui dentro.

hereof, *adv.* di questo.

hereon, *adv.* in questo; su questo.

heresy, *n.* eresìa *f.*

heretic, *n.* erètico *m.*

heretical, *adj.* erètico.

hereto, *adv.* a questo.

heretofore, *adv.* finora.

herewith, *adv.* con questo.

heritage, *n.* eredità *f.*

hermetic, *adj.* ermètico.

hermit, *n.* eremita *m.*

hermitage, *n.* eremitàggio *m.,* romitàggio *m.*

hernia, *n.* èrnia *f.*

hero, *n.* eròe *m.*

heroic, *adj.* eròico.

heroically, *adv.* eroicamente.

heroin, *n.* eroìna *f.*

heroine, *n.* eroìna *f.*

heroism, *n.* eroìsmo *m.*

heron, *n.* airone *m.*

herpes, *n.* èrpete *m.; herpes f.*

herring, *n.* aringa *f.*

herringbone, *n.* lisca d'aringa *f.*

hers, *pron.* suo, di lèi.

herself, *pron.* sè stessa.

hertz, *n.* hertz *m.*

hesitancy, *n.* esitazione *f.*

hesitant, *adj.* esitante.

hesitate, *vb.* esitare.

hesitation, *n.* esitazione *f.*

heterodox, *adj.* eterodòsso.

heterodoxy, *n.* eterodossìa *f.*

heterogeneous, *adj.* eterogèneo.

heterosexual, *adj.* eterosessuale.

hew, *vb.* tagliare.

hex, *n.* strega *f.*

hexagon, *n.* esàgono *m.*

heyday, *n.* apogèo *m.*

hi!, *interj.* ciao.

hiatus, *n.* iato *m.*

hibernate, *vb.* svernare.

hibernation, *n.* ibernazione *f.*

hibiscus, *n.* ibisco *m.*

hiccup, *n.* singulto *m.*

hick, *n.* rùstico.

hickory, *n.* noce americano *m.*

hidden, *adj.* nascosto.

hide, 1. *n.* pèlle *f.* **2.** *vb.* nascóndere *tr.*

hide-and-seek, *n.* nascondino *m.*

hideous, *adj.* spaventoso.

hide-out, *n.* nascondìglio *m.*

hiding place, *n.* nascondìglio *m.*

hierarchical, *adj.* geràrchico.

hierarchy, *n.* gerarchìa *f.*

hieroglyphic, *adj.* geroglìfico.

high, *adj.* alto, elevato; (in price) caro.

highbrow, *n.* and *adj.* intellettuale *(m.* or *f.)*

high fidelity, *n.* alta fedeltà *f.*

high-handed, *adj.* arbitràrio.

high-hat, *vb.* trattare dall'alto in basso.

highland, *n.* regione montuosa *f.*

highlight, *vb.* méttere in rilièvo.

highly, *adv.* altamente, estremamente.

high-minded, *adj.* magnànimo.

Highness, *n.* Altezza *f.*

high noon, *n.* mezzogiorno in punto *m.*

high-pitched, *adj.* acuto; intenso.

high-rise, *n.* costruzione a molti piani *f.*

high school, *n.* licèo *m.,* ginnàsio *m.*

high seas, *n.* alto mare *m. (sg.).*

high-spirited, *adj.* vivace.

high-strung, *adj.* eccitàbile.

high tide, *n.* alta marèa *f.*

high time, *n.* tempo *m.; (it is h.)* é ora.

highway, *n.* strada maestra *f.;* **(h. robber)** grassatore *m.*

hijacker, *n.* dirottatore *m.*

hike, 1. *n.* gita a pièdi *f.* **2.** *vb.* fare una gita a pièdi.

hilarious, *adj.* ìlare.

hilarity, *n*. ilarità *f*.

hill, *n*. collina *f*.

hillside, *n*. pendìo *m*.

hilltop, *n*. cima *f*.

hilly, *adj*. collinoso.

hilt, *n*. èlsa *f*.

him, *pron*. (direct) lo; (indirect) gli; (alone, stressed, or with prep.) lùi.

himself, *pron*. sè stesso; *(refl.)* si.

hind, 1. *n*. cèrva *f*., dàina *f*. 2. *adj*. posteriore.

hinder, *vb*. impedire, ostacolare.

hindmost, *adj*. ùltimo.

hindrance, *n*. impedimento *m*., ostàcolo *m*., intràlcio *m*.

hindsight, *n*. senno di poi *m*.

hinge, *n*. càrdine *m*., gànghero *m*.

hint, 1. *n*. cenno *m*. 2. *vb*. accennare.

hinterland, *n*. retrotèrra *f*.

hip, *n*. anca *f*., fianco *m*.

hippie, *n*. hìppie *m*., capellone *m*.

hippodrome, *n*. ippòdromo *m*.

hippopotamus, *n*. ippopòtamo *m*.

hire, 1. *n*. nòlo *m*. 2. *vb*. noleggiare.

hireling, *n*. mercenàrio *m*.

his, *adj. and pron*. suo, di lùi.

Hispanic, *adj*. ispànico.

hiss, 1. *n*. sìbilo *m*. 2. *vb*. sibilare.

historian, *n*. stòrico *m*.

historic, historical, *adj*. stòrico.

history, *n*. stòria *f*.

histrionic, *adj*. istriònico.

histrionics, *n*. istriònica *f*.

hit, 1. *n*. colpo *m*.; (success) succèsso *m*. 2. *vb*. colpire; percuòtere; picchiare.

hitch, 1. *n*. (obstacle) ostàcolo *m*. 2. *vb*. attaccare.

hitchhike, *vb*. fare l'autostòp.

hitchhiker, *n*. autostoppista *m. and f*.

hither, *adv*. qua.

hitherto, *adv*. finora.

hive, *n*. alveare *m*.

hives, *n*. eruzione cutànea *f*.

hoard, 1. *n*. ammasso *m*. 2. *vb*. ammassare.

hoarse, *adj*. fiòco, ràuco.

hoary, *adj*. canuto, incanutito.

hoax, 1. *n*. inganno *m*. 2. *vb*. ingannare.

hobble, *vb*. zoppicare.

hobby, *n*. passione *f*.

hobby-horse, *n*. cavallo a dòndolo *m*.

hobgoblin, *n*. folletto *m*.

hobnail, *n*. chiòdo gròsso *m*.

hobnob with, *vb*. frequentare.

hobo, *n*. vagabondo *m*.

hock, *vb*. impegnare.

hockey, *n*. hockey *m*.

hocus-pocus, *n*. inganno *m*.

hod, *n*. sècchia *f*.

hodge-podge, *n*. miscùglio *m*.

hoe, 1. *n*. zappa *f*. 2. *vb*. zappare.

hog, *n*. pòrco *m*., maiale *m*.

hog-tie, *vb*. legare bene.

hogshead, *n*. botte *f*.

hoist, *vb*. innalzare.

hold, 1. *n*. presa *f*.; (boat) stiva *f*. 2. *vb*. tenere; (contain) contenere; (**h. up**, support) règgere.

holder, *n*. recipiente *m*.; (**cigarette-h.**) portasigarette *m*.

holdup, *n*. grassazione *f*.

hole, *n*. buco *m*.

holiday, *n*. giorno festivo *m*.; vacanza *f*., fèsta *f*.

holiness, *n*. santità *f*.

Holland, *n*. Olanda *f*.

hollow, *n. and adj*. cavo (*m.*).

holly, *n*. agrifòglio *m*.

hollyhock, *n*. malvaròsa *f*.

holocaust, *n*. olocàusto *m*.

hologram, *n*. ologramma *m*.

holography, *n*. olografìa *f*.

holster, *n*. fondìna *f*.

holy, *adj*. santo.

holy day, *n*. fèsta ecclesiàstica *f*.

Holy See, *n*. Santa Sède *f*.

Holy Spirit, *n*. Spírito Santo *m*.

Holy Week, *n*. settimana santa *f*.

homage, *n*. omàggio *m*.

home, 1. *n*. casa *f*. 2. *adj*. casalingo. 3. *adv*. a casa.

homeland, *n*. pàtria *f*.

homeless, *adj*. sènza tètto.

homelike, *adj*. casalingo.

homely, *adj*. brutto.

home-made, *adj*. fatto in casa.

home rule, *n*. autonomìa *f*.

homesick, be, *vb*. soffrire di nostalgìa.

homesickness, *n*. nostalgìa *f*.

home-spun, *adj*. filato in casa.

homestead, *n*. fattorìa *f*.

homestretch, n. dirittura d'arrivo f.

hometown, n. città natale f.

homeward, adv. vèrso casa.

homework, n. còmpiti m.pl.

homey, adj. ìntimo, còmodo.

homicide, n. (act) omicídio m.; (person) omicida m.

homily, n. omelìa f.

homing pigeon, n. piccione viaggiatore m.

hominy, n. semolino di granturco f.

homogeneity, n. omogeneità f.

homogeneous, adj. omogèneo.

homogenize, vb. omogenizzare.

homonym, n. omònimo m.

homonymous, adj. omònimo.

homosexual, adj. omosessuale.

hone, n. còte f.

honest, adj. onèsto.

honestly, adv. onestamente.

honesty, n. onestà f.

honey, n. mièle m.

honey-bee, n. ape da mièle f.

honeycomb, n. favo m.

honeyed, adj. mielato.

honeymoon, n. luna di mièle m.

honeysuckle, n. caprifòglio m.

honk, vb. (auto horn) suonare.

honor, 1. n. onore m. 2. vb. onorare.

honorable, adj. onorévole.

honorary, adj. onoràrio.

hood, n. cappùccio m.; (auto) còfano m.

hoodlum, n. teppista m.

hoodwink, vb. ingannare.

hoof, n. zòccolo m.

hook, 1. n. uncino m.; **(fishh.)** amo m. 2. vb. uncinare; (catch) prèndere all'amo.

hookworm, n. anchilòstoma m.

hoop, n. cérchio m.

hop, 1. n. (plant) lùppolo m.; (jump) salto m. 2. vb. saltare.

hope, 1. n. speranza f. 2. vb. sperare.

hopeful, adj. pieno di speranza.

hopeless, adj. disperato.

hopelessness, n. disperazione f.

horde, n. òrda f.

horehound, n. marrùbio m.

horizon, n. orizzonte m.

horizontal, adj. orizzontale.

hormone, n. ormone m.

horn, n. còrno m.; (auto) clàcson m.

hornet, n. calabrone m.

horny, adj. calloso.

horoscope, n. oròscopo m.

horrendous, adj. orrèndo.

horrible, adj. orribile.

horrid, adj. òrrido.

horrify, vb. far inorridire; **(be horrified)** inorridire.

horror, n. orrore m.

horse, n. cavallo m.; (cavalry) cavalleria f.

horseback, on, adv. a cavallo.

horsefly, n. mosca cavallina f.

horsehair, n. crine di cavallo f.

horseman, n. cavalière m.

horsemanship, n. equitazione f.

horseplay, n. gièco rozzo m.

horse-power, n. cavallovapore m.

horse-radish, n. ràfano m.

horseshoe, n. fèrro di cavallo m.

horsewhip, n. frustino m.

hortatory, adj. esortatorio.

horticulture, n. orticultura f.

hose, n. (tube) tubo flessìbile m.; (stockings) calze f.pl.

hosiery, n. calzetteria f.

hospitable, adj. ospitale.

hospital, n. ospedale m.

hospitality, n. ospitalità f.

hospitalization, n. ospedalizzazione f.

hospitalize, vb. ospedalizzare.

host, n. (giver of hospitality) òspite m.; (innkeeper) òste m.; (crowd) moltitùdine f.; (Eucharist) òstia f.

hostage, n. ostàggio m.

hostel, n. albérgo m.

hostelry, n. albérgo m.

hostess, n. òspite f.; hostess f.

hostile, adj. ostile.

hostility, n. ostilità f.

hot, adj. caldo; (on water faucets) C.

hotbed, n. terreno concimato m.; (fig.) focolare m.

hot dog, n. salsìccia f.

hotel, n. albérgo m.

hot-headed, adj. eccitàbile.

hothouse, n. sèrra f.

hound, n. cane m.

hour, n. ora f.

hourglass, *n.* clessidra *f.*
hourly, *adv.* ogni ora.
house, *n.* casa *f.;* (legislative) càmera *f.*
housefly, *n.* mosca *f.*
household, *n.* famíglia *f.*
housekeeper, *n.* massaia *f.*
housekeeping, *n.* economía domèstica *f.*
housemaid, *n.* domèstica *f.*
house painter, *n.* imbianchino *m.*
housewarming, *n.* festa di inaugurazione *f.*
housewife, *n.* massaia *f.*
housework, *n.* lavoro domèstico *m.*
housing, *n.* allòggio *m.;* (h. office), *n.* ufficio allocazione alloggi *m.*
hovel, *n.* tugùrio *m.*
hover, *vb.* volteggiare.
hovercraft, *n.* aliscafo *m.*
how, *adv.* come; (h. far) fin dove; (h. long) fino a quando; (h. many, h. much) quanti, quanto.
however, *adv.* comunque, però, tuttavìa.
howitzer, *n.* òbice *m.*
howl, 1. *n.* urlo *m.* 2. *vb.* urlare.
howsoever, *adv.* comunque.
hub, *n.* mòzzo *m.;* (fig.) cèntro *m.*
hubbub, *n.* tumulto *m.*
huckleberry, *n.* mirtillo *m.*
huckster, *n.* trafficante *m.*
huddle, 1. *n.* consultazione *f.* 2. *vb.* rannicchiarsi; (go into a h.) tenere una consultazione.
hue, *n.* sfumatura *f.*
huff, *n.* petulanza *f.*
hug, 1. *n.* abbràccio *m.* 2. *vb.* abbracciare.
huge, *adj.* immane.
hulk, *n.* carcassa *f.*
hulking, *adj.* grosso e goffo.
hull, *n.* (boat) scafo *m.;* (fruit) bùccia *f.*
hullabaloo, *n.* chiasso *m.*
hum, 1. *n.* ronzío *m.* 2. *vb.* (insect) ronzare; (sing) canticchiare.
human, *adj.* umano.
human being, *n.* èssere umano *m.*
humane, *adj.* umanitàrio.
humanism, *n.* umanésimo *m.*
humanist, *n.* umanista *m.*
humanitarian, *adj.* umanitàrio.

humanity, *n.* umanità *f.*
humankind, *n.* gènere umano *m.*
humanly, *adv.* umanamente.
humble, 1. *adj.* ùmile. 2. *vb.* umiliare.
humbug, *n.* impostura *f.*
humdrum, *adj.* monòtono.
humid, *adj.* ùmido.
humidifier, *n.* umidificatore *m.*
humidify, *vb.* inumidire.
humidity, *n.* umidità *f.*
humidor, *n.* scàtola per inumidire i sìgari *f.*
humiliate, *vb.* umiliare.
humiliating, *adj.* umiliante.
humiliation, *n.* umiliazione *f.*
humility, *n.* umiltà *f.*
humor, *n.* umore *m.;* (wit) umorismo *m.*
humorist, *n.* umorista *m.*
humorous, *adj.* umorístico.
hump, *n.* gobba *f.*
humpback, *n.* gobbo *m.,* gobba *f.*
humus, *n.* humus *m.*
hunch, 1. *n.* gobba *f.;* (suspicion) sospètto *m.* 2. *vb.* curvare, *tr.*
hunchback, *n.* gobbo *m.,* gobba *f.*
hundred, *num.* cènto *m.;* (group of a hundred) centinaio *n.m.*
hundredth, *adj.* centésimo.
Hungarian, *adj.* ungherese.
Hungary, *n.* Ungherìa *f.*
hunger, *n.* fame *f.*
hunger strike, *n.* sciòpero della fame *m.*
hungry, be, *vb.* aver fame.
hunk, *n.* pèzzo *m.*
hunt, 1. *n.* càccia *f.* 2. *vb.* cacciare; (h. for) cercare.
hunter, *n.* cacciatore *m.*
hunting, *n.* càccia *f.*
huntress, *n.* cacciatrice *f.*
hurdle, 1. *n.* (hedge) sièpe *f.;* (obstacle) ostàcolo *m.* 2. *vb.* saltare.
hurl, *vb.* lanciare, scagliare.
hurrah for, *interj.* viva, evviva (often written W).
hurricane, *n.* uragàno *m.*
hurry, 1. *n.* fretta *f.* 2. *vb.* affrettare *tr.*
hurt, 1. *n.* danno *m.;* (wound) ferita *f.* 2. *vb.* far male a.
hurtful, *adj.* dannoso.
hurtle, *vb.* precipitarsi.
husband, *n.* marito *m.*

husbandry, *n.* amministrazione *f.*
hush, 1. *vb.* far tacere. **2.** *interj.* zitto!
husk, *n.* bùccia *f.*
husky, *adj.* (strong) fòrte; (hoarse) ràuco.
hustle, 1. *n.* frétta *f.* **2.** *vb.* (shove) spìngere; (hurry) affrettare, *tr.*
hut, *n.* casùpola *f.*
hutch, *n.* coniglièra *f.*
hyacinth, *n.* giacinto *m.*
hybrid, *adj.* ìbrido.
hydrangea, *n.* ortènsia *f.*
hydrant, *n.* idrante *m.*
hydraulic, *adj.* idràulico.
hydrochloric, *adj.* idroclòrico.
hydroelectric, *adj.* idroelèttrico.
hydrogen, *n.* idrògeno *m.*
hydrophobia, *n.* idrofobìa *f.*
hydroplane, *n.* idrovolante *m.*
hydrotherapy, *n.* idroterapèutica *f.*
hyena, *n.* ièna *f.*
hygiene, *n.* igiène *f.*
hygienic, *adj.* igiènico.
hymn, *n.* inno *m.*
hymnal, *n.* innàrio *m.*

hyperacidity, *n.* iperacidità *f.*
hyperbole, *n.* ipèrbole *f.*
hypercritical, *adj.* ipercrìtico.
hypersensitive, *adj.* ipersensitivo.
hypertension, *n.* ipertensione *f.*
hyphen, *n.* tratto d'unione *m.*
hyphenate, *vb.* scrìvere con tratto d'unione.
hypnosis, *n.* ipnòsi *f.*
hypnotic, *adj.* ipnòtico.
hypnotism, *n.* ipnotismo *m.*
hypnotize, *vb.* ipnotizzare.
hypochondria, *n.* ipocondrìa *f.*
hypochondriac, *n. and adj.* ipocondrìaco *(m.)*
hypocrisy, *n.* ipocrisìa *f.*
hypocrite, *n.* ipòcrita *m.*
hypocritical, *adj.* ipòcrito.
hypodermic, *adj.* ipodèrmico.
hypotenuse, *n.* ipotenusa *f.*
hypothesis, *n.* ipòtesi *f.*
hypothetical, *adj.* ipotètico.
hysterectomy, *n.* isterectomìa *f.*
hysteria, hysterics, *n.* isterismo *m.*
hysterical, *adj.* istèrico.

I

I, *pron.* io.
iambic, *adj.* giàmbico.
ice, *n.* ghiàccio *m.*
ice age, *n.* glaciazione *f.,* èra glaciale *f.*
ice-berg, *n.* borgognone *m.*
icebound, *adj.* intrappolato nel ghiaccio.
ice-box, *n.* ghiacciaia *f.*
icebreaker, *n.* rompighiaccio *m.*
ice-cream, *n.* gelato *m.*
ice-skate, *n.* pàttino *m.*
ichthyology, *n.* ittiologìa *f.*
icicle, *n.* ghiacciolo *m.*
icing, *n.* glassa *f.*
icon, *n.* icòne *f.*
icy, *adj.* gelato, ghiacciato.
idea, *n.* idèa *f.*
ideal, *adj.* ideale.
idealism, *n.* idealismo *m.*
idealist, *n.* idealista *m.*
idealistic, *adj.* idealistico.
idealize, *vb.* idealizzare.
ideally, *adv.* idealmente.

identical, *adj.* idèntico.
identifiable, *adj.* identificàbile.
identification, *n.* identificazione *f.*
identify, *vb.* identificare.
identity, *n.* identità *f.*
ideology, *n.* ideologìa *f.*
idiocy, *n.* idiozìa *f.*
idiom, *n.* idiòma *m.*
idiomatic, *adj.* idiomàtico.
idiosyncrasy, *n.* idiosincrasìa *f.*
idiosyncratic, *adj.* idiosincràtico.
idiot, *n.* idiòta *m.*
idiotic, *adj.* idiòta.
idle, *adj.* ozìoso.
idleness, *n.* òzio *m.*
idler, *n.* lazzarone *m.*
idol, *n.* ìdolo *m.*
idolator, *n.* idolatra *m. or f.*
idolatry, *n.* idolatrìa *f.*
idolize, *vb.* idolatrare.
idyl, *n.* idìllio *m.*
idyllic, *adj.* idilliaco.
if, *conj.* se; **(as if)** quasi, como se.

ignite, vb. accèndere.

ignition, n. accensione f.

ignition key, n. chiavetta d'accensione f.

ignoble, adj. ignòbile.

ignominious, adj. ignominioso.

ignoramus, n. ignorantone m.

ignorance, n. ignoranza f.

ignorant, adj. ignorante, ignaro.

ignore, vb. trascurare.

ili, adj. malato.

illegal, adj. illegale.

illegible, adj. illeggìbile.

illegibly, adv. illeggibilmente.

illegitimacy, n. illegittimità f.

illegitimate, adj. illegìttimo.

illicit, adj. illécito.

illiteracy, n. analfabetismo m.

illiterate, n. and adj. analfabèta (m. or f.)

illness, n. malattìa f., malore m.

illogical, adj. illògico.

ill-omened, adj. infàusto.

illuminate, vb. illuminare.

illumination, n. illuminazione f.

illusion, n. illusione f.

illusive, illusory, adj. illusòrio.

illustrate, vb. illustrare.

illustration, n. illustrazione f.

illustrative, adj. illustrativo.

illustrious, adj. illustre.

ill will, n. cattiva volontà f.

image, n. immàgine f.

imagery, n. figure retòriche f.pl.

imaginable, adj. immaginàbile.

imaginary, adj. immaginàrio.

imagination, n. fantasìa f., immaginazione f.

imaginative, adj. immaginativo.

imagine, vb. immaginare, tr., figurarsi.

imam, n. imam m.

imbecile, n. and adj. imbecille (m. or f.)

imitate, vb. imitare.

imitation, n. imitazione f.

imitative, adj. imitativo.

imitator, n. imitatore m.

immaculate, adj. immacolato.

immanent, adj. immanente.

immaterial, adj. immateriale.

immature, adj. immaturo.

immeasurable, adj. non misuràbile, inconmensuràbile.

immediacy, n. immediatezza f.

immediate, adj. immediàto.

immediately, adv. immediatamente, sùbito.

immemorial, adj. immemoràbile.

immense, adj. immènso.

immerse, vb. immèrgere.

immersion, n. immersione f.

immigrant, n. and adj. immigrante.

immigrate, vb. immigrare.

imminent, adj. imminènte.

immobile, adj. immòbile.

immobilize, vb. immobilizzare.

immoderate, adj. immoderato.

immodest, adj. immodèsto, impùdico.

immodesty, n. immodèstia f., impudicìzia f.

immoral, adj. immorale.

immorality, n. immoralità f.

immorally, adv. immoralmente.

immortal, adj. immortale.

immortality, n. immortalità f.

immortalize, vb. immortalare.

immovable, adj. immòbile.

immune, adj. immune, esento.

immunity, n. immunità f.

immunize, vb. immunizzare.

immutable, adj. immutàbile.

imp, n. diavoletto m.

impact, n. urto m.

impair, vb. menomare.

impale, vb. impalare.

impart, vb. impartire.

impartial, adj. imparziale.

impasse, n. impasse f.; vìcolo cieco m.

impassible, adj. impassibile.

impassioned, adj. caloroso, appassionato.

impassive, adj. impassibile.

impatience, n. impaziènza f.

impatient, adj. impaziènte.

impatiently, adv. impazientemente.

impeach, vb. imputare.

impede, vb. impedire.

impediment, n. impedimento m.

impel, vb. impèllere.

impenetrable, adj. impenetràbile.

impenitent, adj. impenitènte.

imperative, n. and adj. imperativo (m.)

imperceptible, adj. impercettìbile.

imperfect, *adj.* imperfètto.
imperfection, *n.* imperfezione *f.*
imperial, *adj.* imperiale.
imperialism, *n.* imperialismo *m.*
imperil, *vb.* méttere in perícolo.
imperious, *adj.* imperioso.
impersonal, *adj.* impersonale.
impersonate, *vb.* impersonare, contraffare.
impersonation, *n.* contraffazione *f.*
impersonator, *n.* impersonatore *m.*
impertinence, *n.* impertinènza *f.*
impertinent, *adj.* impertinènte.
impervious, *adj.* impèrvio.
impetuous, *adj.* impetuoso.
impetus, *n.* ímpeto *m.*
implacable, *adj.* implacàbile.
implant, *vb.* innestare.
implement, *n.* strumento *m.*
implicate, *vb.* implicare.
implication, *n.* implicazione *f.*
implicit, *adj.* implícito.
implied, *adj.* implícito.
implore, *vb.* implorare.
imply, *vb.* implicare; (suggest) suggerire; (insinuate) insinuare.
impolite, *adj.* scortese.
imponderable, *adj.* imponderàbile.
import, 1. *n.* importazione *f.;* (meaning) significato *m.* **2.** *vb.* importare.
importance, *n.* importanza *f.*
important, *adj.* importante; (be i.) importare.
importation, *n.* importazione *f.*
importer, *n.* importatore *m.*
importune, 1. *adj.* importuno. **2.** *vb.* importunare.
impose, *vb.* imporre.
imposition, *n.* imposizione *f.*
impossibility, *n.* impossibilità *f.*
impossible, *adj.* impossíbile.
impotence, *n.* impotènza *f.*
impotent, *adj.* impotènte.
impoverish, *vb.* impoverire.
impregnable, *adj.* inespugnàbile.
impregnate, *vb.* impregnare, ingravidare.
impresario, *n.* impresàrio *m.*
impress, *vb.* (imprint) imprímere; (affect) impressionare.
impression, *n.* impressione *f.*

impressive, *adj.* impressionante.
imprison, *vb.* imprigionare.
imprisonment, *n.* prigionía *f.*
improbable, *adj.* improbàbile.
impromptu, 1. *n.* improvviso *m.* **2.** *adj.* improvvisato; estemporàneo.
improper, *adj.* impròprio, sconveniènte.
improve, *vb.* migliorare.
improvement, *n.* miglioramento *m.*
improvident, *adj.* imprevidente.
improvise, *vb.* improvvisare.
imprudence, *n.* imprudenza *f.*
imprudent, *adj.* imprudente.
impudence, *n.* sfrontatezza *f.;* sfacciatàggine *f.*
impudent, *adj.* impudènte.
impugn, *vb.* impugnare.
impulse, *n.* impulso *m.*
impulsive, *adj.* impulsivo.
impunity, *n.* impunità *f.*
impure, *adj.* impuro.
impurity, *n.* impurità *f.*
impute, *vb.* imputare.
in, *prep.* in; (within, of time) entro.
inadvertent, *adj.* disattento, distratto.
inalienable, *adj.* inalienàbile.
inane, *adj.* inane, fùtile.
inaugural, *adj.* inaugurale; (speech) discorso inaugurale *n.m.*
inaugurate, *vb.* inaugurare.
inauguration, *n.* inaugurazione *f.*
inborn, *adj.* innato, congènito.
inbreeding, *n.* incrocio fra animali e piante affini *m.*
incandescence, *n.* incandescènza *f.*
incandescent, *adj.* incandescènte.
incantation, *n.* incantamento *m.*
incapacitate, *vb.* rèndere incapace.
incapacity, *n.* incapacità *f.*
incarcerate, *vb.* incarcerare.
incarnate, *adj.* incarnato.
incarnation, *n.* incarnazione *f.*
incendiary, *n. and adj.* incendiàrio *(m.).*
incense, *n.* incènso *m.*
incentive, *n.* incentivo *m.*
inception, *n.* inízio *m.*
incessant, *adj.* incessante.

incest, n. incèsto m.

inch, n. pòllice m.

incidence, n. incidènza f.

incident, n. incidènte m.

incidental, adj. incidentale.

incidentally, adv. incidentalmente.

incipient, adj. incipiènte.

incise, vb. incídere.

incision, n. incisione f.

incisive, adj. incisivo.

incisor, n. dènte incisivo m.

incite, vb. incitare.

inclination, n. inclinazione f.

incline, 1. n. pendío m. **2.** vb. inclinare; (fig.) propèndere.

inclined, adj. (disposed) propènso.

inclose, vb. rinchiùdere; (in letter) acclùdere.

include, vb. inclùdere.

including, prep. compreso (adj., agrees with following noun).

inclusive, adj. inclusivo.

incognito, adj. incògnito.

income, n. rèddito m.

incomparable, adj. incomparàbile.

inconsiderate, adj. strafottènte; villano.

inconstant, adj. inconstante.

inconvenience, 1. n. scomodità f. **2.** vb. incomodare.

inconvenient, adj. incòmodo.

incorporate, vb. incorporare tr.

incorrigible, adj. incorreggìbile.

increase, 1. n. aumento m. **2.** vb. accréscere, aumentare.

incredible, adj. incredìbile.

incredulity, n. incredulità f.

incredulous, adj. incrèdulo.

increment, n. incremento m.

incriminate, vb. incriminare.

incrimination, n. incriminazione f.

incrust, vb. incrostare.

incubator, n. incubatrice f.

inculcate, vb. inculcare.

incumbency, n. durata in càrica f.

incumbent, 1. n. titolare m. **2.** adj. incombènte.

incur, vb. incórrere in.

incurable, adj. incuràbile.

indebted, adj. indebitato.

indeed, adv. davvero.

indefatigable, adj. infaticàbile.

indefinite, adj. indefinito.

indefinitely, adv. indefinitamente.

indelible, adj. indelèbile.

indemnify, vb. indennizzare.

indemnity, n. indennità f.

indent, vb. dentellare; (paragraph) allineare all'interno; (coastline) frastagliare.

indentation, n. dentallatura f.

independence, n. indipendènza f.

independent, adj. indipendènte.

in-depth, adj. profondo; esauriente.

index, n. índice m.

India, n. Índia f.

Indian, 1. n. indiano; (American Indian) pellirossa m. **2.** adj. indiano; dei pellirossa.

Indian wrestling, n. braccio di ferro m.

indicate, vb. indicare.

indication, n. indicazione f.

indicative, n. and adj. indicativo (m.)

indicator, n. indicatore m.

indict, vb. accusare.

indictment, n. accusa f.

indifference, n. indifferènza f.

indifferent, adj. indifferènte.

indigenous, adj. indígeno.

indigent, adj. indigènte.

indigestion, n. indigestione f.

indignant, adj. indignato.

indignation, n. indignazione f.

indignity, n. indegnità f., sgarberìa f.

indigo, n. indaco m.

indirect, adj. indiretto.

indiscreet, adj. indiscreto.

indiscretion, n. indiscrezione f.

indispensable, adj. indispensàbile.

indispose, vb. indisporre.

indisposed, adj. indisposto.

indisposition, n. indisposizione f.

indissoluble, adj. indissolùbile.

individual, 1. n. individuo m. **2.** adj. individuale.

individuality, n. individualità f.

individually, adj. individualmente.

indivisible, adj. indivisìbile.

Indochina, n. indocina f.

indoctrinate, vb. indottrinare.
indolent, adj. indolènte.
Indonesia, n. Indonèsia f.
indoor, adj. al coperto.
indoors, adv. al coperto; a casa.
indorse, vb. firmare; (check, etc.) girare.
induce, vb. indurre.
inducement, n. incentivo m.
induct, vb. (into army) arruolare.
induction, n. induzione f.
inductive, adj. induttivo.
indulge, vb. indùlgere.
indulgence, n. indulgènza f.
indulgent, adj. indulgènte.
industrial, adj. industriale.
industrialist, n. industriale m.
industrious, adj. industrioso, operoso.
industry, n. indùstria f.
inebriate, 1. n. ubriacone m. 2. vb. inebriare.
ineligible, adj. ineleggìbile, inàbile.
inept, adj. inètto.
inert, adj. inèrte.
inertia, n. inèrzia f.
inescapable, adj. ineluttàbile.
inevitable, adj. inevitàbile.
inexact, adj. inesatto.
inexorable, adj. inesoràbile.
inexpensive, adj. a buòn mercato.
inexplicable, adj. inesplicàbile.
infallible, adj. infallìbile.
infamous, adj. infame.
infamy, n. infàmia f.
infancy, n. infànzia f.
infant, n. infante m.
infantile, adj. infantile.
infantry, n. fanterìa f.
infantryman, n. fante m.
infatuate, vb. infatuare.
infatuated, adj. innamorato, infatuato.
infect, vb. infettare.
infected, adj. infètto.
infection, n. infezione f.
infectious, adj. infettivo.
infer, vb. inferire, desùmere.
inference, n. inferènza f.
inferior, adj. inferiore.
inferiority, n. inferiorità f.; (i. complex) complesso d'inferiorità.
infernal, adj. infernale.

inferno, n. infèrno m.
infest, vb. infestare.
infidel, n. and adj. infedele; miscredènte.
infidelity, n. infedeltà f.
infiltrate, vb. infiltrare, tr.
infinite, n. and adj. infinito (m.).
infinitesimal, adj. infinitesimale.
infinitive, n. infinito m.
infinity, n. infinità f.
infirm, adj. infèrmo; (weak) dèbole; (unsure) irresoluto.
infirmary, n. infermerìa f.
infirmity, n. infermità f.
inflame, vb. infiammare.
inflammable, adj. infiammàbile.
inflammation, n. infiammazione f.
inflammatory, adj. infiammatòrio.
inflate, vb. gonfiare.
inflation, n. gonfiamento m.; (financial) inflazione f.
inflection, n. inflessione f.; (gram.) flessione f.
inflict, vb. infliggere.
infliction, n. inflizione f.
influence, n. influènza f., influsso m.
influential, adj. influènte.
influenza, n. influènza f.
inform, vb. informare.
informal, adj. senza cerimònie, informale.
information, n. informazioni f.pl.
informed sources, n. fonti accreditate f.pl.
informer, n. informatore m.
infraction, n. infrazione f.
infrared, 1. n. infrarosso m. 2. adj. all'infrarosso.
infrequent, adj. infrequente.
infringe, vb. infràngere.
infuriate, vb. far infuriare; (become i.d) infuriare.
ingenious, adj. ingegnoso.
ingenuity, n. ingegnosità f.
ingredient, n. ingrediènte m.
inhabit, vb. abitare.
inhabitant, n. abitante m.
inhale, vb. inalare.
inherent, adj. inerènte.
inherit, vb. ereditare.
inheritance, n. eredità f., retàggio m.

inhibit, *vb.* inibire.
inhibition, *n.* inibizione *f.*
inhuman, *adj.* inumano.
inimical, *adj.* nemico.
inimitable, *adj.* inimitàbile.
iniquity, *n.* iniquità *f.*
initial, *n. and adj.* iniziale *(f.)*
initiate, *vb.* iniziare.
initiation, *n.* iniziazione *f.*
initiative, *n.* iniziativa *f.*
inject, *vb.* iniettare.
injection, *n.* iniezione *f.*
injunction, *n.* ingiunzione *f.*
injure, *vb.* (harm) danneggiare, nuòcere; (wound) ferire.
injurious, *adj.* dannoso, nocivo.
injury, *n.* danno *m.*, ferita *f.*
injustice, *n.* ingiustizia *f.*
ink, *n.* inchiòstro *m.*
inland, 1. *adj.* intèrno; 2. *adv.* vèrso l'intèrno.
inlet, *n.* pòrto *m.*, canale *m.*
inmate, *n.* paziènte *f.*
inn, *n.* locanda *f.*
inner, *adj.* interiore, intèrno.
innermost, *adj.* più íntimo.
innocence, *n.* innocènza *f.*
innocent, *adj.* innocènte.
innocuous, *adj.* innòcuo.
innovation, *n.* innovazione *f.*
innuendo, *n.* insinuazione *f.*
innumerable, *adj.* innumerévole.
inoculate, *vb.* inoculare.
inoculation, *n.* inoculazione *f.*
input, *n.* entrata *f.*; informazioni fornite *f.pl.*
inquest, *n.* inchièsta *f.*
inquire, *vb.* informarsi.
inquiry, *n.* ricerca d'informazioni *f.*, investigazione *f.*, inchièsta *f.*
inquisition, *n.* inquisizione *f.*
inquisitive, *adj.* eccessivamente curioso.
inroad, *n.* incursione *f.*
insane, *adj.* insano, pazzo.
insanity, *n.* insània *f.*, pazzía *f.*
insatiable, *adj.* insaziàbile.
inscribe, *vb.* iscrivere.
inscription, *n.* iscrizione *f.*
insect, *n.* insètto *m.*
insecticide, *n.* pólvere insetticida *m*
insecure, *adj.* insicuro.
insensible, *adj.* insensíbile.
insensitive, *adj.* insensíbile.

insensitivity, *n.* insensibilità *f.*
inseparable, *adj.* inseparàbile.
insert, 1. *n.* inserto *m.* 2. *vb.* inserire.
insertion, *n.* inserzione *f.*
inshore, *adj. and adv.* presso la spiàggia.
inside, 1. *n.* intèrno *m.* 2. *adj.* intèrno, interiore. 3. *adv., prep.* dentro.
insidious, *adj.* insidioso.
insight, *n.* penetrazione *f.*
insignia, *n.* insegne *f.pl.*
insignificance, *n.* insignificanza *f.*
insignificant, *adj.* insignificante.
insinuate, *vb.* insinuare.
insinuation, *n.* insinuazione *f.*
insipid, *adj.* insípido; (dull) insulso.
insist, *vb.* insistere.
insistence, *n.* insistènza *f.*
insistent, *adj.* insistènte.
insolence, *n.* insolènza *f.*
insolent, *adj.* insolènte.
insolently, *adv.* insolentemente.
insomnia, *n.* insònnia *f.*
inspect, *vb.* ispezionare.
inspection, *n.* ispezione *f.*
inspector, *n.* ispettore *m.*
inspiration, *n.* ispirazione *f.*
inspire, *vb.* ispirare.
install, *vb.* installare; (a person) insediare
installation, *n.* installazione *f.*; (of a person) insediamento *m.*; (industrial) impianto *m.*
installment, *n.* (payment) rata *f.*; (story, etc.) puntata *f.*
instance, *n.* istanza *f.*; (example) esèmpio *m.*; (request) richièsta *f.*; (for i.) per esèmpio.
instant, 1. *n.* istante *m.*, àttimo *m.* 2. *adj.* immediato; (date) corrènte.
instantaneous, *adj.* istantàneo.
instantly, *adv.* immediatamente.
instead, *adv.* invece; (i. of) invece di.
instigate, *vb.* istigare.
instill, *vb.* istillare.
instinct, *n.* istinto *m.*
instinctive, *adj.* istintivo.
institute, *n.* istituto *m.*
institution, *n.* istituzione *f.*
instruct, *vb.* istruire.

instruction, n. istruzione f.

instructive, adj. istruttivo.

instructor, n. istruttore m.

instructress, n. istruttrice f.

instrument, n. strumento m.

instrumental, adj. strumentale.

insufferable, adj. intolleràbile.

insufficient, adj. insufficiènte.

insular, adj. insulare.

insulate, vb. isolare.

insulation, n. isolamento m.

insulator, n. isolatore m.

insulin, n. insulina f.

insult, 1. n. insulto m., ingiùria f. **2.** vb. insultare, ingiurare.

insulting, adj. insultante, ingiurioso.

insuperable, adj. insuperàbile.

insurance, n. assicurazione f.

insure, vb. assicurare, tr.

insurer, n. assicuratore m.

insurgent, n. and adj. ribèlle (m.)

insurmountable, adj. insormontàbile.

insurrection, n. insurrezione f.

intact, adj. intatto.

intake, n. ammissione f.; immissione f.

intangible, adj. intangìbile.

integer, n. nùmero intero m.

integral, adj. integrale.

integrate, vb. integrare.

integrity, n. integrità f.

intellect, n. intellètto m.

intellectual, adj. intellettuale.

intelligence, n. intelligènza f.

intelligent, adj. intelligènte.

intelligentsia, n. intellighènzia f.

intelligible, adj. intelligìbile.

intend, vb. intèndere.

intended, adj. inteso, promesso.

intense, adj. intènso.

intensify, vb. intensificare.

intensity, n. intensità f.

intensive, 1. adj. intensivo.

intent, 1. n. intènto m., intendimento m. **2.** adj. intènto; **(i. on)** intènto a.

intention, n. intenzione f., propòsito m.

intentional, adj. intenzionale.

intentionally, adv. intenzionalmente, apposta.

inter, vb. seppellire.

interact, vb. interagire.

interaction, n. interazione f.

interbreed, vb. incrociare.

intercede, vb. intercèdere.

intercept, vb. intercettare.

interchange, 1. n. interscambio m.; svìncolo m. **2.** vb. interscambiare.

intercourse, n. rappòrto m.

interdict, 1. n. interdetto m. **2.** vb. interdire.

interest, 1. n. interèsse m. **2.** vb. interessare; **(be i.ed in)** interessarsi di.

interesting, adj. interessante.

interface, n. interfàccia f.

interfere, vb. **(i. in)** immischiarsi in, intervenire in; **(i. with)** ostacolare, interferire.

interference, n. ingerènza f.; (physics) interferènza f.

interim, 1. n. frattèmpo m. **2.** adj. provvisòrio.

interior, n. and adj. interiore (m.)

interject, vb. inframettere.

interjection, n. interiezione f.

interlude, n. interlùdio m.

intermarry, vb. fare matrimoni misti.

intermediary, n. and adj. intermediàrio (m.)

intermediate, adj. intermèdio.

interment, n. sepoltura f.

intermission, n. intermissione f., intervallo m.

intermittent, adj. intermittènte.

intern, vb. internare.

internal, adj. intèrno.

Internal Revenue Service, n. Fisco m. (coll.)

international, adj. internazionale.

internationalism, n. internazionalismo m.

interne, n. mèdico intèrno m.

interpose, vb. interporre.

interpret, vb. interpretare.

interpretation, n. interpretazione f.

interpreter, n. intèrprete m.

interrogate, vb. interrogare.

interrogation, n. interrogazione f.

interrogative, adj. interrogativo.

interrupt, vb. interrómpere.

interruption, n. interruzione f.

intersect, vb. intersecare, tr.; (cross) incrociarsi.

intersection, n. intersezione, f.; (crossing) incrócio m.

intersperse, vb. cospàrgere.

interval, n. intervallo m.

intervene, vb. intervenire.

intervention, n. intervènto m.

interview, 1. n. intervista f. **2.** vb. intervistare.

intestine, n. and adj. intestino (m.)

intimacy, n. intimità f.

intimate, adj. intimo.

intimidate, vb. intimidire.

intimidation, n. intimidazione f.

into, prep. in.

intolerant, adj. intollerante.

intonation, n. intonazione f.

intone, vb. intonare.

intoxicant, 1. n. sostanza tossica f.; bevanda alcolica f. **2.** adj. intossicante.

intoxicate, vb. (poison) intossicare; (get drunk) inebriare.

intoxication, n. intossicazione f., ubriachezza f.

intransigent, n.m. and f. and adj. intransigente.

intransitive, adj. intransitivo.

intravenous, adj. endovenoso.

intrepid, adj. intrepido.

intrepidity, n. intrepidità f.

intricacy, n. complicazione f.

intricate, adj. intricato, complicato.

intrigue, 1. n. intrigo m.; (love affair) tresca f. **2.** vb. intrigare.

intrinsic, adj. intrínseco.

introduce, vb. introdurre; (persons) presentare.

introduction, n. introduzione f. presentazione f.

introductory, adj. introduttivo.

introspection, n. introspezione f.

introvert, n.m. introverso.

introverted, adj. introverso, introvertito.

intrude, vb. intrufolarsi, tr.

intruder, n. intruso m.

intuition, n. intuizione f.

intuitive, adj. intuitivo.

inundate, vb. inondare.

invade, vb. invàdere.

invader, n. invasore m.

invalid, n. and adj. invàlido (m.)

invariable, adj. invariàbile.

invasion, n. invasione f.

invective, n. invettiva f.

inveigle, vb. sedurre, adescare.

invent, vb. inventare.

invention, n. invenzione f.

inventive, adj. inventivo.

inventor, n. inventore m.

inventory, n. inventàrio m.

inverse, adj. invèrso.

invertebrate, n. and adj. invertebrato (m.)

invest, vb. investire.

investigate, vb. investigare.

investigation, n. investigazione f.

investment, n. investimento m.

inveterate, adj. inveterato.

invidious, adj. odioso.

invigorate, vb. invigorire.

invincible, adj. invincíbile.

invisible, adj. invisibile.

invitation, n. invito m.

invite, vb. invitare.

invocation, n. invocazione f.

invoice, 1. n. fattura f. **2.** vb. fatturare.

invoke, vb. invocare.

involuntary, adj. involontàrio.

involve, vb. coinvòlgere, implicare.

involved, adj. complicato.

invulnerable, adj. invulneràbile.

inward, 1. adj. íntimo. **2.** adv. vèrso l'interno.

inwardly, adv. intimamente.

iodine, n. iòdio m.

Iran, n. Iran m.

Iraq, n. Iràk m.

irate, adj. irato.

ire, n. ira f.

Ireland, n. Irlanda f.

iridium, n. iridio m.

iris, n. iride f.; (flower) iris f.

Irish, adj. irlandese.

irk, vb. infastidire.

iron, 1. n. fèrro m.; **(flat-i.)** fèrro da stiro. **2.** adj. di fèrro, fèrreo. **3.** vb. stirare.

ironical, adj. irònico.

ironworks, n. ferrièra f.sg.

irony, n. ironia f.

irrational, adj. irrazionale.

irrefutable, adj. irrefutàbile.

irregular, *adj.* irregolare.
irregularity, *n.* irregolarità *f.*
irrelevant, *adj.* non pertinènte, irrilevante.
irreprehensible, *adj.* irreprensíbile.
irreprehensibly, *adv.* irrepren-
síbilmente.
irresistible, *adj.* irresistíbile.
irresponsible, *adj.* irresponsàbile.
irreverent, *adj.* irriverènte.
irrevocable, *adj.* irrevocàbile.
irrigate, *vb.* irrigare.
irrigation, *n.* irrigazióne *f.*
irritability, *n.* irritabilità *f.*
irritable, *adj.* irritàbile.
irritant, *adj.* irritante.
irritate, *vb.* irritare.
irritation, *n.* irritazióne *f.*
island, *n.* ísola *f.*
isolate, *vb.* isolare.
isolation, *n.* isolamento *m.*
isolationist, *n.* isolazionista *m.*
isosceles, *adj.* isòscele.
Israel, *n.* Israèle *m.*
Israeli, *adj.* israeliano.

Israelite, 1. *n.* israelita *m.* **2.** *adj.*
israelítico.
issuance, *n.* emissióne *f.*
issue, 1. *n.* (offspring) pròle *f.;*
(bonds, etc.) emissióne *f.;* (river)
foce *f.;* (magazine) nùmero *m.* **2.**
vb. (come out) uscire; (publish)
pubblicare.
isthmus, *n.* istmo *m.*
it, *pron.* ciò; (subject) esso; (direct
object) lo, la.
Italian, *adj.* italiano.
Italic, *adj.* itàlico.
italics, *n.* corsivo *m.sg.*
Italy, *n.* Itàlia *f.*
itch, 1. *n.* prudore *m.,* prurito *m.* **2.**
vb. prùdere.
itchy, *adj.* che prude.
item, *n.* artícolo *m.*
itemize, *vb.* elencare.
itinerant, *adj.* girovago.
itinerary, *n.* itineràrio *m.*
its, *adj.* suo.
itself, *pron.* esso stesso.
ivory, *n.* avòrio *m.*
ivy, *n.* édera *f.*

J

jab, *vb.* pugnalare.
jabber, *vb.* borbottare.
jack, *n.* binda *f.,* cricco *m.,* martinèllo *m.*
jack-of-all-trades, *n.* factotum
m.
jackal, *n.* sciacallo *m.*
jackass, *n.* àsino *m.*
jacket, *n.* giacca *f.,* giacchetta *f.*
jackhammer, *n.* martello
pneumàtico *m.*
jack-knife, *n.* coltèllo a serramànico *m.*
jade, *n.* giada *f.*
jaded, *adj.* sfinito.
jagged, *adj.* seghettato.
jaguar, *n.* giaguaro *m.*
jail, *n.* càrcere *m.,* prigione *f.*
jailer, *n.* carcerière *m.*
jam, *n.* marmellata *f.;* (trouble)
impíccio *m.*
jamb, *n.* stípite *m.*
jangle, *n.* rumore aspro *m.*
janitor, *n.* bidèllo *m.*
January, *n.* gennaio *m.*

Japan, *n.* il Giappone *m.*
Japanese, *adj.* giapponese.
jar, 1. *n.* giara *f.;* (glass) bottíglia *f.*
2. *vb.* scuòtere; (displease) offèndere.
jargon, *n.* gèrgo *m.*
jasmine, *n.* gelsomino *m.*
jaundice, *n.* itterízia *f.*
jaunt, *n.* escursione *f.*
jaunty, *adj.* disinvolto.
javelin, *n.* giavellòtto *m.*
jaw, *n.* mascèlla *f.*
jawbreaker, *n.* scioglilingua *f.*
jay, *n.* ghiandaia *f.*
jaywalk, *vb.* attraversare la strada
all'infuòri dei passaggi pedonali.
jazz, *n.* jazz *m.* (pronounced
giazz).
jealous, *adj.* geloso.
jealousy, *n.* gelosía *f.*
jeans, *n.* jeans *m.pl.*
jeep, *n.* gip *f.,* jeep *f.*
jeer (at), *vb.* beffarsi (di).
Jehovah's Witnesses, *n.* Tes-
timoni di Gèova *m.pl.*

jelly, n. gelatina f.

jelly-fish, n. medusa f.

jeopardize, vb. méttere in perícolo.

jeopardy, n. perícolo m.

jerk, 1. n. strattone m., sbalzellone m. 2. vb. tirare con strattoni.

jerked beef, n. carne essiccata f.

jerkin, n. giubbotto m.

jerky, adj. a strattoni.

jersey, n. màglia f.

Jerusalem, n. Gerusalèmme f.

jest, 1. n. scherzo m. 2. vb. scherzare.

jester, n. buffone m.

Jesuit, n. gesuita m.

Jesus Christ, n. Gesù Cristo m.

jet, 1. n. (black substance) giavazzo m.; (emission) gètto m.; (plane) reattore m., aviogètto m. 2. adj. a reazione. 3. vb. sgorgare.

jet lag, n. sfasamento prodotto dal passaggio attraverso parecchi fusi orari m., jet lag m.

jetsam, n. relitto m.

jettison, vb. gettare in mare.

jetty, n. mòlo m.

Jew, n. ebrèo m., giudèo m.

jewel, n. gioièllo m.

jewel case, n. scrigno m.; portagiòie m.

jeweler, n. gioiellière m.

jewelry, n. gioiellería f.

Jewish, adj. ebrèo, ebràico.

jib, 1. n. fiòcco m. 2. vb. (horse) recalcitrare; (refuse) rifiutarsi.

jibe, 1. n. bèffa f. 2. vb. (j. at) beffarsi di.

jiffy, n. istante m.

jig, n. giga f.

jigsaw, n. rompicapo m.

jilt, vb. abbandonare.

jingle, vb. tintinnare.

jinx, n. malaugùrio m.

jittery, adj. nervoso.

job, n. impiègo m., occupazione f.

jobber, n. commerciante all'ingròsso m.

jobless, adj. disoccupato.

jockey, n. fantino m.

jocular, adj. umorístico.

jocund, adj. giocondo.

jog, vb. scuòtere.

joggle, n. caletta f.

Johnny-come-lately, n. ritardatario m.

join, 1. n. congiunzione f. 2. vb. congiùngere; (associate with) associarsi con; (j. up) arruolarsi.

joiner, n. (carpenter) falegname m.

joint, 1. n. giuntura f., articolazione f. 2. adj. congiunto, collettivo.

jointly, adv. collettivamente, congiuntamente.

joist, n. travicèllo m.

joke, 1. n. schèrzo m.; (trick) burla f. 2. vb. scherzare.

joker, n. burlone m.

jolly, adj. allegro.

jolt, 1. n. scòssa f., sobbalzo m. 2. vb. sobbalzare.

jonquil, n. giunchiglia f.

josh, vb. canzonare.

jostle, vb. spíngere.

jounce, 1. n. sobbalzo m. 2. vb. sobbalzare.

journal, n. giornale m.

journalism, n. giornalismo m.

journalist, n. giornalista m.

journey, 1. n. viàggio m. 2. vb. viaggiare.

journeyman, n. operaio espèrto m.

jovial, adj. gioviale.

jowl, n. guància f.

joy, n. giòia f.

joyful, adj. gioioso.

joyous, adj. gioioso.

jubilant, adj. giubilante.

jubilee, n. giubilèo m.

Judaism, n. giudaismo m.

judge, 1. n. giùdice m. 2. vb. giudicare.

judgment, n. giudízio m.

judicial, adj. giudiziàrio; (impartial) imparziale.

judiciary, 1. n. magistratura f. 2. adj. giudiziàrio.

judicious, adj. giudizioso.

jug, n. bròcca f.

juggle, vb. far giòchi di prestígio.

juggler, n. prestigiatore m.

jugular, adj. giugulare.

juice, n. succo m.

juicy, adj. succoso.

July, n. lùglio m.

jumble, *n.* confusione *f.*
jumbo, *adj.* enorme.
jump, 1. *n.* salto *m.* **2.** *vb.* saltare.
jump seat, *n.* spuntino *m.*, strapuntino *m.*
junction, *n.* bívio *m.*, diramazione *f.*, biforcazione *f.*
juncture, *n.* giuntura *f.*
June, *n.* giugno *m.*
jungle, *n.* giungla *f.*
junior, *adj.* minore; (in names) iuniore.
junior college, *n.* primo biènnio universitario *m.*
junior high school, *n.* scuola media *f.*
juniper, *n.* ginepro *m.*
junk, *n.* roba vecchia *f.*; cianfrusaglie *f.pl.*

junket, *n.* (food) giuncata *f.*; (trip) escursione *f.*
jurisdiction, *n.* giurisdizione *f.*
jurisprudence, *n.* giurisprudènza *f.*
jurist, *n.* giurista *f.*
juror, *n.* giurato *m.*
jury, *n.* giuría *f.*
just, 1. *adj.* giusto **2.** *adv.* pròprio; (**j. now**) or'ora.
justice, *n.* giustízia *f.*
justifiable, *adj.* giustificàbile.
justification, *n.* giustificazione *f.*
justify, *vb.* giustificare.
jut, *vb.* proiettarsi, spòrgere.
jute, *n.* iuta *f.*
juvenile, *adj.* giovanile.
juxtapose, *vb.* giustapporre.

K

kale, *n.* càvolo *m.*
kaleidoscope, *n.* caleidoscòpio *m.*
kangaroo, *n.* canguro *m.*
karakul, *n.* lince persiana *f.*
karat, *n.* carato *m.*
karate, *n.* karate *m.*
keel, *n.* chíglia *f.*
keen, *adj.* acuto.
keep, *vb.* conservare, serbare, mantenere, tenere; (stay) tenersi.
keeper, *n.* custòde *m.*
keepsake, *n.* ricòrdo *m.*
keg, *n.* barilotto *m.*
kennel, *n.* canile *m.*
kerchief, *n.* fazzoletto *m.*
kernel, *n.* gheríglio *m.*; (fig.) nòcciolo *m.*
kerosene, *n.* petròlio raffinato *m.*, cheroseno *m.*
ketchup, *n.* salsa di pomodoro *f.*
kettle, *n.* péntola *f.*
kettledrum, *n.* tímpano *m.*
key, *n.* chiave *f.*; (piano) tasto *m.*; (musical structure) tonalità *f.*
keyboard, *n.* tastièra *f.*
keyhole, *n.* buco della serratura *f.*
keynote, *n.* (music) tono *m.*; (speech) principio chiave *m.*
keypunch, *vb.* perforare.
keyring, *n.* portachiavi *m.*

keystone, *n.* chiave di volta *f.*
keyword, *n.* parola chiave *f.*
khaki, *n.* cachi *m.*
kick, 1. *n.* càlcio *m.* **2.** *vb.* tirar calci (a).
kid, 1. *n.* (goat) capretto *m.*; (child) ragazzo *m.*, ragazza *f.* **2.** *vb.* prèndere in giro.
kidnap, *vb.* rapire.
kidnapper, *n.* rapitore *m.*
kidnapping, *n.* rapimento *m.*
kidney, *n.* rène *m.*; (as food) rognone *m.*
kidney bean, *n.* fagiolo reniforme *m.*
kill, *vb.* uccídere.
killer, *n.* uccisore *m.*
kiln, *n.* fornace *f.*
kilocycle, *n.* chilociclo *m.*
kilogram, *n.* chilogramma *m.*; chilo *m.*; (abbr.) kg.
kilohertz, *n.* kilohertz *m.*
kilometer, *n.* chilòmetro *m.*; (abbr.) km.
kilowatt, *n.* chilowatt *m.*; (abbr.) kw.
kilt, *n.* gonnellino *m.*; kilt *m.*
kimono, *n.* chimono *m.*
kin, *n.* parentela *f.*
kind, 1. *n.* gènere *m.*, razza *f.* **2.** *adj.* gentile.

kindergarten, *n.* giardino d'infànzia *m.*
kindle, *vb.* accèndere.
kindling, *n.* legna minuta *f.*
kindly, *adj.* benèvolo.
kindness, *n.* gentilezza *f.*
kindred, 1. *n.* parentela *f.* **2.** *adj.* imparentato; (alike) affine.
kinetic, *adj.* cinètico.
king, *n.* re *m.*
kingdom, *n.* regno *m.*
kingly, *adj.* reale, maestoso.
king-size, *adj.* extra grande.
kink, *n.* nodo *m.*
kiosk, *n.* chiòsco *m.*
kiss, 1. *n.* bàcio *m.* **2.** *vb.* baciare.
kitchen, *n.* cucina *f.*
kitchenware, *n.* uténsili da cucina *m.pl.*
kite, *n.* aquilone *m.;* (bird) nìbbio *m.*
kitten, *n.* gattino *m.*
kleptomania, *n.* cleptomanìa *f.*
kleptomaniac, *n.* cleptòmane *m.*
knack, *n.* facoltà *m.*
knapsack, *n.* zàino *m.*
knead, *vb.* impastare.
knee, *n.* ginócchio *m.*
knee-cap, *n.* rotèlla del ginócchio *f.*
kneel, *vb.* inginocchiarsi.
knell, *n.* rintocco *m.*
knickers, *n.* pantaloni *m.pl.*
knife, *n.* coltèllo *m.*
knight, *n.* cavalière *m.;* (chess) cavallo *m.*
knit, *vb.* lavorare a maglia; (**k. one's brows**) aggrottare le ciglia.
knock, *vb.* **1.** *n.* bussata *f.* **2.** *vb.* bussare; (strike) colpire; (**k. down**) abbàttere.
knot, *n.* nodo *m.*
knotty, *adj.* nodoso.
know, *vb.* (from outside in) conóscere; (from inside out) sapere; (**k. how to**) sapere.
knowledge, *n.* conoscènza *f.;* (**without the k. of**) all'insaputa di.
knuckle, *n.* nòcca *f.*
kodak, *n.* kodak *f.*
Korea, *n.* Corèa *f.*
kosher, *adj.* secondo la norma della religione ebraica; (coll.) autèntico.

L

label, *n.* etichetta *f.*
labor, 1. *n.* lavoro *m.;* (workers) manodòpera *f.* **2.** *vb.* lavorare.
laboratory, *n.* laboratòrio *m.*
laborer, *n.* lavoratore *m.*
laborious, *adj.* laborioso.
labor union, *n.* sindacato operaio *m.*
laburnum, *n.* avornièllo *m.*
labyrinth, *n.* labirinto *m.*
lace, *n.* merletto *m.,* pizzo *m.*
lacerate, *vb.* lacerare.
laceration, *n.* lacerazione *f.*
lack, 1. *n.* mancanza *f.* **2.** *vb.* mancare.
lackadaisical, *adj.* lànguido.
lackey, *n.* lacchè *m.*
laconic, *adj.* lacònico.
lacquer, 1. *n.* lacca *f.* **2.** *vb.* laccare.
lactic, *adj.* làttico.
lactose, *n.* lattòsio *m.*
lacy, *adj.* leggèro come merletti.
lad, *n.* ragazzo *m.*
ladder, *n.* scala a pioli *f.;* (stocking) cordiglièra *f.*
ladies, *n.* signore *f.pl.*
ladle, *n.* mèstolo *m.,* ramaiuòlo *m.*
lady, *n.* signora *f.*
ladybug, *n.* coccinèlla *f.*
lag, 1. *n.* ritardo *m.* **2.** *vb.* indugiare.
lag behind, *vb.* restare indiètro.
lager beer, *n.* birra stagionata *f.*
laggard, *n.* pigro *m.*
lagoon, *n.* laguna *f.*
laid-back, *adj.* calmo.
lair, *n.* covo *m.,* tana *f.*
laity, *n.* laicato *m.*
lake, 1. *n.* lago *m.* **2.** *adj.* lacuale.
lamb, *n.* agnèllo *m.;* (meat) abbàcchio *m.*
lambast, *vb.* sferzare, stroncare.
lame, *adj.* zòppo.
lament, 1. *n.* lamento *m.* **2.** *vb.* lamentare.

lamentable, adj. lamentévole.

lamentation, n. lamentazione f.

laminate, vb. laminare.

lamp, n. làmpada f.

lampoon, n. pasquinata f.

lance, 1. n. lància f. 2. vb. tagliare colla lancetta f.

land, 1. n. tèrra f.; (country) paese m. 2. vb. (from boat) sbarcare; (plane) atterrare.

landfall, n. avvistamento di terre m.; (landslide) frana f., slavina f.

landholder, n. proprietàrio di terre m.; latifondista f.

landing, n. sbarco m.; (plane) atterràggio m.

landlady, n. padrona f.

landlord, n. padrone m.

landmark, n. monumento m.

landscape, n. paesaggio m.

landslide, n. frana f.

landward, adv. vèrso tèrra.

lane, n. viòttolo m.

language, n. lingua f.; (manner of talking) linguaggio m.

languid, adj. lànguido.

languish, vb. languire.

languor, n. languore m.

lanky, adj. alto e smilzo.

lanolin, n. lanolina f.

lantern, n. lantèrna f.

lap, 1. n. grembo m. 2. vb. lambire.

lapel, n. risvòlta f.

lapin, n. conìglio m.

lapse, 1. n. (mistake) errore m.; (time) percorso m. 2. vb. decadere.

larceny, n. furto m.

lard, n. strutto m.

large, adj. grande.

largely, adv. in gran parte.

largo, n., adj., adv. largo (m.)

lariat, n. làccio m.

lark, n. allòdola f.; (fun) divertimento m.

larkspur, n. consòlida reale f.

larva, n. larva f.

laryngitis, n. laringite f.

larynx, n. laringe f.

lascivious, adj. lascivo.

laser, n. làser m.

lash, 1. n. frusta f., sfèrza f. 2. vb. frustare, sferzare.

lass, n. ragazza f.

lassitude, n. indolenza f.

lasso, n. làccio m.

last, 1. n. forma f. 2. adj. ùltimo. 3. vb. durare.

lasting, adj. durévole.

latch, n. saliscendi m.

late, 1. adj. tardo, tardivo. 2. adv. tardi; (delayed) in ritardo.

lately, adv. recentemente.

latent, adj. latènte.

lateral, adj. laterale.

lath, n. listèllo m.

lathe, n. tórnio m.

lather, n. schiuma f.

Latin, n. and adj. latino (m.)

latitude, n. latitùdine f.

Latium, n. Làzio m.; (of L.) laziale.

latrine, n. latrina f.

latter, 1. adj. recènte. 2. pron. (opposed to former) questo.

lattice, n. grata f.

laud, vb. lodare.

laudable, adj. lodévole.

laudanum, n. làudano m.

laudatory, adj. elogiativo.

laugh, 1. n. riso m. 2. vb. ridere; (l. at) deridere.

laughable, adj. ridìcolo.

laughter, n. riso m.; (burst of l.) risata f.

launch, 1. n. lància f. 2. vb. (throw) lanciare; (boat) varare.

launching, n. varo m.

launder, vb. lavare.

laundress, n. lavandaia f.

laundry, n. (clothes) bucato m.; (establishment) lavanderìa f.

laundryman, n. lavandaio m.

laureate, adj. laureato.

laurel, n. allòro m.; làuro m.

lava, n. lava f.

lavallière, n. pendènte m.

lavatory, n. latrina f.

lavender, n. lavanda f.

lavish, 1. adj. pròdigo. 2. vb. prodigare.

law, n. legge f., diritto m.

lawful, adj. legale, legìttimo.

lawless, adj. fuori legge.

lawmaker, n. legislatore m.

lawn, n. prato m.

lawn mower, n. falciatrice f.

lawsuit, n. càusa f.

lawyer, n. avvocato m.

lax, adj. rilassato.

laxative, n. and adj. lassativo (m.), purgante (m.).

laxity, n. rilassamento m.

lay, **1.** adj. làico. **2.** vb. méttere, porre, deporre.

lay brother, n. converso m.

layer, n. strato m.

layman, n. làico m.

layout, n. piano m.; menabò m.

lazy, adj. pigro.

laziness, n. pigrizia f.

lead, **1.** n. direzione f.; (metal) piombo m. **2.** vb. menare; condurre.

leaden, adj. di piombo, plùmbeo.

leader, n. capo m.; (Fascist) duce m.

leadership, n. guida f.

lead pencil, n. matita f.

leaf, n. fòglia f.

leafless, adj. privo di foglie.

leaflet, n. fogliolina f.

leafy, adj. fogliuto.

league, n. lega f.

League of Nations, n. Società delle Nazioni f.

leak, **1.** n. falla f. **2.** vb. (lose water) pèrdere; (let water in) far acqua.

leakage, n. infiltrazione f.; (loss) pèrdita f.

leaky, adj. che pèrde, che ha falle.

lean, **1.** adj. magro. **2.** vb. appoggiare, tr.

leaning, adj. inclinato, pendente.

leap, **1.** n. salto m. **2.** vb. saltare.

leap year, n. anno bisestile m.

learn, vb. imparare.

learned, adj. dòtto.

learner, n. apprendista m. and f.

learning, n. dottrina f.

lease, **1.** n. affitto m.; (contract) contratto d'affitto m. **2.** vb. affittare.

leash, n. guinzàglio m.

least, **1.** adj. mínimo. **2.** adv. minimamente.

leather, n. cuòio m.; (artificial l.) similcuòio m.

leathery, adj. tiglioso.

leave, **1.** n. (departure) commiato m., congedo m.; (permission) permesso m.; (furlough) licènza f. **2.** vb. lisciare; (depart) partire; (go away) andàrsene; (l. out) omèttere.

leaven, n. lièvito m.

lecherous, adj. lascivo.

lecture, n. conferènza f.

lecturer, n. conferenzière m.

ledge, n. ripiano m.

ledger, n. libro mastro m.

lee, n. sottovènto m.

leech, n. sanguisuga f.

leek, n. pòrro m.

leer, vb. guardare lascivamente.

leeward, adv. sottovènto.

left, **1.** n. sinistra. **2.** adj. sinistro; (departed) partito. **3.** adv. a sinistra.

left-handed, adj. mancino.

leftist, adj. di sinistra.

left-over, n. avanzo m.

leg, n. gamba f.

legacy, n. làscito m.

legal, adj. legale.

legalize, vb. legalizzare.

legation, n. legazione f.

legend, n. leggènda f.

legendary, adj. leggendàrio.

Leghorn, n. Livorno m.

legible, adj. leggìbile.

legion, n. legione f.

legislate, vb. fare leggi.

legislation, n. legislazione f.

legislator, n. legislatore m.

legislature, n. parlamento m.

legitimate, adj. legìttimo.

legume, n. legume m.

leisure, n. àgio m., riposo m., còmodo m.

leisurely, adj. còmodo.

lemon, n. limone m.

lemonade, n. limonata f.

lend, vb. prestare.

length, n. lunghezza f.

lengthen, vb. allungare, tr.

lengthwise, adv. per il lungo.

lengthy, adj. molto lungo.

lenient, adj. clemènte.

lens, n. lènte f.

Lent, n. quarésima f.

Lenten, adj. di quarésima.

lentil, n. lenticchia f.

lento, adv. lènto.

leopard, n. leopardo m.

leper, n. lebbroso m.

leperous, adj. lebbroso.

leprosy, n. lebbra f.

lesbian, adj. lèsbico m., lèsbica f.; tribade f.

lesion, n. lesione f.

less, 1. *adj.* minore. **2.** *adv. and prep.* meno.

lessen, *vb.* diminuire.

lesser, *adj.* minore.

lesson, *n.* lezione *f.*

lest, *conj.* affinchè . . . non.

let, *vb.* (allow) lasciare, permèttere; (lease) affittare; **(l. alone)** lasciar stare; **(l. up)** diminuire.

letdown, *n.* allentamento *m.*

lethal, *adj.* letale.

lethargic, *adj.* letàrgico.

lethargy, *n.* letargìa *f.*

letter, *n.* léttera *f.*

letter carrier, *n.* postino *m.*

letterhead, *n.* carta intestata *f.*

lettuce, *n.* lattuga *f.*

letup, *n.* pàusa *f.*, sosta *f.*

leukemia, *n.* leucèmia *f.*

levee, *n.* diga *f.*

level, 1. *n.* livèllo *m.* **2.** *adj.* orizzontale, equilibrato. **3.** *vb.* livellare.

lever, *n.* lèva *f.*

leverage, *n.* fozza di una leva *f.*; potere *m.*

levitation, *n.* levitazione *f.*

levity, *n.* leggerezza *f.*

levy, 1. *n.* lèva *f.*; (tax) imposta *f.* **2.** *vb.* arruolare; (tax) imporre.

lewd, *adj.* impùdico.

lexical, *adj.* lessicale.

lexicon, *n.* lèssico *m.*

liability, *n.* responsabilità *f.*

liable, *adj.* responsàbile, soggètto.

liaison, *n.* (mil.) collegamento *m.*; (love affair) relazione *f.*

liar, *n.* bugiardo *m.*

libation, *n.* libagione *f.*

libel, 1. *n.* libèllo *m.* **2.** *vb.* diffamare.

libelous, *adj.* diffamatòrio.

liberal, *n. and adj.* liberale (*m.*)

liberalism, *n.* liberalismo *m.*

liberality, *n.* liberalità *f.*

liberate, *vb.* liberare.

liberation, *n.* liberazione *f.*

liberator, *n.* liberatore *m.*

libertine, *n. and adj.* libertino *m.*

liberty, *n.* libertà *f.*

libidinous, *adj.* libidinoso.

libido, *n.* libido *f.*

librarian, *n.* bibliotecàrio *m.*

library, *n.* bibliotèca *f.*

libretto, *n.* libretto *m.*

license, *n.* licènza *f.*, permesso *m.*; (driver's) patènte *f.*

licentious, *adj.* licenzioso.

lick, *vb.* leccare.

licorice, *n.* liquirizia *f.*

lid, *n.* copèrchio *m.*; (eye) pàlpebra *f.*

lie, 1. *n.* bugia *f.*; menzogna *f.* **2.** *vb.* (tell untruths) mentire; (recline) giacere.

lien, *n.* sequèstro *m.*

lieutenant, *n.* tenènte *f.*; **(second l.)** sottotenènte *m.*

life, 1. *n.* vita *f.* **2.** *adj.* **(for l.)** vitalìzio.

life-boat, *n.* barca di salvatàggio *f.*

life-buoy, *n.* salvagente *m.*

life-guard, *n.* bagnino *m.*

life insurance, *n.* assicurazione sulla vita *f.*

lifeless, *adj.* sènza vita.

life-preserver, *n.* (belt) cintura di salvatàggio *f.*; salvagènte *m.*

life style, *n.* modo di vivere *m.*

life-time, *n.* durata della vita *f.*

lift, 1. *n.* ascensore *m.* **2.** *vb.* sollevare.

ligament, *n.* legamento *m.*

ligature, *n.* legatura *f.*

light, 1. *n.* luce *f.* **2.** *adj.* luminoso; (not heavy) leggièro. **3.** *vb.* accèndere; **(l. up)** illuminare, *tr.*

lighten, *vb.* (make less heavy) alleggerire; (flash) lampeggiare.

lighter, *n.* (cigar, cigarette) accendisigaro *m.*; accendino *m.*

light-house, *n.* faro *m.*

lightly, *adv.* leggiermente.

lightness, *n.* leggerezza *f.*

lightning, *n.* lampo *m.*, fùlmine *m.*; **(l.-rod)** parafùlmine *m.*

lightship, *n.* nave faro *f.*

lignite, *n.* lignite *f.*

Ligurian, *adj.* lìgure.

like, 1. *adj.* simile. **2.** *vb.* (use piacere with English subject as indirect object). **3.** *prep.* come.

likeable, *adj.* amàbile, simpàtico.

likelihood, *n.* probabilità *f.*

likely, *adj.* probàbile.

liken, *vb.* assomigliare.

likeness, *n.* somiglianza *f.*

likewise, *adv.* similmente.

lilac, *n.* lillà *m.*

lilt, n. canto m.

lily, n. giglio m.

lily of the valley, n. mughetto m.

limb, n. (of body) arto m.; mèmbro m.; (of tree) ramo m.

limber, vb. rèndere flessibile.

limbo, n. limbo m.

lime, n. calce f.; **(bird-l.)** vischio f.; (fruit) limone f.; (tree) tiglio m.

limelight, n. bagliore m.

limestone, n. pietra calcare f.

lime-water, n. acqua di calce f.

limit, 1. n. limite m. **2.** vb. limitare.

limitation, n. limitazione f.

limited, adj. (train) ràpido m.

limited company, n. società a responsabilità limitata f.

limited monarchy, n. monarchia costituzionale f.

limitless, adj. illimitato.

limousine, n. limousine f.

limp, 1. n. zoppicamento m. **2.** adj. fiacco, flessibile. **3.** vb. zoppicare.

limpid, adj. limpido.

linden, n. tiglio m.

line, 1. n. linea f.; (row) fila f.; (writing) riga f.; rigo m. **2.** vb. **(l. up)** allineare, tr.

lineage, n. lignàggio m., stirpe f.

lineal, adj. diretto.

linear, adj. lineare.

linen, 1. n. (cloth) tela di lino f.; **(household l.)** biancheria f. **2.** adj. di lino.

liner, n. (boat) transatlàntico m.

linger, vb. indugiare.

lingerie, n. biancheria intima f.

linguist, n. linguista m. and f.

linguistic, adj. linguístico.

linguistics, n. linguística f.

liniment, n. lenitivo m.

lining, n. fòdera f.

link, 1. n. (bond) legame m., vìncolo m.; (in chain) anèllo m. **2.** vb. collegare, tr.

linoleum, n. linòleum m.

linseed, n. seme di lino m.

lint, n. filàccia inglese f.

lion, n. leone m.

lip, n. labbro m.

lipread, vb. lèggere le labbra.

lipservice, n. omaggio ipòcrita m.

lip-stick, n. rossetto m.

liquefy, vb. liquefare, tr.

liqueur, n. liquore m.

liquid, n. and adj. liquido (m.)

liquidate, vb. liquidare.

liquidation, n. liquidazione f.

liquor, n. liquore m.

lira, n. lira f.

lisle, n. filo di cotone mercerizzato m.

lisp, 1. n. pronùncia blesa f. **2.** vb. èssere bleso.

lisping, adj. bleso.

lissome, adj. flessibile, agile.

list, 1. n. lista f., elenco m., ruòlo m.; (slant) inclinazione f. **2.** vb. elencare; (slant) inclinarsi.

listen (to), vb. ascoltare.

listless, adj. svogliato.

litany, n. litanía f.

liter, n. litro m.

literacy, n. alfabetismo m.; alfabetizzazione f.; istruzione f.

literal, adj. letterale.

literary, adj. letteràrio.

literate, adj. letterato.

literature, n. letteratura f.

lithe, adj. flessuoso.

lithograph, 1. n. litografía f. **2.** vb. litografare.

lithography, n. litografía f.

litigant, n. litigante m.

litigation, n. càusa f.

litmus, n. tornasole m.

litter, 1. n. (mess) disórdine m.; (stretcher) barella f.; (animal's bed) lettièra f.; (kittens, puppies) figliata f. **2.** vb. méttere in confusione; (have kittens) figliare.

little, 1. n. poco 2. adj. piccolo **3.** adv. poco.

little finger, n. mignolo m.

little people, n. fate f.pl.; folletti m.pl.

liturgical, adj. litùrgico.

liturgy, n. liturgía f.

livable, adj. abitàbile; sociévole.

live, 1. adj. vivo. **2.** vb. vivere.

livelihood, n. vita f.

lively, adj. vivace, brioso.

liven, vb. ravvivare, tr.

liver, n. fègato m.

livery, n. livrèa f.

livestock, n. bestiame m.

livid, adj. lívido.

living, 1. n. vita f. **2.** adj. vivènte.

lizard, n. lucèrtola f.

lo, interj. ècco.

load, 1. *n.* càrico *m.* **2.** *vb.* caricare.

loaf, 1. *n.* pagnòtta *f.*, pane *m.* **2.** *vb.* oziare.

loafer, *n.* bighellone *m.;* (slipper) pantòfola *f.*

loam, *n.* terríccio *m.*

loan, 1. *n.* prèstito *m.* **2.** *vb.* prestare.

loath, *adj.* riluttante.

loathe, *vb.* abominare.

loathing, *n.* ripugnanza *f.*

loathsome, *adj.* schifoso.

lobby, *n.* corridoio *m.*

lobe, *n.* lòbo *m.*

lobster, *n.* aragosta *f.*

local, 1. *n.* (train) òmnibus *m.;* accelerato *m.* **2.** *adj.* locale.

locale, *n.* località *f.*

locality, *n.* località *f.*

localize, *vb.* localizzare.

locate, *vb.* collocare; (find) trovare; (**be l.d**) trovarsi.

location, *n.* situazione *f.*, posto *m.*

lock, 1. *n.* serratura *f.;* (canal) chiusa *f.* **2.** *vb.* chiùdere a chiave.

locker, *n.* armadietto *m.;* (baggage) depòsito bagagli automatico *m.*

locket, *n.* medaglione *m.*

lockjaw, *n.* tètano *m.*

lockout, *n.* serrata *f.*

locksmith, *n.* fabbro di serrature *m.*

locomotion, *n.* locomozione *f.*

locomotive, *n.* locomotiva *f.*, locomotore *m.*

locust, *n.* locusta *f.*

locution, *n.* locuzione *f.*

lode, *n.* filone *m.*

lodestar, *n.* stella polare *f.*

lodge, 1. *n.* casetta *f.* **2.** *vb.* alloggiare.

lodger, *n.* òspite *m.*

lodging, *n.* allòggio *m.*

loft, *n.* solaio *m.;* (warehouse) magazzino *m.*

lofty, *adj.* alto.

log, *n.* ciòcco *m.*, ceppo *m.;* (treetrunk) tronco d'àlbero *m.*

logarithm, *n.* logaritmo *m.*

loge, *n.* loggione *m.*

logic, *n.* lògica *f.*

logical, *adj.* lògico.

logistic, *adj.* logístico.

logistics, *n.* logística.

loin, *n.* lombo *m.;* (food) lombata *f.*

loincloth, *n.* perizoma *f.*

loiter, *vb.* andare a zonzo.

lollipop, *n.* lecca-lecca *m.*

Lombard, *adj.* lombardo.

Lombardy, *n.* Lombardía *f.*

London, *n.* Londra *f.;* (**of L.**) londinese.

lone, lonely, lonesome, *adj.* solitàrio.

loneliness, *n.* solitùdine *f.*

long, 1. *adj.* lungo. **2.** *vb.* (**l. for**) bramare. **3.** *adv.* lungamente.

long-distance, *adj.* (telephone) interurbano, in teleselezione.

longevity, *n.* longevità *f.*

longing, *n.* brama *f.*

longitude, *n.* longitùdine *f.*

longitudinal, *adj.* longitudinale.

long-lived, *adj.* longèvo.

look, 1. *n.* sguardo *m.;* (appearance) aspètto *m.* **2.** *vb.* guardare; (**l. out,** take care) badare, vigilare.

looking glass, *n.* spècchio *m.*

loom, *n.* telaio *m.*

loop, *n.* càppio *m.*, làccio *m.*

loophole, *n.* feritòia *f.;* (way out) scappatòia *f.*

loose, 1. *adj.* sciòlto. **2.** *vb.* sciògliere.

loosen, *vb.* allentare, *tr.*, sciògliere, *tr.*

loot, *n.* bottino *m.*

lop off, *vb.* mozzare.

lopsided, *adj.* mal equilibrato.

loquacious, *adj.* loquace.

lord, *n.* signore *m.*

lordship, *n.* signoría *f.*

lorry, *n.* autocarro *m.*

lose, *vb.* pèrdere; (mislay) smarrire.

loss, *n.* pèrdita *f.*

lot, *n.* (fate) sòrte *f.;* (drawing) sortéggio *m.;* (group) lotto *m.;* (land) terreno *m.;* (**a l. of, l.s of**) molto *adj.*

lotion, *n.* lozione *f.*

lottery, *n.* lotteria *f.*

lotus, *n.* lòto *m.*

loud, 1. *adj.* alto, fòrte. **2.** *adv.* fòrte.

loud-speaker, *n.* altoparlante *m.*

lounge, 1. *n.* divano *m.*, salone *m.* **2.** *vb.* andare a zonzo.

louse, n. pidòcchio m.

lout, n. zoticone m.

louver, n. ventilatore m.

lovable, adj. amàbile.

love, 1. n. amore m. **2.** vb. amare.

lovely, adj. bèllo, leggiadro.

lover, n. amante m. or f.

low, 1. adj. basso. **2.** vb. mugghiare.

lowbrow, adj. poco intelligènte.

lower, 1. adj. inferiore. **2.** vb. abbassare, tr.

lowly, adj. ùmile.

loyal, adj. leale.

loyalist, n. lealista m.

loyalty, n. lealtà f.

lozenge, n. losanga f.; (pastille) pasticca f.

lubricant, n. and adj. lubrificante (m.)

lubricate, vb. lubrificare.

lucid, adj. chiaro.

luck, n. fortuna f., sòrte f.; **(bad l.)** sfortuna f.

lucky, adj. fortunato.

lucrative, adj. lucroso.

ludicrous, adj. ridícolo.

lug, vb. trascinare.

luggage, n. bagagli m.pl., bagaglio m.

lukewarm, adj. tièpido.

lull, vb. cullare.

lullaby, n. ninna-nanna f.

lumbago, n. lombàggine f.

lumber, n. legname m.

luminous, adj. luminoso.

lump, 1. n. massa f., protuberanza f. **2.** vb. ammassare.

lumpish, adj. grumoso; goffo.

lump sum, n. somma complessiva f., ammontare complessivo m.

lumpy, adj. pieno di protuberanze.

lunacy, n. pazzia f.

lunar, adj. lunare.

lunatic, n. and adj. lunàtico (m.)

lunch, n. colazione f.

luncheon, n. colazione f.

luncheon meat, n. insaccati m.pl.

lung, n. polmone m.

lunge, vb. lanciarsi.

lurch, vb. traballare.

lure, vb. adescare.

lurid, adj. sensazionale.

lurk, vb. nascóndersi.

luscious, adj. saporito.

lush, adj. lussureggiante.

lust, n. concupiscènza f.

luster, n. lustro m.

lustful, adj. concupiscènte.

lustrous, adj. lustro.

lusty, adj. vigoroso.

lute, n. liuto m.

Lutheran, adj. luterano.

luxuriant, adj. lussureggiante, rigoglioso.

luxurious, adj. lussuoso.

luxury, n. lusso m.

lying, adj. menzognèro, bugiardo, mendace.

lymph, n. linfa f.

lymphatic, adj. linfàtico.

lynch, vb. linciare.

lynching, n. linciàggio m.

lynx, n. lince f.

lyre, n. lira f.

lyric, adj. lírico.

lyricism, n. liricismo m.

M

macabre, adj. màcabro.

macaroni, n. pasta asciutta f., maccheroni m.pl.

mace, n. mazza f.

machine, n. màcchina f.

machine gun, n. mitragliatrice, f.

machinery, n. meccanismo m.

machinist, n. macchinista m.

machismo, n. gallismo m.

macho, adj. fallócrate.

mackerel, n. sgombro m.

mackinaw, n. impermeàbile m.

mackintosh, n. impermeàbile m.

mad, adj. pazzo; (angry) furioso.

madam, n. signora f.

madcap, n. and adj. scervellato (m.)

madden, vb. far impazzire.

made-to-order, adj. fatto su misura.

made-up, adj. inventato.

madness, n. pazzia f.

madrigal, n. madrigale m.

maelstrom, n. vòrtice m.

mafia, *n.* mafia *f.*

magazine, *n.* periòdico *m.*, rivista *f.*

magic, 1. *n.* magìa *f.* **2.** *adj.* màgico.

magician, *n.* mago *m.*

magistrate, *n.* magistrato *m.*

magistrature, *n.* magistratura *f.*

magnanimous, *adj.* magnànimo.

magnate, *n.* magnate *m.*

magnesium, *n.* magnèsio *m.*

magnet, *n.* magnète *m.*

magnetic, *adj.* magnètico.

magnificence, *n.* magnificènza *f.*

magnificent, *adj.* magnìfico.

magnify, *vb.* ingrandire.

magnitude, *n.* grandezza *f.*

mahogany, *n.* mògano *m.*

maid, *n.* domèstica *f.;* **(old m.)** zitèlla *f.*

maiden, *n.* fanciulla *f.*

mail, 1. *n.* pòsta *f.* **2.** *vb.* impostare.

mail-box, *n.* buca per lettere *f.*

mailman, *n.* postino *m.*

maim, *vb.* storpiare.

main, *adj.* principale.

mainframe, *n.* parte centrale di una calcolatrice *f.*

mainland, *n.* tèrra ferma *f.*

mainspring, *n.* molla principale *f.*

maintain, *vb.* mantenere; (in argument) sostenere.

maintenance, *n.* mantenimento *m.*

maize, *n.* granturco *m.*

majestic, *adj.* maestoso.

majesty, *n.* maestà *f.*

major, *n. and adj.* maggiore *(m.).*

majority, *n.* maggioranza *f.*

make, *vb.* fare.

make-believe, 1. *n.* finta *f.* **2.** *adj.* finto. **3.** *vb.* fingere.

maker, *n.* fattore *m.*

makeshift, *n.* espediènte *m.*

make-up, *n.* belletto *m.*

malady, *n.* malattìa *f.*

malaria, *n.* malària *f.*

male, *n. and adj.* màschio *(m.).*

malevolent, *adj.* malèvolo.

malice, *n.* malevolènza *f.*

malicious, *adj.* maligno.

malign, 1. *adj.* maligno. **2.** *vb.* diffamare.

malignant, *adj.* maligno.

malleable, *adj.* malleàbile.

malnutrition, *n.* malnutrizione *f.*

malt, *n.* malto *m.*

maltreat, *vb.* maltrattare.

mammal, *n.* mammìfero *m.*

mammoth, *n.* mammut *m.*

man, *n.* uòmo *m.*

manage, *vb.* amministrare, dirigere.

manageable, *adj.* maneggévole; risolvibile.

management, *n.* amministrazione *f.*, direzione *f.*

manager, *n.* amministratore *m.*, direttore *m.*

mandate, *n.* mandato *m.*

mandatory, *adj.* obbligatòrio.

mandolin, *n.* mandolino *m.*

mandrake, *n.* mandràgola *f.*

mane, *n.* crinièra *f.*

maneuver, 1. *n.* manòvra *f.* **2.** *vb.* manovrare.

manganese, *n.* manganese *m.*

manger, *n.* mangiatoia *f.*

mangle, *vb.* tritare.

manhandle, *vb.* malmenare.

manhood, *n.* virilità *f.*

mania, *n.* manìa *f.*

maniac, *n. and adj.* maníaco *(m.).*

manicure, *n.* manicure *f.*

manifest, 1. *adj.* manifèsto. **2.** *vb.* manifestare.

manifesto, *n.* manifèsto *m.*

manifold, *adj.* moltéplice.

manikin, *n.* manichino *m.*

manipulate, *vb.* manipolare.

mankind, *n.* umanità *f.*

manly, *adj.* virile.

manner, *n.* manièra *f.*, mòdo *m.*

mannerism, *n.* manierismo *m.*

manor, *n.* maniero *m.;* fèudo *m.;* proprietà *f.*

mansion, *n.* palazzo *m.*

manslaughter, *n.* omicidio *m.*

mantelpiece, *n.* cornice *f.*

mantle, *n.* mantèllo *m.*

Mantua, *n.* Màntova *f.*

Mantuan, *n. and adj.* mantovano *(m.).*

manual, *n. and adj.* manuale *(m.).*

manufacture, *n.* fabbricazione *f.*

manufacturer, *n.* fabbricante *m.*

manufacturing, *adj.* industriale.

manure, *n.* concime *m.*

manuscript, n. and adj. manoscritto (m.)

many, adj. molti m.pl.; molte f.pl.

map, n. carta f.

maple, n. àcero m.

mar, vb. danneggiare, guastare.

marble, n. marmo m.

march, 1. n. màrcia f. **2.** vb. marciare.

March, n. marzo m.

mare, n. cavalla f.

margarine, n. margarina f.

margin, n. màrgine m.

marginal, adj. marginale.

marijuana, n. marijuana f.

marinate, vb. marinare.

marine, adj. marino, maríttimo.

mariner, n. marinaio m.

marionette, n. marionetta f.

marital, adj. maritale.

maritime, adj. maríttimo.

mark, 1. n. segno m. **2.** vb. marcare, segnare.

market, n. mercato m.

market place, n. piazza del mercato m.

marmalade, n. marmellata f.

maroon, n. (color) marrone m.

marquee, n. pensilina f.

marquis, n. marchese m.

marriage, n. matrimònio m.

marrow, n. midollo m.

marry, vb. sposare, tr.; (woman) maritare, tr.

Marseilles, n. Marsiglia f.

marsh, n. palude f.

marshal, n. maresciallo m.

marital, adj. marziale.

martinet, n. tiranno m.

martyr, n. màrtire m.

martyrdom, n. martírio m.

marvel, 1. n. meraviglia f. **2.** vb. meravigliarsi.

marvelous, adj. meraviglioso.

mascot, n. portafortuna m.

masculine, adj. maschile.

mash, vb. schiacciare.

mask, 1. n. màschera f. **2.** vb. mascherare.

mason, n. muratore m.

masquerade, 1. n. mascherata f. **2.** vb. mascherarsi.

mass, n. massa f.; (church) messa f.

massacre, 1. n. massacro m. **2.** vb. massacrare.

massage, 1. n. massaggio m. **2.** vb. massaggiare.

masseur, n. massaggiatore m.

massive, adj. massiccio.

mass meeting, n. assemblèa f.

mast, n. àlbero m.

master, n. (boss) padrone m.; (great artist) maestro m.; (workman) mastro m.

master-key, n. comunèlla f., passe-par-tout m.

masterpiece, n. capolavoro m.

mastery, n. padronanza f.

masticate, vb. masticare.

mat, n. stuòia f.

match, 1. n. (light) fiammífero m.; (contest) incontro m.; (equal) uguale m.; (marriage) matrimònio m. **2.** vb. uguagliare.

matchless, adj. senza pari.

mate, 1. n. (spouse) consòrte m. or f.; (pal) compagno m.; (second in command) secondo m.; (assistant) assistente m. **2.** vb. accoppiare, tr.

material, n. and adj. materiale (m.).

materialism, n. materialismo m.

materialize, vb. materializzare.

maternal, adj. matèrno.

maternity, n. maternità f.

maternity ward, n. reparto maternità m.

mathematical, adj. matemático.

mathematician, n. matemático m.

mathematics, n. matemàtica f.

matinée, n. mattinata f.

matriarchy, n. matriarcato m.

matricide, n. matricidio m.

matriculation, n. immatricolazione f.

matrimony, n. matrimònio m.

matron, n. matrona f.

matter, 1. n. matèria f.; (pus) pus m. **2.** vb. importare.

matter of fact, n. (as a m.) adv. in realtà.

mattress, n. materasso m.

mature, 1. adj. maturo. **2.** vb. maturare; (fall due) scadere.

maturity, n. maturità f.; (financial) scadènza f.

maudlin, adj. piagnucoloso.

maul, n. percuòtere.

mausoleum, n. mausolèo m.

maxim, n. màssima f.

maximum, n. and adj. màssimo (m.).

may, vb. potere.

May, n. màggio m.

maybe, adv. forse.

mayhem, n. danni m.pl.

mayonnaise, n. maionese f.

mayor, n. síndaco m.

maze, n. labirinto m.

me, pron. me, mi.

meadow, n. prato m.

meadowland, n. prateria f.

meager, adj. magro, scarso.

meal, n. pasto m.; (flour) farina f.

mean, 1. n. mèdia f. 2. adj. (in the middle) mèdio; (base) meschino, spregévole. 3. vb. significare, voler dire.

meander, n. meandro m.

meaning, n. significato m.

meaningful, adj. significativo.

meaningless, adj. insensato.

means, n. mèzzo m.sg.

meantime, meanwhile, n. frattèmpo m.

measles, n. morbillo m.

measurable, adj. misuràbile.

measure, 1. n. misura f. 2. vb. misurare.

measurement, n. misuramento m.

measuring, adj. misuratore.

meat, n. carne f.

meat grinder, n. tritacarne f.

meaty, adj. polposo; in carne.

mechanic, n. meccànico m.

mechanical, adj. meccànico.

mechanism, n. meccanismo m.

mechanize, vb. meccanizzare.

medal, n. medàglia f.

meddle, vb. immischiarsi.

mediaeval, adj. medioevale.

median, adj. mediano.

mediate, vb. fare da intermediàrio.

mediator, n. intermediàrio m.

medical, adj. mèdico.

medicate, vb. medicare.

medicine, n. medicina f.

mediocre, adj. mediòcre.

mediocrity, n. mediocrità f.

meditate, vb. meditare.

meditation, n. meditazione f.

Mediterranean, n. and adj. mediterràneo (m.).

medium, 1. n. mèzzo m. 2. adj. mèdio.; (meat) còtto moderatamente.

medley, n. miscùglio m.

meek, adj. mite.

meekness, n. mitezza f.

meet, vb. incontrare tr.

meeting, n. riunione f., assemblèa f.; (m.-place) ritròvo m.

megahertz, n. megahertz m.

megaphone, n. megàfono m.

melancholy, 1. n. malinconía f. 2. adj. malincònico, melancònico.

mellow, adj. maturato.

melodious, adj. melodioso.

melodrama, n. melodramma m.

melody, n. melodía f.

melon, n. melone m.

melt, vb. fòndere tr., sciògliere tr.

meltdown, n. fusione f.

member, n. sòcio m., membro m.

membership, n. affiliati m.pl.

membrane, n. membrana f.

memento, n. ricòrdo m.

memoir, n. memòria f.

memorable, adj. memoràbile.

memorandum, n. memorandum m.

memorial, 1. n. monumento m., memoriale m. 2. adj. commemorativo.

memorize, vb. imparare a memòria.

memory, n. memòria f.

menace, 1. n. minàccia f. 2. vb. minacciare.

menagerie, n. serràglio m.

mend, vb. accomodare.

mendacious, adj. mendace.

mendicant, 1. n. mèndico m. 2. adj. mendicante.

menial, adj. servile.

menopause, n. menopàusa f.

menses, n. mestruazioni f.pl.

menstruation, n. mestruazione f.; règole f.pl.

menswear, n. abbigliamento maschile m.

mental, adj. mentale.

mentality, n. mentalità f.

menthol, n. mentòlo m.

mention, 1. *n.* menzione *f.* 2. *vb.* menzionare.
menu, *n.* lista *f.*
meow, 1. *n.* miagolio *m.* 2. *vb.* miagolare.
mercantile, *adj.* mercantile.
mercenary, *adj.* mercenàrio.
merchandise, *n.* mercanzia *f.*
merchant, *n.* mercante *m.*
merchant marine, *n.* marina mercantile *f.*
merciful, *adj.* pietoso.
merciless, *adj.* spietato.
mercury, *n.* mercùrio *m.*
mercy, *n.* pietà *f.*, misericòrdia *f.*
mere, *adj.* mèro, sémplice.
merely, *adv.* meramente, semplicemente.
merge, *vb.* assorbire.
merger, *n.* fusione *f.*
meringue, *n.* meringa *f.*
merit, 1. *n.* mèrito *m.* 2. *vb.* meritare.
meritorious, *adj.* meritòrio.
mermaid, *n.* sirena *f.*
merriment, *n.* allegrezza *f.*
merry, *adj.* allegro.
merry-go-round, *n.* carosèllo *m.*
mesh, 1. *n.* (fabric) màglia *f.* 2. *vb.* (gears) ingranare.
mesmerize, *vb.* ipnotizzare.
mess, *n.* pasticcio *m.*, confusione *f.*; (soldiers' meals) ràncio *m.*
message, *n.* messàggio *m.*, ambasciata *f.*
messenger, *n.* messaggèro *m.*
messy, *adj.* confuso, disordinato.
metabolism, *n.* metabolismo *m.*
metal, *n.* metallo *m.*
metallic, *adj.* metàllico.
metamorphosis, *n.* metamòrfosi *f.*
metaphor, *n.* metàfora *f.*
metaphysics, *n.* metafisica *f.*
meteor, *n.* metèora *f.*
meteorology, *n.* meteorologia *f.*
meter, *n.* (recording device) contatore *m.*; (unit of measure) mètro *m.*
method, *n.* mètodo *m.*
meticulous, *adj.* meticoloso.
metric, *adj.* mètrico.
metropolis, *n.* metròpoli *f.*
metropolitan, *adj.* metropolitano.

mettle, *n.* coràggio *m.*
mettlesome, *adj.* briòso.
Mexican, *adj.* messicano.
Mexico, *n.* il Mèssico *m.*
mezzanine, *n.* mezzanino *m.*
microbe, *n.* micròbio *m.*
microfiche, *n.* microscheda *f.*
microfilm, *n.* micròfilm *m.*
microform, *n.* microforma *f.*
microphone, *n.* micròfono *m.*
microscope, *n.* microscòpio *m.*
microscopic, *adj.* microscòpico.
mid-, *adj.* mèdio.
middle, 1. *n.* mèzzo *m.* 2. *adj.* mèdio, intermèdio, mèzzo.
middle-aged, *adj.* di mèzza età.
Middle Ages, *n.* medioèvo *m.*
middle class, *n.* borghesia *f.*, ceto mèdio *m.*, classe mèdia *f.*
Middle East, *n.* Medio Oriente *m.*
midget, *n.* nano *m.*
midnight, *n.* mezzanòtte *f.*
midriff, *n.* diaframma *m.*
midwife, *n.* levatrice *f.*
mien, *n.* aspètto *m.*, cera *f.*
might, 1. *n.* potènza *f.* 2. *vb.* use conditional of potere.
mighty, *adj.* potènte.
migraine, *n.* emicrània *f.*
migrate, *vb.* migrare.
migration, *n.* migrazione *f.*
migratory, *adj.* migratòrio.
Milan, *n.* Milano *f.*
Milanese, *adj.* milanese.
mild, *adj.* mite.
mildew, *n.* muffa bianca *f.*
mildness, *n.* mitezza *f.*
mile, *n.* miglio *m.*
mileage, *n.* chilometràggio *m.*
milestone, *n.* piètra miliare *f.*
militant, *adj.* militante.
militarism, *n.* militarismo *m.*
military, *adj.* militare.
militia, *n.* milízia *f.*
milk, 1. *n.* latte *m.* 2. *vb.* mùngere.
milk-bar, *n.* latteria *f.*
milkman, *n.* lattaio *m.*
milky, *adj.* làtteo.
Milky Way, *n.* Via Latea *f.*
mill, 1. *n.* mulino *m.*; (factory) fàbbrica *f.* 2. *vb.* macinare.
millenium, *n.* millènio *m.*
miller, *n.* mugnaio *m.*
milligram, *n.* milligrammo *m.*
millimeter, *n.* millimetro *m.*

milliner, n. modista m. or f.

millinery, n. modisteria f.

milling, n. macinatura f.; **(m. machine)** n. fresatrice f.

million, n. milione m.

millionaire, n. milionàrio m.

mimic, 1. n. imitatore m. **2.** adj. imitato. **3.** vb. imitare.

mimicry, n. mimetismo m.

minaret, n. minareto m.

mince, vb. triturare.

mind, 1. n. mente f., ànimo m. **2.** vb. badare a; (obey) ubbidire a; **(never m.)** non impòrta.

mindful, adj. mèmore.

mine, 1. n. minièra f.; (explosive) mina f. **2.** adj. mio. **3.** vb. minare.

mine field, n. campo minato m.

miner, n. minatore m.

mineral, n. and adj. minerale (m.).

mine-sweeper, n. nave spazzamine f.

mingle, vb. mescolare, tr.

miniature, n. miniatura f.

miniaturize, vb. miniaturizzare.

minimal, adj. mínimo.

minimize, vb. ridurre al mínimo.

minimum, n. and adj. mínimo (m.).

minimum wage, n. salàrio mínimo m.

mining, 1. n. coltivazione delle minière f. **2.** adj. mineràrio.

miniskirt, n. minigonna f.

minister, 1. n. ministro m. **2.** vb. ministrare.

ministry, n. ministèro m.

mink, n. visone m.

minnow, n. pesciolino m.

minor, 1. n. (person under 21) minorènne. **2.** adj. minore, minorènne.

minority, n. minoranza f.; (age) minor età f.

minstrel, n. menestrèllo m.

mint, 1. n. (plant) menta f.; (coin factory) zecca f. **2.** vb. coniare.

minus, prep. meno.

minute, 1. n. minuto m.; (of meeting) verbale m. **2.** adj. minuto.

miracle, n. miràcolo m.

miraculous, adj. miracoloso.

mirage, n. miràggio m.

mire, n. fango m.

mirror, n. spècchio m.

mirth, n. allegria f.

misadventure, n. disgràzia f.

misappropriate, vb. appropriare indebitamente.

misbehave, vb. comportarsi male.

miscalculation, n. càlcolo sbagliato m.

miscarriage, n. (justice) errore giudiziario m.; (medicine) aborto spontàneo m.

miscellaneous, adj. miscellàneo.

mischief, n. cattivèria f., malízia f.

mischievous, adj. cattivo, malizioso.

misconception, n. fraintendimento m.

misconstrue, vb. fraintèndere.

miscreant, n. and adj. miscredènte.

misdemeanor, n. contravvenzione f.

miser, n. avaro m.

miserable, adj. mísero.

miserly, adj. avaro.

misery, n. misèria f.

misfit, n. persona inadatta f.

misfortune, n. sfortuna f.

misgiving, n. apprensione f., dùbbio m.

mishap, n. disgràzia f.

mislay, vb. smarrire.

mislead, vb. ingannare.

misplace, vb. smarrire.

misplaced, adj. fuòri di propòsito.

mispronounce, vb. pronunziar male.

miss, 1. n. (unsuccessful shot) colpo mancato m. **2.** vb. mancare, pèrdere; (feel the lack of) sentire la mancanza di.

Miss, n. signorina f.

missile, n. missile m.

mission, n. missione f.

missionary, n. and adj. missionàrio (m.).

misspell, vb. scrívere scorrettamente.

mist, n. nébbia f.

mistake, 1. n. sbàglio m. **2.** vb. sbagliare.

mistaken, adj. errato, erròneo, sbagliato.

mister, *n.* signore *m.*

mistletoe, *n.* vischio *m.*

mistreat, *vb.* maltrattare, bistrattare.

mistress, *n.* padrona *f.;* (lover) amante *f.*

mistrust, 1. *n.* sfidùcia *f.* **2.** *vb.* diffidare di.

misty, *adj.* nebbioso.

misunderstand, *vb.* fraintèndere.

misuse, *vb.* abusare di.

mite, *n.* (coin) òbolo *m.;* (small piece) pezzettino *m.;* (tot) piccino *m.*

mitigate, *vb.* mitigare.

mitten, *n.* guanto *m.*

mix, *vb.* mescolare, *tr.*

mixed, *adj.* misto, assortito.

mixed feelings, *n.* ambivalenza *f.*

mixture, *n.* mescolanza *f.,* mistura *f.*

mix-up, *n.* confusione *f.*

moan, 1. *n.* gèmito *m.* **2.** *vb.* gèmere.

moat, *n.* fòssa *f.*

mob, *n.* fòlla *f.,* plebàglia *f.*

mobile, *adj.* mòbile.

mobility, *n.* mobilità *f.*

mobilization, *n.* mobilitazione *f.*

mobilize, *vb.* mobilitare.

mobster, *n.* criminale *m.;* gangster *m.*

moccasin, *n.* mocassino *m.*

mock, 1. *adj.* finto. **2.** *vb.* derìdere, beffarsi di, schernire.

mockery, *n.* derisione *f.,* scherno *m.*

mod, *adj.* moderno.

mode, *n.* (way) mòdo *m.;* (fashion) mòda *f.*

model, 1. *n.* modèllo *m.* **2.** *vb.* modellare.

moderate, 1. *adj.* moderato. **2.** *vb.* moderare.

moderation, *n.* moderazione *f.*

modern, *adj.* modèrno.

modernize, *vb.* rimodernare, *tr.*

modest, *adj.* modèsto.

modesty, *n.* modèstia *f.*

modify, *vb.* modificare.

modish, *adj.* alla mòda.

modulate, *vb.* modulare.

moist, *adj.* ùmido.

moisten, *vb.* inumidire.

moisture, *n.* umidità *f.*

molar, *adj.* molare.

molasses, *n.* melassa *f.*

mold, 1. *n.* forma *f.,* stampo *m.;* (must) muffa *f.* **2.** *vb.* formare, modellare.

moldy, *adj.* ammuffito.

mole, *n.* (animal) talpa *f.;* (pier) mòlo *m.*

molecule, *n.* molècola *f.*

molest, *vb.* molestare.

mollify, *vb.* ammollire.

molten, *adj.* fuso.

moment, *n.* momènto *m.*

momentary, *adj.* momentàneo.

momentous, *adj.* importante.

monarch, *n.* monarca *m.*

monarchy, *n.* monarchìa *f.*

monastery, *n.* monastèro *m.*

Monday, *n.* lunedì *m.*

monetary, *adj.* monetàrio.

money, *n.* denaro *m.*

money-order, *n.* vàglia *f.*

mongrel, *n. and adj.* bastardo (*m.*).

monitor, *n.* monitore *m.*

monk, *n.* mònaco *m.*

monkey, *n.* scimmia *f.*

monocle, *n.* monòcolo *m.*

monologue, *n.* monòlogo *m.*

monoplane, *n.* monoplano *m.*

monopolize, *vb.* monopolizzare.

monopoly, *n.* monopòlio *m.*

monosyllable, *n.* monosìllabo *m.*

monotone, *n.* tono uniforme *m.*

monotonous, *adj.* monòtono.

monotony, *adj.* monotonìa *f.*

monoxide, *n.* monòssido *m.*

monsoon, *n.* monsone *m.*

monster, 1. *n.* mostro *m.* **2.** *adj.* (huge) immènso.

monstrosity, *n.* mostruosità *f.*

monstrous, *adj.* mostruoso.

month, *n.* mese *m.*

monthly, *adj.* mensile.

monument, *n.* monumento *m.*

monumental, *adj.* monumentale.

mood, *n.* stato d'ànimo *m.*

moody, *adj.* triste.

moon, *n.* luna *f.*

moonlight, *n.* chiaro di luna *m.*

moor, 1. *n.* brughièra *f.* **2.** *vb.* ormeggiare.

mooring, *n.* ormèggio *m.*

moot, *adj.* discusso.

mop, *n.* scopa di stracci *f.*

moped, n. ciclomotore m.

moral, n. and adj. morale (f.).

morale, n. morale m.

moralist, n. moralista m.

morality, n. moralità f.

morally, adv. moralmente.

morbid, adj. morboso.

more, adv. più; (m. and m.) sempre più.

moreover, adv. per di più.

mores, n. costumi m.pl.

morgue, n. càmera mortuària f.

morning, n. mattina f., mattino m.

moron, n. imbecille m.

morose, adj. poco sociévole.

morphine, n. morfina f.

Morse code, n. còdice Morse m.

morsel, n. (food) boccone m.; (piece) frammento m.

mortal, n. and adj. mortale (m.).

mortality, n. mortalità f.

mortar, n. calcina f.

mortgage, 1. n. ipotèca f. **2.** vb. ipotecare.

mortician, n. imprenditore di pompe funebri m.

mortify, vb. mortificare.

mortuary, adj. mortuàrio.

mosaic, n. mosàico m.

Moscow, Mosca.

Moslem, n. and adj. mussulmano (m.)

mosque, n. moschèa f.

mosquito, n. zanzara f.; (m. net) zanzarièra f.

moss, n. mùschio m.

most, 1. adj. la maggior parte di. **2.** adj. maggiormente.

mostly, adv. per lo più.

motel, n. motèl m.

moth, n. tarma f.

moth-eaten, adj. tarmato m.

mother, n. madre f., mamma f.

mother country, n. màdre patria f.

motherhood, n. maternità f.

mother-in-law, n. suòcera f.

motif, n. motivo m.

motion, n. mòto m.; (parliamentary) mozione f.

motionless, adj. immòbile.

motion-picture, n. pellìcola f.

motivate, vb. motivare.

motive, 1. n. motivo m. **2.** adj.

motore; **(m. power)** fòrza motrice.

motley, n. eterogèneo, multicolore.

motor, n. motore m.

motorboat, n. motoscafo m.

motorcycle, n. motocicletta f.

motorist, n. automobilista m.

motorize, vb. motorizzare.

motorized farming, n. motocultura f.

motto, n. motto m.

mound, n. tùmulo m.

mount, vb. montare, salire.

mountain, n. montagna f., monte m.

mountaineer, n. montanaro m.

mountainous, adj. montagnoso, montuoso.

mountebank, n. ciarlatano m.

mourn, vb. piàngere.

mournful, adj. doloroso.

mourning, n. lutto m.

mouse, n. sórcio m., tòpo m.

mouth, n. bocca f.

mouthpiece, n. (instrument) imboccatura f.; (spokesman) portavoce m.

movable, adj. mòbile.

move, 1. n. (household goods) traslòco m. **2.** vb. muòvere, tr.

movement, n. movimento m.

movie, n. cinema m., film m.

moving, 1. n. (household goods) traslòco m. **2.** adj. commovènte.

moving staircase, n. scala mòbile f.

mow, vb. falciare.

Mr., n. Sig. m. (abbr. for Signore).

Mrs., n. Sra. f. (abbr. for Signora).

much, adj. and adv. molto.

mucilage, n. gomma liquida f.

muck, n. letame m., melma f.

muckrake, vb. sollevare scàndali.

mucous, adj. mucoso.

mucus, n. muco m.

mud, n. fango m., lòto m.

muddy, adj. fangoso.

mudslide, n. smottamento m.

muff, 1. n. manicotto m. **2.** vb. sbagliare.

muffle, vb. (wrap up) imbaccucare, tr.; (silence) attutire.

muffler, n. (scarf) sciarpa f.; (auto) silenziatore dello scàrico m.

mug, n. coppa f.

mulatto, n. mulatto m.

mulberry, n. gelso m.

mule, n. mulo m.

mullah, n. mulla(h) m.

multicolored, adj. multicolore.

multinational, adj. multinazionale.

multiple, adj. mùltiplo.

multiplication, n. moltiplicazione f.

multiplicity, n. molteplicità f.

multiply, vb. moltiplicare, tr.

multitude, n. moltitùdine f.

mummy, n. mùmmia f.

mumps, n. orecchioni m.pl.

munch, vb. sgranocchiare.

Munich, n. Mònaco di Bavièra m.

municipal, adj. municipale.

munificent, adj. munificènte.

munition, n. munizione f.

mural, adj. murale.

murder, n. assassinio m.

murderer, n. assassino m.

murmur, 1. n. mormorío m. 2. vb. mormorare.

muscle, n. mùscolo m.

muscular, adj. muscolare.

muse, 1. n. rausa f. 2. vb. meditare.

museum, n. musèo m.

mushroom, n. fungo m.

music, n. mùsica f.

musical, adj. musicale.

musical comedy, n. operetta f., rivista f.

music hall, n. sala da concerti f.

musician, n. musicista f.

musk, n. mùschio m.

muslin, n. mussolina f.

must, n. use present of dovere.

mustache, n. baffi m.pl.

mustard, n. sènape f., mostarda f.

muster, 1. n. rivista f. 2. vb. radunare.

musty, adj. ammuffito.

mutation, n. mutazione f.

mute, adj. muto.

mutilate, vb. mutilare.

mutiny, 1. n ammutinamento m. 2. vb. ammutinarsi.

mutter, vb. borbottare.

mutton, n. carne di montone f.

mutual, adj. mùtuo.

mutual fund, n. fondo comune d'investimento m.

muzzle, n. (gun) bocca f.; (animal's mouth) muso m.; (mouth covering) museruòla f.

my, adj. mìo.

myopia, n. miopìa f.

myriad, 1. n. mirìade f. 2. adj. innumerévole.

myrrh, n. mirra f.

myrtle, n. mirto m.

myself, pron. me stesso; (I m.) ìo stesso.

mysterious, adj. misterioso.

mystery, n. mistèro m.

mystic, adj. místico.

mysticism, n. misticismo m.

mystification, n. mistificazione f.

mystify, vb. mistificare.

myth, n. mìto m.

mythical, adj. mítico.

mythology, n. mitologìa f.

N

nag, 1. n. ronzino m. 2. vb. tormentare.

nail, 1. n. chiòdo m.; (of finger, toe) unghia f. 2. vb. inchiodare.

naïve, adj. ingènuo.

naked, adj. nudo.

name, 1. n. nome m.; (family n.) cognome m. 2. vb. chiamare; (nominate) nominare.

namely, adv. cioè.

namesake, n. omònimo m.

nap, 1. n. pisolino m., sonnellino m. 2. vb. sonnecchiare.

naphtha, n. nafta f.

napkin, n. tovagliòlo m.

Naples, n. Nàpoli f.

narcissus, n. narciso m.

narcotic, n. and adj. narcòtico (m.).

narrate, vb. narrare.

narrative, 1. n. racconto m. 2. adj. narrativo.

narration, n. narrazione f.

narrow, adj. stretto.

nasal, adj. nasale.

nasty, adj. disgustoso, antipàtico.

natal, _adj._ natale.
nation, _n._ nazione _f._
national, _adj._ nazionale.
nationalism, _n._ nazionalismo _m._
nationality, _n._ nazionalità _f._
nationalization, _n._ nazionalizzazione _f._
nationalize, _vb._ nazionalizzare.
native, 1. _n._ indigeno _m._ **2.** _adj._ nativo, indígeno.
nativity, _n._ natività _f._
natural, _adj._ naturale.
naturalist, _n._ naturalista _m._
naturalize, _vb._ naturalizzare.
naturalness, _n._ naturalezza _f._
nature, _n._ natura _f._
naughty, _adj._ birichino.
nausea, _n._ nàusea _f._
nauseating, _adj._ nauseante.
nautical, _adj._ náutico.
naval, _adj._ navale.
nave, _n._ navata _f._
navel, _n._ ombellico _m._
navigable, _adj._ navigàbile.
navigate, _vb._ navigare.
navigation, _n._ navigazione _f._
navigator, _n._ navigatore _m._
navy, _n._ marina _f._
navy yard, _n._ arsenale _m._
Neapolitan, _adj._ napoletano.
near, 1. _adj._, _adv._ vicino. **2.** _prep._ vicino a.
nearby, _adj._ vicino.
nearly, _adv._ quasi.
near-sighted, _adj._ miope.
neat, _adj._ lindo, pulito.
neatness, _n._ pulizia _f._
nebula, _n._ nebulosa _f._
nebulous, _adj._ nebuloso.
necessary, _adj._ necessàrio; **(be n.)** bisognare, volerci.
necessity, _n._ necessità _f._
neck, _n._ collo _m._
necklace, _n._ collana _f._
necktie, _n._ cravatta _f._
nectar, _n._ néttare _m._
need, 1. _n._ bisogno _m._ **2.** _vb._ aver bisogno di.
needful, _adj._ necessário.
needle, _n._ ago _m._; (phonograph) puntina _f._
needless, _adj._ inútile.
needy, _adj._ bisognoso.
nefarious, _adj._ malvàgio, sùbdolo.

negate, _vb._ negare.
negation, _n._ negazione _f._
negative, 1. _n._ negativa _f._ **2.** _adj._ negativo.
neglect, _vb._ trascurare.
neglectful, _adj._ negligente, trascurato.
negligée, _n._ vestàglia _f._
negligent, _adj._ trascurato.
negligible, _adj._ trascuràbile.
negotiable, _adj._ negoziàbile.
negotiate, _vb._ negoziare.
negotiation, _n._ negoziazione _f._
Negro, _n._ negro _m._
neighbor, _n._ vicino _m._, próssimo _m._
neighborhood, _n._ vicinanza _f._
neither, _conj._ nè.
neologism, _n._ neologismo _m._
neon, _n._ nèon _m._
neophyte, _n._ neòfita _m._
nephew, _n._ nipote _m._
nepotism, _n._ nepotismo _m._
nerve, _n._ nèrvo _m._; (effrontery) sfrontatezza _f._
nervous, _adj._ nervoso.
nest, _n._ nido _m._
nest egg, _n._ grùzzolo _m._
nestle, _vb._ annidarsi.
net, _n._ rete _f._
netting, _n._ rete _f._
nettle, 1. _n._ ortica _f._ **2.** _vb._ irritare.
network, _n._ rete _f._
neuralgia, _n._ nevralgía _f._
neurology, _n._ neurologia _f._
neurotic, _adj._ nevròtico.
neutral, _n. and adj._ nèutro (_m._).
neutrality, _n._ neutralità _f._
neutralize, _vb._ neutralizzare.
neutron, _n._ neutrone _m._
neutron bomb, _n._ bomba al neutrone _f._
never, _adv._ mai.
nevertheless, _adv._ nondimeno.
new, _adj._ nuòvo.
newborn, _n._ neonato _m._
news, _n._ notízie _f.pl._
news-boy, _n._ giornalaio _m._
newscast, _n._ radiocorrière _m._
newspaper, _n._ giornale _m._
newsreel, _n._ attualità _f.pl._
next, _adj._ próssimo, seguènte.
nibble, _vb._ rosicchiare.
nice, _adj._ gentile, buòno.
nick, _n._ tacca _f._

nickel, n. níchel m.

nickname, n. nomígnolo m.

nicotine, n. nicotina f.

niece, n. nipote f.

niggardly, adj. taccagno.

night, n. nòtte f.

night club, n. ritròvo notturno m., nightclub m.

nightgown, n. camícia da nòtte f.

nightingale, n. usignuòlo m.

nightly, adv. ogni nòtte.

nightmare, n. íncubo m.

night-stick, n. clava f.

nimble, adj. àgile.

nine, num. nòve.

nineteen, num. diciannòve.

nineteenth, adj. dècimo nòno, diciannovèsimo.

ninetieth, adj. novantèsimo.

ninety, num. novanta.

ninth, adj. nòno.

nip, n. pizzicotto m.

nipple, n. capézzolo m.

nitrate, n. nitrato m.

nitrogen, n. nitrògeno m.

no, 1. adj. nessuno. 2. interj. nò.

nobility, n. nobiltà f.

noble, n. and adj. nòbile (m.).

nobleman, n. nobiluòmo m.

nobly, adv. nobilmente.

nobody, pron. nessuno.

nocturnal, adj. notturno.

nocturne, n. notturno m.

nod, 1. n. cenno d'assenso col capo m. 2. fare un cenno col capo.

node, n. nòdo m.

no-frills, adj. sémplice.

noise, n. rumore m.

noiseless, adj. silenzioso.

noisome, adj. puzzolènte.

noisy, adj. rumoroso.

nomad, n. nòmade m.

nominal, adj. nominale.

nominate, vb. nominare, designare.

nomination, n. nòmina f.

nominee, n. designato m., candidato m.

nonaligned, adj. non allineato.

nonchalant, adj. incurante.

noncombatant, n. and adj. non combattènte (m.).

non-commissioned officer, n. sottufficiale m.

noncommittal, adj. che non si compromette, disimpegnato.

nondescript, adj. sènza caratteristiche speciali.

none, adj. and pron. nessuno.

nonentity, n. nullità f.

nonpartisan, adj. nèutro.

nonresident, adj. non residènte.

nonsense, n. assurdità f., fandònie f.pl.

nonstop, adj. sènza fermate.

noodles, n. tagliatélle f.pl.

nook, n. cantùccio m.

noon, n. mezzogiorno m.

no one, pron. nessuno.

noose, n. nodo scorsoio m.

nor, conj. nè.

norm, n. nòrma f.

normal, adj. normale.

normally, adv. normalmente.

north, 1. n. nord m. 2. adj. settentrionale.

northeast, n. nord-èst m.

northern, adj. settentrionale.

North Pole, n. polo nord m.

northwest, n. nord-òvest m.

Norway, n. Norvègia f.

Norwegian, adj. norvegese.

nose, n. naso m.

nosebleed, n. emorragía nasale f.

nose dive, n. picchiata f.

nostalgia, n. nostalgía f.

nostril, n. narice f.

nostrum, n. rimèdio empírico m.

nosy, adj. ficcanaso.

not, adv. non.

notable, adj. notévole.

notary, n. notaio m.

notation, n. notazione f.

notch, 1. n. tacca f. 2. vb. intaccare.

note, 1. n. nòta f.; (short letter) biglietto m. 2. vb. notare.

notebook, n. agènda f., taccuino m.

noted, adj. nòto.

notepaper, n. carta da léttera f.

noteworthy, adj. rimarchévole.

nothing, pron. niènte, nulla.

notice, 1. n. avviso m., attenzione f. 2. vb. osservare.

noticeable, adj. notévole.

notification, n. notificazione f., avviso m.

notify, vb. notificare.

notion, *n.* nozione *f.*

notoriety, *n.* notorietà *f.*

notorious, *adj.* famigerato, notòrio.

notwithstanding, *prep.* nonostante.

nougat, *n.* torrone *m.*

noun, *n.* sostantivo *m.*

nourish, *vb.* nutrire.

nourishment, *n.* nutrimento *m.*

novel, 1. *n.* romanzo *m.* **2.** *adj.* originale.

novelist, *n.* romanzière *m.*

novelty, *n.* novità *f.*

November, *n.* novèmbre *m.*

novena, *n.* novèna *f.*

novice, *n.* novízio *m.*

Novocaine, *n.* novocaína *f.*

now, *adv.* ora, adèsso.

nowadays, *adv.* di questi tempi.

noway(s), *adv.* in nessun modo.

nowhere, *adv.* in nessun luògo.

noxious, *adj.* nocivo.

nozzle, *n.* imboccatura *f.*

nuance, *n.* sfumatura *f.*

nuclear, *adj.* nucleare.

nuclear warhead, *n.* testata càrica nucleare *f.*

nuclear waste, *n.* rifiuti nucleari *m.pl.*

nucleus, *n.* nùcleo *m.*

nude, *adj.* nudo.

nudge, *n.* colpetto di gòmito *m.*

nugget, *n.* pepita *f.*

nudist, *n. and adj.* nudista *m. and f.*

nuisance, *n.* fastídio *m.*, seccatura *f.*

nuke, 1. *n.* arma atòmica *f.* **2.** *vb.* bombardare con l'atòmica.

nullify, *vb.* annullare.

numb, *adj.* intorpidito.

number, 1. *n.* nùmero *m.* **2.** *vb.* numerare.

numerical, *adj.* numèrico.

numerous, *adj.* numeroso.

nun, *n.* mònaca *f.*, suòra *f.*

nuncio, *n.* nùnzio *m.*

nuptial, 1. *adj.* nuziale.

nurse, 1. *n.* (hospital) infermièra *f.*; (wet-nurse) nutrice *f.*, bàlia *f.*; (baby-tender) bambinaia *f.* **2.** *vb.* curare.

nursery, *n.* stanza dei bambini *f.*; (plants) vivaio *m.*

nurture, *vb.* allevare, curare.

nut, *n.* nocciòla *f.*

nut-cracker, *n.* schiaccianoci *m.*

nutrition, *n.* nutrizione *f.*

nutritious, *adj.* nutriènte.

nutshell, *n.* gùscio di noce *m.*

nylon, *n.* nàilon *m.*

nymph, *n.* ninfa *f.*

O

oak, *n.* quèrcia *f.*

oar, *n.* remo *m.*

oasis, *n.* òasi *f.*

oath, *n.* (solemn) giuramento *m.*; (swear-word) bestémmia *f.*

oatmeal, *n.* fiocchi d'avena *m.pl.*

oats, *n.* avena *f.sg.*

obdurate, *adj.* ostinato.

obedience, *n.* obbediènza *f.*

obedient, *adj.* obbediènte.

obeisance, *n.* riverènza *f.*

obelisk, *n.* obelisco *m.*

obese, *adj.* obèso.

obey, *vb.* ubbidire, obbedire.

obfuscate, *vb.* offuscare.

obituary, *n.* necrològio *m.*

object, 1. *n.* oggètto *m.* **2.** *vb.* opporsi, obiettare.

objection, *n.* obiezione *f.*

objectionable, *adj.* offensivo.

objective, *n. and adj.* obiettivo (*m.*)

obligate, *vb.* obbligare.

obligation, *n.* òbbligo *m.*, obbligazione *f.*

obligatory, *adj.* obbligatòrio.

oblige, *vb.* obbligare.

obliging, *adj.* servizièvole.

oblique, *adj.* obliquo.

obliterate, *vb.* cancellare.

oblivion, *n.* oblìo *m.*

oblivious, *adj.* dimèntico, ignaro.

oblong, *adj.* oblungo.

obnoxious, *adj.* odioso.

oboe, *n.* òboe *m.*

obscene, *adj.* oscèno.

obscenity, *n.* oscenità *f.*

obscure, *adj.* oscuro.

obscurity, *n.* oscurità *f.*

obsequious, *adj.* ossequioso.

observance, *n.* osservanza *f.*

observation, *n.* osservazione *f.*

observatory, *n.* osservatòrio *m.*

observe, *vb.* osservare.

observer, *n.* osservatore *m.*

obsess, *vb.* ossessionare.

obsession, *n.* ossessione *f.*

obsolete, *adj.* caduto in disuso.

obstacle, *n.* ostàcolo *m.*

obstetrical, *adj.* ostètrico.

obstetrician, *n.* ostètrico *m.*

obstinate, *adj.* ostinato.

obstreperous, *adj.* clamoroso, chiassoso.

obstruct, *vb.* ostruire, ostacolare.

obstruction, *n.* ostruzione *f.*

obtain, *vb.* ottenere.

obtrude, *vb.* intrùdersi.

obtuse, *adj.* ottuso.

obviate, *vb.* evitare.

obvious, *adj.* òvvio.

occasion, 1. *n.* occasione *f.* **2.** *vb.* cagionare.

occasional, *adj.* occasionale.

occasionally, *adv.* di quando in quando.

Occident, *n.* occidènte *m.*

occidental, *adj.* occidentale.

occlusion, *n.* occlusione *f.*

occult, *adj.* occulto.

occupant, *n.* occupante *m.,* inquilino *m.*

occupation, *n.* occupazione *f.,* professione *f.*

occupy, *vb.* occupare.

occur, *vb.* accadere, succèdere.

occurrence, *n.* avvenimento *m.*

ocean, *n.* ocèano *m.*

ocean liner, *n.* transatlàntico *m.*

o'clock, *n.* ora *f.*

octagon, *n.* ottàgono *m.*

octave, *n.* ottava *f.*

October, *n.* ottobre *m.*

octopus, *n.* ottòpode *m.,* pòlipo *m.*

ocular, *adj.* oculare.

oculist, *n.* oculista *m.*

odd, *adj.* (numbers) dispari; (queer) strano.

oddity, *n.* stranezza *f.*

odds, *n.* probabilità *f.*

odious, *adj.* odioso.

odor, *n.* odore *m.*

of, *prep.* di; (from) da.

off, *adv.* via.

offend, *vb.* offèndere.

offender, *n.* responsàbile *m.;* (accused) imputato *m.*

offense, *n.* offesa *f.*

offensive, 1. *n.* offensiva *f.* **2.** *adj.* offensivo.

offer, 1. *n.* offèrta *f.* **2.** *vb.* offrire.

offering, *n.* offèrta *f.*

offhand, *adv.* estemporaneamente.

office, *n.* ufficio *m.;* (dentist's, doctor's) gabinetto *m.;* (**o. supplies**) oggetti di cancellería *m.pl.*

officer, *n.* ufficiale.

official, 1. *adj.* ufficiale (*m.*).

officiate, *vb.* officiare.

officious, *adj.* inframmettènte.

offshore, *adv.* vicino alla tèrra.

offspring, *n.* pròle *f.*

often, *adv.* spesso.

oil, 1. *n.* òlio *m.* **2.** *vb.* ùngere, lubrificare.

oil-cloth, *n.* tela cerata *f.*

oily, *adj.* oleoso.

ointment, *n.* unguènto *m.*

okay, *interj.* va bene.

old, *adj.* vècchio.

old-fashioned, *adj.* passato di mòda.

olfactory, *adj.* olfattòrio.

oligarchy, *n.* oligarchía *f.*

olive, *n.* (tree) olivo *m.;* (fruit) oliva *f.*

ombudsman, *n.* mediatore *m.*

omelet, *n.* frittata *f.*

omen, *n.* presàgio *m.*

ominous, *adj.* infàusto.

omission, *n.* omissione *f.*

omit, *vb.* omèttere.

omnibus, *n.* àutobus *m.*

omnipotent, *adj.* onnipotènte.

on, *adv. and prep.* su, sopra.

once, *adv.* una vòlta; (formerly) un tèmpo.

one, *num.* uno.

onerous, *adj.* oneroso.

oneself, *pron.* sè stesso (*sg.*); sè stessi (*pl.*).

one-sided, *adj.* unilaterale.

one-way, *adj.* (fare) di corsa semplice; (street) a sènso ùnico.

onion, *n.* cipolla *f.*

onion-skin, *n.* carta velina *f.*

onlooker, *n.* presente *m.,* testimone *m.*

only, 1. *adj.* único. **2.** *adv.* solamente, soltanto; (but) ma.
onslaught, *n.* attacco *m.*
onset, *n.* attacco *m.*, princìpio *m.*
onto, *prep.* su, sopra a.
onus, *n.* ònere *m.*
onward, *adv.* avanti.
ooze, 1. *n.* melma *f.* **2.** *vb.* trasudare.
opacity, *n.* opacità *f.*
opal, *n.* opale *m.*
opaque, *adj.* opaco.
open, 1. *adj.* apèrto. **2.** *vb.* aprire.
opening, *n.* (breach) apertura *f.*; (start) inízio *m.*; inaugurazione *f.*
open-minded, *adj.* imparziale, aperto.
opera, *n.* òpera *f.*
opera-glasses, *n.* binòcolo da teatro *m.* (*sg.*)
operate, *vb.* operare.
operatic, *adj.* lírico.
operation, *n.* operazione *f.*
operative, *adj.* operativo.
operator, *n.* operatore *m.*
operetta, *n.* operetta *f.*
ophthalmic, *adj.* oftàlmico.
opinion, *n.* opinione *f.*, parere *m.*
opium, *n.* òppio *m.*
opponent, *n.* antagonista *m.*
opportune, *adj.* opportuno.
opportunism, *n.* opportunismo *m.*
opportunity, *n.* occasione *f.*
oppose, *vb.* opporre, *tr.*
opposite, 1. *n. and adj.* oppòsto (*m.*). **2.** *adv.* dirimpètto. **3.** *prep.* dirimpètto a.
opposition, *n.* opposizione *f.*
oppress, *vb.* opprímere.
oppression, *n.* oppressione *f.*
oppressive, *adj.* oppressivo.
oppressor, *n.* oppressore *m.*
optic, *adj.* òttico.
optician, *n.* òttico *m.*
optics, *n.* òttica *f.*
optimism, *n.* ottimismo *m.*
optimistic, *adj.* ottimístico.
option, *n.* opzione *f.*
optional, *adj.* facoltativo.
optometrist, *n.* optometrista *m.*
optometry, *n.* optometría *f.*
opulence, *n.* opulènza *f.*

opulent, *adj.* opulènto.
or, *conj.* o (before *o*, od); sía, ossía.
oracle, *n.* oràcolo *m.*
oral, *adj.* orale.
orange, n. (tree) aràncio *m.*; (fruit) arància *f.*
orangeade. *n.* aranciata *f.*
oration, *n.* orazione *f.*
orator, *n.* oratore *m.*
oratory, *n.* oratòria *f.*
orbit, *n.* òrbita *f.*
orchard, *n.* òrto *m.*, frutteto *m.*
orchestra, *n.* orchèstra *f.*
orchid, *n.* orchidèa *f.*
ordain, *vb.* ordinare.
ordeal, *n.* ordàlia *f.*; (fig.) pròva *f.*
order, 1. *n.* òrdine *m.* **2.** *vb.* ordinare.
orderly, *adj.* ordinato.
ordinance, *n.* ordinanza *f.*
ordinary, *adj.* ordinàrio.
ordination, *n.* ordinazione *f.*
ore, *n.* minerale *m.*
organ, *n.* òrgano *m.*
organdy, *n.* organza *f.*
organic, *adj.* orgànico.
organism, *n.* organismo *m.*
organist, *n.* organista *m.*
organization, *n.* organizzazione *f.*
organize, *vb.* organizzare.
orgy, *n.* òrgia *f.*
orient, *vb.* orientare.
Orient, *n.* Orènte *m.*
Oriental, *adj.* orientale.
orientation, *n.* orientazione *f.*
origin, *n.* orígine *f.*
original, *adj.* originale; (former) primitivo.
originality, *n.* originalità *f.*
ornament, 1. *n.* ornamento *m.* **2.** *vb.* ornare.
ornamental, *adj.* ornamentale.
ornate, *adj.* ornato.
ornithology, *n.* ornitología *f.*
orphan, *n. and adj.* òrfano (*m.*).
orphanage, *n.* orfanotròfio *m.*
orthodox, *adj.* ortodòsso.
orthography, *n.* ortografía *f.*
orthopedic, *adj.* ortopèdico.
oscillate, *vb.* oscillare.
osmosis, *n.* osmòsi *f.*
ostensible, *adj.* ostensíbile.

ostentation, *n.* ostentazione *f.*

ostentatious, *adj.* ostentato.

ostracize, *vb.* ostracizzare.

ostrich, *n.* struzzo *m.*

other, *adj.* altro.

otherwise, *adv.* altrimenti.

otter, *n.* lontra *f.*

ouch, *interj.* ahi!

ought, *vb.* use conditional of dovere.

ounce, *n.* óncia *f.*

our, *adj.* nòstro.

ours, *pron.* nòstro.

ourselves, *pron.* noi stessi *m.,* noi stesse *f.*

oust, *vb.* spèllere.

ouster, *n.* espulsione *f.*

out, *adv.* fuòri.

outbid, *vb.* offrire di più

outbreak, *n.* scòppio *m.*

outburst, *n.* scòppio *m.*

outcast, *n.* pària *m.*

outcome, *n.* evènto *m.*

outdoors, *adv.* all'apèrto.

outer, *adj.* esteriore.

outfit, 1. *n.* corredo *m.* 2. *vb.* corredare, fornire.

outgoing, *adj.* espansivo.

outgrow, *vb.* crescere oltre una certa misura.

outgrowth, *n.* risultato *m.*

outing, *n.* escursione *f.,* gita *f.*

outlandish, *adj.* curioso, strano.

outlast, *vb.* sopravvivere a.

outlaw, *n.* bandito *m.*

outlet, *n.* sbocco *m.,* sfògo *m.;* (electrical) presa elèttrica *f.*

outline, *n.* schizzo *m.*

outlive, *vb.* sopravvivere a.

outlook, *n.* propsettiva *f.;* previsioni *f.pl.*

outnumber, *vb.* essere in maggior nùmero.

out of, *prep.* fuòri di; (motion) fuòri da.

out-of-date, *adj.* arretrato.

out-of-print, *adj.* esaurito.

out-of-tune, *adj.* stonato.

out-of-work, *adj.* senza lavoro.

outpost, *n.* avamposto *m.*

output, *n.* produzione *f.;* rendimento *m.*

outrage, *n.* oltràggio *m.*

outrageous, *adj.* oltraggioso.

outrank, *vb.* precédere.

outright, *adv.* completamente.

outrun, *vb.* oltrepassare.

outside, 1. *n.* and *adj.* estèrno (*m.*). 2. *adv.* fuòri. 3. *prep.* fuòri di; (except) all'infuòri di.

outskirts, *n.* sobborghi *m.pl.,* periferia *f.*

outstanding, *adj.* eccellente; (debt) arretrato.

outward, 1. *adj.* esteriore. 2. *adv.* vèrso l'estèrno.

outwardly, *adv.* esteriormente.

oval, *n.* and *adj.* ovale (*m.*)

ovary, *n.* ovàia *f.*

ovation, *n.* ovazione *f.*

oven, *n.* forno *m.*

over, *adv.* and *prep.* sopra; (o. again) di nuòvo; (o. and o.) ripetutamente.

overbearing, *adj.* prepotènte.

overcoat, *n.* sopràbito *m.*

overcome, *vb.* sopraffare, superare.

overdue, *adj.* scaduto.

overflow, *vb.* stripare, traboccare.

overhaul, *vb.* rimèttere a nuòvo.

overhead, 1. *n.* spese ordinàrie *f.pl.* 2. *adj.* and *adv.* in alto.

overkill, *n.* esagerazione retòrica *f.;* reazione sproporzionata *f.*

overlook, *vb.* omèttere, trascurare.

overnight, 1. *adj.* notturno. 2. *adv.* durante la nòtte.

overpass, *n.* cavalcavia *m.*

overpower, *vb.* vincere.

overrule, *vb.* decídere contro; (law) cassare.

overrun, *vb.* invàdere.

oversee, *vb.* sorvegliare.

oversight, *n.* negligènza *f.*

overstuffed, *adj.* imbottito.

overt, *adj.* apèrto.

overtake, *vb.* raggiùngere.

overthrow, 1. *n.* sconvolgimento *m.* 2. *vb.* sconvòlgere, sovvertire.

overtime, *adj.* straordinàrio.

overture, *n.* sinfonía *f.*

overturn, *vb.* capovòlgere.

overview, *n.* quadro generale *m.*

overweight, *n.* peso eccessivo *m.*

overwhelm, *vb.* sopraffare.

overwork, 1. *n.* lavoro eccessivo *m.* **2.** *vb.* lavorare troppo.

owe, *vb.* dovere.

owing, *adj.* dovuto; **(o. to)** dovuto a.

owl, *n.* civetta *f.,* gufo *m.;* **(o. service)** servizio notturno *m.*

own, 1. *adj.* pròprio. **2.** *vb.* possedere.

owner, *n.* possessore *m.*

ox, *n.* bue *m.*

oxygen, *n.* ossìgeno *m.*

oyster, *n.* òstrica *f.*

P

pa, *n.* babbo *m.*

pace, *n.* passo *m.*

pacific, *adj.* pacifico.

pacifier, *n.* pacificatore *m.*

pacifism, *n.* pacifismo *m.*

pacifist, *n.* pacifista *m.*

pacify, *vb.* pacificare.

pack, 1. *n.* pacco *m.;* (gang) banda *m.;* (cards) mazzo *m.;* (dogs) muta *f.* **2.** *vb.* imballare; (suitcases) fare le valigie.

package, *n.* pacco *m.*

packer, *n.* imballatore *m.*

packing, *n.* imballàggio *m.*

pact, *n.* patto *m.*

pad, 1. *n.* cuscinetto *m.* **2.** *vb.* imbottire.

padding, *n.* imbottitura *f.*

paddle, 1. *n.* remo *m.* **2.** *vb.* remare; (splash) spruzzare; (spank) sculacciare.

paddock, *n.* campo *m.*

padlock, *n.* lucchetto *m.*

Padua, *n.* Pàdova *f.*

Paduan, *adj.* padovano.

pagan, *n. and adj.* pagano (*m.*).

page, 1. *n.* pàgina *f.;* (servant) pàggio *m.* **2.** *vb.* chiamare.

pageant, *n.* cortèo *m.*

pageantry, *n.* pompa *f.,* fasto *m.*

paginate, *vb.* impaginare.

pagoda, *n.* pagòda *f.*

pail, *n.* sécchia *f.*

pain, *n.* dolore *m.,* pena *f.*

painful, *adj.* doloroso.

painkiller, *n.* analgèsico *m.*

painless, *adj.* indolore.

painstaking, *adj.* coscienzoso.

paint, 1. *n.* colore *m.;* (make-up) belletto *m.* **2.** *vb.* dipingere.

painter, *n.* pittore *m.*

painting, *n.* pittura *f.,* dipinto *m.*

pair, *n.* paio *m.*

pajamas, *n.* pigiama *m.pl.*

pal, *n.* compagno *m.,* amico *m.*

palace, *n.* palazzo *m.*

palatable, *adj.* gustoso.

palate, *n.* pàlato *m.*

palatial, *adj.* magnifico.

pale, 1. *adj.* pàllido **2.** *vb.* impallidire.

paleness, *n.* pallore *m.*

palette, *n.* tavolòzza *f.*

pall, *vb.* perder sapore *m.*

pallbearer, *n.* persona che règge i cordoni *f.*

pallid, *adj.* pàllido.

palm, *n.* palma *f.*

palpitate, *vb.* palpitare.

paltry, *adj.* meschino.

pamper, *vb.* viziare.

pamphlet, *n.* opùscolo *m.*

pan, 1. *n.* padèlla *f.* **2.** *vb.* criticare aspramente; **(p. out)** riuscire.

panacea, *n.* panacèa *f.*

pancake, *n.* frittèlla *f.*

pancreas, *n.* pancreas *m.*

pane, *n.* **(p. of glass)** vetro *m.*

panel, *n.* pannèllo *m.*

panelist, *n.* relatore a un convegno *m.*

pang, *n.* spàsimo *m.*

panic, *n.* pànico *m.*

panorama, *n.* panorama *m.*

pant, *vb.* anelare, ansare.

panther, *n.* pantèra *f.*

panties, *n.* mutandine (da dònna) *f.pl.*

pantomime, *n.* pantomima *f.*

pantry, *n.* dispènsa *f.*

pants, *n.* pantaloni *m.pl.*

panty hose, *n.* collant *m.* (*Italy*); ghette *f.pl.* (*Switzerland*)

pap, *n.* pappa *f.*

papa, *n.* papà *m.*

papacy, *n.* papato *m.*

papal, *adj.* papale.

paper, *n.* carta *f.;* **(newsp.)** giornale *m.;* **(wall-p.)** carta da parati *f.*

paperback, *n.* libro in brossura *m.*

paper-hanger, *n.* tappezzière in carta *m.*

paperwork, *n.* trafila burocràtica *f.*

paprika, *n.* pàprika *f.*

par, *n.* pari *f.*

parable, *n.* paràbola *f.*

parachute, *n.* paracadute *m.*

parade, *n.* parata *f.*

paradise, *n.* paradiso *m.*

paradox, *n.* paradòsso *m.*

paradoxical, *adj.* paradossale.

paraffin, *n.* paraffina *f.*

paragraph, *n.* paràgrafo *m.*

parakeet, *n.* pappagallo *m.*

parallel, *n. and adj.* parallèlo *(m.)*.

paralysis, *n.* paràlisi *f.*

paralyze, *vb.* paralizzare.

paramedic, *n.* paramèdico *m.;* assistente mèdico *m.*

parameter, *n.* paràmetro *m.*

paramount, *adj.* suprèmo.

paraphrase, 1. *n.* paràfrasi *f.* 2. *vb.* parafrasare.

parasite, *n.* parassita *f.*

parcel, *n.* pacco *m.*

parch, *vb.* inaridire.

parchment, *n.* pergamena *f.*

pardon, 1. *n.* perdono *m.* 2. *vb.* perdonare.

pare, *vb.* (nails) tagliare; (fruit) sbucciare.

parent, *n.* genitore *m.*

parentage, *n.* paternità *f.*

parenthesis, *n.* parèntesi *f.*

pariah, *n.* pària *m.*

Paris, *n.* Parigi *f.*

parish, *n.* parròcchia *f.;* **(p. priest)** pàrroco *m.*

Parisian, *adj.* parigino.

parity, *n.* parità *f.*

park, 1. *n.* parco *m.* 2. *vb.* parcheggiare.

parking, *n.* postéggio *m.* **(p. area)** autoparchéggio *m.;* **(p. lights)** luci di posizione *f.pl.*

parkway, *n.* viale *m.;* (superhighway) autostrada *f.*

parley, 1. *n.* parlamento *m.* 2. *vb.* parlamentare.

parliament, *n.* parlamento *m.*

parliamentary, *adj.* parlamentare.

parlor, *n.* salòtto *m.*

Parmesan, *adj.* parmigiano.

parochial, *adj.* parrocchiale.

parody, 1. *n.* parodìa *f.* 2. *vb.* parodiare.

parole, *n.* paròla d'onore *f.*

paroxysm, *n.* parossismo *m.*

parricide, *n.* patricìdio *m.*

parrot, *n.* pappagallo *m.*

parse, *vb.* analizzare grammaticalmente.

parsimonious, *adj.* parsimonioso.

parsimony, *n.* parsimònia *f.*

parsley, *n.* prezzémolo *m.*

parson, *n.* pàrroco *m.*

part, 1. *n.* parte *f.* 2. *vb.* separare, *tr.*

partake, *vb.* partecipare.

partial, *adj.* parziale.

partiality, *n.* parzialità *f.*

participant, *n.* partecipante *m.*

participate, *vb.* partecipare.

participation, *n.* partecipazione *f.*

participle, *n.* participio *m.*

particle, *n.* particèlla *f.*

particular, *adj.* particolare; (fussy) esigènte.

parting, *n.* separazione *f.*

partisan, *n. and adj.* partigiano *(m.)*.

partition, *n.* partizione *f.;* (wall) muro divisòrio *m.*

partly, *adv.* in parte.

partner, *n.* compagno *m.,* sòcio *m.*

partnership, *n.* associazione *f.;* società *f.*

part of speech, *n.* parte del discorso *f.*

partridge, *n.* pernice *f.*

party, *n.* (political) partito *m.;* (social) ricevimento *m.;* (legal) parte in càusa *f.;* (person) indivìduo *m.;* (group) gruppo *m.*

pass, 1. *n.* passo *m.* 2. *vb.* passare; (auto) sorpassare; (exam.) superare; (go beyond) oltrepassare.

passable, *adj.* (road) praticàbile; (work) passàbile.

passage, n. passàggio m.

passé, adj. fuòri di mòda; (faded) appassito.

passenger, n. passeggèro m.

passer-by, n. passante m.

passing, n. (auto) sorpasso m.

passion, n. passione f.

passionate, adj. appassionato.

passive, n. and adj. passivo (m.).

Passover, n. Pasqua ebràica f.

passport, n. passapòrto m.

past, n. and adj. passato (m.).

paste, 1. n. pasta f., còlla f. **2.** vb. incollare.

pastel, n. pastèllo m.

pasteurize, vb. pasteurizzare.

pastille, n. pastìglia f., pasticca f.

pastime, n. passatèmpo m.

pastor, n. pastore m.

pastry, n. pasticcerìa f.

pastry shop, n. pasticcerìa f.

pasture, n. pàscolo m.

pasty, 1. n. pasticcio m. **2.** adj. (color) pàllido.

pat, 1. n. colpetto m.; (butter, etc.) panetto m. **2.** vb. bàttere leggieramente.

patch, 1. n. pèzza f. **2.** vb. rappezzare, rattoppare.

patchwork, n. raffazzonamento m.

patent, 1. n. brevetto m. **2.** vb. brevettare.

patent leather, n. pèlle verniciata f.

paternal, adj. patèrno.

paternity, n. paternità f.

path, n. sentièro m., pista f.

pathetic, adj. patètico.

path finder, n. esploratore m.

pathology, n. patologìa f.

pathos, n. pàtos m.

pathway, n. sentiero m.

patience, n. paziènza f.

patient, adj. paziènte.

patio, n. cortile m.

patriarch, n. patriarca f.

patrician, n. and adj. patrìzio m.

patricide, n. patricidio m.

patrimony, n. patrimònio m.

patriot, n. patriòta m.

patriotic, adj. patriòttico.

patriotism, n. patriottismo m.

patrol, n. pattùglia f.

patrolman, n. poliziòtto m.

patron, n. patròno m.

patronage, n. patronato m.

patronize, vb. comprare da.

pattern, n. modèllo m.

pauper, n. pòvero m.

pause, n. pàusa f.

pave, vb. pavimentare.

pavement, n. selciato m.

pavilion, n. padiglione m.

paw, n. zampa f.

pawn, 1. n. pegno m.; (chess) pedìna f. **2.** impegnare.

pay, 1. n. paga f. **2.** vb. pagare; **(p. in)** versare.

payable, adj. pagàbile.

paycheck, n. assegno-paga m.

payday, n. giorno-paga m.

payment, n. pagamento m., versamento m.

payoff, n. pagamento m.; profitto m.

payroll, n. libro paga m.

pea, n. pisèllo m.

peace, n. pace f.

peaceable, adj. pacìfico.

peaceful, adj. tranquillo.

peach, n. (tree) pèsco m.; (fruit) pèsca f.

peacock, n. pavone m.

peak, n. cima f., picco m.

peak hour, n. ora di punta f.

peal, 1. n. scampanìo m. **2.** vb. scampanare.

peanut, n. aràchide f.

peanut butter, n. pasta d'arachidi f.

pear, n. (tree) pero m.; (fruit) pera f.

pearl, n. pèrla f.

peasant, n. contadino m.

pea soup, n. minestra di piselli f., (fig.) grande nebbia f.

peat, n. torba f.

pebble, n. ciòttolo m.

peck, vb. beccare.

peculiar, adj. (special) peculiare; (queer) strano.

peculiarity, n. peculiarità f.

pecuniary, adj. pecuniàrio.

pedagogue, n. pedagògo m.

pedagogy, n. pedagogìa f.

pedal, 1. n. pedale m. **2.** vb. pedalare.

pedant, n. pedante m.

peddle, vb. vèndere al minuto.

peddler, *n.* venditore ambulante *m.*

pedestal, *n.* piedestallo *m.*

pedestrian, 1. *n.* pedone *m.* **2.** *adj.* pedèstre; (pertaining to pedestrians) pedonale.

pediatrician, *n.* pediàtra *m.*

pedigree, *n.* genealogia *f.*

peek, *vb.* sbirciare.

peel, *vb.* sbucciare, pelare.

peep, 1. *n.* occiata *f.* **2.** *vb.* (look) dare un' occhiata; (appear) spuntare.

peephole, *n.* spioncino *m.*

Peeping Tom, *n.* guardone *m.*

peer, 1. *n.* pari *m.* **2.** *vb.* guardare curiosamente.

peevish, *adj.* stizzoso.

peg, *n.* piolo *m.*

pelt, 1. *n.* (skin) pèlle *f.* **2.** *vb.* assalire.

pelvis, *n.* pèlvi *f.*

pen, 1. *n.* penna *f.;* **(fountain p.)** penna stilogràfica. **2.** *vb.* scrivere.

penalty, *n.* pena *f.*

penance, *n.* penitènza *f.*

penchant, *n.* inclinazione *f.*

pencil, *n.* làpis *m.,* matita *f.*

pendant, *n.* pendènte *m.*

pending, 1. *adj.* pendènte. **2.** *prep.* in attesa di.

penetrate, *vb.* penetrare.

penetration, *n.* penetrazione *f.*

penicillin, *n.* penicillina *f.*

peninsula, *n.* penisola *f.*

penitence, *n.* penitènza *f.*

penitent, *n. and adj.* penitènte *(m.).*

pen-knife, *n.* temperino *m.*

penniless, *adj.* al verde.

penny, *n.* sòldo *m.*

pension, *n.* pensione *f.*

pensive, *adj.* pensoso.

pent-up, *adj.* rinchiuso.

penury, *n.* penùria *f.*

people, *n.* (folks) gènte *f.;* (nation) pòpolo *m.*

pepper, *n.* pepe *m.*

per, *prep.* per.

perambulator, *n.* carrozzèlla *f.*

perceive, *vb.* scòrgere.

per cent, *adv.* per cènto.

percentage, *n.* percentuale *m.*

perceptible, *adj.* percettìbile.

perception, *n.* percezione *f.*

perch, 1. *n.* (fish) pesce pèrsico *m.;* (pole) pèrtica *f.;* (for birds) posatòio *m.* **2.** *vb.* posarsi; (roost) appollaiarsi.

perdition, *n.* perdizione *f.*

peremptory, *adj.* perentòrio.

perennial, *adj.* perènne.

perfect, 1. *adj.* perfètto. **2.** *vb.* perfezionare.

perfection, *n.* perfezione *f.*

perforation, *n.* perforazione *f.*

perform, *vb.* eseguire; (a play) rappresentare; (sing) cantare; (instrumental music) suonare.

performance, *n.* esecuzione *f.,* rappresentazione *f.*

perfume, 1. *n.* profumo *m.* **2.** *vb.* profumare.

perfunctory, *adj.* casuale.

perhaps, *adv.* forse; **(p. even)** magari.

peril, *n.* pericolo *m.*

perilous, *adj.* pericoloso.

perimeter, *n.* perìmetro *m.*

period, *n.* perìodo *m.*

periodic, *adj.* periòdico.

periodical, *n. and adj.* periòdico *(m.).*

periphery, *n.* periferia *f.*

periscope, *n.* periscòpio *m.*

perish, *vb.* perire.

perishable, *adj.* deperìbile.

perjure oneself, *vb.* spergiurare.

perjury, *n.* spergiuro *m.*

perk, *vb.* alzare; **(p. oneself up)** mettersi in ghingheri.

permanent, *adj.* permanènte.

permeate, *vb.* permeare.

permissible, *adj.* permissìbile.

permission, *n.* permesso *m.*

permit, 1. *n.* permesso *m.* **2.** *vb.* permèttere.

permute, *vb.* permutare.

pernicious, *adj.* pernicioso.

perpendicular, *n. and adj.* perpendicolare *(m.).*

perpetrate, *vb.* perpetrare.

perpetual, *adj.* perpètuo.

perplex, 1. *adj.* perplèsso. **2.** *vb.* rèndere perplèsso.

perplexity, *n.* perplessità *f.*

per se, *adv.* di per sè.

persecute, *vb.* perseguitare.

persecution, *n.* persecuzione *f.*

perseverance, *n.* perseveranza *f.*

persevere, vb. perseverare.
Perisan Gulf, n. Golfo Pèrsico m.
persimmon, n. cachi m.pl.
persist, vb. persistere.
persistent, adj. persistènte.
person, n. persona f.
personage, n. personàggio m.
personal, adj. personale.
personality, n. personalità f.
personally, adv. personalmente.
personnel, n. personale m.
perspective, n. prospettiva f.
perspiration, n. sudore m.
perspire, vb. sudare.
persuade, vb. persuadere.
persuasive, adj. persuasivo.
pertain, vb. appartenere.
pertinent, adj. pertinènte.
perturb, vb. perturbare.
peruse, vb. scórrere.
pervade, vb. pervàdere.
perverse, adj. pervèrso.
perversion, n. perversione f.
pervert, vb. pervertire.
pessimism, n. pessimismo m.
pestilence, n. pestilènza f.
pet, 1. n. and adj. favorito (m.);
(animal) animale domèstico m. 2.
vb. vezzeggiare.
petal, n. pètalo m.
petition, n. petizione f.
petrify, vb. pietrificare.
petrol, n. benzina f.
petroleum, n. petròlio m.
petticoat, n. sottana f.
petty, adj. meschino, píccolo.
petulance, n. petulanza f.
petulant, adj. petulante.
pew, n. banco in chièsa m.
phantom, n. fantasma m.
pharmacist, n. farmacista m.
pharmacy, n. farmacía f.
phase, n. fase f.
pheasant, n. fagiano m.
phenomenal, adj. fenomenale.
phenomenon, n. fenòmeno m.
philanthropy, n. filantropía f.
philately, n. filatèlica f.
philosopher, n. filòsofo m.
philosophical, adj. filosòfico.
philosophy, n. filosofía f.
phlegm, n. flèmma m.
phlegmatic, adj. flemmàtico.
phobia, n. fobía f.
phonetic, adj. fonètico.

phonograph, n. grammòfono m.
phosphorus, n. fòsforo m.
photocopier, n. fotocopiatore m.
photocopy, n. fotocopia f.
photoelectric, adj. fotoelèttrico.
photogenic, adj. fotogènico.
photograph, 1. n. fotografía f. 2.
vb. fotografare.
photographer, n. fotògrafo m.
photography, n. fotografía f.
photostat, n. riproduzione ana-
stàtica f.
phrase, n. frase f.
physical, adj. fisico.
physician, n. mèdico m.
physicist, n. fisico m.
physics, n. fisica f.
physiology, n. fisiología f.
physiotherapy, n. fisioterapía f.
physique, n. fisico m.
pianist, n. pianista m.
piano, n. pianofòrte m.
picayune, adj. meschino.
piccolo, n. ottavino m.
pick, 1. n. piccone m. 2. vb.
(gather) raccògliere; (select) scégliere.
picket, n. picchetto m.
pickle, n. salamòia f.; (trouble)
impiccio m.
pickpocket, n. borsaiòlo m.
picnic, n. gita f.
picture, n. quadro m.
picturesque, adj. pittoresco.
pie, n. tòrta f.
piece, n. pèzzo m.
Piedmont, n. Piemonte m.
Piedmontese, adj. piemontese.
pier, n. (dock) banchina f., mòlo
m.; (pillar) pilone m.
pierce, vb. forare, traforare.
piercing, adj. lancinante, acuto.
piety, n. pietà f.
pig, n. pòrco m.; maiale m.
pigeon, n. piccione m.
pigeonhole, n. casèlla f.
pigment, n. pigmènto m.
pigsty, n. porcile m.
pigtail, n. codino m.
pike, n. picca f.; autostrada f.
pile, n. (heap) ammasso m.,
mucchio m.; (post) palafitta f. 2.
vb. ammucchiare.
pilfer, vb. rubacchiare.
pilgrim, n. pellegrino m.

pilgrimage, n. pellegrinàggio m.

pill, n. pillola f.

pillage, 1. n. sacchéggio m. 2. vb. saccheggiare.

pillar, n. pilastro m., pilone m.

pillow, n. guanciale m.

pillowcase, n. fèdera f.

pilot, n. pilòta m.

pimp, n. ruffiano m.; lenone m.

pimple, n. forùncolo m.

pin, n. spillo m.

pinch, 1. n. pizzicòtto m. 2. vb. pizzicare.

pine, 1. n. pino m. 2. vb. languire.

pineapple, n. ananàs m.

pine cone, n. pigna f.

ping-pong, n. tennis da tàvola m.

pink, adj. ròsa.

pinnacle, n. pinnàcolo m.

pint, n. pinta f.

pioneer, n. pionière m.

pious, adj. pío.

pipe, n. tubo m.; (tobacco) pipa f.

piper, n. piffero m.

piquant, adj. piccante.

pirate, n. pirata m.

pistol, n. pistola f.

piston, n. pistone m., stantuffo m.

pit, n. buca f.

pitch, 1. n. (tar) pece f.; (throw) làncio m.; (music) tòno m. 2. vb. (hurl) lanciare.

pitchblende, n. pechblenda f., uraninite f.

pitcher, n. bròcca f.; (thrower) lanciatore m.

pitchfork, n. forca f.

pitfall, n. tràppola f.

pitiful, adj. pietoso.

pitiless, adj. spietato.

pity, n. pietà f.; (shame) peccato m.; **(what a p.)** che peccato!

pivot, n. pèrnio m.

pizza, n. pizza f.

placard, n. cartèllo m.

placate, vb. placare.

place, 1. n. posto m., luògo m.; **(take p.)** aver luògo; accadere. 2. vb. méttere; porre.

placid, adj. plàcido.

plagiarism, n. plàgio m.

plague, n. pèste f.

plain, 1. n. pianura f. 2. adj. (clear) chiaro; (simple) sémplice, modèsto.

plaintiff, n. attore m.

plan, 1. n. piano m., progètto m.; (map) pianta f. 2. vb. progettare.

plane, 1. n. (airplane) aeroplano m.; (carpenter's) pialla f. 2. vb. piallare.

planet, n. pianeta m.

planetarium, n. planetàrio m.

planetary, adj. planetàrio.

plank, n. asse f., tàvola f.

plant, 1. n. pianta f.; (factory; installation) impianto m. 2. vb. piantare.

plantation, n. piantagione f.

planter, n. piantatore m.; (plantation owner) proprietàrio di piantagione m.

plasma, n. plasma m.

plaster, 1. n. intònaco m.; (medical) empiastro m. 2. vb. intonacare.

plastic, 1. n. plàstica f. 2. adj. plàstico.

plate, n. piatto m.; (photographic) lastra f.; (auto) targa f.

plateau, n. altopiano m.

platform, n. piattaforma f.

platinum, n. plàtino m.

platitude, n. banalità f.

platoon, n. drappèllo m., plotone m.

platter, n. piatto grande m.

plaudit, n. applàuso m.

plausible, adj. plausibile.

play, 1. n. (game) giòco m.; (joke) schèrzo m.; (theater) dramma m. 2. vb. giocare; (on stage) recitare; (instrument) suonare.

player, n. (game) giocatore m.; (instrument) suonatore m.

playful, adj. scherzoso.

playground, n. campo per ricreazione m.

playmate, n. compagno di giòchi m.

playwright, n. drammaturgo m.

plea, n. preghièra f.; (excuse) scusa f.

plead, vb. esortare, implorare; (give as excuse) addurre come scusa.

pleasant, adj. piacévole.

please, 1. vb. piacere a. 2. adv., interj. per favore.

pleasing, adj. piacévole, grato.

pleasure, n. piacere m.

pleat, n. piega f.

plebiscite, n. plebiscito m.

pledge, 1. n. pegno m. 2. vb. impegnare.

plentiful, adj. abbondante.

plenty, 1. n. abbondanza f. 2. adj. **(p. of)** molto.

pleurisy, n. pleurite f.

pliable, pliant, adj. pieghévole.

pliers, n. pinze f.pl., pinzette f.pl.

plight, n. situazione f.

plot, 1. n. (conspiracy) complòtto m.; (story) intréccio m.; (land) appezzamento m.; (plan) pianta f.

plow, 1. n. aratro m. 2. vb. arare.

plowman, n. bracciante m.; contadino m.

pluck, 1. n. fégato m. 2. vb. cògliere.

plucky, adj. coraggioso.

plug, 1. n. tappo m.; (electric) spina f. 2. vb. tappare.

plum, n. (tree) susino m.; (fruit) susina f., prugna f.

plumage, n. piumàggio m.

plumber, n. trombaio m., stagnino m.; idràulico m.

plumbing, n. impianto idràulico m.

plume, n. penna f.

plummet, vb. precipitare.

plump, adj. grassòccio.

plum tree, n. susino m.

plunder, 1. n. bottino m., prèda f. 2. vb. saccheggiare, predare.

plunge, 1. n. tuffo m. 2. vb. tuffare, tr.

plural, 1. n. and adj. plurale (m.).

plus, prep. più.

plutocrat, n. plutòcrate m.

plywood, n. legno compensato m.

pneumatic, adj. pneumàtico.

pneumonia, n. polmonite f.

poach, vb. (hunt illegally) andare a càccia di fròdo; (eggs) cuòcere in camicia; (poached eggs) uòva affogate.

poacher, n. cacciatore di fròdo m.

pocket, 1. n. tasca f. 2. vb. intascare.

pocket-book, n. portafògli m.

pocket-size, adj. tascàbile.

pod, n. bacello m.

podiatry, n. cura dei pièdi f.

poem, n. poesia f., poèma m.

poet, n. poèta m., poetéssa f.

poetic, adj. poètico.

poetry, n. poesia f.

poignant, adj. doloroso.

point, 1. n. punto m. 2. vb. puntare; **(p. to)** indicare; **(p. out)** additare.

pointed, adj. acuto.

pointless, adj. privo di senso.

poise, n. equilibrio m.

poison, 1. n. veleno m. 2. vb. avvelenare.

poisonous, adj. velenoso.

poke, vb. spingere; (fire) attizzare.

Poland, n. Polònia f.

polar, adj. polare.

pole, n. (post) palo m.; (rod) pertica f.; (wagon) timone m.; (electrical, geographical) pòlo m.

police, n. polizia f.

policeman, n. vígile m., poliziòtto m.

policy, n. política f.; (insurance) polizza f.

polish, 1. n. (material) lùcido m.; (gloss) lucidatura f. 2. vb. lucidare.

Polish, adj. polacco.

polite, adj. cortese.

politeness, n. cortesia f.

politic, political, adj. político.

politician, n. político m.

politics, n. política f.

poll, 1. n. (head) tèsta f.; (voting) votazione f.; **(p.-tax)** capitazione f. 2. vb. (get, in voting) ottenere.

pollen, n. pòlline m.

pollute, vb. contaminare.

polonaise, n. polacca f.

polygamy, n. poligamía f.

polygon, n. polígono m.

pomp, n. pompa f., fasto m.

pompous, adj. pomposo, fastoso.

poncho, n. impermeàbile m.

pond, n. stagno m.

ponder, vb. ponderare.

ponderous, adj. ponderoso.

pontiff, n. pontéfice m.

pontoon, n. pontone m.

pony, n. cavallino m.

pool, n. stagno m.; (money) fondo comune m.

poor, adj. pòvero.

pop, 1. *n.* scòppio *m.;* (father) babbo *m* **2.** *vb.* scoppiettare.

popcorn, *n.* pop-corn *m.*

pope, *n.* papa *m.*

popeyed, *adj.* con gli occhi fuori dalle òrbite.

poppy, *n.* papavero *m.*

popular, *adj.* popolare.

popularity, *n.* popolarità *f.*

populate, *vb.* popolare.

population, *n.* popolazione *f.*

porcelain, *n.* porcellana *f.*

porch, *n.* veranda *f.;* (church) pòrtico *m.*

pore, *n.* pòro *m.*

pork, *n.* maiale *m.*

pornography, *n.* pornografìa *f.*

porous, *adj.* poroso.

port, *n.* pòrto *m.*

portable, *adj.* portàtile.

portal, *n.* portale *m.*

portend, *vb.* presagire.

portent, *n.* presàgio *m.*

porter, *n.* facchino *m.,* portabagagli *m.;* (hotel) portière *m.*

portfolio, *n.* cartèlla *f.,* portafòglio *m.*

porthole, *n.* oblò *m.*

portico, *n.* pòrtico *m.*

portion, *n.* porzione *f.*

portly, *adj.* corpulènto.

portrait, *n.* ritratto *m.*

portray, *vb.* ritrattare.

Portugal, *n.* il Portogallo *m.*

Portuguese, *adj.* portoghese.

pose, 1. *n.* pòsa *f.* **2.** *vb.* posare; **(p. as)** atteggiarsi a.

position, *n.* posizione *f.*

positive, *adj.* positivo.

possess, *vb.* possedere.

possession, *n.* possèsso *m.*

possessive, *adj.* possessivo.

possessor, *n.* possessore *m.*

possibility, *n.* possibilità *f.*

possible, *adj.* possìbile.

possibly, *adv.* possibilmente, forse.

possum, *n.* opòssum *m.*

post, 1. *n.* (pole) palo *m.;* (place) posto *m.;* (mail) pòsta *f.* **2.** *vb.* (put up) affiggere; (mail) impostare.

postage, *n.* affrancatura *f.;* **(p.-stamp)** francobollo *m.*

postal, *adj.* postale.

post card, *n.* cartolina postale *f.*

poster, *n.* cartèllo *m.*

poste restante, *adv.* fermo pòsta.

posterior, 1. *n.* culo *m.* **2.** *adj.* posteriore.

posterity, *n.* posterità *f.,* pòsteri *m.pl.*

postgraduate, *adj.* di perfezionamento.

postman, *n.* postino *m.*

postmark, *n.* timbro postale, *m.*

postmortem, 1. *adj.* postumo. **2.** *n.* autopsìa *f.*

post office, *n.* ufficio postale *m.*

postpone, *vb.* posporre, rimandare.

postscript, *n.* poscritto *m.*

posture, *n.* posizione *f.*

pot, *n.* pèntola *f.;* (marijuana) marijuana *f.*

potassium, *n.* potàssio *m.*

potato, *n.* patata *f.*

potent, *adj.* potènte.

potential, *n. and adj.* potenziale *(m.)*

pot-hole, *n.* buca *f.*

potion, *n.* pozione *f.*

pottery, *n.* stovìglie *f.pl.*

pouch, *n.* borsa *f.*

poultry, *n.* pollame *m.*

pound, 1. *n.* libbra *f.;* **(p. sterling)** sterlina *f.* **2.** *vb.* pestare.

pour, *vb.* versare; **(p. off)** travasare.

poverty, *n.* povertà *f.,* misèria *f.*

powder, 1. *n.* pòlvere *m.;* **(face-p.)** cìpria *f.;* **(p.-puff)** fiòcco da cìpria *f.* **2.** *vb.* polverizzare; (one's face) incipriare, *tr.*

power, *n.* potere *m.,* potènza *f.*

powerful, *adj.* possènte.

powerless, *adj.* impotènte.

practicable, *adj.* praticàbile.

practical, *adj.* pràtico.

practically, *adv.* praticamente.

practice, 1. *n.* pràtica *f.* **2.** *vb.* praticare, esercitare, *tr.*

practiced, *adj.* espèrto.

practitioner, *n.* professionista *m.*

pragmatic, *adj.* prammàtico.

prairie, *n.* prateria *f.*

praise, 1. *n.* lòde *f.* **2.** *vb.* lodare.

prank, *n.* birichinata *f.,* burla *f.*

pray, *vb.* pregare.

prayer, *n.* preghièra *f.*

preach, *vb.* predicare.

preacher, *n.* predicatore *m.*

preamble, *n.* preàmbolo *m.*

precarious, *adj.* precàrio.

precaution, *n.* precauzione *f.*

precede, *vb.* precèdere.

precedence, *n.* precedènza *f.*

precedent, *n.* precedènte *m.*

precept, *n.* precètto *m.*

precinct, *n.* distretto *m.*, circoscrizione *f.*

precious, *adj.* prezioso.

precipice, *n.* precipízio *m.*

precipitate, *vb.* precipitare.

precipitous, *adj.* precipitoso.

precise, *adj.* preciso.

precision, *n.* precisione *f.*

preclude, *vb.* preclùdere.

precocious, *adj.* precòce.

precursor, *n.* precursore *m.*

predatory, *adj.* predatòrio, di prèda.

predecessor, *n.* predecessore *m.*

predestination, *n.* predestinazione *f.*

predicament, *n.* impíccio *m.*

predicate, *n.* predicato *m.*

predict, *vb.* predire.

prediction, *n.* predizione *f.*

predilection, *n.* predilezione *f.*

predispose, *vb.* predisporre.

predominant, *adj.* predominante.

preeminent, *adj.* preminente.

preempt, *vb.* preacquisire.

prefabricated, *adj.* prefabbricato.

preface, *n.* prefazione *f.*

prefect, *n.* prefètto *m.*

prefer, *vb.* preferire.

preferable, *adj.* preferíbile.

preference, *n.* preferènza *f.*

prefix, *n.* prefisso *m.*

pregnancy, *n.* gravidanza *f.*

pregnant, *adj.* gràvida *f.*, incinta *f.*; (animals only) prègna *f.*

prehistoric, *adj.* preistòrico.

prejudice, 1. *n.* pregiudízio *m.* 2. *vb.* pregiudicare.

prejudiced, *adj.* pregiudicato.

prelate, *n.* prelato *m.*

preliminary, *adj.* preliminare.

prelude, *n.* prelùdio *m.*

premature, *adj.* prematuro.

premeditate, *vb.* premeditare.

premier, *n.* primo ministro *m.*

premiere, *n.* prima *f.*

premise, *n.* premessa *f.*

premium, *n.* prèmio *m.*

premonition, *n.* premonizione *f.*

prenatal, *adj.* prenatale.

prepaid, *adj.* saldato in anticipo, prepagato.

preparation, *n.* preparazione *f.*

preparatory, *adj.* preparatòrio.

prepare, *vb.* preparare.

prepay, *vb.* pagare in anticipo.

preponderant, *adj.* preponderante.

preposition, *n.* preposizione *f.*

preposterous, *adj.* assurdo.

prerecorded, *adj.* preregistrato.

prerequisite, *n.* primo requisito *m.*

prerogative, *n.* prerogativa *f.*

presage, 1. *n.* presagio *m.* 2. *vb.* presagire.

prescribe, *vb.* prescrivere.

prescription, *n.* prescrizione *f.*

presence, *n.* presènza *f.*

present, 1. *n.* dono *m.*, regalo *m.*, omàggio *m.* 2. *adj.* presènte; (be p.) assistere. 3. *vb.* presentare; regalare.

presentable, *adj.* presentàbile.

presentation, *n.* presentazione *f.*

presently, *adv.* fra pòco, immediatamente.

preservation, *n.* conservazione *f.*

preservative, *adj.* conservativo.

preserve, *vb.* preservare, conservare, serbare.

preside, *vb.* presièdere.

presidency, *n.* presidènza *f.*

president, *n.* presidènte *m.*

press, 1. *n.* prèssa *f.*; (newspapers) stampa *f.* 2. *vb.* prèmere; stríngere; (urge) insístere.

pressing, *adj.* urgènte.

pressure, *n.* pressione *f.*

pressure cooker, *n.* pèntola a pressione *f.*

prestige, *n.* prestígio *m.*

presume, *vb.* presùmere.

presumption, *n.* presunzione *f.*

presumptuous, *adj.* presuntuoso.

presumptuousness, *n.* presuntuosità *f.*

presuppose, *vb.* presupporre.

pretend, *vb.* fingere, far finta; (claim) pretèndere.

pretense, *n.* finta *f.*

pretension, *n.* pretesa *f.*

pretentious, *adj.* pretenzioso.

pretext, *n.* pretèsto *m.*

pretty, *adj.* grazioso, bellino.

prevail, *vb.* prevalere.

prevalent, *adj.* prevalènte.

prevent, *vb.* impedire.

prevention, *n.* prevenzione *f.*

preventive, *adj.* preventivo.

preview, *n.* anteprima *f.*

previous, *adj.* precedènte.

prey, *n.* prèda *f.*

price, *n.* prèzzo *m.*

priceless, *adj.* inestimàbile.

prick, *vb.* pùngere.

pride, *n.* orgóglio *m.*

priest, *n.* prète *m.*

prim, *adj.* affettato.

primary, *adj.* primàrio.

prime, *adj.* primo, principale.

prime minister, *n.* primo ministro *m.*

primitive, *adj.* primitivo.

prince, *n.* prìncipe *m.*

princess, *n.* principessa *f.*

principal, 1. *n.* capo *m.,* direttore *m.* 2. *adj.* principale.

principally, *adv.* principalmente.

principle, *n.* princípio *m.*

print, 1. *n.* stampa *f.;* (impression) impronta *f.* 2. *vb.* stampare.

printed matter, *n.* (mail) stampe *f.pl.*

printer, *n.* stampante *f.*

printing, *n.* stampa *f.;* (press-run) tiratura *f.*

printing-press, *n.* màcchina per stampare *f.*

printout, *n.* foglio stampato prodotto da un calcolatore elettrònico *m.*

prior, 1. *adj.* anteriore. 2. *adv.* prima; (p. to) prima di.

priority, *n.* priorità *f.*

prism, *n.* prisma *m.*

prison, *n.* prigione *f.*

prison van, *n.* cellulare *m.*

prisoner, *n.* prigionièro *m.*

privacy, *n.* intimità *f.,* solitùdine *f.*

private, 1. *n.* soldato sémplice *m.* 2. *adj.* privato.

private eye, *n.* investigatore privato *m.*

privation, *n.* privazione *f.*

privet, *n.* ligustro *m.*

privilege, *n.* privilègio *m.*

privy, *n.* latrina *f.*

prize, 1. *n.* prèmio *m.* 2. *vb.* apprezzare.

probability, *n.* probabilità *f.*

probable, *adj.* probàbile.

probate, 1. *n.* omologazione *f.* 2. *vb.* omologare.

probation, *n.* pròva *f.*

probe, *vb.* sondare.

probity, *n.* probità *f.*

problem, *n.* problèma *m.*

procedure, *n.* procedimento *m.;* (legal) procedura *f.*

proceed, *vb.* procèdere.

process, *n.* procèsso *m.*

procession, *n.* processione *f.*

proclaim, *vb.* proclamare.

proclamation, *n.* proclamazione *f.*

procrastinate, *vb.* procrastinare.

procure, *vb.* procurare.

prod, 1. *n.* pùngolo *m.;* stìmolo *m.* 2. *vb.* stimolare.

prodigal, *adj.* pròdigo.

prodigy, *n.* prodígio *m.*

produce, 1. *n.* prodotti agrìcoli *m.pl.* 2. *vb.* produrre.

producer, *n.* produttore *m.;* impressario *m.*

product, *n.* prodotto *m.*

production, *n.* produzione *f.*

productive, *adj.* produttivo.

profane, 1. *adj.* profano. 2. *vb.* profanare.

profanity, *n.* bestémmie *f.pl.*

profess, *vb.* professare.

profession, *n.* professione *f.*

professional, 1. *n.* professionista *m.* 2. *adj.* professionale.

professor, *n.* professore *m.*

proficient, *adj.* espèrto.

profile, *n.* profilo *m.*

profit, 1. *n.* guadagno *m.,* profitto *m.,* vantàggio *m.* 2. *vb.* approfittare.

profitable, *adj.* vantaggioso.

profiteer, *n.* pescecane *m.*

profligate, *n. and adj.* prodigo *m.,* dissoluto *m.*

profound, *adj.* profondo.

profoundly, *adv.* profondamente.

profundity, *n.* profondità *f.*

profuse, *adj.* profuso.

progeny, *n.* prole *f.*

prognosis, n. prògnosi f.
program, n. programma m.
progress, 1. n. progrèsso m. 2. vb. progredire.
progressive, adj. progressivo.
prohibit, vb. proibire.
prohibition, n. proibizione f., divièto m.
prohibitive, adj. proibitivo.
project, 1. n. progètto m. 2. vb. (plan) progettare; (stick out) spòrgere.
projectile, n. proièttile m.
projection, n. proiezione f.
projector, n. proiettore m.
proliferation, n. proliferazione f.
prolific, adj. prolifico.
prologue, n. pròlogo m.
prolong, vb. prolungare.
prolongation, n. prolungamento m.
prominent, adj. prominènte.
promiscuous, adj. promiscuo.
promise, 1. n. promessa f. 2. vb. prométtere.
promote, vb. promuòvere.
promotion, n. promozione f.
prompt, adj. pronto.
prompter, n. suggeritore m.
promulgate, vb. promulgare.
pronoun, n. pronome m.
pronounce, vb. pronunciare.
pronunciation, n. pronùncia f.
proof, n. pròva f.; (printing) bòzze f.pl.
proof-read, vb. corrèggere le bòzze di.
prop, 1. n. puntèllo m. 2. vb. puntellare.
propaganda, n. propaganda f.
propagate, vb. propagare.
propel, vb. spíngere innanzi.
propeller, n. èlica f.
propensity, n. propensione f.
proper, adj. pròprio.
property, n. proprietà f.
prophecy, n. profezia f.
prophesy, vb. profetizzare.
prophet, n. profèta m.
prophetic, adj. profètico.
propitiate, vb. propiziare.
propitious, adj. propízio.
proponent, n. proponènte m.
proportion, n. proporzione f.

proportionate, adj. proporzionato.
proposal, n. propòsta f.
propose, vb. proporre, tr.
proposition, n. propòsta f.
proprietor, n. proprietàrio m.
propriety, n. conveniènza f.
propulsion, n. propulsione f.
prorate, vb. rateizzare.
prosaic, adj. prosàico.
proscribe, vb. proscrívere.
prose, n. pròsa f.
prosecute, vb. intentare giudízio contro.
prosecutor, n. esecutore m.; (law) pùbblico ministero m.
proselyte, n. prosèlite m. and f.
prosody, n. prosodia f., mètrica f.
prospect, n. prospètto m.
prospective, adj. prospettivo.
prosper, vb. prosperare.
prosperity, n. prosperità f.
prosperous, adj. pròspero.
prostitute, n. prostituta f.
prostrate, 1. adj. prostrato. 2. vb. prostrare.
protagonist, n. protagonista m.
protect, vb. protèggere.
protection, n. protezione f.
protective, adj. protettivo.
protector, n. protettore m.
protégé, n. protètto m.
protein, n. proteína f.
pro tempore, adj. provvisorio, ad interim.
protest, 1. n. protèsta f. 2. vb. protestare.
Protestant, n. and adj. protestante (m.).
Protestantism, n. protestantésimo m.
protocol, n. protocòllo m.
proton, n. protone m.
protoplasma, n. protoplasma m.
protract, vb. protrarre.
protrude, vb. spíngere fuòri, tr.
protuberance, n. protuberanza f.
proud, adj. orgoglioso.
prove, vb. comprovare.
proverb, n. provèrbio m.
proverbial, adj. proverbiale.
provide, vb. provvedere.
provided, conj. purchè.
providence, n. provvidènza f.
province, n. província f.

provincial, *adj.* provinciale.

provision, *n.* provvista *f.*

provocation, *n.* provocazione *f.*

provoke, *vb.* provocare.

prowess, *n.* prodezza *f.*

prowl, *vb.* vagare intorno.

proximity, *n.* prossimità *f.*

proxy, *n.* (person) procuratore *m.*; (document) procura *f.*

prudence, *n.* prudènza *f.*

prudent, *adj.* prudènte.

prune, *n.* prugna secca *f.*

pry, *vb.* ficcare il naso.

psalm, *n.* salmo *m.*

pseudonym, *n.* pseudònimo *m.*

psychedelic, *adj.* psichedèlico.

psychiatrist, *n.* psichiatra *m.*

psychiatry, *n.* psichiatrìa *f.*

psychoanalysis, *n.* psicoanàlisi *f.*

psychological, *adj.* psicològico.

psychology, *n.* psicologìa *f.*

psychosis, *n.* psicòsi *f.*

ptomaine, *n.* ptomaìna *f.*

public, *n. and adj.* pùbblico (*m.*).

publication, *n.* pubblicazione *f.*

publicity, *n.* pubblicità *f.*

publish, *vb.* pubblicare.

publisher, *n.* editore *m.*

pudding, *n.* budino *m.*

puddle, *n.* pozzànghera *f.*

puff, 1. *n.* sbuffo *m.*; (powder-p.) fiòcco da cipria *m.* **2.** *vb.* sbuffare.

pugnacious, *adj.* pugnace.

pull, 1. *n.* tirata *f.* **2.** *vb.* tirare.

pulley, *n.* puléggia *f.*

pulmonary, *adj.* polmonare.

pulp, *n.* polpa *f.*

pulpit, *n.* pùlpito *m.*

pulsar, *n.* pùlsar *m.*

pulsate, *vb.* pulsare.

pulse, *n.* polso *m.*

pump, 1. *n.* pompa *f.* **2.** *vb.* pompare.

pumpkin, *n.* zucca *f.*

pun, *n.* freddura *f.*

punch, 1. *n.* (drink) pònce *m.*; (blow) pugno *m.* **2.** *vb.* (make hole) perforare; (hit) colpire; dar pugni a.

punctual, *adj.* puntuale.

punctuate, *vb.* punteggiare.

punctuation, *n.* punteggiatura *f.*

puncture, 1. *n.* puntura *f.*; (tire) foratura *f.* *vb.* forare.

pungent, *adj.* pungènte.

punish, *vb.* punire.

punishment, *n.* punizione *f.*

punitive, *adj.* punitivo.

puny, *adj.* débole.

pupil, *n.* alunno *m.*, scolaro *m.*

puppet, *n.* burattino *m.*

puppy, *n.* cùcciolo *m.*

purchase, 1. *n.* compra *f.*; (grasp) presa *f.* **2.** *vb.* comprare.

purchasing power, *n.* potere d'acquisto *m.*

pure, *adj.* puro.

purée, *n.* passato *m.*

purgative, *n. and adj.* purgante *f.*

purge, 1. *n.* purga *f.* **2.** *vb.* purgare.

purify, *vb.* purificare.

puritan, *n. and adj.* puritano (*m.*)

puritanical, *adj.* da puritano.

purity, *n.* purezza *f.*, purità *f.*

purple, *n.* pórpora *f.*

purport, 1. *n.* significato *m.* **2.** *vb.* use future of verb which in English is dependent on "purport".

purpose, *n.* fine *m.*, scòpo *m.*, propòsito *m.*; (on p.) appòsta.

purposely, *adv.* appòsta.

purr, *vb.* fare le fusa.

purse, *n.* borsa *f.*

pursue, *vb.* inseguire, perseguire.

pursuit, *n.* inseguimento *m.*

pus, *n.* pus *m.*

push, 1. *n.* spinta *f.* **2.** *vb.* spíngere.

pusher, *n.* spacciatore *m.*

pushy, *adj.* aggressivo, insistente.

put, *vb.* méttere, porre, ficcare; (p. back) rimméttere; (p. down, suppress) sopprímere; (p. in) inserire; (p. off) rimandare; (p. on) indossare; (p. out, extinguish) spégnere; (p. up with) soffrire.

putrid, *adj.* pùtrido.

putsch, *n.* insurrezione *f.*

puzzle, *n.* indovinello *m.*; (crossword p.) crucivèrba *m.*

puzzling, *adj.* di difficile soluzione.

pygmy, *n.* pigmèo *m.*

pyramid, *n.* piràmide *f.*

pyre, *n.* pira *f.*

python, *n.* pitone *m.*

Q

quadrangle, n. quadràngolo m.

quadraphonic, adj. quadrofònico.

quadruped, n. quadrùpede m.

quail, 1. n. quàglia f. **2.** vb. scoraggiarsi.

quaint, adj. strano.

quake, 1. n. trèmito m. **2.** vb. tremare.

qualification, n. qualificazione f., qualifica f., requisito m.

qualified, adj. idòneo.

qualify, vb. qualificare; (be fit) essere idòneo.

quality, n. qualità f.

qualm, n. nàusea f.; (fig.) scrùpolo m.

quandary, n. perplessità f.

quantity, n. quantità f., somma f.

quarantine, n. quarentena f.

quarrel, 1. n. lite f. **2.** vb. litigare.

quarry, n. cava f.

quarter, n. (one fourth) quarto m.; (region; mercy) quartiere m.; (three months) trimèstre m.

quarterly, adj. trimestrale.

quartet, n. quartetto m.

quartz, n. quarzo m.

quasar, n. quàsar m.

quaver, vb. tremolare.

queen, n. regina f.

queer, adj. strano.

quell, vb. sopprimere.

quench, vb. estínguere; (q. one's thirst) dissetare.

query, 1. n. domanda f. **2.** vb. domandare.

quest, n. ricerca f.

question, 1. n. domanda f., questione f. **2.** vb. interrogare; (doubt) dubitare di.

questionable adj. dùbbio.

question mark, n. punto interrogativo m.

questionnaire, n. questionàrio m.

quick, 1. adj. ràpido, pronto, svelto. **2.** adv. prèsto.

quicken, vb. affrettare, tr.

quicksand, n. sàbbie mòbili f.pl.

quiet, 1. n. quiète f. **2.** adj. quièto; (be, keep q.) tacere.

quilt, n. trapunta f.

quinine, n. chinino m.

quintet, n. quintètto m.

quip, n. motto m.

quit, vb. (leave) lasciare; (stop) cessare, smèttere; (resign) diméttersi.

quite, adv. completamente, pròprio.

quiver, 1. n. farètra f. **2.** vb. tremare; (shiver) rabbrividire.

quixotic, adj. donchisciottesco.

quiz, 1. n. esame m. **2.** vb. esaminare.

quorum, n. quorum m.

quota, n. quòta f.

quotation, n. citazione f.

quote, vb. citare.

R

rabbi, n. rabbino m.

rabbit, n. conìglio m.

rabble, n. plebàglia f., volgo m.

rabid, adj. rabbioso.

rabies, n. ràbbia f.

raccoon, n. procione m.

race, 1. n. (contest) corsa f.; (breed) razza f. **2.** vb. córrere.

race-track, n. ippòdromo m.

racial, adj. razziale.

racism, n. razzismo m.

racist, adj. razzista.

rack, 1. n. (torture) ruòta f.; (for feed) rastrellièra f.; (luggage) reticella f.; (railroad) cremaglièra f. **2.** vb. torturare.

racket, n. (tennis) racchetta f.; (uproar) frastuòno m., baccano m.

radar, n. (instrument) radiotelèmetro m.; (science) radiotelemetría f.

radiance, n. fulgore m.

radiant, adj. raggiante.

radiate, vb. irradiare, tr.

radiation, n. irradiazione f.

radiator, *n.* radiatore *m.*

radical, *n. and adj.* radicale (*m.*).

radio, 1. *n.* ràdio *f.* **2.** *adj.* (**pertaining to r.**) radiofònico.

radioactive, *adj.* radioattivo.

radiology, *n.* radiologia *f.*

radish, *n.* ramolàccio *m.,* ravanèllo *m.*

radium, *n.* ràdio *m.*

radius, *n.* ràggio *m.*

raffle, *n.* lotteria *f.*

raft, *n.* zàttera *f.*

rafter, *n.* travicèllo *m.*

rag, *n.* cèncio *m.,* stràccio *m.*

ragamuffin, *n.* straccione *m.*

rage, 1. *n.* ràbbia *f.* **2.** *vb.* infuriare.

ragged, *adj.* cencioso.

raid, *n.* incursione *f.*

rail, *n.* rotaia *f.;* (bar) sbarra *f.*

railcar, *n.* automotrice *f.;* (**electric r.**) elettromotrice *f.*

railing, *n.* ringhièra *f.*

railroad, 1. *n.* ferrovia *f.* **2.** *adj.* (**pertaining to r.s**) ferroviàrio.

railway, *n.* ferrovia *f.*

rain, 1. *n.* piòggia *f.* **2.** *vb.* piòvere; (**r. cats and dogs**) diluviare.

rainbow, *n.* arcobaleno *m.*

raincoat, *n.* impermeàbile *m.*

rainfall, *n.* precipitazione atmosfèrica *f.*

rainy, *adj.* piovoso.

raise, *vb.* (bring up) allevare; (erect) erigere; (grow) coltivare; (increase) aumentare; (hoist) inalzare; (lift) levare; (collect) raccògliere; (intensify) alzare.

raisin, *n.* uva secca *f.;* (**sultana r.**) uva sultanina *f.*

rake, 1. *n.* rastrèllo *m.* **2.** *vb.* rastrellare.

rally, 1. *n.* (recovery) ricùpero di fòrze *m.;* (meeting) raduno *m.* **2.** *vb.* riunire, *tr.*

ram, 1. *n.* (animal) montone *m.;* (post) battipalo *m.* **2.** *vb.* bàttere; cacciare.

ramble, *vb.* divagare.

ramify, *vb.* ramificare.

ramp, *n.* piano inclinato *m.*

rampage, *n.* stato d'eccitazione *m.*

rampart, *n.* bastione *m.*

ranch, *n.* fattoria *f.*

rancid, *adj.* ràncido.

rancor, *n.* rancore *m.*

random, *n.* (**at r.**) a casàccio.

range, 1. *n.* (distance) portata *f.;* (mountains) catena *f.;* (scope) estensione *f.;* (sphere) sfèra *f.;* (stove) cucina econòmica *f.* **2.** *vb.* (arrange) disporre; (vary) variare.

rank, *n.* (position) rango *m.;* (line) fila *f.;* (position) grado *m.*

ransack, *vb.* frugare dappertutto.

ransom, 1. *n.* riscatto *m.* **2.** *vb.* riscattare.

rap, 1. *n.* colpo *m.,* picchio *m.* **2.** *vb.* colpire, picchiare.

rapacious, *adj.* rapace.

rape, *n.* violare.

rapid, *adj.* ràpido.

rapport, *n.* rappòrto *m.*

rapture, *n.* èstasi *f.*

rare, *adj.* raro; (underdone) pòco còtto, al sangue.

rarely, *adv.* raramente.

rascal, *n.* briccone *m.*

rash, 1. *n.* eruzione *f.* **2.** *adj.* inconsiderato.

raspberry, *n.* lampone *m.;* (Bronx cheer) pernàcchia *f.*

rat, *n.* ratto *m.*

rate, 1. *n.* (price) prèzzo *m.;* (speed) velocità *f.* **2.** *vb.* classificare, *tr.*

rather, *adv.* piuttosto.

ratify, *vb.* ratificare.

ratio, *n.* rappòrto *f.*

ration, 1. *n.* razione *f.;* (**r.-card**) tèssera annonària *f.* **2.** *vb.* razionare.

rational, *adj.* razionale.

rattle, *n.* ràntolo *m.,* rumore secco *m.*

raucous, *adj.* ràuco.

ravage, *n.* devastazione *f.* **2.** *vb.* devastare.

rave, *vb.* delirare.

ravel, *n.* groviglio *m.*

raven, 1. *n.* corvo *m.* **2.** *adj.* corvino.

ravenous, *adj.* affamato.

ravine, *n.* canalone *m.,* burrone *m.*

ravish, *vb.* incantare, entusiasmare; rapire.

raw, *adj.* grezzo, crudo.

raw material, *n.* materie prime *f.pl.*

ray, *n.* ràggio *m.*

rayon, *n.* ràion *m.*

razor, n. rasòio m.

reach, 1. n. portata f. **2.** vb. (get to) arrivare a; raggiùngere; (extend) allungare.

react, vb. reagire.

reaction, n. reazione f.

reactionary, adj. reazionàrio.

reactor, n. reattore m.

read, vb. lèggere.

reader, n. (person) lettore m.; (book) libro di lettura m.

readily, adj. prontamente.

reading, n. lettura f.

ready, adj. pronto; (r.-made) già fatto.

real, adj. reale, vero.

real estate, n. beni immòbili m.pl.

realist, n. realista m.

realtor, n. agente immobiliare m.

reality, n. realtà f.

realization, n. realizzazione f.

realize, vb. (make real) realizzare; (be, become aware of) rendersi conto di.

really, adv. realmente, veramente, davvero.

realm, n. reame m., regno m.

ream, n. risma f.

reap, vb. miètere, reccògliere.

rear, 1. n. (back) parte posteriore f.; (r.-guard) retroguàrdia f. **2.** vb. (bring up) allevare; (raise) alzare; (erect) èrgere, tr.; (lift) sollevare; (of horse) impennarsi.

rearmament, n. riarmo m.

rear-view mirror, n. spècchio retrovisore m.

reason, 1. n. ragione f. **2.** vb. ragionare.

reasonable, adj. ragionévole.

reassessment, n. rivalutazione f.

reassure, vb. rassicurare.

rebate, n. sconto m.

rebel, 1. n. and adj. ribèlle (m.). **2.** vb. ribellarsi.

rebellion, n. ribellione f.

rebellious, adj. ribèlle.

rebirth, n. rinàscita f.

reborn, be, vb. rinàscere.

rebound, 1. n. rimbalzo m. **2.** vb. rimbalzare.

rebuff, n. ripulsa f.

rebuild, vb. ricostruire.

rebuke, 1. n. rimpròvero m. **2.** vb. rimproverare.

rebuttal, n. confutazione f.

recalcitrant, adj. ricalcitrante.

recall, vb. richiamare.

recant, vb. ritrattare.

recapitulate, vb. ricapitolare.

recede, vb. recèdere.

receipt, n. ricevuta f.; (document) quietanza f.

receive, vb. ricévere.

receiver, n. ricevitore m.

recent, adj. recènte.

recently, adv. recentemente.

receptacle, n. ricettàcolo m., recipiènte m.

reception, n. accogliènza f.; (party) ricevimento m.

receptive, adj. ricettivo.

recess, n. (in wall) rientranza f.; (vacation) vacanze f.

recipe, n. ricètta f.

recipient, n. ricevènte f.

reciprocate, vb. ricambiare.

recitation, n. recitazione f.

recite, vb. recitare.

reckless, adj. avventato.

reckon, vb. (count) contare; (deem) stimare; (think) pensare.

reclaim, vb. redimere; (land) bonificare.

reclamation, n. bonifica f.

recline, vb. reclinare.

recognition, n. riconoscimento f.

recognize, vb. riconóscere.

recoil, vb. indietreggiare.

recollect, vb. ricordare, rammentarsi.

recommend, vb. raccomandare.

recommendation, n. raccomandazione f.

recompense, 1. n. ricompènsa f. **2.** vb. ricompensare.

reconcile, vb. riconciliare.

recondition, vb. riparare.

reconsider, vb. riprèndere in esame.

reconstruct, vb. ricostruire.

record, 1. n. memòria f., ricordo m.; registro m.; (top achievement) primato m.; (phonograph) disco m.; (r. library) discoteca f.; (r. player) giradischi m. **2.** vb. registrare; (phonograph) incidere.

recording, n. incisione f.

recount, vb. (tell) raccontare; (count again) contare di nuòvo.

recourse, n. ricorso m.; **(have r.)** ricórrere.

recover, vb. ricuperare.

recovery, n. ricúpero m.; **(medical)** guarigione f.

recreation, n. ricreazione f.

recruit, 1. n. rècluta f. **2.** vb. reclutare.

rectangle, n. rettàngolo m.

rectifier, n. rettificatrice f.

rectify, vb. rettificare.

rectitude, n. rettitùdine f.

rectum, n. retto m.

recuperate, vb. ricuperare.

recur, vb. ricórrere, ritornare.

recurrent, adj. ricorrente.

recycle, vb. riciclare.

red, adj. rosso.

red cell, n. glòbulo rosso m.

redeem, vb. redìmere.

redeemer, n. redentore m.

redemption, n. redenzione f.

red-light district, n. quartiere a luci rosse m.

redress, n. riparazione f.

reduce, vb. ridurre.

reduction, n. riduzione f.

reed, n. canna f.; **(for instrument)** ància f.

reef, n. scòglio m.

reel, 1. n. (bobbin) naspo m.; (spool) rocchetto m.; (dance) trescone m. **2.** vb. traballare; **(r. off)** dipanare.

refer, vb. riferire, tr.

referee, n. àrbitro m.

reference, n. allusione f., riferimento m.; **(cross-r.)** rimando m.; **(r. room)** sala di consultazione f.

referendum, n. referendum m.

refill, vb. riempire di nuòvo.

refine, vb. raffinare.

refinement, n. raffinatezza f.

refinery, n. raffineria f.

reflect, vb. riflèttere.

reflection, n. riflessione f., riflèsso m.

reflex, n. riflèsso m.

reflexive, adj. riflessivo.

reform, 1. n. riforma f. **2.** vb. riformare.

reformation, n. riforma f.

refractory, adj. ribèlle.

refrain, vb. trattenere, tr.

refresh, vb. rinfrescare, ristorare.

refreshment, n. ristòro m.

refrigerator, n. frigorífero m.

refuge, n. rifùgio m.; **(take r.)** rifugiarsi.

refugee, n. rifugiato m.

refund, vb. restituire.

refusal, n. rifiuto m.

refuse, **1.** n. (waste matter) rifiuti m. pl. **2.** vb. rifiutare.

refutation, n. confutazione f.

refute, vb. confutare.

regain, vb. ritornare a.

regal, adj. regale.

regard, 1. n. riguardo m., rispètto m.; **(look at)** guardare; **(concern)** riguardare; **(consider)** considerare.

regarding, prep. riguardo a.

regardless, adv. ciò nonostante; **(r. of)** malgrado.

regent, n. reggènte m.

regime, n. regime m.

regiment, n. reggimento m.

region, n. regione f.

register, 1. n. registro m. **2.** vb. registrare.

registration, n. registrazione f.

regret, 1. n. rimpianto m., rincrescimento m. **2.** vb. rimpiàngere, rincréscere (with English subject in dative).

regular, adj. regolare.

regularity, n. regolarità f.

regulate, vb. regolare.

regulation, n. regolamento m.

regulator, n. regolatore m.

rehabilitate, vb. riabilitare.

rehearsal, n. pròva f.

rehearse, vb. provare.

reign, 1. n. regno m. **2.** vb. regnare.

reimburse, vb. rimborsare.

reins, n. rèdini f. pl.

reincarnation, n. nuòva incarnazione f.

reindeer, n. rènna f.

reinforce, vb. rinforzare.

reinforcement, n. rinfòrzo m.

reinstate, vb. ripristinare.

reiterate, vb. reiterare.

reject, vb. rigettare, respingere.

rejoice, vb. rallegrare, tr.

rejoin, vb. (answer) replicare; (join again) ricongiùngersi.

rejoinder, n. rèplica f.

rejuvenate, vb. ringiovanire.

relapse, 1. n. ricaduta f. **2.** vb. ricadere.

relate, vb. (tell) narrare; (be connected with) riferirsi a; riguardare; (connect) méttere in relazione. **r. to,** entrare in rapporto con.

related, adj. affine, connèsso.

relation, n. (story) narrazione f.; (connection) rappòrto m.; relazione f.; (person) parènte m.

relationship, n. rappòrto m.; (kinship) parentela f.

relative, 1. n. parènte m. **2.** adj. relativo.

relativity, n. relatività f.

relax, vb. allentare, tr.

relaxation, n. distensione f.

relaxing, adj. distensivo.

relay, vb. ritrasméttere.

release, 1. n. liberazione f. **2.** vb. liberare, sprigionare.

relent, vb. aver pietà.

relentless, adj. implacàbile.

relevant, adj. pertinènte.

reliable, adj. affidàbile.

reliant, adj. fiducioso.

relic, n. avanzo m.; (religious) relíquia f.

relief, n. sollièvo m.; (social work) assistènza f.; (diversion) diversivo m.; (replacement) càmbio m.; (help) soccorso m.

relieve, vb. sollevare; (help) soccórrere; (free) liberare; (alleviate) alleviare.

religion, n. religione f.

religious, adj. religioso.

relinquish, vb. abbandonare.

relish, 1. n. gusto m.; (sauce) condimento m. **2.** vb. gustare.

reluctance, n. riluttanza f.

reluctant, adj. riluttante.

rely, vb. confidare.

remain, vb. restare, rimanere.

remainder, n. rèsto m.

remark, 1. n. osservazione f. **2.** vb. osservare.

remarkable, adj. notévole, rimarchévole.

remarry, vb. risposarsi (refl.), prèndere in seconde nozze.

remedy, 1. n. rimèdio m. **2.** vb. rimediare a.

remember, vb. ricordarsi di.

remembrance, n. ricòrdo m.

remind, vb. rammentare.

reminiscence, n. reminiscènza f.

remiss, adj. negligènte.

remit, vb. (send) spedire; (forgive) riméttere.

remittance, n. spedizione f.

remnant, n. rèsto m., rimanènte m.

remonstrance, n. remostranza f.

remorse, n. rimòrso m.

remorseful, adj. pentito.

remote, adj. remòto.

remote control, n. telecomando. m.

removable, adj. mòbile, rimuovìbile.

removal, n. rimozione f.

remove, vb. tògliere, rimuòvere.

remuneration, n. rimunerazion f.

renaissance, n. rinascimento m.

rend, vb. strappare.

render, vb. rèndere.

rendezvous, n. appuntamento m.

rendition, n. esecuzione f.

renege, vb. rifiutare.

renew, vb. rinnovare.

renewal, n. rinnovamento m.

renounce, vb. rinunciare a.

renovate, vb. rimodernare.

renown, n. rinomanza f.

renowned, adj. rinomato.

rent, 1. n. affitto m., pigione f. **2.** vb. affittare, noleggiare.

rental, n. nolèggio m.

repair, 1. n. riparazione f. **2.** vb. riparare.

reparation, n. riparazione f.

repatriate, vb. rimpatriare.

repay, vb. ripagare, rimborsare.

repeal, 1. n. abrogazione f., rèvoca f. **2.** vb. abrogare, revocare.

repeat, 1. n. (music) ripresa f. **2.** vb. ripètere, replicare.

repel, vb. respíngere.

repent, vb. pentirsi di.

repentance, n. pentimento m.

repercussion, n. ripercussione f.

repertoire, n. repertòrio m.

repetition, n. ripetizione f.; (theater) rèplica f.

replace, vb. sostituire, rimpiazzare.

replenish, vb. riempire di nuòvo.

reply, 1. *n.* risposta *f.;* (rebuttal) rèplica *f.* **2.** *vb.* rispóndere; replicare.

report, 1. *n.* (bang) detonazione *f.;* (news) notízia *f.;* (rumor) voce *f.;* (memoir) rappòrto *m.* **2.** *vb.* dare notízia di; (complain of) denunciare.

reporter, *n.* cronista *m.,* giornalista *m.*

repose, 1. *n.* ripòso *m.* **2.** *vb.* riposare.

reprehend, *vb.* riprèndere.

reprehensible, *adj.* rimproveràbile.

represent, *vb.* rappresentare.

representation, *n.* rappresentazione *f.*

representative, 1. *n.* deputato *m.* **2.** *adj.* rappresentativo.

repress, *vb.* reprímere.

repression, *vb.* repressione *f.*

reprimand, 1. *n.* rimpròvero *m.* **2.** *vb.* rimproverare.

reprisal, *n.* rappresàglia *f.*

reproach, 1. *n.* rimpròvero *m.* **2.** *vb.* rimproverare.

reproduce, *vb.* riprodurre, *tr.*

reproduction, *n.* riproduzione *f.*

reproof, *n.* rimpròvero *m.*

reprove, *vb.* rimproverare.

reptile, *n.* rèttile *m.*

republic, *n.* repúbblica *f.*

republican, *adj.* repubblicano.

repudiate, *vb.* ripudiare.

repudiation, *n.* ripùdio *m.*

repulse, 1. *n.* ripulsa *f.* **2.** *vb.* respíngere.

repulsive, *adj.* repellènte.

reputation, *n.* reputazione *f.*

repute, *vb.* reputare.

reputedly, *adv.* secondo l'opinione generale.

request, 1. *n.* richièsta *f.,* domanda *f.* **2.** *vb.* richièdere, domandare.

require, *vb.* richièdere, esígere.

requirement, *n.* esigènza *f.,* requisito *m.*

requisite, 1. *n.* requisito *m.* **2.** *adj.* necessàrio.

requisition, 1. *n.* requisizione *f.* **2.** *vb.* requisire.

requite, *n.* contraccambiare.

resale, *n.* rivèndita *f.*

rescind, *vb.* rescíndere.

rescue, 1. *n.* liberazione *f.* **2.** *vb.* liberare.

research, *n.* ricerche *f.pl.*

resell, *vb.* rivèndere.

resemblance, *n.* rassomiglianza *f.*

resemble, *vb.* rassomigliare a.

resent, *vb.* offèndersi di.

resentful, *adj.* risentito, offeso.

resentment, *n.* risentimento *m.*

reservation, *n.* risèrva *f.;* (tickets) prenotazione *f.*

reserve, 1. *n.* risèrva *f.* **2.** *vb.* riservare; (tickets) prenotare.

reservist, *n.* riservista *m.*

reservoir, *n.* serbatòio *m.*

reset, *vb.* regolare; rimettere nella condizione originale.

reside, *vb.* risièdere, abitare.

residence, *n.* residènza *f.,* abitazione *f.*

resident, 1. *n.* abitante *m.* **2.** *adj.* residènte.

residue, *n.* resíduo *m.*

resign, *vb.* dimèttersi; **(r. oneself, give up hope)** rassegnarsi.

resignation, *n.* dimissione *f.;* (loss of hope) rassegnazione *f.*

resist, *vb.* resístere.

resistance, *n.* resistènza *f.*

resolute, *adj.* risoluto.

resolution, *n.* risoluzione *f.*

resolve, 1. *n.* decisione *f.* **2.** *vb.* risòlvere, sciògliere; (decide) decidersi.

resonance, *n.* risonanza *f.*

resonant, *adj.* risonante.

resort, 1. *n.* (recourse) ricorso *m.;* (vacation place) stazione *f.;* luògo di soggiorno *m.* **2.** *vb.* ricórrere.

resound, *vb.* risonare, risuonare.

resource, *n.* risorsa *f.*

respect, 1. *n.* rispètto *m.* **2.** *vb.* rispettare.

respectable, *adj.* rispettàbile.

respectful, *adj.* rispettoso.

respective, *adj.* rispettivo.

respiration, *n.* respirazione *f.*

respite, *n.* trégua *f.*

respond, *vb.* rispóndere.

response, *n.* risposta *f.*

responsibility, *n.* responsabilità *f.*

responsible, *adj.* responsàbile.

responsive, *adj.* rispondènte, sensìbile.

rest, 1. *n.* (remainder) rimanènte *m.;* (repose) ripòso *m.* **2.** *vb.* riposare.

restaurant, *n.* ristorante *m.,* ristoratore *m.,* trattoria *f.;* **(r.-keeper)** trattore *m.*

restful, *adj.* riposante.

restitution, *n.* restituzione *f.*

restless, *adj.* irrequièto.

restoration, *n.* restaurazione *f.*

restore, *vb.* restaurare.

restrain, *vb.* trattenère.

restraint, *n.* contròllo *m.*

restrict, *vb.* restringere.

restriction, *n.* restrizione *f.*

result, 1. *n.* risultato *m.* **2.** *vb.* risultare.

resume, *vb.* riassùmere, riprèndere.

résumé, *n.* riassunto *m.*

resurgent, *adj.* risorgènte.

resurrect, *vb.* risuscitare.

resurrection, *n.* resurrezione *f.*

retail, 1. *adv.* al minuto, al dettàglio. **2.** *vb.* vèndere al minuto, véndere al dettàglio.

retain, *vb.* ritenère, conservare.

retake, *vb.* riprèndere.

retaliate, *vb.* ricambiare.

retaliation, *n.* rappresàglia *f.*

retard, *vb.* ritardare.

retention, *n.* ritenzione *f.;* (remembering ability) memòria *f.*

reticence, *n.* reticènza *f.*

reticent, *adj.* reticènte.

retina, *n.* rètina *f.*

retinue, *n.* sèguito *m.*

retire, *vb.* ritirare, *tr.*

retort, *vb.* replicare, ribàttere.

retract, *vb.* (pull back) ritrarre; (withdraw) ritrattare.

retreat, 1. *n.* ritirata *f.* **2.** *vb.* ritirarsi.

retribution, *n.* retribuzione *f.*

retributive, *adj.* retributivo.

retrieve, *vb.* recuperare.

retriever, *n.* cane da presa.

retroactive, *adj.* retroattivo.

retrospect, *n.* sguardo retrospettivo *m.*

retrospective, *adj.* retrospettivo.

retry, *vb.* ritentare; (law) processare una seconda volta.

return, 1. *n.* ritorno *m.;* **(r. ticket)** biglietto d'andata e ritorno *m.* **2.** *vb.* tornare; ritornare.

return address, *n.* mittente *m.*

reunion, *n.* riunione *f.*

reunite, *vb.* riunire.

revamp, *vb.* rinnovare.

reveal, *vb.* rivelare.

revel, 1. *n.* (noisy good time) baldòria *f.;* (drunken rout) gozzovìglia *f.* **2.** *vb.* far baldòria; gozzovigliare.

revelation, *n.* rivelazione *f.*

revelry, *n.* baldòria *f.*

revenge, 1. *n.* vendetta *f.* **2.** *vb.* vendicare.

revengeful, *adj.* vendicativo.

revenue, *n.* entrata *f.*

reverberate, *vb.* riverberare.

revere, *vb.* riverire.

reverence, *n.* riverènza *f.*

reverend, *adj.* reverèndo.

reverent, *adj.* riverènte.

reverie, *n.* fantasticheria *f.*

reverse, 1. *n.* rovèscio *m.,* contràrio *m.;* (auto) màrcia indiètro *f.* **2.** *vb.* rovesciare; (direction) invertire.

revert, *vb.* ritornare.

review, 1. *n.* rivista *f.,* riesame *m.;* **(book r.)** recensione *f.* **2.** *vb.* passare in rivista; riesaminare; (book) recensire.

revise, *vb.* rivedere.

revision, *n.* revisione *f.*

revival, *n.* ravvivamento *m.;* (theater) ripresa *f.*

revive, *vb.* ravvivare.

revocation, *n.* rèvoca *f.*

revoke, *vb.* revocare.

revolt, 1. *n.* rivòlta *f.* **2.** *vb.* rivoltare. *tr.*

revolting, *adj.* rivoltante.

revolution, *n.* rivoluzione *f.;* (turn) giro *m.*

revolutionary, *adj.* rivoluzionàrio.

revolve, *vb.* girare.

revolver, *n.* rivoltèlla *f.*

revue, *n.* rivista *f.*

reward, 1. *n.* ricompènsa *f.* **2.** *vb.* ricompensare.

rewind, *vb.* riavvòlgere, ribobinare.

rewinding, n. riavvolgimento m., ribobninatura f.

rhetoric, n. retòrica f.

rhetorical, adj. retòrico.

rheumatic, adj. reumàtico.

rheumatism, n. reumatismo m.

rhinoceros, n. rinoceronte m.

rhubarb, n. rabàrbaro m.

rhyme, 1. n. rima f. **2.** vb. rimare.

rhythm, n. ritmo m.

rhythmical, adj. ritmico.

rib, n. còstola f.

ribbon, n. nastro m.

rice, n. riso m.

rich, adj. ricco.

riches, n. ricchezza f.

rid, vb. sbarazzare.

riddle, n. enigma m., indovinello m.

ride, 1. n. corsa f. **2.** vb. (on horse) cavalcare; (other transport) andare.

rider, n. cavalière m.

ridge, n. (mountain) cresta f., crinale m.; (between furrows) pòrca f.

ridicule, 1. n. ridicolo m. **2.** vb. deridere.

ridiculous, adj. ridìcolo.

rifle, n. fucile m.

rig, 1. n. equipàggio m.; (ship) atrezzatura f. **2.** vb. equipaggiare; attrezzare.

right, 1. n. (side) dèstra f.; (justice) giusto m. **2.** adj. (side) dèstro; (straight) diretto; (correct) corrètto; (**be r.**) aver ragione. **3.** vb. (set upright) drizzare; (correct) corrèggere.

righteous, adj. giusto.

righteousness, n. giustízia f.

right of way, n. precedènza f.

rigid, adj. rìgido.

rigidity, n. rigidezza f.

rigor, n. rigore m.

rigorous, adj. rigoroso.

rim, n. bordo m., orlo m.

ring, 1. n. (circle) cérchio m.; (for finger) anèllo m.; (boxing) quadrato m.; (on bell) suòno m., scampanellata f. **2.** vb. suonare; (**r. out**) risuonare; (**form a r. around**) accerchiare.

rinse, vb. risciacquare.

riot, 1. n. tumulto m. **2.** vb. creare disordini.

rip, vb. strappare.

ripe, adj. maturo.

ripen, vb. maturare.

ripoff, 1. n. furto m. **2.** vb. rubare.

ripple, n. increspatura f.

rise, 1. n. (increase) aumènto m.; (origin) origine f. **2.** vb. alzarsi, levarsi, sorgere.

risk, 1. n. rischio m. **2.** vb. arrischiare, rischiare.

risky, adj. rischiòso.

rite, n. rito m.

ritual, n. and adj. rituale (m.).

rival, 1. n. and adj. rivale. **2.** vb. rivaleggiare con.

rivalry, n. rivalità f.

river, n. fiume m.

rivet, 1. n. chiòdo ribadito m. **2.** vb. ribadire.

roach, n. scarafàggio m.

road, 1. n. cammino m., strada f., vía f. **2.** adj. (pertaining to roads) stradale.

roam, vb. vagare.

roar, 1. n. ruggito m. **2.** vb. ruggire.

roast, 1. n. arròsto m. **2.** vb. arrostire.

roast beef, n. roastbeef, m., rosbif m.

roasting, n. (of coffee) torrefazione f.

rob, vb. derubare; (**r. completely**) svaligiare.

robber, n. ladrone m.

robbery, n. furto m.

robe, n. vèste f.

robin, n. pettirosso m.

robot, n. autòma m.

robust, adj. robusto.

rock, 1. n. ròccia f.; (music) (musicaccia) rock f.; (fortress) ròcca f.; (pertaining to r.) roccioso. **2.** vb. dondolare.

rocker, n. (rocking-chair) sèdia a dòndolo f.

rocket, n. razzo m.

rocking, adj. dondolante; (**r. chair**) sedia a dòndolo f.; (**r. horse**) cavallo a dòndolo f.

rocky, adj. roccioso.

rod, n. verga f.

rodent, n. roditore m.

roe, n. cèrva f.

rogue, n. briccone m.

roguish, adj. bricconesco.

rôle, n. ruòlo m.

roll, 1. n. ròtolo m.; (bread) panino m.; (list) ruòlo m.; (of ship) rullìo m. **2.** vb. rotolare; (ship) rullare.

roll call, n. chiamata f., appello m.

roller, n. rotèlla m., rullo m.

roller-bearing, n. cuscinetto a rotolamento m.

roller coaster, n. ottovolante m., montagne russe f. pl.

roller skate, 1. n. pàttini a rotelle m. pl. **2.** vb. pattinare coi pàttini a rotelle.

Roman, adj. romano.

Roman Catholic Church, n. Chiesa Cattòlica Apostòlica Romana f.

romance, n. romanzo m.

romantic, adj. romàntico.

Rome, n. Roma f.

romp, vb. giocare vigorosamente.

roof, n. tètto m.

roof garden, n. giardino pènsile m.

room, n. (in house) càmera f., stanza f.; (space) posto m., spàzio f.

roommate, n. compagno di stanza m., compagna di stanza f.

rooster, n. gallo m.

root, n. radice f.

rope, n. còrda f., fune f.

rosary, n. rosàrio m.

rose, n. ròsa f.

rosin, n. rèsina f.

rosy, adj. ròseo.

rot, 1. n. putrefazione f. **2.** vb. marcire, imputridire f.

rotary, adj. rotatòrio.

rotate, vb. rotare.

rotation, n. rotazione f.

rotten, adj. pùtrido.

rouge, n. rossetto m.

rough, adj. rùvido, rozzo.

round, 1. n. giro m. **2.** adj. rotondo, tondo. **3.** adv. intorno. **4.** prep. intorno a.

rouse, vb. svegliare, risvegliare.

rout, n. rotta f.

route, n. percorso m.

routine, n. routine f., abitùdini f. pl.

rove, vb. errare.

row, n. (fight) lite f.; (uproar) baccano m.; (series) fila f.; (boat ride) remata f. **2.** vb. (raise a row) litigare; (use oars) remare.

rowboat, n. battèllo a remi m.

rowdy, adj. litigioso.

royal, adj. reale, règio.

royalty, n. regalità f.

rub, 1. n. fregata f. **2.** vb. fregare, strofinare.

rubber, n. gomma f.; (overshoe) scarpa di gomma f.

rubbish, n. scarti m. pl.; (nonsense) fandònie f. pl.

ruby, n. rubino m.

rudder, n. timone m.

ruddy, adj. rubicondo.

rude, adj. rude.

rudiment, n. rudimento m.

rue, vb. pentirsi di.

ruffian, n. malfattore m.

ruffle, 1. n. increspatura f. **2.** vb. increspare.

rug, n. (for floor) tappeto m.; (blanket) copèrta f.

rugged, adj. scabroso.

ruin, 1. n. rovina f.; (remain) rùdere m. **2.** vb. rovinare.

ruinous, adj. ravinoso.

rule, 1. n. règola f. **2.** vb. regolare; (reign) regnare.

ruler, n. (lawgiver) sovrano m.; (measuring-stick) righello m.

ruling, 1. n. òrdine m., decreto m. **2.** adj. al governo, governante.

rum, n. rum m.

rumble, 1. n. brontolìo m. **2.** vb. brontolare.

ruminate, vb. ruminare.

rummage, vb. frugare, rovistare.

rumor, n. diceria f., voce f.

run, 1. n. (in stocking) cordiglièra f. **2.** vb. córrere; (work) funzionare; (flow) scórrere; (**r. across**) incontrare; (**r. away**) fuggire; (**r. into**) investire.

runaway, n. evaso m., fuggiasco m.

run-down, adj. indebolito, esgusto.

rung, n. piolo m.

runner, n. corridore m.

runner-up, *n.* finalista *m.*
runoff, *n.* ballottaggio *m.*
run-of-the-mill, *adj.* ordinario.
runway, *n.* pista *f.*
rupture, *n.* rottura *f.*
rural, *adj.* rurale.
rush, 1. *n.* afflusso *m.;* (hurry) fretta *f.;*(reed) giunco *m.* **2.** *vb.* affluire; precipitarsi.
rush hour, *n.* ora di punta *f.*
Russia, *n.* Rùssia *f.*

Russian, *adj.* russo.
rust, 1. *n.* rùggine *f.* **2.** *vb.* arrugginire, *tr.*
rustic, *n. and adj.* rùstico *(m.).*
rustle, 1. *n.* fruscìo *m.* **2.** *vb.* frusciare.
rust-proof, *adj.* inossidàbile.
rusty, *adj.* arrugginito, rugginoso.
rut, *n.* solco *m.*
ruthless, *adj.* spietato.
rye, *n.* ségale *f.*

S

Sabbath, *n.* giorno di ripòso *m.*
saber, *n.* sciàbola *f.*
sable, *n.* zibellino *m.*
sabotage, 1. *n.* sabotàggio *m.* **2.** *vb.* sabotare.
saboteur, *n.* sabotatore *m.*
saccharine, 1. *n.* saccarina *f.* **2.** *adj.* saccarino.
sachet, *n.* sacchetto di profumo *m.*
sack, 1. *n.* sacco *m.;* (pillage) sacchèggio *m.* **2.** *vb.* (discharge) licenziare; (plunder) saccheggiare.
sacrament, *n.* sacramento *m.*
sacred, *adj.* sacro.
sacrifice, 1. *n.* sacrificio *m.* **2.** *vb.* sacrificare.
sacrilege, *n.* sacrilègio *m.*
sacrilegious, *adj.* sacrìlego.
sacristan, *n.* sagrestano *m.*
sacristy, *n.* sagrestìa *f.*
sad, *adj.* triste.
sadden, *vb.* rattristare.
saddle, 1. *n.* sèlla *f.* **2.** *vb.* sellare.
sadism, *n.* sadismo *m.*
safe, 1. *n.* cassafòrte *f.* **2.** *adj.* sicuro, salvo; (s. and sound) sano e salvo.
safeguard, 1. *n.* salvaguàrdia *f.* **2.** *vb.* salvaguardare.
safety, *n.* sicurezza *f.*
safety island, *n.* isolòtto salvagente *m.*
safety-pin, *n.* spilla di sicurezza *f.*
sage, *n. and adj.* sàggio *(m.).*
sail, 1. *n.* vela *f.* **2.** *vb.* navigare; (depart) salpare.
sailboat, *n.* battèllo a vela *m.*
sailor, *n.* marinaio *m.*
saint, *n.* santo *m.*

sake, *n.* motivo *m.*
salad, *n.* insalata *f.*
salary, *n.* stipèndio *m.*
sale, *n.* véndita *f.,* spàccio *m.*
salesman, *n.* commesso *m.;* (traveling s.) commesso viaggiatore *m.*
sales tax, *n.* tassa di scambio *f.*
saliva, *n.* saliva *f.*
salmon, *n.* salmone *m.*
salon, *n.* salone *m.*
salt, 1. *n.* sale *m.* **2.** *vb.* salare.
salty, *adj.* salato.
salutation, *n.* saluto *m.*
salute, 1. *n.* saluto *m.* **2.** *vb.* salutare.
salvage, 1. *n.* salvatàggio *m.* **2.** *vb.* salvare.
salvation, *n.* salvezza *f.*
salve, *n.* unguento *m.*
same, *adj.* stesso.
sample, *n.* campione *m.;* (s. fair) fièra campionària *f.*
sanatorium, *n.* sanatòrio *m.*
sanctify, *vb.* santificare.
sanction, 1. *n.* sanzione *f.* **2.** *vb.* sanzionare.
sanctity, *n.* santità *f.*
sanctuary, *n.* santuàrio *m.*
sand, *n.* rena *f.,* sàbbia *f.*
sandal, *n.* sàndalo *m.*
sandwich, *n.* tramezzino *m.*
sandy, *adj.* renoso, sabbioso.
sane, *adj.* sano.
sanguinary, *adj.* sanguinàrio.
sanitary, *adj.* igiènico, sanitàrio; (s. napkin) assorbente igiènico *m.*
sanitation, *n.* igiène *f.*
sanity, *n.* sanità *f.*

Santa Claus, *n.* Befana *f.* (old woman who brings presents on Twelfth Night).

sap, 1. *n.* linfa *f.;* (fool) citrullo *m.* 2. *vb.* (weaken) indebolire.

sapling, *n.* alberello *m.*

sapling, *n.* alberello *m.*

sapphire, *n.* zaffiro *m.*

sarcasm, *n.* sarcasmo *m.*

sarcastic, *adj.* sarcàstico.

sardine, *n.* sardèlla *f.*

Sardinia, *n.* Sardegna *f.*

Sardinian, *adj.* sardo.

sash, *n.* cintura *f.*

sassy, *adj.* impertinente, vivace.

sassy, *adj.* impertinente, vivace.

satellite, *n.* satèllite *m.*

satin, *n.* raso *m.*

satire, *n.* sàtira *f.*

satirize, *vb.* satireggiare.

satisfaction, *n.* soddisfazione *f.*

satisfactory, *adj.* soddisfacènte *f.*

satisfy, *vb.* soddisfare.

saturate, *vb.* saturare.

saturation, *n.* saturazione *f.*

Saturday, *n.* sàbato *m.*

sauce, *n.* salsa *f.*

saucepan, *n.* casseruola *f.*

saucer, *n.* piattino *m.*

saucy, *adj.* impertinènte.

sausage, *n.* salsíccia *f.*

savage, *n. and adj.* selvàggio *m.*

save, 1. *vb.* (preserve) salvare; (economize) risparmiare. 2. *prep.* salvo.

savings, *adj.* salvatore; **(s. account)** conto di risparmio *m.*

savings, *n.* risparmio *m.;* **(s.-bank)** cassa di risparmio *f.*

savior, *n.* salvatore *m.*

savor, 1. *n.* sapore *m.* 2. *vb.* sapere.

savory, *adj.* saporito.

saw, 1. *n.* sega *f.;* (proverb) provèrbio *m.* 2. *vb.* segare.

sawmill, *n.* segheria *f.*

saxophone, *n.* sassòfono *m.*

say, *vb.* dire; **(s. again)** ridire.

saying, *n.* provèrbio *m.*

scab, 1. *n.* crosta *f.;* (nonstriker) crumiro *m.*

scabby, *adj.* crostoso; rognoso.

scaffold, *n.* patíbolo *m.*

scaffolding, *n.* impalcatura *f.*

scald, 1. *n.* scottatura *f.* 2. *vb.* scottare.

scale, 1. *n.* scala *f.;* (balance) bilància *f.;* (fish, etc.) squama *f.;* (music) gamma *f.* 2. *vb.* scrostare; (climb) arrampicarsi su.

scallop, *n.* (seafood) conchiglia *f.,* pettine *m.;* (meat) scaloppina *f.*

scalp, *n.* pèlle del crànio *f.;* scalpo *m.*

scalper, *n.* bagarino *m.*

scan, *vb.* scrutare; (poetry) scandire.

scandal, *n.* scàndalo *m.;* (gossip) maldicènza *f.*

scandalous, *adj.* scandaloso.

scant, *adj.* scarso.

scar, 1. *n.* cicatrice *f.* 2. *vb.* cicatrizzare, *tr.*

scarce, *adj.* scarso; **(be s.)** scarseggiare.

scarcely, *adv.* appena.

scarcity, *n.* scarsità *f.*

scare, 1. *n.* spavento *m.* 2. *vb.* spaventare.

scarecrow, *n.* spauràcchio *m.*

scarf, *n.* sciarpa *f.*

scarlet, *n. and adj.* scarlatto *(m.).*

scarlet fever, *n.* scarlattina *f.*

scathing, *adj.* mordace.

scatter, *vb.* spàrgere.

scavenger, *n.* spazzino *m.*

scenario, *n.* scenàrio *m.*

scene, *n.* scèna *f.*

scenery, *n.* paesàggio *m.*

scent, *n.* odore *m.,* fiuto *m.,* profumo *m.;* (track) pista *f.*

schedule, *n.* oràrio *m.*

scheme, *n.* progètto *m.*

scholar, *n.* dòtto *m.,* erudito *m.*

scholarship, *n.* borsa di stùdio *f.;* (knowledge) erudizione *f.*

school, *n.* scuòla *f.*

sciatica, *n.* sciàtica *f.*

science, *n.* sciènza *f.*

science fiction, *n.* fantascienza *f.*

scientific, *adj.* scientífico.

scientist, *n.* scienziato *m.*

scissors, *n.* fòrbici *f.pl.*

scoff, *vb.* schernire, farsi beffe.

scold, *vb.* sgridare.

scolding, *n.* ramanzina *f.*

scoop, 1. *n.* cucchiàio *m.,* ramaiuòlo *m.* 2. *vb.* travasare.

scope, *n.* (extent) portata *f.;* (outlet) sfògo *m.*

scorch, *vb.* bruciare.

score, 1. *n.* (points) punti *m.pl.;* (twenty) ventina *f.;* (music) partitura *f.* **2.** *vb.* segnare.

scorn, 1. *n.* disprèzzo *m.,* disdegno *m.* **2.** *vb.* disprezzare, disdegnare.

scornful, *adj.* sprezzante, sdegnoso.

Scotch, *adj.* scozzese.

Scotland, *n.* Scòzia *f.*

scoundrel, 1. *n.* birbante *m.;* farabutto *m.*

scour, *vb.* lavare strofinando.

scourge, 1. *n.* sfèrza *f.* **2.** *vb.* sferzare.

scout, *n.* esploratore *m.*

scowl, *vb.* aggrottare le ciglia.

scramble, 1. *n.* parapìglia *m.* **2.** *vb.* (climb) arrampicarsi.

scrambled eggs, *n.* uòva strapazzate *f.pl.*

scrap, 1. *n.* pezzetto *m.;* (fight) tafferùglio *m.* **2.** *vb.* scartare; (fight) azzuffarsi.

scrapbook, *n.* albo di ritagli *m.*

scrape, 1. *n.* (trouble) impìccio *m.* **2.** *vb.* raschiare.

scraper, *n.* raschietto *m.*

scrap paper, *n.* carta straccia *f.*

scratch, 1. *n.* graffiatura *f.* **2.** *vb.* graffiare.

scream, 1. *n.* strillo *m.* **2.** *vb.* strillare.

screech, 1. *n.* stridìo *m.* **2.** *vb.* stridere.

screen, 1. *n.* (furniture) paravènto *m.;* (sieve) crivèllo *m.;* (movie) schèrmo *m.* **2.** *vb.* (protect) protèggere; (sift) crivellare.

screen test, *n.* provino *m.*

screw, 1. *n.* vite *f.* **2.** *vb.* avvitare.

screw-driver, *n.* cacciavite *m.*

scribble, *vb.* scribacchiare.

scribe, *n.* scriba *m.*

scriptwriter, *n.* soggettista *m. and f.*

scripture, *n.* scrittura *f.*

scroll, *n.* ròtolo *m.*

scrub, *vb.* strofinare.

scruple, *n.* scrùpolo *m.*

scrupulous, *adj.* scrupoloso.

scrutinize, *vb.* scrutare.

skull, *n.* remo a bratto *m.;* canotto *m.*

sculptor, *n.* scultore *m.*

sculpture, *n.* scultura *f.*

scum, *n.* schiuma *f.;* (rabble) feccia *f.*

scythe, *n.* falce *f.*

sea, *n.* mare *m.*

seabed, *n.* letto del mare *m.*

seafood, *n.* frutti di mare *m.pl.*

seal, 1. *n.* sigillo *m.;* suggèllo *m.* (animal) fòca *f.* **2.** *vb.* sigillare.

sealing-wax, *n.* ceralacca *f.*

seam, *n.* cucitura *f.*

seaport, *n.* pòrto di mare *m.*

search, 1. *n.* ricerca *f.* **2.** *vb.* ricercare.

seasick, *adj.* (be s.) soffrire di mal di mare.

seasickness, *n.* mal di mare *m.*

season, 1. *n.* stagione *f.;* (s. ticket) bigliètto d'abbonamento *m.* **2.** *vb.* condire.

seasoning, *n.* condimento *m.*

seat, 1. *n.* (chair) sèdia *f.;* (place) posto *m.;* (headquarters) sede *f.;* (s. belt) cintura di sicurezza *f.* **2.** *vb.* far sedere.

second, *n. and adj.* secondo (*m.*).

secondary, *adj.* secondàrio.

secret, *n. and adj.* segreto (*m.*).

secretary, *n.* segretàrio *m.,* -ia *f.*

section, *n.* sezione *f.*

sectional, *adj.* sezionale, secante.

secular, *adj.* secolare.

secure, *adj.* sicuro.

security, *n.* sicurezza *f.*

sedative, *n. and adj.* sedativo (*m.*).

seduce, *vb.* sedurre.

seductive, *adj.* seducènte.

see, *vb.* vedere.

seed, *n.* seme *m.*

seek, *vb.* cercare.

seem, *vb.* parere, sembrare.

seep, *vb.* trasudare.

seesaw, *n.* altalena *f.*

segment, *n.* segmento *m.*

segregate, *vb.* segregare.

seize, *vb.* afferrare.

seldom, *adv.* di rado, raramente.

select, 1. *adj.* scelto. **2.** *vb.* scégliere.

selection, *n.* scelta *f.,* selezione *f.*

selective, *adj.* selettivo.

self, *pron.* stesso; **self-,** di sè stesso.

selfish, *adj.* egoístico.

selfishness, n. egoismo m.

sell, vb. véndere.

semantic, adj. semàntico.

semantics, n. semàntica f.

semester, n. semèstre m.

semicircle, n. semicérchio m.

semicolon, n. punto e virgola, m.

seminary, n. seminàrio m.

senate, n. senato m.

senator, n. senatore m.

send, vb. mandare, spedire, inviare.

senile, adj. senile.

senior, adj. maggiore; (father) padre.

senior citizen, n. persona anziana f.

sensation, n. sensazione f.

sensational, adj. sensazionale.

sense, 1. n. sènso m.; (intelligence) senno m. **2.** vb. intuire.

sensible, adj. assennato.

sensitive, adj. sensitivo, sensìbile.

sensual, adj. sensuale.

sentence, 1. n. frase f., proposizione f.; (court) condanna f. **2.** vb. condannare.

sentiment, n. sentimento m.

sentimental, adj. sentimentale.

separate, 1. adj. separato. **2.** vb. separare.

separation, n. separazione f.

September, n. settèmbre m.

septic, adj. infettato, sèttico.

sequence, n. sèrie f.

sequester, vb. isoalre; sequestrare.

serenade, n. serenata f.

serene, adj. sereno.

sergeant, n. sergènte m.

serial, adj. in sèrie, periòdico.

series, n. sèrie f.

serious, adj. sèrio.

seriousness, n. serietà f.

sermon, n. sermone m.

serpent, n. serpènte m.

serum, n. sièro m.

servant, n. domèstico m., sèrvo m.; (s.s, collectively) servitù f.

serve, vb. servire.

service, n. servízio m.

service station, n. stazione di servízio m., benzinàio m.

servile, adj. servile.

servitude, n. servitù f.

sesame, n. sèsamo m.

session, n. sessione f.

set, 1. n. sèrie f.; (clique) cricca f. **2.** adj. fisso. **3.** vb. (put) méttere; (regulate) regolare; (fix) fissare; (mount) montare.

setback, n. rovèscio m.

setting, n. ambiente m.; (theater) scenario m.; (sun) tramonto m.

settle, vb. (establish) stabilire, tr.; (fix) fissare; (decide) decídere; (arrange) sistemare; (pay) saldare; **(s. down to)** méttersi a.

settlement, n. (colony) colònia f.; (hamlet) borgo m.; (accounts) regolamento m.; (affairs) sistemazione f.

setup, n. organizzazione f.

settler, n. colòno m.

seven, num. sètte.

seventeen, num. diciassètte.

seventeenth, adj. diciassettésimo.

seventh, adj. sèttimo.

seventieth, adj. settantésimo.

seventy, num. settanta.

sever, vb. staccare, tr.

several, adj. parecchi.

severance, n. interruzione f.; **(s. pay)** liquidazione f., buonuscita f., indennità di fine contratto f.

severe, adj. sevèro.

severity, n. severità f.

sew, vb. cucire.

sewer, n. fogna f.

sex, n. sèsso m.

sexism, n. sessismo m.

sexist, n. and adj. sessista.

sexton, n. sagrestano m.

sexual, adj. sessuale.

shabby, adj. (worn-out) lògoro; (mean) gretto, meschino.

shack, n. capanna f.

shade, 1. n. ombra f.; (color) tinta f.; (against light) paralume m. **2.** vb. ombreggiare; (darken) oscurare.

shadow, n. ombra f.

shady, adj. ombroso.

shaft, n. (mine) pozzo m.; (transmission) àlbero m.; (wagon) stanga f.; (ray) ràggio m.; (arrow) strale m.

shaggy, adj. ispido.

shake, 1. n. scòssa f.; **(hand-s.)**

stretta di mano *f.* 2. *vb.* scuòtere, *tr.;* (quiver) tremare; **(s. hands with)** stringere la mano a.

shall, *vb.* dovere; or use future tense of verb.

shallow, *adj.* pòco profondo.

shame, 1. *n.* vergogna *f.;* (pity) peccato *m.;* **(what a s.)** che peccato! 2. *vb.* gettar vergogna su.

shameful, *adj.* vergognoso.

shampoo, *n.* sciampò *m.*

shape, 1. *n.* forma *f.,* fòggia *f.* 2. *vb.* formare, foggiare.

share, 1. *n.* parte *f.;* (stock) azione *f.* 2. *vb.* condivídere.

shark, *n.* pescecane *m.*

sharp, 1. *n.* (music) dièsis *m.* 2. *adj.* acuto.

sharpen, *vb.* aguzzare.

sharply, *adv.* acutamente; (harshly) aspramente.

sharpness, *n.* acutezza *f.*

shatter, *vb.* frantumare.

shave, *vb.* ràdere, *tr.,* fare la barba a, *tr.*

shaving cream, *n.* crema da barba *f.*

shawl, *n.* scialle *m.*

she, *pron.* ella *f.,* essa *f.,* lèi *f.*

sheaf, *n.* fàscio *m.,* covone *m.*

shear, *vb.* tosare.

shears, *n.* cesòie *f.pl.*

sheath, *n.* fòdero *m.,* guaina *f.*

shed, 1. *n.* tettòia *f.* 2. *vb.* versare; (lose) lasciar cadere.

sheep, *n.* pècora *f.*

sheet, *n.* (bed) lenzuòlo *m.;* (paper) fòglio *m.;* (metal) lastra *f.*

shelf, *n.* scaffale *m.*

shell, 1. *n.* (egg) gùscio *m.;* (pod) baccèllo *m.;* (conch) conchíglia *f.;* (explosive) bomba *f.* 2. *vb.* bombardare.

shellac, *n.* gomma lacca *f.*

shellfish, *n.* frutto di mare *m.*

shelter, 1. *n.* ricòvero *m.* 2. *vb.* ricoverare, *tr.*

shelve, *vb.* mèttere sullo scaffale; (politics) archiviare, insabbiare.

shepherd, *n.* pastore *m.*

sherbet, *n.* sorbetto *m.*

sherry, *n.* vino di Xeres *m.*

shield, 1. *n.* scudo *m.* 2. *vb.* protèggere.

shift, 1. *n.* (change) cambiamento

m.; (turn) turno *m.* 2. *vb.* cambiare.

shin, *n.* stinco *m.*

shine, *vb.* brillare, splèndere; (shoes) lucidare.

shingles, *n.* erpes *f.*

shining, *adj.* brillante, luminoso.

shiny, *adj.* lùcido.

ship, 1. *n.* nave *f.* 2. *vb.* spedire.

shipment, *n.* spedizione *f.*

shipper, *n.* speditore *m.*

shipping agent, *n.* spedizionière *m.*

shipside, *n.* molo *m.*

shipwreck, *n.* naufràgio *m.*

shipyard, *n.* cantiere navale *m.*

shirk, *vb.* sottrarsi a.

shirt, *n.* camícia *f.*

shiver, 1. *n.* brívido *m.* 2. *vb.* rabbrividire.

shoal, *n.* secca *f.,* banco sabbioso *m.*

shock, 1. *n.* scòssa *f.,* urto *m.* 2. *vb.* urtare.

shocking, *adj.* scioccante, disgustoso.

shock therapy, *n.* terapìa d'urto *f.*

shoddy, *adj.* scadente.

shoe, 1. *n.* scarpa *f.* 2. *vb.* calzare; (horse) terrare.

shoelace, *n.* làccio per scarpe *m.*

shoemaker, *n.* calzolaio *m.*

shoot, 1. *n.* (sprout) germóglio *m.* 2. *vb.* (gun) sparare; (a person) fucilare; **(s. down)** abbàttere.

shop, 1. *n.* bottega *f.,* negòzio *m.,* spàccio *m.* 2. *vb.* far còmpere.

shopping, *n.* còmpere *f.pl.,* spese *f.pl.*

shore, *n.* spiàggia *f.,* sponda *f.*

short, *adj.* brève, corto; **(s. circuit)** corto circùito *m.;* **(run s.)** scarseggiare.

shortage, *n.* mancanza *f.*

shorten, *vb.* abbreviare, *tr.*

shorthand, *n.* stenografìa *f.*

shortly, *adv.* fra pòco.

shorts, *n.* calzoncini corti *m.pl.*

shot, *n.* colpo *m.,* sparo *m.;* (bullets) pallini *m.pl.;* (distance) portata *f.*

should, *vb.* use conditional of dovere.

shoulder, *n.* spalla *f.*

shout, 1. *n.* grido *m.* 2. *vb.* gridare.

shove, 1. *n.* spinta *f.* 2. *vb.* spíngere.

shovel, *n.* pala *f.*

show, 1. *n.* mostra *f.,* esposizione *f.;* (theater) spettàcolo *m.* 2. *vb.* mostrare.

shower, *n.* (rain) acquazzone *m.;* (bath) dóccia *f.*

shrapnel, *n.* shrápnel *m.*

shrewd, *adj.* acuto, furbo.

shriek, 1. *n.* strillo *m.* 2. *vb.* strillare.

shrill, *adj.* strídulo.

shrimp, *n.* gamberetto *m.;* (small person) nano *m.*

shrine, *n.* santuàrio *m.*

shrink, *vb.* contrarsi; **(s. from)** rifuggire da.

shroud, *n.* sudàrio *m.*

shrub, *n.* arbusto *m.*

shudder, 1. *n.* brívido *m.* 2. *vb.* rabbrividire.

shun, *vb.* schivare.

shut, *vb.* chiùdere.

shutter, *n.* persiane *f.pl.,* scuri *m.pl.* (camera) otturatore *m.*

shy, *adj.* tímido.

Sicilian, *adj.* siciliano.

Sicily, *n.* Sicília *f.*

sick, *adj.* ammalato, malato.

sickness, *n.* malattía *f.*

side, *n.* lato *m.,* fianco *m.*

side-car, *n.* carrozzino *m.*

side-dish, *n.* contorno *m.*

sidewalk, *n.* marciapiède *m.*

siege, *n.* assèdio *m.*

sieve, *n.* crivèllo *m.,* setàccio *m.,* vàglio *m.*

sift, *vb.* setacciare; crivellare.

sigh, 1. *n.* sospiro *m.* 2. *vb.* sospirare.

sight, *n.* vista *f.*

sightseeing, *n.* turismo *m.*

sign, 1. *n.* segno *m.* 2. *vb.* firmare, sottoscrívere.

signal, 1. *n.* segnale *m.;* **(directional s.)** fréccia *f.* 2. *vb.* segnalare.

signature, *n.* firma *f.*

significance, *n.* significato *m.*

significant, *adj.* significativo.

signify, *vb.* significare.

silence, 1. *n.* silènzio *m.* 2. *vb.* azzittire, far tacere.

silencer, *n.* silenziatore *m.*

silent, *adj.* silenzioso, zitto.

silk, *n.* seta *f.*

silken, silky, *adj.* di seta, setàceo.

silkworm, *n.* baco da seta *m.*

sill, *n.* davanzale *m.*

silo, *n.* silo *m.*

silt, *n.* sedimento *m.*

silver, 1. *n.* argènto *m.* 2. *adj.* argènteo.

silver lining, *n.* spiraglio di speranza *m.*

silverware, *n.* posateria d'argento *m.*

silvery, *adj.* d'argento; argèneto.

similar, *adj.* símile.

similarity, *n.* somiglianza *f.*

similarly, *adv.* similmente.

simmer, *vb.* cuòcere a fuoco lento.

simple, *adj.* sémplice.

simple-minded, *adj.* sciocco.

simplicity, *n.* semplicità *f.*

simplify, *vb.* semplificare.

simply, *adv.* semplicemente.

simulate, *vb.* simulare.

simultaneous, *adj.* simultàneo.

sin, 1. *n.* peccato *m.* 2. *vb.* peccare.

since, 1. *prep.* sino da. 2. *conj.* da quando; (because) giacché, poiché.

sincere, *adj.* sincèro.

sincerely, *adv.* sinceramente.

sincerity, *n.* sincerità *f.*

sinew, *n.* nèrbo *m.*

sinful, *adj.* peccaminoso.

sing, *vb.* cantare.

singe, *vb.* strinare.

singer, *n.* cantatore *m.,* cantatrice *f.*

single, *adj.* solo, ùnico; (unmarried) cèlibe.

single file, *n.* fila indiana *f.*

single-handedly, *adv.* da solo.

single-phase, *adj.* monofase.

singsong, 1. *adj.* monòtono 2. *n.* cantilena *f.*

singular, *adj.* singolare.

sinister, *adj.* sinistro.

sink, 1. *n.* acquaio *m.,* lavandino *m.* 2. *vb.* affondare; (ground) sprofondarsi.

sinner, *n.* peccatore *m.*

sinuous, *adj.* sinuoso.

sinus, *n.* seno frontale *m.*

sinusitis, *n.* sinusite *f.*

sip, 1. *n.* sorso *m.* **2.** *vb.* sorseggiare.

siphon, *n.* sifone *m.*

sir, *n.* signore *m.*

siren, *n.* sirèna *f.*

sirloin, *n.* lombo *m.*

sister, *n.* sorèlla *f.*

sister-in-law, *n.* cognata *f.*

sit, *vb.* sedere.

site, *n.* sito *m.*

sitting, *n.* seduta *f.*

situate, *vb.* situare.

situation, *n.* situazione *f.*

six, *num.* sèi.

sixteen, *num.* sédici.

sixteenth, *adj.* sedicésimo, decimosèsto.

sixth, *adj.* sèsto.

sixtieth, *adj.* sessantésimo.

sixty, *num.* sessanta.

size, *n.* grandezza *f.; (apparel)* misura *f.*

sizing, *n.* incollatura *f.*

skate, *n.* **1.** pàttino *m.* **2.** *vb.* pattinare.

skateboard, *n.* asse a rotelle *m.*

skein, *n.* matassa *f.*

skeleton, *n.* schèletro *m.*

skeptic, *n.* scèttico *m.*

skeptical, *adj.* scèttico.

sketch, 1. *n.* abbozzo *m.,* schizzo *m.* **2.** *vb.* abbozzare, schizzare.

ski, 1. *n.* sci *m.* **2.** *vb.* sciare.

skid, *n.* slittamento *m.* **2.** *vb.* slittare.

ski-lift, *n.* seggiovia *f.*

skill, *n.* abilità *f.,* destrezza *f.*

skillful, *adj.* àbile, dèstro.

skim, *vb.* (remove cream) scremare; (go over lightly) sfiorare, rasentare.

skin, 1. *n.* pèlle *f.* **2.** *vb.* pelare; (fruit) sbucciare.

skip, *vb.* saltare.

skirmish, 1. *n.* scaramùccia *f.* **2.** *vb.* scontrarsi.

skirt, 1. *n.* gònna *f.,* sottana *f.* **2.** *vb.* rasentare.

skull, *n.* crànio *m.*

skunk, *n.* moffetta *f.,* pùzzola *f.; (person)* puzzone *m.*

sky, *n.* cièlo *m.*

skylight, *n.* lucernàrio *m.*

skyscraper, *n.* grattacièlo *m.*

slab, *n.* lastra *f.*

slack, *adj.* lento.

slacken, *vb.* rallentare.

slacks, *n.* calzoni *m.pl.*

slam, *vb.* sbàttere.

slander, 1. *n.* calùnnia *f.* **2.** *vb.* calunniare.

slang, *n.* gèrgo *m.*

slant, 1. *n.* pendìo *m.* **2.** *adj.* oblìquo. **3.** *vb.* inclinarsi.

slap, 1. *n.* schiaffo *m.* **2.** *vb.* schiaffeggiare.

slash, 1. *n.* squàrcio *m.* **2.** *vb.* squarciare.

slat, *n.* stecca *f.*

slate, *n.* ardèsia *f.,* lavagna *f.*

slaughter, 1. *n.* massacro *m.,* carneficina *f.;* macèllo *m.* **2.** *vb.* massacrare, macellare.

slave, *n.* schiavo *m.*

slavery, *n.* schiavitù *f.*

slave trade, *n.* tratta degli schiavi *f.*

Slavic, *adj.* slavo.

slay, *vb.* trucidare.

sled, *n.* slitta *f.*

sledge hammer, *n.* mazza *f.*

sleek, *adj.* liscio.

sleep, 1. *n.* sonno *m.* **2.** *vb.* dormire.

sleeping bag, *n.* sacco a pelo *m.*

sleeping car, *n.* vagone lètti *m.*

sleeping pill, *n.* sonnifero *m.*

sleepless, *adj.* insonne.

sleepwalker, *n.* sonnàmbulo *m.*

sleepy, *adj.* sonnolento.

sleet, *n.* nevischio *m.*

sleeve, *n.* mànica *f.*

sleigh, *n.* slitta *f.*

slender, *adj.* svelto.

sleuth, *n.* segùgio *m.*

slice, 1. *n.* fetta *f.* **2.** *vb.* affettare.

slide, *vb.* scivolare, sdrucciolare.

slide rule, *n.* règolo calcolatore *m.*

sliding door, *n.* porta scorrèvole *f.*

sliding scale, *n.* scala mòbile *f.*

slight, 1. *n.* disprezzo *m.* (thin) èsile, esiguo, insufficiènte; *adj.* **2.** *vb.* **slim,** *adj.* sottile.

slime, *n.* melma *f.*

slimy, *adj.* bavoso; melmoso.

sling, 1. *n.* fionda *f.* **2.** *vb.* lanciare, scagliare.

slink, *vb.* andare furtivamente.

slip, 1. *n.* scivolone *m.;* (mistake) errore *m.;* (paper) striscia *f.;* (underwear) sottovèste *f.* **2.** *vb.* scivolare, sdrucciolare; (make a mistake) sbagliare.

slipper, *n.* pantòfola *f.*

slippery, *adj.* sdrucciolévole.

slit, *n.* fessura *f.*

slogan, *n* paròla d'òrdine *f.;* (advertising) motto *m.*

slope, *n.* pendènza *f.,* pendío *m.*

sloppy, *adj.* trasandato.

slot, *n.* fessura *f.*

slot machine, *n.* distributore automàtico *m.*

slouch, *vb.* stare scomposto.

slovenly, *adj.* trascurato.

slow, *adj.* lento; (behind time) indiètro, in ritardo.

slowly, *adv.* lentamente.

slowness, *n.* lentezza *f.*

sluggish, *adj.* lento.

slum, *n.* bassofondo *m.*

slumber, *n.* sonno *m.*

slur, 1. *n.* calùnnia *f.;* (music) legatura *f.* **2.** *vb.* calunniare.

slush, *n.* fanghíglia *f.*

sly, *adj.* furbo.

smack, 1. *n.* (blow) pacca *f.;* (boat) battèllo *m.* **2.** *vb.* (hit) schiaffeggiare; (taste) sapere.

small, *adj.* piccolo.

smallpox, *n.* vaiòlo *m.*

smart, *adj.* elegante, intelligènte.

smash, *vb.* fracassare, frantumare.

smear, *vb.* spalmare.

smell, 1. *n.* odore *m.;* (stench) puzzo *m.;* (sense) fiuto *m.* **2.** *vb.* fiutare; (stink) puzzare.

smelt, 1. *n.* (fish) eperlano *m.* **2.** *vb.* (melt) fòndere.

smile, 1. *n.* sorriso *m.* **2.** *vb.* sorrìdere.

smite, *vb.* colpire.

smock, *n.* (workman's) camiciòtto *m.;* (hospital) càmice *m.*

smoke, 1. *n.* fumo *m.* **2.** *vb.* fumare.

smokestack, *n.* fumaiòlo *m.*

smolder, *vb.* covare.

smooth, 1. *adj.* levigato, líscio. **2.** *vb.* levigare, lisciare.

smother, *vb.* asfissiare, soffocare.

smug, *adj.* contento di sè stesso.

smuggler, *n.* contrabbandière *m.*

smuggling, *n.* contrabbando *m.*

snack, *n.* spuntino *m.*

snag, *n.* ostàcolo *m.*

snail, *n.* lumaca *f.*

snake, *n.* sèrpe *m.*

snap, *vb.* schioccare; (break) rómpere.

snapshot, *n.* istantànea *f.*

snare, *n.* tràppola *f.*

snarl, 1. *n.* (growl) rínghio *m.;* (tangle) groviglio *m.* **2.** *vb.* ringhiare, aggrovigliare, *tr.*

snatch, *vb.* afferrare, ghermire.

sneak, *vb.* andare furtivamente.

sneaker, *n.* scarpa di tela *f.*

sneer, 1. *n.* sogghigno *m.* **2.** *vb.* sogghignare.

sneeze, 1. *n.* starnuto *m.* **2.** *vb.* starnutire.

snicker, *n.* risatina *f.*

snob, *n.* snob *m.*

snore, *n.* russare.

snow, 1. *n* neve *f.* **2.** *vb.* nevicare.

snowdrift, *n.* ammasso di neve *m.*

snub, *vb.* non salutare.

snug, *adj.* còmodo.

so, *adv.* così; **(so far,** in time) finora; **(so far,** in space) fin qui; **(so as to)** così da.

soak, *vb.* bagnare, inzuppare.

so-and-so, *n.* tal dei tali *m.*

soap, *n.* sapone *m.*

soap opera, *n.* telenovela *f.*

soapy, *adj.* saponoso.

soar, *vb.* volare in alto.

sob, 1. *n.* singhiozzo *m.* **2.** *vb.* singhiozzare.

sober, *adj.* moderato, non ubriaco; (serious) sòbrio.

sobriety, *n.* sobrietà *f.*

so-called, *adj.* cosidetto.

soccer, *n.* calcio *m.*

sociable, *adj.* sociévole.

social, *adj.* sociale; **(s. work)** assistènza sociale *m. f.*

socialism, *n.* socialismo *m.*

socialist, *n. and adj.* socialista.

social worker, *n.* assistente sociale *m. and f.*

society, *n.* società *f.*

sociology, *n.* sociología *f.*

sock, 1. *n.* calzino *m.;* (blow) pugno *m.* **2.** *vb.* (hit) colpire.

socket, n. òrbita f.; (electric) presa f.

sod, n. piòta f., zòlla f.; (with grass) zòlla erbosa f.

soda, n. sòda f.

sodium, n. sòdio m.

sofa, n. sofà m.

soft, adj. mòlle, mòrbido.

soft-boiled egg, n. uovo alla coque m.

soft drink, n. bíbita non alcoòlica f.

soften, vb. ammollire.

softener, n. ammorbidente m.

soil, 1. n. suòlo m., terreno m. 2. vb. sporcare.

soiled, adj. spòrco.

sojourn, 1. n. soggiorno m. 2. vb. soggiornare.

solace, 1. n. consolazione f. 2. vb. consolare.

solar, adj. solare.

solder, 1. n. saldatura f. 2. vb. saldare.

soldier, n. soldato m.

sole, 1. n. (of foot, shoe) suòla f.; (fish) sògliola f. 2. adj. único.

solemn, adj. solènne.

solemnity, n. solennità f.

solicit, vb. sollecitare.

solicitous, adj. sollécito.

solid, n. and adj. sòlido (m.).

solidify, vb. solidificare, tr.

solidity, n. solidità f.

solitary, adj. solitàrio.

solitude, n. solitúdine f.

solo, n. assolo m.

soloist, n. solista m. or f.

so long, interj. ciao.

soluble, adj. solùbile.

solution, n. soluzione f.

solve, vb. risòlvere.

solvent, n. and adj. solvènte (m.).

somber, adj. fosco, sòbrio.

some, 1. pron. ne. 2. adj. qualche, alcuni; (a little) un po'.

somebody, pron. qualcuno.

somehow, adv. in qualche mòdo.

someone, pron. qualcuno.

somersault, n. capriòla f., salto mortale m.

something, pron. qualcosa, qualche cosa.

sometime, adj. (former) già.

sometimes, adv. qualche vòlta.

somewhat, adv. un po'.

somewhere, adv. in qualche luògo.

son, n. figlio m.

song, n. canto m., canzone f.

son-in-law, n. gènero m.

soon, adv. prèsto, fra pòco.

soot, n. fuliggine f.

soothe, vb. calmare.

soothingly, adv. dolcemente.

sophisticated, adj. sofisticato.

soprano, n. soprano m.

sorcery, n. stregoneria f.

sordid, adj. sòrdido.

sore, 1. n. piaga f. 2. adj. dolènte; (angry) adirato.

sorrow, 1. n. dolore m. 2. vb. addolorarsi.

sorrowful, adj. addolorato.

sorry, adj. spiacente.

sort, 1. n. sòrta f. 2. vb. assortire.

soul, n. ànima f.

sound, 1. n. suòno m. 2. adj. sano, giusto. 3. vb. suonare; (take soundings) sondare.

soup, n. minèstra f., zuppa f.

sour, adj. àcido; (unripe) acèrbo.

source, n. fonte f., sorgènte f.

south, n. sud m., mezzogiorno m.

southeast, n. sud-èst m.

southern, adj. meridionale.

South Pole, n. pòlo sud m.

southwest, n. sud-òvest m.

souvenir, n. ricòrdo m.

sovereign, n. and adj. sovrano (m.).

soviet, 1. n. sovièt m. 2. adj. soviético.

sow, 1. n. scrofa f., tròia f. 2. vb. seminare.

space, n. spàzio m.

space shuttle, n. spola spaziale f.

spacious, adj. spazioso.

spade, n. vanga f.

spaghetti, n. spaghetti m.pl.

Spain, n. Spagna f.

span, 1. n. (measure) spanna f.; (bridge) ponte m. 2. vb. stèndersi su.

Spaniard, n. spagnolo m.

Spanish, adj. spagnolo.

spank, vb. sculacciare.

spanking, n. sculacciata f.

spar, 1. n. àlbero m. 2. vb. (box) fare il pugilato.

spare, 1. *n.* pèzzo di ricàmbio *m.* **2.** *adj.* (extra) di ricàmbio; (thin) magro; (available) disponíbile. **3.** *vb.* aver disponíbile; (save) risparmiare.

spare parts, *n.* pezzi di ricambio *m.pl.*

spare room, *n.* camera per gli òspiti *f.*

spare tire, *n.* ruota di scorta *f.*

spark, *n.* scintilla *f.*

sparkle, *vb.* scintillare.

sparkling, *adj.* scintillante; **(s. water)** acqua gasata *f.* **(s. wine)** vino frizzante *m.*

spark-plug, *n.* candela d'accensione *f.*

sparrow, *n.* pàssero *m.*

sparse, *adj.* rado.

spasm, *n.* spàsimo *m.*

spasmodic, *adj.* spasmòdico.

spatial, *adj.* spaziale.

spatter, 1. *n.* spuzzo *m.* **2.** *vb.* spruzzare.

spatula, *n.* spatola *f.*

spawn, 1. *n.* prole *f.*, progenie *f.* **2.** *vb.* generare.

speak, *vb.* parlare; **(s. ill)** sparlare.

speaker, *n.* oratore *m.*; (presiding officer) presidènte *m.*

spear, 1. *n.* lància *f.* **2.** *vb.* trafiggere.

spearhead, 1. *n.* punta di lancia *f.* **2.** *vb.* condurre.

special, *adj.* speciale.

special delivery, *n.* espresso *m.*

specialist, *n.* specialista *m.*

specially, *adv.* specialmente.

specialty, *n.* specialità *f.*

species, *n.* spècie *f.*

specific, *adj.* specífico.

specify, *vb.* specificare.

specimen, *n.* sàggio *m.*

spectacle, *n.* spettàcolo *m.*; *(pl.,* eyeglasses) occhiali *m.pl.*

spectacular, *adj.* spettacolare.

spectator, *n.* spettatore *m.*

spectrum, *n.* spèttro *m.*

speculate, *vb.* speculare.

speculation, *n.* speculazione *f.*

speech, *n.* discorso *m.*

speechless, *adj.* interdetto.

speed, 1. *n.* velocità *f.* **2.** *vb.* affrettare, *tr.*; **(s. up)** accelerare, *tr.*

speedometer, *n.* tachímetro *m.*

speedy, *adj.* veloce.

spell, 1. *n.* incantèsimo *m.* **2.** *vb.* scrivere.

spelling, *n.* ortografia *f.*

spend, *vb.* (money) spèndere; (time) passare.

spendthrift, *n.* sciupone *m.*

sphere, *n.* sfèra *f.*

spice, *n.* spèzie, *f.pl.*

spider, *n.* ragno *m.*; **(s.-web)** ragnatela *f.*

spike, *n.* chiòdo *m.*

spill, *vb.* rovesciare.

spillway, *n.* scàrico *m.*

spin, 1. *n.* (excursion) giretto *m.* **2.** *vb.* filare; (whirl) girare.

spinach, *n.* spinaci *m.pl.*

spine, *n.* spina dorsale *f.*

spinet, *n.* spinetta *f.*

spinster, *n.* zitella *f.*

spiral, *n. and adj.* spirale *(m.)*

spire, *n.* gùglia *f.*

spirit, *n.* spirito *m.*

spiritual, *adj.* spirituale.

spiritualism, *n.* spiritismo *m.*

spit, *vb.* sputare.

spite, 1. *n.* dispètto *m.*; **(in s. of)** malgrado. **2.** *vb.* contrariare.

splash, 1. *n.* tonfo *m.*, spruzzo *m.* **2.** *vb.* spruzzare.

splendid, *adj.* splèndido.

splendor, *n.* splendore *m.*

splice, *vb.* congiùngere.

splint, *n.* stecca *f.*

splinter, 1. *n.* schéggia *f.* **2.** *vb.* scheggiare, *tr.*

split, 1. *n.* (crack) fessura *f.*; (division) scissione *f.* **2.** *vb.* (wood) spaccare; (crack) fèndere, *tr.*; (divide) dividere, *tr.*, scíndere, *tr.*

splurge, *vb.* spèndere molto denaro.

spoil, *vb.* guastare.

spoke, *n.* ràggio *m.*

spokesman, *n.* portavoce *m.*

sponge, *n.* spugna *f.*

sponsor, *n.* mallevadore *m.*; (backer) sostenitore *m.*

spontaneity, *n.* spontaneità *f.*

spontaneous, *adj.* spontàneo.

spool, *n.* bobina *f.*; (film) rocchetto *m.*

spoon, *n.* (large) cucchiaio *m.*; (small) cucchiaino *m.*

spoonful, *n.* cucchiaiata *f.*

sporadic, *adj.* sporàdico.

spore, *n.* spòra *f.*

sport, 1. *n.* sport *m.,* dipòrto *m.* 2. *adj.* sportivo.

sportsman, *n.* sportivo *m.*

spot, *n.* (place) posto *m.;* (blot) màcchia *f.*

spouse, *n.* sposo *m.,* sposa *f.*

spout, 1. *n.* becco *m.* 2. *vb.* spruzzare.

sprain, 1. *n.* stòrta *f.* 2. *vb.* stòrcere.

sprawl, *vb.* sdraiarsi.

spray, *vb.* sprizzare, nebulizzare.

sprayer, *n.* nebulizzatore *m.*

spray paint, *n.* vernice a spruzzo *f.*

spread, 1. *n.* distesa *f.;* (food) banchetto *m.* 2. *adj.* disteso, spiegato. 3. *vb.* stèndere, *tr.,* spiegare, *tr.;* (diffuse) diffóndere, *tr.*

spree, *n.* baldòria *f.*

sprig, *n.* ramoscèllo *m.*

sprightly, *adj.* brioso.

spring, 1. *n.* (season) primavera *f.;* (source) fonte *f.,* sorgènte *f.;* (leap) salto *m.;* (metal) mòlla *f.* 2. *vb.* sórgere, saltare; (leap up) scattare.

springboard, *n.* trampolino *m.*

springtime, *n.* primavera *f.*

sprinkle, *vb.* cospàrgere.

sprinkling, *n.* spruzzo *m.*

sprint, 1. *n.* corsa veloce. 2. *vb.* córrere velocemente.

sprinter, *n.* velocista *m.*

sprout, 1. *n.* germóglio *m.* 2. *vb.* germogliare.

spry, *adj.* arzillo.

spur, 1. *n.* sprone *m.,* sperone *m.* 2. *vb.* spronare.

spurious, *adj.* spùrio.

spurn, *vb.* disdegnare.

spurt, 1. *n.* scatto *m.* 2. *vb.* scattare; (pour out) spruzzare.

spy, 1. *n.* spione *m.* 2. *vb.* spiare; (perceive) scòrgere.

spyglass, *n.* canocchiale *m.*

spying, *n.* spionaggio *m.*

squabble, *n.* battibecco *m.*

squad, *n.* squadra *f.*

squadron, *n.* squadrone *f.*

squalid, *adj.* squàllido.

squall, *vb.* sbraitare.

squalor, *n.* squallore *m.*

squander, *vb.* scialacquare.

square, 1. *n.* quadrato *m.;* (open place) piazza *f.* 2. *adj.* quadrato. 3. *vb.* quadrare.

square root, *n.* radice quadrata *f.*

squash, 1. *n.* (drink) spremuta *f.;* (vegetable) zucca *f.* 2. *vb.* spiaccicare.

squashy, *adj.* tènero; (fruit) maturo.

squat, 1. *adj.* tarchiato. 2. *vb.* accosciarsi.

squeak, 1. *n.* cigolìo *m.* 2. *vb.* cigolare.

squeamish, *adj.* schizzinoso.

squeeze, 1. *n.* stretta *f.* 2. *vb.* stringere; (juice) sprèmere.

squeezer, *n.* spremiagrumi *m.*

squirrel, *n.* scoiàttolo *m.*

squirt, *vb.* schizzare, zampillare.

stab, 1. *n.* pugnalata *f.* 2. *vb.* pugnalare.

stability, *n.* stabilità *f.*

stabilize, *vb.* stabilizzare.

stable, 1. *n.* stalla *f.* 2. *adj.* stàbile.

stack, 1. *n.* mùcchio *m.* 2. *vb.* ammucchiare.

stadium, *n.* stàdio *m.*

staff, *n.* (stick) bastone *m.;* (personnel) personale *m.;* (music) rigo *m.*

stag, *n.* cèrvo *m.*

stage, *n.* (theater) palcoscènico *m.;* (phase) fase *f.,* stàdio *m.*

stagflation, *n.* inflazione in un'economia stagnante *f.*

stagger, *vb.* barcollare.

stagnant, *adj.* stagnante.

stagnate, *vb.* stagnare.

stain, 1. *n.* màcchia *f.;* (color) colore *m.* 2. *vb.* colorare; macchiare.

staircase, stairs, *n.* scala *f.*

stake, 1. *n.* (post) palo *m.;* (sum, bet) posta *f.* 2. *vb.* rischiare; (bet) puntare.

stale, *adj.* raffermo.

stalemate, 1. *n.* punto mòrto *m.*

stalk, *n.* gambo *m.*

stall, 1. *n.* stallo *m.;* (vendor's) banco *m.* 2. *vb.* (stop) arrestarsi.

stallion, *n.* stallone *m.*

stalwart, *adj.* robusto.

stamen, *n.* stame *m.*

stamina, *n.* vigore *m.*

stammer, *vb.* balbettare.

stamp, 1. *n.* (adhesive) bollo *m.;* (embossed, impressed) timbro *m.;* **(postage-s.)** francobollo *m.* **2.** *vb.* bollare, timbrare.

stampede, *n.* fuga precipitosa *f.*

stamp pad, *n.* cuscinetto *m.*

stand, 1. *n.* (position) posizione *f.;* (vendor's) padiglione *m.;* (grandstand) tribuna *f.* **2.** *vb.* stare; (put) méttere; (suffer) soffrire, tollerare; **(s. up)** stare in pièdi.

standard, 1. *n.* nòrma *f.* **2.** *adj.* normale.

standardize, *vb.* standardizzare.

standing, 1. *n.* riputazione *f.* **2.** *adj.* permanènte; **(s. up)** in pièdi.

standpoint, *n.* punto di vista *m.*

staple, *n.* (fiber) fibra *f.; (comm.)* prodotto principale *m.*

star, *n.* stella *f.*

starboard, *n.* tribordo *m.*

starch, 1. *n.* àmido *m.* **2.** *vb.* inamidare.

starchy, *adj.* inamidato.

stare, *vb.* guardare fisso.

starfish, *n.* stella marina *f.*

stark, *adv.* completamente.

starlet, *n.* piccola celebrità *f.*

start, 1. *n.* inízio *m.;* (departure) partènza *f.;* (jump) sussulto *m.* **2.** *vb.* cominciare, iniziare; (depart) partire; (jump) sussultare, trasalire.

starter, *n.* (beginner) iniziatore *m.;* (auto) avviamento *m.*

startle, *vb.* allarmare, far trasalire.

startling, *adj.* allarmante, sorpredente.

star system, *n.* divismo *m.*

starvation, *n.* fame *f.*

starve, *vb.* morire di fame.

state, 1. *n.* stato *m.* **2.** *vb.* affermare.

statement, *n.* affermazione *f.;* (bank) rendiconto *m.;* (legal) deposizione *f.*

stateroom, *n.* cabina *f.*

statesman, *n.* uòmo di stato *m.;* statista *m.*

static, *adj.* stàtico.

station, *n.* stazione *f.*, fattoría *f.*

stationary, *adj.* stazionàrio.

stationer, *n.* cartolaio *m.*

stationery, *n.* oggetti di cancelería *m.pl.;* **(s. store)** cartoleria *f.*

station wagon, *n.* giardinetta *f.*

statistics, *n.* (science) statística *f.;* (data) statístiche *f.pl.*

statue, *n.* stàtua *f.*

stature, *n.* statura *f.*

status, *n.* condizione *f.*

statute, *n.* statuto *m.*

statutory, *adj.* legale.

staunch, *adj.* fedele.

stay, 1. *n.* (sojourn) permanènza *f.;* (delay) sospensione *f.* **2.** *vb.* restare; (hold back) fermare.

steadfast, *adj.* saldo.

steady, *adj.* fermo, saldo.

steak, *n.* bistecca *f.*

steal, *vb.* rubare; (go furtively) andare di soppiatto.

stealth, *n.* **(by s.)** furtivamente.

stealthily, *adv.* di soppiatto.

stealthy, *adj.* furtivo.

steam, *n.* vapore *m.*

steamboat, *n.* piròscafo *m.*

steamship, *n.* piròscafo *m.*

steel, 1. *n.* acciàio *m.* **2.** *vb.* indurire.

steel wool, *n.* lana di acciàio *f.*, pàglia di acciàio *f.*

steep, *adj.* èrto, rípido, scosceso.

steeple, *n.* campanile *m.*

steeplechase, *n.* corsa ad ostàcoli *f.*

steer, *vb.* dirígere.

steering wheel, *n.* volante *m.*, sterzo *m.;* (boat) timone *m.*

stellar, *adj.* stellare.

stem, *n.* stelo *m.*

stencil, *n.* stampino *m.*

stenographer, *n.* stenògrafa *f.*

stenography, *n.* stenografía *f.*

step, 1. *n.* (pace) passo *m.;* (footprint) orma *f.;* (stair) gradino *m.* **2.** *vb.* camminare.

stepfather, *n.* patrigno *m.*

stepladder, *n.* scalèo *m.*

stepmother, *n.* matrigna *f.*

stereotype, *n.* stereotípia *f.*

stereophonic, *adj.* stereofònico.

sterile, *adj.* stèrile.

sterility, *n.* sterilità *f.*

sterilize, *vb.* sterilizzare.

sterling, *adj.* puro; **(pound s.)** sterlina *f.*

stern, 1. *n.* poppa *f.* **2.** *adj.* sevèro.

stethoscope, n. stetoscòpio m.

stevedore, n. stivatore m.

stew, 1. n. stufato m. **2.** vb. stufare.

steward, n. camerière m.

stewardess, n. (boat) camerièra f.; (plane) assistente di volo f.

stick, 1. n. bastone m. **2.** vb. (adhere) aderire; (attach) appiccicare, attaccare; (shove) cacciare, ficcare.

sticker, n. etichetta f.

sticky, adj. attaccatíccio, viscoso.

stiff, adj. rígido.

stiffen, vb. irrigidire, tr.

stiffness, n. rigidezza f.

stifle, vb. soffocare.

stigma, n. stigma m.

stigmata, n. stigmate f.pl.

still, 1. n. alambicco m. **2.** adj. calmo. **3.** vb. calmare. **4.** adv. ancora.

still-born, adj. nato mòrto.

still life, n. natura mòrta f.

stillness, n. quiète f., calma f.

stilted, adj. ampolloso.

stimulant, n. and adj. stimolante (m.)

stimulate, vb. stimolare.

stimulus, n. stímolo m.

sting, 1. n. (body-part) pungiglione m.; (wound) puntura f. **2.** vb. pùngere.

stingy, adj. avaro, tírchio.

stipulate, vb. stipulare.

stir, 1. n. agitazione f., commozione f. **2.** vb. agitare, tr., muòvere, tr.

stirring, adj. commovente.

stitch, 1. n. punto m. **2.** vb. cucire.

stock, 1. n. (supply) provvista f.; (lineage) stirpe f.; (animals) bestiame m.; (of gun) càlcio m.; (financial) azioni f. **2.** vb. tenere in magazzino.

stockbroker, n. agènte di càmbio m.

stock exchange, n. borsa f.

stockfish, n. stocafisso m.

stockholder, n. azionista m.

Stockholm, n. Stoccolma f.

stocking, n. calza f.

stockpile, 1. n. riserva f.; scorta f. **2.** vb. far scorta.

stockroom, n. magazzino m.; depòsito m.

stockyard, n. mattatòio m.

stodgy, adj. ottuso.

stoic, n. stòico m.

stoical, adj. stòico.

stole, n. stòla f.

stolid, adj. stòlido.

stomach, 1. n. stòmaco m. **2.** vb. tollerare.

stone, 1. n. piètra f., sasso m. **2.** vb. lapidare.

stooge, n. (theater) spalla f.; (crime) còmplice m.

stool, n. sgabello m.

stoop, vb. curvarsi; (demean oneself) abbassarsi.

stooped, adj. curvo.

stop, 1. n. fermata f. **2.** vb. fermare, tr.; (close) otturare, tappare; (cease) smèttere; (cease moving) sostare.

stopgap, n. temporàneo m.

stop-over, n. fermata intermèdia f.

stopper, n. tappo m.

stopping, n. sosta f.

storage, n. magazzinàggio m.

store, 1. n. negòzio m.; (supply) provvista f. **2.** vb. immagazzinare, conservare; (fill) riempire.

storehouse, n. magazzino m.

stork, n. cicogna f.

storm, n. tempèsta f.

storm troops, n. truppe d'assalto f.pl.

stormy, adj. tempestoso.

story, n. racconto m., stòria f.

storyteller, n. narratore m.

stout, adj. grasso; (strong) fòrte.

stove, n. fornèllo m., stufa f.

strafe, 1. n. attacco violento m. **2.** vb. attaccare violentemente, bombardare pesantemente.

straight, 1. adj. diritto, rètto. **2.** adv. direttamente, diritto.

straight-away, n. rettilineo m.

straighten, vb. raddrizzare.

straightforward, adj. franco.

strain, 1. n. tensione f. **2.** vb. sforzare, tr.; (filter) colare.

strainer, n. colino m.

strait, n. stretto m.

strand, 1. n. riva f. **2.** vb. arenarsi.

strange, adj. strano; (foreign) stranièro.

stranger, n. stranièro m.

strangle, *vb.* strangolare.

strap, *n.* cinghia *f.*

stratagem, *n.* stratagèmma *m.*

strategic, *adj.* stratègico.

strategy, *n.* strategia *f.*

stratosphere, *n.* stratosfèra *f.*

stratum, *n.* strato *m.*

straw, *n.* pàglia *f.*; (for drinking) cannùccia di pàglia *f.*

strawberry, *n.* fràgola *f.*

stray, 1. *adj.* smarrito. 2. *vb.* allontanarsi.

streak, *n.* ramo *m.*, vena *f.*, venatura *f.*

stream, *n.* corrènte *f.*, fiòtto *m.*

streamlined, *adj.* aerodinàmico.

street, *n.* via *f.*, strada *f.*

streetcar, *n.* tram *m.*

strength, *n.* fòrza *f.*

strengthen, *vb.* rafforzare.

strenuous, *adj.* strènuo.

streptococcus, *n.* streptococco *m.*

stress, 1. *n.* sfòrzo *m.*, tensione *f.*; (accent) accènto *m.* 2. *vb.* accentare.

stretch, 1. *n.* tratto *m.* 2. *vb.* tèndere.

stretcher, *n.* barèlla *f.*

strew, *vb.* cospàrgere.

stricken, *adj.* colpito.

strict, *adj.* sevèro.

stride, 1. *n.* passo lungo *m.* 2. *vb.* camminare a passi lunghi.

strident, *adj.* strídulo.

strife, *n.* conflitto *m.*

strike, 1. *n.* (workers') sciòpero *m.* 2. *vb.* scioperare; (hit) colpire.

strike-breaker, *n.* crumiro *m.*

string, 1. *n.* filo *m.*, còrda *f.* 2. *vb.* infilare.

string bean, *n.* fagiòlo *m.*

stringent, *adj.* rigoroso.

strip, 1. *n.* stríscia *f.* 2. *vb.* spogliare, *tr.*

stripe, *n.* lista *f.*, stríscia *f.*

strive, *vb.* sforzarsi.

stroke, 1. *n.* colpo *m.* 2. *vb.* accarezzare.

stroll, 1. *n.* passeggiata *f.* 2. *vb.* passeggiare.

stroller, *n.* passeggiatore *m.*

strong, *adj.* fòrte.

strongbox, *n.* cassaforte *f.*

strong drink, *n.* bevanda alcòlica *f.*

stronghold, *n.* roccafòrte *f.*

structure, *n.* struttura *f.*

struggle, 1. *n.* lotta *f.* 2. *vb.* lottare.

strut, *vb.* pavoneggiarsi.

stub, *n.* mozzicone *m.*; (checkbook) madre *f.*

stubborn, *adj.* testardo.

stucco, *n.* stucco *m.*

stuck, *adj.* infisso, attaccato.

student, *n.* studènte *m.*, studentessa *f.*

student body, *n.* scolaresca *f.*

studio, *n.* stùdio *m.*

studious, *adj.* studioso.

study, 1. *n.* stùdio *m.* 2. *vb.* studiare.

stuff, 1. *n.* (cloth) stoffa *f.*; (junk) ròba *f.* 2. *vb.* rimpinzare, imbottire; (food) infarcire.

stuffed, *adj.* ripièno.

stuffing, *n.* ripièno *m.*

stuffy, *adj.* opprimente; (nose) chiuso.

stumble, *vb.* inciampare.

stump, *n.* (tree) ceppo *m.*; (arm, leg) moncone *m.*

stun, *vb.* stordire.

stunning, *adj.* stordente, sbalorditivo.

stunt, *n.* impresa fuòri del consuèto *f.*

stunt man, *n.* controfigura *f.*, stuntman, *m.*

stupendous, *adj.* stupèndo.

stupid, *adj.* stùpido.

stupidity, *n.* stupidità *f.*

stupor, *n.* stupore *m.*

sturdy, *adj.* gagliàrdo.

stutter, *vb.* tartagliare.

Stuttgart, *n.* Stoccarda *f.*

sty, *n.* porcile *m.*; (eye) orzaiòlo *m.*

style, *n.* stile *m.*

stylish, *adj.* di mòda.

suave, *adj.* blando.

subconscious, *adj.* subcosciènte.

subdivide, *vb.* suddividere.

subdue, *vb.* soggiogare.

subdued, *adj.* soggiogato; (light) tènue; (voice) sommesso.

subject, 1. *n.* soggètto *m.*; (of king) suddito *m.* 2. *adj.* soggètto. 3. *vb.* sottoporre, assoggettare.

subjugate, *vb.* soggiogare.
subjunctive, *n.* and *adj.* congiuntivo (*m.*)
sublimate, 1. *n.* and *adj.* sublimato (*m.*) **2.** *vb.* sublimare.
sublime, *adj.* sublime.
submarine, 1. *n.* sommergibile *m.* **2.** *adj.* sottomarino.
submerge, *vb.* sommèrgere.
submersion, *n.* sommersione *f.*
submission, *n.* sottomissione *f.*
submit, *vb.* sottométtere, *tr.*
subnormal, *adj.* subnormale.
subordinate, *n.* and *adj.* subordinato (*m.*)
subscribe, *vb.* (write name) sottoscrivere; (take regularly) abbonarsi; (agree with) aderire.
subscription, *n.* abbonamento *m.*
subsequent, *adj.* successivo.
subservient, *adj.* servile.
subside, *vb.* diminuire; (building) sprofondarsi; (earth) cédere; (water) abbassarsi.
subsidy, *n.* sussidio *m.*
substance, *n.* sostanza *f.*
substantial, *adj.* sostanziale.
substitute, 1. *n.* sostituto *m.* **2.** *vb.* sostituire.
substitution, *n.* sostituzione *f.*
subterfuge, *n.* sotterfùgio *m.*
subtle, *adj.* sottile.
subtract, *vb.* sottrarre.
suburb, *n.* sobborgo *m.*
subvention, *n.* sovvenzione *f.*
subversive, *adj.* sovversivo.
subvert, *vb.* sovvertire.
subway, *n.* metropolitana *f.*
succeed, *vb.* (come after) succèdere a; (be successful) riuscire.
success, *n.* successo *m.*, riuscita *f.*
successful, *adj.* riuscito.
succession, *n.* successione *f.*, sèrie *f.*
successive, *adj.* successivo.
successor, *n.* successore *m.*
succor, 1. *n.* soccorso *m.* **2.** *vb.* soccórrere.
succumb, *vb.* soccómbere.
such, *adj.* tale.
suck, *vb.* succhiare.
suction, *n.* aspirazione *f.*
sudden, *adj.* improvviso.
suds, *n.* schiuma *f.*
sue, *vb.* citare in giudizio.

suffer, *vb.* soffrire.
suffice, *vb.* bastare.
sufficient, *adj.* sufficiènte.
suffocate, *vb.* soffocare.
sugar, *n.* zùcchero *m.*
suggest, *vb.* suggerire.
suggestion, *n.* suggerimento *m.*
suicide, *n.* suicidio *m.*; (commit s.) suicidarsi.
suit, 1. *n.* (clothes) àbito *m.*; (cards) colore *m.*; (request) domanda *f.*; (law) càusa *f.* **2.** *vb.* convenire a, andar bène a.
suitable, *adj.* conveniènte.
suitcase, *n.* valìgia *f.*
suite, *n.* sèrie *f.*; (followers) sèguito *m.*; (music) suite *f.*
suitcase, *n.* valìgia *f.*
suitor, *n.* corteggiatore *m.*; (law) querelante *m.*
sulky, *adj.* imbronciato.
sullen, *adj.* cupo.
sultana raisin, *n.* uva sultanina *f.*
sultry, *adj.* soffocante, afoso.
sum, 1. *n.* somma *f.* **2.** *vb.* sommare; (s. up) riassùmere.
summarize, *vb.* riassùmere.
summary, *n.* and *adj.* sommàrio (*m.*)
summer, 1. *n.* estate *f.* **2.** *adj.* estivo.
summit, *n.* sommità *f.*, cima *f.*
summon, *vb.* chiamare, citare.
summons, *n.* chiamata *f.*; (court) citazione *f.*
sumptuous, *adj.* sontuoso.
sun, *n.* sole *m.*
sunbathe, *vb.* prendere la tintarella.
sunburn, *n.* abbronzatura *f.*
sunburned, *adj.* abbronzato.
Sunday, *n.* doménica *f.*
Sunday school, *n.* sciola di catechismo *f.*
sunflower, *n.* girasole *m.*
sunglasses, *n.* occhiale da sole *m.pl.*
sunken, *adj.* infossato.
sunny, *adj.* assolato.
sunset, *n.* tramonto *m.*
sunshine, *n.* sole *m.*
sunstroke, *n.* insolazione *f.*
suntan cream, *n.* crema solare *f.*
superb, *adj.* supèrbo.

superficial, *adj.* superficiale.
superfluous, *adj.* supèrfluo.
super-highway, *n.* autostrada *f.*
superhuman, *adj.* sovrumano.
superintendent, *n.* sovrintendènte *m.*
superior, *adj.* superiore.
superiority, *n.* superiorità *f.*
superlative, *n. and adj.* superlativo (*m.*)
superman, *n.* superuòmo *m.*
supernatural, *adj.* soprannaturale.
supersede, *vb.* soppiantare.
superstar, *n.* superstar *m.*
superstition, *n.* superstizione *f.*
superstitious, *adj.* superstizioso.
supervise, *vb.* sorvegliare.
supper, *n.* cena *f.*
supplant, *vb.* soppiantare.
supplement, *n.* supplemento *m.*
supply, 1. *n.* fornitura *f.*, provvista *f.* **2.** *vb.* fornire, provvedere.
support, 1. *n.* sostegno *m.* **2.** *vb.* appoggiare, sostenere.
suppose, *vb.* supporre.
suppress, *vb.* supprimere.
suppression, *n.* soppressione *f.*
supreme, *adj.* suprèmo.
sure, *adj.* sicuro.
surely, *adv.* sicuramente.
surety, *n.* sicurezza *f.*
surf, *n.* frangènti *m.pl.*
surface, *n.* superficie *f.*
surge, *vb.* ondare.
surgeon, *n.* chirurgo *m.*
surgery, *n.* chirurgia *f.*
surmise, 1. *n.* congettura *f.* **2.** *vb.* congetturare.
surmount, *vb.* sormontare.
surname, *n.* cognome *m.*
surpass, *vb.* sorpassare.
surplus, *n.* avanzo *m.*
surprise, 1. *n.* sorpresa *f.* **2.** *vb.* sorprèndere.
surrender, *vb.* (hand over) cédere; (yield) arrèndersi.
surround, *vb.* circondare.
surroundings, *n.* dintorni *m.pl.*
surveillance, *n.* sorveglianza *f.*
survey, 1. *n.* esame *m.*; (geographical) rilevamento *m.* **2.** *vb.* esaminare.
surveyor, *n.* agrimensore *m.*
survival, *n.* sopravvivènza *f.*

survive, *vb.* sopravvivere.
susceptible, *adj.* suscettibile.
suspect, 1. *n.* sospètto. **2.** *vb.* sospettare.
suspend, *vb.* sospèndere.
suspense, *n.* incertezza *f.*
suspension, *n.* sospensione *f.*
suspension bridge, *n.* ponte sospeso *m.*
suspicion, *n.* sospètto *m.*
suspicious, *adj.* sospettoso; (questionable) sospètto.
sustain, *vb.* sostenere.
swallow, 1. *n.* (bird) ròndine *f.*; (food) beccone *m.*; (drink) sorso *m.* **2.** *vb.* inghiottire.
swamp, 1. *n.* palude *f.* **2.** *vb.* inondare.
swan, *n.* cigno *m.*
swap, 1. *n.* baratto *m.* **2.** *vb.* barattare.
swarm, 1. *n.* sciame *m.* **2.** *vb.* sciamare; (be crowded) formicolare.
sway, *vb.* oscillare; (influence) dominare.
swear, *vb.* giurare; (curse) bestemmiare; (s.-word) bestèmmia *f.*
sweat, 1. *n.* sudore *f.* **2.** *vb.* sudare.
sweater, *n.* golf *m.*
Swede, *n.* svedese *m.*
Sweden, *n.* Svèzia *f.*
Swedish, *adj.* svedese.
sweep, *vb.* spazzare.
sweeper, *n.* spazzino *m.*
sweeping, *adj.* travolgente, completo.
sweepstakes, *n.* lotteria *f.*
sweet, *adj.* dolce.
sweeten, *vb.* addolcire; zuccherare.
sweetheart, *n.* innamorato *m.*, innamorata *f.*
sweetness, *n.* dolcezza *f.*
sweet tooth, *n.* dèbole per i dolciumi *m.*
swell, 1. *adj.* magnífico. **2.** *vb.* gonfiare, *tr.*
swelter, *vb.* sudare.
swift, *adj.* veloce.
swim, *vb.* nuotare.
swimming, *n.* nuoto *m.*
swimsuit, *n.* costume da bagno *m.*
swindle, *vb.* truffare.

swindler, n. truffatore m.
swine, n. pòrco m.
swing, 1. n. (children's) altalena f. **2.** vb. dondolare, penzolare.
swirl, vb. turbinare.
swirling, adj. vorticoso.
Swiss, adj. svizzero.
switch, 1. n. (rod) verga f.; (railway) scàmbio m.; (electric) interruttore m. **2.** vb. (whip) sferzare; **(s. on)** accèndere; **(s. off)** spègnere.
switchboard, n. centralino m.
Switzerland, vb. Svìzzera f.
swivel, n. perno m.
sword, n. spada f.
sword-fish, n. pesce spada m.
syllable, n. sìllaba f.
symbol, n. sìmbolo m.
symbolic, adj. simbòlico.
sympathetic, adj. sensìbile.

sympathize, vb. simpatizzare.
sympathy, n. simpatìa f.
symphonic, adj. sinfònico.
symphony, n. sinfonìa f.; **(s. orchestra)** orchèstra sinfònica f.
symptom, n. sìntomo m.
symptomatic, adj. sintomàtico.
synchronous, adj. sìncrono.
synchronize, vb. sincronizzare.
syndicate, n. consòrzio m.
syndrome, n. sìndrome f.
synonym, n. sinònimo m.
synonymous, adj. sinònimo.
synthesis, n. sìntesi f.
synthetic, adj. sintètico.
syphilis, n. sìfilide f.
syphilitic, adj. sifilìtico.
syringe, n. siringa f.
syrup, n. sciròppo m.
system, n. sistèma m.
systematic, adj. sistemàtico.

T

tabernacle, n. tabernàcolo m.
table, n. tàvola f.
tablecloth, n. tovàglia f.
tablespoon, n. cucchiaio m.
tablespoonful, n. cucchiaiata f.
tablet, n. tavoletta f.; (pastille) pastiglia f., pastìcca f.
tack, 1. n. bulletta f. **2.** vb. attaccare; (turn) virare.
tact, n. tatto m.
tag, n. etichetta f.
tail, n. coda f.
tailor, n. sarto m.
take, vb. prèndere; (carry) portare; (lead) condurre.
tale, n. racconto m.
talent, n. talènto m.
talk, 1. n. discorso m. **2.** vb. parlare.
talkative, adj. loquace.
tall, adj. alto.
tallow, n. sego m.
tame, 1. adj. addomesticato, mansuèto. **2.** vb. addomesticare, domare.
tamper, vb. immischiarsi.
tan, 1. n. (sun) abbronzatura f. **2.** adj. castagno. **3.** vb. abbronzare; (leather) conciare.
tangible, adj. tangìbile.

tangle, 1. n. garbùglio m. **2.** vb. ingarbugliare.
tank, n. serbatòio m.; (armored vehicle) carro armato m.
tap, 1. n. (blow) colpetto m.; (faucet) rubinetto m. **2.** vb. percuòtere.
tape, n. nastro m.
tape recorder, n. magnetòfono m., registratore magnético m.
tapestry, n. tappezzerìa f.
tar, 1. n. catrame m. **2.** vb. incatramare.
target, n. bersàglio m.
tariff, n. tariffa f.
tarnish, 1. n. appannatura f. **2.** vb. appannare, tr.
tart, 1. n. tòrta f.; (harlot) puttana f. **2.** adj. acre.
task, n. cómpito m., incàrico m.
taste, 1. n. gusto m. **2.** vb. gustare.
tasty, adj. gustoso, saporito.
taunt, vb. schernire.
taut, adj. teso.
tavern, n. osterìa f., tavèrna f.
tax, n. imposta f., tassa f.
taxi, n. taxi m., tassì m.; **(t. driver)** tassista m.
taxpayer, n. contribuènte m.
tax rate, n. aliquota f.
tea, n. thè (tè) m.

teach, *vb.* insegnare.

teacher, *n.* insegnante *m. or f.*, maestro *m.*, maestra *f.*

teaching aids, *n.* sussidi didàttici *m.pl.*

team, *n.* squadra *f.*

teamwork, *n.* lavoro di squadra *m.*

tea-pot, *n.* teièra *f.*

tear, 1. *n.* làcrima *f.* **2.** *vb.* strappare.

tease, *vb.* tormentare.

teaspoon, *n.* cucchiaino da thè *m.*

technical, *adj.* tècnico.

technique, *n.* tècnica *f.*

teddy bear, *n.* orsacchiotto *m.*

tedious, *adj.* tedioso.

tedium, *n.* tèdio *m.*

telegram, *n.* telegramma *m.*

telegraph, 1. *n.* telègrafo *m.* **2.** *vb.* telegrafare.

telephone, 1. *n.* telèfono *m.;* **(t.-call)** telefonata *f.* **2.** *vb.* telefonare.

telescope, *n.* telescòpio *m.*

teletype, *n.* telescrivènte *f.*

televise, *vb.* trasméttere per televisione.

television, *n.* televisione *f.;* **(t. screen)** teleschermo *m.;* **(t. set)** televisore *m.*

tell, *vb.* raccontare.

teller, *n.* cassière *m.*

temper, 1. *n.* (anger) còllera *f.* **2.** *vb.* temperare.

temperament, *n.* temperamento *m.*

temperamental, *adj.* capriccioso.

temperance, *n.* temperanza *f.*

temperate, *adj.* temperato.

temperature, *n.* temperatura *f.*

tempest, *n.* tempèsta *f.*

tempestuous, *adj.* tempestoso.

temple, *n.* tèmpio *m.;* (forehead) tèmpia *f.*

temporary, *adj.* provvisòrio.

tempt, *vb.* tentare.

temptation, *n.* tentazione *f.*

tempting, *adj.* tentatore, tentatrice.

ten, *num.* dièci.

tenable, *adj.* difendìbile.

tenacious, *adj.* tenace.

tenant, *n.* inquilino *m.*

tend, *vb.* tèndere; (care for) curare.

tendency, *n.* tendènza *f.*

tender, 1. *n.* carro di scòrta *m.* **2.** *adj.* tènero. **3.** *vb.* offrire.

tenderly, *adv.* teneramente.

tenderness, *n.* tenerezza *f.*

tendon, *n.* tèndine *m.*

tenet, *n.* principio *m.;* dogma *m.*

tennis, *n.* tènnis *m.*

tenor, *n.* tenore *m.*

tense, *adj.* teso.

tension, *n.* tensione *f.*

tent, *n.* tènda *f.*

tentacle, *n.* tentàcolo *m.*

tentative, 1. *n.* tentativo *m.* **2.** *adj.* sperimentale, tentativo.

tenth, *adj.* dècimo.

term, *n.* período *m.;* (school) trimèstre *m.*

terminal, *adj.* terminale.

terminate, *vb.* terminare.

terminus, *n.* capolínea *m.*, tèrmine *m.*

terrace, *n.* terrazza *f.*

terrible, *adj.* terribile.

terribly, *adv.* terribilmente.

terrify, *vb.* atterrire.

territory, *n.* territòrio *m.*

terror, *n.* terrore *m.*

test, 1. *n.* pròva *f.* **2.** *vb.* provare, collaudare.

testament, *n.* testamento *m.*

testify, *vb.* testimoniare.

testimony, *n.* testimonianza *f.*

text, *n.* tèsto *m.*

textile, 1. *n.* tessuto *m.* **2.** *adj.* tèssile.

texture, *n.* tessitura *f.*

than, *prep.* (before nouns, pronouns) di; (elsewhere) che.

thank, *vb.* ringraziare.

thankful, *adj.* grato.

that, 1. *adj.* quel, quello, quella. **2.** *pron.* quello, quella. **3.** *conj.* che.

the, *def. art.* il, lo, la, l'; i, gli, gl', le.

theater, *n.* teatro *m.*

thee, *pron.* te, ti.

theft, *n.* furto *m.*

their, *adj.* loro.

theirs, *pron.* loro.

them, *pron.* li, le; loro.

theme, *n.* tèma *m.*

themselves, *pron.* si, sè; essi, stessi.

then, *adv.* (at that time) allora; (therefore) dunque; (afterward) pòi.

thence, *adv.* di là.

theologian, *n.* teòlogo *m.*

theology, *n.* teología *f.*

theoretical, *adj.* teòrico.

theory, *n.* teoría *f.*

therapy, *n.* terapía *f.*

there, *adv.* lí, là; ci, vi.

therefore, *adv.* perciò.

thermometer, *n.* termòmetro *m.*

these, *adj. and pron.* questi *m.pl.;* queste *f.pl.*

thesis, *n.* tesi *m.*

they, *pron.* loro; essi *m.pl.;* esse *f.pl.*

thick, *adj.* spesso, folto, dènso, fitto.

thicken, *vb.* infoltire, condensare.

thickness, *n.* spessore *m.*

thief, *n.* ladro *m.*

thieve, *vb.* rubare.

thigh, *n.* còscia *f.*

thimble, *n.* ditale *m.*

thin, *adj.* sottile; (meager) magro.

thing, *n.* còsa *f.*

thingumajig, *n.* còso *m.*

think, *vb.* pensare.

thinkable, *adj.* pensàbile.

thinker, *n.* pensatore *m.*

third, *adj.* tèrzo.

Third World, *n.* Tèrzo Mondo *m.*

thirst, *n.* sete *f.*

thirsty, *adj.* (be t.) aver sete.

thirteen, *num.* trédici.

thirteenth, *adj.* tredicèsimo, decimotèrzo.

thirtieth, *adj.* trentésimo.

thirty, *num.* trenta.

this, *adj. and pron.* questo *m.sg.,* questa *f.sg.;* (**t. man**) questi *pron.m.sg.*

thorax, *n.* torace *m.*

thorn, *n.* spina *f.*

thorny, *adj.* spinoso.

thorough, *adj.* complèto.

those, **1.** *adj.* quei, quegli *m.pl.;* quelle *f.pl.* **2.** *pron.* quelli *m.pl.;* quelle *f.pl.*

thou, *pron.* tu.

though, **1.** *adv.* però. **2.** *conj.* sebbène.

thought, *n.* pensièro *m.*

thoughtful, *adj.* pensoso; (careful) attènto.

thoughtless, *adj.* incurante.

thousand, *num.* mille.

thread, **1.** *n.* filo *m.* **2.** *vb.* infilare.

threat, *n.* minàccia *f.*

threaten, *vb.* minacciare.

three, *num.* tre.

threshold, *n.* sòglia *f.*

thrift, *n.* economía *f.*

thrill, *n.* frèmito *m.*

thrilling, *adj.* emozionante; eccitante.

thrive, *vb.* prosperare.

throat, *n.* gola *f.*

throne, *n.* tròno *m.*

through, **1.** *adj.* (direct) dirètto. **2.** *prep.* per, attravèrso; (**go t., pass t.**) attraversare.

throughout, *adv.* dappertutto, completamente.

throw, *vb.* gettare, lanciare, buttare.

thrust, **1.** *n.* spinta *f.* **2.** *vb.* spíngere.

thumb, *n.* pòllice *m.*

thunder, **1.** *n.* tuòno *m.* **2.** *vb.* tuonare.

Thursday, *n.* giovedí *m.*

thus, *adv.* cosí.

thwart, *vb.* frustrare.

thy, *adj.* tuo.

ticket, *n.* biglietto *m.*

tickle, *vb.* solleticare.

ticklish, *adj.* delicato.

tide, *n.* marèa *f.*

tidy, **1.** *adj.* ordinato. **2.** *vb.* ordinare.

tie, **1.** *n.* (bond) legame *m.;* (necktie) cravatta *f.* **2.** *vb.* legare; (make equal score) èssere pari con.

tier, *n.* fila *f.*

tiger, *n.* tigre *m.*

tight, *adj.* stretto, teso.

tighten, *vb.* stríngere.

tile, *n.* tégola *f.*

till, **1.** *n.* cassetto *m.* **2.** *vb.* coltivare. **3.** *prep.* fino a; sino a. **4.** *conj.* finchè.

tilt, **1.** *n.* inclinazione *f.* **2.** *vb.* inclinare.

timber, *n.* legname *m.*

time, *n.* tèmpo *m.;* (o'clock) ora *f.;* (occasion) vòlta *f.*

timetable, n. oràrio m.

timid, adj. tímido.

timidity, n. timidezza f.

timidly, adv. timidamente.

tin, n. stagno m.; (metal can) latta f.

tint, n. tinta f.

tiny, adj. minùscolo.

tip, 1. n. (end) punta f.; (reward) mància f. **2.** vb. (tilt) inclinare; (give money to) dare una mància a.

tire, 1. n. pneumàtico m. **2.** vb. stancare.

tired, adj. stanco.

tissue, n. tessuto m.; (facial) fazzoletti detergenti m.pl.; scottex m.; carta assorbente f.

title, n. tìtolo m.

to, prep. a, ad (before a and, optionally, before other vowels).

toast, 1. n. pane abbrustolito m.; (health) toast m., bríndisi m. **2.** vb. abbrustolire; (drink health) brindare.

tobacco, n. tabacco m.; **(t. shop)** tabacchería f.

today, n. and adv. òggi (m.)

toe, n. dito del pìede m.; **(big t.)** pòllice m.

together, adv. insìeme.

toil, 1. n. fatica f. **2.** vb. faticare.

toilet, n. latrina f., gabinetto m.; **(t. paper)** carta igienica f.

token, n. segno m.; (metal) gettone m.

tolerance, n. tolleranza f.

tolerant, adj. tollerante.

tolerate, vb. tollerare.

toll, n. pedaggio m.

tomato, n. pomodoro m.

tomb, n. tomba f.

tombstone, n. làpide f.

tomorrow, n. and adv. domani (m.)

ton, n. tonnellata f.

tone, n. tòno m.

tongue, n. lingua f.

tongue twister, n. scioglilingua m.

tonic, n. and adj. tònico (m.)

tonight, adv. stasera.

tonnage, n. stazza f.

tonsil, n. tonsilla f.

too, adv. (also) anche; (excessively) troppo.

tool, n. utensile m.

too many, too much, adj. troppo.

tooth, n. dènte m.

toothache, n. mal di denti m.

toothbrush, n. spazzolino per i denti m.

toothless, adj. sdentato.

tooth paste, n. dentifricio m.

toothpick, n. stuzzicadenti m.

top, 1. n. sommità f. **2.** vb. superare.

topcoat, n. sopràbito m.

topic, n. argomento m.

topical, adj. d'attualità.

topless, adj. topless.

top-secret, adj. top secret, segretissimo.

topsy-turvy, adv. sottosopra.

torch, n. fiàccola f.

torment, 1. n. tormento m. **2.** vb. tormentare.

tornado, n. tornado m., tromba d'aria f.

torrent, n. torrènte m.

torture, 1. n. tortura f. **2.** vb. torturare.

toss, vb. buttare, agitare, tr.

total, n. and adj. totale (m.)

totalitarian, adj. totalitàrio.

totter, vb. barcollare.

touch, 1. n. tocco m. **2.** vb. toccare.

tough, adj. (meat) tiglioso; (hard) difficile.

tour, 1. n. vìaggio m. **2.** vb. viaggiare.

touring, tourism, n. turismo m.

tourist, 1. n. turista m. or f. **2.** adj. turístico.

tournament, n. concorso m.

tow, vb. rimorchiare.

toward, prep. vèrso.

towel, n. asciugatòio m.; **(hand-t.)** asciugamani m.

tower, n. torre f.

town, n. città f.; **(small t.)** cittadina f.

toy, 1. n. giocàttolo m., trastullo m. **2.** vb. trastullarsi.

trace, 1. n. tràccia f. **2.** vb. rintracciare.

track, n. binàrio m.; (for running) pista f.

tract, n. tratto m.

tractor, *n.* trattore *m.*
trade, 1. *n.* commèrcio *m.* **2.** *vb.* commerciare.
trader, *n.* commerciante *m.*
tradition, *n.* tradizione *f.*
traditional, *adj.* tradizionale.
traffic, *n.* tràffico *m.*
traffic light, *n.* semàforo *m.*
tragedy, *n.* tragèdia *f.*
tragic, *adj.* tràgico.
trail, *n.* sentièro *m.*
trailer, *n.* rimòrchio *m.;* **(house-t.)** carovana *f.;* **(t. truck)** autotreno *m.*
train, 1. *n.* treno *m.* **2.** *vb.* allenare.
traitor, *n.* traditore *m.*
tram, *n.* tram *m.*
tramway, *n.* tranvìa *f.*
tramp, *n.* vagabondo *m.*
tranquil, *adj.* tranquillo.
tranquilizer, *n.* calmante *m.*
tranquillity, *n.* tranquillità *f.*
transaction, *n.* operazione *f.*
transfer, 1. *n.* trasferimento *m.* **2.** *vb.* trasferire.
transfix, *vb.* trafiggere.
transform, *vb.* trasformare.
transfusion, *n.* trasfusione *f.*
transition, *n.* transizione *f.*
translate, *vb.* tradurre.
translation, *n.* traduzione *f.*
transmit, *vb.* trasméttere.
transparent, *adj.* trasparènte.
transport, 1. *n.* traspòrto *m.* **2.** *vb.* trasportare.
transportation, *n.* traspòrto *m.*
transsexual, *adj.* trans-sessuale *m.*
transvestite, *adj.* travestito.
trap, *n.* tràppola *f.*
trash, *n.* cianfrusàglia *f.*
travel, 1. *n.* viàggio *m.;* **(t. agency)** agenzìa viaggi *f.* **2.** *vb.* viaggiare.
traveler, *n.* viaggiatore *m.*
traveler's check, *n.* assegno (per) viaggiatori *m.*
travesty, *n.* parodìa *f.*
tray, *n.* vassòio *m.*
treacherous, *adj.* a tradimento, proditòrio; (deceptive) ingannévole.
treachery, *n.* tradimento *m.*
tread, 1. *n.* passo *m.* **2.** *vb.* calpestare.
treason, *n.* tradimento *m.*

treasure, *n.* tesòro *m.*
treasurer, *n.* tesorière *m.*
treasury, *n.* tesòro *m.*
treat, *vb.* trattare.
treatise, *n.* trattato *m.*
treatment, *n.* trattamento *m.*
treaty, *n.* trattato *m.*
tree, *n.* àlbero *m.*
treetop, *n.* cima dell'àlbero *f.*
tremble, *vb.* tremare.
tremendous, *adj.* tremèndo.
tremor, *n.* trèmito *m.*
trench, *n.* trincèa *f.*
trend, *n.* tendènza *f.*
trespass, *n.* violazione di confine *f.*
triage, *n.* scelta *f.*
trial, *n.* pròva *f.;* (law) procèsso *m.*
triangle, *n.* triàngolo *m.*
tribe, *n.* tribù *m.*
tribulation, *n.* tribolazione *f.*
tributary, *n. and adj.* tributàrio *(m.);* (river) affluènte *(m.)*
tribute, *n.* tributo *m.*
trick, 1. *n.* tiro *m.;* trucco *m.* **2.** *vb.* ingannare.
trickle, 1. *n.* gocciolìo *m.* **2.** *vb.* gocciolare.
tricky, *adj.* ingannévole.
trifle, *n.* bazzècola *f.*
trigger, *n.* grilletto *m.*
trim, 1. *adj.* ordinato *m.* **2.** *vb.* (clip) cimare; (make neat) ordinare.
trimming, *n.* guarnizione *f.*
trinket, *n.* ninnolo *m.*
trip, 1. *n.* viàggio *m.* **2.** *vb.* incespicare.
tripe, *n.* trippa *f.*
triple, 1. *adj.* trìplice. **2.** *vb.* triplicare, *tr.*
tripod, *n.* treppiede *m.*
trite, *adj.* trito.
triumph, 1. *n.* trionfo *m.* **2.** *vb.* trionfare.
triumphal, *adj.* trionfale.
triumphant, *adj.* trionfante.
trivial, *adj.* meschino.
trolley-bus, *n.* filobus *m.;* **(t.-b. line)** filovìa *f.*
trolley-car, *n.* tram *m.*
troop, *n.* truppa *f.*
trophy, *n.* trofèo *m.*
tropic, *n.* tròpico *m.*
tropical, *adj.* tròpico.
trot, 1. *n.* tròtto *m.* **2.** *vb.* trottare.

trouble, 1. *n.* guaio *m.;* (jam) impíccio *m.;* (bother) disturbo *m.;* fastídio *m.* **2.** *vb.* disturbare, infastidire.

troublesome, *adj.* fastidioso.

trough, *n.* trògolo *m.*

trousers, *n.* calzoni *m.pl.*

trousseau, *n.* corredo nuziale *m.*

trout, *n.* tròta *f.*

truce, *n.* trégua *f.*

truck, *n.* càmion *m.,* autocarro *m.*

true, *adj.* vero; (loyal) fedele.

truly, *adv.* veramente; **(yours t.)** Vostro devmo.

trumpet, *n.* tromba *f.*

trumpeter, *n.* trombettière *m.*

trunk, *n.* (tree) tronco *m.;* (luggage) baùle *m.*

trust, *n.* fidùcia *f.;* (comm.) consòrzio *m.*

trustworthy, *adj.* affidàbile.

truth, *n.* verità *f.*

truthful, *adj.* verídico; fedele.

try, *vb.* provare, tentare.

tryst, *n.* appuntamento *m.*

T-shirt, *n.* maglietta *f.*

tub, *n.* vasca *f.*

tube, *n.* tubo *m.;* (radio) vàlvola *f.*

tuberculosis, *n.* tubercolòsi *f.*

tuck, 1. *n.* pièga *f.* **2.** *vb.* rimboccare.

Tuesday, *n.* martedí *m.*

tuft, *n.* ciuffo *m.*

tug, *vb.* tirare.

tug-boat, *n.* rimorchiatore *m.*

tuition, *n.* (fee) tassa scolàstica *f.*

tulip, *n.* tulipano *m.*

tumble, 1. *n.* capitómbolo *m.* **2.** *vb.* capitombolare.

tumor, *n.* tumore *m.*

tumult, *n.* tumulto *m.*

tuna, *n.* tonno *m.*

tune, 1. *n.* melodía *f.* **2.** *vb.* accordare; **(t. in)** sintonizzare.

tuneful, *adj.* melodioso.

tunnel, 1. *n.* galleria *f.,* traforo *m.* **2.** *vb.* traforare.

turban, *n.* turbante *m.*

turbine, *n.* turbina *f.*

turbo-jet, *n.* turboreattore *m.*

turbo-prop, *n.* turbo-èlica *f.*

turf, *n.* zolla erbosa *f.;* pàscolo *m.*

Turin, *n.* Torino *f.*

Turinese, *adj.* torinese.

Turk, *n.* Turco *m.*

turkey, *n.* tacchino *m.*

Turkey, *n.* Turchia *f.*

Turkish, *adj.* turco.

turmoil, *n.* confusione *f.*

turn, 1. *n.* giro *m.;* (vehicle) svòlta *f.;* (time around) turno *m.* **2.** *vb.* girare.

turncoat, *n.* voltagabbana *m.*

turning point, *n.* svolta cruciale *f.*

turnip, *n.* rapa *f.*

turnout, *n.* (gathering) folla *f.*

turnover, *n.* rovesciamento *m.;* (comm.) giro *m.*

turnpike, *n.* autostrada a pedaggio *f.*

turn signal, *n.* fréccia *f.*

turret, *n.* torretta *f.*

turtle, *n.* tartaruga *f.*

Tuscan, *adj.* toscano.

Tuscany, *n.* Toscana *f.*

tutor, *n.* insegnante privato *m.*

tuxedo, *n.* smoking *m.*

twelfth, *adj.* dodicèsimo.

twelve, *num.* dódici.

twentieth, *adj.* ventèsimo.

twenty, *num.* venti.

twice, *adv.* due vòlte.

twig, *n.* ramoscèllo *m.*

twilight, *n.* crepùscolo *m.*

twin, *n.* gemèllo *m.*

twine, *n.* spago *m.*

twinkle, *vb.* luccicare.

twist, *vb.* tòrcere, *tr.*

two, *num.* due.

tycoon, *n.* magnate *m.*

type, 1. *n.* tipo *m.* **2.** *vb.* dattilografare.

typewriter, *n.* màcchina da scrìvere *f.*

typhoid fever, *n.* febbre tifoidèa *f.*

typhoon, *n.* tifone *m.*

typhus, *n.* tifo *m.*

typical, *adj.* típico.

typist, *n.* dattilógrafa *f.*

tyranny, *n.* tirannía *f.*

tyrant, *n.* tiranno *m.*

udder, n. mammèlla f.

ugliness, n. bruttezza f.

ugly, adj. brutto.

ulcer, n. ùlcera f.

ulterior, adj. ulteriore.

ultimate, adj. ùltimo.

umbrella, n. ombrèllo m.

Umbrian, adj. umbro.

umpire, n. àrbitro m.

un-, 1. with adjectives, non, in-, a-, s-. 2. with verbs, s-, dis-.

unable, adj. incapace.

unanimous, adj. unànime.

unbecoming, adj. sconvenènte.

unbounded, adj. sconfinato.

uncertain, adj. incèrto.

uncertainty, n. incertezza f.

uncle, n. zio m.

unconscious, adj. incònscio.

uncork, vb. sturare.

uncouth, adj. gòffo.

uncover, vb. scoprire, tr.

under, 1. adj. inferiore. 2. adv. and prep. sotto.

underestimate, vb. sottovalutare.

undergo, vb. subire.

underground, adj. sotterràneo.

underline, vb. sottolineare.

underneath, adv. and prep. sotto.

underpass, n. sottopassàggio m.

undershirt, n. camiciòla f.; canuttièra f.

undersigned, adj. sottoscritto.

understand, vb. capire.

understanding, n. comprensione f.

undertake, vb. intraprèndere.

undertaker, n. imprenditore di pompe fùnebri m.

underwear, n. biancheria intima f.

underworld, n. malavita f.

undo, vb. disfare.

undress, vb. svestire, tr.

undulate, vb. ondeggiare.

unearth, vb. dissotterrare.

uneasy, adj. inquièto.

unemployed, adj. disoccupato.

unequal, adj. ineguale.

uneven, adj. disuguale.

unexpected, adj. inaspettato.

unexpectedly, adv. inaspettatamente.

unfair, adj. ingiusto.

unfamiliar, adj. pòco nòto.

unfavorable, adj. sfavorévole.

unfit, adj. inàbile, disadatto.

unfold, vb. spiegare, tr.

unforgettable, adj. indimenticàbile.

unfortunate, adj. disgraziato, sfortunato.

unfurl, vb. spiegare.

unhappy, adj. infelice.

uniform, 1. n. divisa f., unifórme m. 2. adj. unifórme.

unify, vb. unificare.

unilateral, adj. unilaterale.

union, n. unione f.

unique, adj. ùnico.

unisex, adj. ùnisex.

unit, n. unità f.

unite, vb. unire.

United Nations, n. Nazioni Unite f.pl.

United States, n. Stati Uniti m.pl.

unity, n. unità f.

universal, adj. universale.

universe, n. univèrso m.

university, n. università f.

unjust, adj. ingiusto.

unjustified, adj. ingiustificato.

unknowingly, adv. inconsapevolmente.

unknown, adj. ignòto, sconosciuto.

unleaded, adj. senza piombo.

unleash, vb. sguinzagliare; scatenare.

unless, conj. a meno che . . . non.

unlike, adj. dissímile.

unlikely, adj. improbàbile.

unload, vb. scaricare.

unlock, vb. aprire.

unlucky, adj. disgraziato, infelice.

unmarried, adj. cèlibe.

unmask, vb. smascherare.

unmistakable, adj. inconfondìbile.

unofficial, adj. ufficioso.

unorthodox, adj. non ortodosso.

unpack, vb. disimballare.

unpleasant, adj. spiacévole.

unqualified, adj. (unfit) incompetènte; (unreserved) incondizionato.

unravel, vb. districare, tr.

unrecognizable, adj. irriconoscibile.

unrighteous, adj. iniquo.

unsafe, adj. pericoloso.

unsavory, adj. insìpido; disgustoso.

unscathed, adj. incolume.

unseemly, adj. sconveniènte.

unsettle, vb. sconvólgere.

unsteady, adj. instàbile.

unsuccessful, adj. infruttuoso.

untie, vb. sciògliere.

until, 1. prep. fino a, sino a. **2.** conj. finchè . . . non.

untruth, n. menzogna f.

untruthful, adj. menzognèro.

unusable, adj. inservìbile.

unusual, adj. insòlito.

unwarranted, adj. ingiustificato.

unwell, adj. indisposto.

unwind, vb. dipanare.

unworthiness, n. indegnità f.

unworthy, adj. indegno.

up, 1. adv. su. **2.** prep. su per.

upbraid, vb. rimproverare.

upbringing, n. educazione f.

uphill, 1. adj. (hard) àrduo. **2.** adv. all'insù.

uphold, vb. sostenere.

upholder, n. sostenitore m.

upholster, vb. tappezzare.

upholsterer, n. tappezzière m.

upon, prep. sopra, su.

upper, adj. superiore.

upright, adj. and adv. diritto.

uprising, n. sollevazione f.

uproar, n. baccano m.

uproot, vb. sradicare.

upset, 1. n. sconvolgimento m. **2.** vb. sconvólgere. **3.** adj. sconvolto.

upside down, adv. sottosopra.

upstairs, adv. su dalle scale.

uptight, adj. teso.

upward, adv. in alto.

urban, adj. urbano.

urchin, n. monèllo m.

urge, vb. spìngere, sollecitare.

urgency, n. urgènza f.

urgent, adj. urgènte.

urinal, n. urinale m.; (public) vespasiano m.

urinate, vb. urinare.

urine, n. urina f.

urn, n. urna f.

us, pron. noi, ci.

usage, n. usanza f.

use, 1. n. uso m. **2.** vb. usare, adoperare, servirsi di.

useful, adj. ùtile.

useless, adj. inùtile.

user, n. utènte m.

usher, n. màschera f.

usual, adj. sòlito, usuale; **(as u.)** come di sòlito.

usurp, vb. usurpare.

usury, n. usura f.

utensil, n. utensìle m.

uterus, n. ùtero m.

utility, n. utilità f.; (light truck) camioncino m.

utilize, vb. utilizzare.

utmost, adj. estrèmo.

utter, 1. adj. complèto. **2.** vb. proferire, emèttere.

utterance, n. espressione f.

utterly, adv. completamente.

uvula, n. ùgola f.

V

vacancy, n. posto vacante m.; (hotel) stanza lìbera f.

vacant, adj. vacante, vuòto.

vacate, vb. abbondanare, lasciar lìbero.

vacation, n. vacanze f.pl.; (rest) ripòso m.

vaccinate, vb. vaccinare.

vaccination, n. vaccinazione f.

vaccine, n. vaccino m.

vacillate, vb. vacillare.

vacuous, adj. vàcuo.

vacuum, n. vuòto m.

vacuum cleaner, n. aspirapolvere m.

vagrant, n. and adj. vagabondo (m.).

vague, adj. vago.

vain, adj. vano; **(in v.)** invano.

valet, n. camerière m.

valiant, *adj.* valoroso.

valid, *adj.* vàlido.

valise, *n.* valigia *f.*

valley, *n.* valle *f.*

valor, *n.* valore *m.*

valuable, *adj.* prezioso; (expensive) costoso.

value, 1. *n.* valore *m.* 2. *vb.* stimare, valutare.

value-added tax, *n.* imposta sul valore aggiunto *f.*

valueless, *adj.* privo di valore.

valve, *n.* vàlvola *f.*

vampire, *n.* vampiro *m.*

van, *n.* (vehicle) carro *m.;* furgone *m.;* (front) avanguàrdia *f.;* **(moving v.)** furgone per traslòchi *m.*

vandal, *n.* vàndalo *m.*

vanguard, *n.* avanguàrdia *f.*

vanilla, *n.* vaniglia *f.*

vanish, *vb.* svanire.

vanity, *n.* vanità *f.*

vanquish, *vb.* vìncere.

vapid, *adj.* insìpido.

vapor, *n.* vapore *m.*

variance, *n.* disaccòrdo *m.*

variation, *n.* variazione *f.*

varied, *adj.* svariato.

variety, *n.* varietà *f.*

various, *adj.* vàrio.

varnish, *n.* vernice *f.*

vary, *vb.* variare.

vase, *n.* vaso *m.*

vasectomy, *n.* vasectomìa *f.*

vassal, *n.* vassallo *m.*

vast, *adj.* vasto.

vat, *n.* tino *m.*

Vatican City, *n.* Città del Vaticano *f.*

vaudeville, *n.* spettàcolo di varietà *m.*

vault, 1. *n.* (of roof) vòlta *f.;* (jump) salto *m.* 2. *vb.* saltare.

veal, *n.* vitèllo *m.*

vegetable, 1. *n.* legume *m.;* **(v.s)** verdura *f.* 2. *adj.* vegetale.

vehemence, *n.* veemènza *f.*

vehement, *adj.* veemènte.

vehicle, *n.* veìcolo *m.*

veil, *n.* velo *m.*

vein, *n.* vena *f.;* (geology) filone *m.*

velocity, *n.* velocità *f.*

velvet, 1. *n.* velluto *m.* 2. *adj.* di velluto.

veneer, 1. *n.* piallàccio *m.* 2. *vb.* impiallacciare.

venereal, *adj.* venèreo.

Venetian, *adj.* veneziano.

vengeance, *n.* vendetta *f.*

vengeful, *adj.* vendicativo.

Venice, *n.* Venèzia *f.*

venom, *n.* veleno *m.*

venomous, *adj.* velenoso.

vent, 1. *n.* foro *m.;* (expression) sfògo *m.* 2. *vb.* sfogare.

ventilate, *vb.* ventilare.

ventilation, *n.* ventilazione *f.*

ventriloquist, *n.* ventrìloquo *m.*

venture, 1. *n.* ventura *f.;* (risk) rischio *m.* 2. *vb.* rischiare; (dare) osare.

venturesome, *adj.* avventuroso.

veracity, *n.* veridicità *f.*

verb, *n.* vèrbo *m.*

verbal, *adj.* verbale.

verbose, *adj.* verboso.

verdict, *n.* verdetto *m.*

verge, 1. *n.* orlo *m.* 2. *vb.* **(v. on)** confinare con.

verify, *vb.* verificare.

vermilion, *adj.* vermìglio.

vermin, *n.* insetti *m.pl.*

vernacular, *n. and adj.* vernàcolo *(m.),* volgare *(m.).*

versatile, *adj.* versàtile.

verse, *n.* vèrso *m.*

versify, *vb.* versificare.

version, *n.* versione *f.*

versus, *prep.* contro.

vertebrate, *n. and adj.* vertebrato *(m.)*

vertical, *adj.* verticale.

vertigo, *n.* vertìgine *f.*

verve, *n.* brìo *m.*

very, 1. *adj.* vero; (selfsame) stesso. 2. *adv.* molto; or add suffix -ìssimo.

vespers, *n.* vèspri *m.pl.*

vessel, *n.* (container) recipiènte *m.;* (boat) nave *f.*

vest, *n.* gilè *m.,* panciòtto *m.*

vestige, *n.* vestigia *f.pl.*

vestry, *n.* sagrestìa *f.*

Vesuvius, *n.* Vesùvio *m.*

veteran, *n.* veterano *m.*

veterinary, *n. and adj.* veterinàrio *(m.)*

veto, 1. *n.* vèto *m.* 2. *vb.* vietare.

vex, *vb.* irritare.

vexing, *adj.* noioso.
via, *prep.* via.
viaduct, *n.* viadotto *m.*
vibrate, *vb.* vibrare.
vibration, *n.* vibrazione *f.*
vicar, *n.* vicário *m.*
vice, *n.* vízio *m.*
vice versa, *adv.* viceversa.
vicinity, *n.* vicinanza *f.*
vicious, *adj.* vizioso.
victim, *n.* vittima *f.*
victorious, *adj.* vittorioso.
victory, *n.* vittòria *f.*
victuals, *n.* vettovàglie *f.pl.,* vitto *m.*
videodisc, *n.* videodisco *m.*
videotape, *n.* videocassetta *f.*
view, *n.* vista *f.,* veduta *f.*
vigil, *n.* véglia *f.,* vigília *f.*
vigilant, *adj.* vigilante.
vigor, *n.* vigore *m.*
vigorous, *adj.* vigoroso.
vile, *adj.* vile.
vilify, *vb.* vilificare.
villa, *n.* villa *f.*
village, *n.* villàggio *m.*
villain, *n.* furfante *m.;* (in play) antagonista *m.*
vim, *n.* brio *m.*
vindicate, *vb.* rivendicare.
vine, *n.* vite *f.*
vinegar, *n.* aceto *m.*
vineyard, *n.* vigna *f.*
vintage, *n.* vendémmia *f.*
viol, viola, *n.* viòla *f.*
violate, *vb.* violare.
violation, *n.* violazione *f.,* contravvenzione *f.*
violator, *n.* violatore *m.,* contraventore *m.*
violence, *n.* violènza *f.*
violent, *adj.* violènto.
violet, *n.* viola *f.*
violin, *n.* violino *m.*
violinist, *n.* violinista *m.*
viper, *n.* vìpera *f.*
virgin, *n.* vérgine *f.*
virginity, *n.* verginità *f.*

virile, *adj.* virile.
virility, *n.* virilità *f.*
virtual, *adj.* virtuale.
virtue, *n.* virtù *f.*
virtuous, *adj.* virtuoso.
virulence, *n.* virolenza *f.*
virus, *n.* virus *m.*
visa, 1. *n.* visto *m.* **2.** *vb.* vistare.
viscous, *adj.* viscoso.
vise, *n.* mòrsa *f.*
visible, *adj.* visíbile.
vision, *n.* visione *f.;* (of v.) visivo.
visit, 1. *n.* visita *f.* **2.** *vb.* visitare.
visiting card, *n.* biglietto da vísita *m.*
visitor, *n.* òspite *m. or f.*
vista, *n.* vista *f.;* panorama *m.*
visual, *adj.* visuale.
vital, *adj.* vitale.
vitality, *n.* vitalità *f.*
vitamin, *n.* vitamina *f.*
vitiate, *vb.* viziare.
vivacious, *adj.* vivace.
vivid, *adj.* vívido.
vocabulary, *n.* vocabolàrio *m.*
vocal, *adj.* vocale.
vociferate, *vb.* vociare.
vogue, *n.* voga *f.*
voice, *n.* voce *f.*
void, *adj.* nullo; (devoid) privo.
volcano, *n.* vulcano *m.*
voltage, *n.* voltàggio *m.*
volume, *n.* volume *m.*
voluntary, *adj.* volontàrio.
volunteer, *n.* volontàrio *m.*
vomit, 1. *n.* vòmito *m.* **2.** *vb.* vomitare.
vote, 1. *n.* voto *m.* **2.** *vb.* votare.
voter, *n.* votante *m.*
voting, *n.* votazione *f.*
vouch for, *vb.* attestare.
vow, *n.* voto *m.*
vowel, *n.* vocale *f.*
voyage, 1. *n.* viàggio *f.* **2.** *vb.* viaggiare.
vulgar, *adj.* volgare.
vulgarity, *n.* volgarità *f.*
vulnerable, *adj.* vulneràbile.

W

wad, *n.* batùffolo *m.;* (roll) ròtolo *m.*
wadding, *n.* ovatta *f.*

wade, *vb.* attraversare a guado.
wag, 1. *n.* buonumore *m.* **2.** *vb.* dimenare, scuòtere.

wage, vb. (war) fare.

wager, 1. n. scommessa f. **2.** vb. scomméttere.

wages, n. salàrio m.

wagon, n. carro m.

wail, vb. lamentarsi.

waist, n. cintura f., vita f.

waistcoat, n. gilè m., panciòtto m.

wait, vb. aspettare.

waiter, n. camerière m.

waitress, n. camerièra f.

waive, vb. rinunciare a.

waiver, n. rinùncia f.

wake, 1. n. (vigil) vèglia f.; (of boat) scia f. **2.** vb. svegliare; (be awake) vegliare.

walk, 1. n. passeggiata f. **2.** vb. camminare, passeggiare.

wall, n. muro m.

wallcovering, n. tapezzeria f.

wallet, n. portafògli m.

wallpaper, n. carta da parati f.

walnut, n. noce f.

walrus, n. trichèco m.

waltz, n. vàlzer m.

wan, adj. smunto, smorto.

wand, n. bacchetta f.

wander, vb. vagare.

wane, 1. n. decadenza f. **2.** vb. declinare.

want, 1. n. bisogno m.; (poverty) misèria f. **2.** vb. desiderare.

war, n. guèrra f.

ward, n. pupillo m.; (city) rione m.

wardrobe, n. guardaroba m.

ware, n. mèrce f.

warehouse, n. depòsito m., magazzino m.

warlike, adj. guerresco.

warlord, n. capofazione m., signore della guerra m.

warm, adj. caldo, caloroso.

warmonger, n. guerrafondàio m.

warmth, n. calore m.

warn, vb. ammonire, avvertire.

warning, n. avviso m., ammonimento m.

warp, vb. curvare tr., viziare.

warrant, n. mandato m.

warranty, n. garanzia f.

warrior, n. guerrièro m.

warship, n. nave da guerra f.

wash, 1. n. (laundry) biancheria f. **2.** vb. lavare.

wash-basin, n. lavabo m.

washing machine, n. lavabiancheria m.

washroom, n. lavatòio m.

wasp, n. vèspa f.

waste, 1. n. sprèco m. **2.** vb. sprecare.

wastebasket, n. cestino rifiùti m.

watch, 1. n. (timepiece) orològio m.; (guard) guàrdia f. **2.** vb. guardare.

watchful, adj. vigilante.

watchmaker, n. orologiaio m.

watchman, n. guardiano m.

water, 1. n. acqua f. **2.** vb. innaffiare.

waterbed, n. letto ad acqua m.

water-color, n. acquarèllo m.

waterfall, n. cascata f.

waterproof, adj. impermeàbile.

wave, 1. n. onda f. **2.** vb. sventolare.

waver, vb. esitare, vacillare.

wax, 1. n. cera f. **2.** vb. incerare.

way, n. via f.; (manner) manièra f.

we, pron. noi.

weak, adj. dèbole.

weaken, vb. indebolire.

weakly, adv. debolmente.

weakness, n. debolezza f.

wealth, n. ricchezza f.

wealthy, adj. ricco.

weapon, n. arma f.

wear, 1. n. consumo m. **2.** vb. portare; **(w. out)** consumare; logorare.

weary, adj. stanco.

weasel, n. dònnola f.

weather, n. tèmpo m.; **(w. report)** bollettino metereologico m.

weave, vb. tèssere.

weaver, n. tessitore m.

weaving, n. tessitura f.

web, n. tela f.

wedding, n. nòzze f.pl.

wedge, 1. n. bietta f., cùneo m. **2.** vb. incuneare.

Wednesday, n. mercoledì m.

weed, n. erbàccia f.

week, n. settimana f.

weekday, n. giorno feriale m.

week end, n. fine di settimana f.

weekly, n.; adj. settimanale (m.)

weep, vb. piàngere.

weigh, vb. pesare.

weight, n. peso m.

weird, *adj.* strano.

welcome, *adj.* benvenuto.

welfare, *n.* benèssere *m.*

well, 1. *n.* pozzo *m.* 2. *vb.* sgorgare. 3. *adv., interj.* bène.

well-known, *adj.* nòto.

west, *n.* òvest *m.*

western, *adj.* occidentale.

westward, *adv.* vèrso òvest.

wet, 1. *adj.* ùmido. 2. *vb.* inumidire.

whale, *n.* balena *f.*

what, *pron.* che?, che còsa?

whatever, 1. *adj.* qualunque. 2. *pron.* qualunque còsa.

wheat, *n.* frumento *m.*

wheel, *n.* ruòta *f.; (w. chair)* sèdia a rotelle *f.*

when, *adv.* quando.

whence, *adv.* donde.

whenever, *adv.* ogniqualvòlta.

where, *adv.* dove.

wherever, *adv.* dovunque.

whether, *conj.* se.

which, 1. *interrog. pron., adj.* quale. 2. *rel. pron.* che, il quale; *(after prep.)* cùi; **(to w.)** cùi.

whichever, *adj.; pron.* qualunque.

while, *conj.* mentre.

whim, *n.* capríccio *m.*

whip, 1. *n.* frusta *f.* 2. *vb.* frustare.

whirl, *vb.* girare.

whirlpool, *n.* vòrtice *m.*

whirlwind, *n.* túrbine *m.*

whisk broom, *n.* scopetta *f.*

whisker, *n.* basetta *f.*

whiskey, *n.* whiskey *m.*

whisper, 1. *n.* bisbíglio *m.* 2. *vb.* bisbigliare.

whistle, 1. *n.* fischio *m.* 2. *vb.* fischiare.

white, *adj.* bianco.

whiten, *vb.* imbiancare.

white plague, *n.* tubercolosi *f.*

white slavery, *n.* la tratta delle bianche *f.*

who, whom, *pron.* 1. *interrog.* chi. 2. *rel.* che, il quale; *(after prep.)* cùi.

whoever, whomever, *pron.* chiunque.

whole, *adj.* intèro, tutto.

wholehearted, *adj.* di gran cuore, sincero.

wholesale, *adj., adv.* all'ingròsso.

wholesome, *adj.* sano.

wholly, *adv.* completamente.

whom, see **who.**

whore, *n.* puttana *f.*

whose, *pron.* 1. *interrog.* di chi?. 2. *rel.* cùi.

why, *adv.* perchè.

wicked, *adj.* malvàgio.

wickedness, *n.* malvagità *f.*

wide, *adj.* largo.

wide-angle, *adj.* grandangolare.

widen, *vb.* allargare, *tr.*

widespread, *adj.* diffuso.

widow, *n.* védova *f.*

widower, *n.* védovo *m.*

width, *n.* larghezza *f.*

wield, *vb.* règgere.

wife, *n.* móglie *f.*

wig, *n.* parrucca *f.*

wild, *adj.* selvàggio; *(plants)* selvàtico; *(mad)* furioso.

wilderness, *n.* desèrto *m.*

wildlife, *n.* fàuna selvàtica *f.*

will, 1. *n.* volontà *f.; (testament)* testamento *m.* 2. *vb. (leave)* lasciare; *(future)* use future tense.

willful, *adj.* capàrbio, ostinato.

willing, *adj.* pronto.

willow, *n.* sàlice *m.*

wilt, *vb.* appassire.

win, *vb.* vincere.

wind, 1. *n.* vènto *m.* 2. *vb.* avvòlgere; *(watch)* caricare.

windmill, *n.* mulino a vento *m.*

window, *n.* finèstra *f.*

window dressing, *n.* vetrinística *f.;* facciata *f.*

windshield, *n.* parabrezza *m.;* paravènto *m.; (w.-wiper)* tergicristallo *m.*

windy, *adj.* ventoso.

wine, *n.* vino *m.*

wing, *n.* ala *f.*

wink, *vb.* ammiccare.

winner, *n.* vincitore *m.*

winter, 1. *n.* invèrno *m.* 2. *adj.* **(of w.)** invernale.

wintry, *adj.* invernale.

wipe, *vb.* asciugare.

wire, 1. *n.* filo *m.; (telegram)* telegramma *m.* 2. *vb.* telegrafare.

wireless, 1. *n. (radio)* ràdio *f.* 2. *adj.* sènza fili.

wire recorder, *n.* registratore a filo *m.*

wiretap, vb. intercettare.

wisdom, n. saggezza f.

wise, adj. sàggio.

wish, 1. n. desidèrio m. **2.** vb. desiderare.

wit, n. intelligènza f.; (humor) spírito m. (wag) buonumore m.

witch, n. strega f.

witch hunt, n. caccia alle streghe f.

with, prep. con.

withdraw, vb. ritirare, tr.

wither, vb. avvizzire.

withhold, vb. trattenere.

within, 1. adv. dentro. **2.** prep. entro.

without, prep. sènza.

witness, n. testimone m.

witty, adj. spiritoso.

wizard, n. stregone m.

woe, n. calamità f., guaio m.

wolf, n. lupo m., lupa f.

woman, n. dònna f.

womb, n. ùtero m.

wonder, 1. n. meravíglia f. **2.** vb. meravigliarsi, domandarsi.

wonderful, adj. meraviglioso.

woo, vb. corteggiare.

wood, n. legno m.; (forest) bosco m., forèsta f.

wooded, adj. boscoso.

wooden, adj. di legno.

wool, n. lana f.

woolen, adj. di lana.

word, n. paròla f.

wordy, adj. verboso.

work, 1. n. lavoro m., òpera f. **2.** vb. lavorare; (function) funzionare.

worker, n. lavoratore m.

workman, n. operaio m.

world, n. mondo m.

worldly, adj. mondano.

world-wide, adj. mondiale.

worm, n. vèrme m.

worn-out, adj. lògoro.

worry, 1. n. preoccupazione f. **2.** vb. preoccupare, tr.

worse, 1. adj. peggiore. **2.** adv. pèggio.

worship, 1. n. adorazione f., culto m. **2.** vb. adorare.

worst, 1. adj. il peggiore. **2.** adv. il pèggio.

worth, 1. n. valore m. **2.** adj. (be w.) valere.

worthless, adj. sènza valore.

worthy, adj. degno.

would, vb. use conditional tense.

would-be, adj. millantато, preteso.

wound, 1. n. ferita f. **2.** vb. ferire.

wrap, 1. n. mantèllo m. **2.** vb. avvòlgere.

wrapping, n. involucro m.

wrath, n. ira f.

wreath, n. ghirlanda f.

wreck, 1. n. (ship) naufràgio m.; (ruin) rovina f. **2.** vb. naufragare, rovinare.

wrench, 1. n. (tool) chiave inglese f. **2.** vb. strappare.

wrestle, vb. lottare.

wrestling, n. lotta f.

wretched, adj. mísero.

wring, vb. tòrcere.

wrinkle, 1. n. ruga f. **2.** vb. corrugare.

wrist, n. polso m.

wrist-watch, n. orològio da polso m.

write, vb. scrívere.

writer, n. scrittore m.

writhe, vb. contòrcersi.

writing, n. scrittura f., scritto m.

wrong, 1. n. tòrto m. **2.** adj. errato; (be w.) aver tòrto.

wrongdoing, n. malefatta f., trasgressione f.

wry, adj. storto, sbieco.

X, Y, Z

x-rays, n. raggi x (pron. ics) m. pl.

xylophone, n. xilòfono m.

yacht, n. pànfilo m.

yard, n. cortile m.; (railroad) scalo di smistamento m.; (measure) jarda f.

yarn, n. filato m.; (tale) stòria f.

yawn, 1. n. sbadíglio m. **2.** vb. sbadigliare.

year, n. anno m.

yearbook, *n.* annuàrio *m.*
yearly, 1. *adj.* annuale. **2.** *adv.* ogni anno.
yearn, *vb.* bramare.
yell, 1. *n.* urlo *m.* **2.** *vb.* urlare.
yellow, *adj.* giallo.
yelp, *vb.* guaire.
yes, *interj.* sì.
yes-man, *n.* leccapiedi *m.*
yesterday, *n. and adv.* ièri *(m.)*
yet, 1. *adv.* ancora. **2.** *conj.* tuttavia.
yield, 1. *n.* produzione *f.* **2.** *vb.* cèdere; (produce) produrre.
yoke, *n.* giogo *m.*
yolk, *n.* tuòrlo *m.*
you, *pron.* tu, te, ti; voi, vi, Lei; La, Lo, Loro.
young, *adj.* gióvane.
your, *adj.* tuo; vòstro; Suo; Loro.
yours, *pron.* tuo; vòstro; Suo; Loro.
yourself, *pron.* tu stesso; te stesso; voi stessi, Lei stesso; Loro stessi.

youth, *n.* giovinezza *f.*
youthful, *adj.* giovanile.
yowl, 1. *n.* urlo *m.* **2.** *vb.* urlare.
Yugoslav, *adj.* jugoslavo.
Yugoslavia, *n.* Jugoslàvia *f.*

zap, *vb.* colpire repentinamente e inaspettatamente.
zeal, *n.* zèlo *m.*
zealous, *aj.* zelante.
zebra, *n.* zèbra *f.*
zephyr, *n.* zèffiro *m.*, zaffiro *m.*
zero, *n.* zèro *m.*
zest, *n.* entusiasmo *m.*
zinc, *n.* zinco *m.*
zip code, *n.* còdice di avviamento postale *m.*
zipper, *n.* chiusura lampo *f.*
zodiac, *n.* zodiaco *m.*
zone, *n.* zòna *f.*
zoo, *n.* giardino zoològico *m.*
zoological, *adj.* zoològico.
zoology, *n.* zoología *f.*
Zurich, *n.* Zurigo *m.*

Useful Words and Phrases

Good day.	Buòn giorno.
Good afternoon.	Buòna sera.
Good evening.	Buòna sera.
Good night.	Buòna nòtte.
Good-bye.	Arrivederci.
How are you?	Come sta?
Fine, thank you.	Bène, gràzie.
Glad to meet you.	Piacere.
Thank you very much.	Molte gràzie.
You're welcome.	Prègo.
Please.	Per favore.
Pardon me.	Mi scusi.
Good luck.	Buòna fortuna.
To your health.	Salute.
As soon as possible.	Quanto prima.
Look out!	Attenzione!
Who is it?	Chi è?
Just a minute!	Un momento.
Please help me.	M'aiuti, per favore.
Do you understand?	Capisce?
I don't understand.	Non capisco.
Speak slowly, please.	Parli adàgio, per favore.
Please repeat.	Ripeta, per favore.
I don't speak Italian.	Non parlo italiano.
Do you speak English?	Parla inglese?
Does anyone here speak English?	C'è qualcuno che parla inglese?
How do you say . . . in Italian?	Come si dice . . . in italiano?
What do you call this?	Come si chiama questo?
What is your name?	Come si chiama?
My name is . . .	Mi chiamo . . .
I am an American.	Sono americano.
May I introduce . . . ?	Vorrèi presentare. . . .
How is the weather?	Che tèmpo fa?
What time is it?	Che ora è?
What is it?	Che còsa è?
Please help me with my luggage.	Per favore, mi aiuti con i miei bagagli.
Is there any mail for me?	C'è posta per me?
May I have the bill, please?	Potrei avere il conto, per favore?
Where can I get a taxi?	Dove posso trovare un tassi?
What is the fare to . . . ?	Qual'è il prezzo della corsa fino a . . . ?

Please take me to this address.	Per favore, mi porti a questo indirizzo.
Please let me off at . . .	Per favore, mi faccia scéndere a . . .
How much does this cost?	Quanto còsta questo?
It is too expensive.	È troppo caro.
May I see something cheaper?	Potrei vedere qualcosa di più económico?
May I see something better?	Potrei vedere qualcosa di migliore?
It is not exactly what I want.	Non è esattamente quel che vorrèi.
I want to buy . . .	Vorrèi comprare . . .
I want to eat.	Vorrèi mangiare.
I would like . . .	Vorrèi . . .
Can you recommend a restaurant?	Può raccomandare un ristorante?
I am hungry.	Ho fame.
I am thirsty.	Ho sete.
I have a reservation.	Ho una prenotazione.
May I see the menu?	Potrei vedere il menù?
Please give me . . .	Per favore, mi dia . . .
Please bring me . . .	Per favore, mi porti . . .
Is service included in the bill?	Il servizio è compreso nel conto?
Check, please.	Il conto, per favore.
Do you accept traveler's checks?	Si accettano assegni per viaggiatori?
Is there a hotel here?	C'è un albèrgo qui?
Where is the men's (women's) room?	Dov'è il gabinetto per signori (signore)?
Please call the police.	Per favore, chiami la polizia.
Where is the nearest drugstore?	Dov'è la farmacia più vicina?
Where can I mail this letter?	Dove posso impostare questa léttera?
I am lost.	Mi sono smarrito (*m.*); mi sono smarrita (*f.*).
Where is . . . ?	Dov'è . . . ?
What is the way to . . . ?	Qual'è la strada per . . . ?
Take me to . . .	Mi conduca a . . .
I need . . .	Ho bisogno di . . .
I am ill.	Sono malato (*m.*); sono malata (*f.*).
Please call a doctor.	Chiami un mèdico, per favore.

I want to send a telegram.	Vorrèi spedire un telegramma.
Where is the nearest bank?	Dov'è la banca più vicina?
Where can I change money?	Dove posso far cambiare del denaro?
Will you accept checks?	Accètta assegni?
What is the postage?	Quanto còsta l'affrancatura?
Right away.	Sùbito.
Help!	Aiuto!
Come in.	Avanti.
Hello (on telephone).	Pronto.
Stop.	Si fermi.
Hurry.	Fàccia prèsto.
Go on.	Avanti.
Right.	A dèstra.
Left.	A sinistra.
Straight ahead.	Sèmpre diritto.

Signs

Attenzione	Caution	**Sènso ùnico**	One way (street)
Pericolo	Danger		
Uscita	Exit	**È vietato fumare**	No smoking
Entrata	Entrance	**È vietato entrare**	No admittar
Alt, Alto	Stop	**Signore**	Women
Chiuso	Closed	**Signori, Uòmini**	Men
Apèrto	Open	**Gabinetto (di decènza), Cèsso**	Toilet
Rallentate, Rallentare	Slow down		

Weights and Measures

The Italians use the *Metric System* of weights and measures, which is a decimal system in which multiples are shown by the prefixes: deci- (one tenth); centi- (one hundredth); milli- (one thousandth); deca- (ten); etto- (hundred); chilo- (abbreviated *k.*) (thousand).

1 centimetro =	.3937 inches
1 mètro =	39.37 inches
1 chilòmetro (abbr. *km.*) =	.621 mile
1 centigramma =	.1543 grain
1 gramma =	15.432 grains
1 ettogramma (abbr. *etto*) =	3.527 ounces
1 chilogramma (abbr. *kg.*) =	2.2046 pounds
1 tonnellata =	2,204 pounds
1 centilitro =	.338 ounces
1 litro =	1.0567 quart (liquid); .908 quart (dry)
1 chilolitro =	264.18 gallons

Town & Country

The Daily Telegraph

MINI
MATT
Town & Country

ORION

Orion Books
A division of the Orion Publishing Group Ltd
Orion House
5 Upper St Martin's Lane
London
WC2H 9EA

This collected edition first published by
Orion Books Ltd in 2003

A CIP catalogue record for this book
is available from the British Library

ISBN 0 75285 842 4

Printed and bound in Great Britain by
Clays Ltd, St Ives plc

FOREWORD

The Government keeps itself busy finding new things to ban and, wherever we live, our way of life is under attack. Motorists in London are now charged £5 to drive into the capital, while people in the countryside feel that politicians do not understand or appreciate their traditional pursuits.

Now cartoons are under threat. It is rumoured that the Culture Secretary has commissioned a study to discover if humans actually feel pain when they see a cartoon they don't 'get'. The Antis claim that readers have been seen to wince when they are faced with a dying joke. Cartoonists argue that it is all over very quickly and that they are providing a service by filling up space in newspapers which somebody has to do. The alternatives might cause even more suffering.

A protest is being organised. Cartoonists, wearing their distinctive corduroy jackets, will march on the capital (thus avoiding the £5 charge) to defy the ban. They will be joined by thousands of employees of the correction fluid industry, who depend on them, and by practitioners of the ancient craft of pen felt-tipping, whose livelihood is also threatened.

Town & Country

'He's captured brilliantly
the lack of facilities,
transport and cheap
housing in rural areas'

'Darling, your season
ticket has arrived'

'Did you have a good day at
the railway station, dear?'

'We've had reports that your sheep are worrying French farmers'

'...and on that farm he had
an overdraft, ee-i-ee-i-oh'

'It's amazing to think
some city kids have never
seen a burglary'

'It's very sad – this used to be a tyre and exhaust centre before all the car thefts'

'Police? Can you see with
your High Street video
camera if the greengrocer
has any broccoli'

'There goes the
neighbourhood'

'You can tell the age of a
road scheme by the number
of protesters in the tree'

'To avoid overcrowding
we won't be announcing
which platform the 7.53
will be arriving at'

'And how long has this lamb
been stalking you, Mary?'

'Our speed camera has run out
of film so I've done this
artist's impression of you'

'You don't understand London ways. They have to be controlled and it's all over very quickly'

'Their numbers have to be controlled and this is the most humane way'

'I have several bank accounts
and I use a system of
overdraft rotation'

'I've become a vegetarian – I
can't bear the cruel way some
supermarkets treat farmers'

'Mowing the lawn
isn't "playing God"'

'Go past the derelict farm, turn right at the boarded-up post office and it's opposite the closed-down Barclays'

'LOOK! A rural post office'

'It's cheaper than parking it'

'We're going walkies but,
remember, NO HUNTING'

'Your Agriculture Minister has
been worrying my sheep'

'And how would sir like his
steak vaccinated?'

'One forgets that all trains
used to go as fast as this'

'I'm afraid the 8.17 has had a
near-miss with the timetable'

'Just think how much later they'd be if they stopped at every red light'

'It's a new breed of
non-working dog'

'An asylum centre? I was
hoping it was a post office'

'I'm arresting you for driving
in miles instead of kilometres'

'Just a minute! This breaches
EC fishing regulations'

'We've got a problem – a veal
calf farm is being closed down
to make way for a motorway'

'I see you've picked up those
smart London ways'

'Is this supper or
a Countryside Protest?'

'The trouble is, you don't
know what you're
pollinating these days'

'European railways are terrible –
if you show up at the station
just ten minutes late the
train has already gone'

'It's not really, but I'm hoping
Greenpeace will break in
and mow it'

'Eat your vegetables or you'll never grow up to be big, strong and mildew resistant'